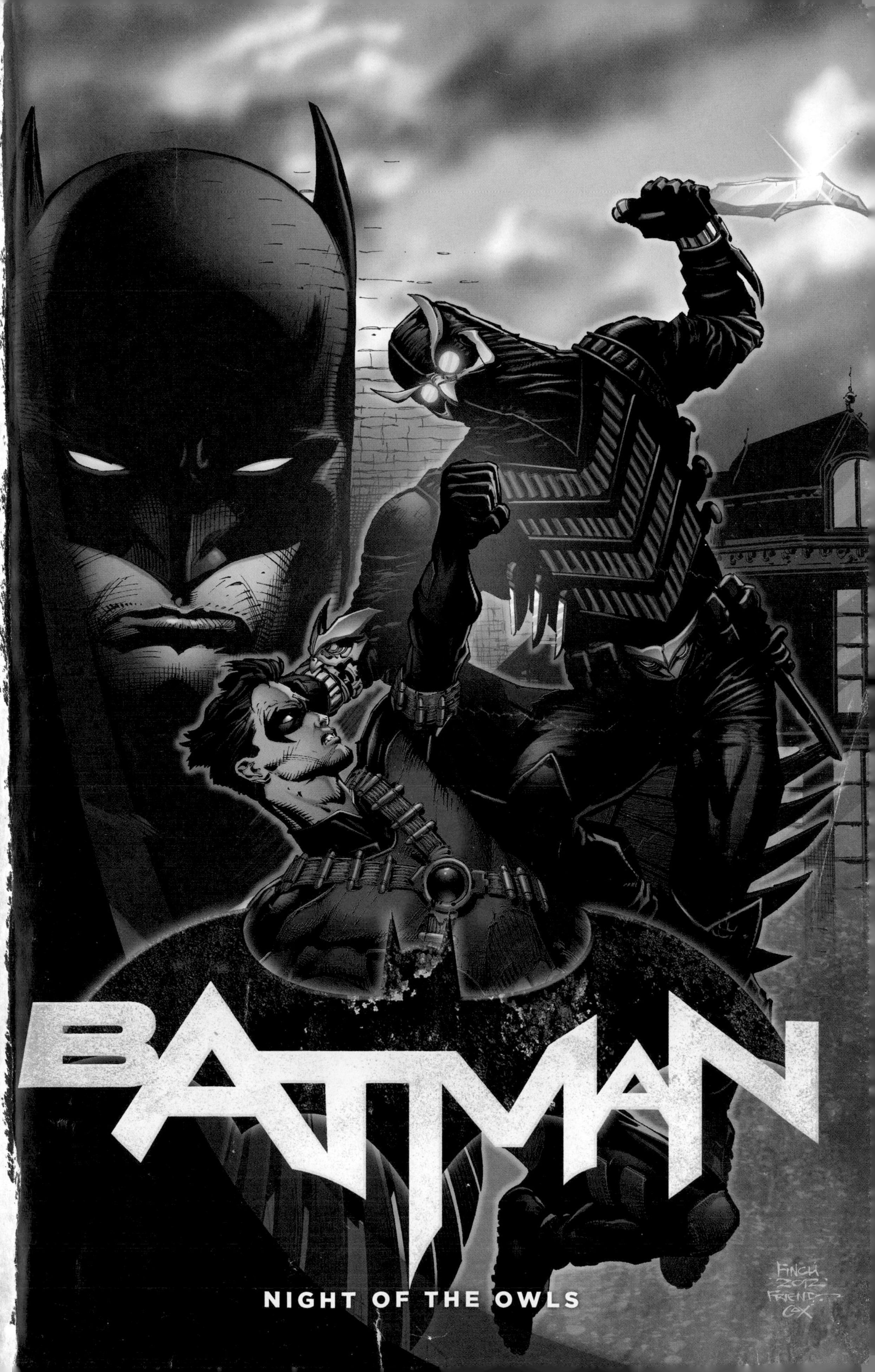
BATMAN
NIGHT OF THE OWLS
FINCH 2012 FRIEND COX

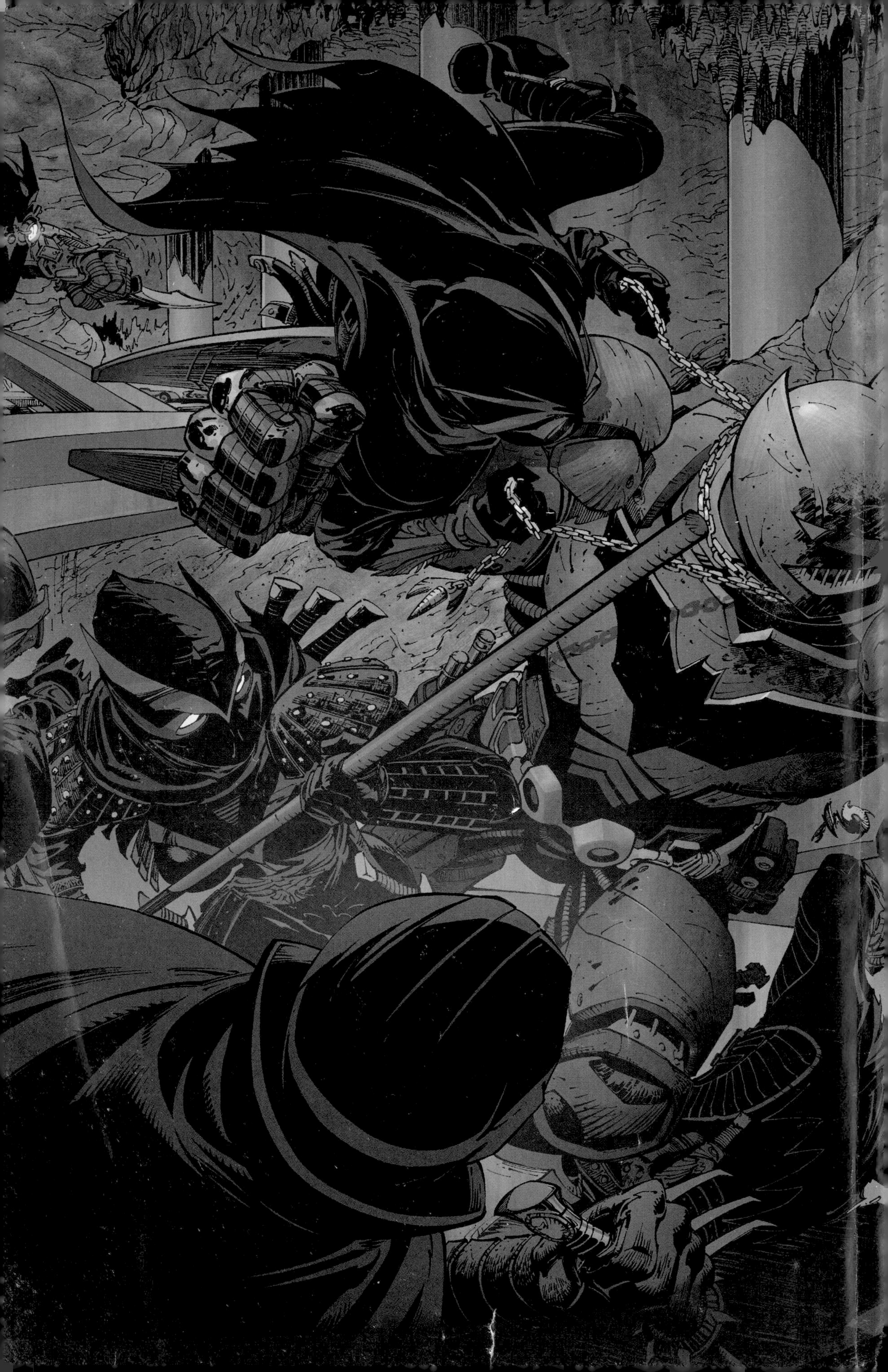

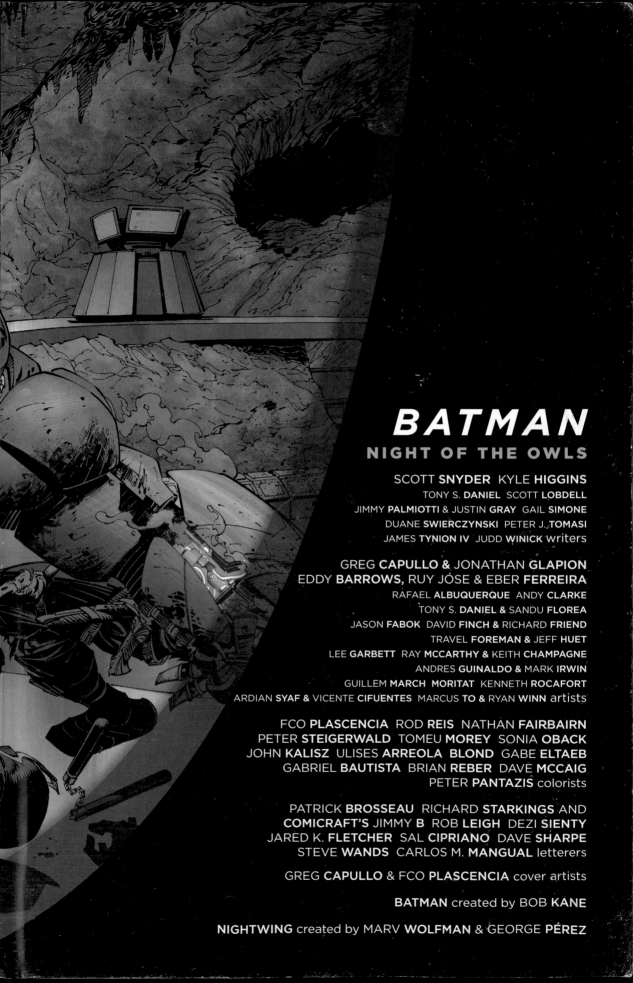

BATMAN
NIGHT OF THE OWLS

SCOTT **SNYDER**   KYLE **HIGGINS**
TONY S. **DANIEL**   SCOTT **LOBDELL**
JIMMY **PALMIOTTI** & JUSTIN **GRAY**   GAIL **SIMONE**
DUANE **SWIERCZYNSKI**   PETER J. **TOMASI**
JAMES **TYNION IV**   JUDD **WINICK** writers

GREG **CAPULLO** & JONATHAN **GLAPION**
EDDY **BARROWS,** RUY **JÓSE** & EBER **FERREIRA**
RAFAEL **ALBUQUERQUE**   ANDY **CLARKE**
TONY S. **DANIEL** & SANDU **FLOREA**
JASON **FABOK**   DAVID **FINCH** & RICHARD **FRIEND**
TRAVEL **FOREMAN** & JEFF **HUET**
LEE **GARBETT**   RAY **MCCARTHY** & KEITH **CHAMPAGNE**
ANDRES **GUINALDO** & MARK **IRWIN**
GUILLEM **MARCH**   **MORITAT**   KENNETH **ROCAFORT**
ARDIAN **SYAF** & VICENTE **CIFUENTES**   MARCUS **TO** & RYAN **WINN** artists

FCO **PLASCENCIA**   ROD **REIS**   NATHAN **FAIRBAIRN**
PETER **STEIGERWALD**   TOMEU **MOREY**   SONIA **OBACK**
JOHN **KALISZ**   ULISES **ARREOLA**   **BLOND**   GABE **ELTAEB**
GABRIEL **BAUTISTA**   BRIAN **REBER**   DAVE **MCCAIG**
PETER **PANTAZIS** colorists

PATRICK **BROSSEAU**   RICHARD **STARKINGS** AND
COMICRAFT'S JIMMY **B**   ROB **LEIGH**   DEZI **SIENTY**
JARED K. **FLETCHER**   SAL **CIPRIANO**   DAVE **SHARPE**
STEVE **WANDS**   CARLOS M. **MANGUAL** letterers

GREG **CAPULLO** & FCO **PLASCENCIA** cover artists

BATMAN created by BOB **KANE**

NIGHTWING created by MARV **WOLFMAN** & GEORGE **PÉREZ**

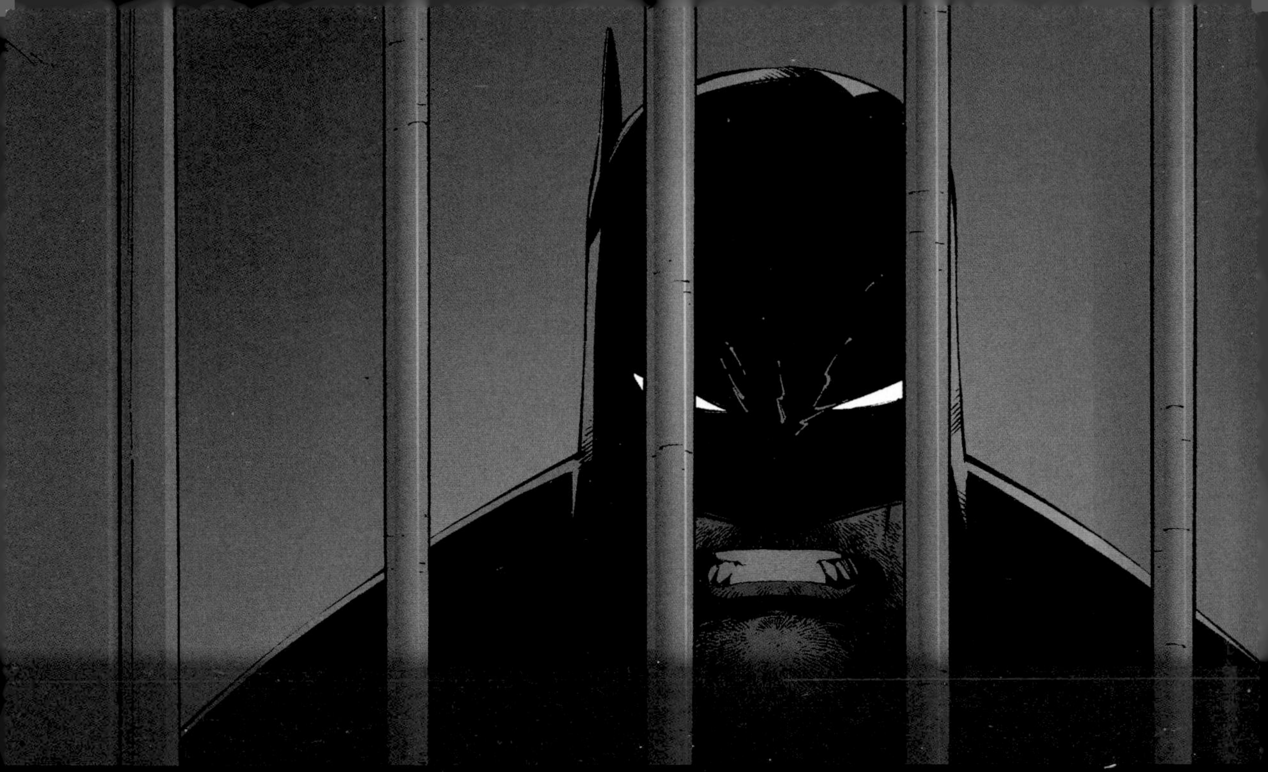

MIKE MARTS JOEY CAVALIERI BOBBIE CHASE BRIAN CUNNINGHAM RACHEL GLUCKSTERN HARVEY RICHARDS Editors – Original Series
KATIE KUBERT RICKEY PURDIN KATE STEWART Assistant Editors – Original Series PETER HAMBOUSSI Editor
ROBBIN BROSTERMAN Design Director – Books ROBBIE BIEDERMAN Publication Design

BOB HARRAS VP – Editor-in-Chief

DIANE NELSON President DAN DIDIO and JIM LEE Co-Publishers
GEOFF JOHNS Chief Creative Officer
JOHN ROOD Executive VP – Sales, Marketing and Business Development
AMY GENKINS Senior VP – Business and Legal Affairs NAIRI GARDINER Senior VP – Finance
JEFF BOISON VP – Publishing Operations MARK CHIARELLO VP – Art Direction and Design
JOHN CUNNINGHAM VP – Marketing TERRI CUNNINGHAM VP – Talent Relations and Services
ALISON GILL Senior VP – Manufacturing and Operations HANK KANALZ Senior VP – Digital
JAY KOGAN VP – Business and Legal Affairs, Publishing JACK MAHAN VP – Business Affairs, Talent
NICK NAPOLITANO VP – Manufacturing Administration SUE POHJA VP – Book Sales
COURTNEY SIMMONS Senior VP – Publicity BOB WAYNE Senior VP – Sales

BATMAN: NIGHT OF THE OWLS

DC Comics, 1700 Broadway, New York, NY 10019
A Warner Bros. Entertainment Company.
Printed by RR Donnelley, Salem, VA, USA. 12/28/12. First Printing.

HC ISBN: 978-1-4012-3773-8
SC ISBN: 978-1-4012-4252-7

SUSTAINABLE FORESTRY INITIATIVE
Certified Chain of Custody
At Least 20% Certified Forest Content
www.sfiprogram.org
SFI-01042
APPLIES TO TEXT STOCK ONLY

Library of Congress Cataloging-in-Publication Data

Snyder, Scott.
Batman : night of the owls / Scott Snyder, Kyle Higgins, Greg Capullo, Eddy Barrows.
p. cm.
"Originally published in single magazine form in Batman 8-11, Nightwing 8-9, All-Star Western 9, Catwoman 9, Batgirl 9, Batman: The Dark Knight 9, Batman and Robin 9, Batwing 9, Birds Of Prey 9, Red Hood and The Outlaws 9, Batman Annual 1."
ISBN 978-1-4012-3773-8
1. Graphic novels. I. Higgins, Kyle, 1985- II. Capullo, Greg. III. Barrows, Eddy. IV. Title. V. Title: Night of the owls.
PN6728.B36S666 2012
741.5'973—dc23
2012040574

PREVIOUSLY...

Batman had believed the Court of Owls was just a nursery rhyme. As a young boy, he'd even honed his detective skills trying to prove that they existed, but despite careful investigation, he never found any proof that a secret, owl-obsessed cabal ruled Gotham City.

That was before the Talon, the Court's legendary assassin, tried to kill Bruce Wayne in the middle of his meeting with mayoral candidate Lincoln March. It took all of his wits and skills as the Dark Knight to survive the deadly plummet from the top of Old Wayne Tower.

Batman uncovered the Court's nests, hidden in secret floors of Wayne-constructed buildings, dating as far back as the 19th century. The Talon ambushed the Caped Crusader while he was investigating a lead, thereby capturing him—and proceeded to hunt the Dark Knight through a labyrinth for the Court's sadistic amusement!

While trapped in the Court's maze, he discovered evidence of a longstanding rivalry between the Owls and the Wayne family... even proof that they were responsible for the death of his great-great-grandfather, the architect Alan Wayne. After a strenuous battle with the Talon, only Batman's incredible perseverance allowed him to make a harrowing escape—almost at the cost of his own life.

In defeat, the Court abandoned their champion. Upon examining his bested enemy, Batman made several shocking discoveries. The Talon he'd fought was William Cobb, Dick Grayson's great-grandfather—the Court recruited their killers from Haly's Circus—and they had intended to make Dick their next executioner! Even more worrisome was the fact that the process by which Cobb had been reanimated endowed him with metahuman regenerative abilities, which only extreme cold could suppress.

The Court unleashed their ultimate offensive. They awakened all of the Talons from previous generations who, like William Cobb, had been kept in suspended animation—and set them all loose on Gotham City! Against a plague of nearly undying assassins, Batman and his allies are in for one LONG night...

...THE NIGHT OF THE OWLS HAS BEGUN!

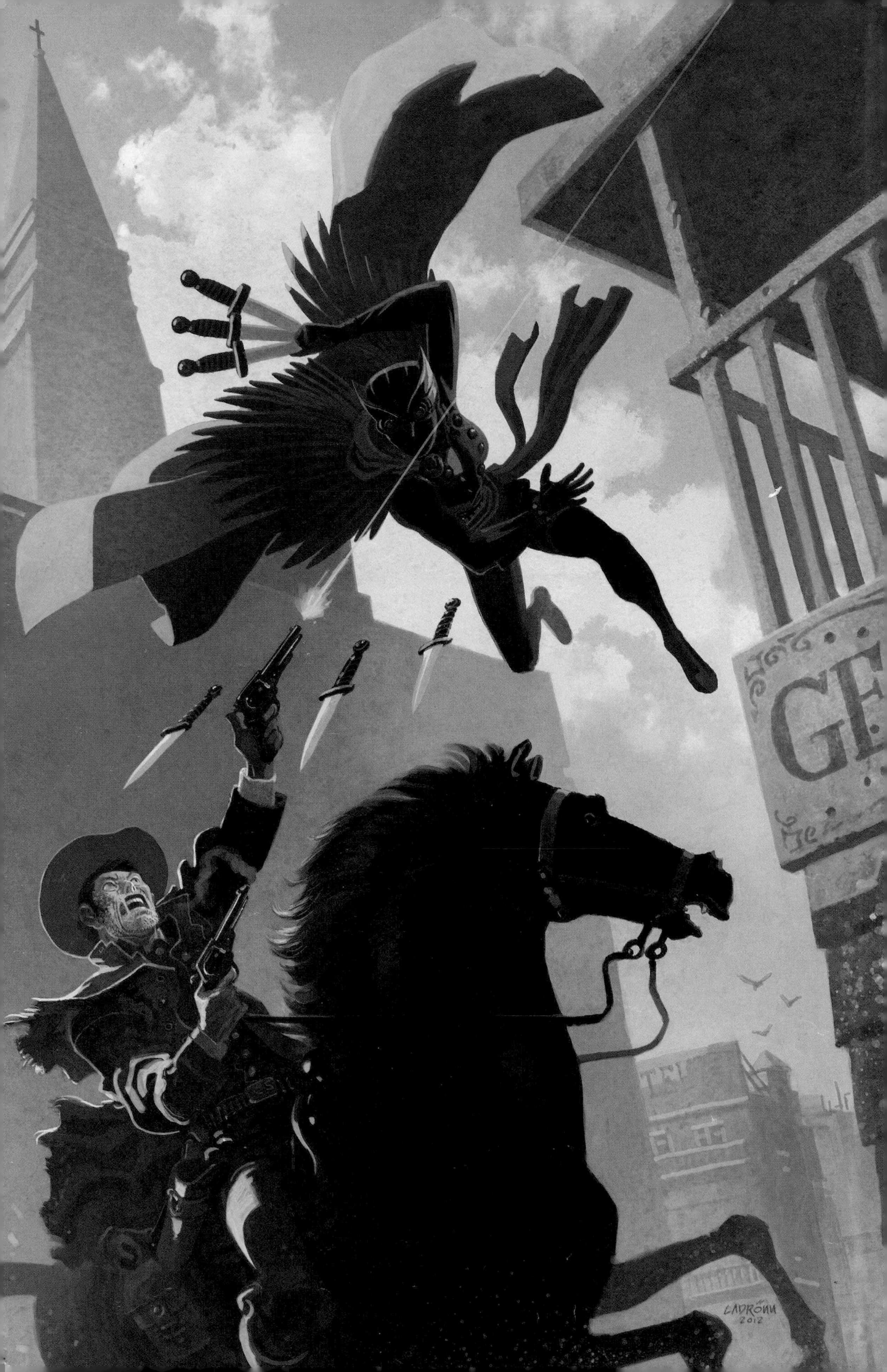
LADRÖNN
2012

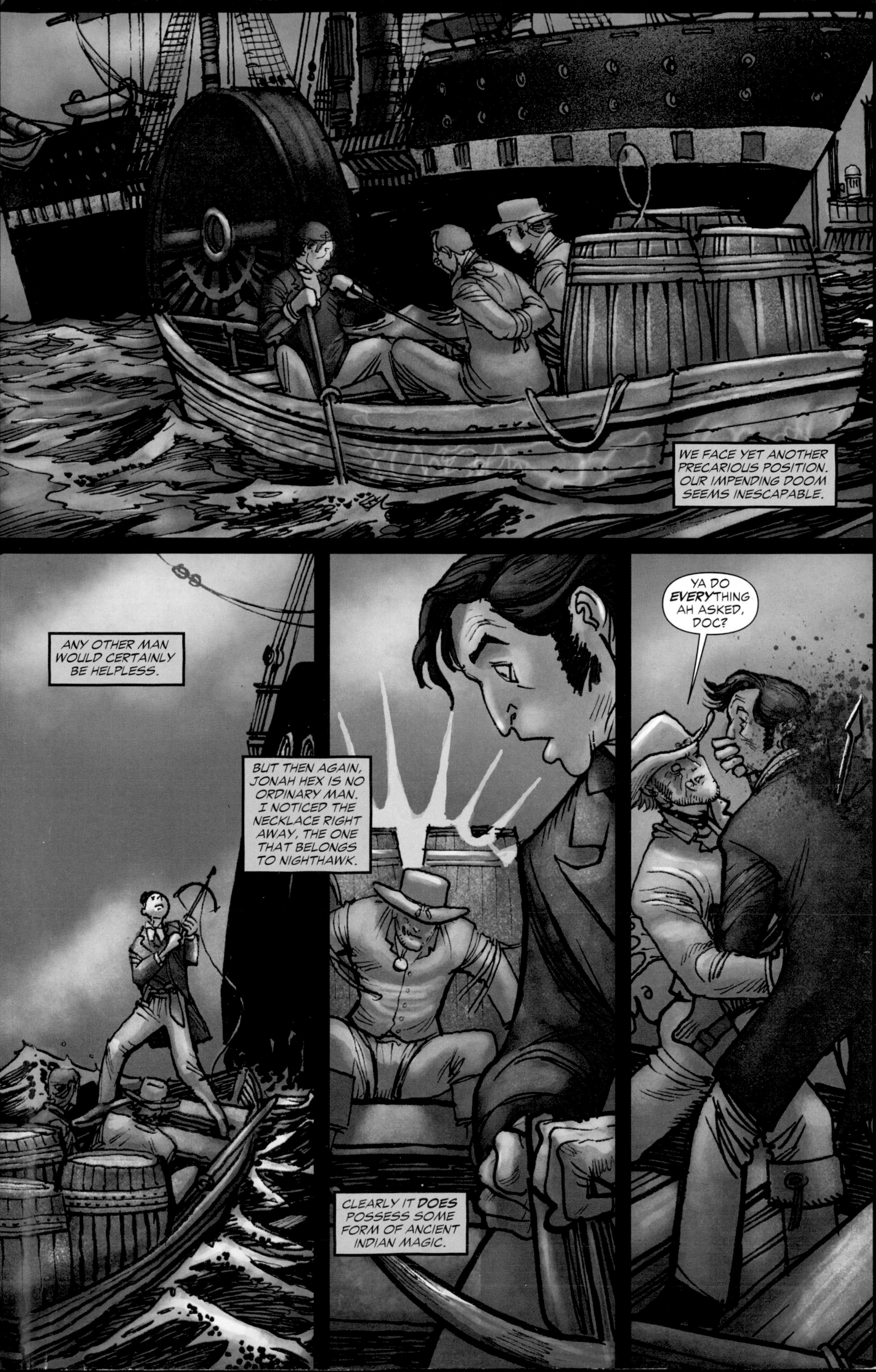
WE FACE YET ANOTHER PRECARIOUS POSITION. OUR IMPENDING DOOM SEEMS INESCAPABLE.
ANY OTHER MAN WOULD CERTAINLY BE HELPLESS.
BUT THEN AGAIN, JONAH HEX IS NO ORDINARY MAN. I NOTICED THE NECKLACE RIGHT AWAY, THE ONE THAT BELONGS TO NIGHTHAWK.
CLEARLY IT DOES POSSESS SOME FORM OF ANCIENT INDIAN MAGIC.
YA DO EVERYTHING AH ASKED, DOC?

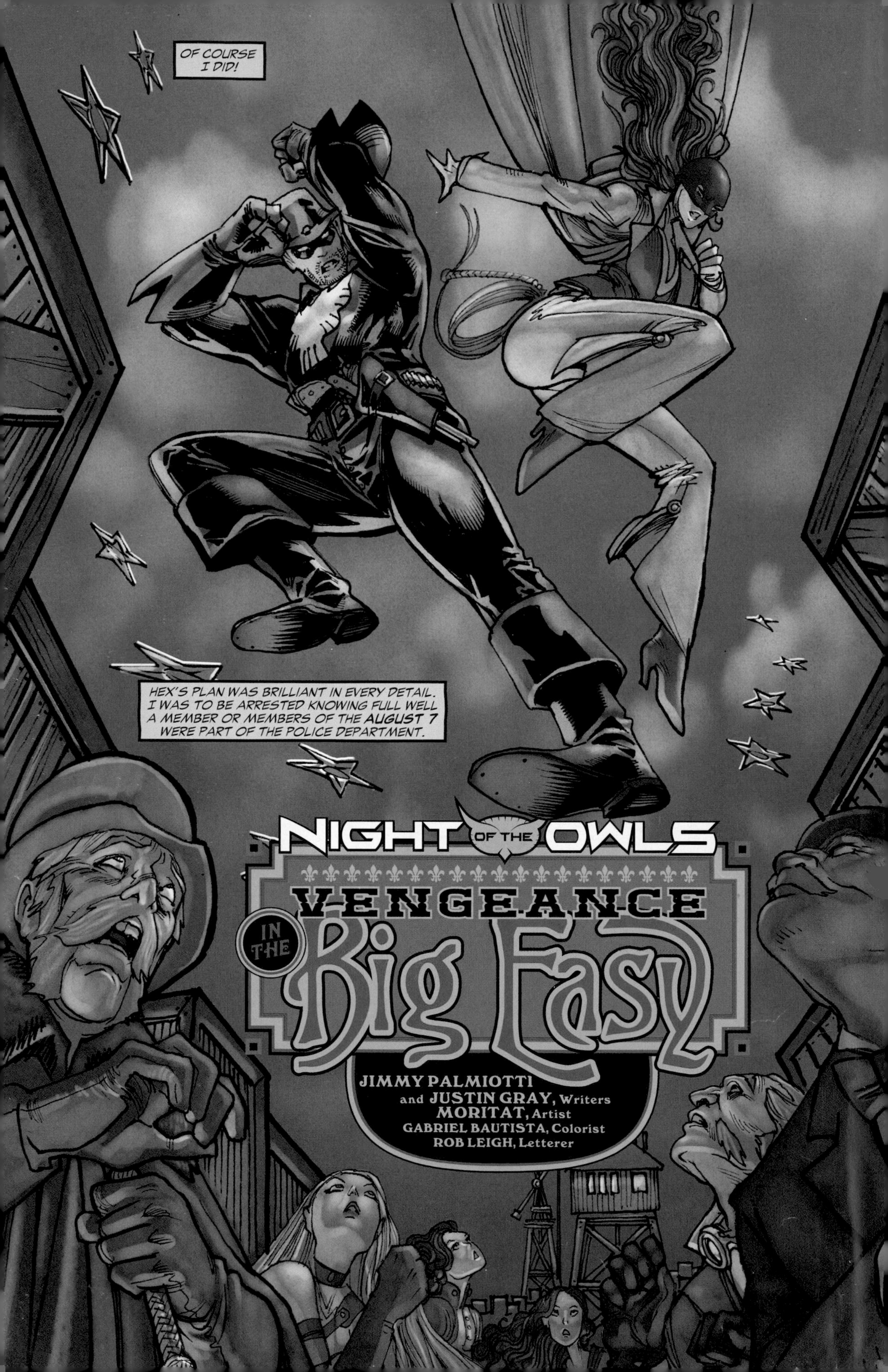
OF COURSE I DID!
HEX'S PLAN WAS BRILLIANT IN EVERY DETAIL. I WAS TO BE ARRESTED KNOWING FULL WELL A MEMBER OR MEMBERS OF THE AUGUST 7 WERE PART OF THE POLICE DEPARTMENT.
NIGHT OF THE OWLS
VENGEANCE IN THE Big Easy
JIMMY PALMIOTTI and JUSTIN GRAY, Writers
MORITAT, Artist
GABRIEL BAUTISTA, Colorist
ROB LEIGH, Letterer

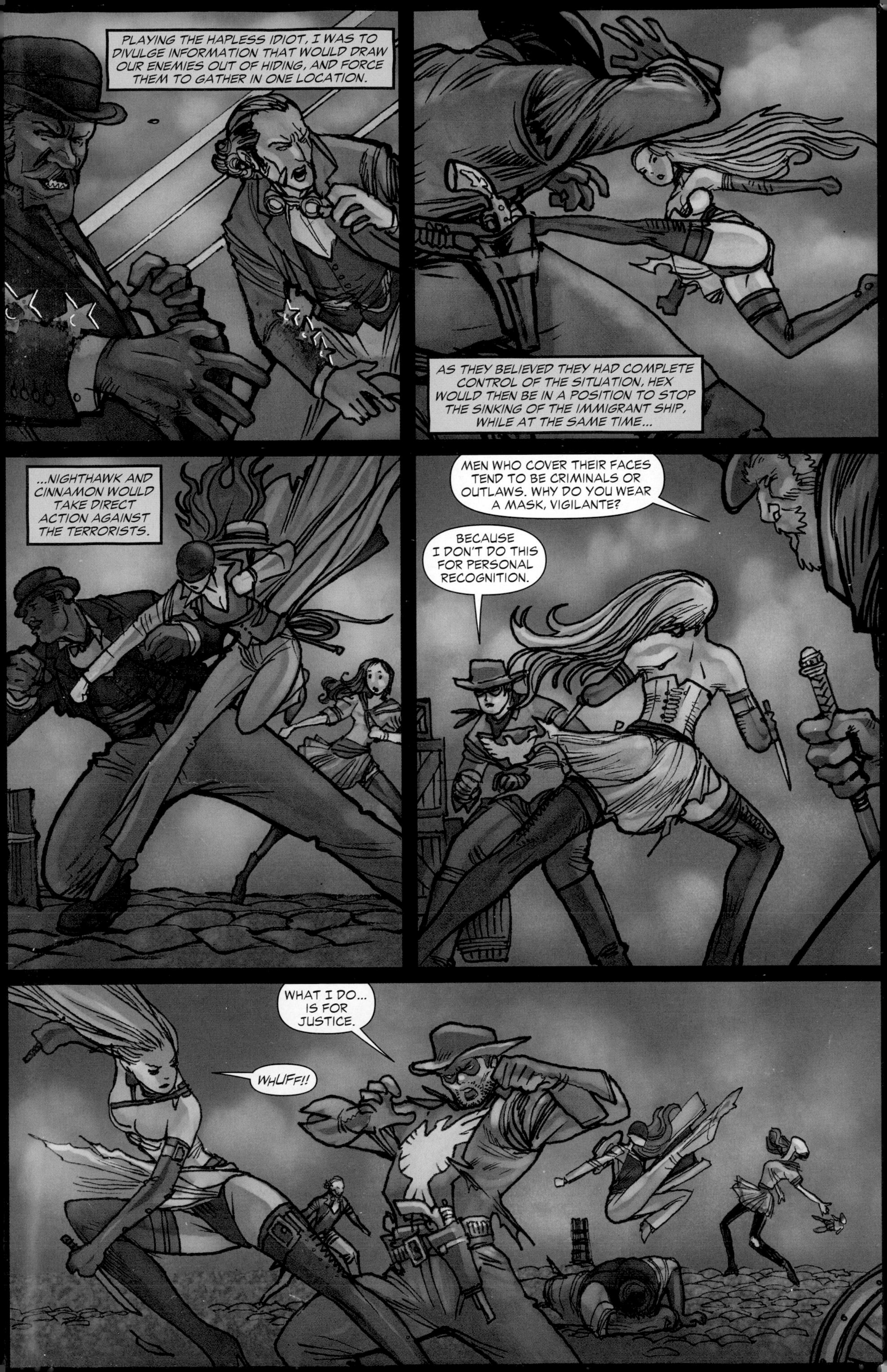
PLAYING THE HAPLESS IDIOT, I WAS TO DIVULGE INFORMATION THAT WOULD DRAW OUR ENEMIES OUT OF HIDING, AND FORCE THEM TO GATHER IN ONE LOCATION.
AS THEY BELIEVED THEY HAD COMPLETE CONTROL OF THE SITUATION, HEX WOULD THEN BE IN A POSITION TO STOP THE SINKING OF THE IMMIGRANT SHIP, WHILE AT THE SAME TIME...
...NIGHTHAWK AND CINNAMON WOULD TAKE DIRECT ACTION AGAINST THE TERRORISTS.
MEN WHO COVER THEIR FACES TEND TO BE CRIMINALS OR OUTLAWS. WHY DO YOU WEAR A MASK, VIGILANTE?
BECAUSE I DON'T DO THIS FOR PERSONAL RECOGNITION.
WHAT I DO... IS FOR JUSTICE.
WHUFF!!

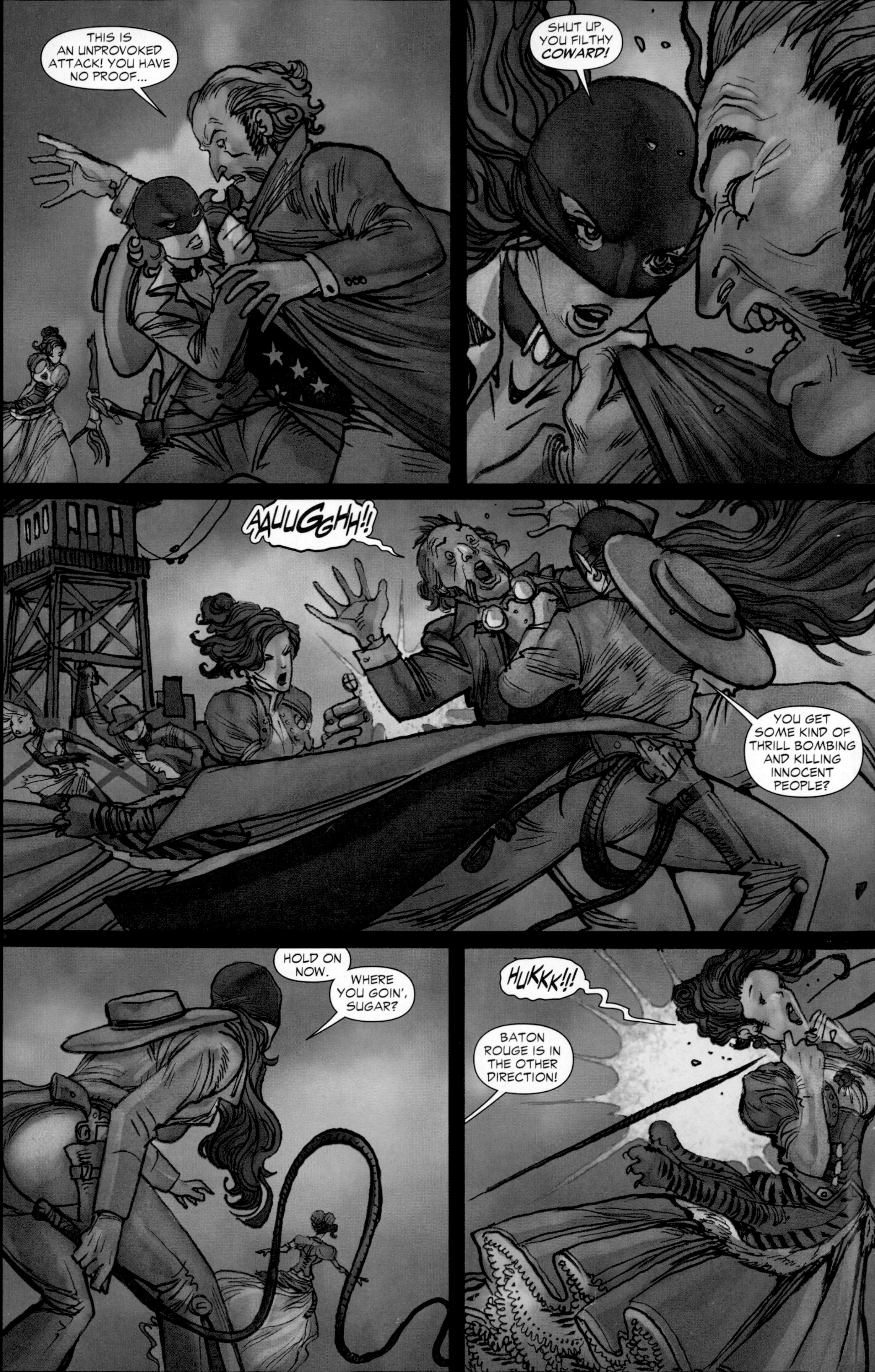
THIS IS AN UNPROVOKED ATTACK! YOU HAVE NO PROOF...
SHUT UP, YOU FILTHY COWARD!
AAUUGGHH!!
YOU GET SOME KIND OF THRILL BOMBING AND KILLING INNOCENT PEOPLE?
HOLD ON NOW.
WHERE YOU GOIN', SUGAR?
HUKKK!!!
BATON ROUGE IS IN THE OTHER DIRECTION!

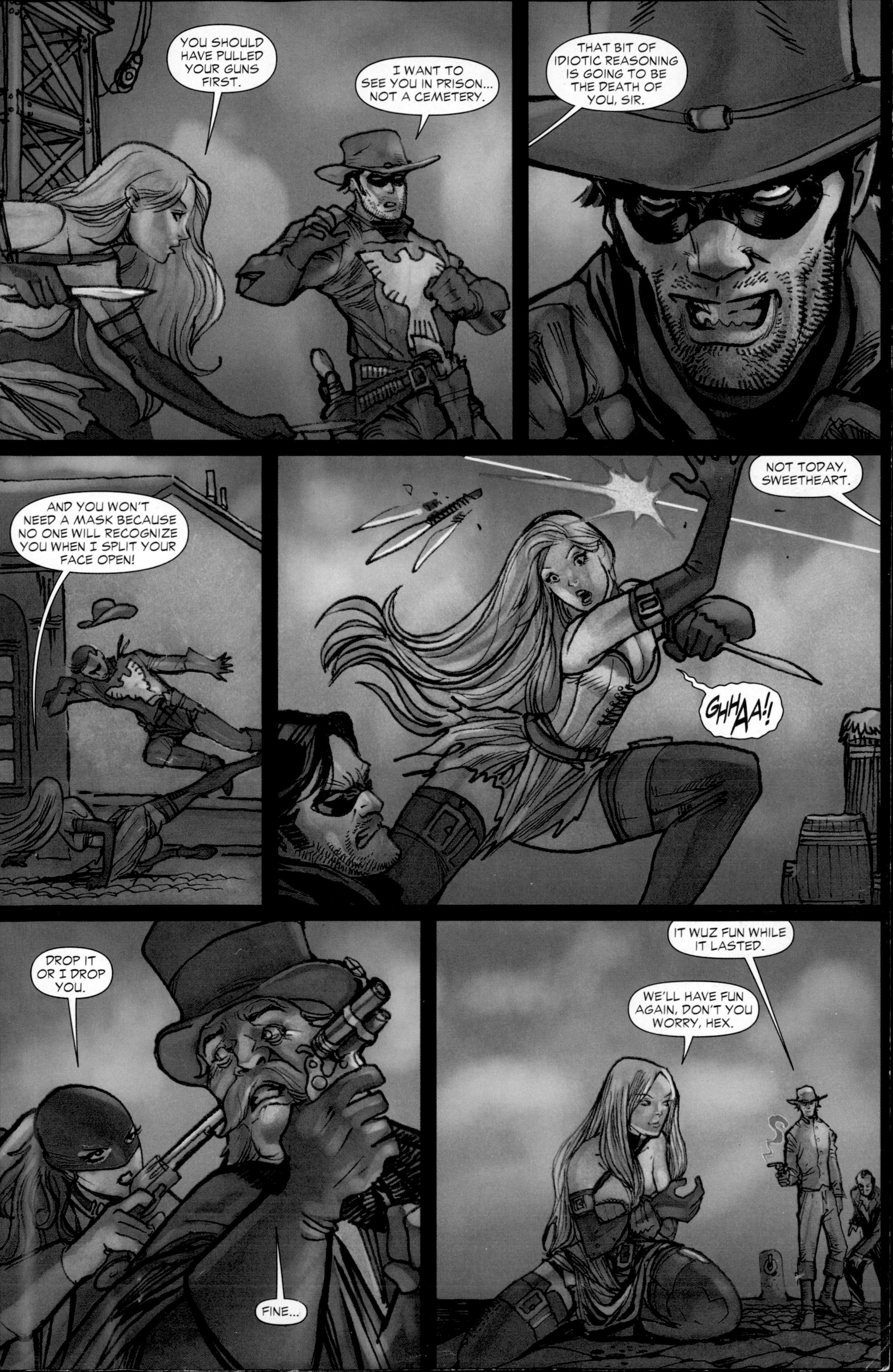
YOU SHOULD HAVE PULLED YOUR GUNS FIRST.
I WANT TO SEE YOU IN PRISON... NOT A CEMETERY.
THAT BIT OF IDIOTIC REASONING IS GOING TO BE THE DEATH OF YOU, SIR.
AND YOU WON'T NEED A MASK BECAUSE NO ONE WILL RECOGNIZE YOU WHEN I SPLIT YOUR FACE OPEN!
NOT TODAY, SWEETHEART.
GHHAA!!
DROP IT OR I DROP YOU.
FINE...
IT WUZ FUN WHILE IT LASTED.
WE'LL HAVE FUN AGAIN, DON'T YOU WORRY, HEX.

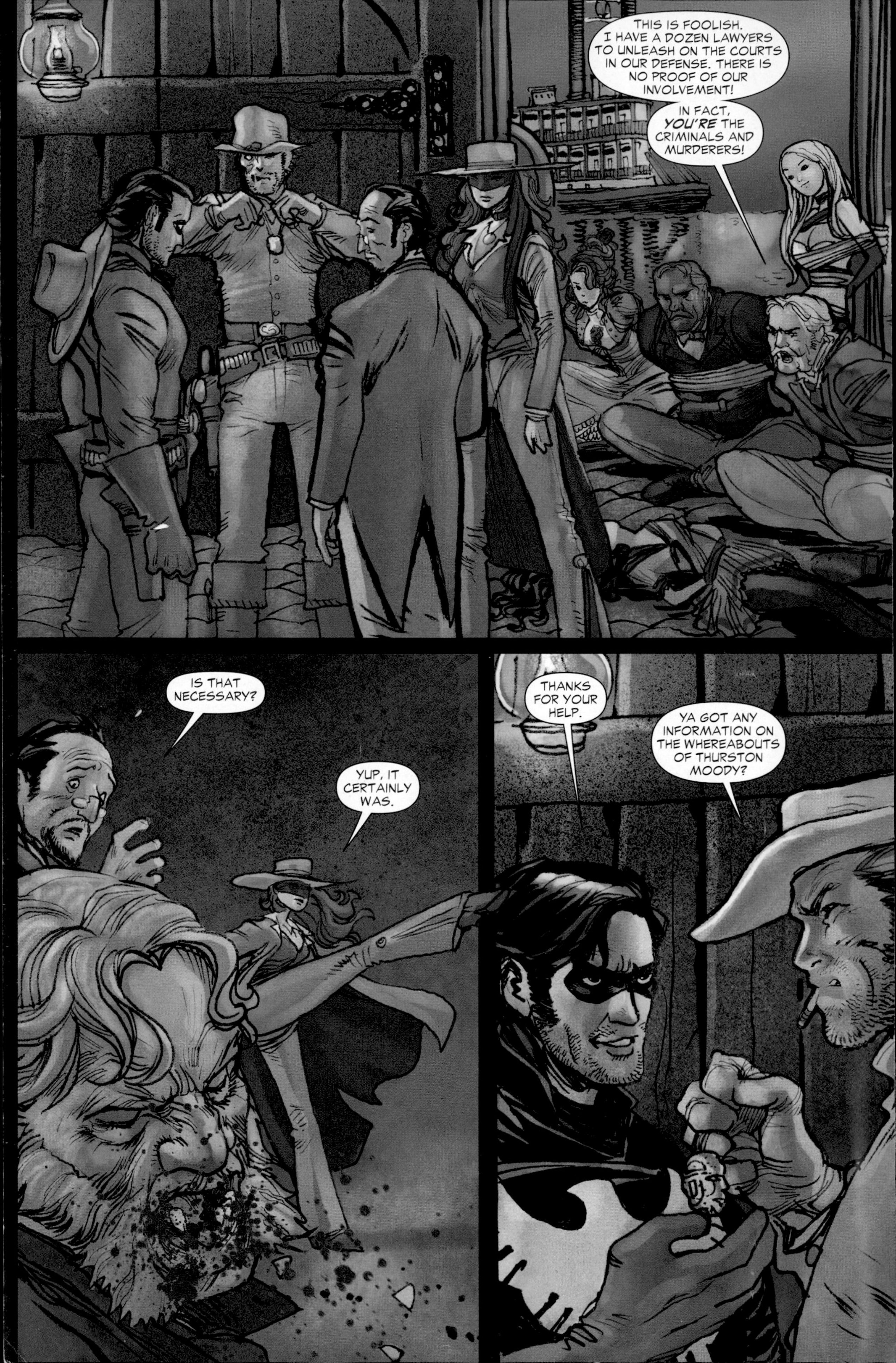
THIS IS FOOLISH. I HAVE A DOZEN LAWYERS TO UNLEASH ON THE COURTS IN OUR DEFENSE. THERE IS NO PROOF OF OUR INVOLVEMENT!
IN FACT, *YOU'RE* THE CRIMINALS AND MURDERERS!
IS THAT NECESSARY?
YUP, IT CERTAINLY WAS.
THANKS FOR YOUR HELP.
YA GOT ANY INFORMATION ON THE WHEREABOUTS OF THURSTON MOODY?

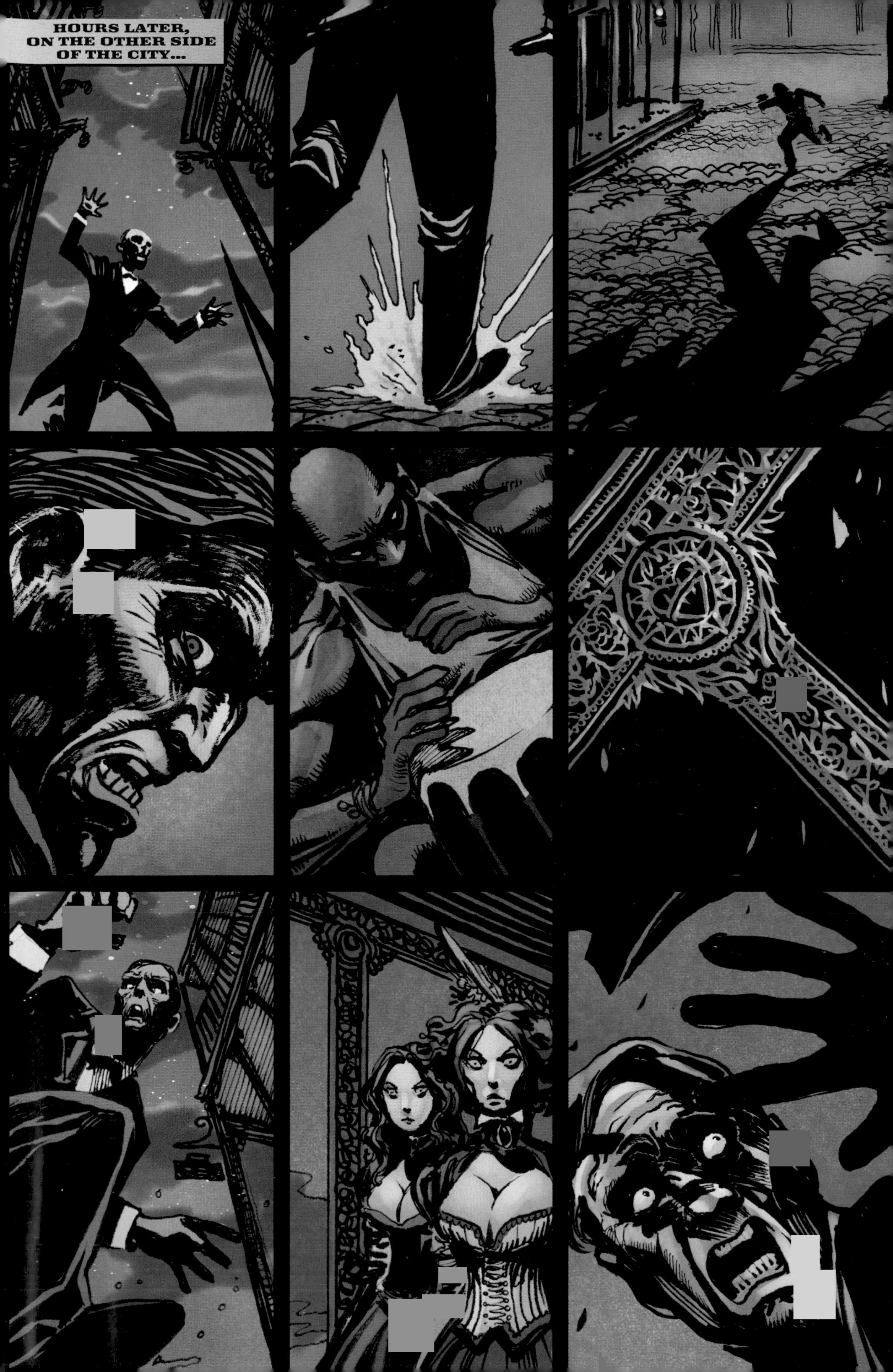
HOURS LATER, ON THE OTHER SIDE OF THE CITY...

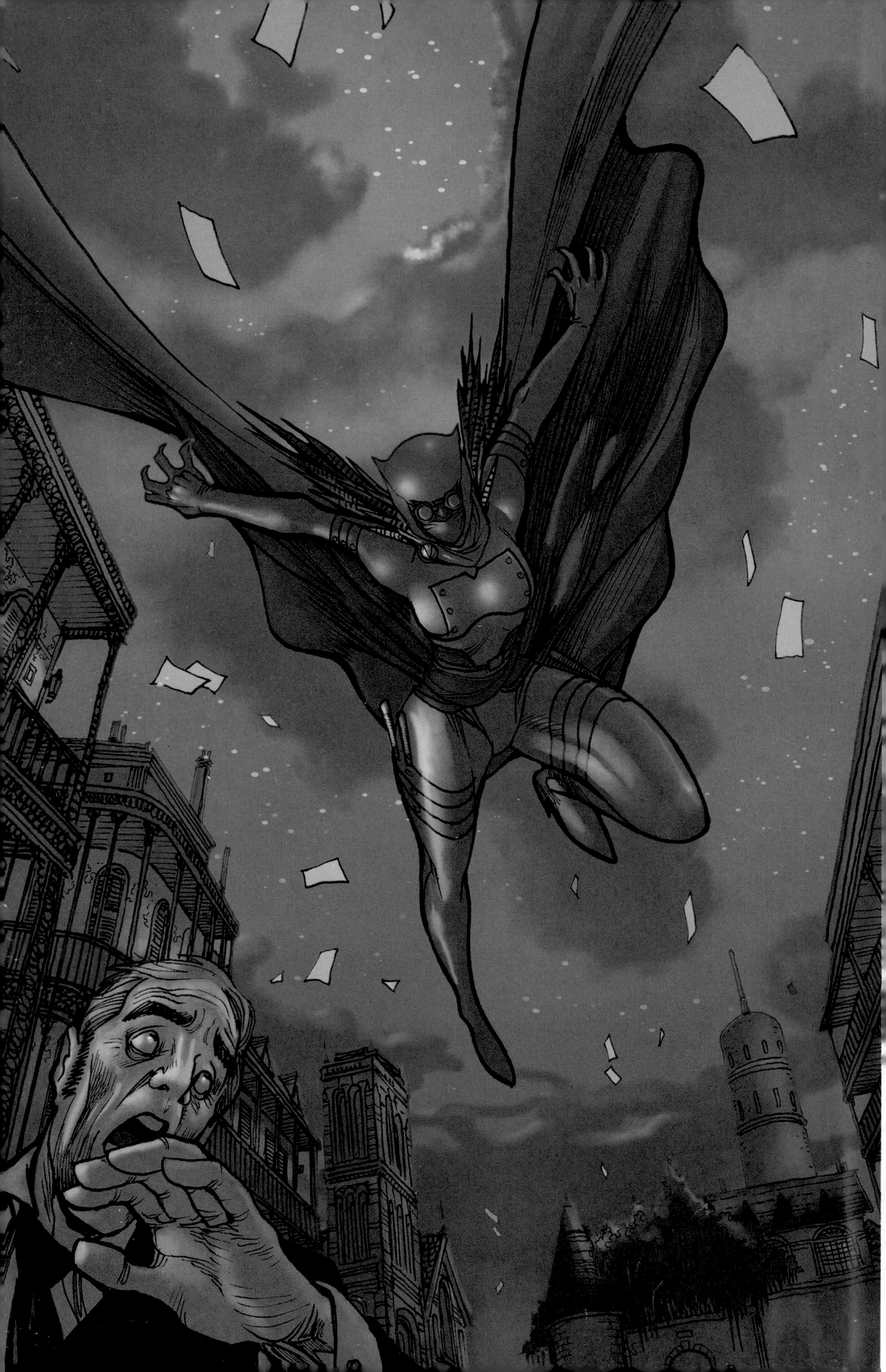

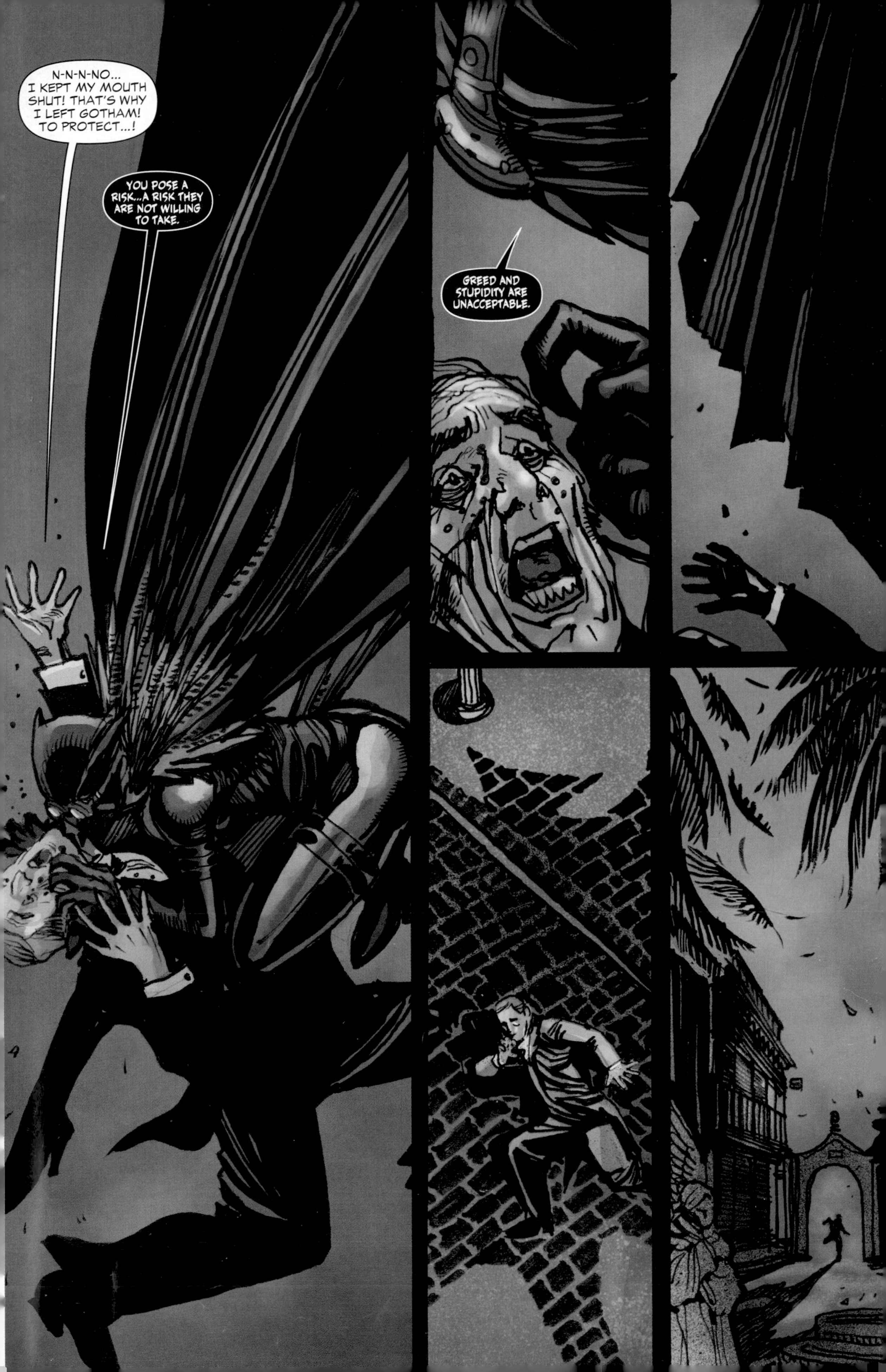
N-N-N-NO... I KEPT MY MOUTH SHUT! THAT'S WHY I LEFT GOTHAM! TO PROTECT...!
YOU POSE A RISK...A RISK THEY ARE NOT WILLING TO TAKE.
GREED AND STUPIDITY ARE UNACCEPTABLE.

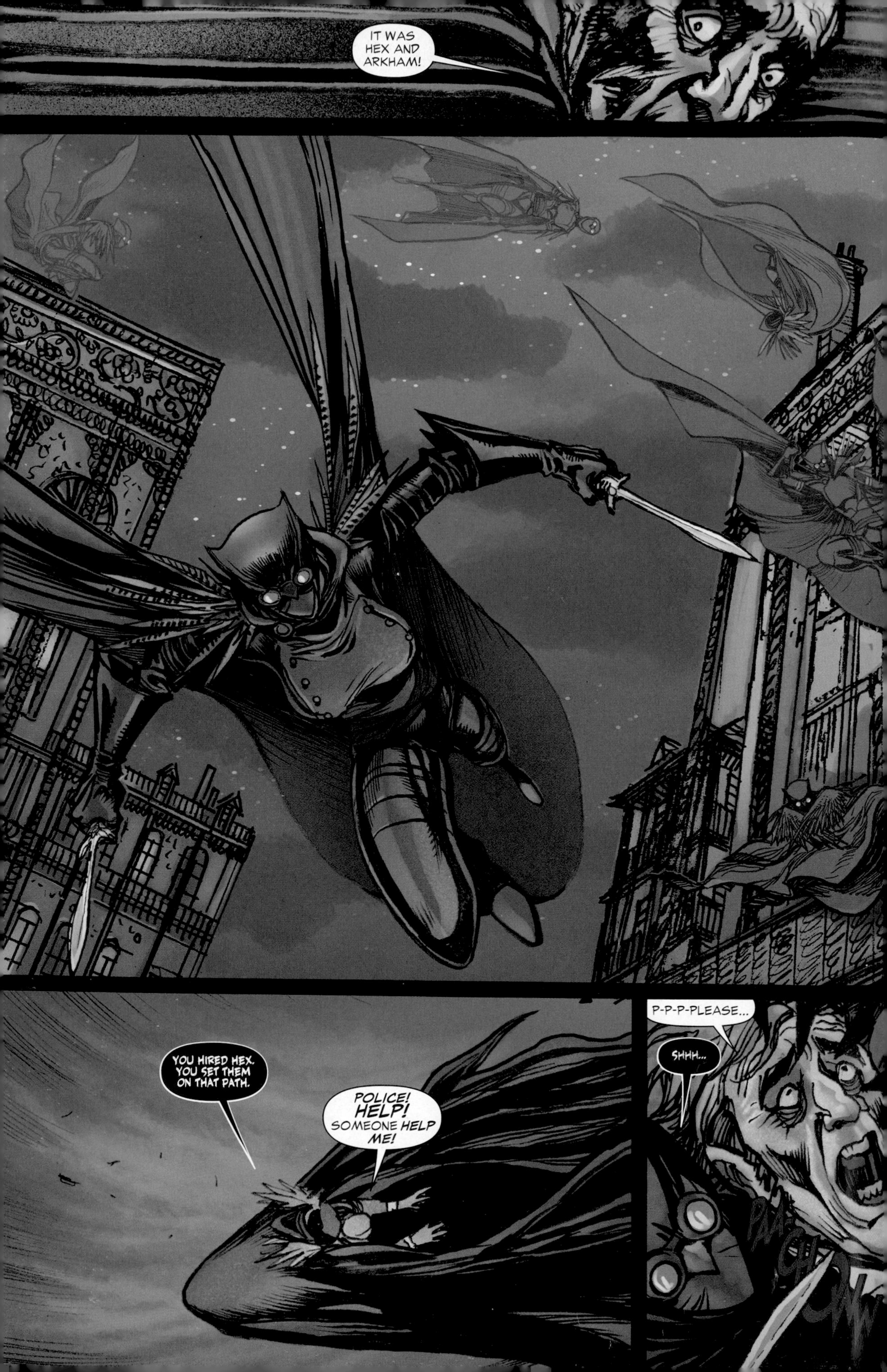
IT WAS HEX AND ARKHAM!
YOU HIRED HEX. YOU SET THEM ON THAT PATH.
POLICE! HELP! SOMEONE HELP ME!
P-P-P-PLEASE...
SHHH...
PAKCHOW

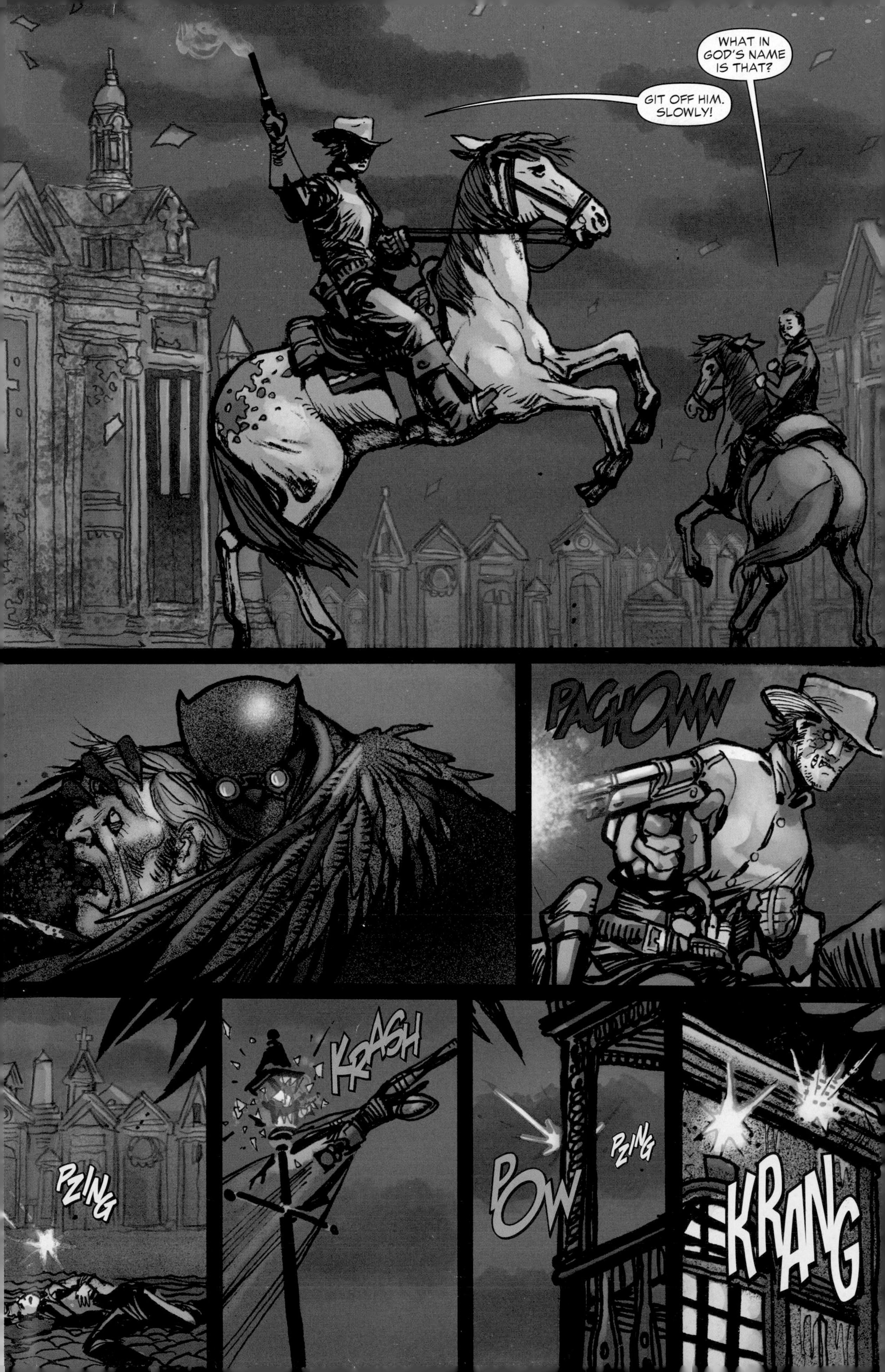
WHAT IN GOD'S NAME IS THAT?
GIT OFF HIM. SLOWLY!
PACHOWW
PZING
KRASH
POW
PZING
KRANG

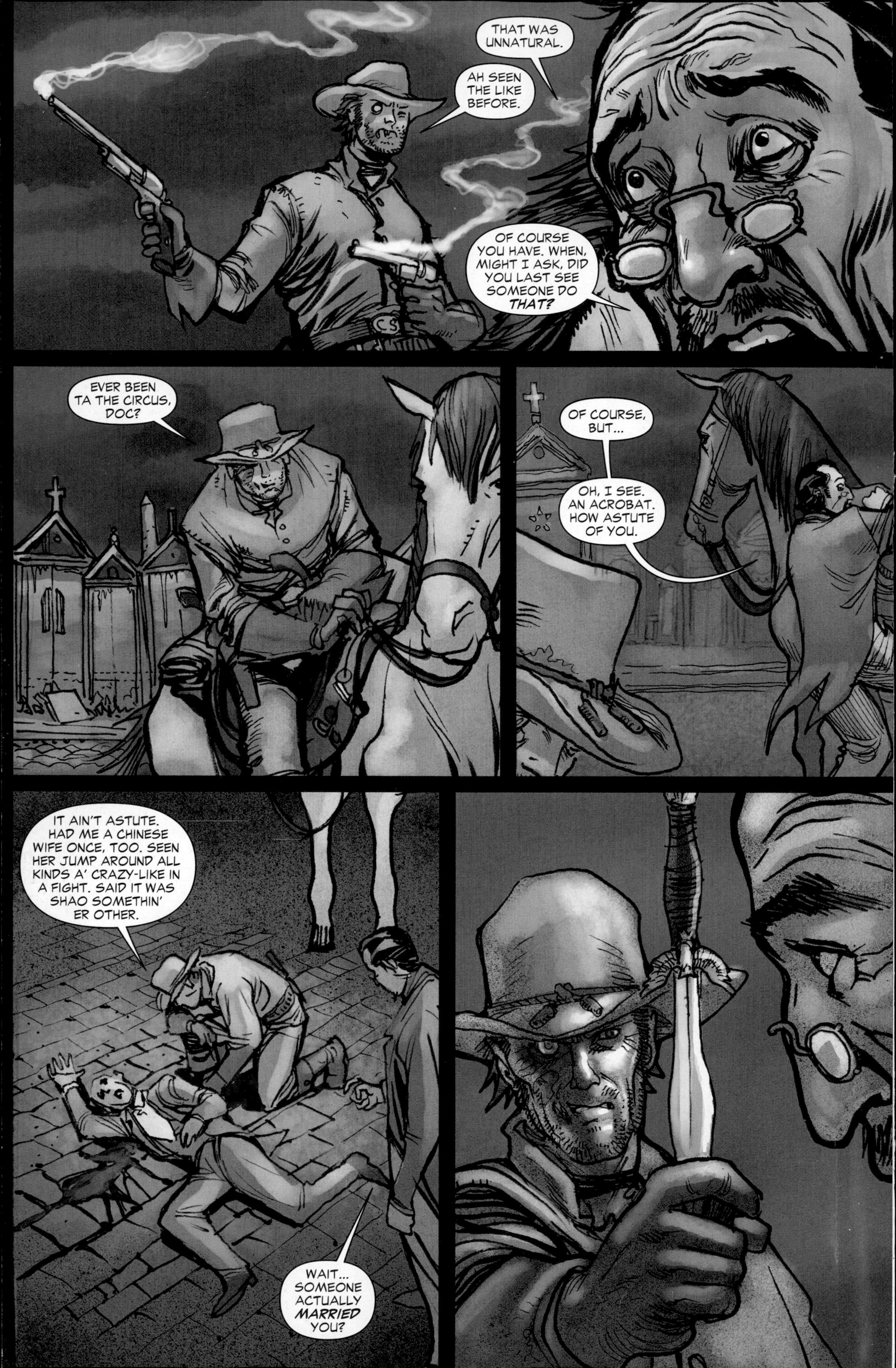
THAT WAS UNNATURAL.
AH SEEN THE LIKE BEFORE.
OF COURSE YOU HAVE. WHEN, MIGHT I ASK, DID YOU LAST SEE SOMEONE DO *THAT?*
EVER BEEN TA THE CIRCUS, DOC?
OF COURSE, BUT...
OH, I SEE. AN ACROBAT. HOW ASTUTE OF YOU.
IT AIN'T ASTUTE. HAD ME A CHINESE WIFE ONCE, TOO. SEEN HER JUMP AROUND ALL KINDS A' CRAZY-LIKE IN A FIGHT. SAID IT WAS SHAO SOMETHIN' ER OTHER.
WAIT... SOMEONE ACTUALLY *MARRIED* YOU?

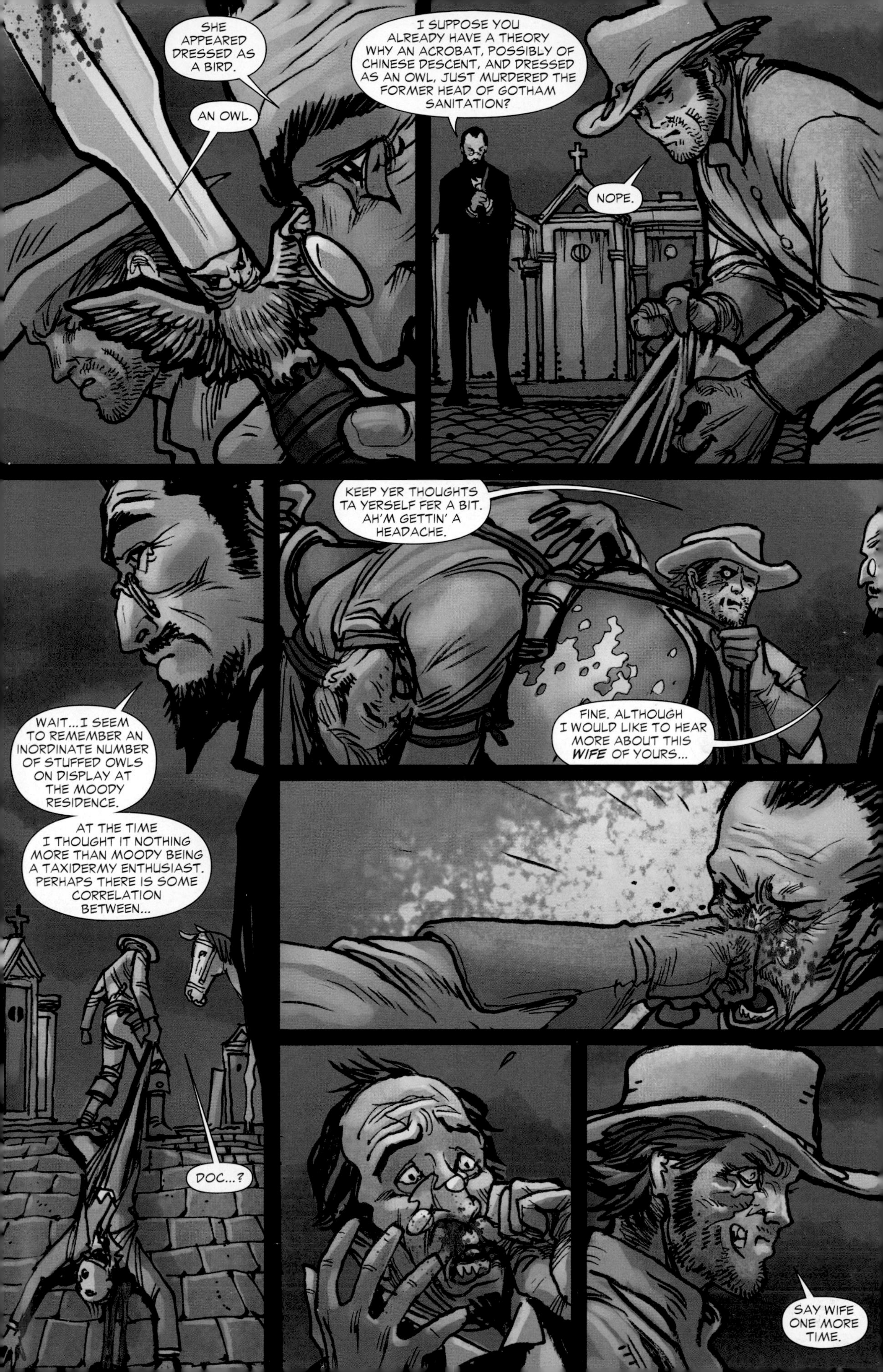
SHE APPEARED DRESSED AS A BIRD.
AN OWL.
I SUPPOSE YOU ALREADY HAVE A THEORY WHY AN ACROBAT, POSSIBLY OF CHINESE DESCENT, AND DRESSED AS AN OWL, JUST MURDERED THE FORMER HEAD OF GOTHAM SANITATION?
NOPE.
WAIT...I SEEM TO REMEMBER AN INORDINATE NUMBER OF STUFFED OWLS ON DISPLAY AT THE MOODY RESIDENCE.
AT THE TIME I THOUGHT IT NOTHING MORE THAN MOODY BEING A TAXIDERMY ENTHUSIAST. PERHAPS THERE IS SOME CORRELATION BETWEEN...
KEEP YER THOUGHTS TA YERSELF FER A BIT. AH'M GETTIN' A HEADACHE.
FINE. ALTHOUGH I WOULD LIKE TO HEAR MORE ABOUT THIS WIFE OF YOURS...
DOC...?
SAY WIFE ONE MORE TIME.

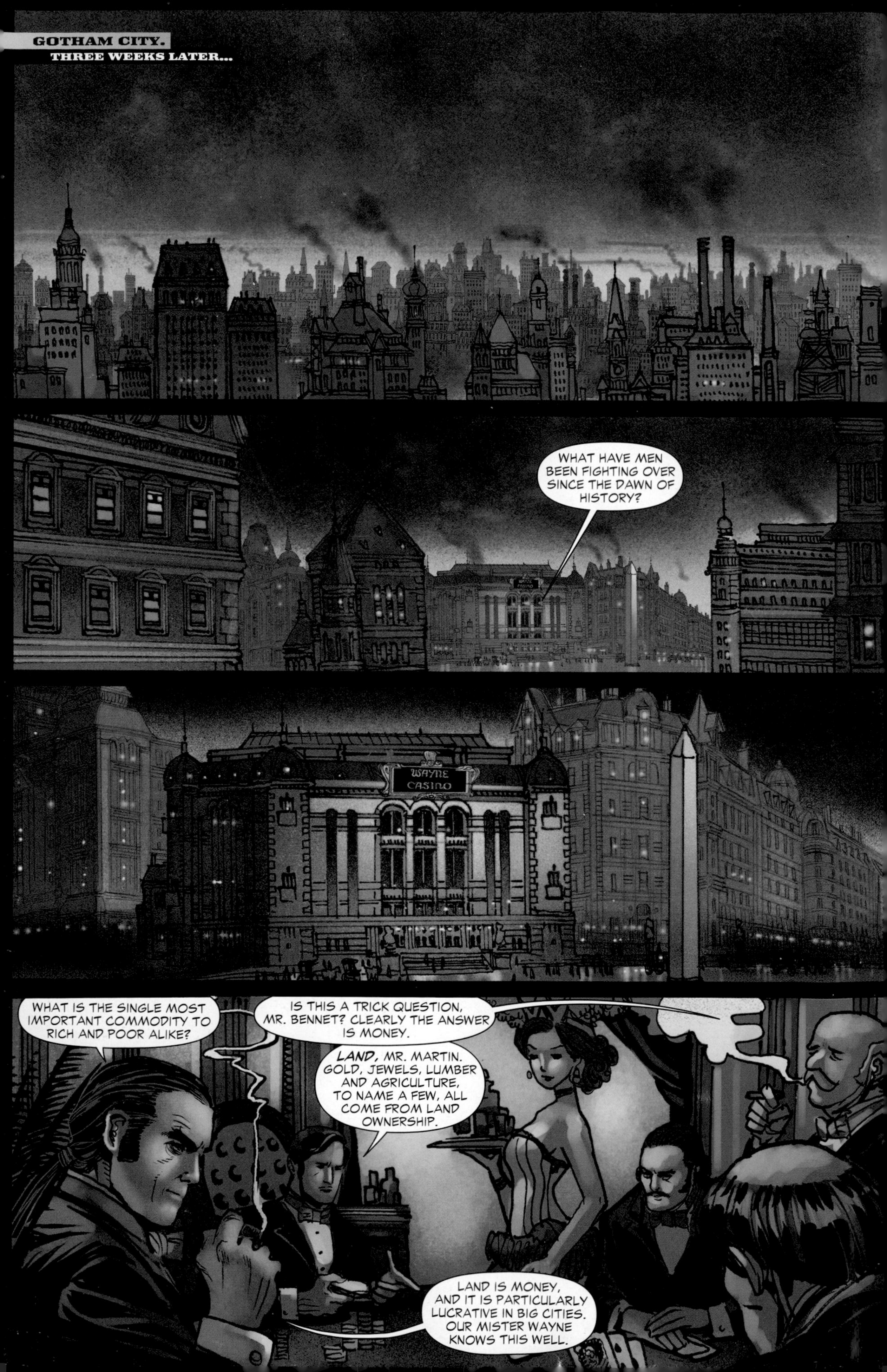
GOTHAM CITY.
THREE WEEKS LATER...
WHAT HAVE MEN BEEN FIGHTING OVER SINCE THE DAWN OF HISTORY?
WAYNE CASINO
WHAT IS THE SINGLE MOST IMPORTANT COMMODITY TO RICH AND POOR ALIKE?
IS THIS A TRICK QUESTION, MR. BENNET? CLEARLY THE ANSWER IS MONEY.
LAND, MR. MARTIN. GOLD, JEWELS, LUMBER AND AGRICULTURE, TO NAME A FEW, ALL COME FROM LAND OWNERSHIP.
LAND IS MONEY, AND IT IS PARTICULARLY LUCRATIVE IN BIG CITIES. OUR MISTER WAYNE KNOWS THIS WELL.

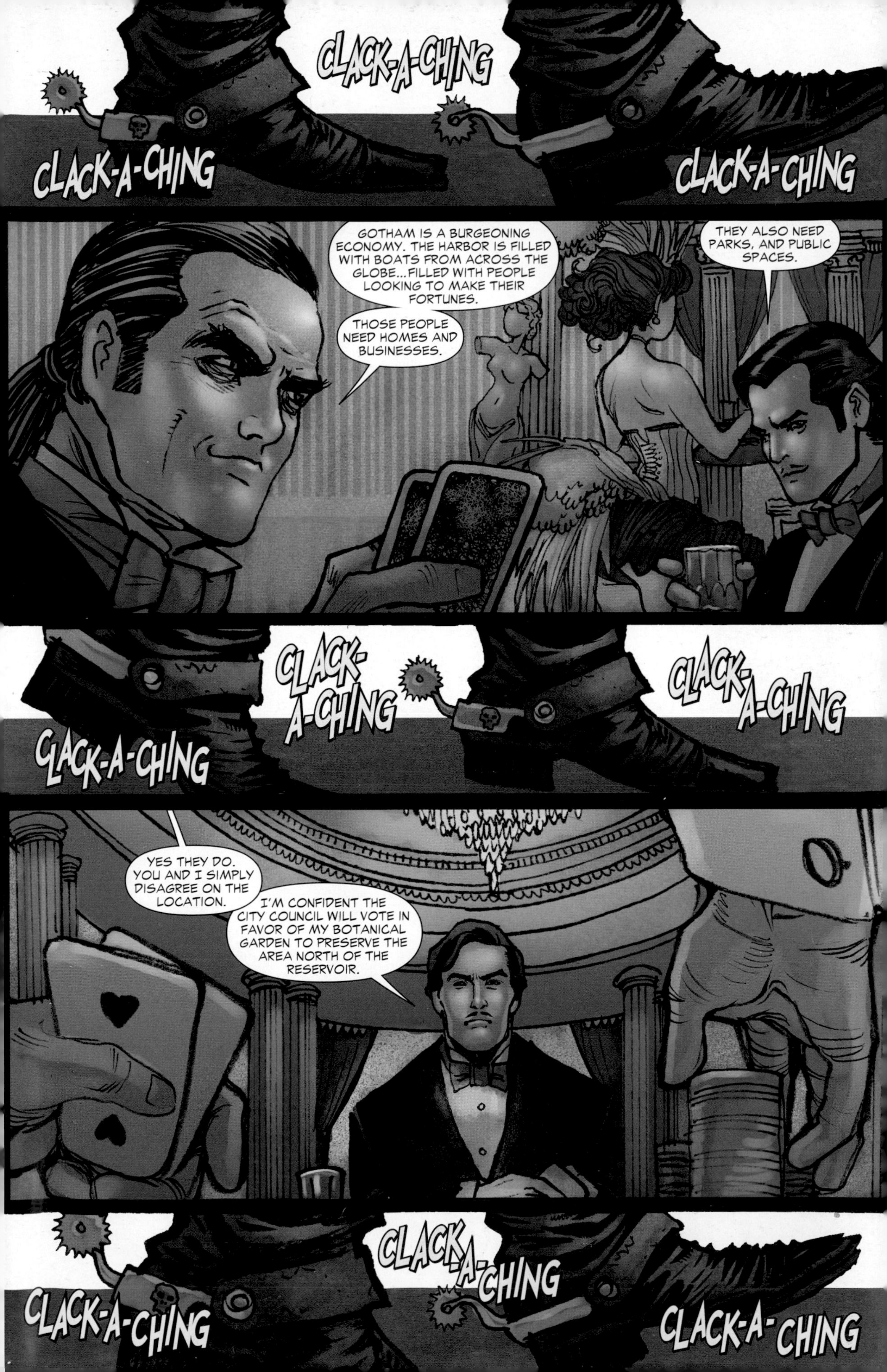
CLACK-A-CHING
CLACK-A-CHING
CLACK-A-CHING
GOTHAM IS A BURGEONING ECONOMY. THE HARBOR IS FILLED WITH BOATS FROM ACROSS THE GLOBE...FILLED WITH PEOPLE LOOKING TO MAKE THEIR FORTUNES.
THOSE PEOPLE NEED HOMES AND BUSINESSES.
THEY ALSO NEED PARKS, AND PUBLIC SPACES.
CLACK-A-CHING
CLACK-A-CHING
CLACK-A-CHING
YES THEY DO. YOU AND I SIMPLY DISAGREE ON THE LOCATION.
I'M CONFIDENT THE CITY COUNCIL WILL VOTE IN FAVOR OF MY BOTANICAL GARDEN TO PRESERVE THE AREA NORTH OF THE RESERVOIR.
CLACK-A-CHING
CLACK-A-CHING
CLACK-A-CHING

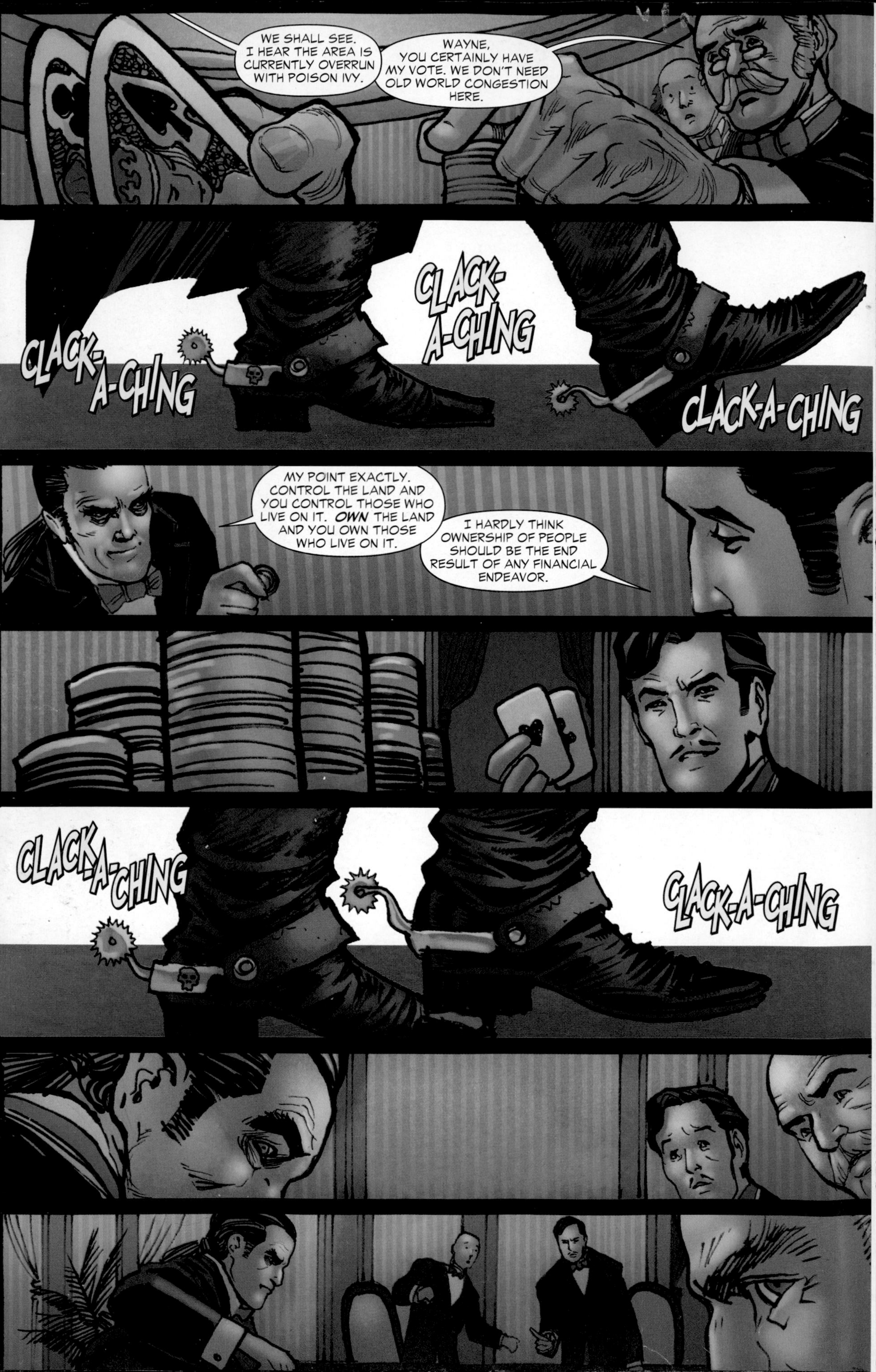

WE SHALL SEE. I HEAR THE AREA IS CURRENTLY OVERRUN WITH POISON IVY.
WAYNE, YOU CERTAINLY HAVE MY VOTE. WE DON'T NEED OLD WORLD CONGESTION HERE.
CLACK-A-CHING
CLACK-A-CHING
CLACK-A-CHING
MY POINT EXACTLY. CONTROL THE LAND AND YOU CONTROL THOSE WHO LIVE ON IT. OWN THE LAND AND YOU OWN THOSE WHO LIVE ON IT.
I HARDLY THINK OWNERSHIP OF PEOPLE SHOULD BE THE END RESULT OF ANY FINANCIAL ENDEAVOR.
CLACK-A-CHING
CLACK-A-CHING

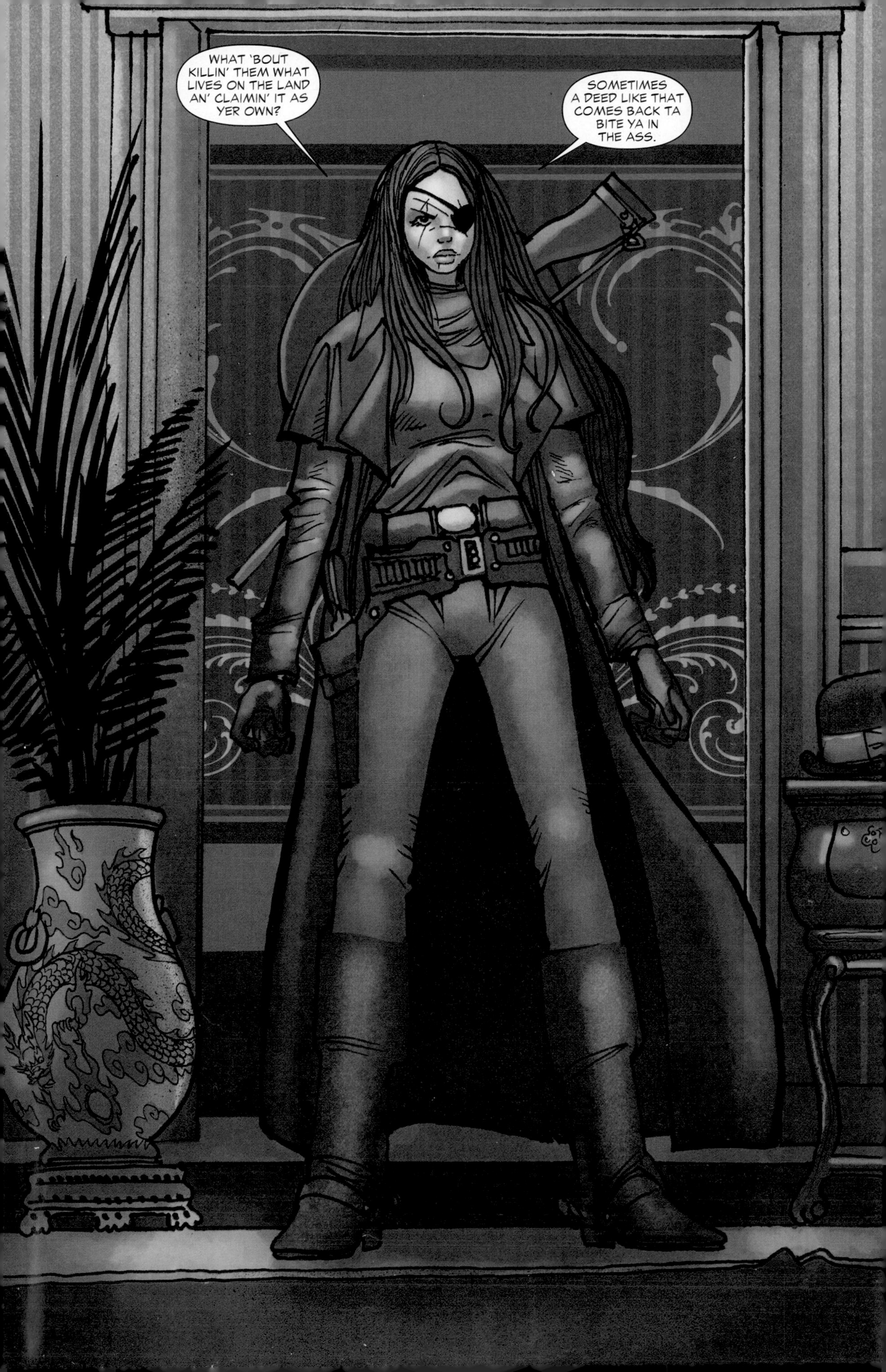
WHAT 'BOUT KILLIN' THEM WHAT LIVES ON THE LAND AN' CLAIMIN' IT AS YER OWN?
SOMETIMES A DEED LIKE THAT COMES BACK TA BITE YA IN THE ASS.

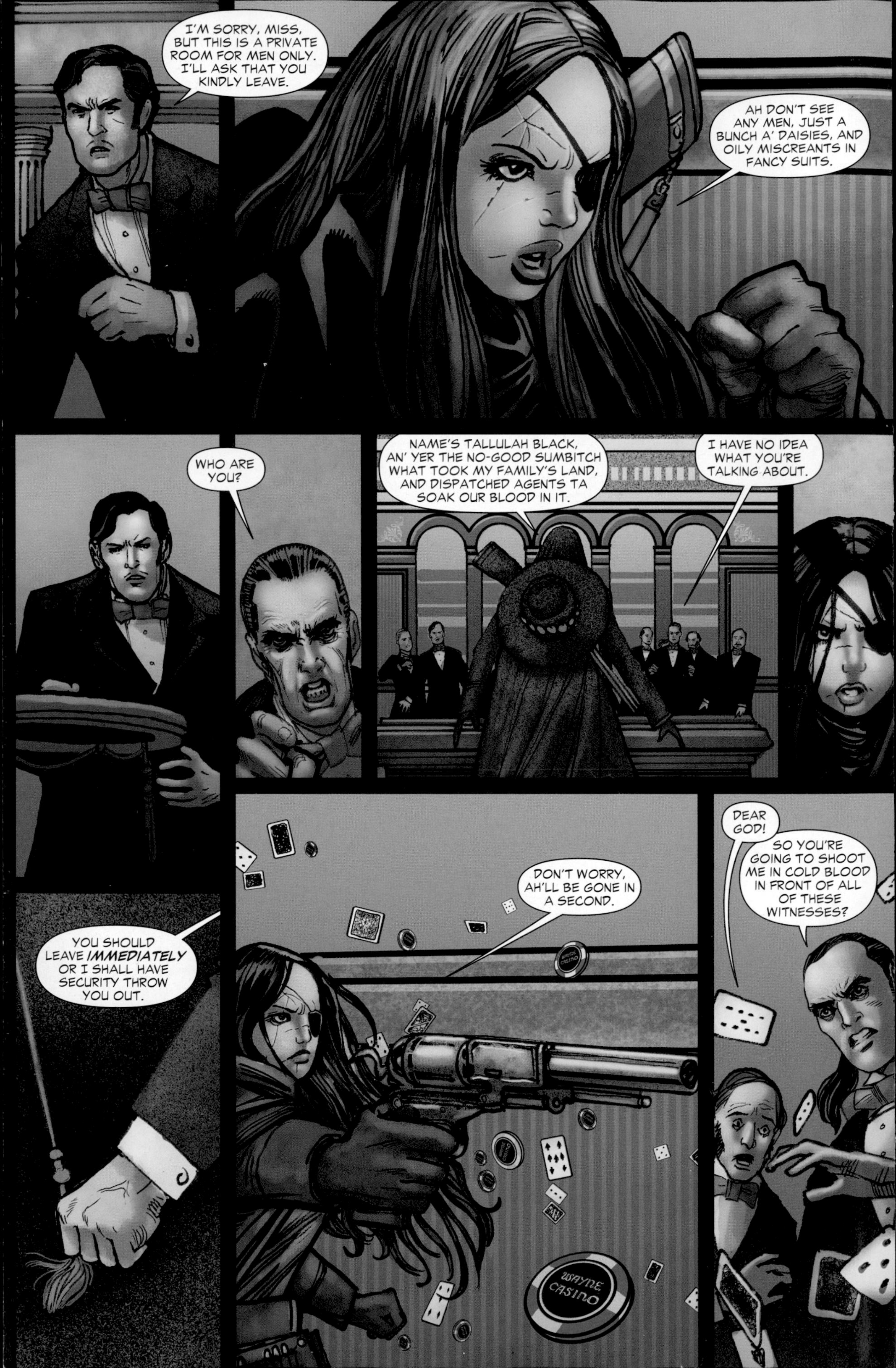
I'M SORRY, MISS, BUT THIS IS A PRIVATE ROOM FOR MEN ONLY. I'LL ASK THAT YOU KINDLY LEAVE.
AH DON'T SEE ANY MEN, JUST A BUNCH A' DAISIES, AND OILY MISCREANTS IN FANCY SUITS.
WHO ARE YOU?
NAME'S TALLULAH BLACK, AN' YER THE NO-GOOD SUMBITCH WHAT TOOK MY FAMILY'S LAND, AND DISPATCHED AGENTS TA SOAK OUR BLOOD IN IT.
I HAVE NO IDEA WHAT YOU'RE TALKING ABOUT.
YOU SHOULD LEAVE *IMMEDIATELY* OR I SHALL HAVE SECURITY THROW YOU OUT.
DON'T WORRY, AH'LL BE GONE IN A SECOND.
DEAR GOD!
SO YOU'RE GOING TO SHOOT ME IN COLD BLOOD IN FRONT OF ALL OF THESE WITNESSES?
WAYNE CASINO

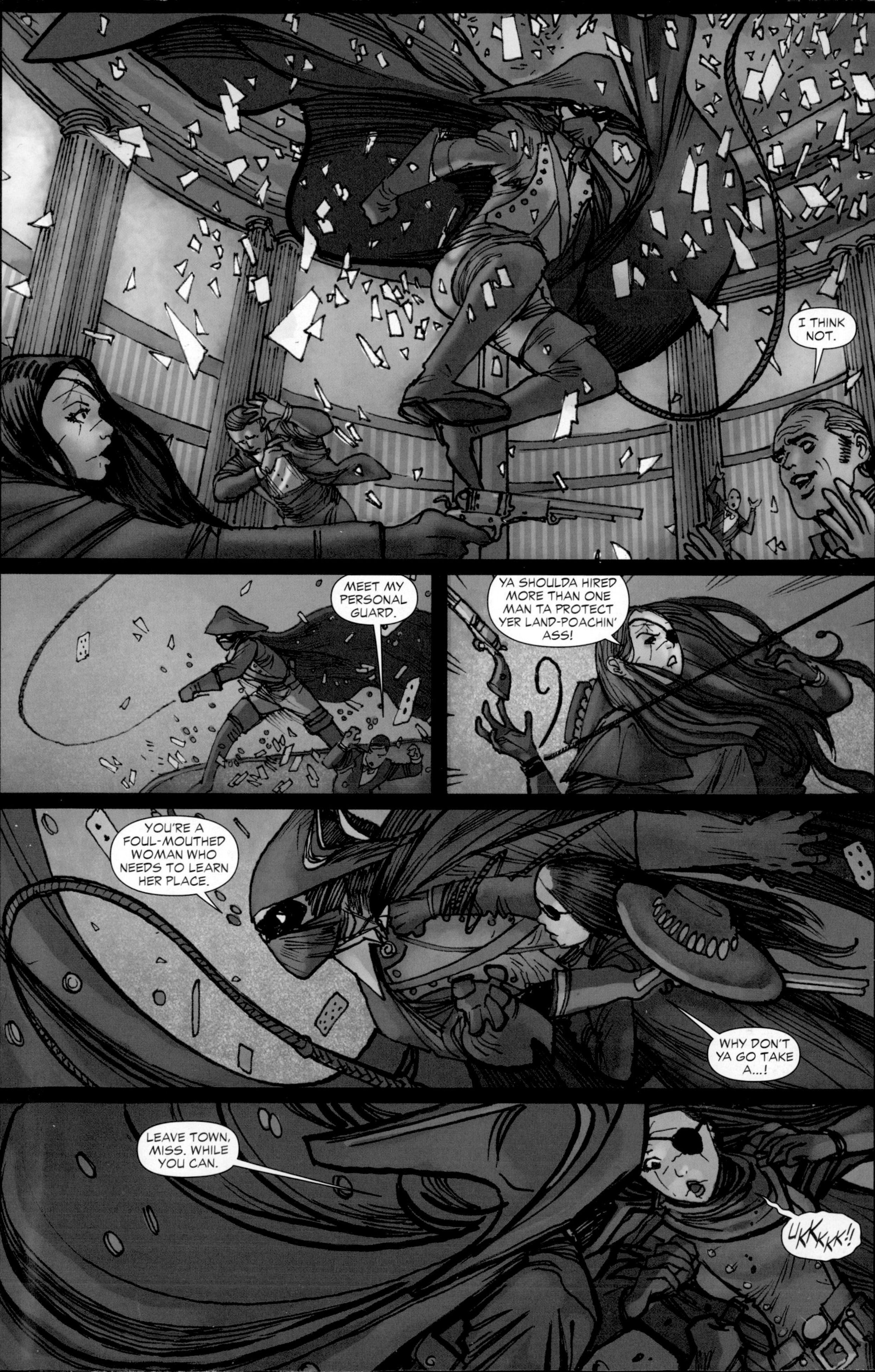
I THINK NOT.
MEET MY PERSONAL GUARD.
YA SHOULDA HIRED MORE THAN ONE MAN TA PROTECT YER LAND-POACHIN' ASS!
YOU'RE A FOUL-MOUTHED WOMAN WHO NEEDS TO LEARN HER PLACE.
WHY DON'T YA GO TAKE A...!
LEAVE TOWN, MISS. WHILE YOU CAN.
UKKKKK!!

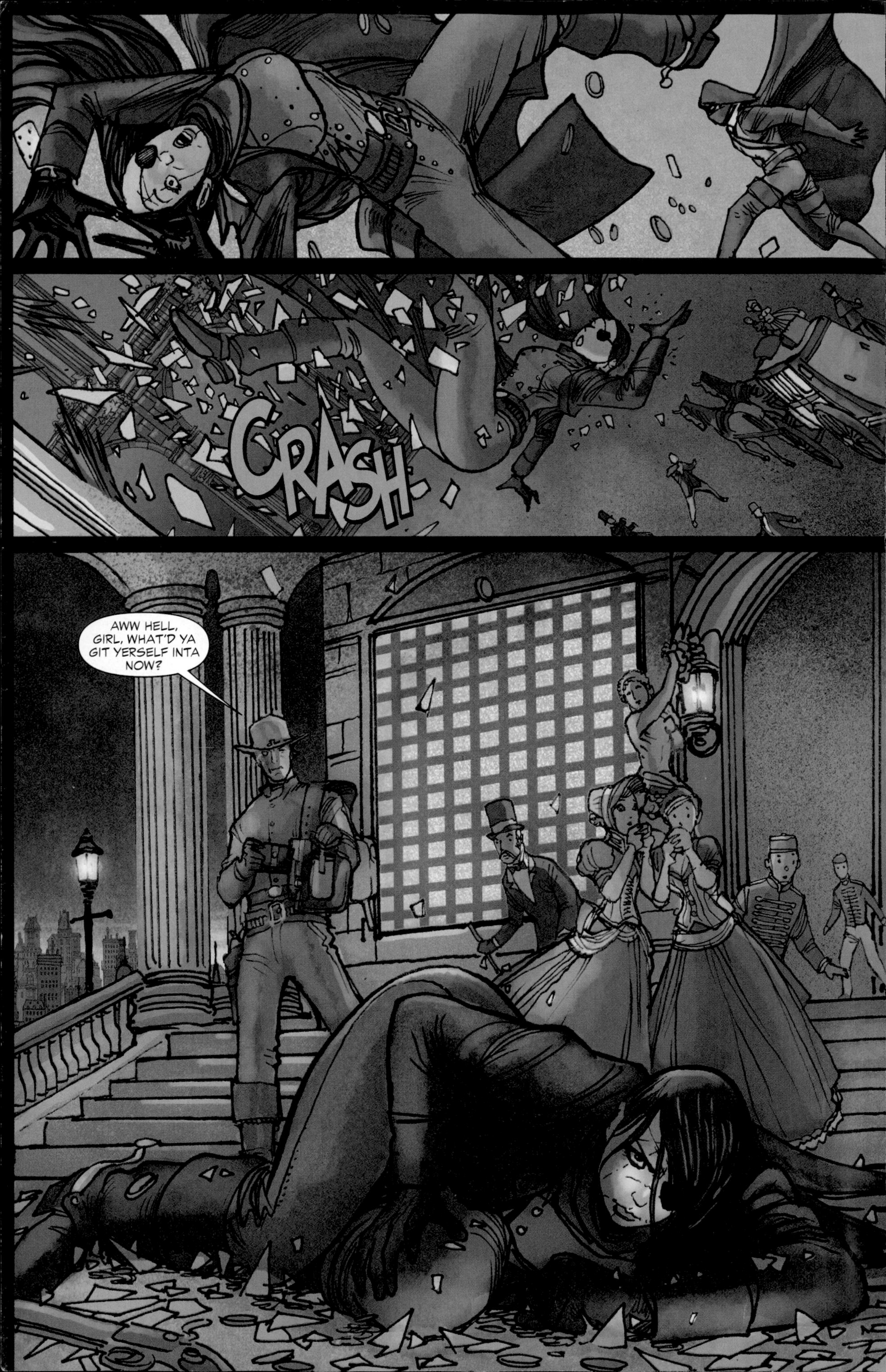
CRASH
AWW HELL, GIRL, WHAT'D YA GIT YERSELF INTA NOW?

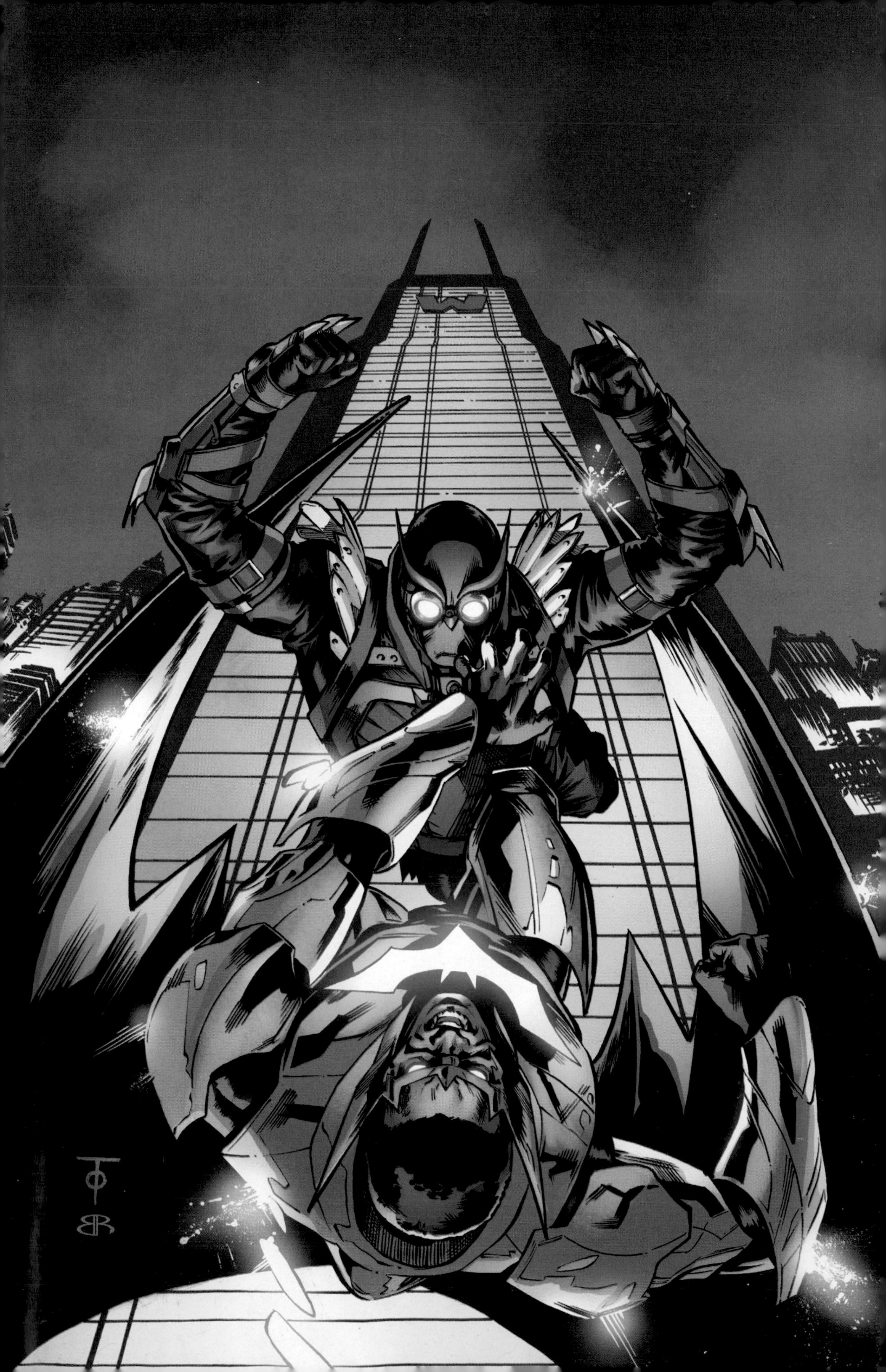

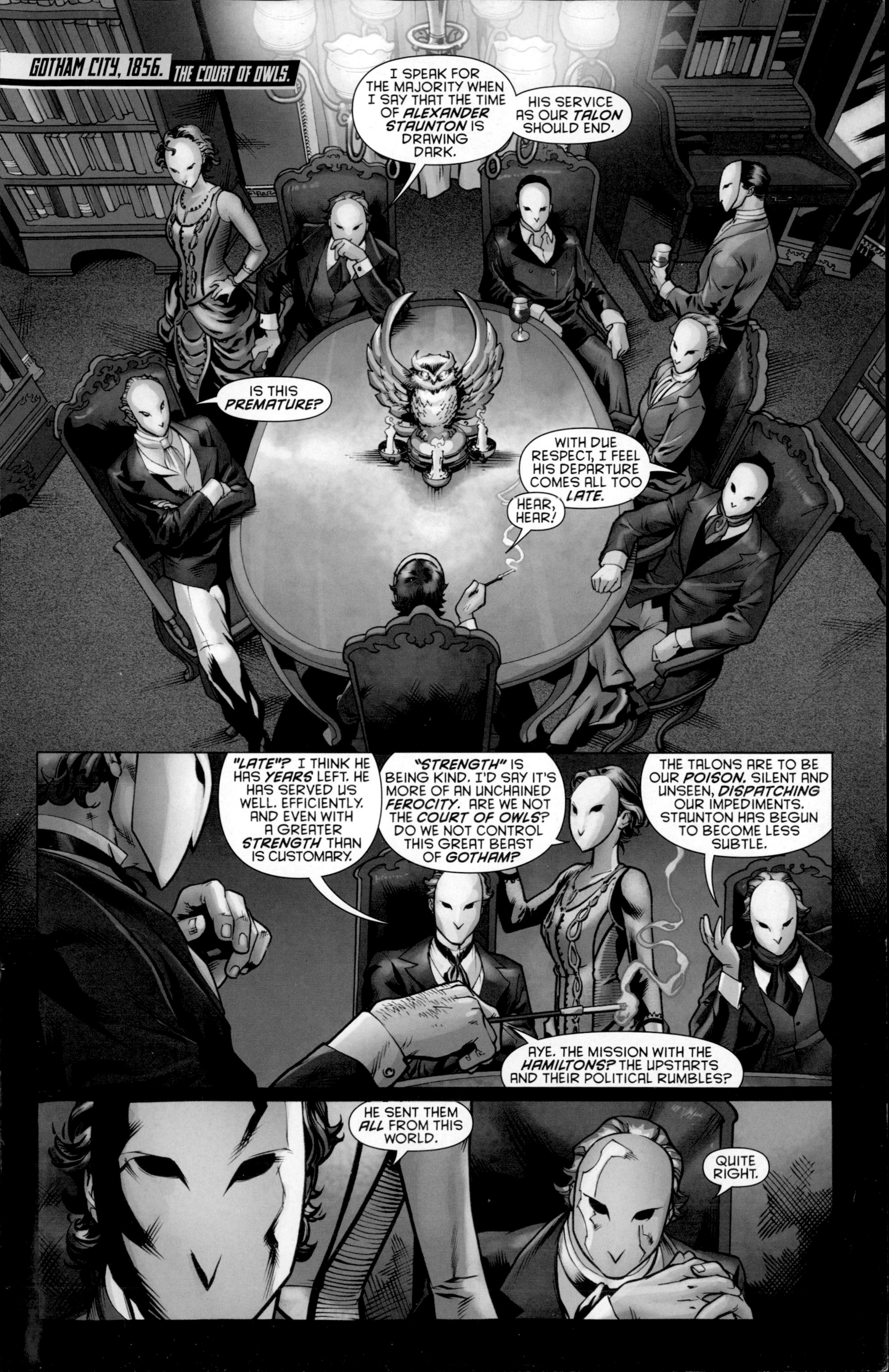
GOTHAM CITY, 1856. THE COURT OF OWLS.
I SPEAK FOR THE MAJORITY WHEN I SAY THAT THE TIME OF ALEXANDER STAUNTON IS DRAWING DARK.
HIS SERVICE AS OUR TALON SHOULD END.
IS THIS PREMATURE?
WITH DUE RESPECT, I FEEL HIS DEPARTURE COMES ALL TOO LATE.
HEAR, HEAR!
"LATE"? I THINK HE HAS YEARS LEFT. HE HAS SERVED US WELL. EFFICIENTLY. AND EVEN WITH A GREATER STRENGTH THAN IS CUSTOMARY.
"STRENGTH" IS BEING KIND. I'D SAY IT'S MORE OF AN UNCHAINED FEROCITY. ARE WE NOT THE COURT OF OWLS? DO WE NOT CONTROL THIS GREAT BEAST OF GOTHAM?
THE TALONS ARE TO BE OUR POISON. SILENT AND UNSEEN, DISPATCHING OUR IMPEDIMENTS. STAUNTON HAS BEGUN TO BECOME LESS SUBTLE.
AYE. THE MISSION WITH THE HAMILTONS? THE UPSTARTS AND THEIR POLITICAL RUMBLES?
HE SENT THEM ALL FROM THIS WORLD.
QUITE RIGHT.

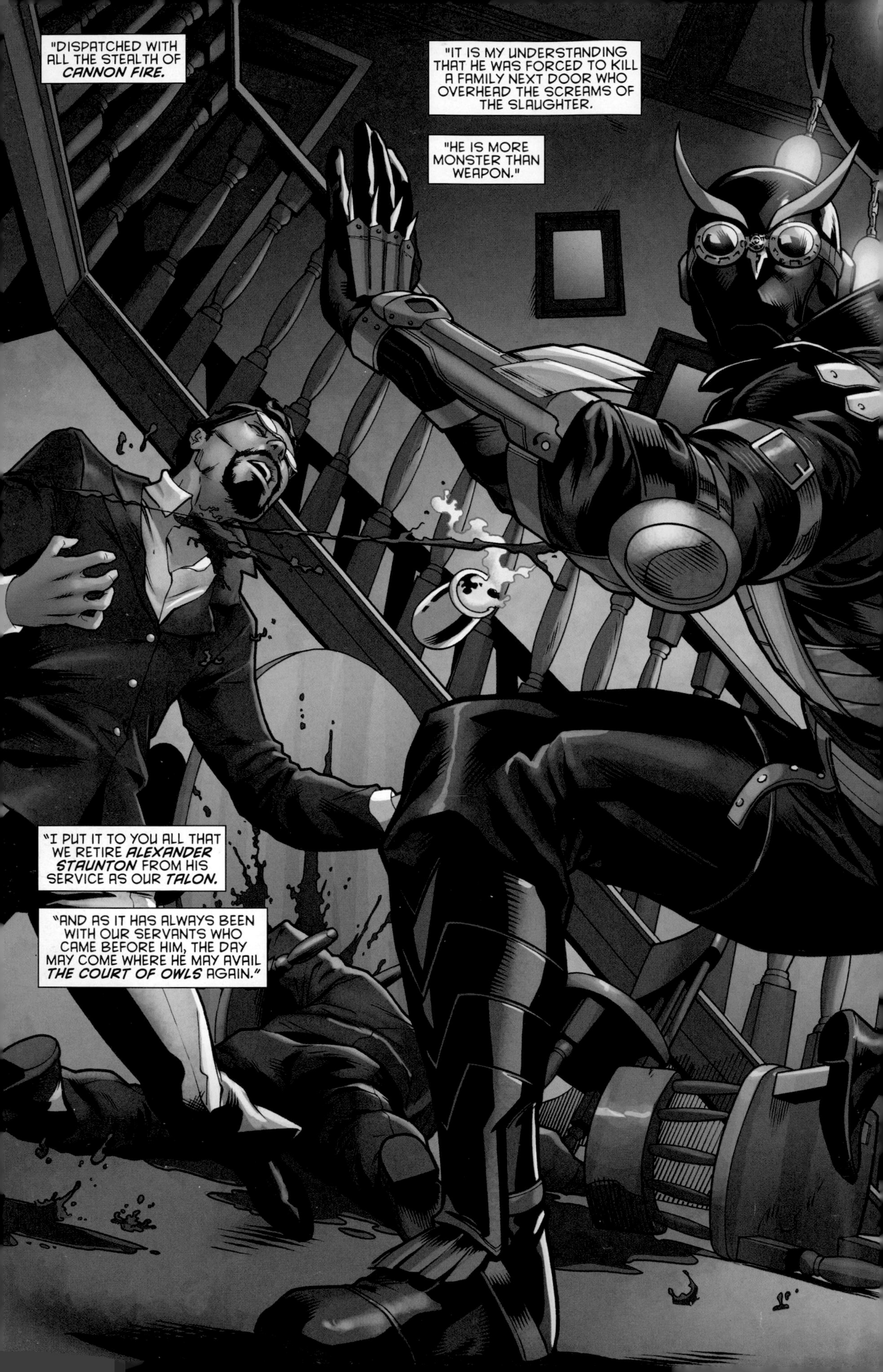
"DISPATCHED WITH ALL THE STEALTH OF *CANNON FIRE.*
"IT IS MY UNDERSTANDING THAT HE WAS FORCED TO KILL A FAMILY NEXT DOOR WHO OVERHEAD THE SCREAMS OF THE SLAUGHTER.
"HE IS MORE MONSTER THAN WEAPON."
"I PUT IT TO YOU ALL THAT WE RETIRE *ALEXANDER STAUNTON* FROM HIS SERVICE AS OUR *TALON.*
"AND AS IT HAS ALWAYS BEEN WITH OUR SERVANTS WHO CAME BEFORE HIM, THE DAY MAY COME WHERE HE MAY AVAIL *THE COURT OF OWLS* AGAIN."

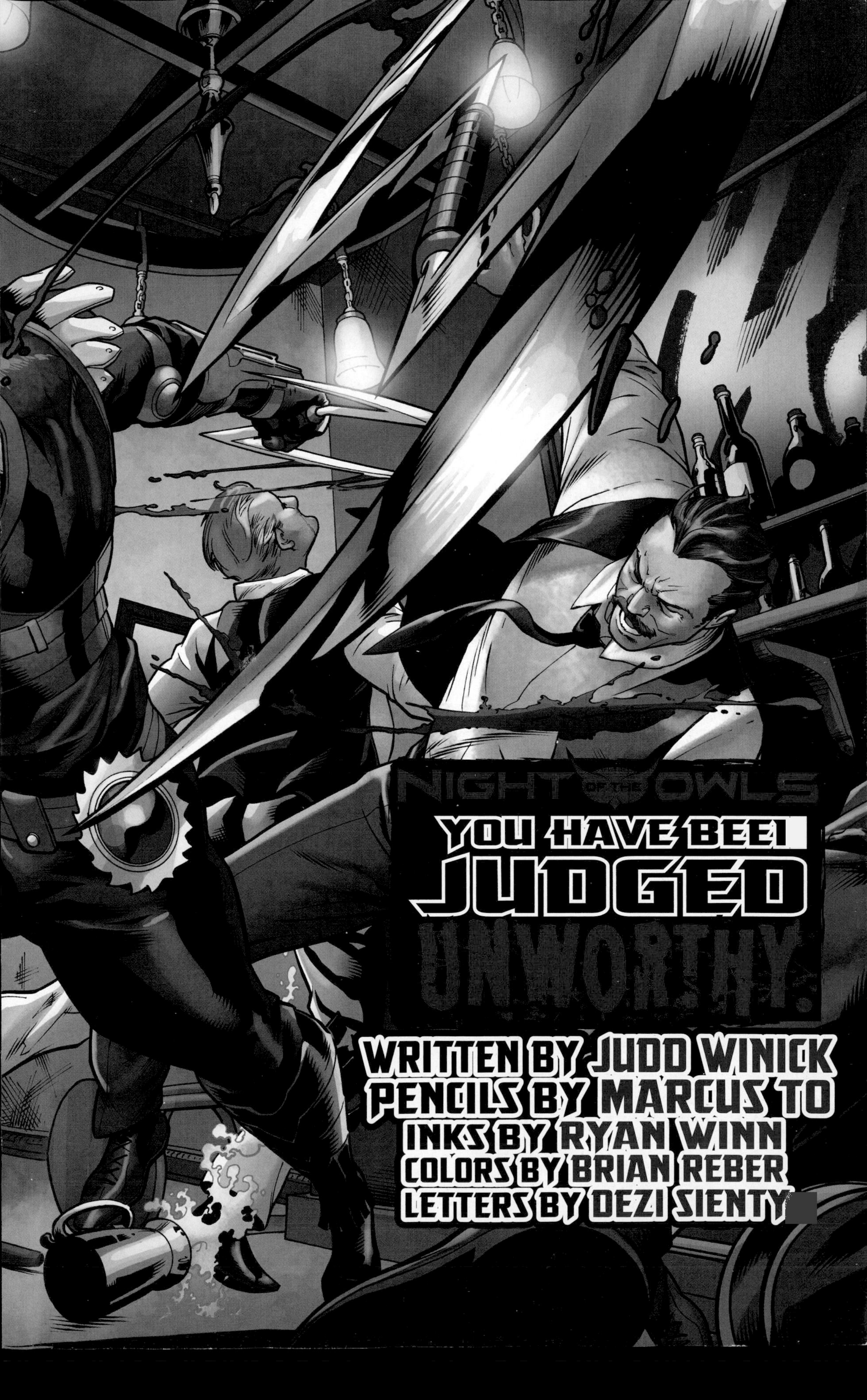
NIGHT OF THE OWLS
YOU HAVE BEE
JUDGED
UNWORTHY.
WRITTEN BY JUDD WINICK
PENCILS BY MARCUS TO
INKS BY RYAN WINN
COLORS BY BRIAN REBER
LETTERS BY DEZI SIENTY

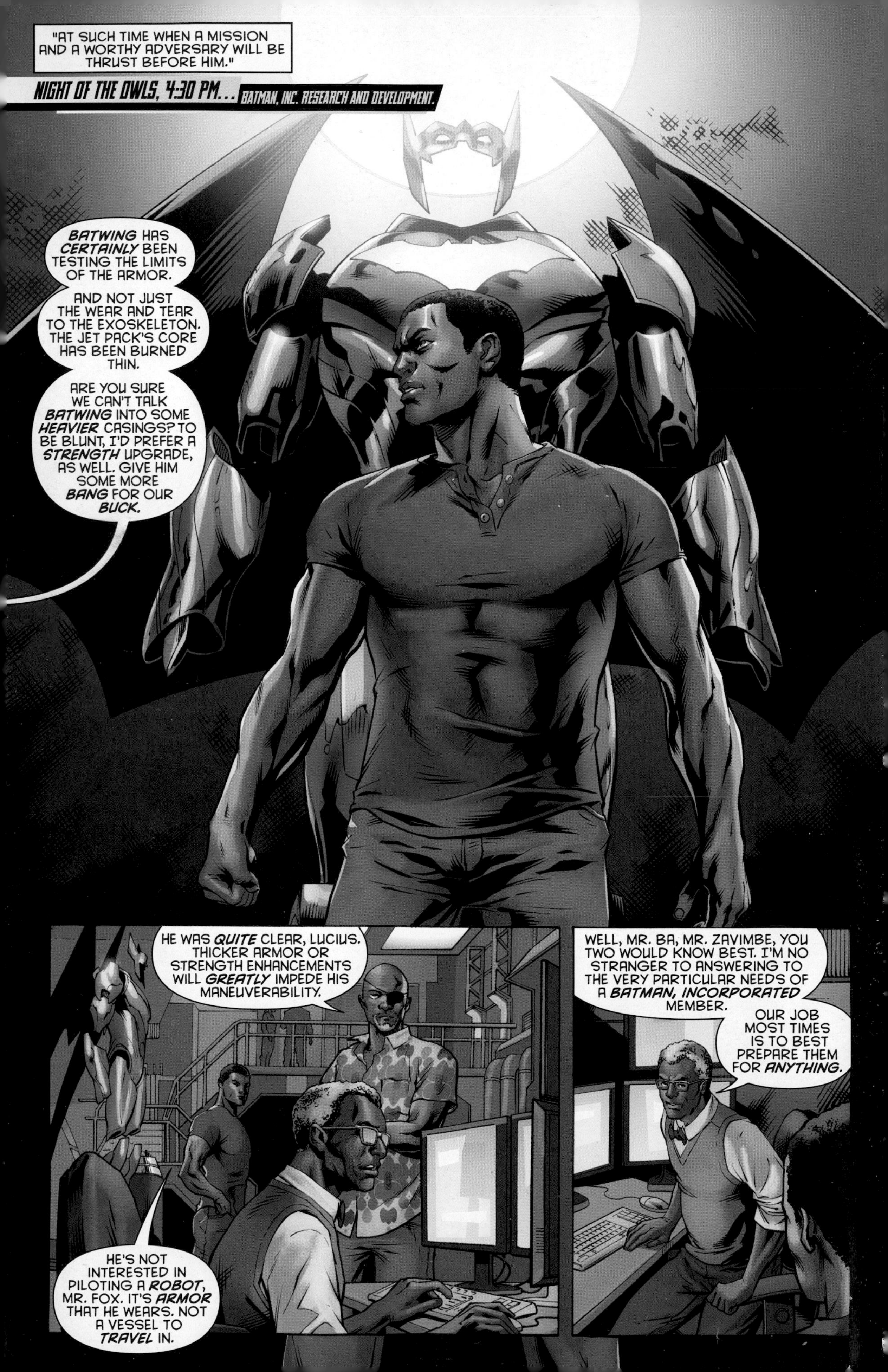
"AT SUCH TIME WHEN A MISSION AND A WORTHY ADVERSARY WILL BE THRUST BEFORE HIM."
NIGHT OF THE OWLS, 4:30 PM...
BATMAN, INC. RESEARCH AND DEVELOPMENT.
BATWING HAS CERTAINLY BEEN TESTING THE LIMITS OF THE ARMOR.
AND NOT JUST THE WEAR AND TEAR TO THE EXOSKELETON. THE JET PACK'S CORE HAS BEEN BURNED THIN.
ARE YOU SURE WE CAN'T TALK BATWING INTO SOME HEAVIER CASINGS? TO BE BLUNT, I'D PREFER A STRENGTH UPGRADE, AS WELL. GIVE HIM SOME MORE BANG FOR OUR BUCK.
HE WAS QUITE CLEAR, LUCIUS. THICKER ARMOR OR STRENGTH ENHANCEMENTS WILL GREATLY IMPEDE HIS MANEUVERABILITY.
HE'S NOT INTERESTED IN PILOTING A ROBOT, MR. FOX. IT'S ARMOR THAT HE WEARS. NOT A VESSEL TO TRAVEL IN.
WELL, MR. BA, MR. ZAVIMBE, YOU TWO WOULD KNOW BEST. I'M NO STRANGER TO ANSWERING TO THE VERY PARTICULAR NEEDS OF A BATMAN, INCORPORATED MEMBER.
OUR JOB MOST TIMES IS TO BEST PREPARE THEM FOR ANYTHING.

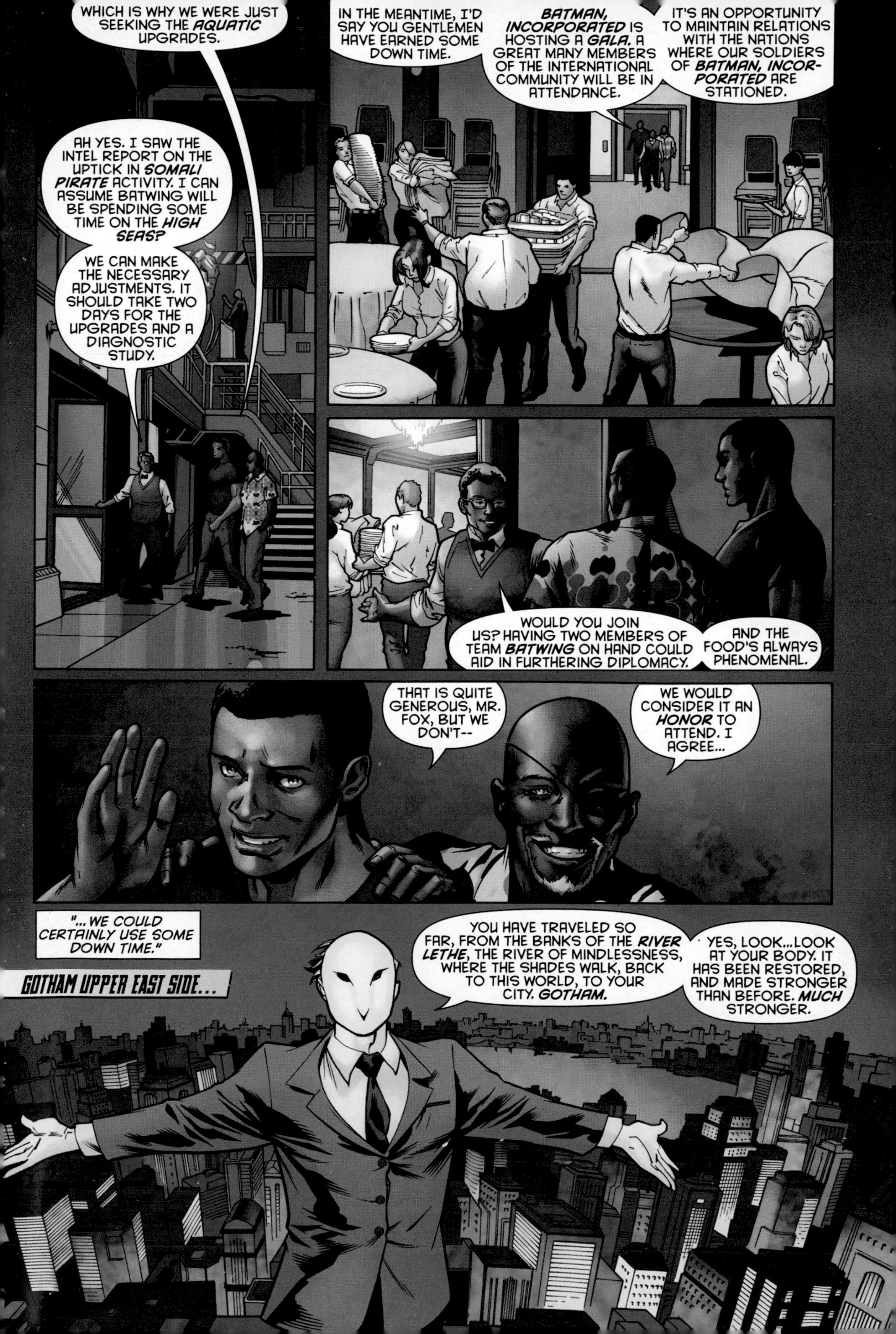
WHICH IS WHY WE WERE JUST SEEKING THE AQUATIC UPGRADES.
AH YES. I SAW THE INTEL REPORT ON THE UPTICK IN SOMALI PIRATE ACTIVITY. I CAN ASSUME BATWING WILL BE SPENDING SOME TIME ON THE HIGH SEAS?
WE CAN MAKE THE NECESSARY ADJUSTMENTS. IT SHOULD TAKE TWO DAYS FOR THE UPGRADES AND A DIAGNOSTIC STUDY.
IN THE MEANTIME, I'D SAY YOU GENTLEMEN HAVE EARNED SOME DOWN TIME.
BATMAN, INCORPORATED IS HOSTING A GALA. A GREAT MANY MEMBERS OF THE INTERNATIONAL COMMUNITY WILL BE IN ATTENDANCE.
IT'S AN OPPORTUNITY TO MAINTAIN RELATIONS WITH THE NATIONS WHERE OUR SOLDIERS OF BATMAN, INCORPORATED ARE STATIONED.
WOULD YOU JOIN US? HAVING TWO MEMBERS OF TEAM BATWING ON HAND COULD AID IN FURTHERING DIPLOMACY.
AND THE FOOD'S ALWAYS PHENOMENAL.
THAT IS QUITE GENEROUS, MR. FOX, BUT WE DON'T--
WE WOULD CONSIDER IT AN HONOR TO ATTEND. I AGREE...
"...WE COULD CERTAINLY USE SOME DOWN TIME."
GOTHAM UPPER EAST SIDE...
YOU HAVE TRAVELED SO FAR, FROM THE BANKS OF THE RIVER LETHE, THE RIVER OF MINDLESSNESS, WHERE THE SHADES WALK, BACK TO THIS WORLD, TO YOUR CITY. GOTHAM.
YES, LOOK...LOOK AT YOUR BODY. IT HAS BEEN RESTORED, AND MADE STRONGER THAN BEFORE. MUCH STRONGER.

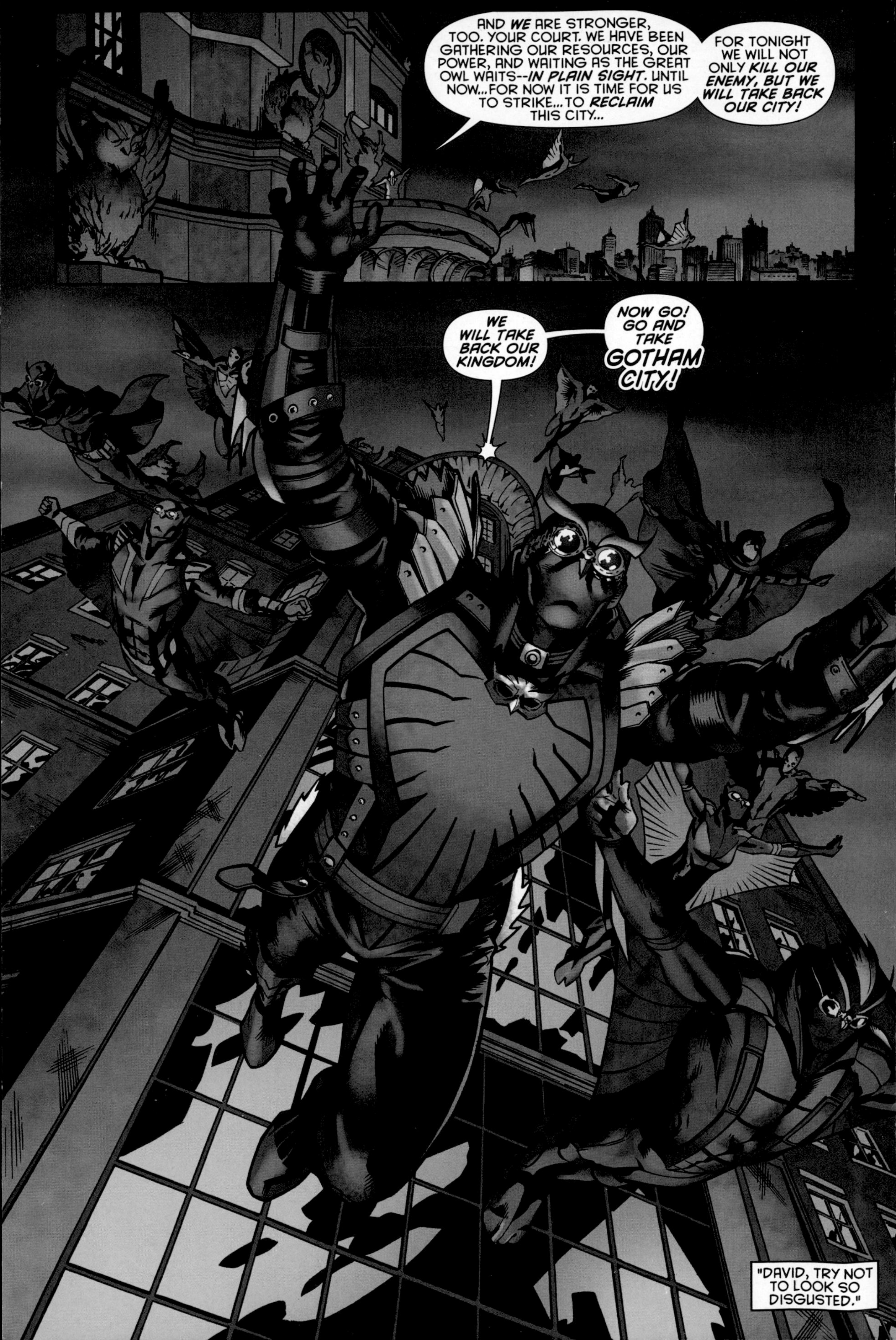
AND *WE* ARE STRONGER, TOO. YOUR COURT. WE HAVE BEEN GATHERING OUR RESOURCES, OUR POWER, AND WAITING AS THE GREAT OWL WAITS--*IN PLAIN SIGHT*. UNTIL NOW...FOR NOW IT IS TIME FOR US TO STRIKE...TO *RECLAIM* THIS CITY...
FOR TONIGHT WE WILL NOT ONLY *KILL OUR ENEMY, BUT WE WILL TAKE BACK OUR CITY!*
WE WILL TAKE BACK OUR KINGDOM!
NOW GO! GO AND TAKE GOTHAM CITY!
"DAVID, TRY NOT TO LOOK SO DISGUSTED."

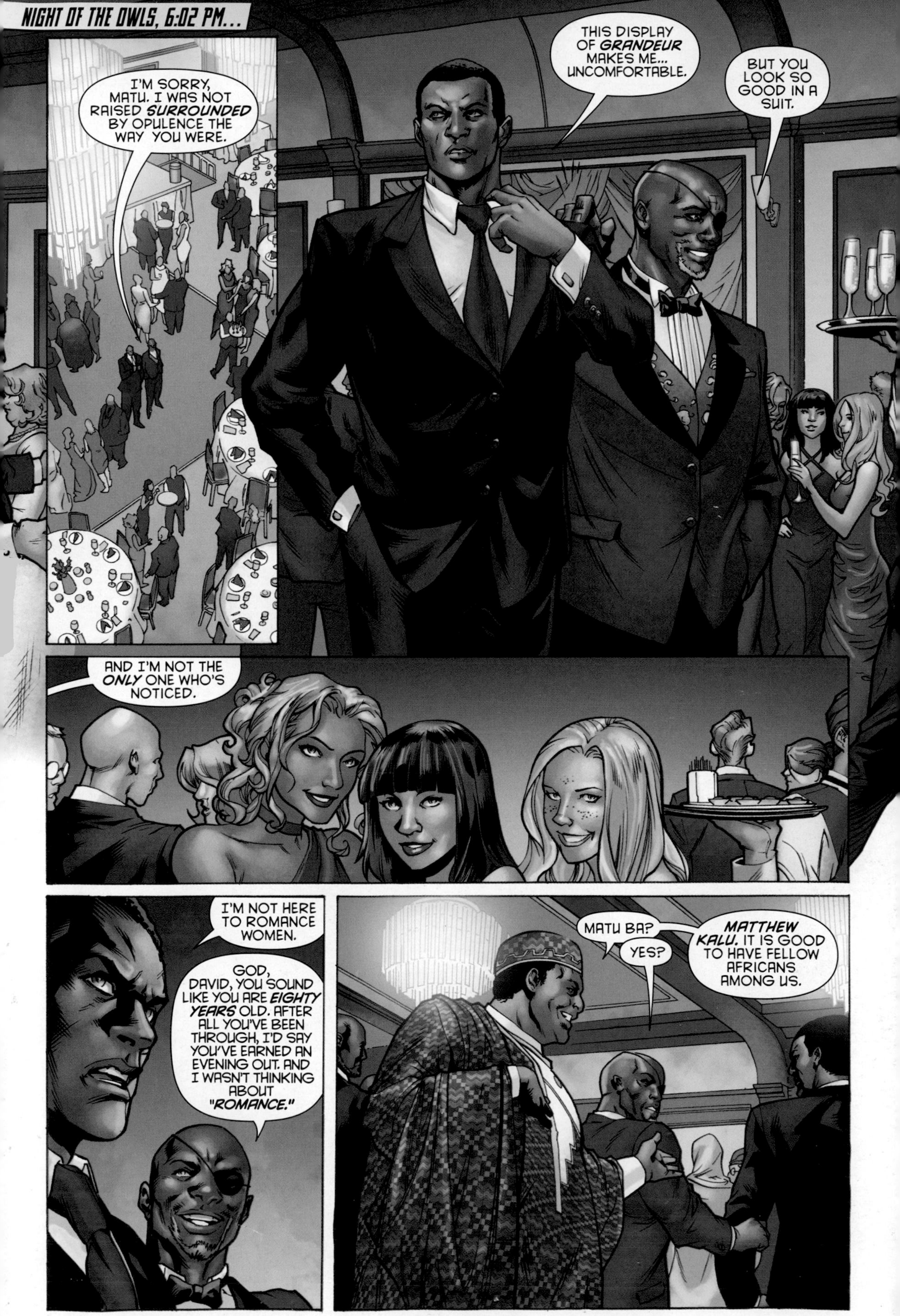
NIGHT OF THE OWLS, 6:02 PM...
I'M SORRY, MATU. I WAS NOT RAISED SURROUNDED BY OPULENCE THE WAY YOU WERE.
THIS DISPLAY OF GRANDEUR MAKES ME... UNCOMFORTABLE.
BUT YOU LOOK SO GOOD IN A SUIT.
AND I'M NOT THE ONLY ONE WHO'S NOTICED.
I'M NOT HERE TO ROMANCE WOMEN.
GOD, DAVID, YOU SOUND LIKE YOU ARE EIGHTY YEARS OLD. AFTER ALL YOU'VE BEEN THROUGH, I'D SAY YOU'VE EARNED AN EVENING OUT. AND I WASN'T THINKING ABOUT "ROMANCE."
MATU BA?
YES?
MATTHEW KALU. IT IS GOOD TO HAVE FELLOW AFRICANS AMONG US.

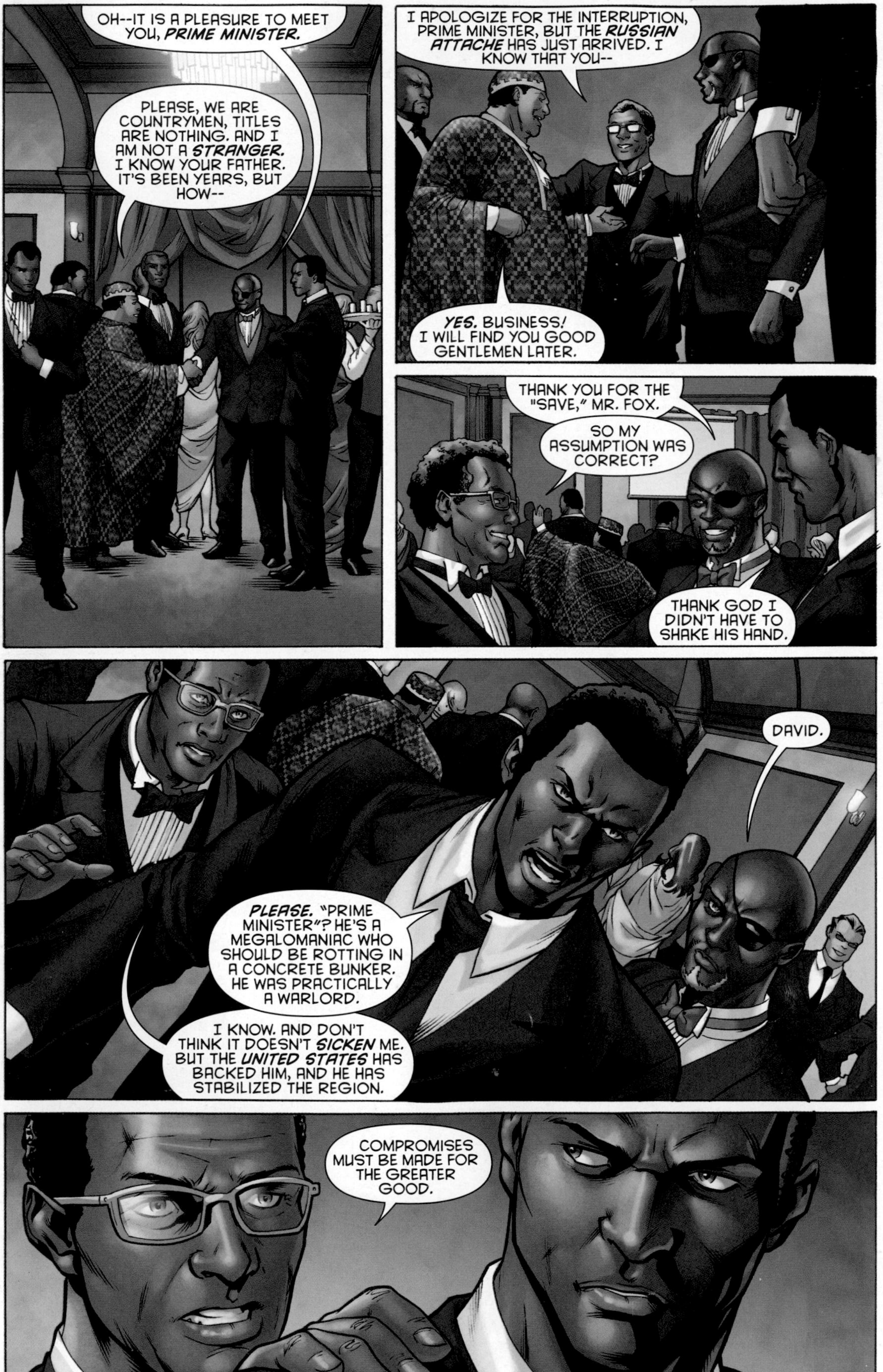
OH--IT IS A PLEASURE TO MEET YOU, PRIME MINISTER.
PLEASE, WE ARE COUNTRYMEN, TITLES ARE NOTHING. AND I AM NOT A STRANGER. I KNOW YOUR FATHER. IT'S BEEN YEARS, BUT HOW--
I APOLOGIZE FOR THE INTERRUPTION, PRIME MINISTER, BUT THE RUSSIAN ATTACHE HAS JUST ARRIVED. I KNOW THAT YOU--
YES. BUSINESS! I WILL FIND YOU GOOD GENTLEMEN LATER.
THANK YOU FOR THE "SAVE," MR. FOX.
SO MY ASSUMPTION WAS CORRECT?
THANK GOD I DIDN'T HAVE TO SHAKE HIS HAND.
DAVID.
PLEASE. "PRIME MINISTER"? HE'S A MEGALOMANIAC WHO SHOULD BE ROTTING IN A CONCRETE BUNKER. HE WAS PRACTICALLY A WARLORD.
I KNOW. AND DON'T THINK IT DOESN'T SICKEN ME. BUT THE UNITED STATES HAS BACKED HIM, AND HE HAS STABILIZED THE REGION.
COMPROMISES MUST BE MADE FOR THE GREATER GOOD.

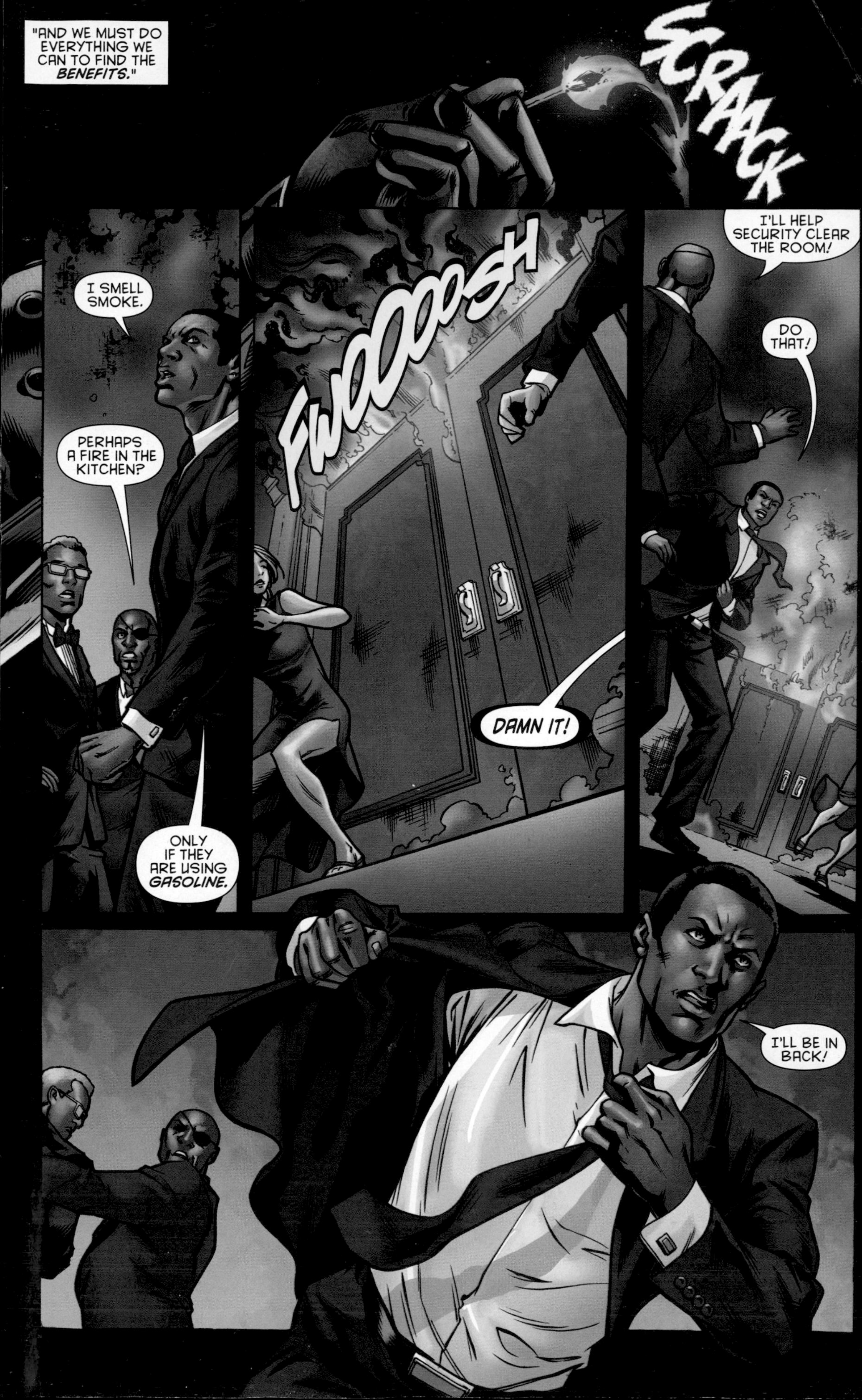
"AND WE MUST DO EVERYTHING WE CAN TO FIND THE *BENEFITS.*"
SCRAACK
I SMELL SMOKE.
PERHAPS A FIRE IN THE KITCHEN?
ONLY IF THEY ARE USING *GASOLINE.*
FWOOOOSH
DAMN IT!
I'LL HELP SECURITY CLEAR THE ROOM!
DO THAT!
I'LL BE IN BACK!

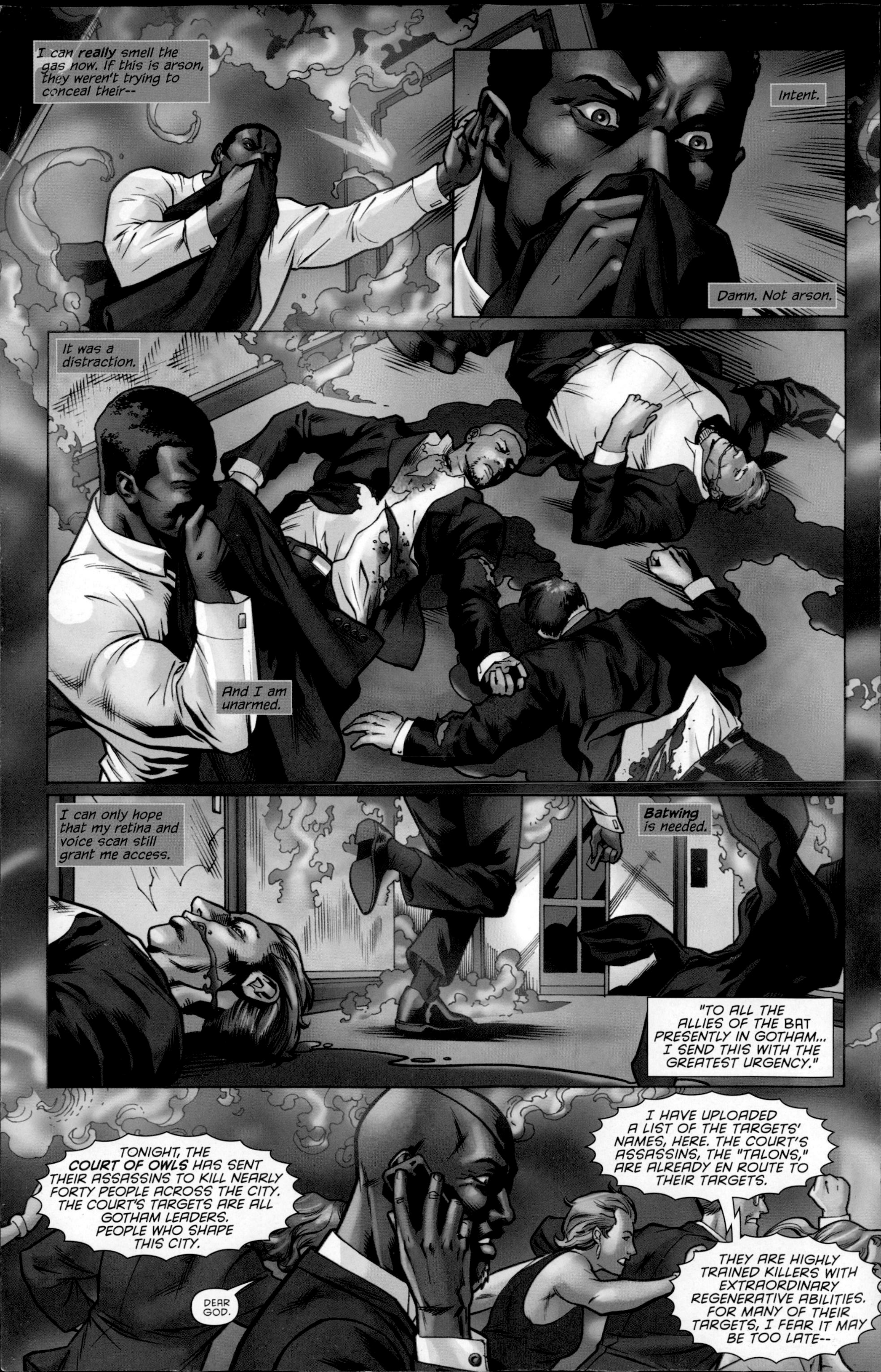

I can really smell the gas now. If this is arson, they weren't trying to conceal their--
Intent.
Damn. Not arson.
It was a distraction.
And I am unarmed.
I can only hope that my retina and voice scan still grant me access.
Batwing is needed.
"TO ALL THE ALLIES OF THE BAT PRESENTLY IN GOTHAM... I SEND THIS WITH THE GREATEST URGENCY."
TONIGHT, THE COURT OF OWLS HAS SENT THEIR ASSASSINS TO KILL NEARLY FORTY PEOPLE ACROSS THE CITY. THE COURT'S TARGETS ARE ALL GOTHAM LEADERS. PEOPLE WHO SHAPE THIS CITY.
I HAVE UPLOADED A LIST OF THE TARGETS' NAMES, HERE. THE COURT'S ASSASSINS, THE "TALONS," ARE ALREADY EN ROUTE TO THEIR TARGETS.
DEAR GOD.
THEY ARE HIGHLY TRAINED KILLERS WITH EXTRAORDINARY REGENERATIVE ABILITIES. FOR MANY OF THEIR TARGETS, I FEAR IT MAY BE TOO LATE--

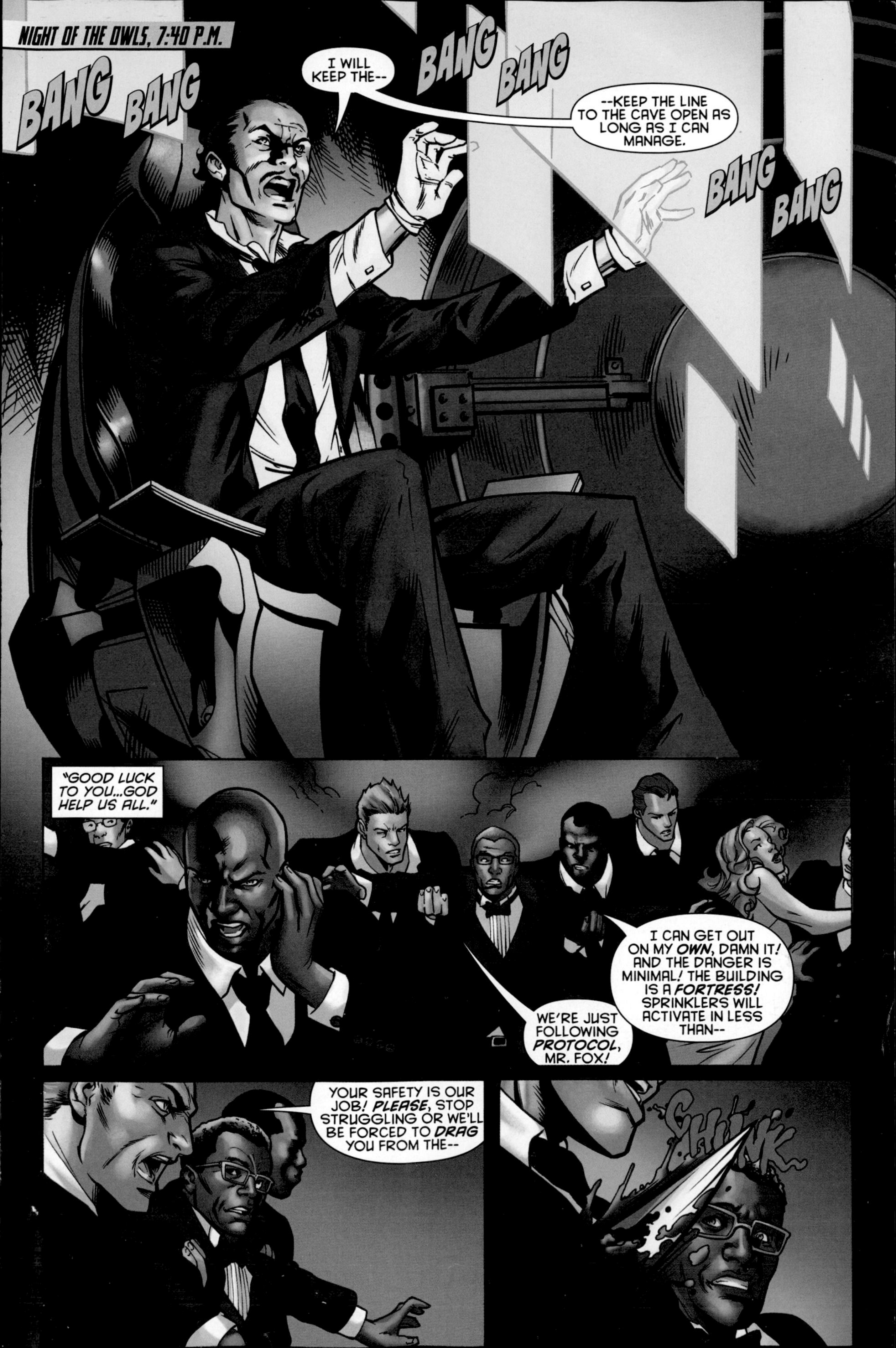
NIGHT OF THE OWLS, 7:40 P.M.
BANG BANG
I WILL KEEP THE--
BANG BANG
--KEEP THE LINE TO THE CAVE OPEN AS LONG AS I CAN MANAGE.
BANG BANG
"GOOD LUCK TO YOU...GOD HELP US ALL."
I CAN GET OUT ON MY OWN, DAMN IT! AND THE DANGER IS MINIMAL! THE BUILDING IS A FORTRESS! SPRINKLERS WILL ACTIVATE IN LESS THAN--
WE'RE JUST FOLLOWING PROTOCOL, MR. FOX!
YOUR SAFETY IS OUR JOB! PLEASE, STOP STRUGGLING OR WE'LL BE FORCED TO DRAG YOU FROM THE--
CHUNK

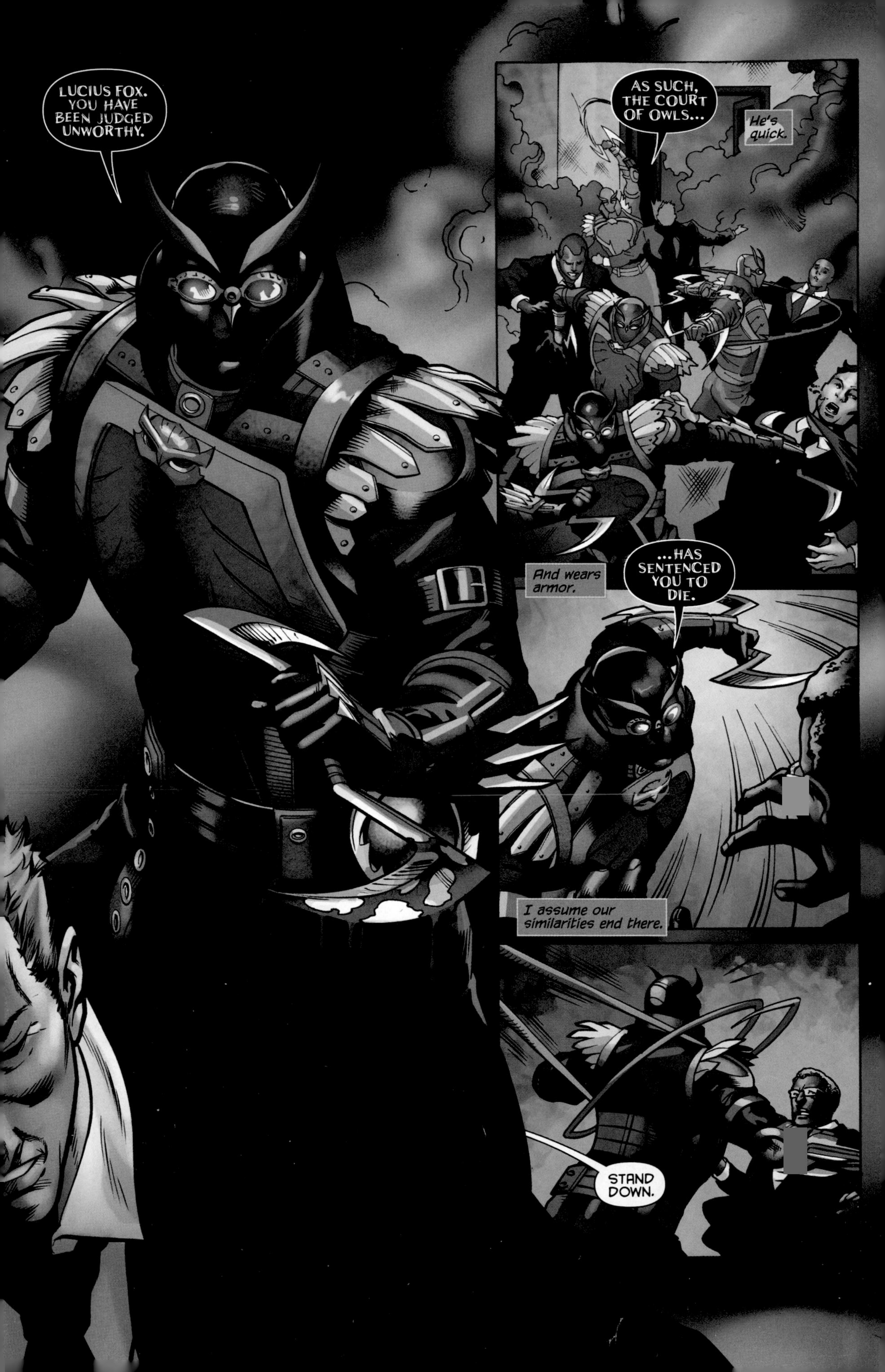
LUCIUS FOX. YOU HAVE BEEN JUDGED UNWORTHY.
AS SUCH, THE COURT OF OWLS...
He's quick.
And wears armor.
...HAS SENTENCED YOU TO DIE.
I assume our similarities end there.
STAND DOWN.

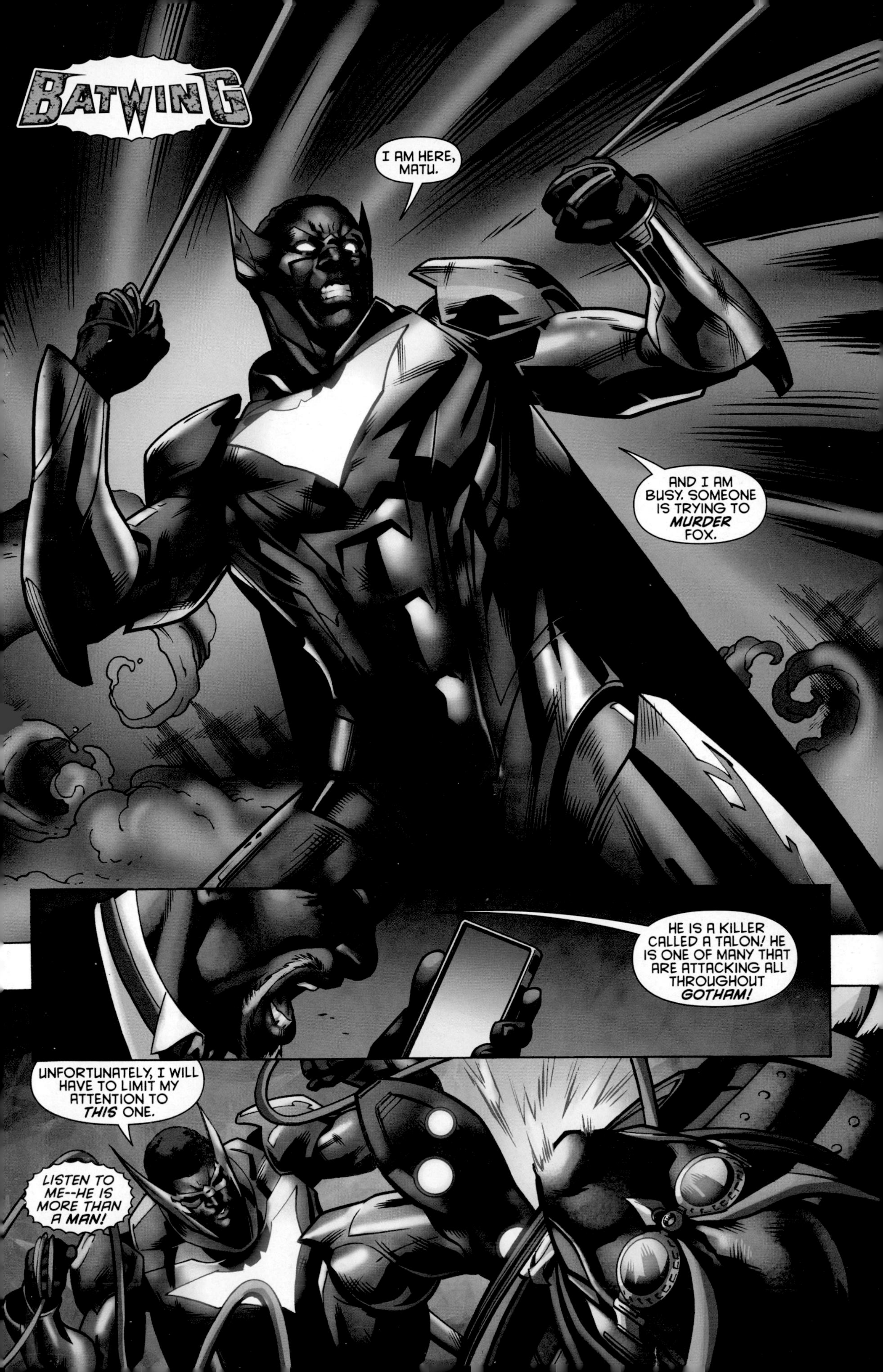
BATWING
I AM HERE, MATU.
AND I AM BUSY. SOMEONE IS TRYING TO MURDER FOX.
HE IS A KILLER CALLED A TALON! HE IS ONE OF MANY THAT ARE ATTACKING ALL THROUGHOUT GOTHAM!
UNFORTUNATELY, I WILL HAVE TO LIMIT MY ATTENTION TO THIS ONE.
LISTEN TO ME--HE IS MORE THAN A MAN!

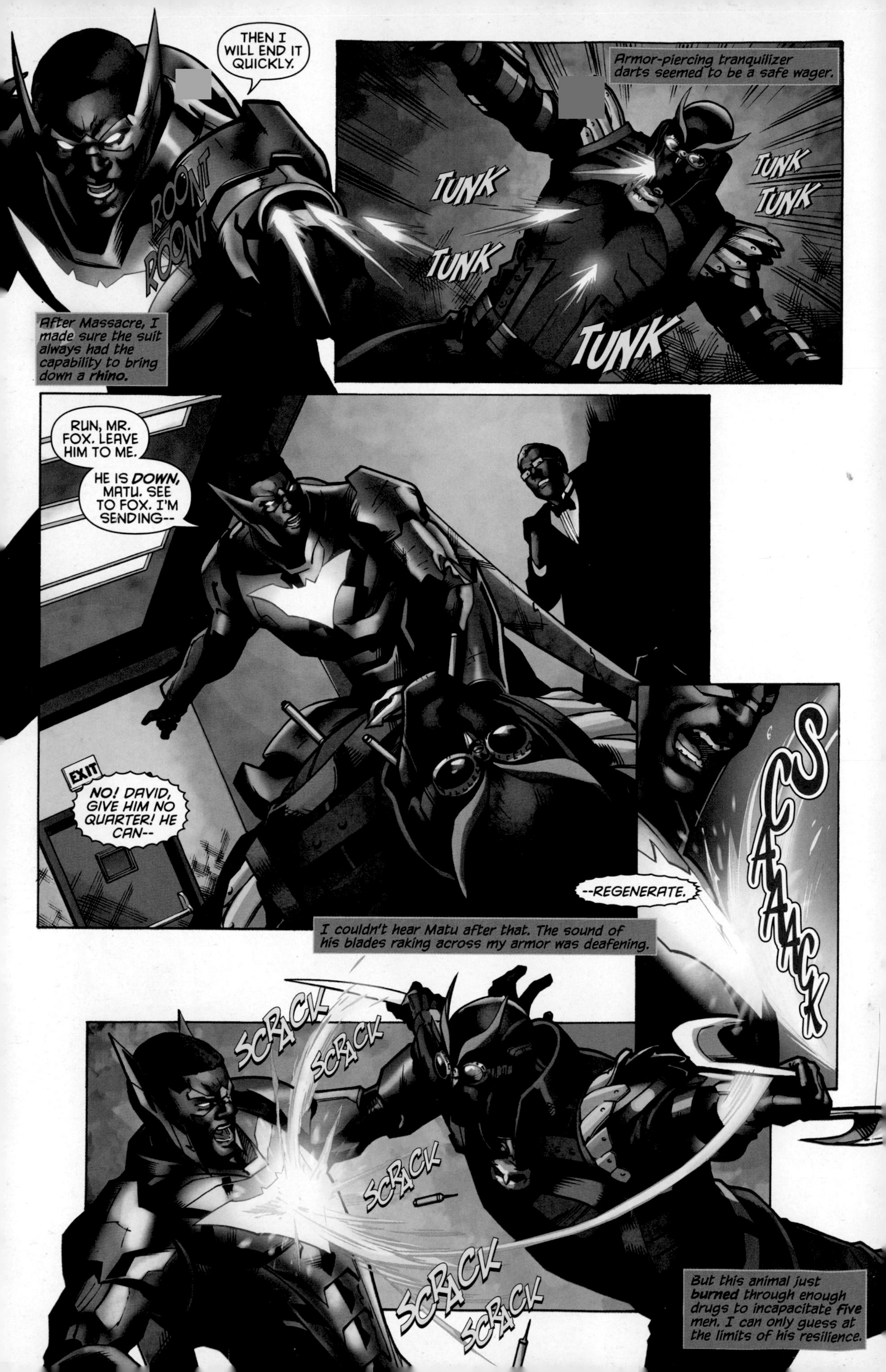
THEN I WILL END IT QUICKLY.
ROONT
ROONT
After Massacre, I made sure the suit always had the capability to bring down a *rhino*.
Armor-piercing tranquilizer darts seemed to be a safe wager.
TUNK
TUNK
TUNK
TUNK
TUNK
RUN, MR. FOX. LEAVE HIM TO ME.
HE IS *DOWN*, MATU. SEE TO FOX. I'M SENDING--
EXIT
NO! DAVID, GIVE HIM NO QUARTER! HE CAN--
--REGENERATE.
SCAAACK
I couldn't hear Matu after that. The sound of his blades raking across my armor was deafening.
SCRACK
SCRACK
SCRACK
SCRACK
SCRACK
But this animal just **burned** through enough drugs to incapacitate **five** men. I can only guess at the limits of his resilience.

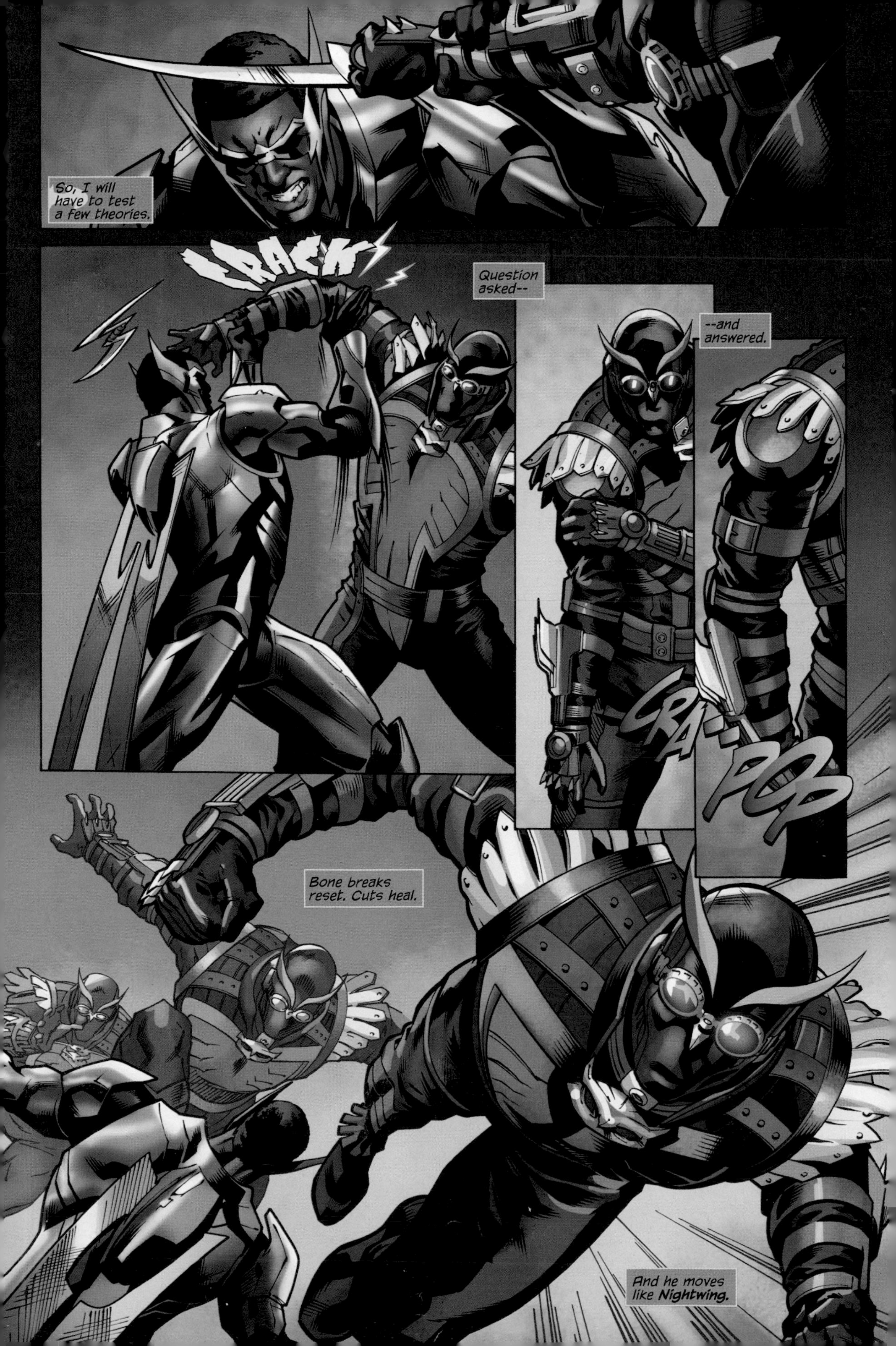
So, I will have to test a few theories.
CRACK
Question asked--
--and answered.
CRA--POP
Bone breaks reset. Cuts heal.
And he moves like **Nightwing**.

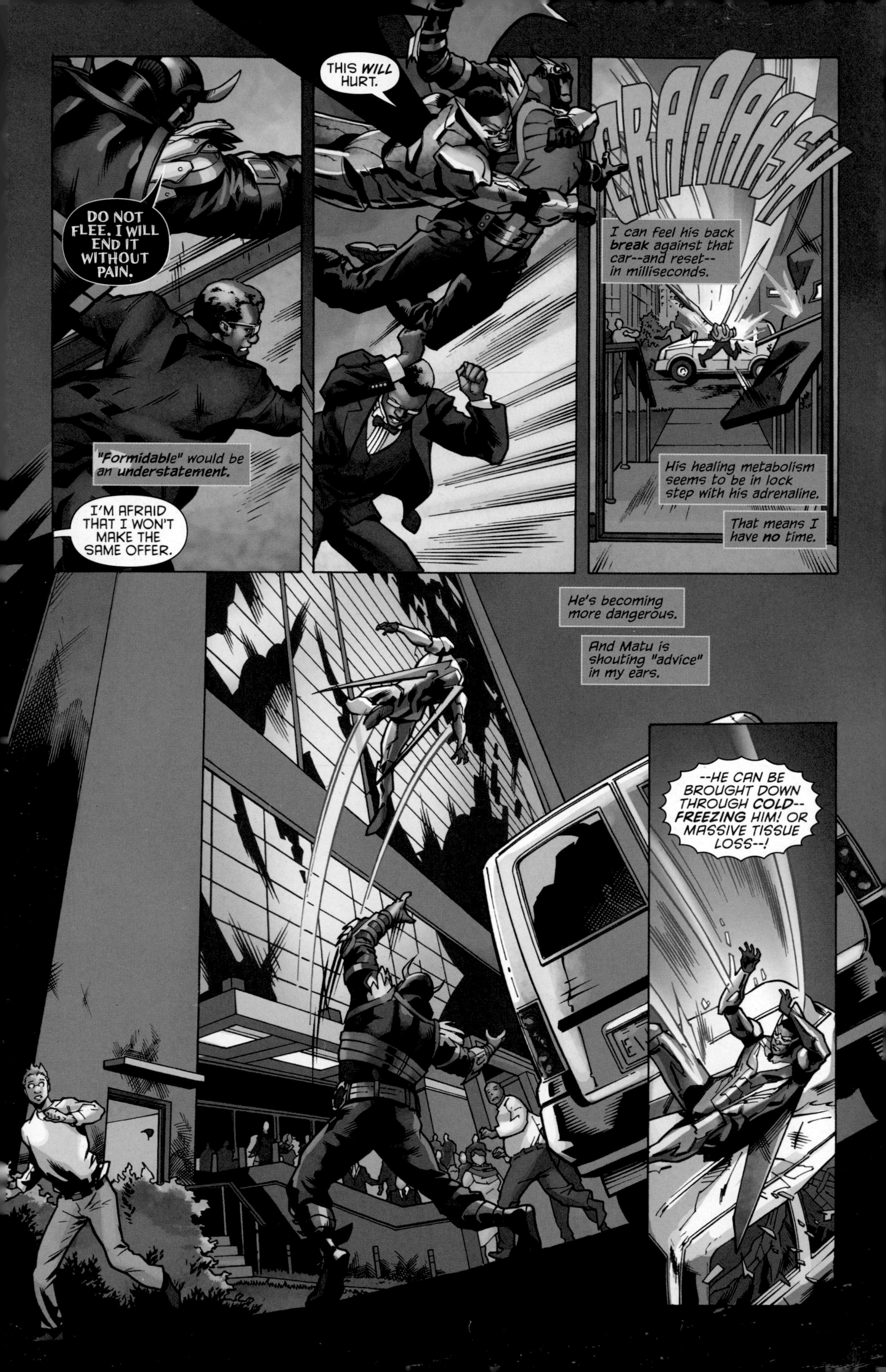
DO NOT FLEE. I WILL END IT WITHOUT PAIN.
"Formidable" would be an understatement.
I'M AFRAID THAT I WON'T MAKE THE SAME OFFER.
THIS WILL HURT.
CRAAAAASH
I can feel his back break against that car--and reset--in milliseconds.
His healing metabolism seems to be in lock step with his adrenaline.
That means I have no time.
He's becoming more dangerous.
And Matu is shouting "advice" in my ears.
--HE CAN BE BROUGHT DOWN THROUGH COLD--FREEZING HIM! OR MASSIVE TISSUE LOSS--!

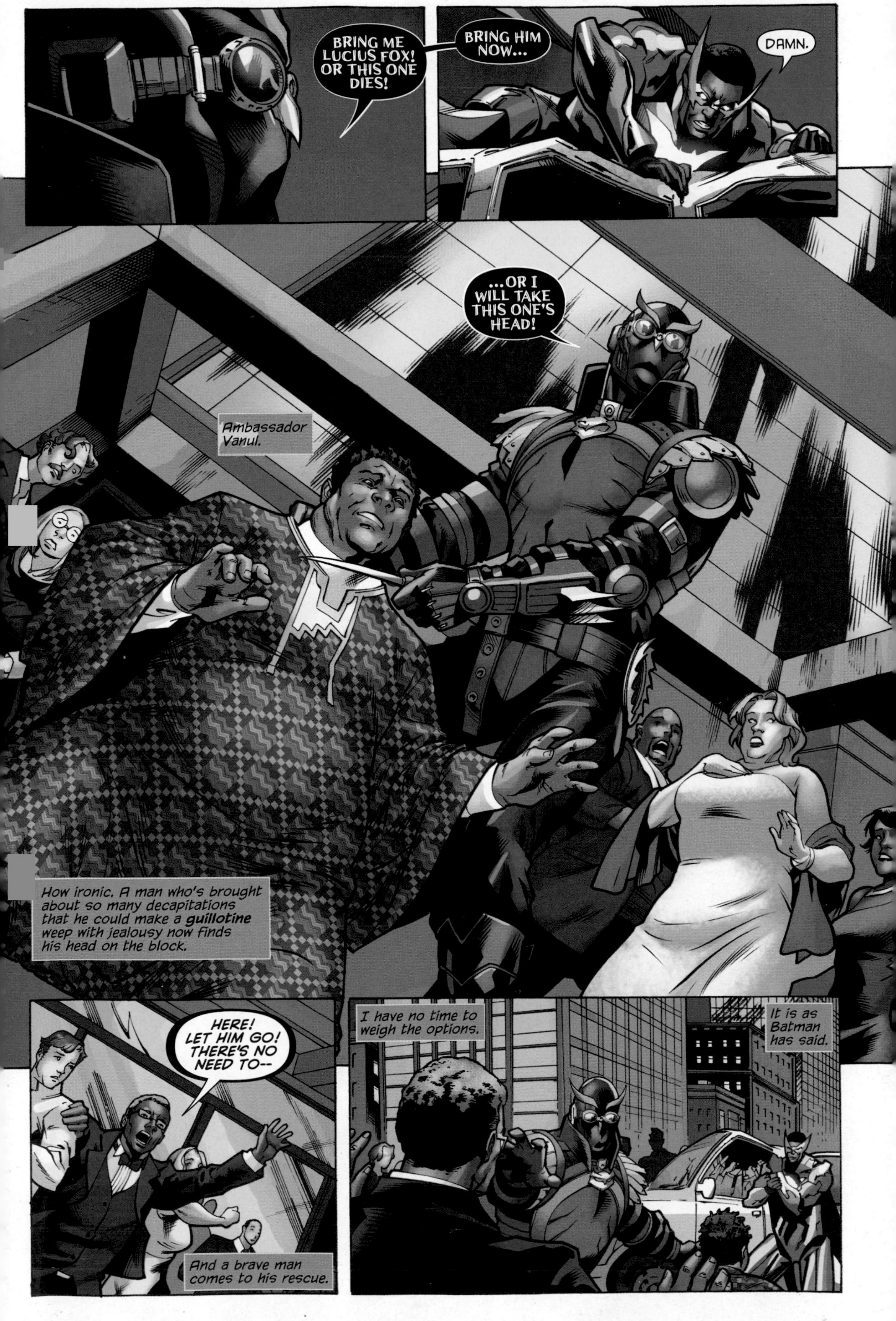
BRING ME LUCIUS FOX! OR THIS ONE DIES!
BRING HIM NOW...
DAMN.
...OR I WILL TAKE THIS ONE'S HEAD!
Ambassador Vanul.
How ironic. A man who's brought about so many decapitations that he could make a guillotine weep with jealousy now finds his head on the block.
HERE! LET HIM GO! THERE'S NO NEED TO--
And a brave man comes to his rescue.
I have no time to weigh the options.
It is as Batman has said.

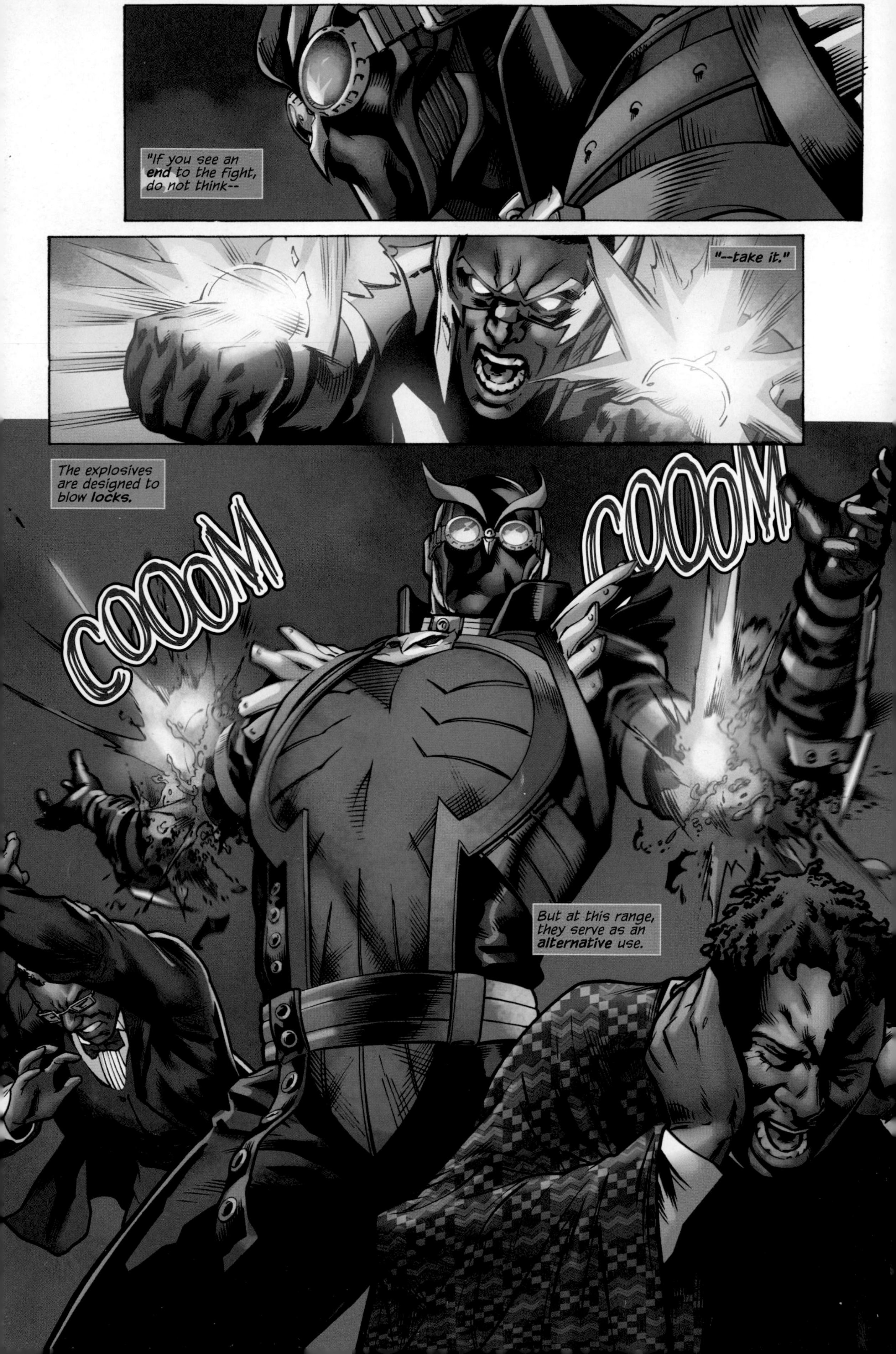
"If you see an end to the fight, do not think--
"--take it."
The explosives are designed to blow locks.
COOOM
COOOM
But at this range, they serve as an alternative use.

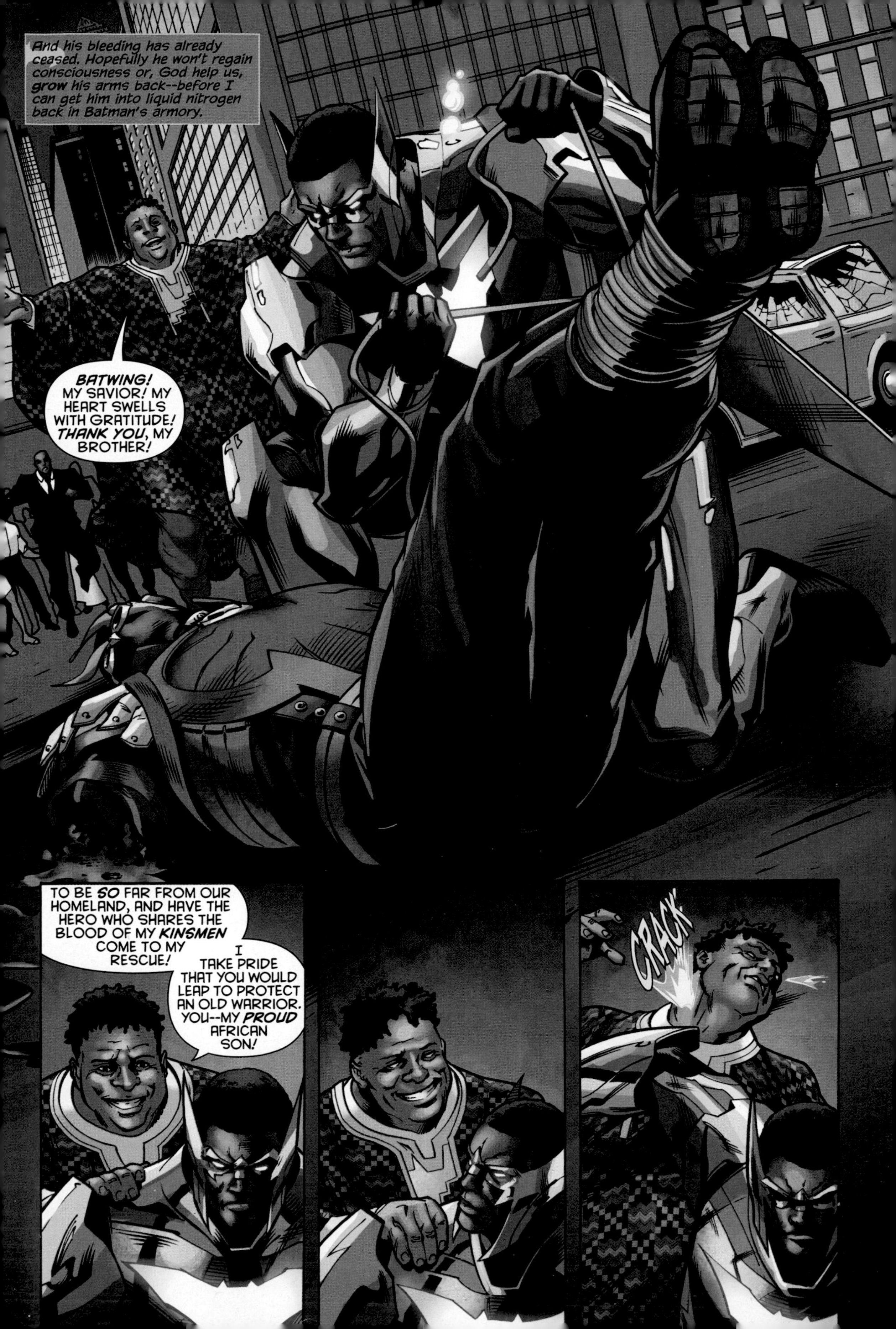
And his bleeding has already ceased. Hopefully he won't regain consciousness or, God help us, grow his arms back--before I can get him into liquid nitrogen back in Batman's armory.
BATWING! MY SAVIOR! MY HEART SWELLS WITH GRATITUDE! THANK YOU, MY BROTHER!
TO BE SO FAR FROM OUR HOMELAND, AND HAVE THE HERO WHO SHARES THE BLOOD OF MY KINSMEN COME TO MY RESCUE!
I TAKE PRIDE THAT YOU WOULD LEAP TO PROTECT AN OLD WARRIOR. YOU--MY PROUD AFRICAN SON!
CRACK

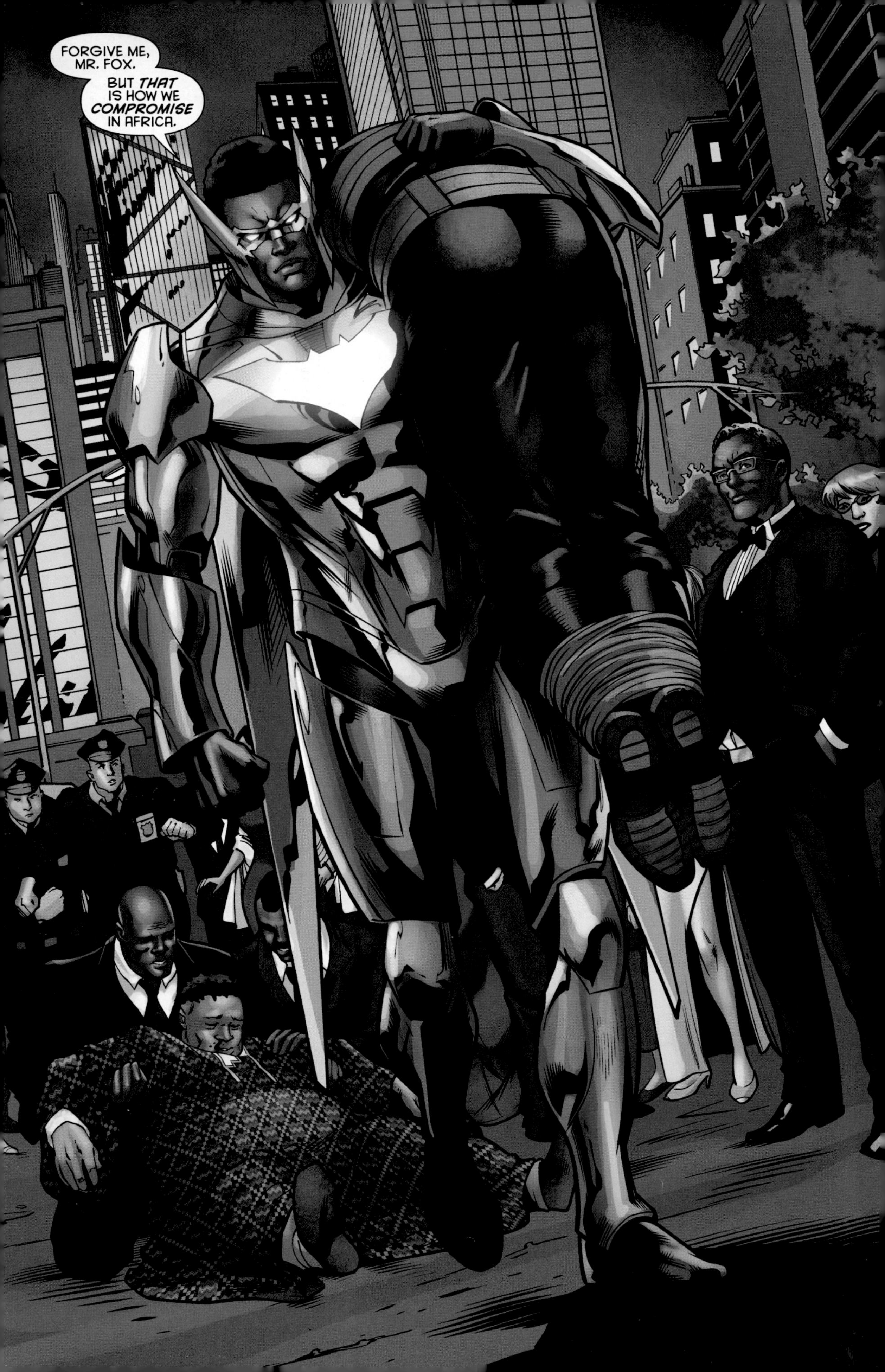

FORGIVE ME, MR. FOX.
BUT *THAT* IS HOW WE *COMPROMISE* IN AFRICA.

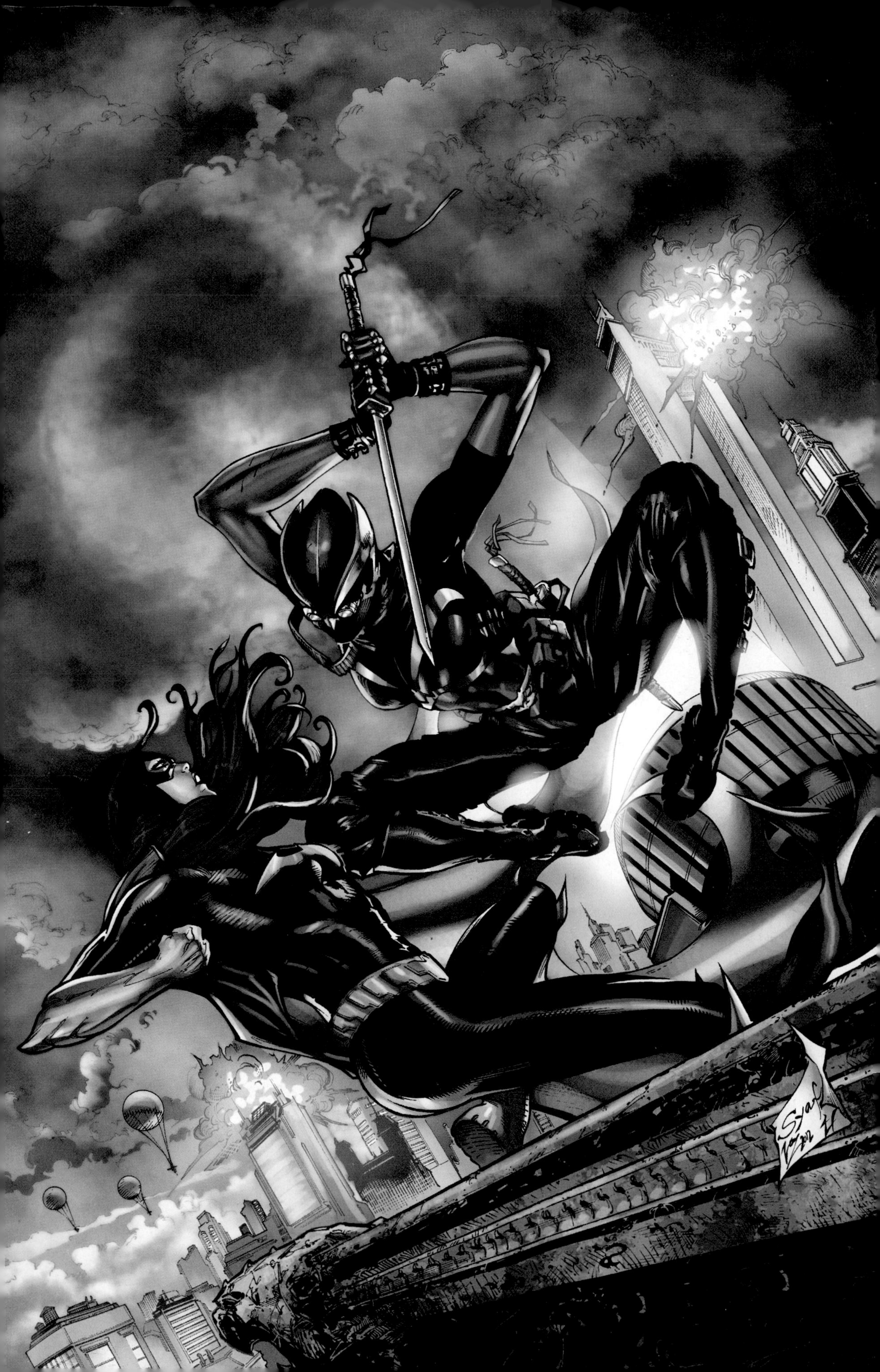

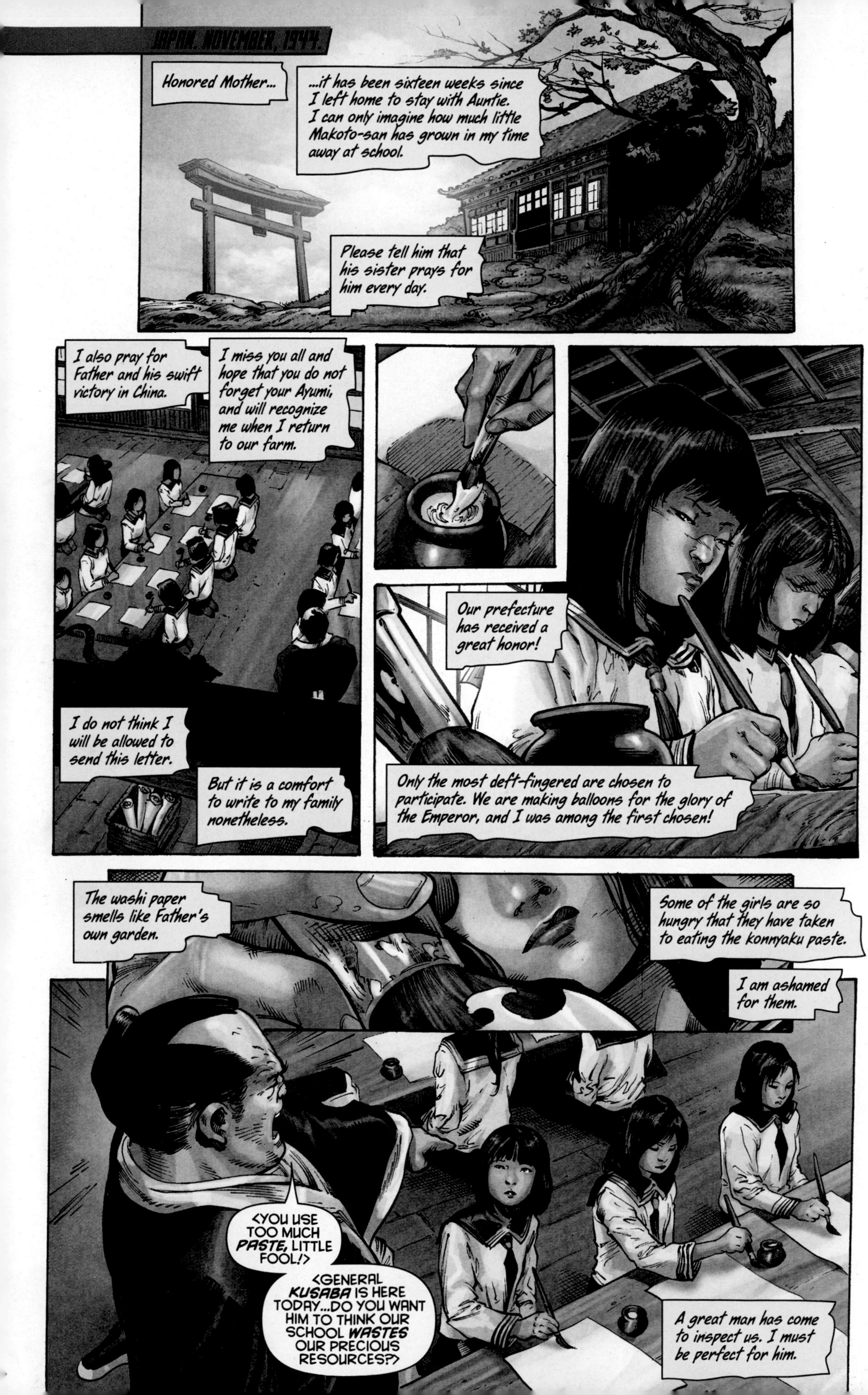
JAPAN, NOVEMBER, 1944.
Honored Mother...
...it has been sixteen weeks since I left home to stay with Auntie. I can only imagine how much little Makoto-san has grown in my time away at school.
Please tell him that his sister prays for him every day.
I also pray for Father and his swift victory in China.
I miss you all and hope that you do not forget your Ayumi, and will recognize me when I return to our farm.
I do not think I will be allowed to send this letter.
But it is a comfort to write to my family nonetheless.
Our prefecture has received a great honor!
Only the most deft-fingered are chosen to participate. We are making balloons for the glory of the Emperor, and I was among the first chosen!
The washi paper smells like Father's own garden.
Some of the girls are so hungry that they have taken to eating the konnyaku paste.
I am ashamed for them.
<YOU USE TOO MUCH PASTE, LITTLE FOOL!>
<GENERAL KUSABA IS HERE TODAY...DO YOU WANT HIM TO THINK OUR SCHOOL WASTES OUR PRECIOUS RESOURCES?>
A great man has come to inspect us. I must be perfect for him.

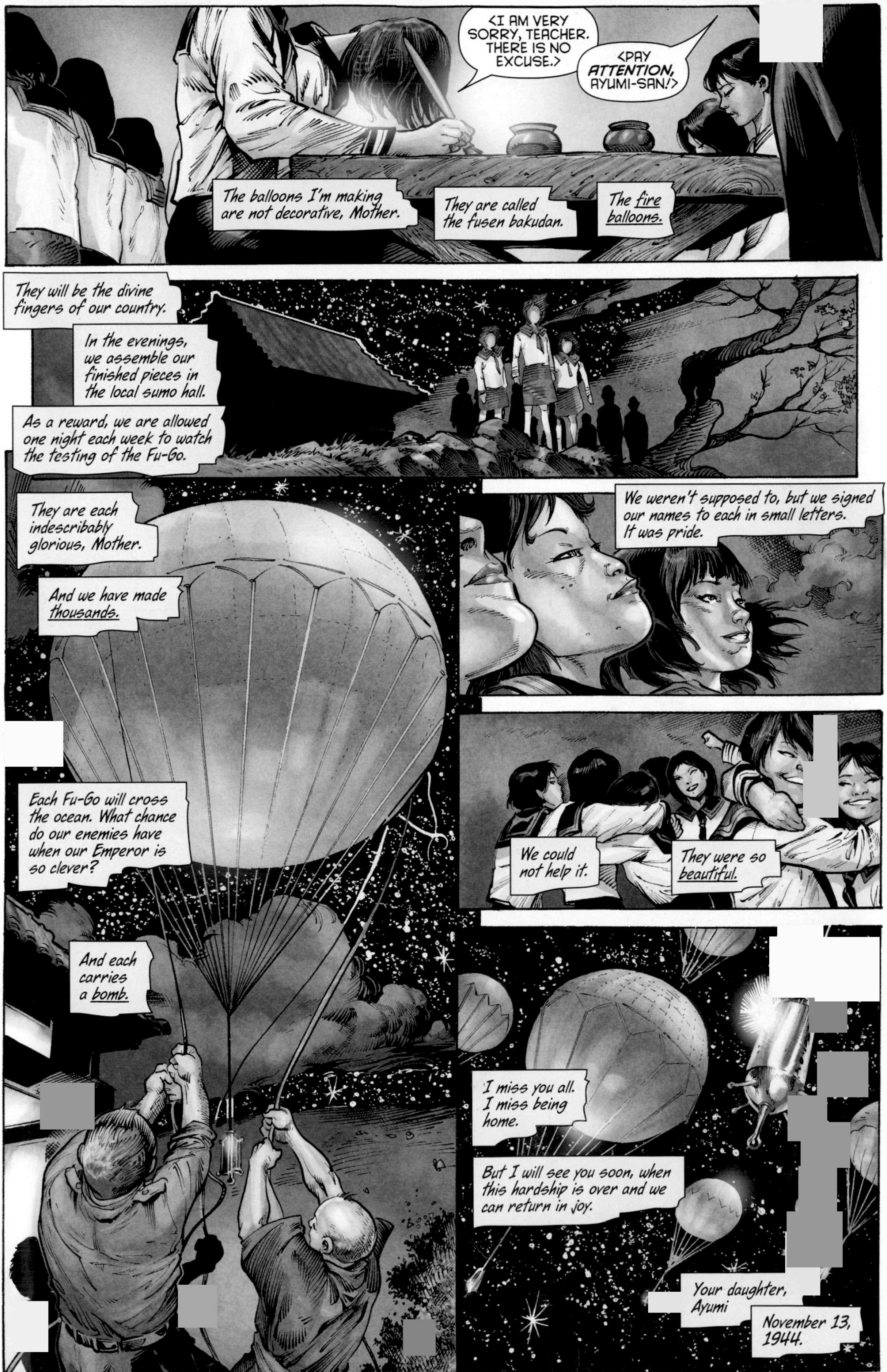

<I AM VERY SORRY, TEACHER. THERE IS NO EXCUSE.>
<PAY ATTENTION, AYUMI-SAN!>
The balloons I'm making are not decorative, Mother.
They are called the fusen bakudan.
The fire balloons.
They will be the divine fingers of our country.
In the evenings, we assemble our finished pieces in the local sumo hall.
As a reward, we are allowed one night each week to watch the testing of the Fu-Go.
They are each indescribably glorious, Mother.
And we have made thousands.
We weren't supposed to, but we signed our names to each in small letters. It was pride.
Each Fu-Go will cross the ocean. What chance do our enemies have when our Emperor is so clever?
We could not help it.
They were so beautiful.
And each carries a bomb.
I miss you all. I miss being home.
But I will see you soon, when this hardship is over and we can return in joy.
Your daughter, Ayumi
November 13, 1944.

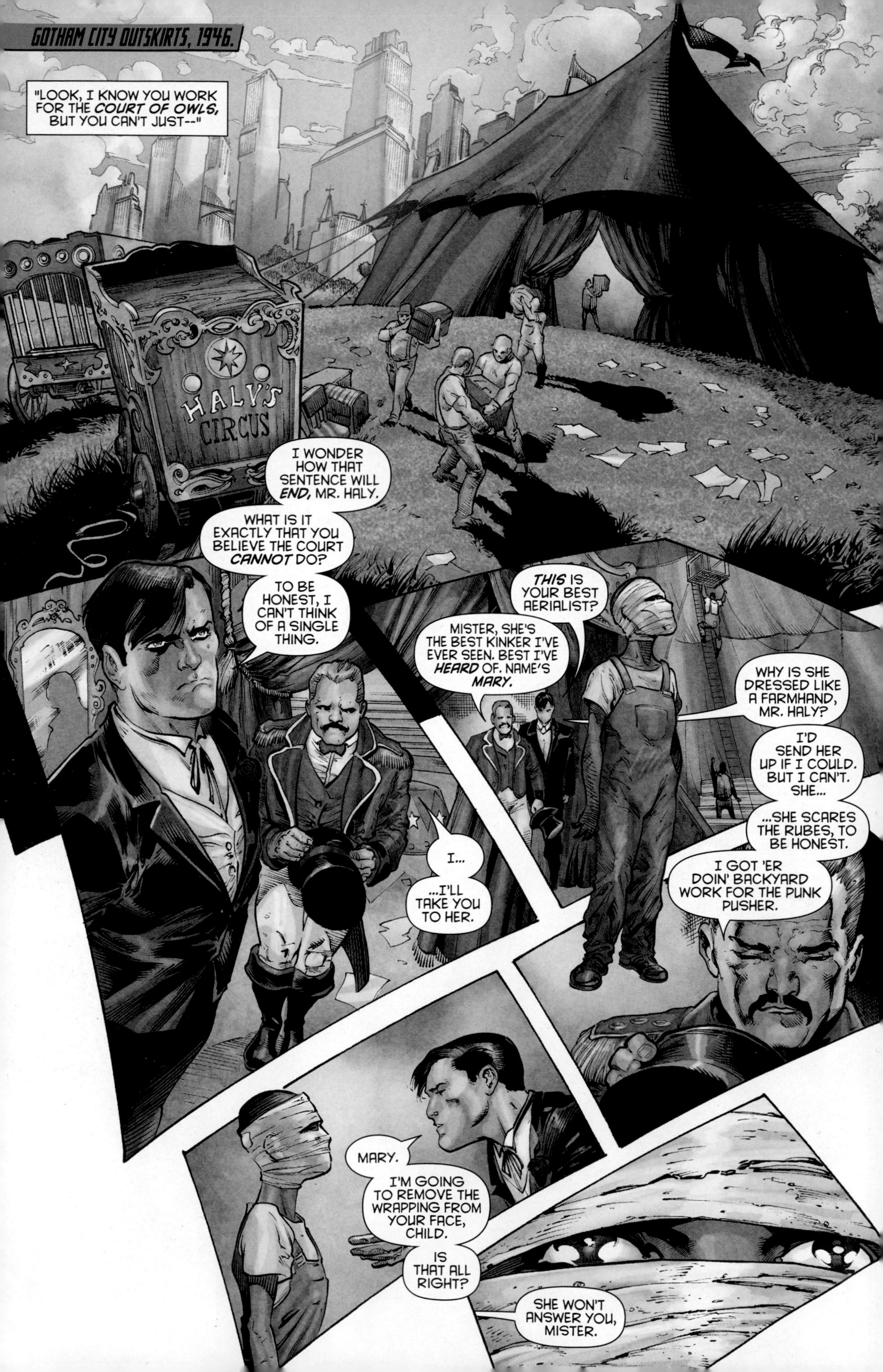
GOTHAM CITY OUTSKIRTS, 1946.
"LOOK, I KNOW YOU WORK FOR THE COURT OF OWLS, BUT YOU CAN'T JUST--"
HALY'S CIRCUS
I WONDER HOW THAT SENTENCE WILL END, MR. HALY.
WHAT IS IT EXACTLY THAT YOU BELIEVE THE COURT CANNOT DO?
TO BE HONEST, I CAN'T THINK OF A SINGLE THING.
I...
...I'LL TAKE YOU TO HER.
THIS IS YOUR BEST AERIALIST?
MISTER, SHE'S THE BEST KINKER I'VE EVER SEEN. BEST I'VE HEARD OF. NAME'S MARY.
WHY IS SHE DRESSED LIKE A FARMHAND, MR. HALY?
I'D SEND HER UP IF I COULD. BUT I CAN'T. SHE...
...SHE SCARES THE RUBES, TO BE HONEST.
I GOT 'ER DOIN' BACKYARD WORK FOR THE PUNK PUSHER.
MARY.
I'M GOING TO REMOVE THE WRAPPING FROM YOUR FACE, CHILD.
IS THAT ALL RIGHT?
SHE WON'T ANSWER YOU, MISTER.

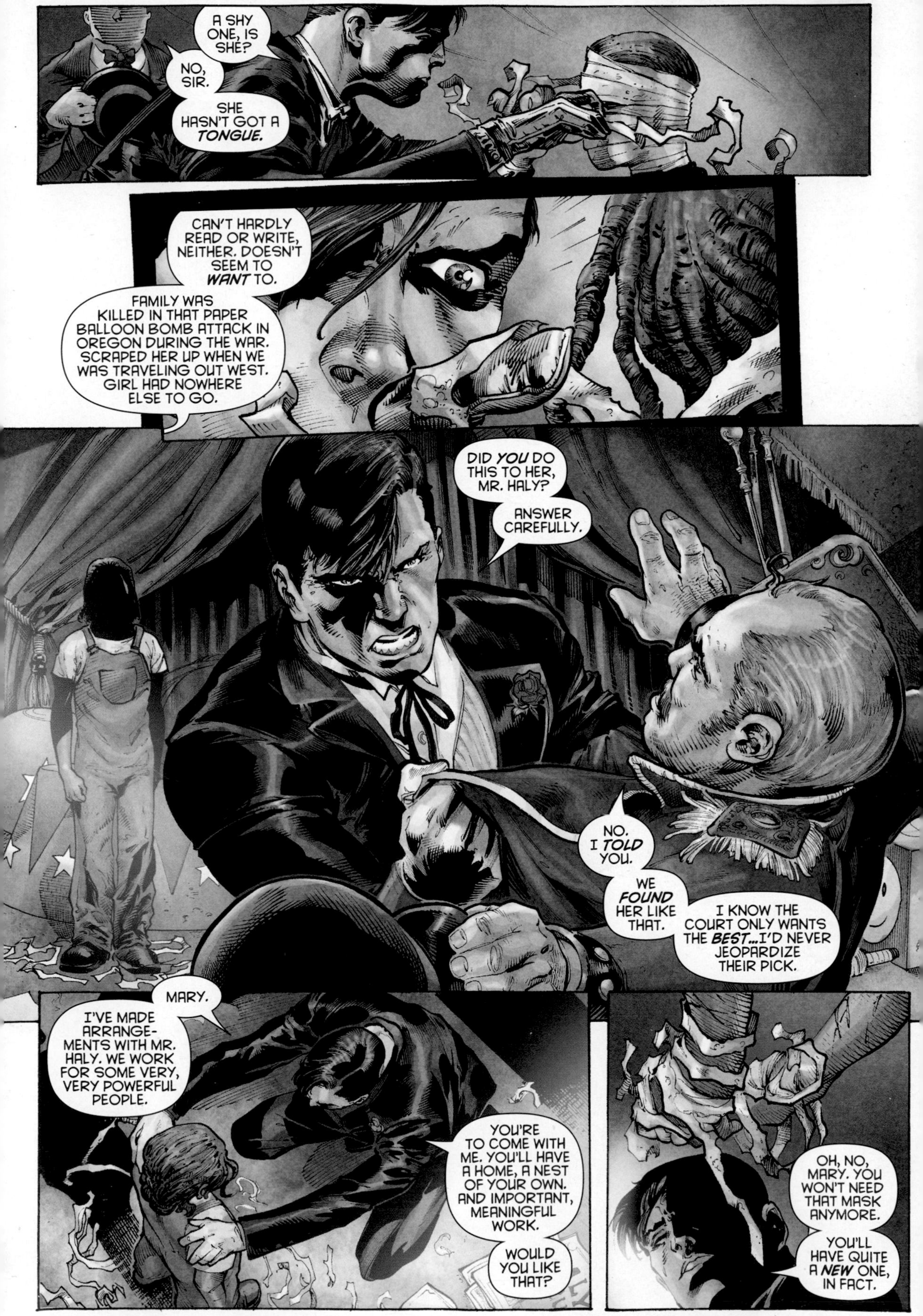
A SHY ONE, IS SHE?
NO, SIR.
SHE HASN'T GOT A *TONGUE.*
CAN'T HARDLY READ OR WRITE, NEITHER. DOESN'T SEEM TO *WANT* TO.
FAMILY WAS KILLED IN THAT PAPER BALLOON BOMB ATTACK IN OREGON DURING THE WAR. SCRAPED HER UP WHEN WE WAS TRAVELING OUT WEST. GIRL HAD NOWHERE ELSE TO GO.
DID *YOU* DO THIS TO HER, MR. HALY?
ANSWER CAREFULLY.
NO. I *TOLD* YOU.
WE *FOUND* HER LIKE THAT.
I KNOW THE COURT ONLY WANTS THE *BEST*...I'D NEVER JEOPARDIZE THEIR PICK.
MARY.
I'VE MADE ARRANGE-MENTS WITH MR. HALY. WE WORK FOR SOME VERY, VERY POWERFUL PEOPLE.
YOU'RE TO COME WITH ME. YOU'LL HAVE A HOME, A NEST OF YOUR OWN. AND IMPORTANT, MEANINGFUL WORK.
WOULD YOU LIKE THAT?
OH, NO, MARY. YOU WON'T NEED THAT MASK ANYMORE.
YOU'LL HAVE QUITE A *NEW* ONE, IN FACT.

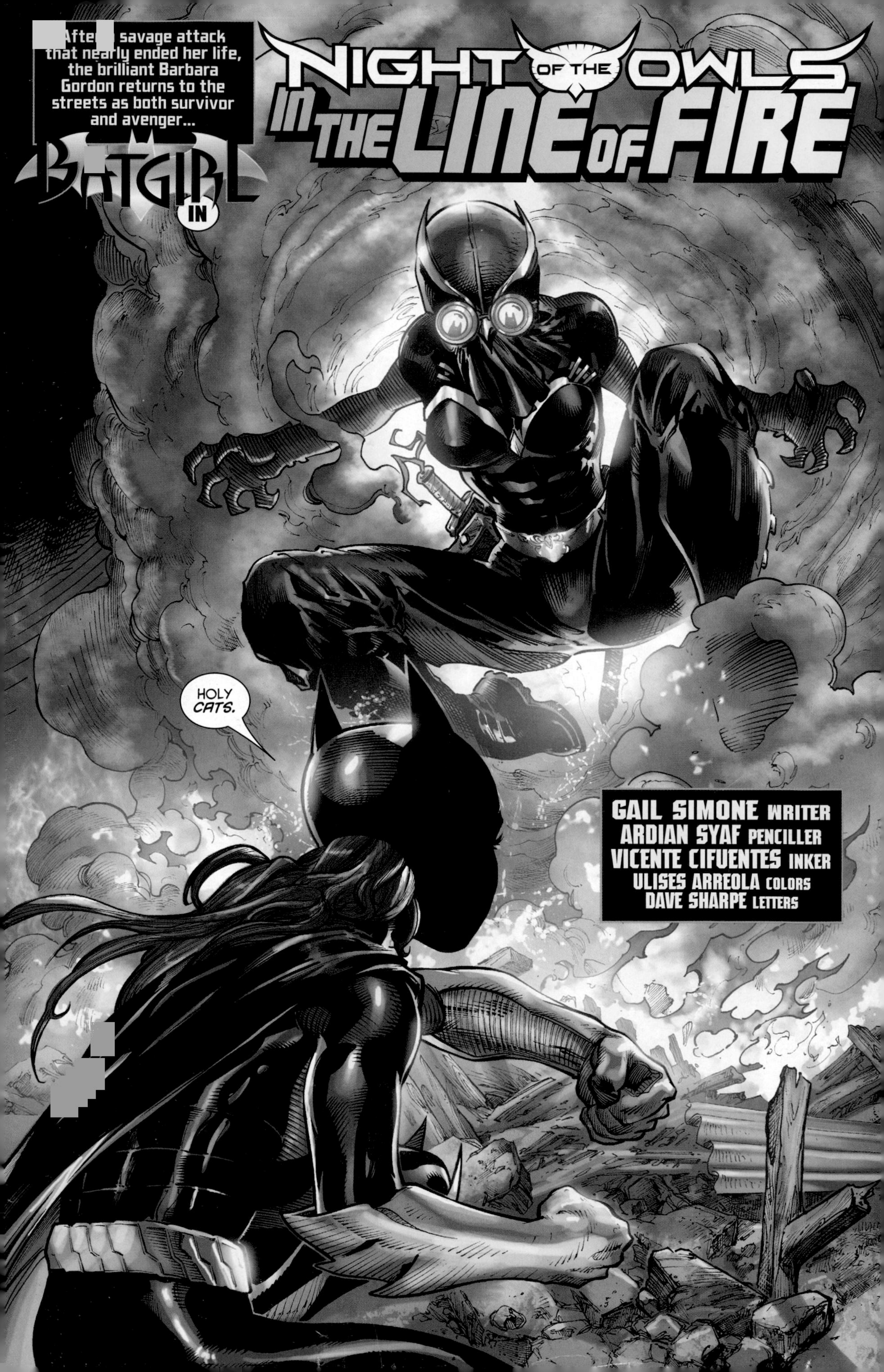
Afte savage attack that nearly ended her life, the brilliant Barbara Gordon returns to the streets as both survivor and avenger...
BATGIRL
IN
NIGHT OF THE OWLS
IN THE LINE OF FIRE
HOLY CATS.
GAIL SIMONE WRITER
ARDIAN SYAF PENCILLER
VICENTE CIFUENTES INKER
ULISES ARREOLA COLORS
DAVE SHARPE LETTERS

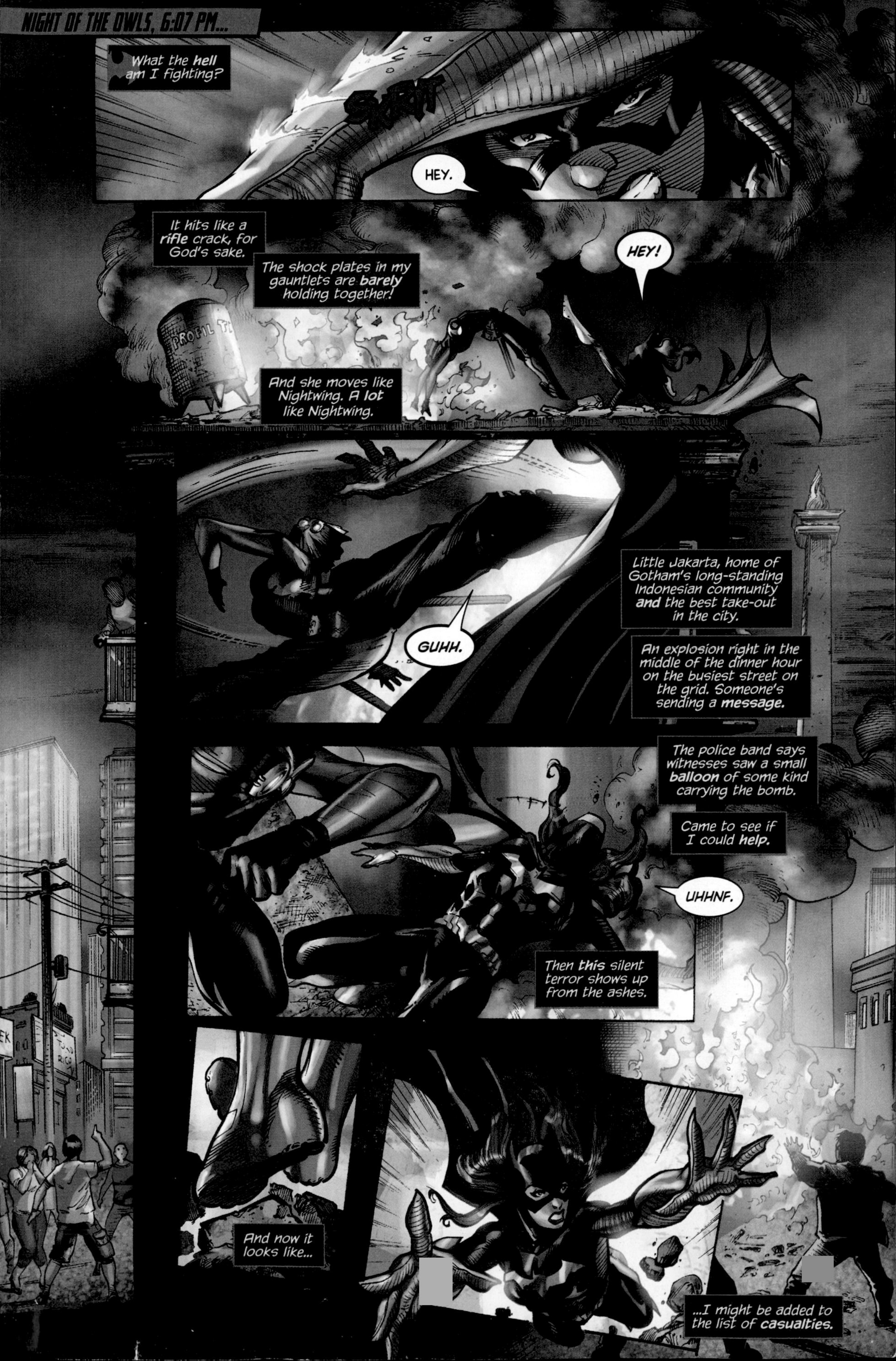
NIGHT OF THE OWLS, 6:07 PM...
What the hell am I fighting?
SKRIT
HEY.
It hits like a rifle crack, for God's sake.
The shock plates in my gauntlets are barely holding together!
HEY!
And she moves like Nightwing. A lot like Nightwing.
GUHH.
Little Jakarta, home of Gotham's long-standing Indonesian community and the best take-out in the city.
An explosion right in the middle of the dinner hour on the busiest street on the grid. Someone's sending a message.
The police band says witnesses saw a small balloon of some kind carrying the bomb.
Came to see if I could help.
UHHNF.
Then this silent terror shows up from the ashes.
And now it looks like...
...I might be added to the list of casualties.

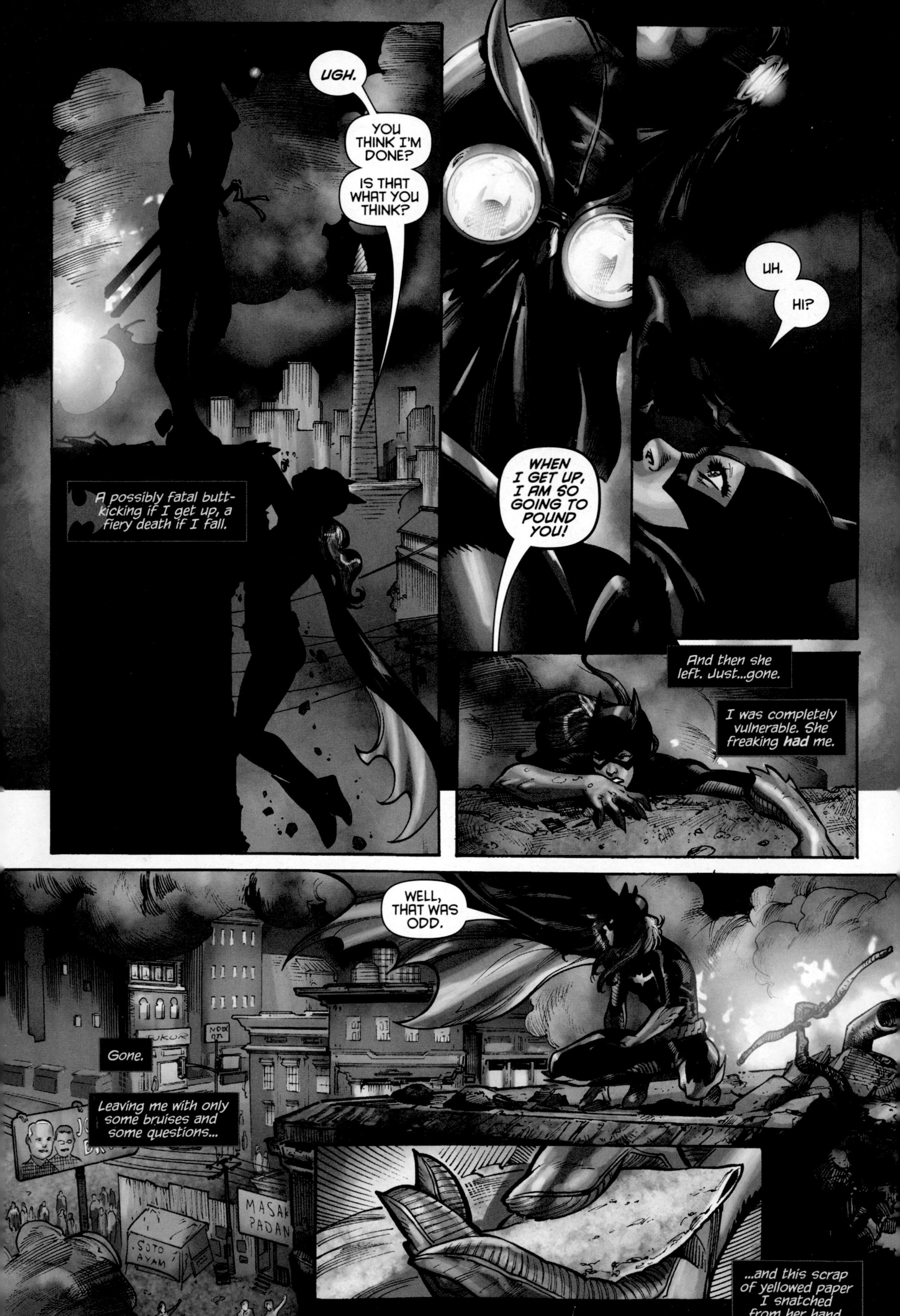
UGH.
YOU THINK I'M DONE?
IS THAT WHAT YOU THINK?
A possibly fatal butt-kicking if I get up, a fiery death if I fall.
WHEN I GET UP, I AM SO GOING TO POUND YOU!
UH.
HI?
And then she left. Just...gone.
I was completely vulnerable. She freaking **had** me.
WELL, THAT WAS ODD.
Gone.
Leaving me with only some bruises and some questions...
MASAK PADAN
SOTO AYAM
...and this scrap of yellowed paper I snatched from her hand.

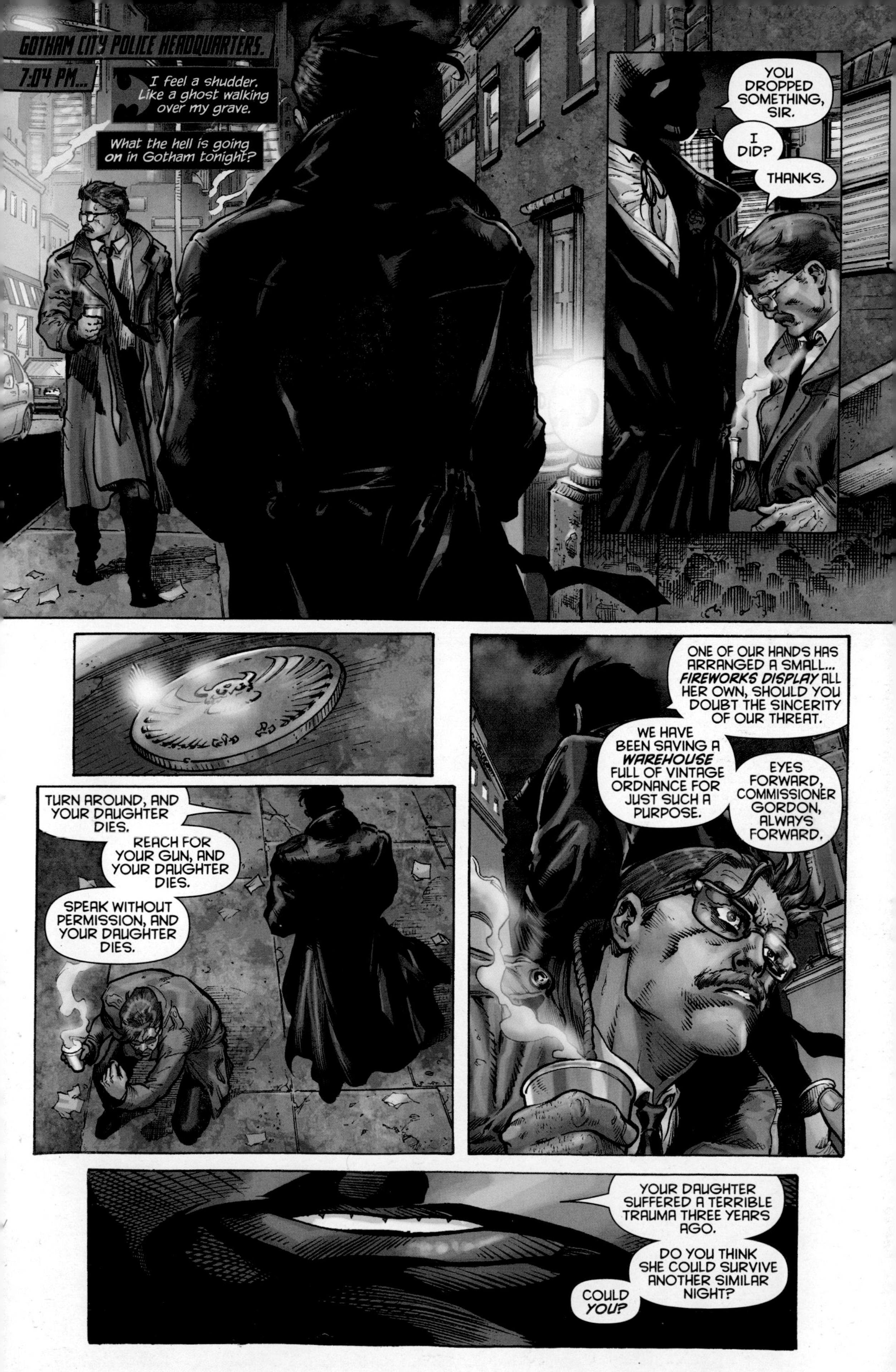
GOTHAM CITY POLICE HEADQUARTERS.
7:04 PM...
I feel a shudder. Like a ghost walking over my grave.
What the hell is going on in Gotham tonight?
YOU DROPPED SOMETHING, SIR.
I DID?
THANKS.
TURN AROUND, AND YOUR DAUGHTER DIES.
REACH FOR YOUR GUN, AND YOUR DAUGHTER DIES.
SPEAK WITHOUT PERMISSION, AND YOUR DAUGHTER DIES.
ONE OF OUR HANDS HAS ARRANGED A SMALL... FIREWORKS DISPLAY ALL HER OWN, SHOULD YOU DOUBT THE SINCERITY OF OUR THREAT.
WE HAVE BEEN SAVING A WAREHOUSE FULL OF VINTAGE ORDNANCE FOR JUST SUCH A PURPOSE.
EYES FORWARD, COMMISSIONER GORDON, ALWAYS FORWARD.
YOUR DAUGHTER SUFFERED A TERRIBLE TRAUMA THREE YEARS AGO.
DO YOU THINK SHE COULD SURVIVE ANOTHER SIMILAR NIGHT?
COULD YOU?

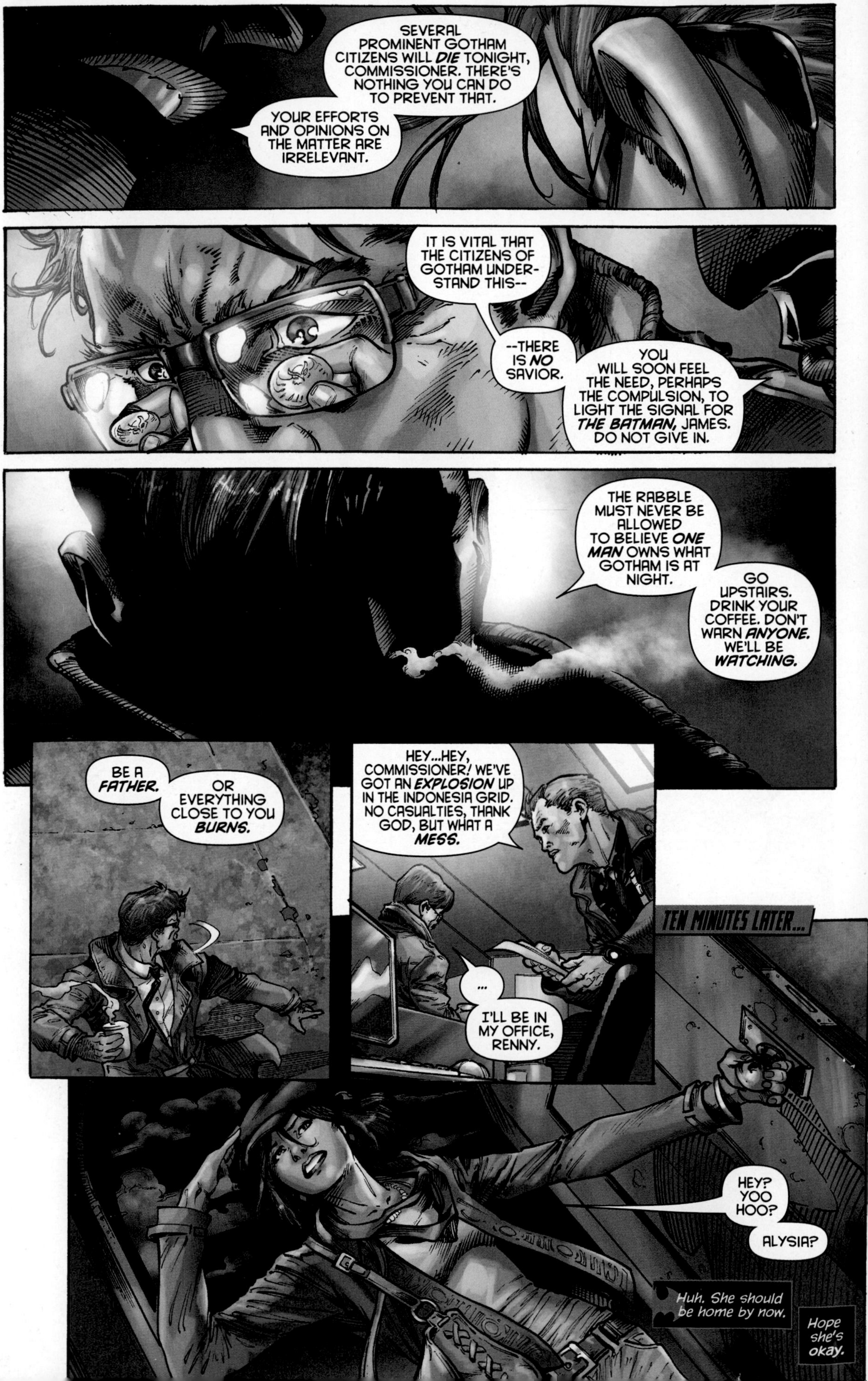
SEVERAL PROMINENT GOTHAM CITIZENS WILL *DIE* TONIGHT, COMMISSIONER. THERE'S NOTHING YOU CAN DO TO PREVENT THAT.
YOUR EFFORTS AND OPINIONS ON THE MATTER ARE IRRELEVANT.
IT IS VITAL THAT THE CITIZENS OF GOTHAM UNDER-STAND THIS--
--THERE IS *NO* SAVIOR.
YOU WILL SOON FEEL THE NEED, PERHAPS THE COMPULSION, TO LIGHT THE SIGNAL FOR *THE BATMAN,* JAMES. DO NOT GIVE IN.
THE RABBLE MUST NEVER BE ALLOWED TO BELIEVE *ONE MAN* OWNS WHAT GOTHAM IS AT NIGHT.
GO UPSTAIRS. DRINK YOUR COFFEE. DON'T WARN *ANYONE.* WE'LL BE *WATCHING.*
BE A *FATHER.*
OR EVERYTHING CLOSE TO YOU *BURNS.*
HEY...HEY, COMMISSIONER! WE'VE GOT AN *EXPLOSION* UP IN THE INDONESIA GRID. NO CASUALTIES, THANK GOD, BUT WHAT A *MESS.*
...
I'LL BE IN MY OFFICE, RENNY.
TEN MINUTES LATER...
HEY? YOO HOO?
ALYSIA?
Huh. She should be home by now.
Hope she's okay.

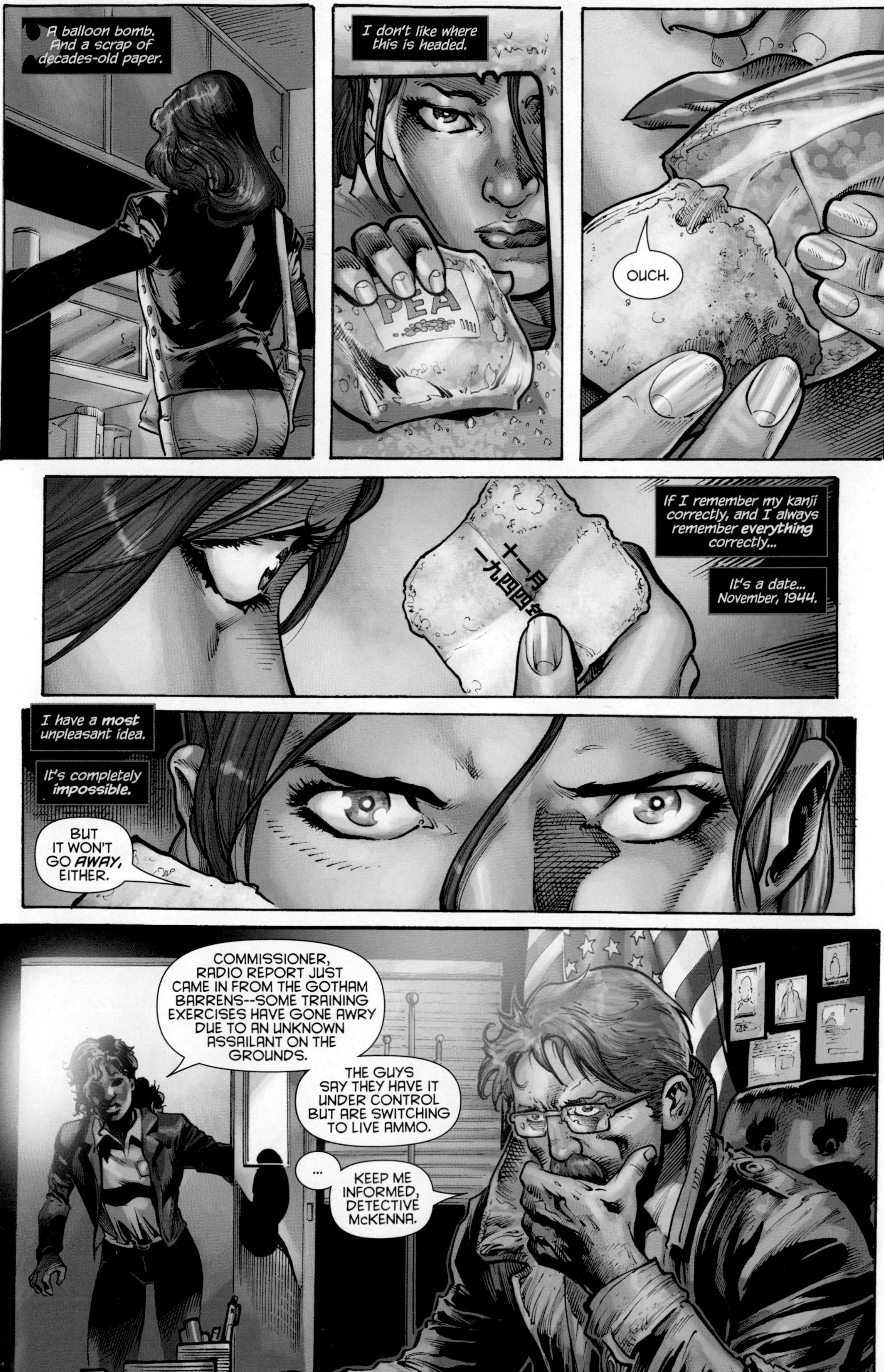

A balloon bomb. And a scrap of decades-old paper.
I don't like where this is headed.
PEA
OUCH.
十一月
一九四四年
If I remember my kanji correctly, and I always remember everything correctly...
It's a date... November, 1944.
I have a most unpleasant idea.
It's completely impossible.
BUT IT WON'T GO AWAY, EITHER.
COMMISSIONER, RADIO REPORT JUST CAME IN FROM THE GOTHAM BARRENS--SOME TRAINING EXERCISES HAVE GONE AWRY DUE TO AN UNKNOWN ASSAILANT ON THE GROUNDS.
THE GUYS SAY THEY HAVE IT UNDER CONTROL BUT ARE SWITCHING TO LIVE AMMO.
...
KEEP ME INFORMED, DETECTIVE McKENNA.

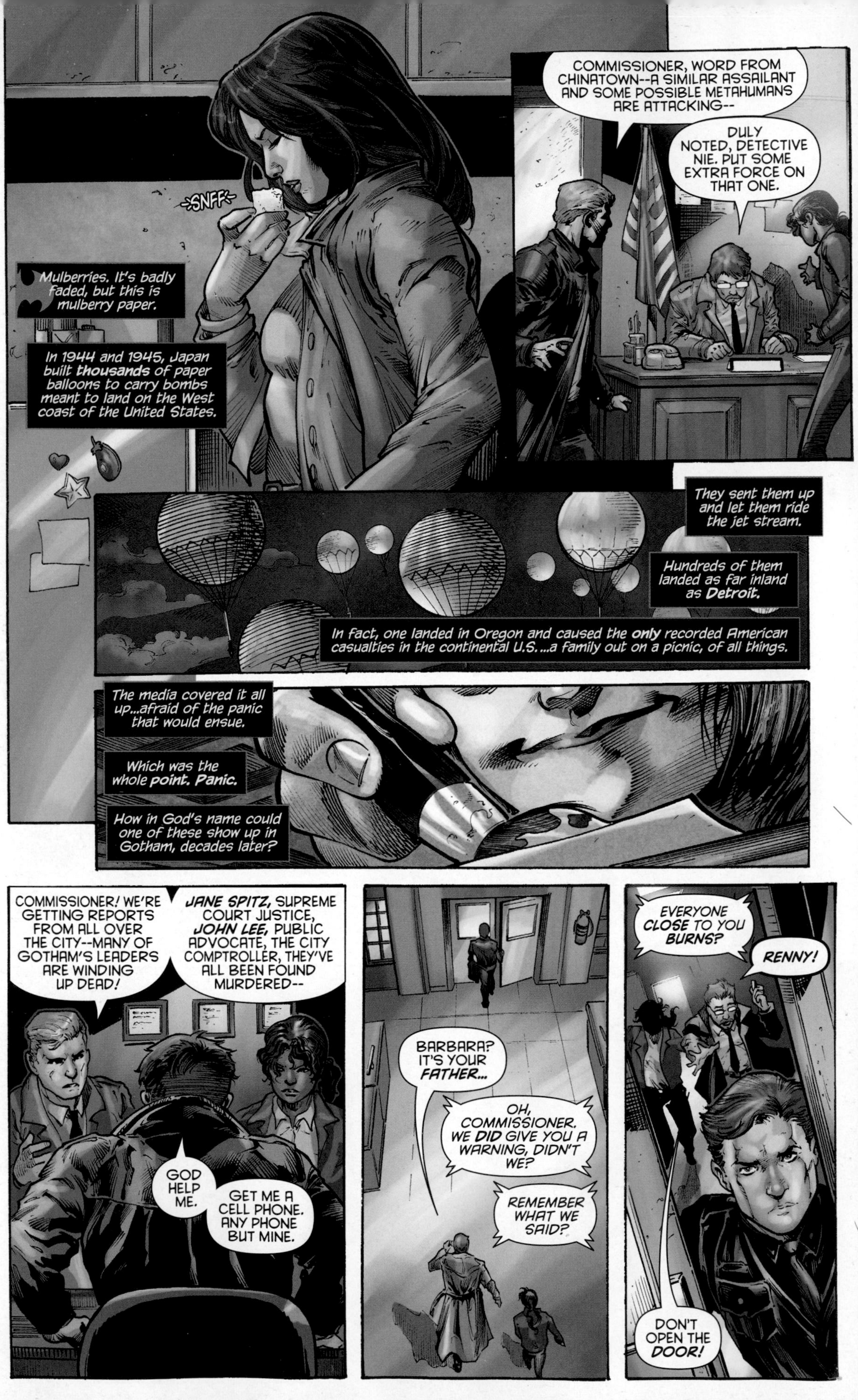

COMMISSIONER, WORD FROM CHINATOWN--A SIMILAR ASSAILANT AND SOME POSSIBLE METAHUMANS ARE ATTACKING--
DULY NOTED, DETECTIVE NIE. PUT SOME EXTRA FORCE ON THAT ONE.
SNFF
Mulberries. It's badly faded, but this is mulberry paper.
In 1944 and 1945, Japan built thousands of paper balloons to carry bombs meant to land on the West coast of the United States.
They sent them up and let them ride the jet stream.
Hundreds of them landed as far inland as Detroit.
In fact, one landed in Oregon and caused the only recorded American casualties in the continental U.S. ...a family out on a picnic, of all things.
The media covered it all up...afraid of the panic that would ensue.
Which was the whole point. Panic.
How in God's name could one of these show up in Gotham, decades later?
COMMISSIONER! WE'RE GETTING REPORTS FROM ALL OVER THE CITY--MANY OF GOTHAM'S LEADERS ARE WINDING UP DEAD!
JANE SPITZ, SUPREME COURT JUSTICE, JOHN LEE, PUBLIC ADVOCATE, THE CITY COMPTROLLER, THEY'VE ALL BEEN FOUND MURDERED--
GOD HELP ME.
GET ME A CELL PHONE. ANY PHONE BUT MINE.
BARBARA? IT'S YOUR FATHER...
OH, COMMISSIONER. WE DID GIVE YOU A WARNING, DIDN'T WE?
REMEMBER WHAT WE SAID?
EVERYONE CLOSE TO YOU BURNS?
RENNY!
DON'T OPEN THE DOOR!

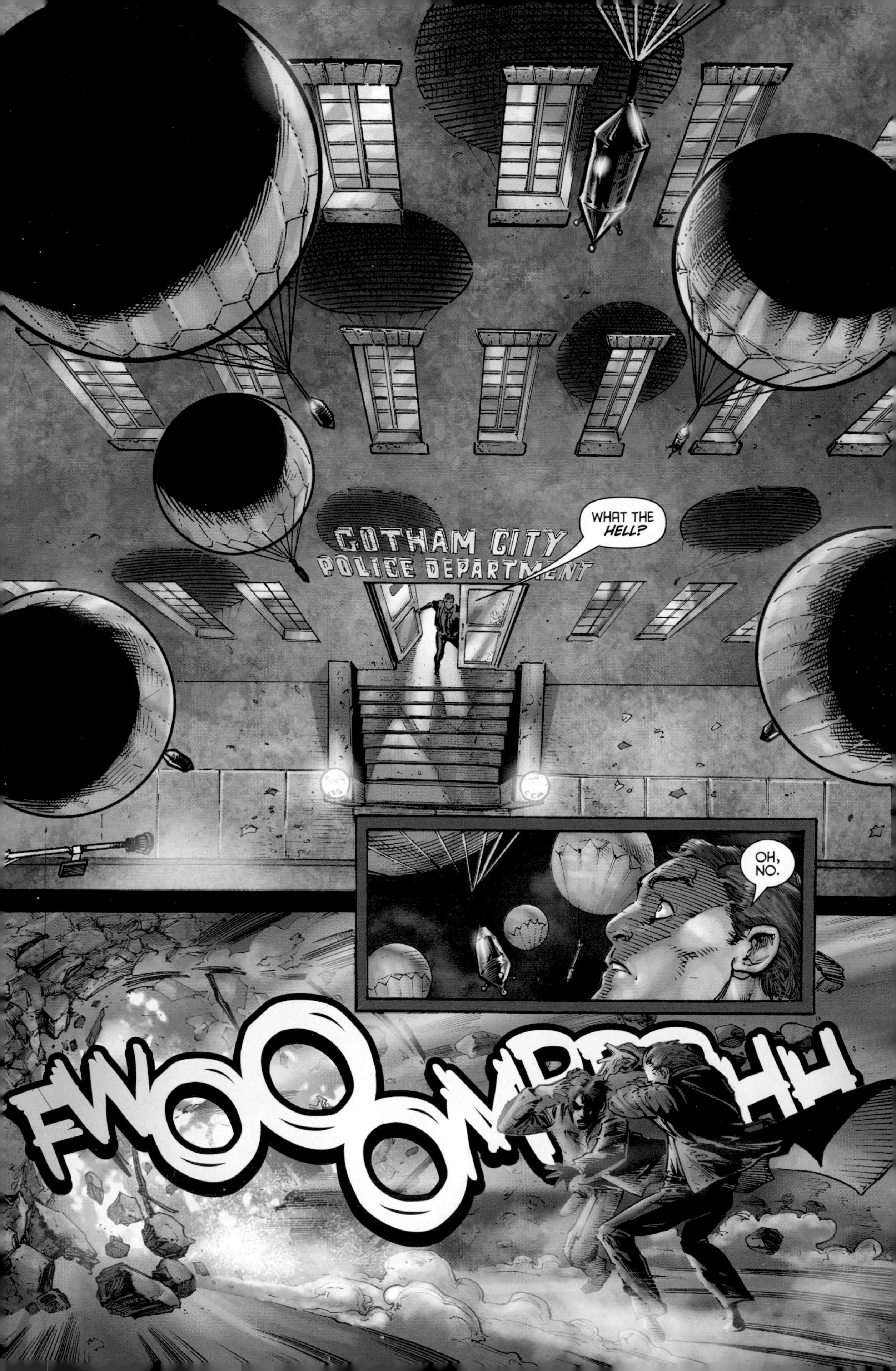
GOTHAM CITY
POLICE DEPARTMENT
WHAT THE HELL?
OH, NO.
FWOOOOMPPHH

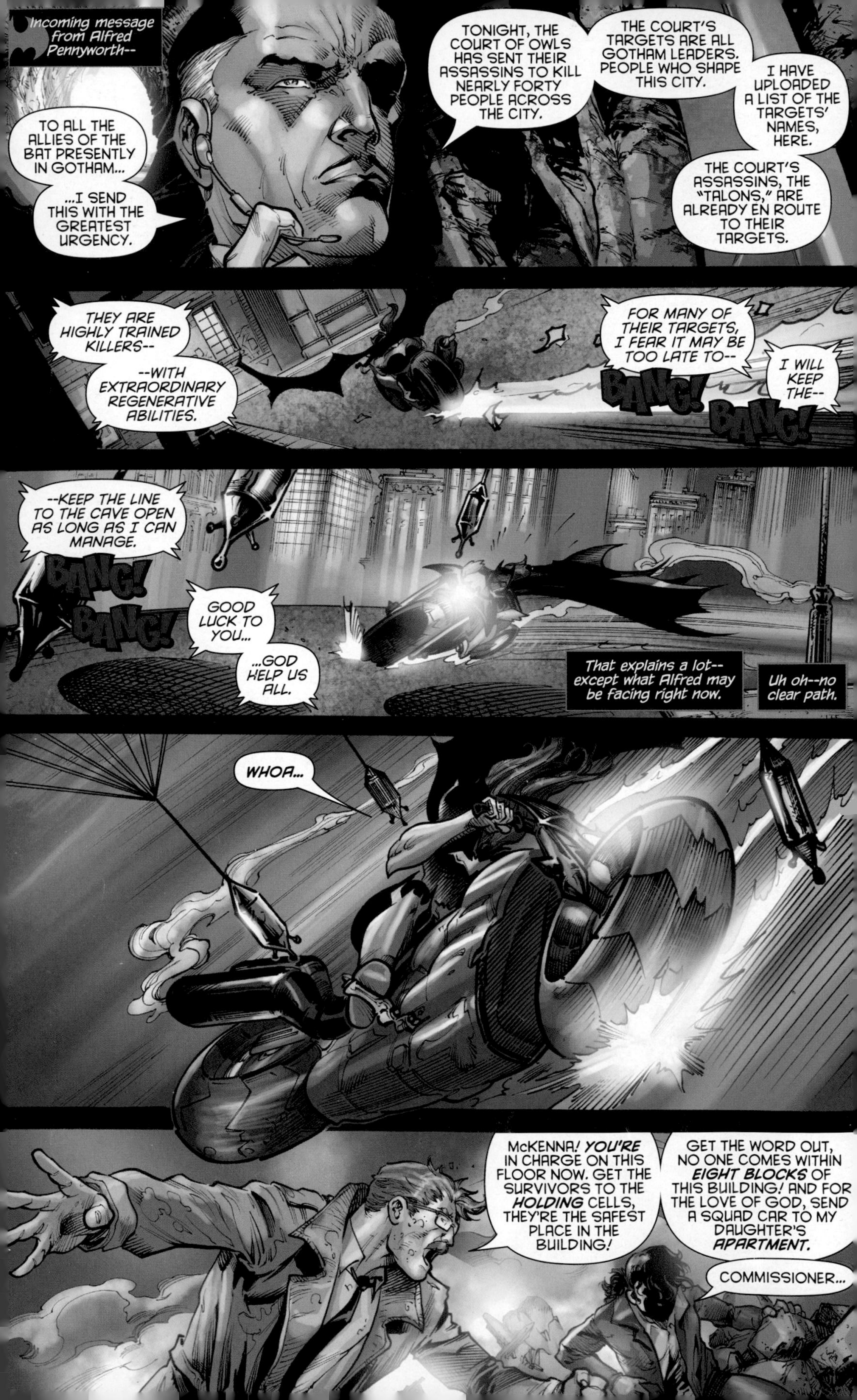
Incoming message from Alfred Pennyworth--
TO ALL THE ALLIES OF THE BAT PRESENTLY IN GOTHAM...
...I SEND THIS WITH THE GREATEST URGENCY.
TONIGHT, THE COURT OF OWLS HAS SENT THEIR ASSASSINS TO KILL NEARLY FORTY PEOPLE ACROSS THE CITY.
THE COURT'S TARGETS ARE ALL GOTHAM LEADERS. PEOPLE WHO SHAPE THIS CITY.
I HAVE UPLOADED A LIST OF THE TARGETS' NAMES, HERE.
THE COURT'S ASSASSINS, THE "TALONS," ARE ALREADY EN ROUTE TO THEIR TARGETS.
THEY ARE HIGHLY TRAINED KILLERS--
--WITH EXTRAORDINARY REGENERATIVE ABILITIES.
FOR MANY OF THEIR TARGETS, I FEAR IT MAY BE TOO LATE TO--
BANG!
I WILL KEEP THE--
BANG!
--KEEP THE LINE TO THE CAVE OPEN AS LONG AS I CAN MANAGE.
BANG!
BANG!
GOOD LUCK TO YOU...
...GOD HELP US ALL.
That explains a lot--except what Alfred may be facing right now.
Uh oh--no clear path.
WHOA...
McKENNA! YOU'RE IN CHARGE ON THIS FLOOR NOW. GET THE SURVIVORS TO THE HOLDING CELLS, THEY'RE THE SAFEST PLACE IN THE BUILDING!
GET THE WORD OUT, NO ONE COMES WITHIN EIGHT BLOCKS OF THIS BUILDING! AND FOR THE LOVE OF GOD, SEND A SQUAD CAR TO MY DAUGHTER'S APARTMENT.
COMMISSIONER...

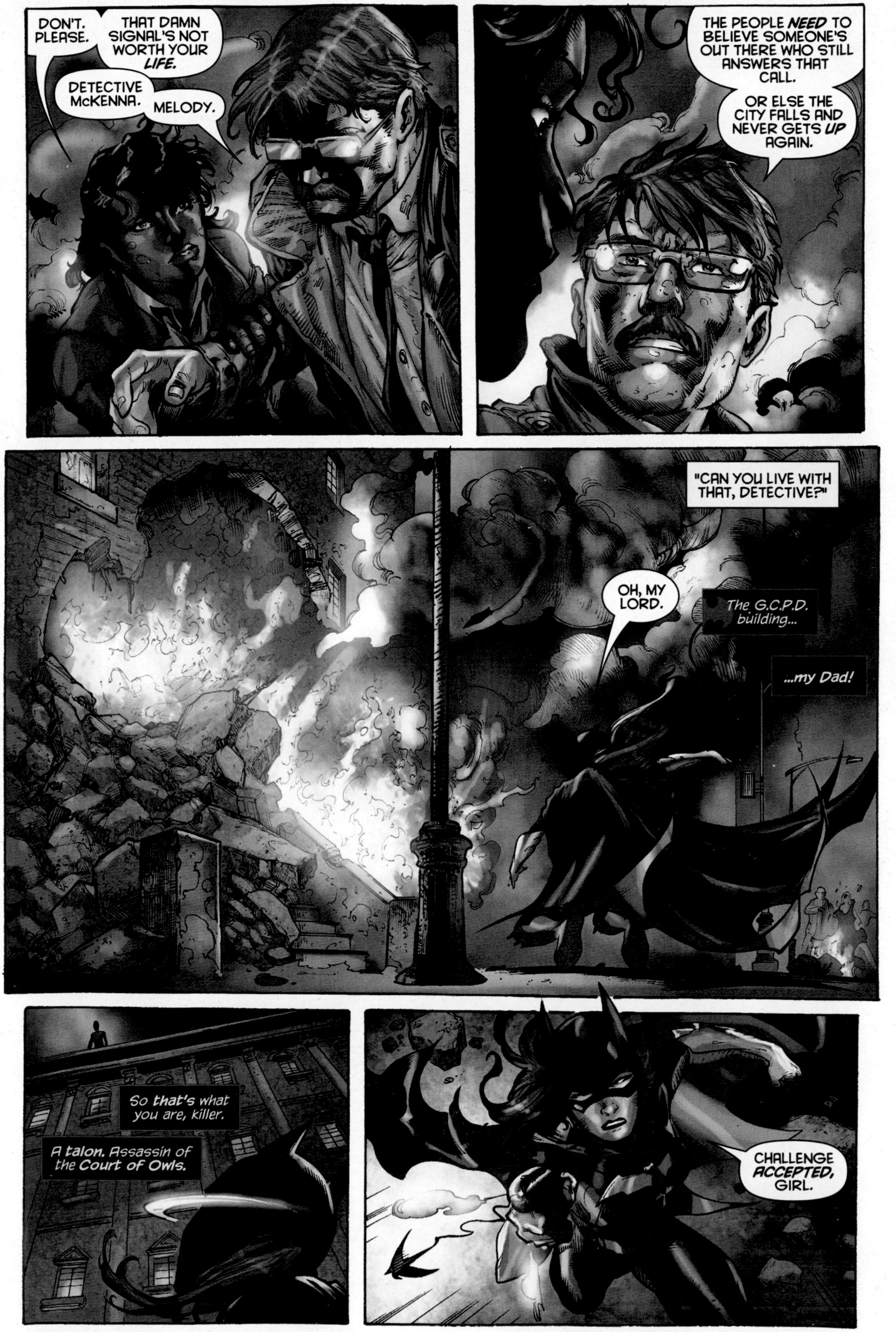

DON'T. PLEASE.
THAT DAMN SIGNAL'S NOT WORTH YOUR LIFE.
DETECTIVE McKENNA.
MELODY.
THE PEOPLE NEED TO BELIEVE SOMEONE'S OUT THERE WHO STILL ANSWERS THAT CALL.
OR ELSE THE CITY FALLS AND NEVER GETS UP AGAIN.
"CAN YOU LIVE WITH THAT, DETECTIVE?"
OH, MY LORD.
The G.C.P.D. building...
...my Dad!
So that's what you are, killer.
A talon. Assassin of the Court of Owls.
CHALLENGE ACCEPTED, GIRL.

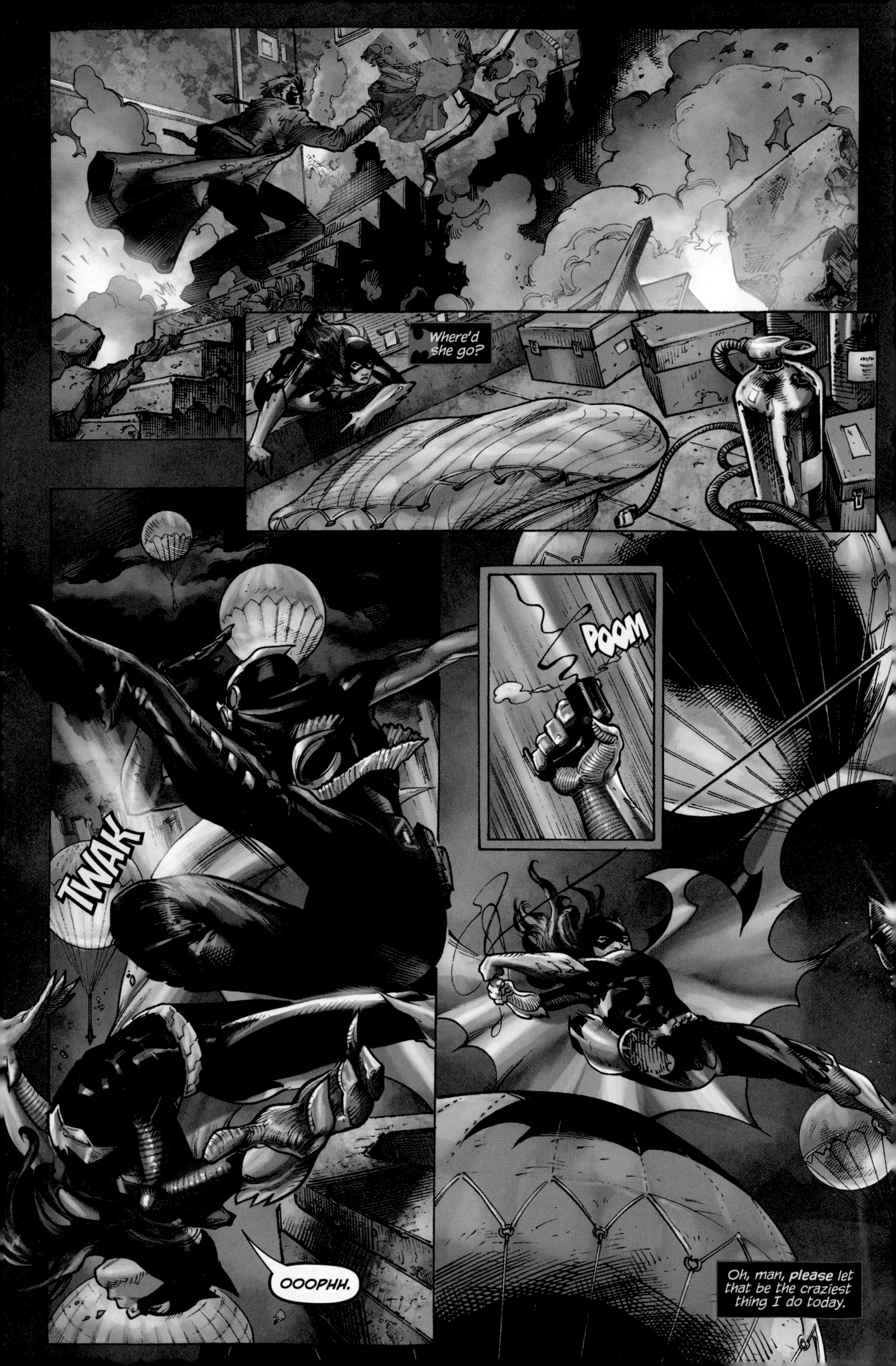
Where'd she go?
POOM
TWAK
OOOPHH.
Oh, man, **please** let that be the craziest thing I do today.

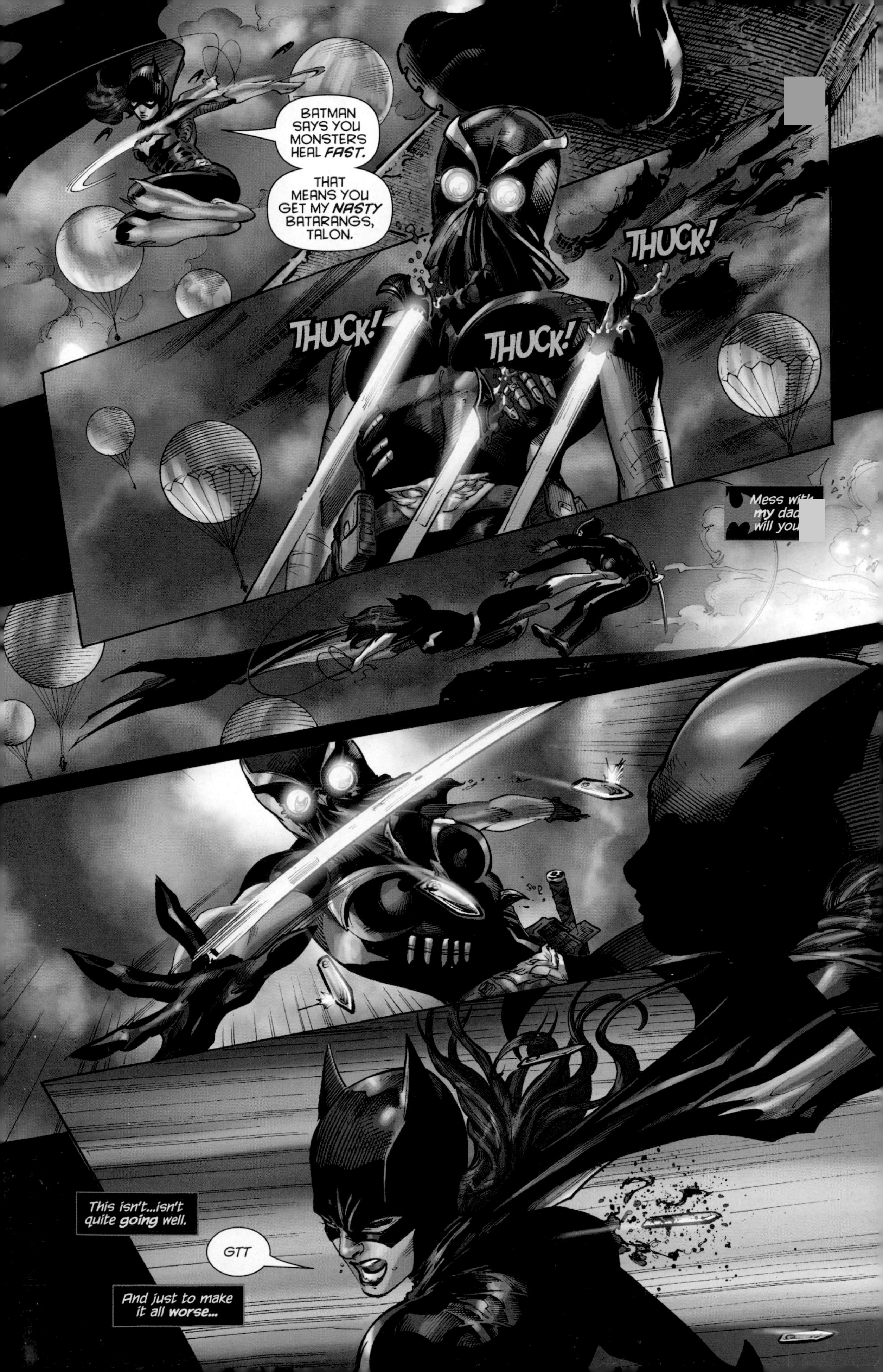

BATMAN SAYS YOU MONSTERS HEAL *FAST.*
THAT MEANS YOU GET MY *NASTY* BATARANGS, TALON.
THUCK!
THUCK!
THUCK!
Mess wit
my dad
will you
This isn't...isn't quite *going* well.
GTT
And just to make it all *worse...*

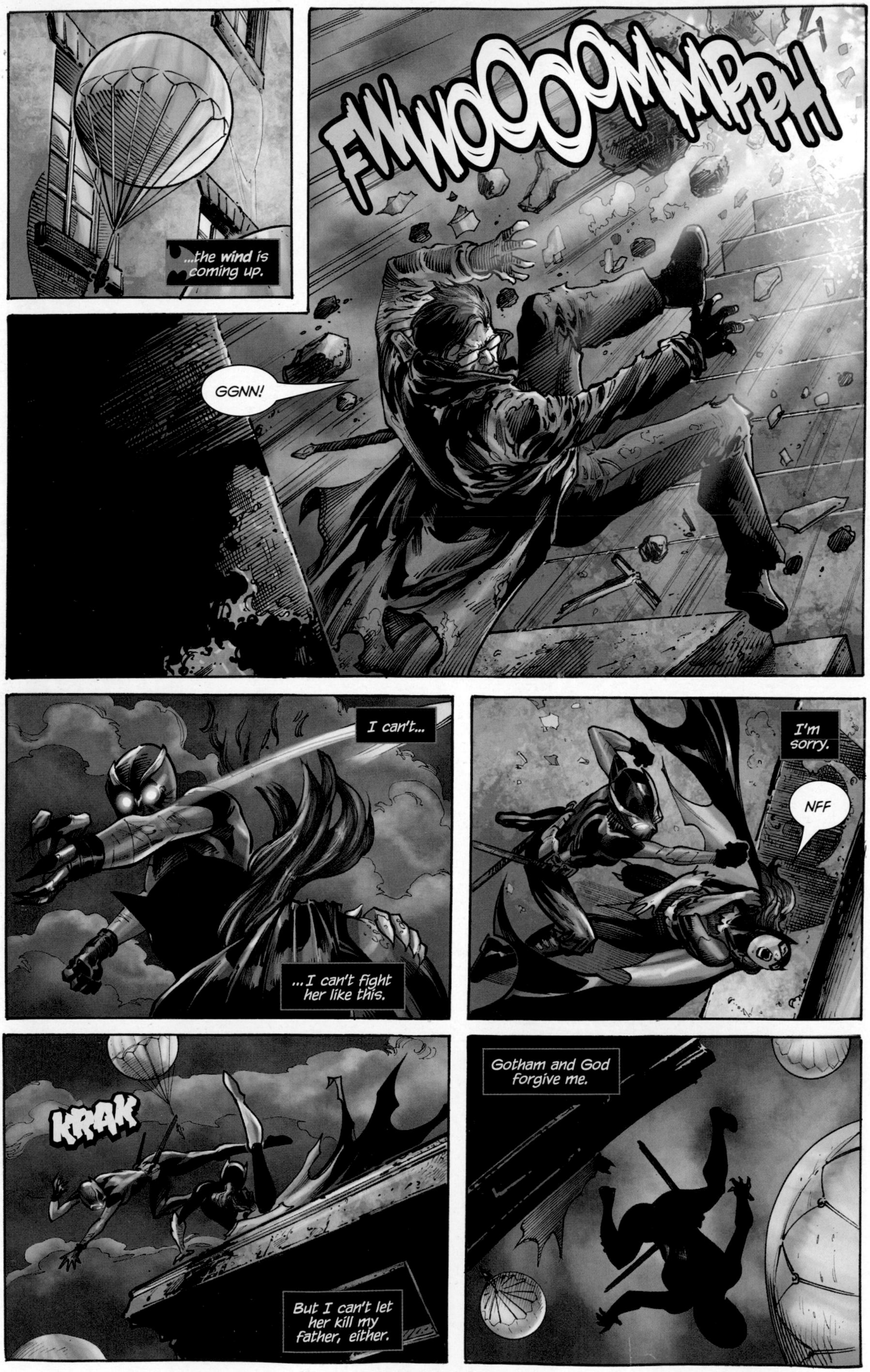

...the wind is coming up.
FWOOOOMMPPH
GGNN!
I can't...
...I can't fight her like this.
I'm sorry.
NFF
KRAK
But I can't let her kill my father, either.
Gotham and God forgive me.

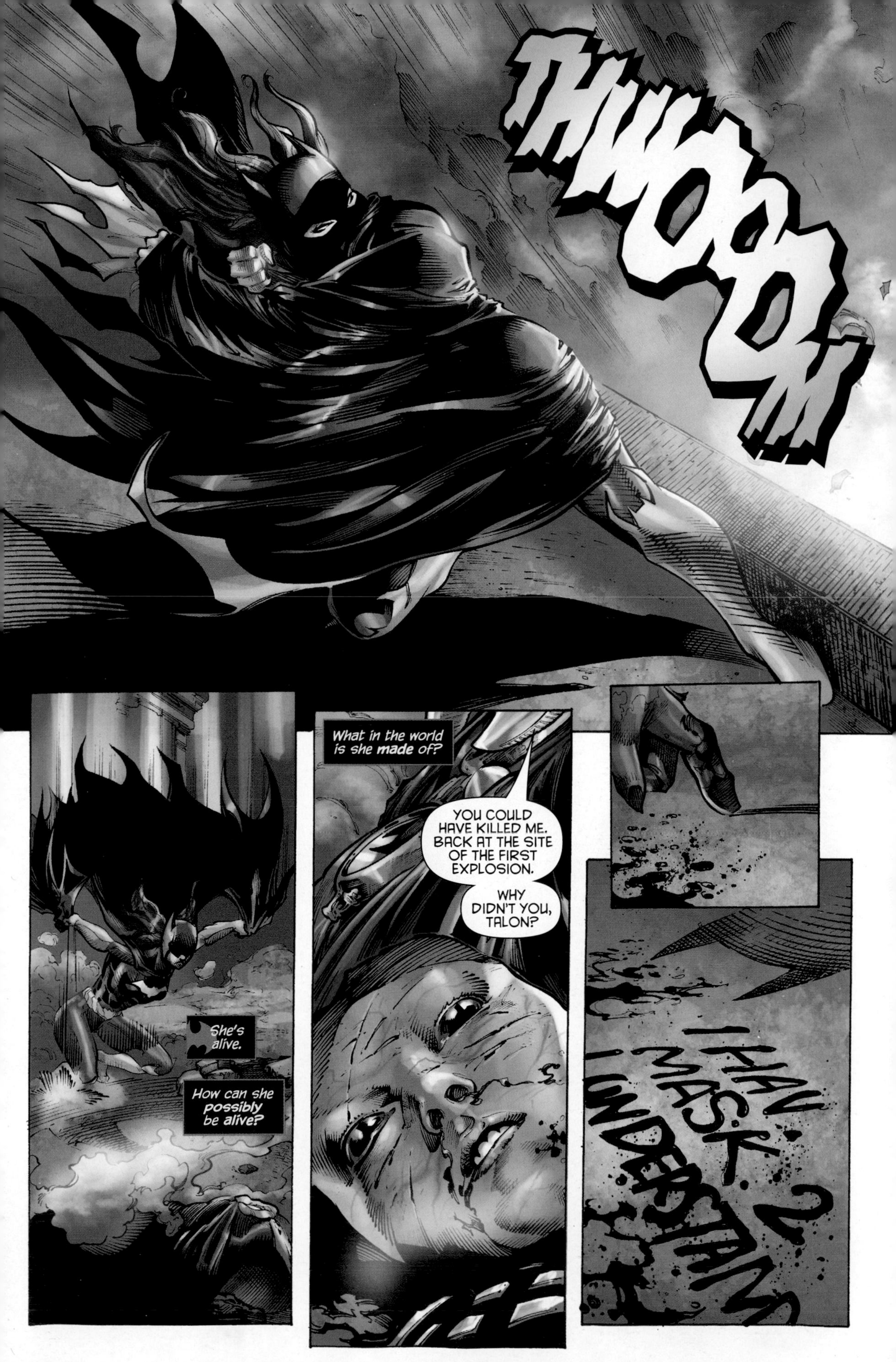
THWOOOM
She's alive.
How can she possibly be alive?
What in the world is she made of?
YOU COULD HAVE KILLED ME. BACK AT THE SITE OF THE FIRST EXPLOSION.
WHY DIDN'T YOU, TALON?
I HAV
MASK
UNDERSTAN?

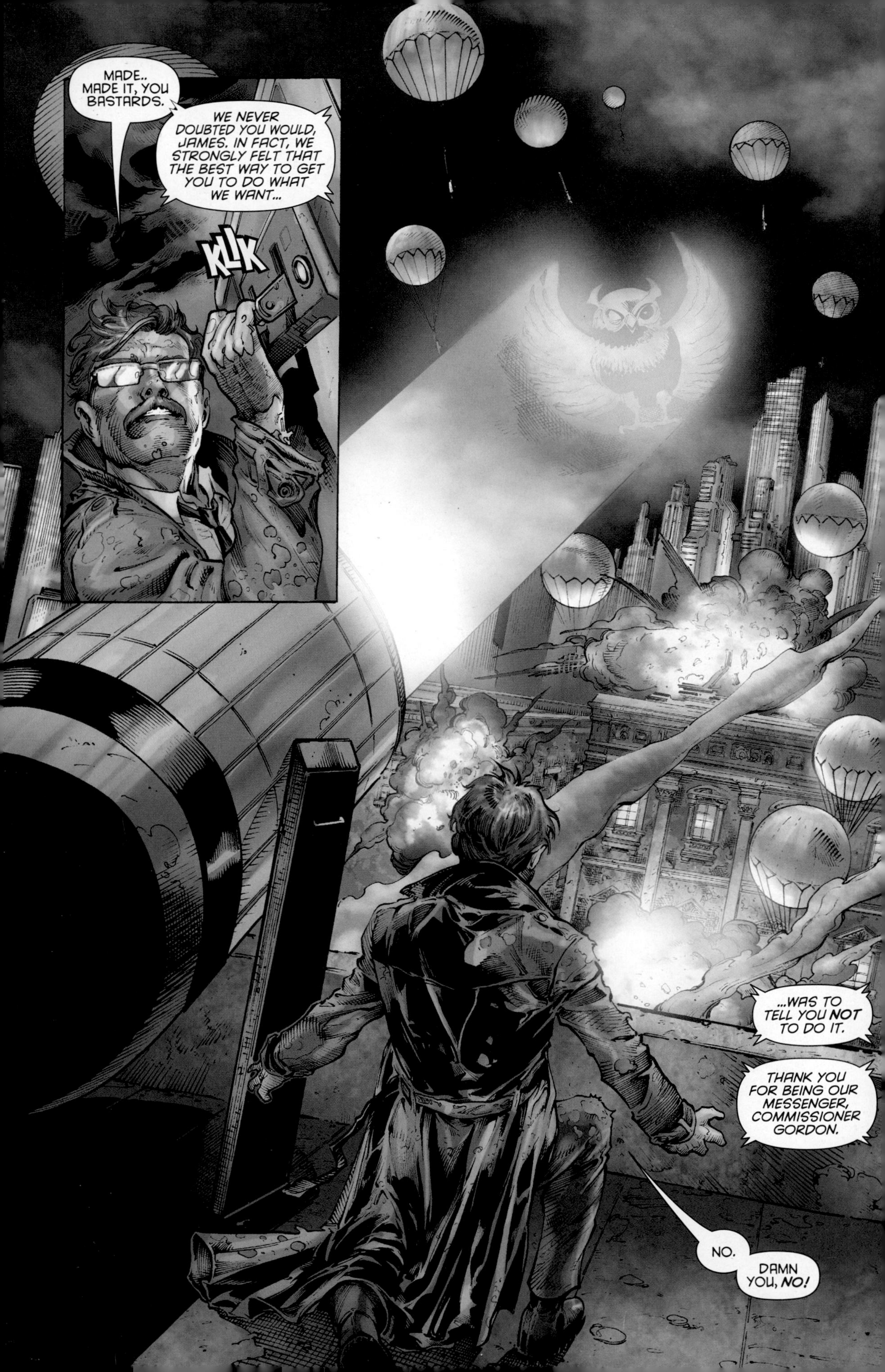
MADE.. MADE IT, YOU BASTARDS.
WE NEVER DOUBTED YOU WOULD, JAMES. IN FACT, WE STRONGLY FELT THAT THE BEST WAY TO GET YOU TO DO WHAT WE WANT...
KLIK
...WAS TO TELL YOU NOT TO DO IT.
THANK YOU FOR BEING OUR MESSENGER, COMMISSIONER GORDON.
NO.
DAMN YOU, NO!

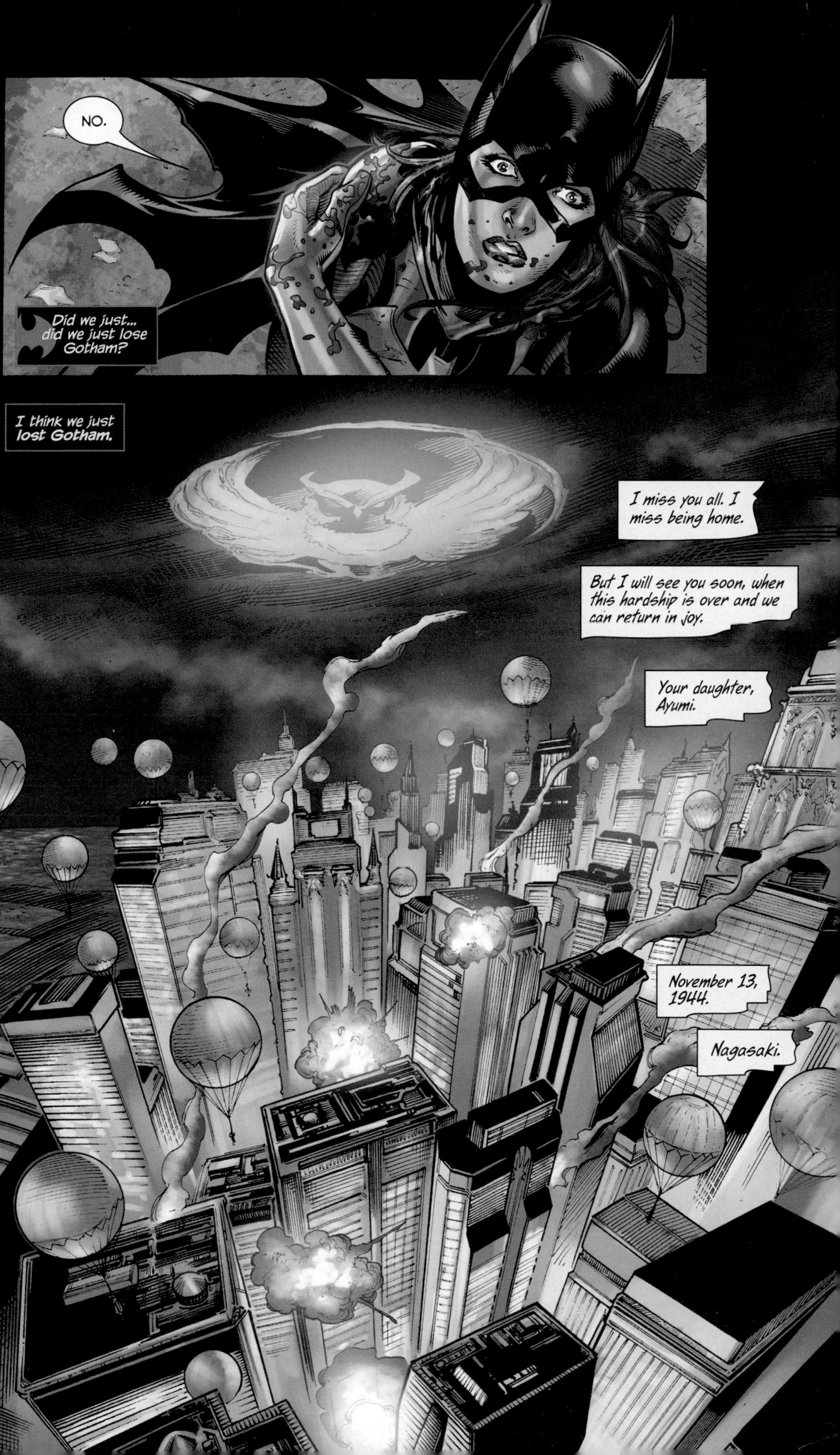
NO.
Did we just... did we just lose Gotham?
I think we just lost Gotham.
I miss you all. I miss being home.
But I will see you soon, when this hardship is over and we can return in joy.
Your daughter, Ayumi.
November 13, 1944.
Nagasaki.

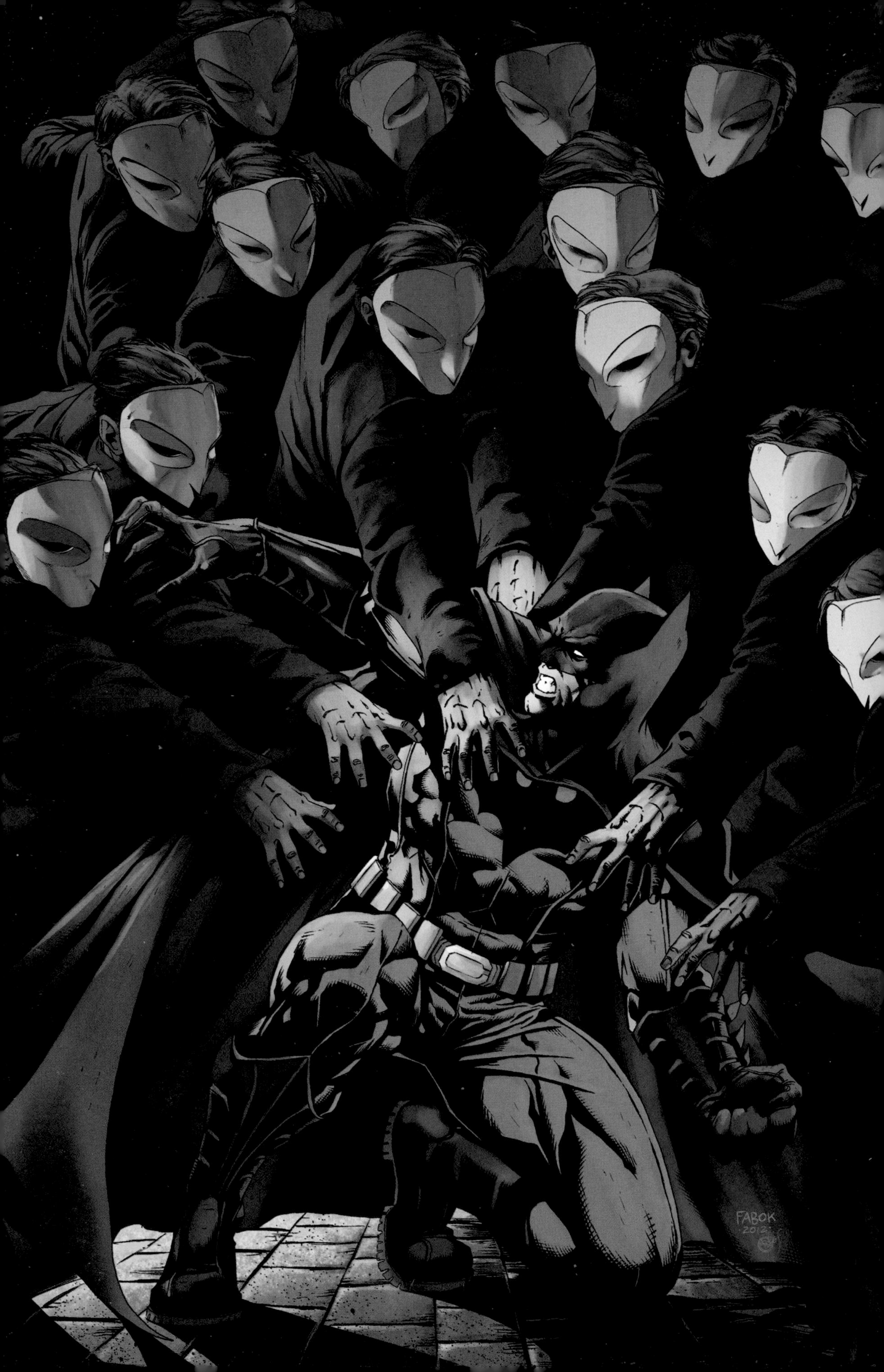
FABOK
2012

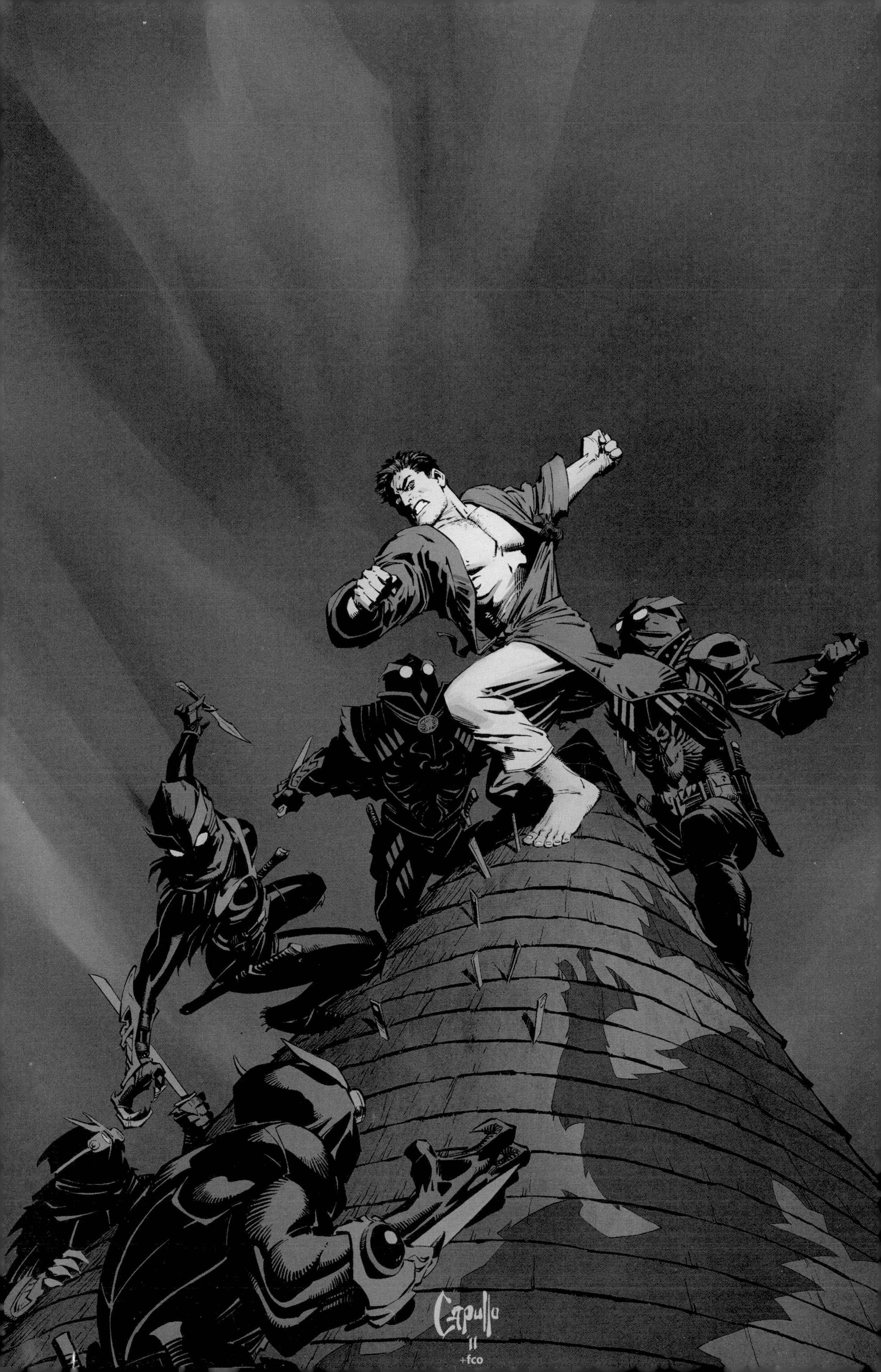
Capullo
'11
+fco

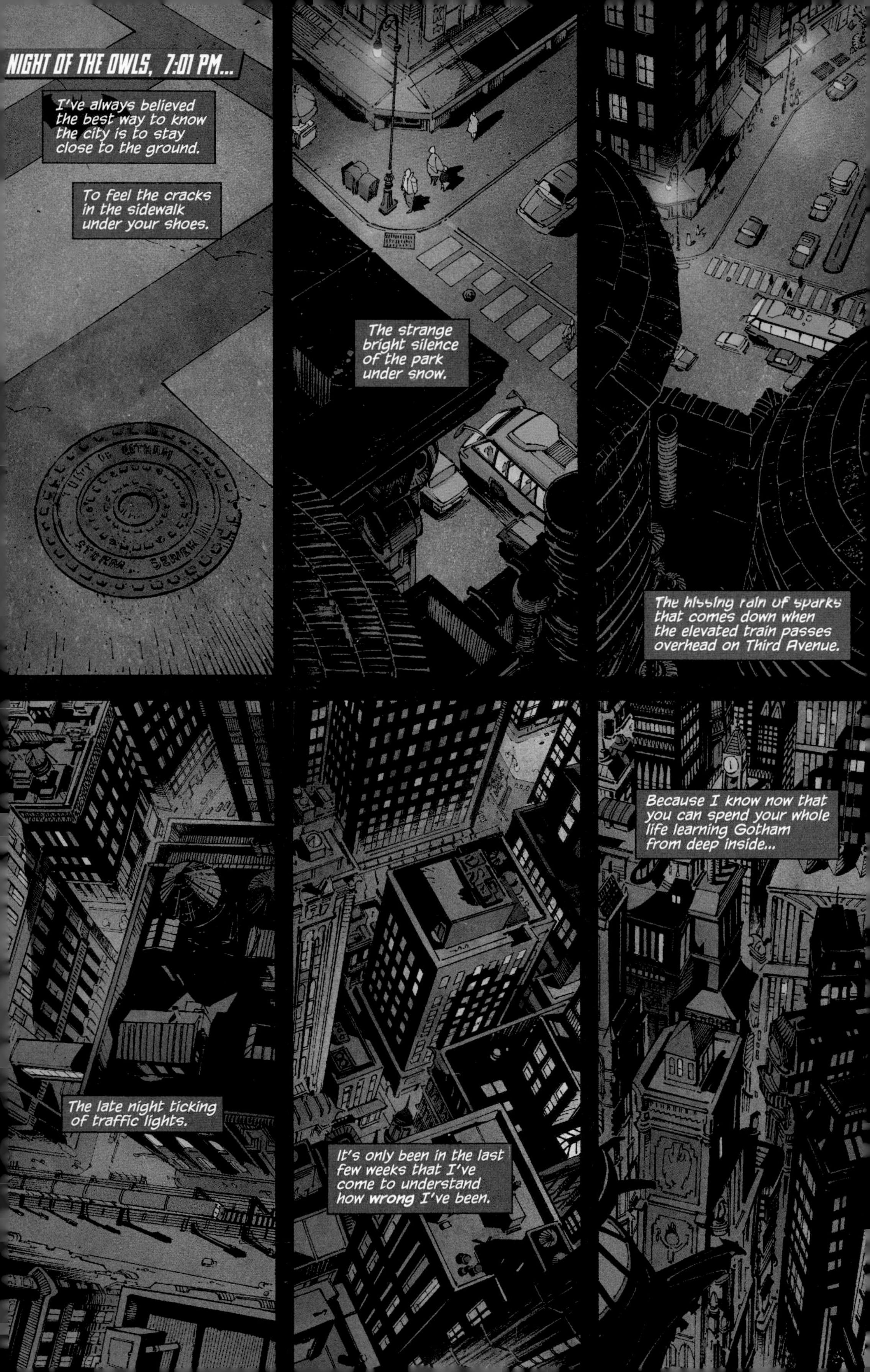
NIGHT OF THE OWLS, 7:01 PM...
I've always believed the best way to know the city is to stay close to the ground.
To feel the cracks in the sidewalk under your shoes.
The strange bright silence of the park under snow.
The hissing rain of sparks that comes down when the elevated train passes overhead on Third Avenue.
The late night ticking of traffic lights.
It's only been in the last few weeks that I've come to understand how **wrong** I've been.
Because I know now that you can spend your whole life learning Gotham from deep inside...

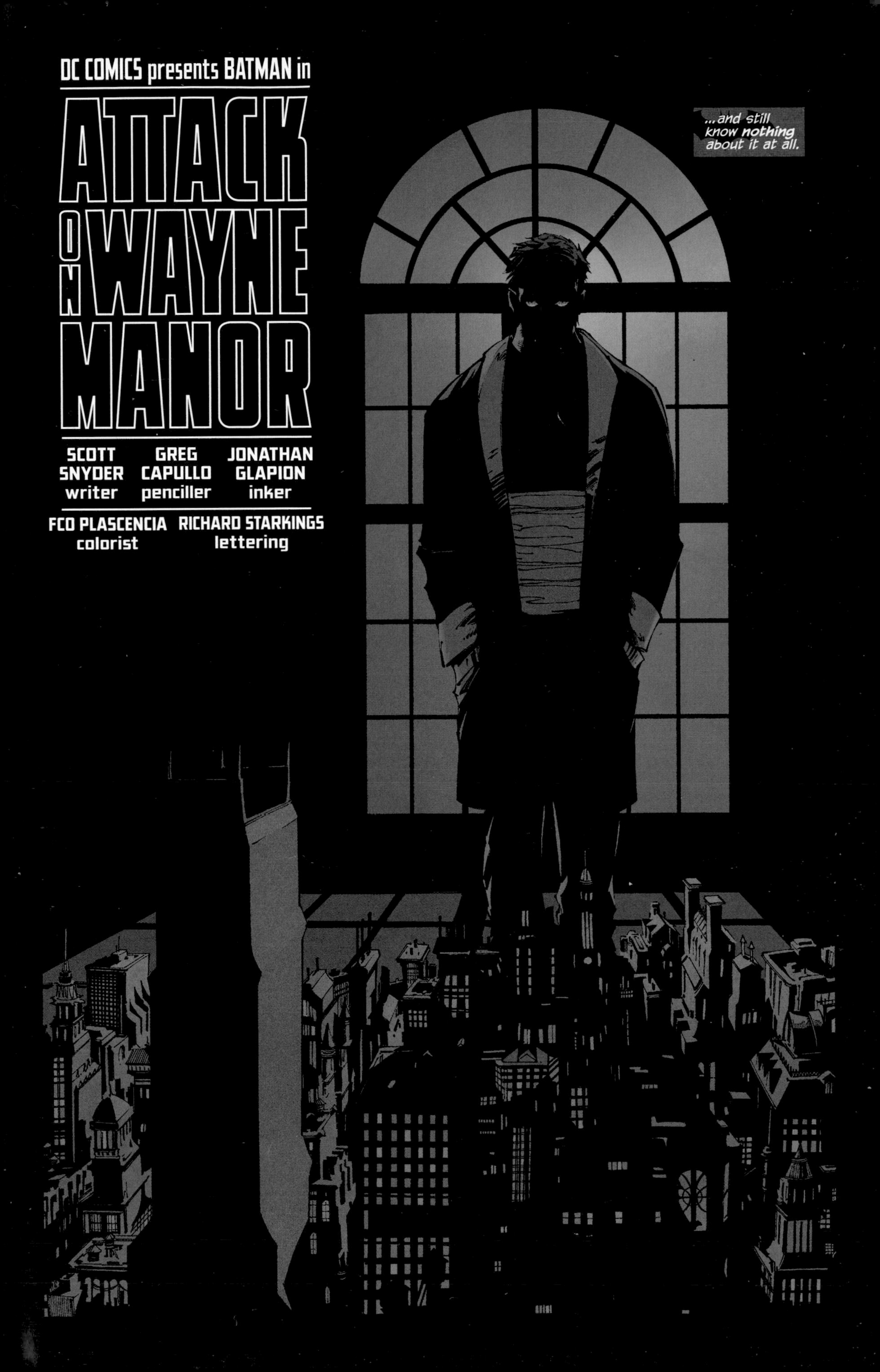
DC COMICS presents BATMAN in
ATTACK ON WAYNE MANOR
SCOTT SNYDER writer
GREG CAPULLO penciller
JONATHAN GLAPION inker
FCO PLASCENCIA colorist
RICHARD STARKINGS lettering
...and still know nothing about it at all.

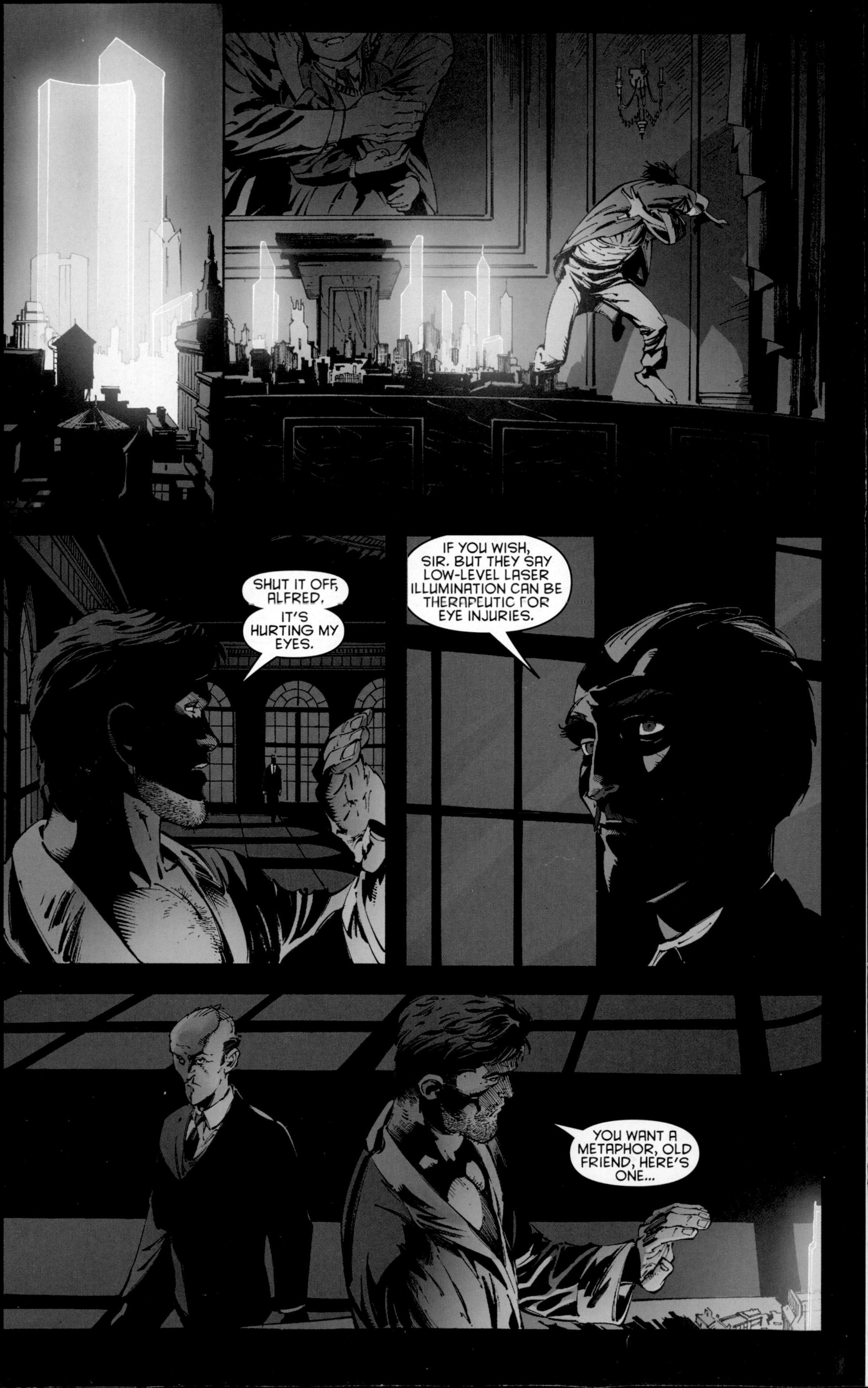

SHUT IT OFF, ALFRED. IT'S HURTING MY EYES.
IF YOU WISH, SIR. BUT THEY SAY LOW-LEVEL LASER ILLUMINATION CAN BE THERAPEUTIC FOR EYE INJURIES.
YOU WANT A METAPHOR, OLD FRIEND, HERE'S ONE...

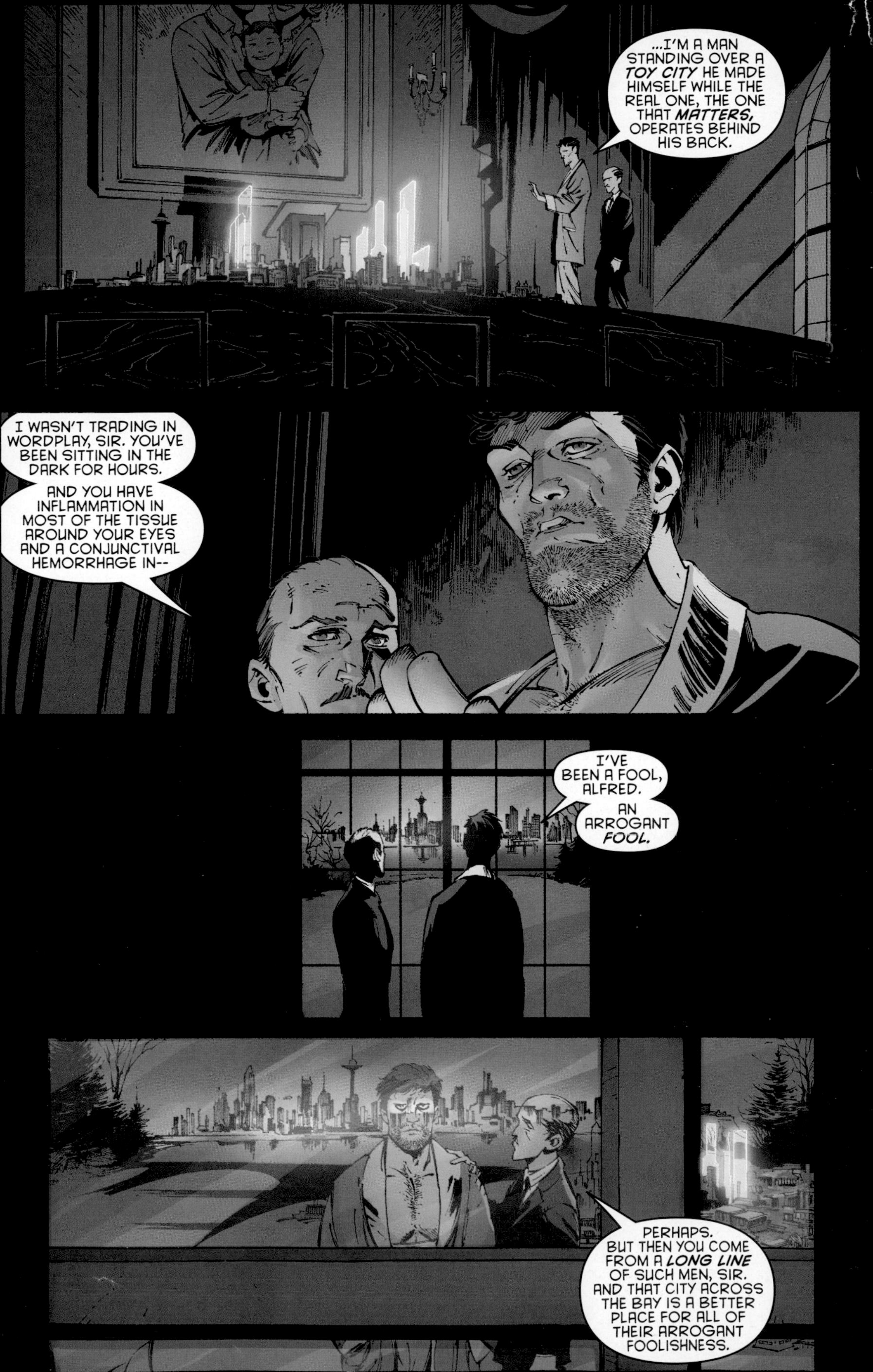
...I'M A MAN STANDING OVER A TOY CITY HE MADE HIMSELF WHILE THE REAL ONE, THE ONE THAT MATTERS, OPERATES BEHIND HIS BACK.
I WASN'T TRADING IN WORDPLAY, SIR. YOU'VE BEEN SITTING IN THE DARK FOR HOURS.
AND YOU HAVE INFLAMMATION IN MOST OF THE TISSUE AROUND YOUR EYES AND A CONJUNCTIVAL HEMORRHAGE IN--
I'VE BEEN A FOOL, ALFRED.
AN ARROGANT FOOL.
PERHAPS. BUT THEN YOU COME FROM A LONG LINE OF SUCH MEN, SIR. AND THAT CITY ACROSS THE BAY IS A BETTER PLACE FOR ALL OF THEIR ARROGANT FOOLISHNESS.

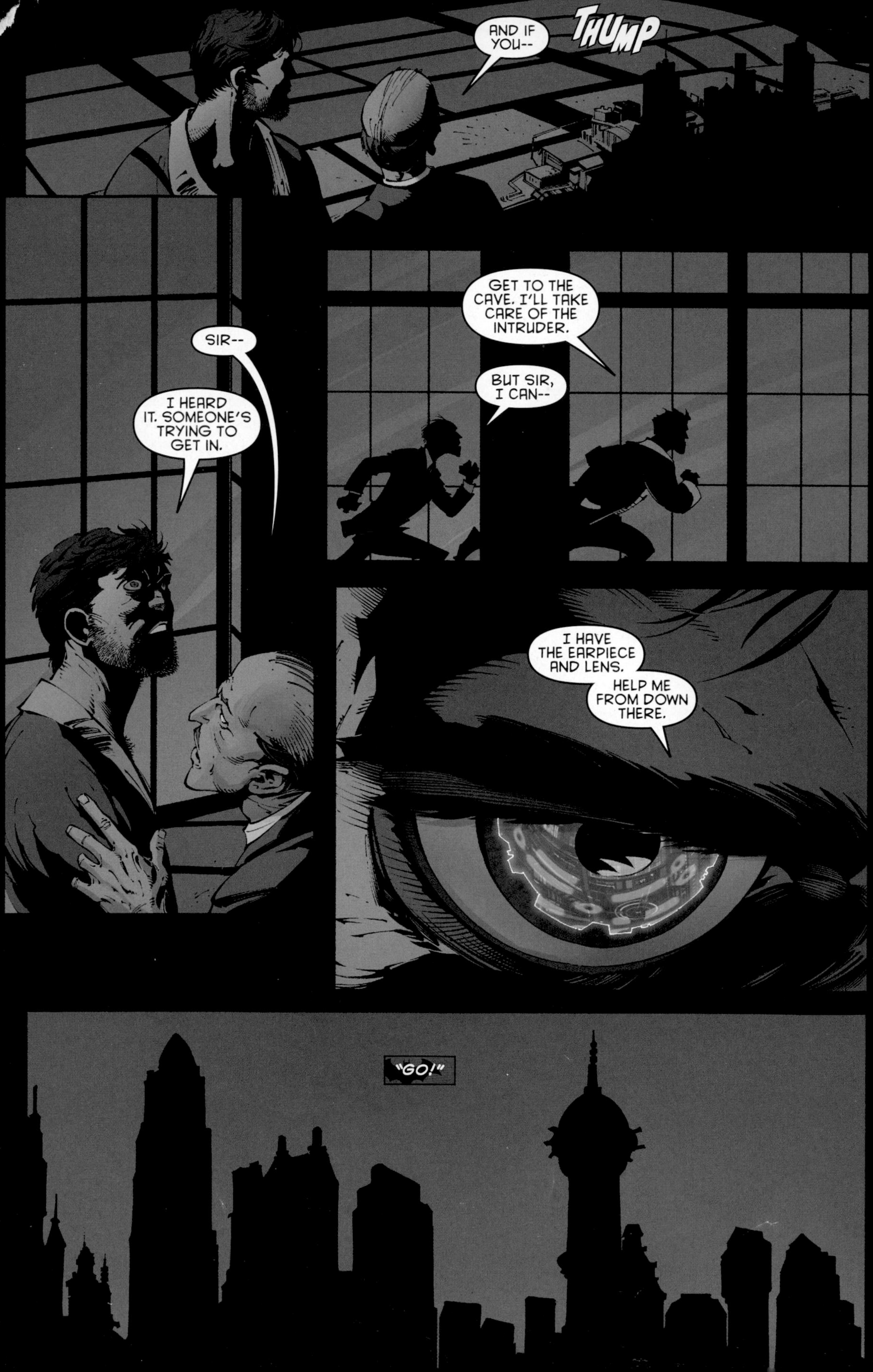
AND IF YOU--
THUMP
SIR--
I HEARD IT. SOMEONE'S TRYING TO GET IN.
GET TO THE CAVE. I'LL TAKE CARE OF THE INTRUDER.
BUT SIR, I CAN--
I HAVE THE EARPIECE AND LENS.
HELP ME FROM DOWN THERE.
"GO!"

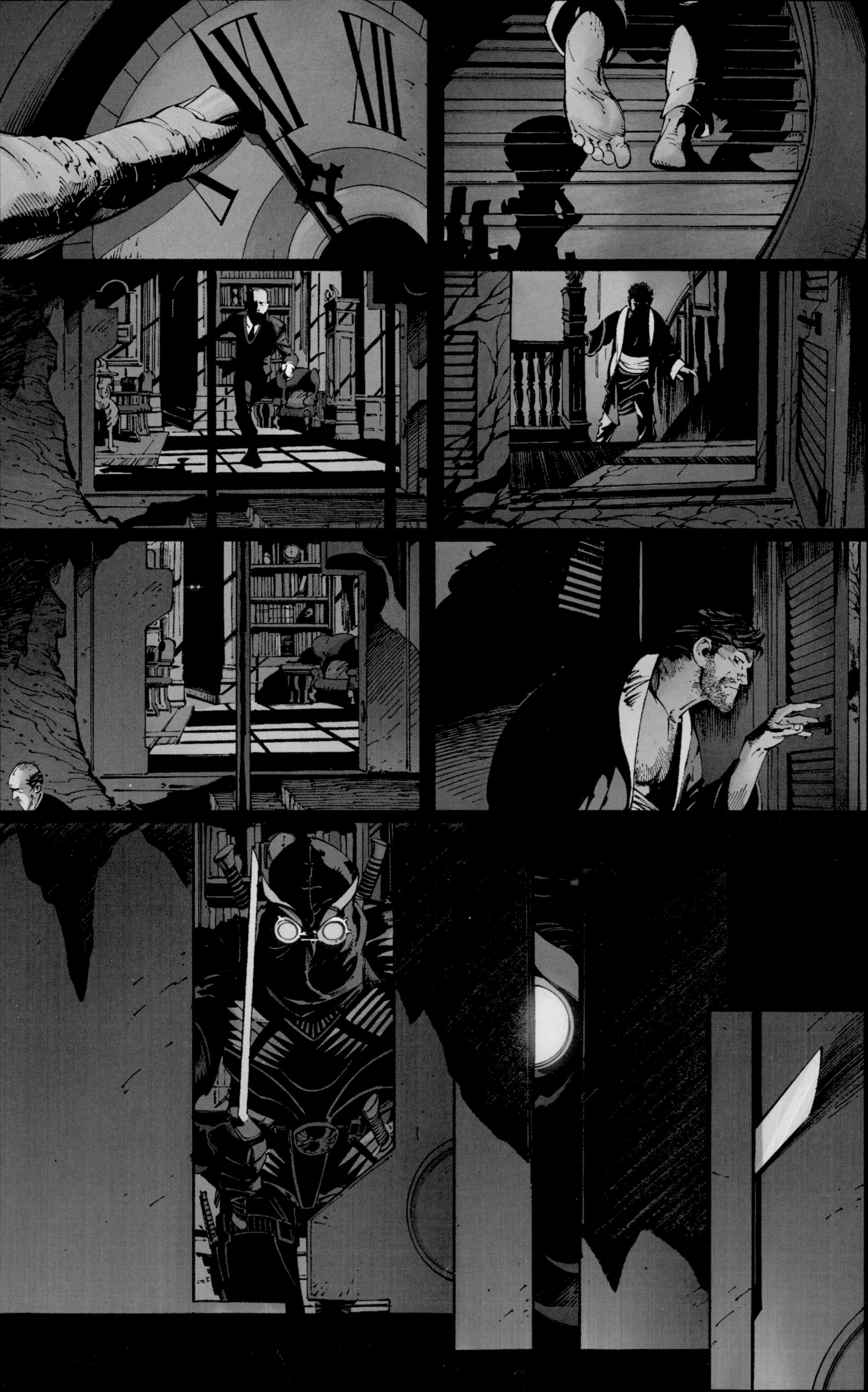

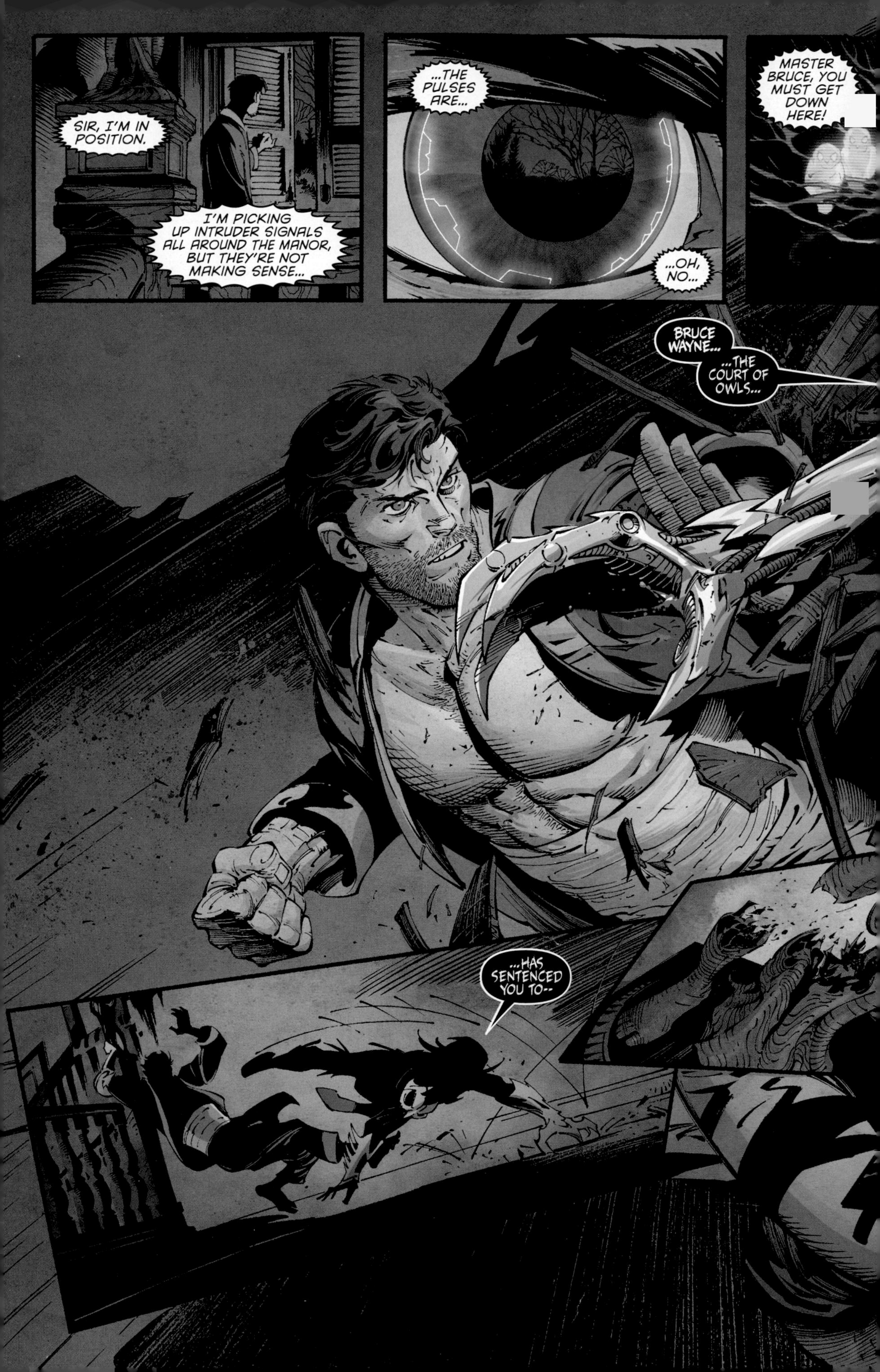
SIR, I'M IN POSITION.
I'M PICKING UP INTRUDER SIGNALS ALL AROUND THE MANOR, BUT THEY'RE NOT MAKING SENSE...
...THE PULSES ARE...
...OH, NO...
MASTER BRUCE, YOU MUST GET DOWN HERE!
BRUCE WAYNE...
...THE COURT OF OWLS...
...HAS SENTENCED YOU TO--

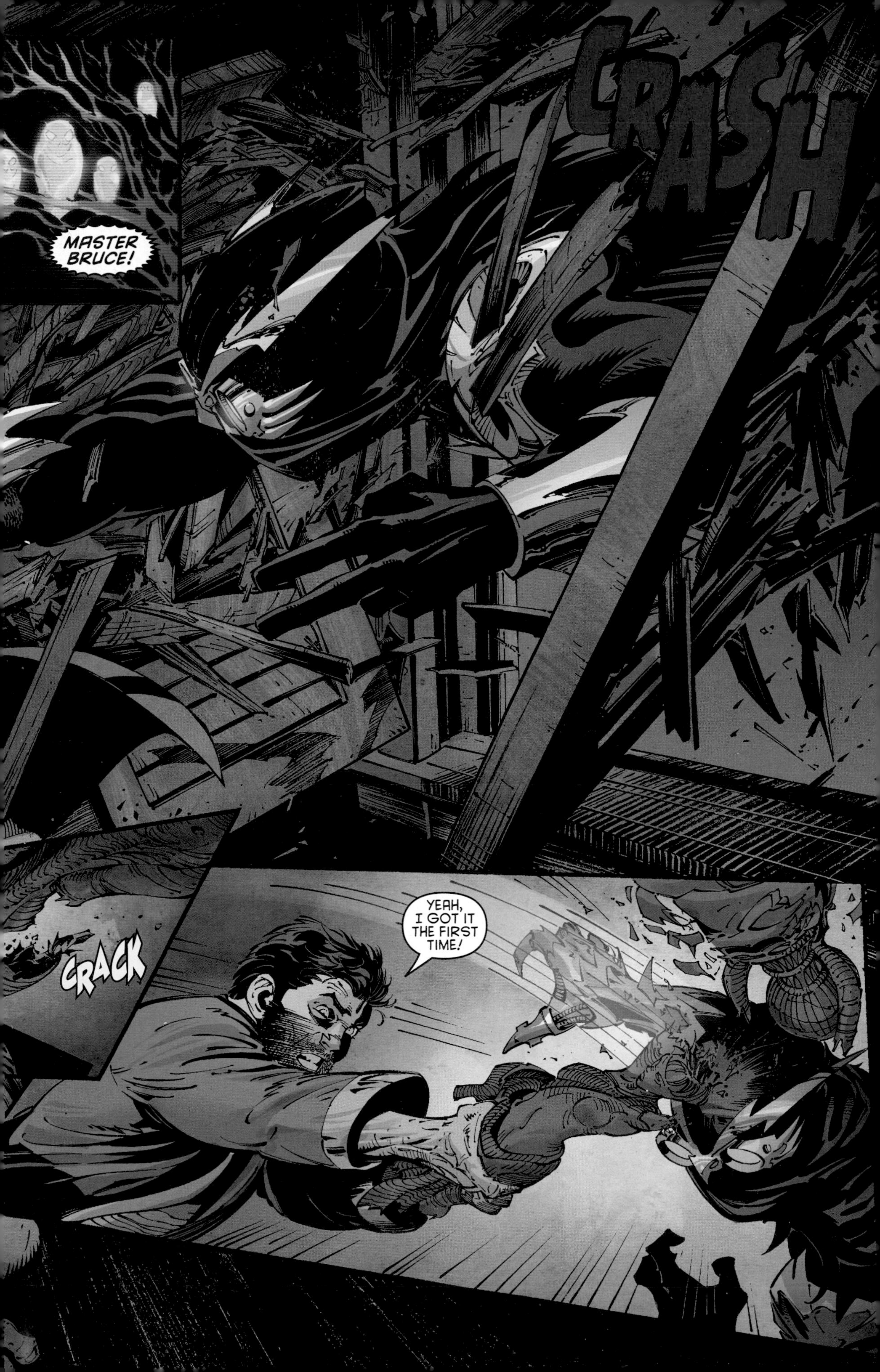
MASTER BRUCE!
CRASH
CRACK
YEAH, I GOT IT THE FIRST TIME!

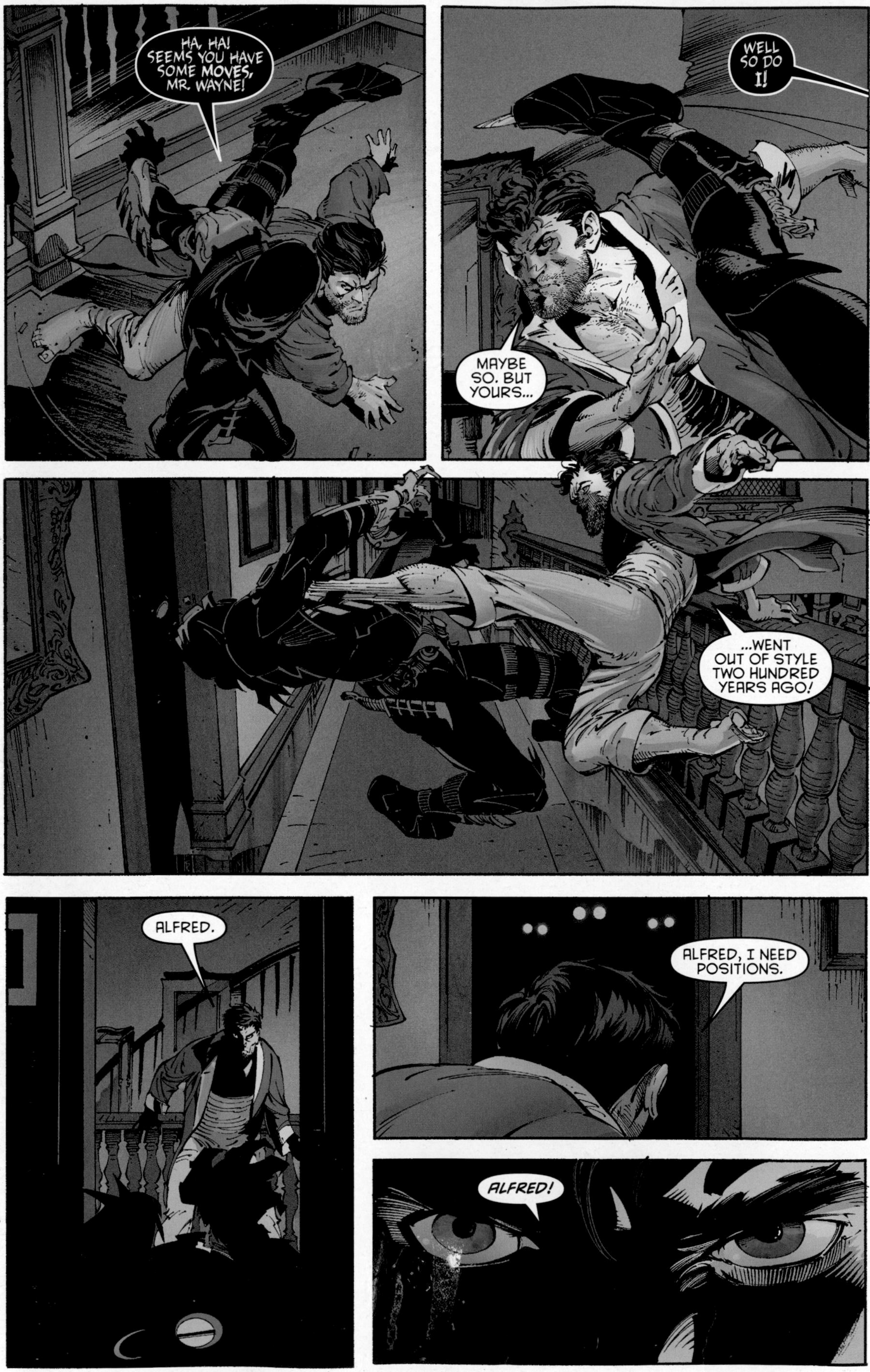
HA, HA! SEEMS YOU HAVE SOME MOVES, MR. WAYNE!
WELL SO DO I!
MAYBE SO. BUT YOURS...
...WENT OUT OF STYLE TWO HUNDRED YEARS AGO!
ALFRED.
ALFRED, I NEED POSITIONS.
ALFRED!

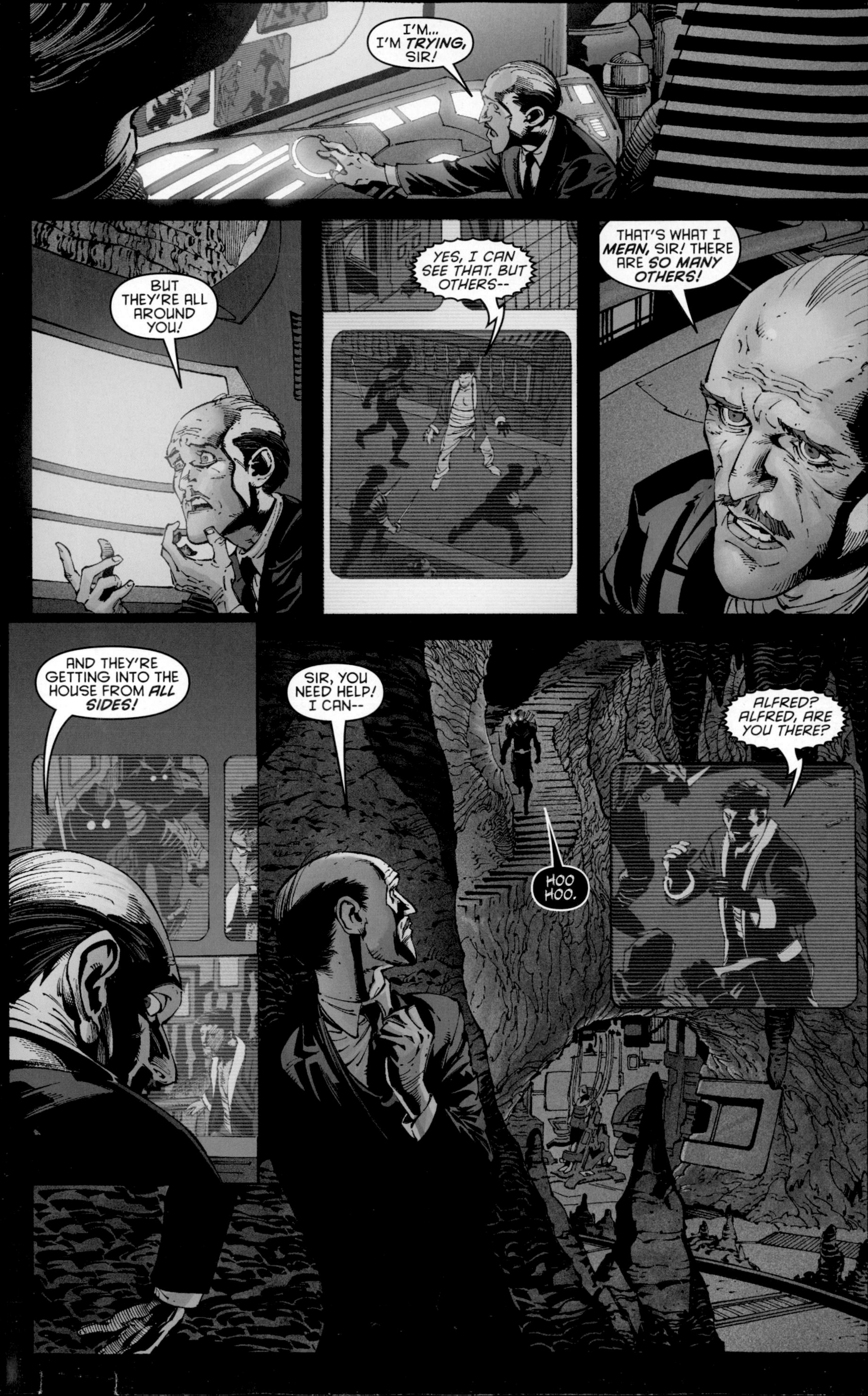
I'M... I'M *TRYING,* SIR!
BUT THEY'RE ALL AROUND YOU!
YES, I CAN SEE THAT. BUT OTHERS--
THAT'S WHAT I *MEAN,* SIR! THERE ARE *SO MANY OTHERS!*
AND THEY'RE GETTING INTO THE HOUSE FROM *ALL SIDES!*
SIR, YOU NEED HELP! I CAN--
ALFRED? ALFRED, ARE YOU THERE?
HOO HOO.

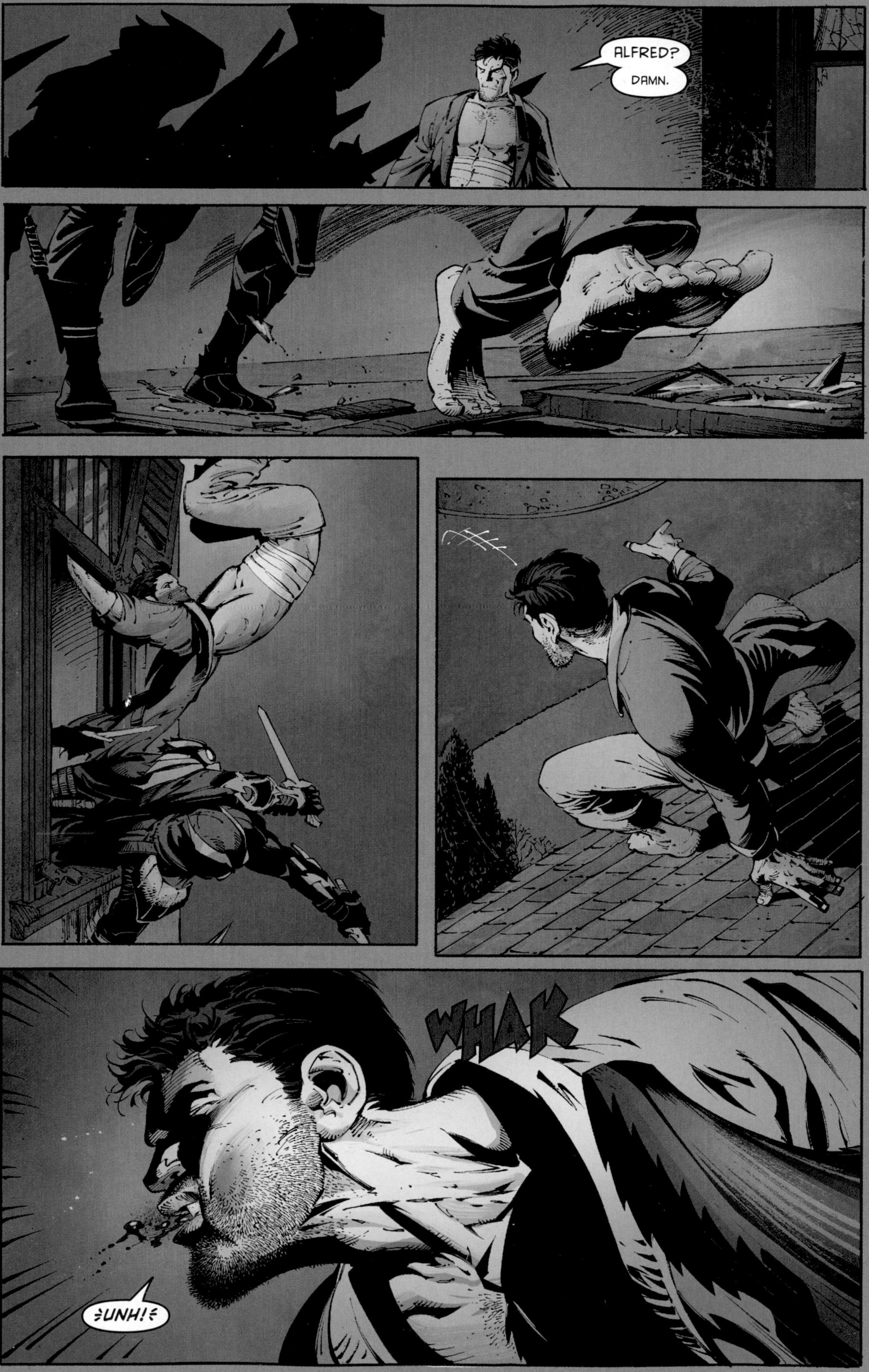
ALFRED?
DAMN.
WHAK
UNH!

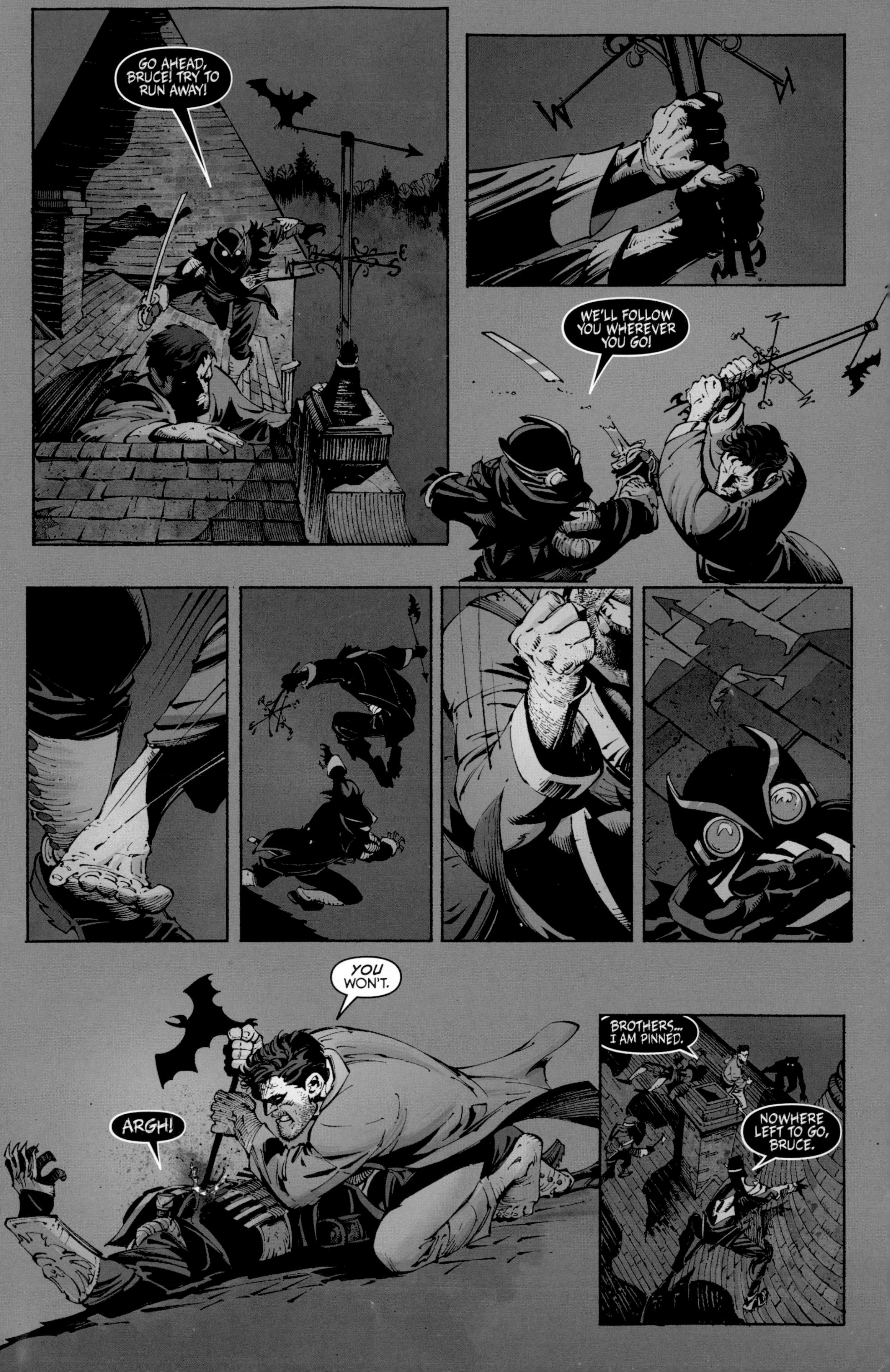
GO AHEAD, BRUCE! TRY TO RUN AWAY!
WE'LL FOLLOW YOU WHEREVER YOU GO!
YOU WON'T.
ARGH!
BROTHERS... I AM PINNED.
NOWHERE LEFT TO GO, BRUCE.

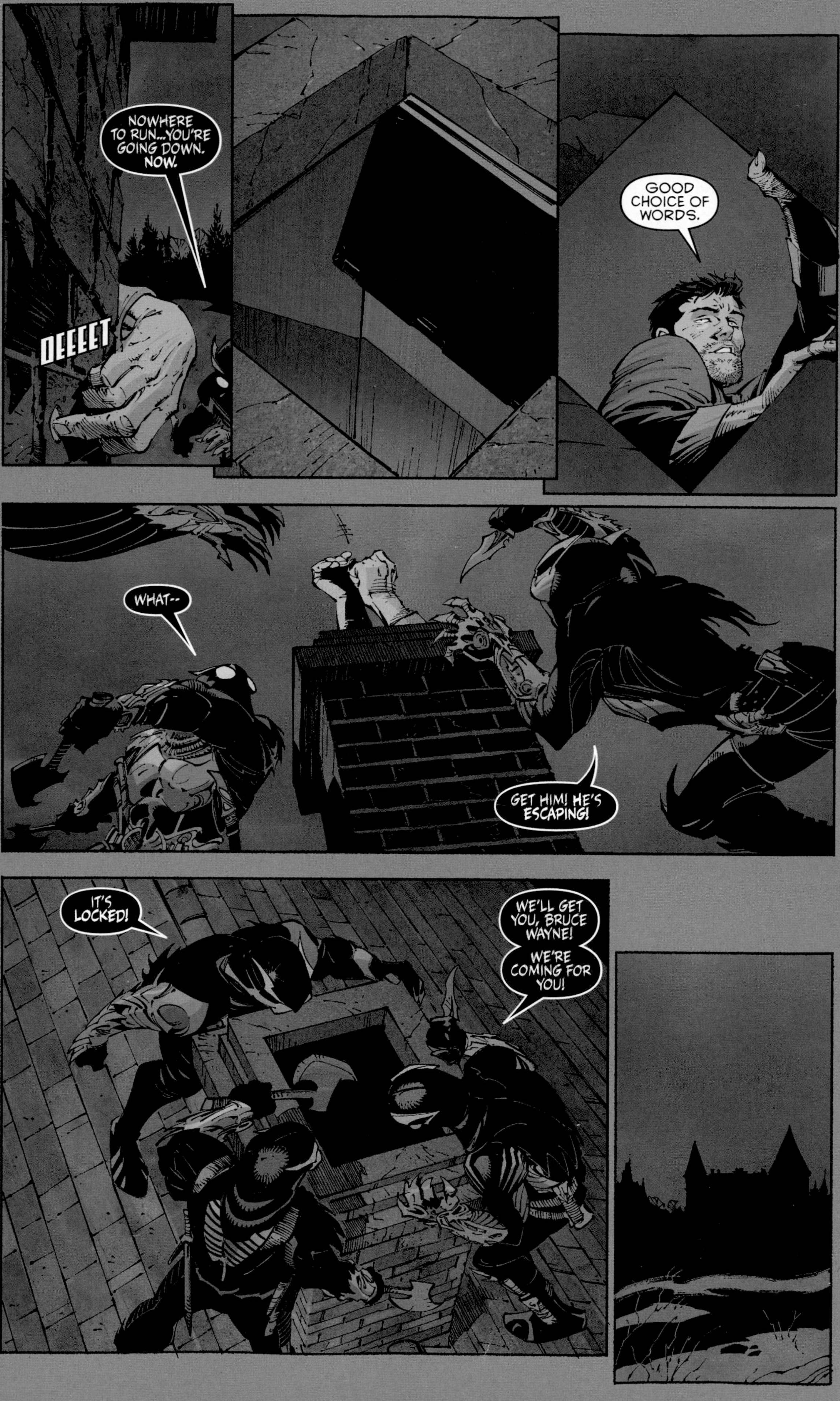
NOWHERE TO RUN...YOU'RE GOING DOWN. NOW.
DEEEET
GOOD CHOICE OF WORDS.
WHAT--
GET HIM! HE'S ESCAPING!
IT'S LOCKED!
WE'LL GET YOU, BRUCE WAYNE!
WE'RE COMING FOR YOU!

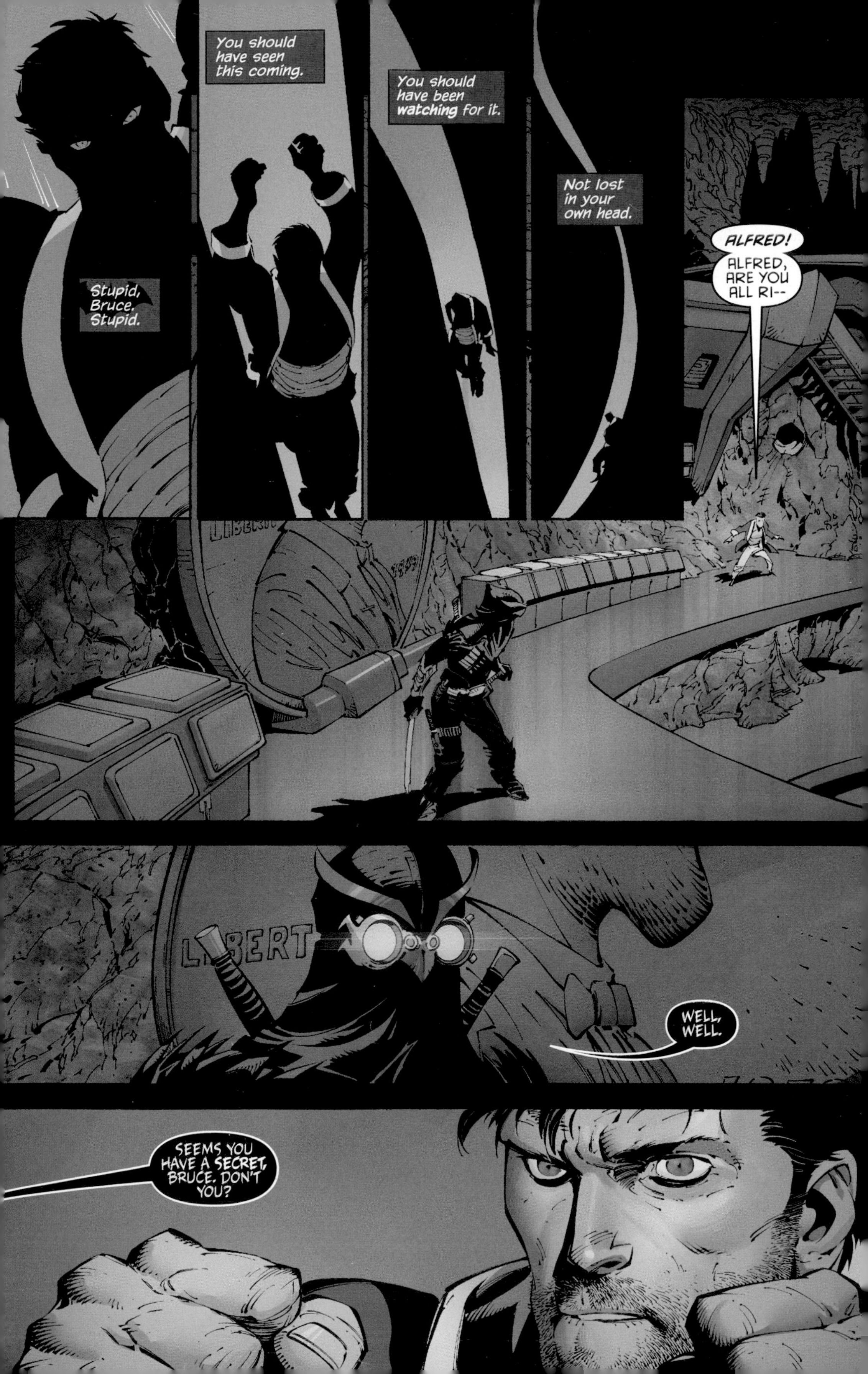

Stupid, Bruce. Stupid.
You should have seen this coming.
You should have been **watching** for it.
Not lost in your own head.
ALFRED!
ALFRED, ARE YOU ALL RI--
LIBERT
WELL, WELL.
SEEMS YOU HAVE A **SECRET**, BRUCE. DON'T YOU?

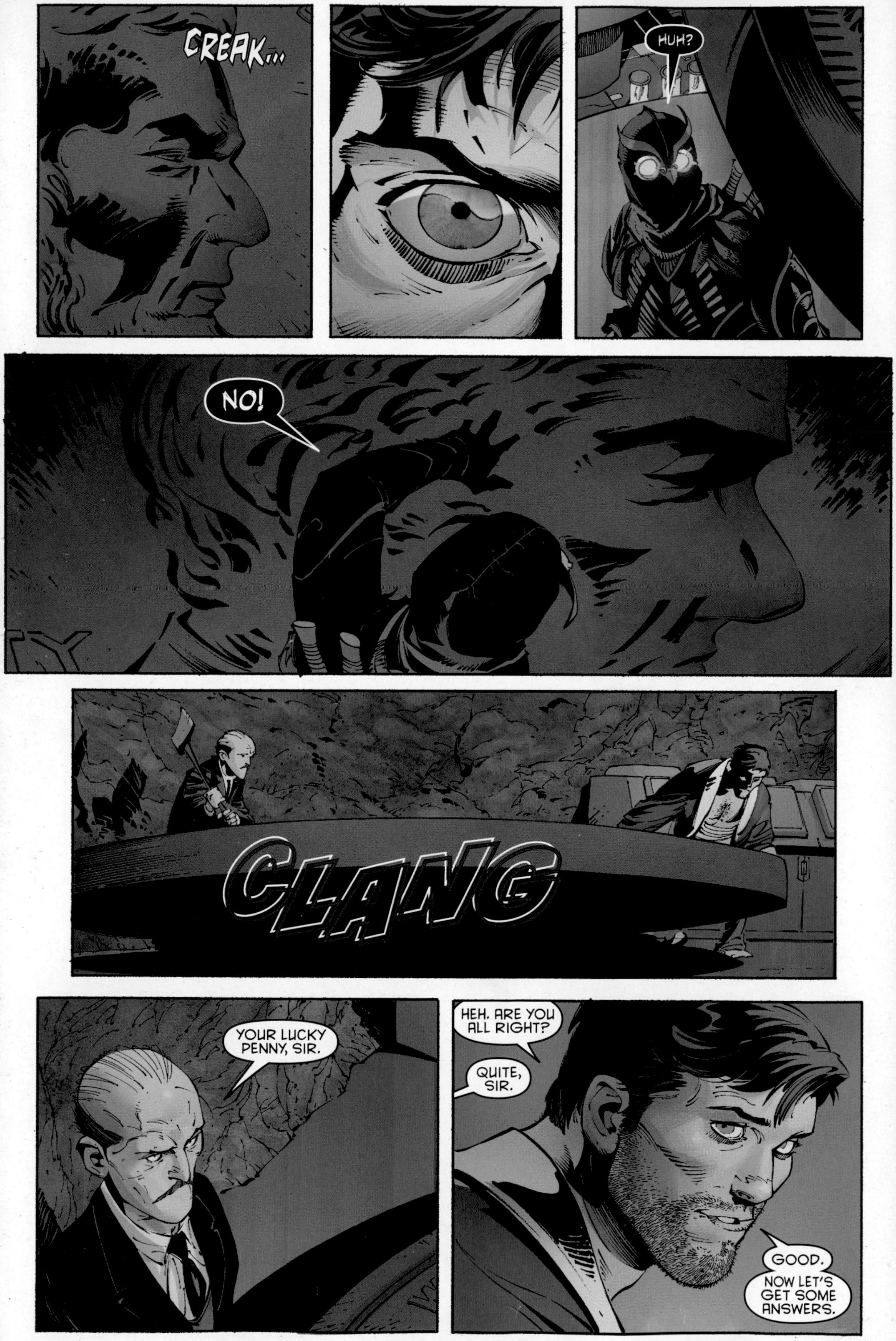
CREAK...
HUH?
NO!
CLANG
YOUR LUCKY PENNY, SIR.
HEH. ARE YOU ALL RIGHT?
QUITE, SIR.
GOOD. NOW LET'S GET SOME ANSWERS.

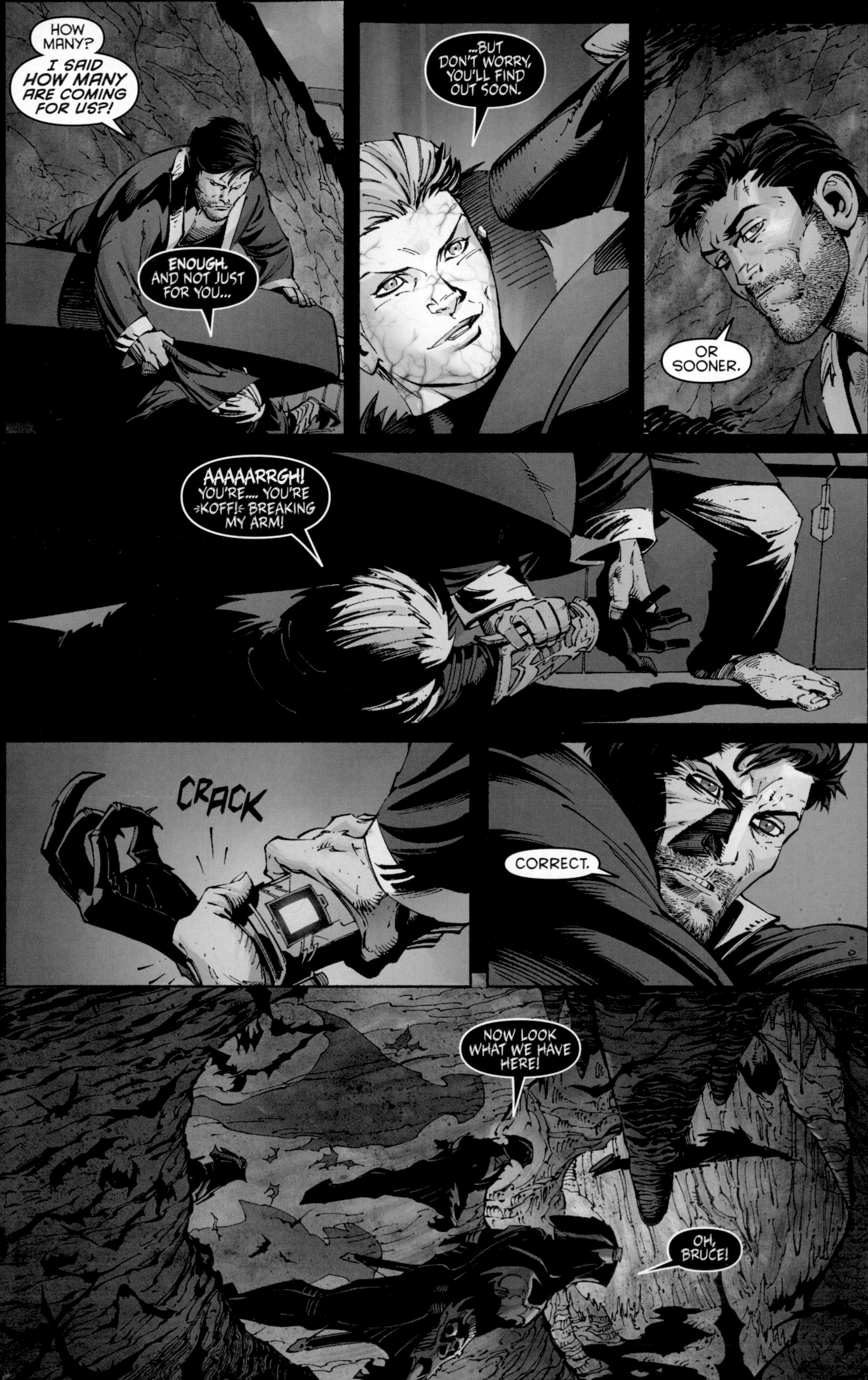
HOW MANY?
I SAID HOW MANY ARE COMING FOR US?!
ENOUGH. AND NOT JUST FOR YOU...
...BUT DON'T WORRY, YOU'LL FIND OUT SOON.
OR SOONER.
AAAAARRGH! YOU'RE... YOU'RE *KOFF!* BREAKING MY ARM!
CRACK
CORRECT.
NOW LOOK WHAT WE HAVE HERE!
OH, BRUCE!

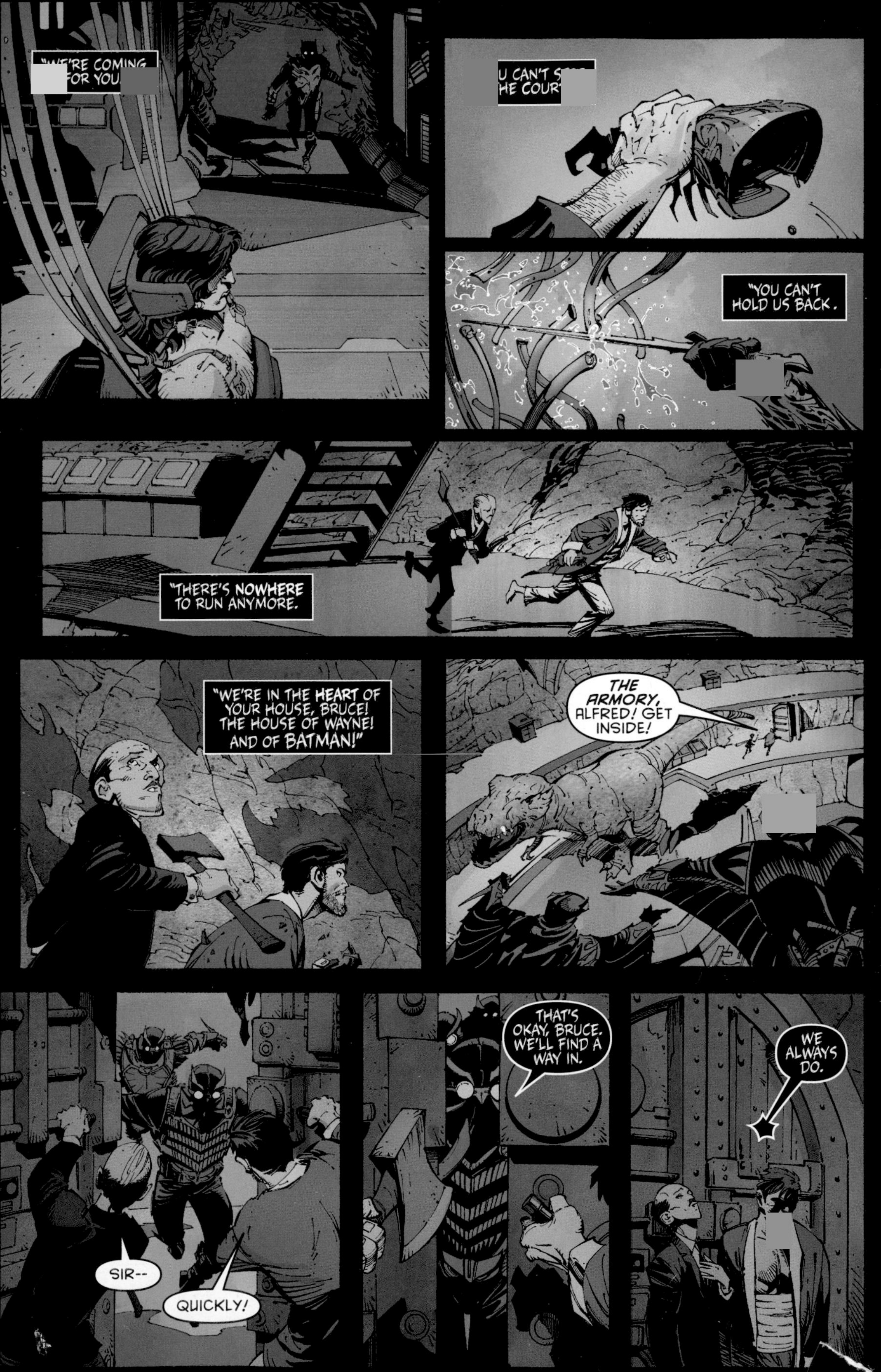
"WE'RE COMING
FOR YOU
U CAN'T S
HE COUR
"YOU CAN'T HOLD US BACK.
"THERE'S NOWHERE TO RUN ANYMORE.
"WE'RE IN THE HEART OF YOUR HOUSE, BRUCE! THE HOUSE OF WAYNE! AND OF BATMAN!"
THE ARMORY, ALFRED! GET INSIDE!
SIR--
QUICKLY!
THAT'S OKAY, BRUCE. WE'LL FIND A WAY IN.
WE ALWAYS DO.

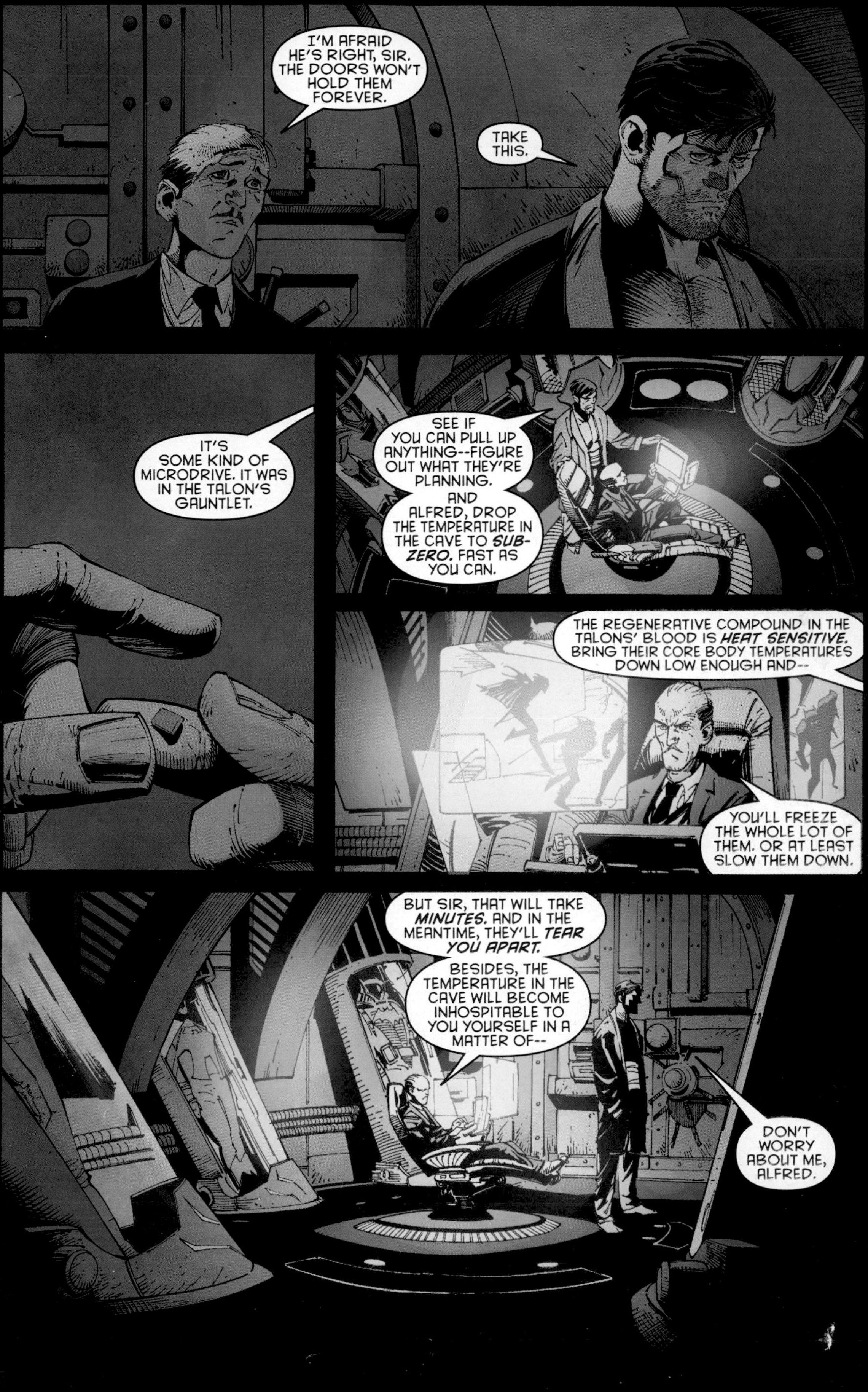

I'M AFRAID HE'S RIGHT, SIR. THE DOORS WON'T HOLD THEM FOREVER.
TAKE THIS.
IT'S SOME KIND OF MICRODRIVE. IT WAS IN THE TALON'S GAUNTLET.
SEE IF YOU CAN PULL UP ANYTHING--FIGURE OUT WHAT THEY'RE PLANNING.
AND ALFRED, DROP THE TEMPERATURE IN THE CAVE TO *SUB-ZERO.* FAST AS YOU CAN.
THE REGENERATIVE COMPOUND IN THE TALONS' BLOOD IS *HEAT SENSITIVE.* BRING THEIR CORE BODY TEMPERATURES DOWN LOW ENOUGH AND--
YOU'LL FREEZE THE WHOLE LOT OF THEM. OR AT LEAST SLOW THEM DOWN.
BUT SIR, THAT WILL TAKE *MINUTES.* AND IN THE MEANTIME, THEY'LL *TEAR YOU APART.*
BESIDES, THE TEMPERATURE IN THE CAVE WILL BECOME INHOSPITABLE TO YOU YOURSELF IN A MATTER OF--
DON'T WORRY ABOUT ME, ALFRED.

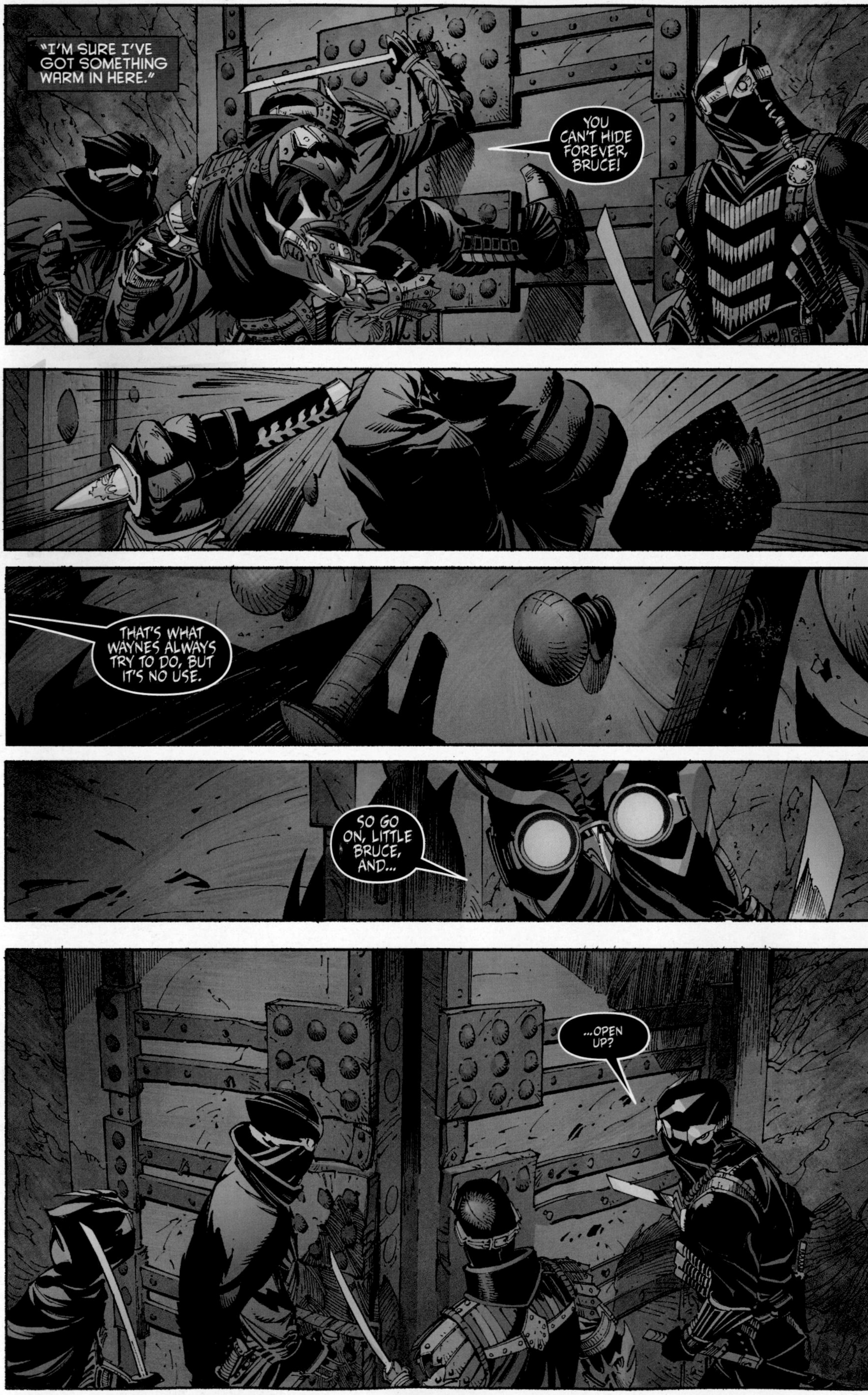
"I'M SURE I'VE GOT SOMETHING WARM IN HERE."
YOU CAN'T HIDE FOREVER, BRUCE!
THAT'S WHAT WAYNES ALWAYS TRY TO DO, BUT IT'S NO USE.
SO GO ON, LITTLE BRUCE, AND...
...OPEN UP?

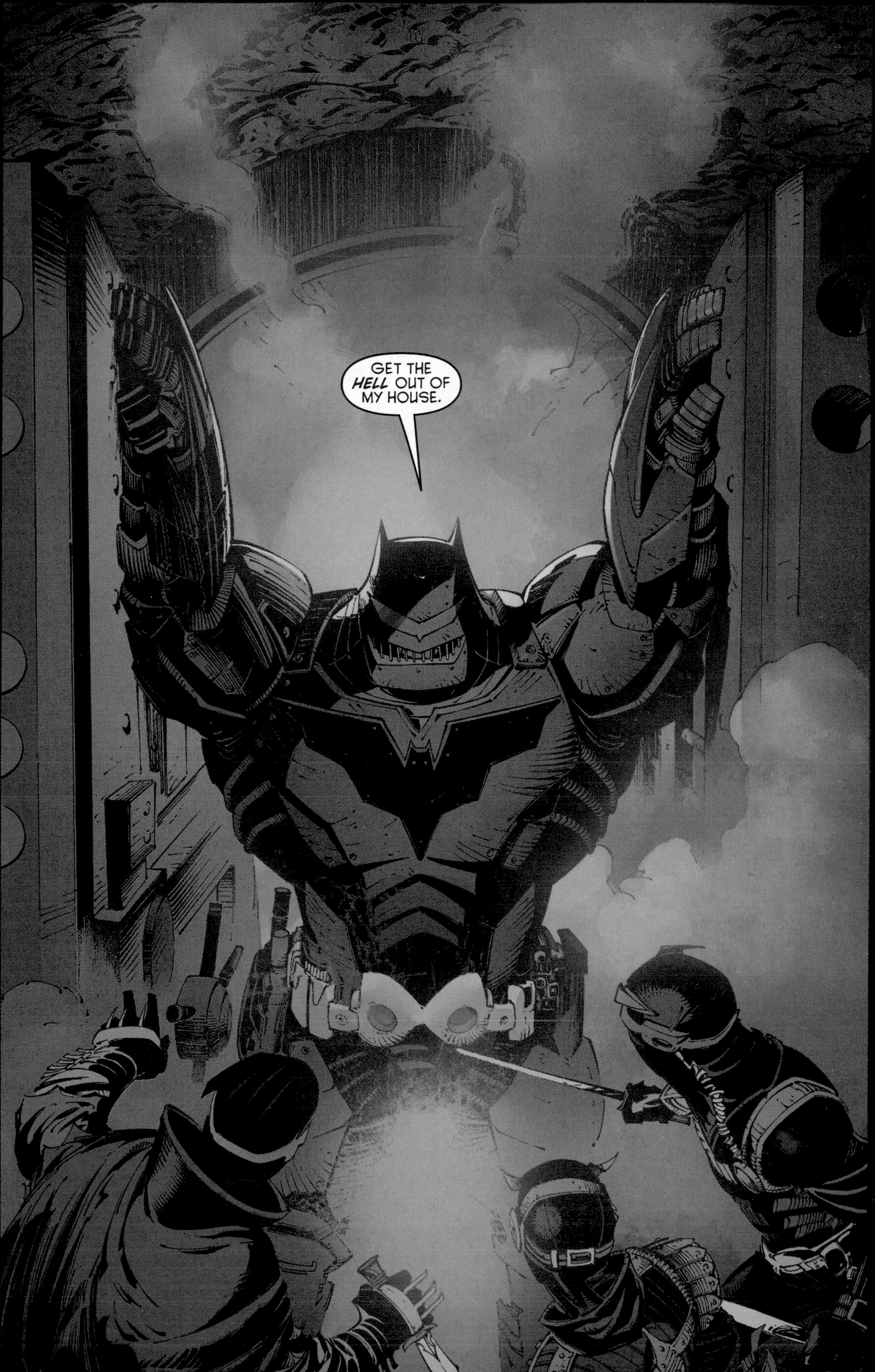
GET THE HELL OUT OF MY HOUSE.

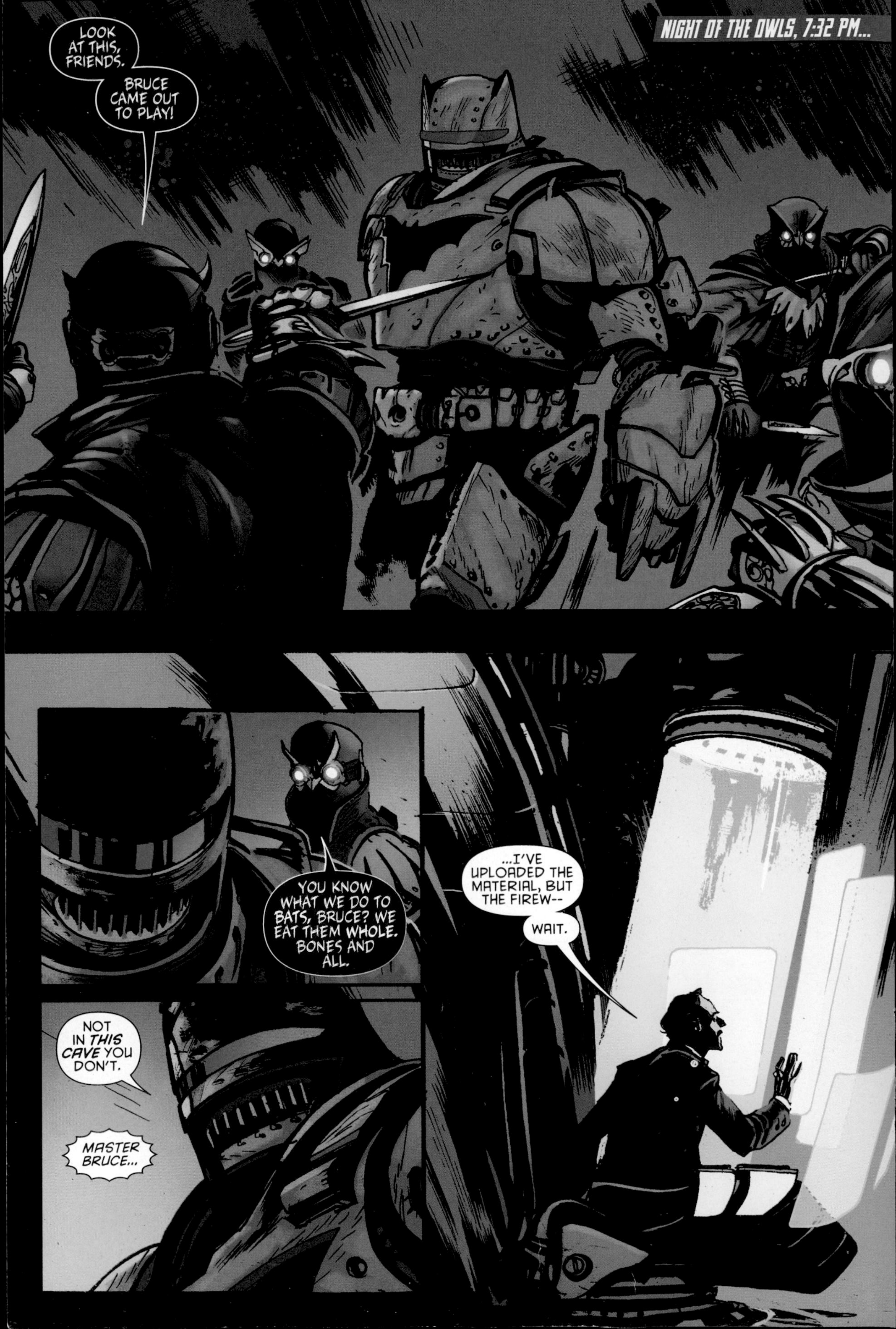
NIGHT OF THE OWLS, 7:32 PM...
LOOK AT THIS, FRIENDS.
BRUCE CAME OUT TO PLAY!
YOU KNOW WHAT WE DO TO BATS, BRUCE? WE EAT THEM WHOLE. BONES AND ALL.
...I'VE UPLOADED THE MATERIAL, BUT THE FIREW--
WAIT.
NOT IN THIS CAVE YOU DON'T.
MASTER BRUCE...

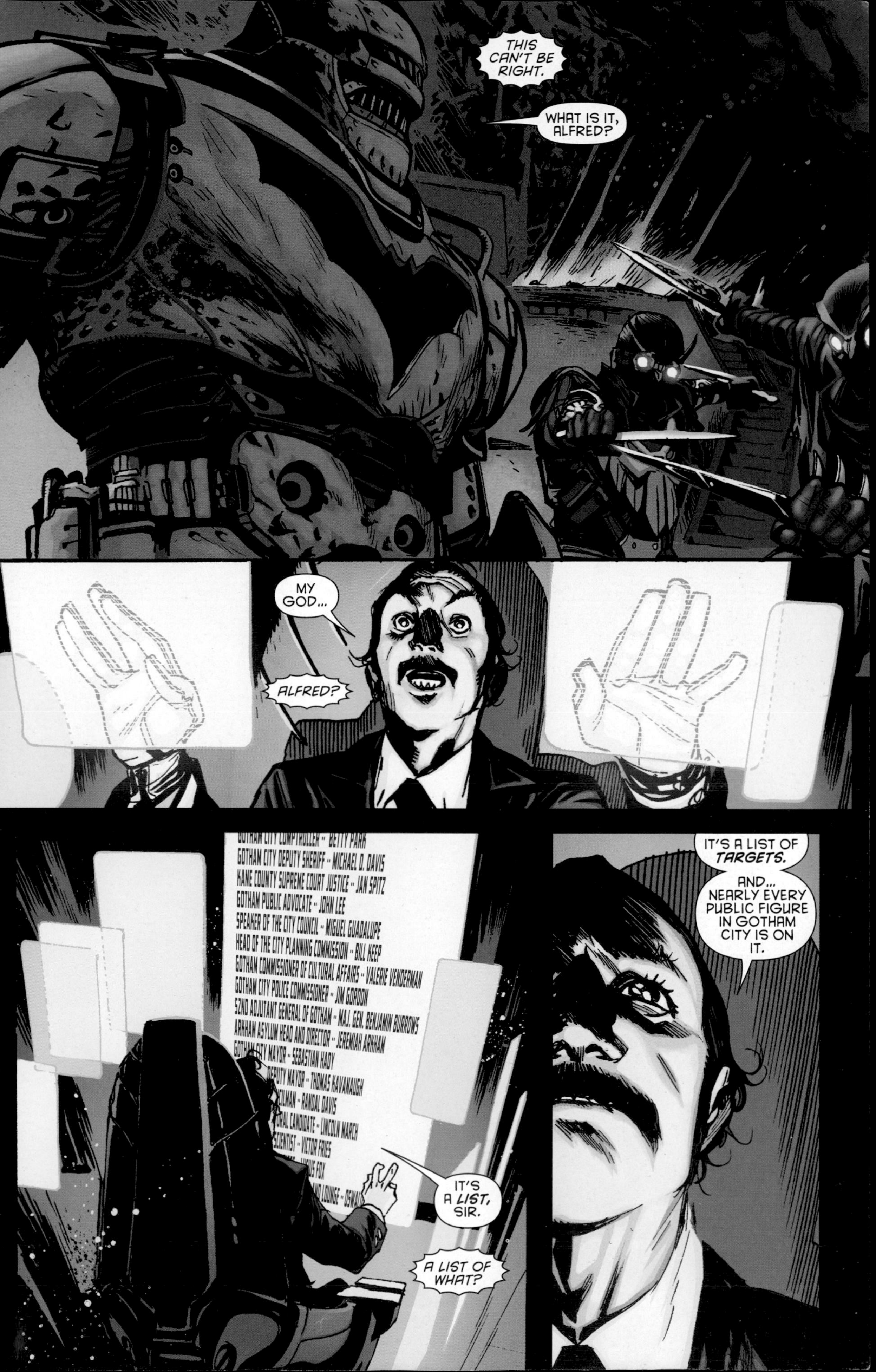
THIS CAN'T BE RIGHT.
WHAT IS IT, ALFRED?
MY GOD...
ALFRED?
GOTHAM CITY COMPTROLLER -- BETTY PARK
GOTHAM CITY DEPUTY SHERIFF -- MICHAEL D. DAVIS
KANE COUNTY SUPREME COURT JUSTICE -- JAN SPITZ
GOTHAM PUBLIC ADVOCATE -- JOHN LEE
SPEAKER OF THE CITY COUNCIL -- MIGUEL GUADALUPE
HEAD OF THE CITY PLANNING COMMISSION -- BILL KEEP
GOTHAM COMMISSIONER OF CULTURAL AFFAIRS -- VALERIE VENDERMAN
GOTHAM CITY POLICE COMMISSIONER -- JIM GORDON
52ND ADJUTANT GENERAL OF GOTHAM -- MAJ. GEN. BENJAMIN BURROWS
ARKHAM ASYLUM HEAD AND DIRECTOR -- JEREMIAH ARKHAM
GOTHAM CITY MAYOR -- SEBASTIAN HADY
DEPUTY MAYOR -- THOMAS KAVANAUGH
IT'S A LIST, SIR.
A LIST OF WHAT?
IT'S A LIST OF TARGETS.
AND... NEARLY EVERY PUBLIC FIGURE IN GOTHAM CITY IS ON IT.

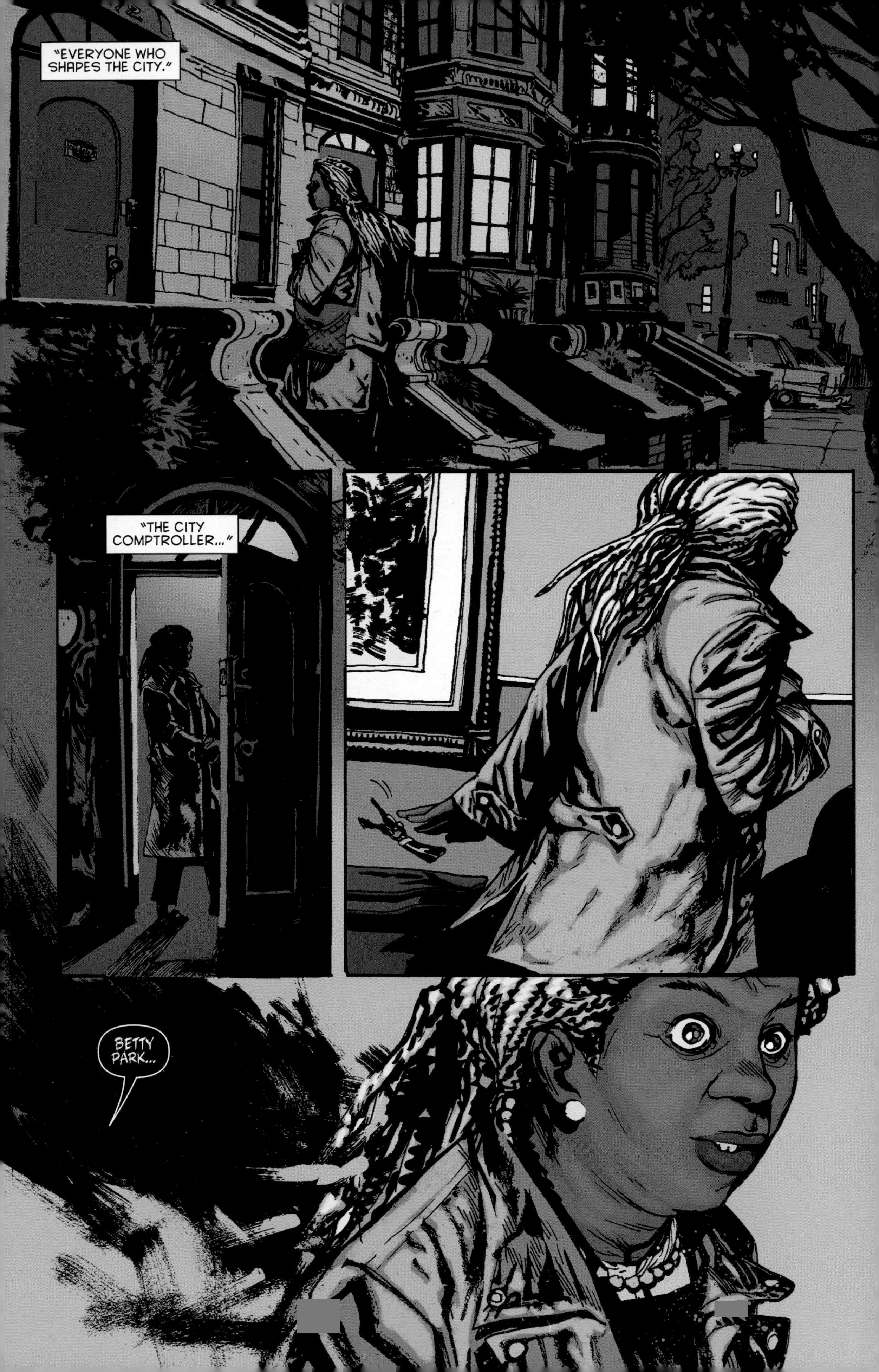
"EVERYONE WHO SHAPES THE CITY."
"THE CITY COMPTROLLER..."
BETTY PARK...

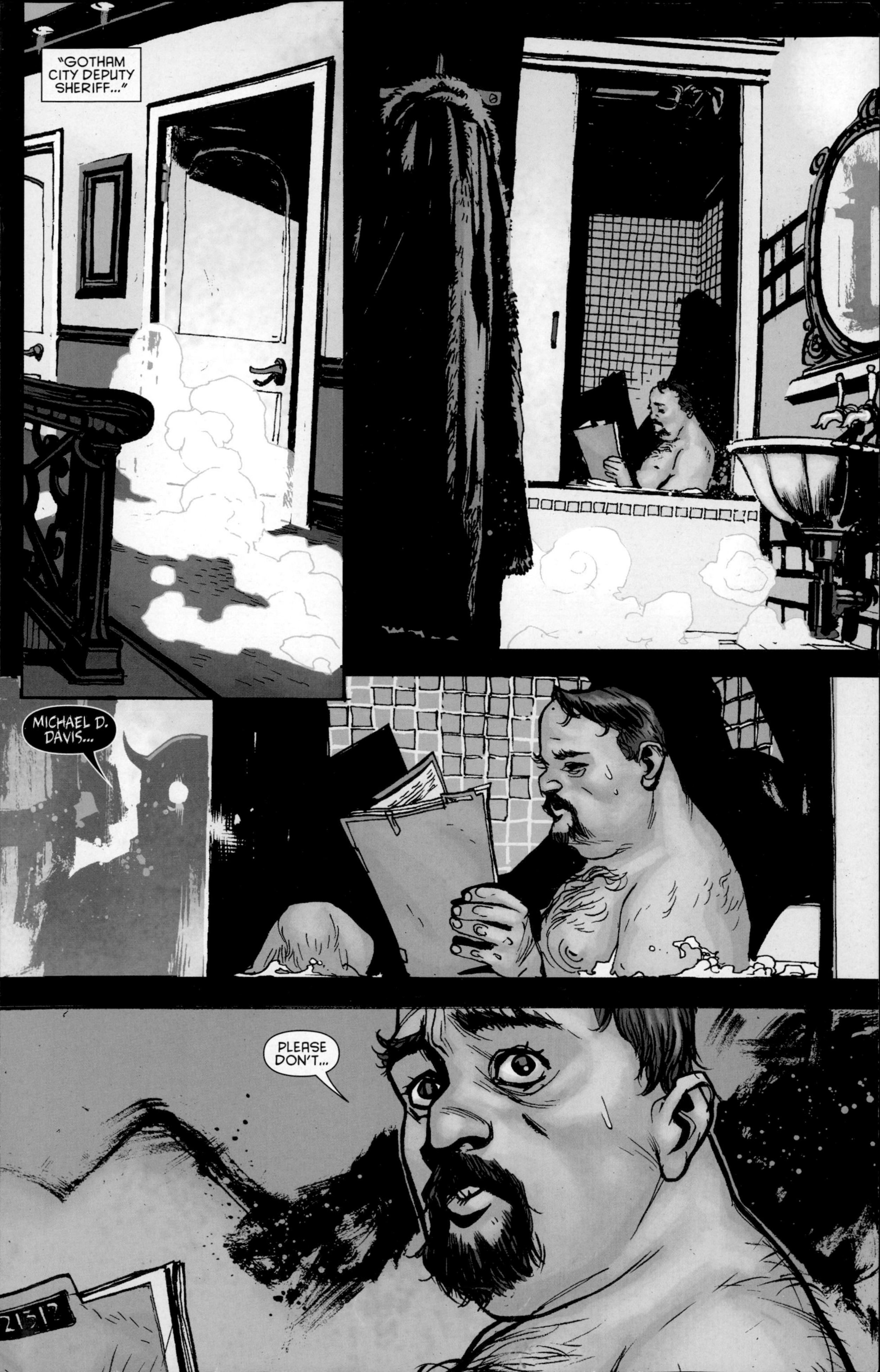
"GOTHAM CITY DEPUTY SHERIFF..."
MICHAEL D. DAVIS...
PLEASE DON'T...

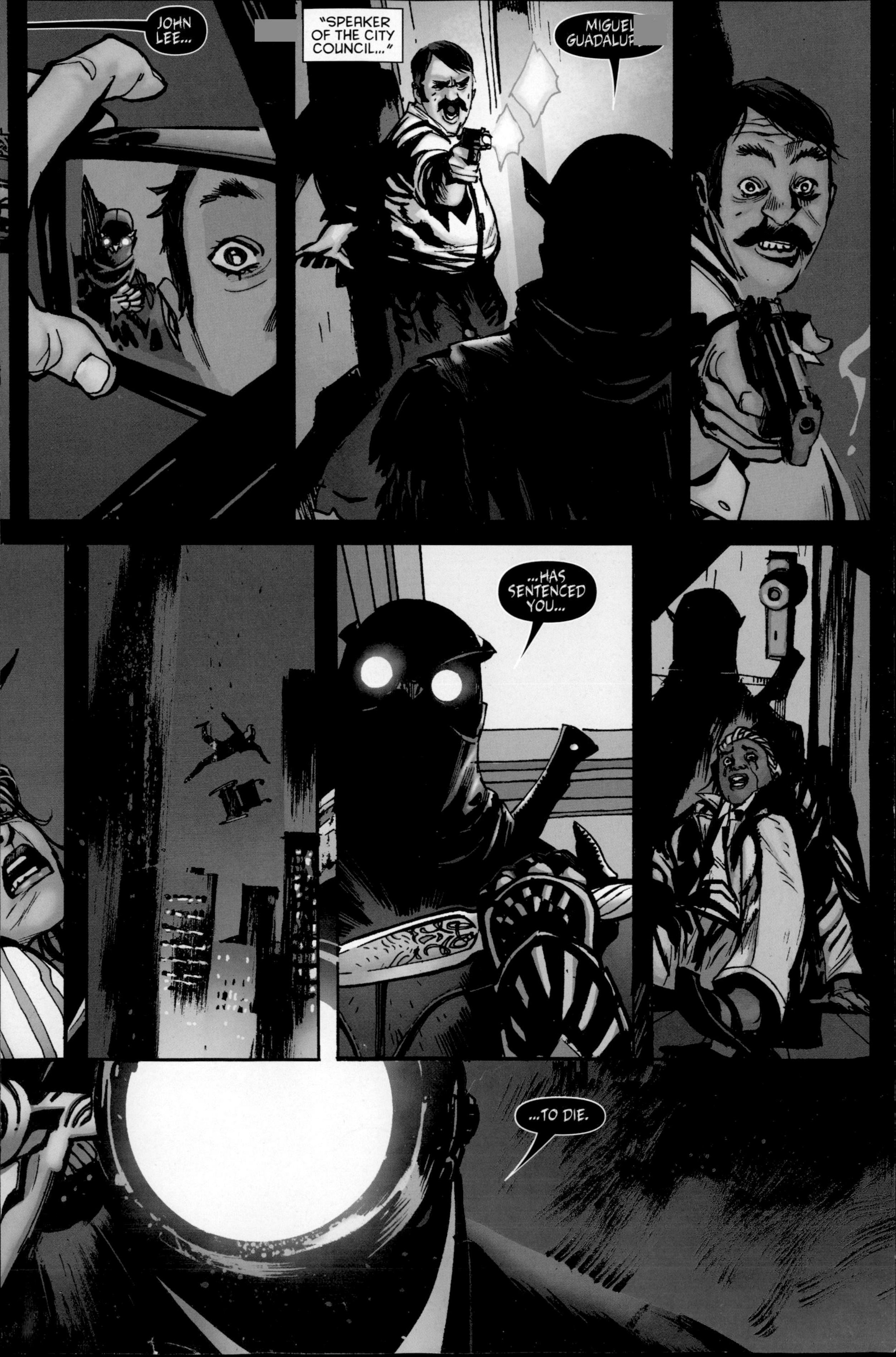
JOHN LEE...
"SPEAKER OF THE CITY COUNCIL..."
MIGUEL GUADALUP
...HAS SENTENCED YOU...
...TO DIE.

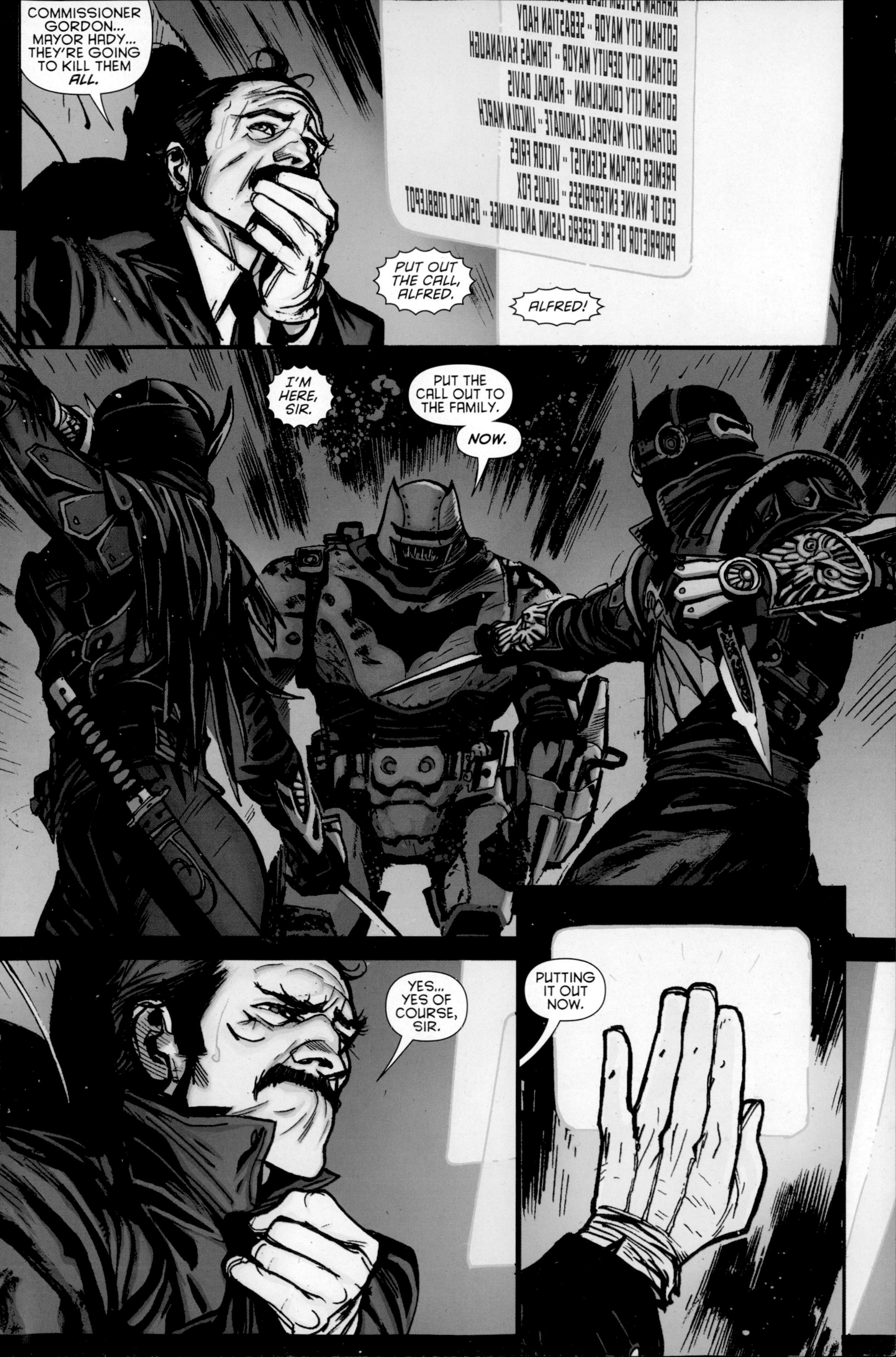
COMMISSIONER GORDON... MAYOR HADY... THEY'RE GOING TO KILL THEM *ALL.*
GOTHAM CITY MAYOR -- SEBASTIAN HADY
GOTHAM CITY DEPUTY MAYOR -- THOMAS KAVANAUGH
GOTHAM CITY COUNCILMAN -- RANDAL DAVIS
GOTHAM CITY MAYORAL CANDIDATE -- LINCOLN MARCH
PREMIER GOTHAM SCIENTIST -- VICTOR FRIES
CEO OF WAYNE ENTERPRISES -- LUCIUS FOX
PROPRIETOR OF THE ICEBERG CASINO AND LOUNGE -- OSWALD COBBLEPOT
PUT OUT THE CALL, ALFRED.
ALFRED!
I'M HERE, SIR.
PUT THE CALL OUT TO THE FAMILY.
NOW.
YES... YES OF COURSE, SIR.
PUTTING IT OUT NOW.

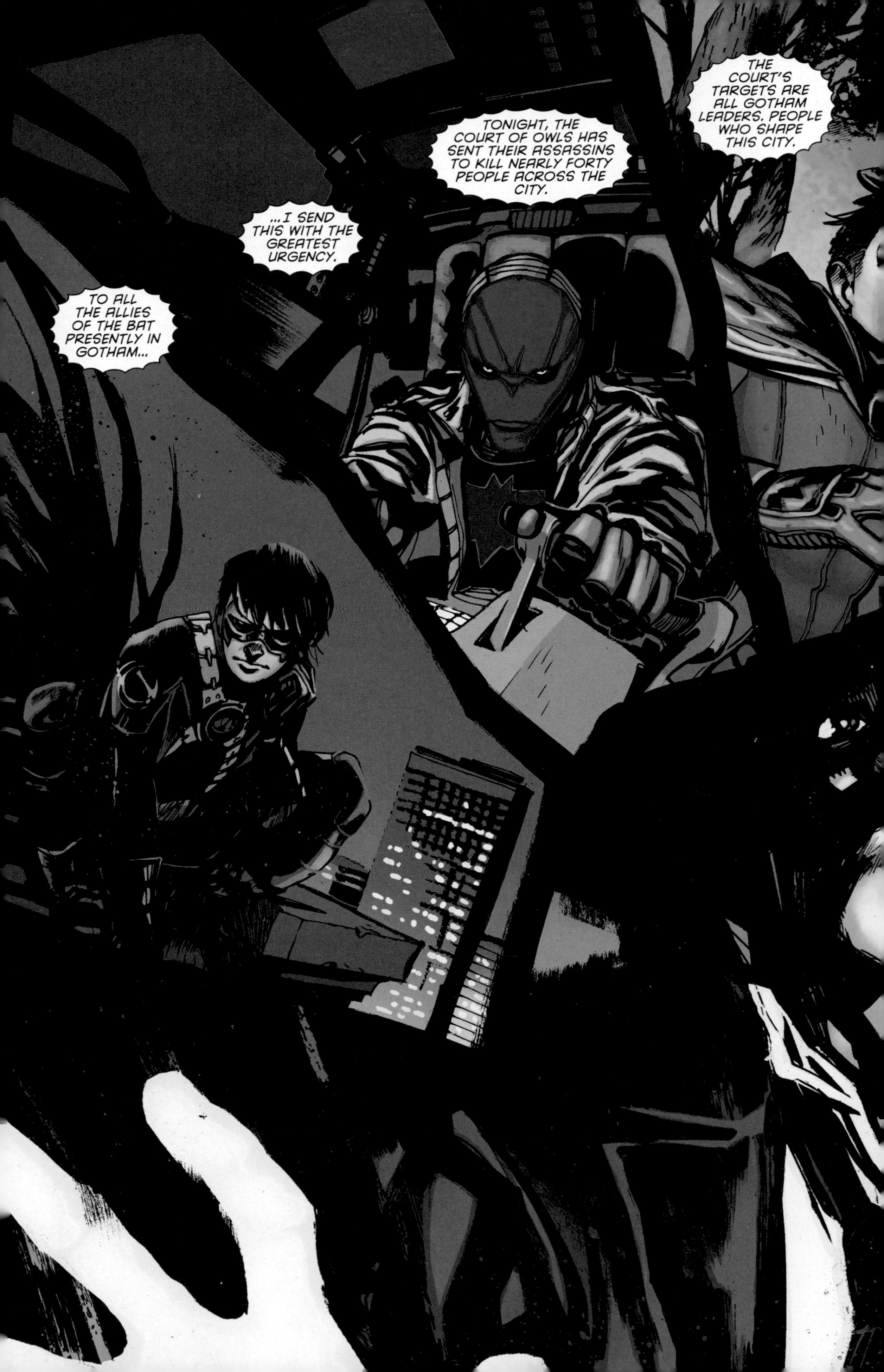
TO ALL THE ALLIES OF THE BAT PRESENTLY IN GOTHAM...
...I SEND THIS WITH THE GREATEST URGENCY.
TONIGHT, THE COURT OF OWLS HAS SENT THEIR ASSASSINS TO KILL NEARLY FORTY PEOPLE ACROSS THE CITY.
THE COURT'S TARGETS ARE ALL GOTHAM LEADERS. PEOPLE WHO SHAPE THIS CITY.

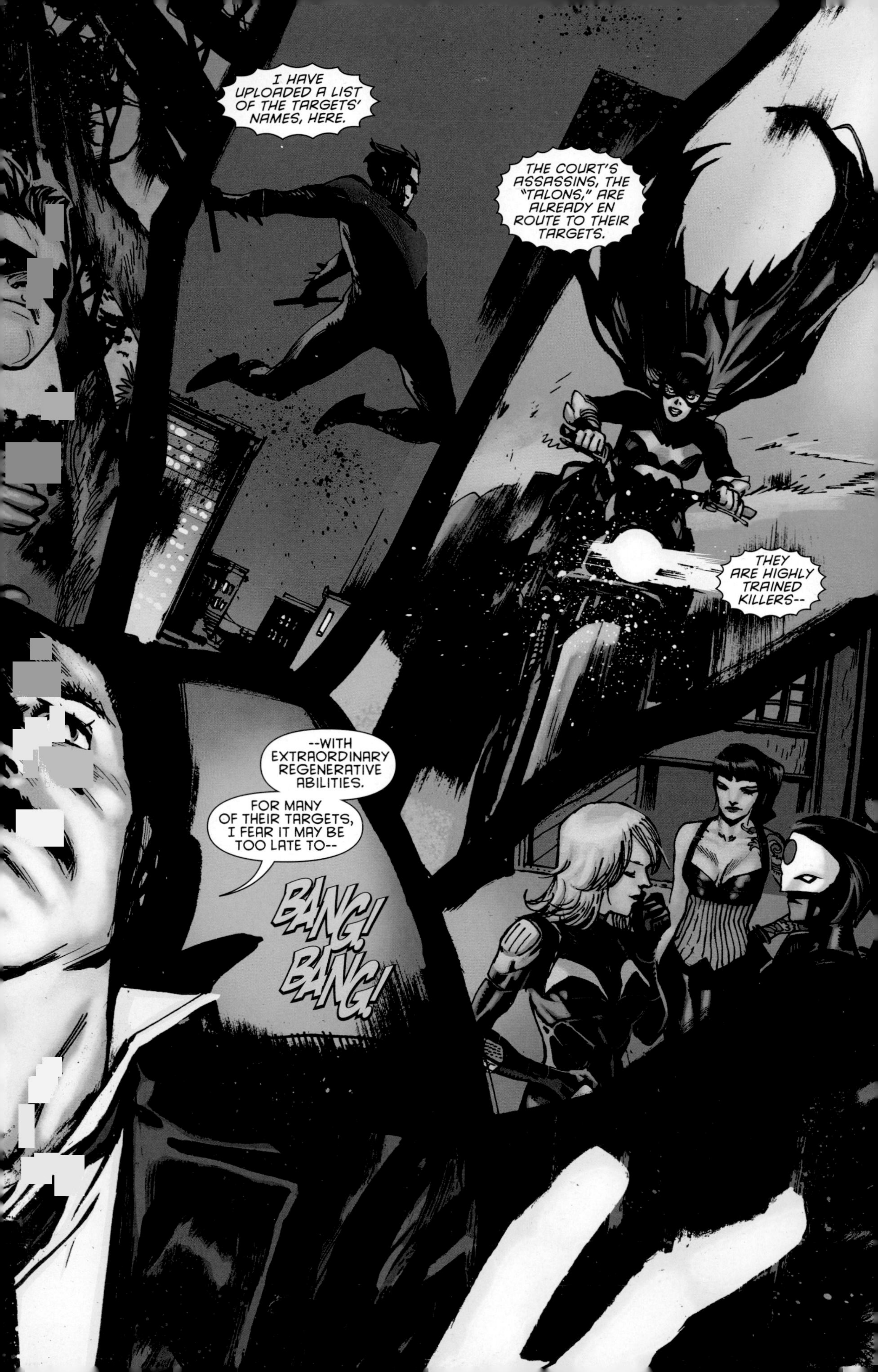
I HAVE UPLOADED A LIST OF THE TARGETS' NAMES, HERE.
THE COURT'S ASSASSINS, THE "TALONS," ARE ALREADY EN ROUTE TO THEIR TARGETS.
THEY ARE HIGHLY TRAINED KILLERS--
--WITH EXTRAORDINARY REGENERATIVE ABILITIES.
FOR MANY OF THEIR TARGETS, I FEAR IT MAY BE TOO LATE TO--
BANG! BANG!

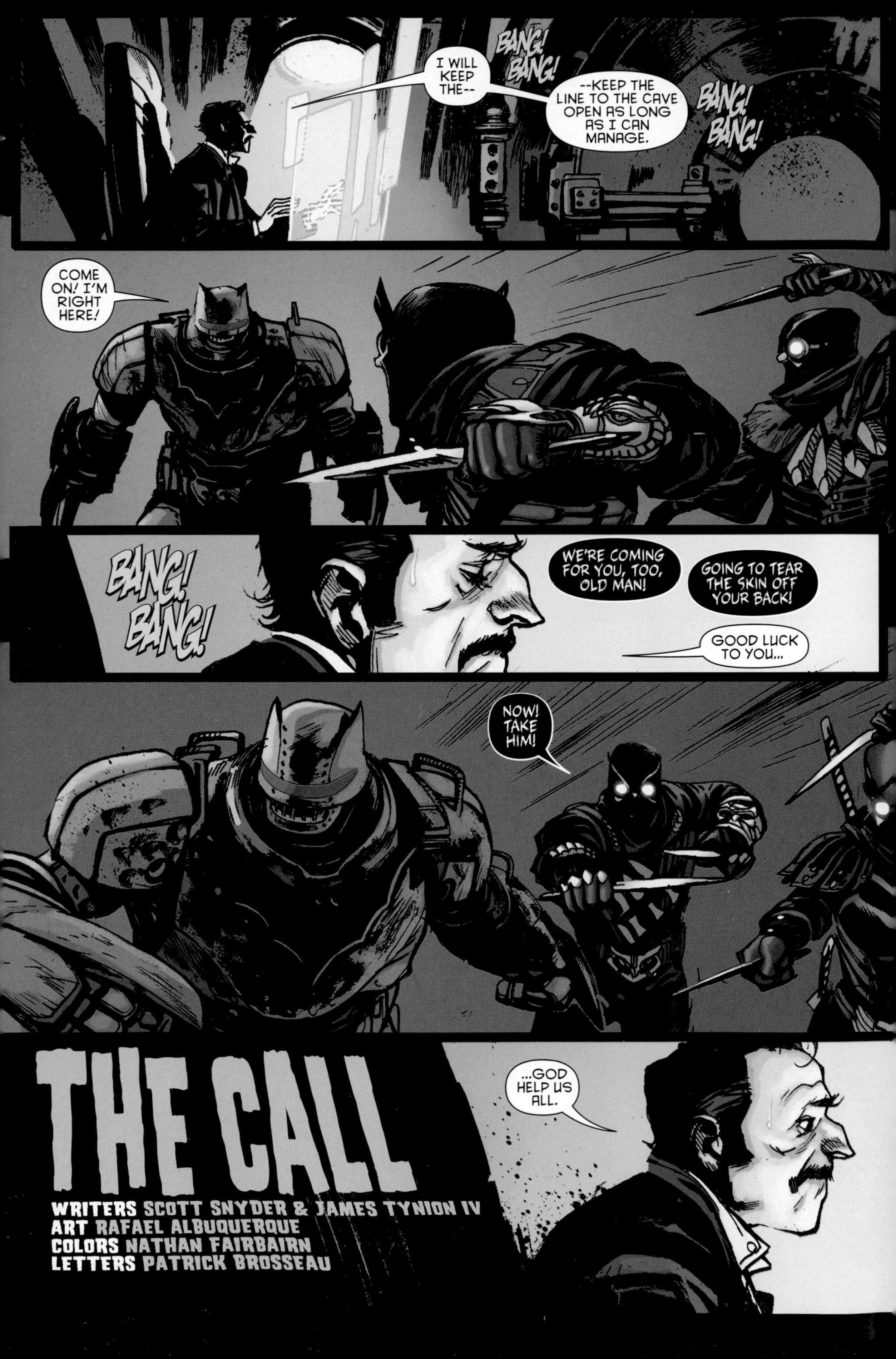
I WILL KEEP THE--
BANG! BANG!
--KEEP THE LINE TO THE CAVE OPEN AS LONG AS I CAN MANAGE.
BANG! BANG!
COME ON! I'M RIGHT HERE!
BANG! BANG!
WE'RE COMING FOR YOU, TOO, OLD MAN!
GOING TO TEAR THE SKIN OFF YOUR BACK!
GOOD LUCK TO YOU...
NOW! TAKE HIM!
THE CALL
WRITERS SCOTT SNYDER & JAMES TYNION IV
ART RAFAEL ALBUQUERQUE
COLORS NATHAN FAIRBAIRN
LETTERS PATRICK BROSSEAU
...GOD HELP US ALL.

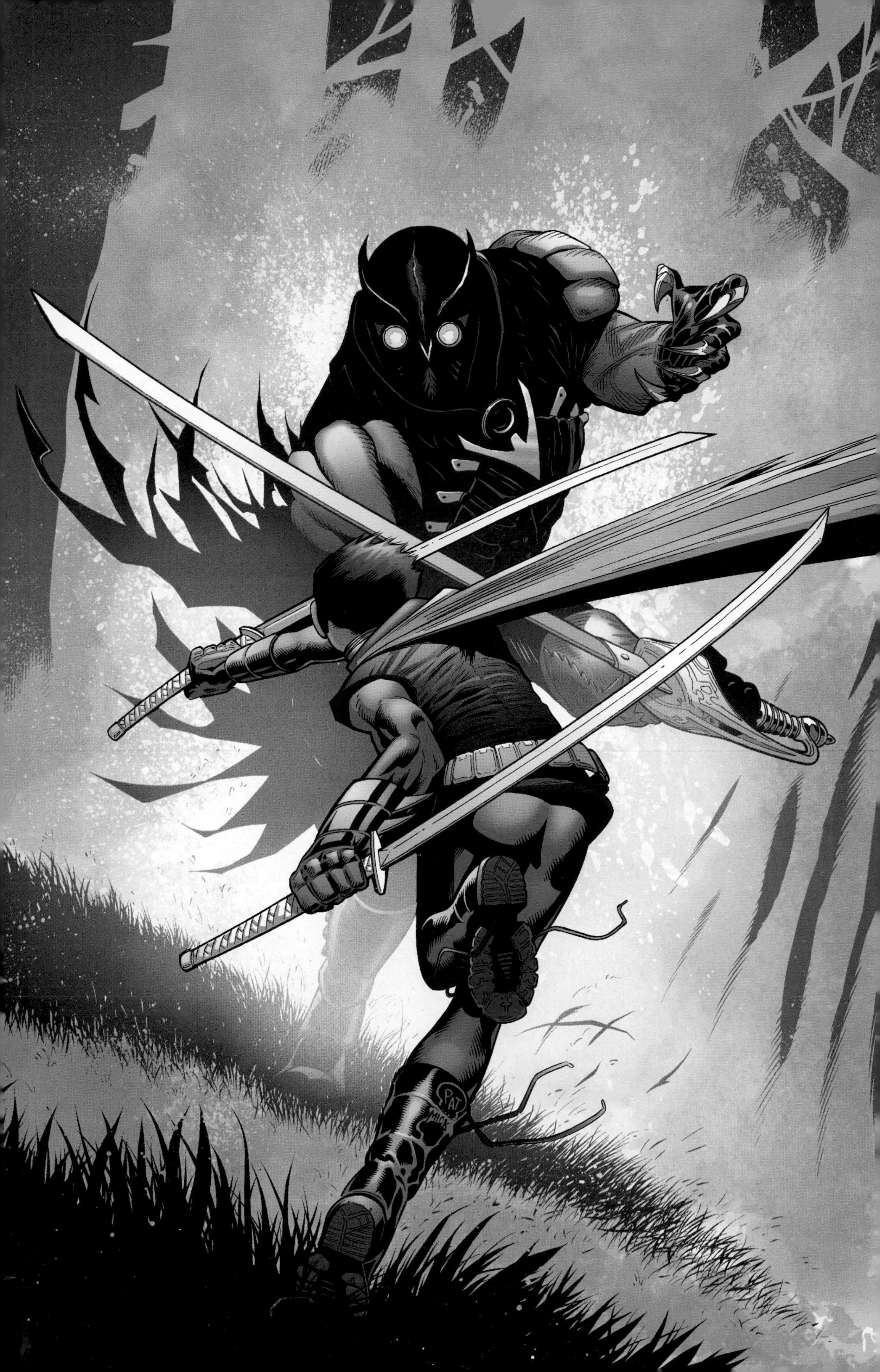
PAT
MICK

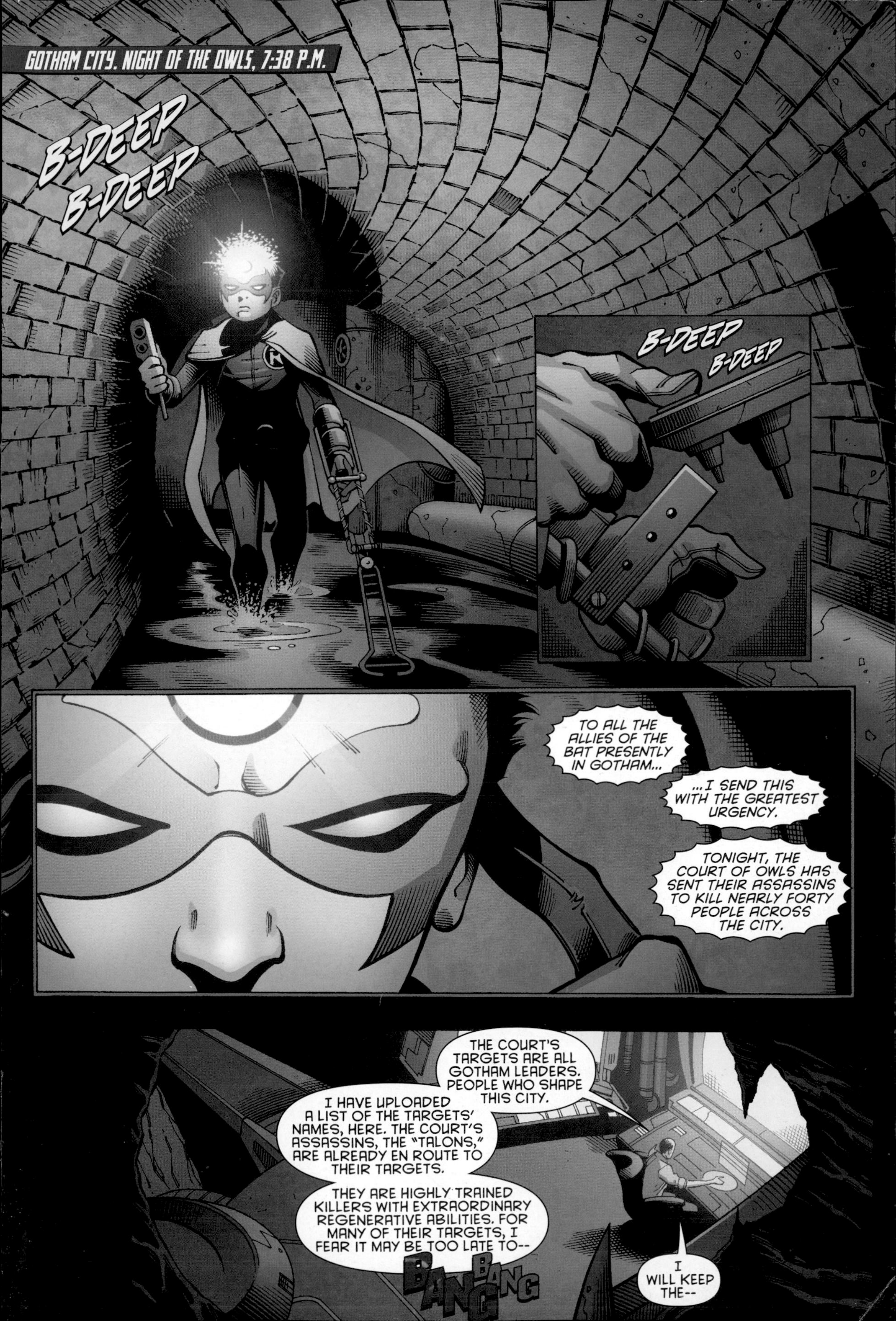

GOTHAM CITY. NIGHT OF THE OWLS, 7:38 P.M.
B-DEEP B-DEEP
B-DEEP B-DEEP
TO ALL THE ALLIES OF THE BAT PRESENTLY IN GOTHAM...
...I SEND THIS WITH THE GREATEST URGENCY.
TONIGHT, THE COURT OF OWLS HAS SENT THEIR ASSASSINS TO KILL NEARLY FORTY PEOPLE ACROSS THE CITY.
THE COURT'S TARGETS ARE ALL GOTHAM LEADERS. PEOPLE WHO SHAPE THIS CITY.
I HAVE UPLOADED A LIST OF THE TARGETS' NAMES, HERE. THE COURT'S ASSASSINS, THE "TALONS," ARE ALREADY EN ROUTE TO THEIR TARGETS.
THEY ARE HIGHLY TRAINED KILLERS WITH EXTRAORDINARY REGENERATIVE ABILITIES. FOR MANY OF THEIR TARGETS, I FEAR IT MAY BE TOO LATE TO--
BANG BANG BANG
I WILL KEEP THE--

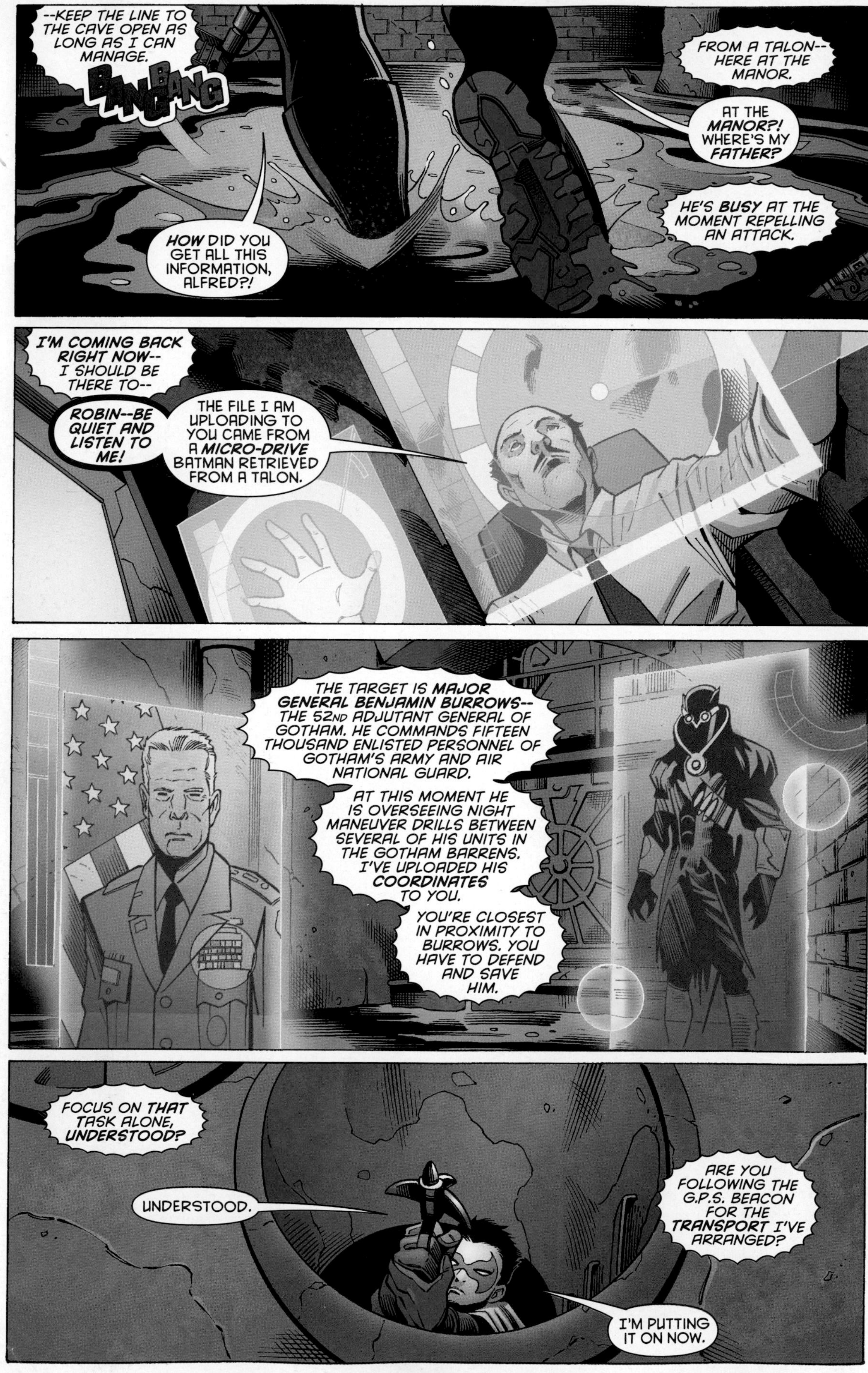
--KEEP THE LINE TO THE CAVE OPEN AS LONG AS I CAN MANAGE.
BANG BANG BANG
HOW DID YOU GET ALL THIS INFORMATION, ALFRED?!
FROM A TALON-- HERE AT THE MANOR.
AT THE MANOR?! WHERE'S MY FATHER?
HE'S BUSY AT THE MOMENT REPELLING AN ATTACK.
I'M COMING BACK RIGHT NOW-- I SHOULD BE THERE TO--
ROBIN--BE QUIET AND LISTEN TO ME!
THE FILE I AM UPLOADING TO YOU CAME FROM A MICRO-DRIVE BATMAN RETRIEVED FROM A TALON.
THE TARGET IS MAJOR GENERAL BENJAMIN BURROWS-- THE 52ND ADJUTANT GENERAL OF GOTHAM. HE COMMANDS FIFTEEN THOUSAND ENLISTED PERSONNEL OF GOTHAM'S ARMY AND AIR NATIONAL GUARD.
AT THIS MOMENT HE IS OVERSEEING NIGHT MANEUVER DRILLS BETWEEN SEVERAL OF HIS UNITS IN THE GOTHAM BARRENS. I'VE UPLOADED HIS COORDINATES TO YOU.
YOU'RE CLOSEST IN PROXIMITY TO BURROWS. YOU HAVE TO DEFEND AND SAVE HIM.
FOCUS ON THAT TASK ALONE, UNDERSTOOD?
UNDERSTOOD.
ARE YOU FOLLOWING THE G.P.S. BEACON FOR THE TRANSPORT I'VE ARRANGED?
I'M PUTTING IT ON NOW.

NIGHT OF THE OWLS

ROBIN HEARS A HOO

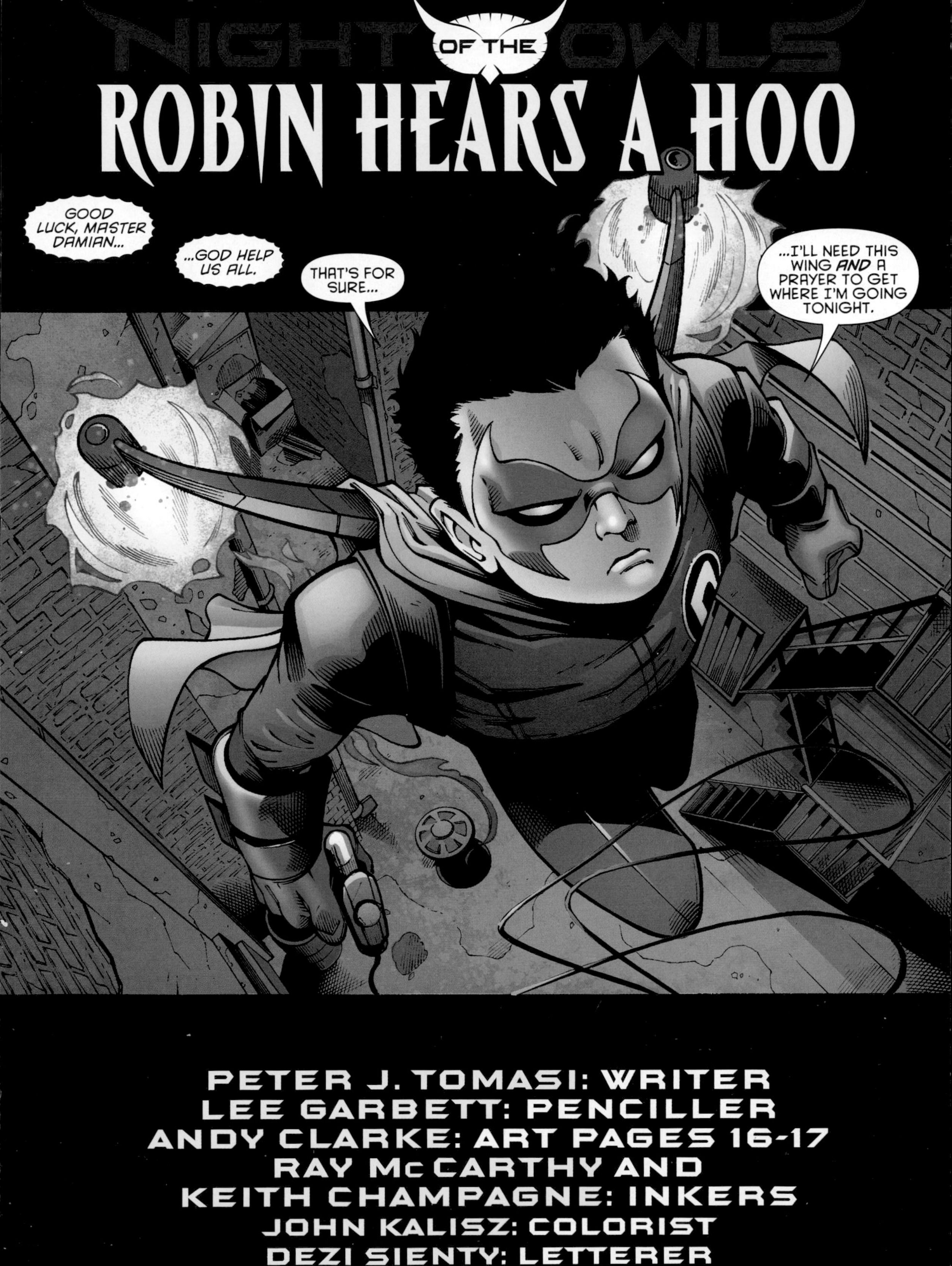
GOOD LUCK, MASTER DAMIAN...
...GOD HELP US ALL.
THAT'S FOR SURE...
...I'LL NEED THIS WING *AND* A PRAYER TO GET WHERE I'M GOING TONIGHT.

PETER J. TOMASI: WRITER
LEE GARBETT: PENCILLER
ANDY CLARKE: ART PAGES 16-17
RAY McCARTHY AND
KEITH CHAMPAGNE: INKERS
JOHN KALISZ: COLORIST
DEZI SIENTY: LETTERER

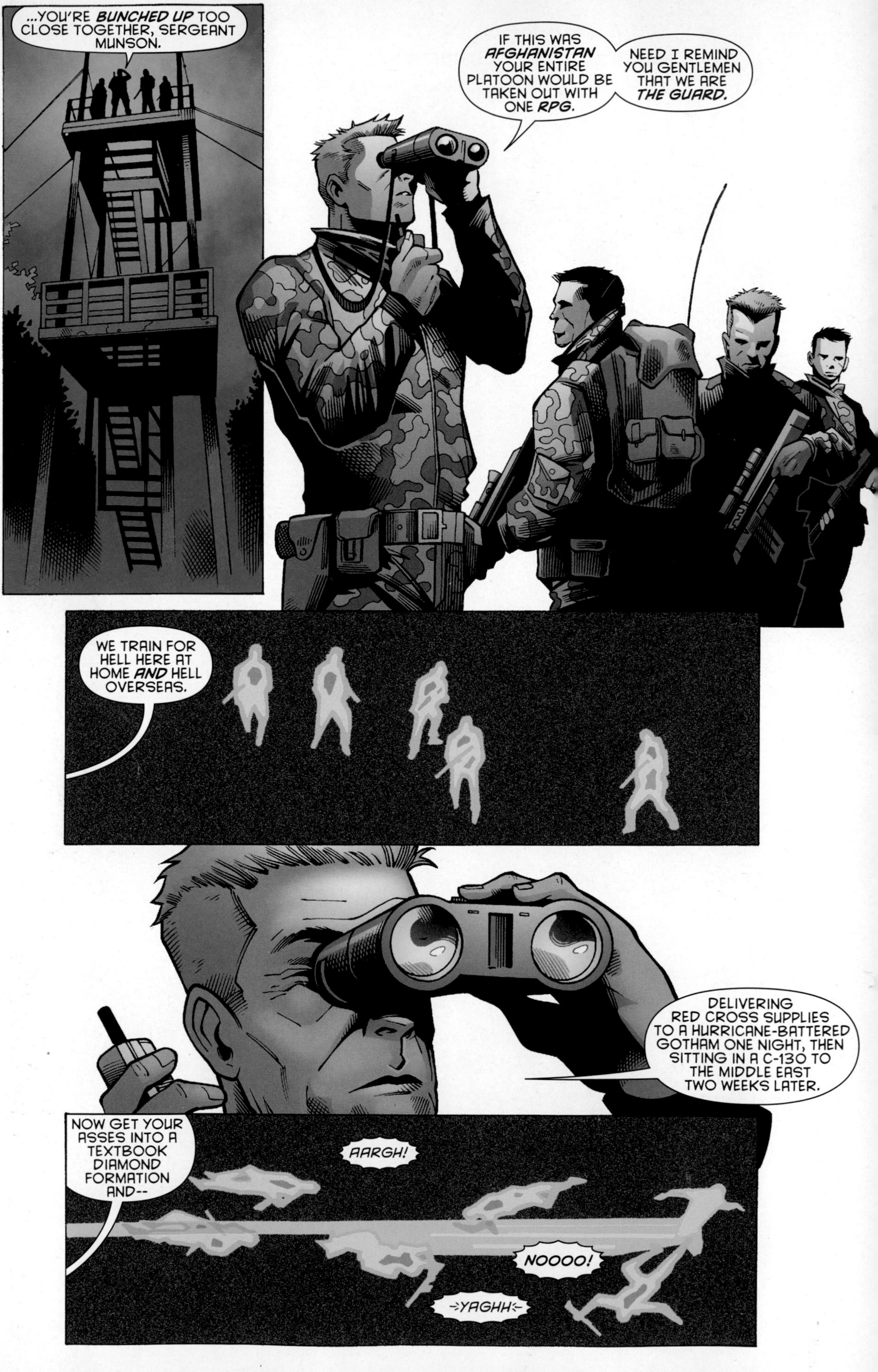
...YOU'RE BUNCHED UP TOO CLOSE TOGETHER, SERGEANT MUNSON.
IF THIS WAS AFGHANISTAN YOUR ENTIRE PLATOON WOULD BE TAKEN OUT WITH ONE RPG.
NEED I REMIND YOU GENTLEMEN THAT WE ARE THE GUARD.
WE TRAIN FOR HELL HERE AT HOME AND HELL OVERSEAS.
DELIVERING RED CROSS SUPPLIES TO A HURRICANE-BATTERED GOTHAM ONE NIGHT, THEN SITTING IN A C-130 TO THE MIDDLE EAST TWO WEEKS LATER.
NOW GET YOUR ASSES INTO A TEXTBOOK DIAMOND FORMATION AND--
AARGH!
NOOOO!
YAGHH

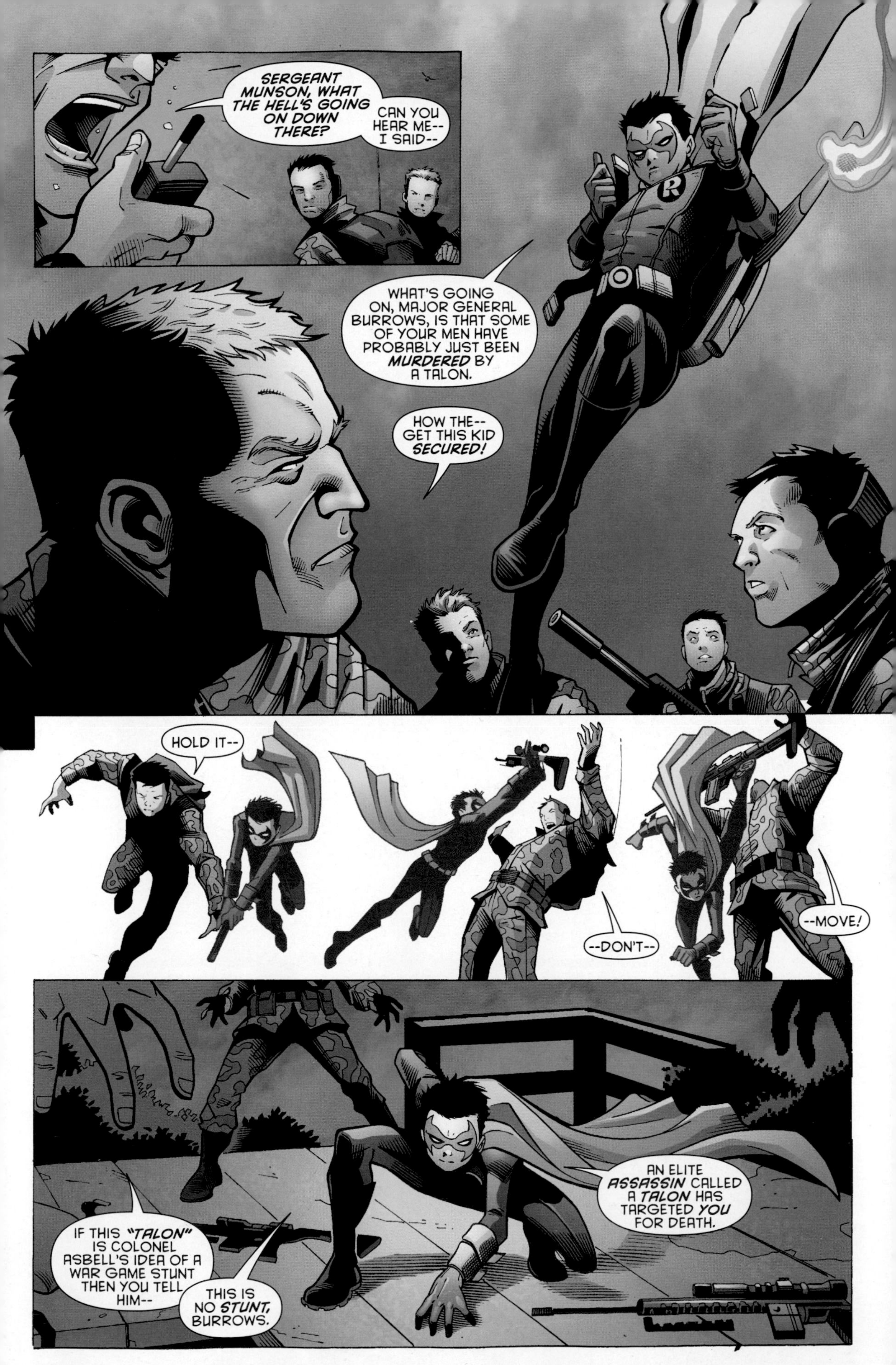
SERGEANT MUNSON, WHAT THE HELL'S GOING ON DOWN THERE?
CAN YOU HEAR ME-- I SAID--
WHAT'S GOING ON, MAJOR GENERAL BURROWS, IS THAT SOME OF YOUR MEN HAVE PROBABLY JUST BEEN MURDERED BY A TALON.
HOW THE-- GET THIS KID SECURED!
HOLD IT--
--DON'T--
--MOVE!
AN ELITE ASSASSIN CALLED A TALON HAS TARGETED YOU FOR DEATH.
IF THIS "TALON" IS COLONEL ASBELL'S IDEA OF A WAR GAME STUNT THEN YOU TELL HIM--
THIS IS NO STUNT, BURROWS.

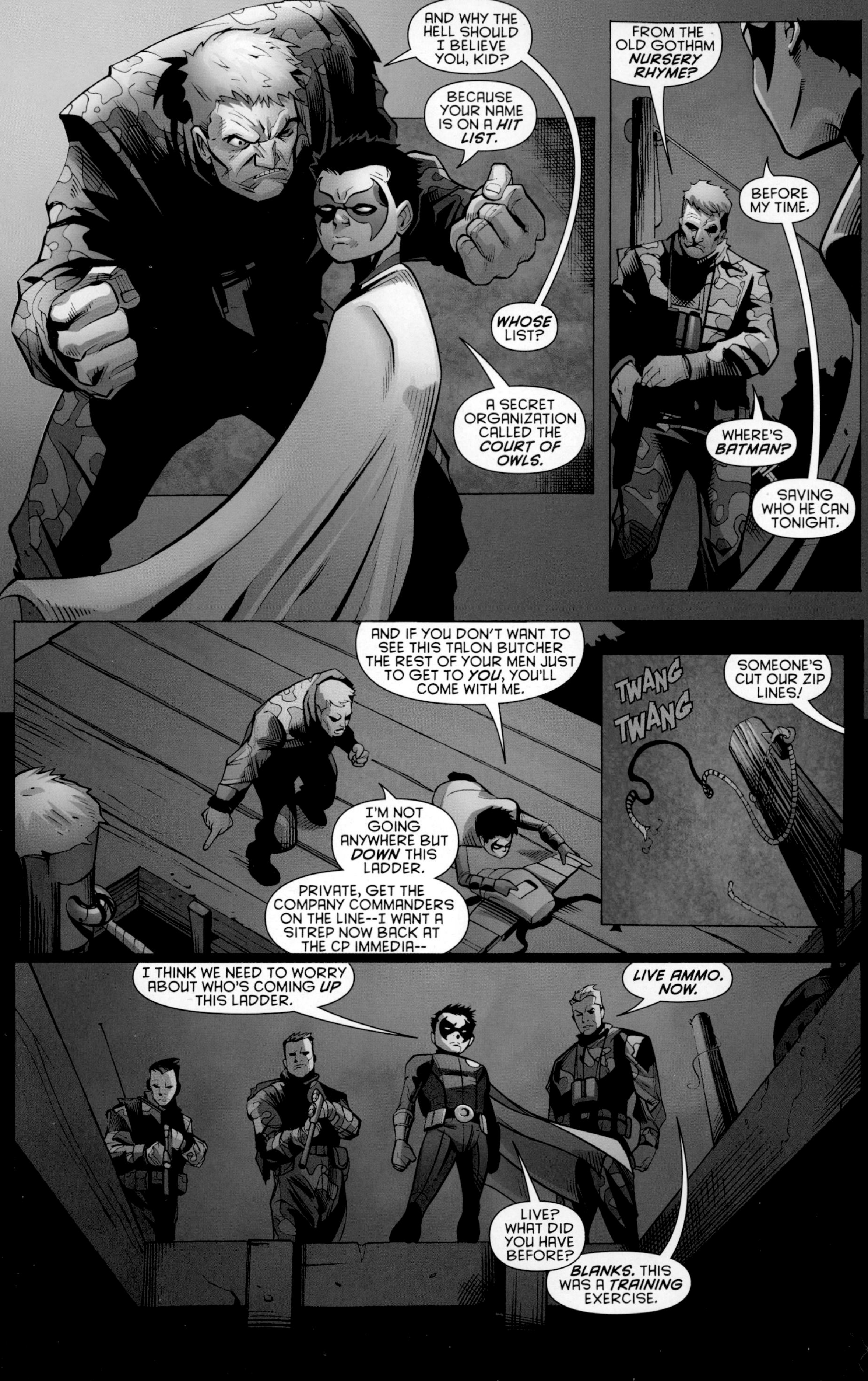
AND WHY THE HELL SHOULD I BELIEVE YOU, KID?
BECAUSE YOUR NAME IS ON A HIT LIST.
WHOSE LIST?
A SECRET ORGANIZATION CALLED THE COURT OF OWLS.
FROM THE OLD GOTHAM NURSERY RHYME?
BEFORE MY TIME.
WHERE'S BATMAN?
SAVING WHO HE CAN TONIGHT.
AND IF YOU DON'T WANT TO SEE THIS TALON BUTCHER THE REST OF YOUR MEN JUST TO GET TO YOU, YOU'LL COME WITH ME.
I'M NOT GOING ANYWHERE BUT DOWN THIS LADDER.
PRIVATE, GET THE COMPANY COMMANDERS ON THE LINE--I WANT A SITREP NOW BACK AT THE CP IMMEDIA--
TWANG
TWANG
SOMEONE'S CUT OUR ZIP LINES!
I THINK WE NEED TO WORRY ABOUT WHO'S COMING UP THIS LADDER.
LIVE AMMO. NOW.
LIVE? WHAT DID YOU HAVE BEFORE?
BLANKS. THIS WAS A TRAINING EXERCISE.

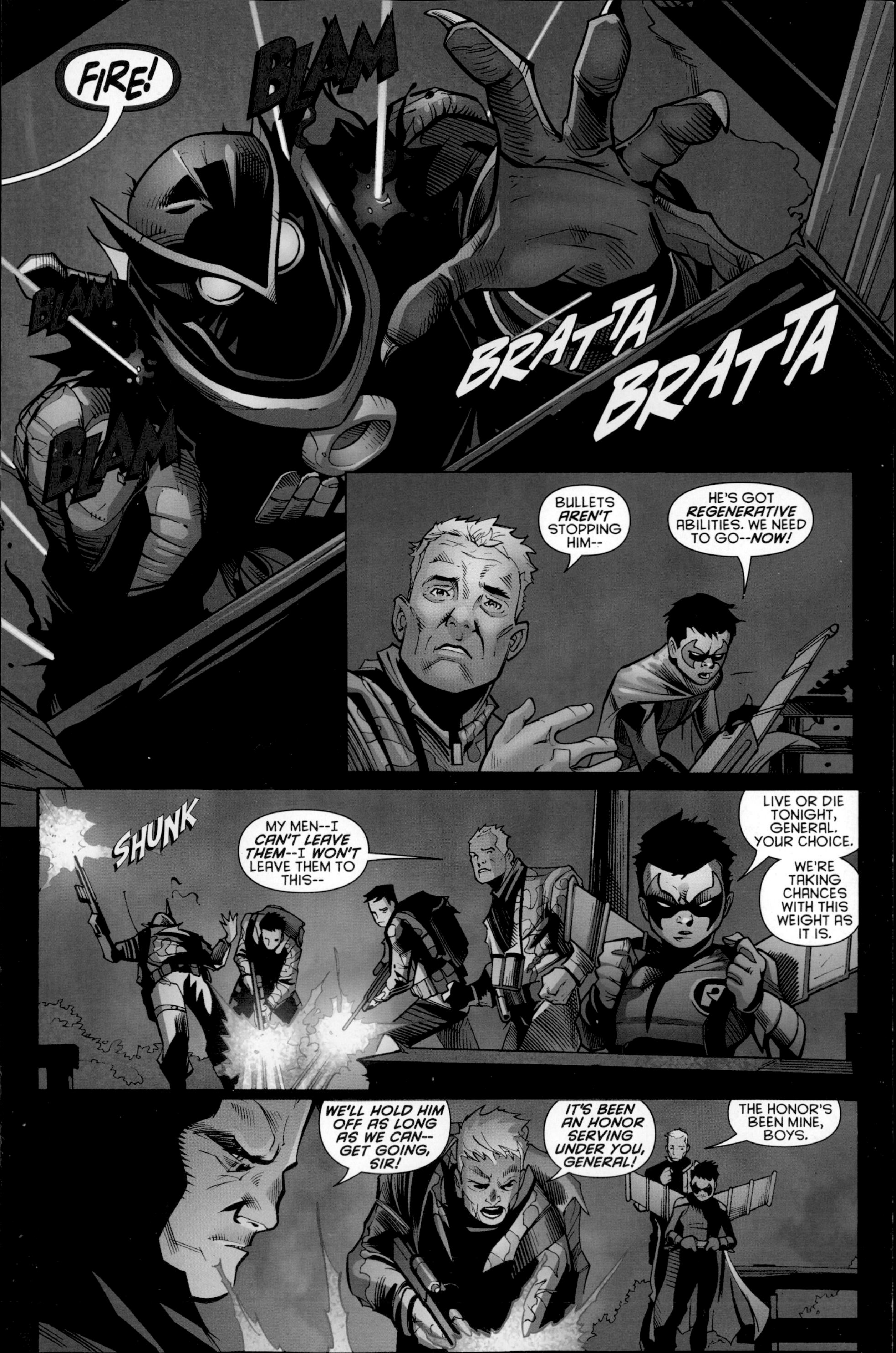
FIRE!
BLAM
BLAM
BLAM
BRATTA
BRATTA
BULLETS AREN'T STOPPING HIM--
HE'S GOT REGENERATIVE ABILITIES. WE NEED TO GO--NOW!
SHUNK
MY MEN--I CAN'T LEAVE THEM--I WON'T LEAVE THEM TO THIS--
LIVE OR DIE TONIGHT, GENERAL. YOUR CHOICE.
WE'RE TAKING CHANCES WITH THIS WEIGHT AS IT IS.
WE'LL HOLD HIM OFF AS LONG AS WE CAN-- GET GOING, SIR!
IT'S BEEN AN HONOR SERVING UNDER YOU, GENERAL!
THE HONOR'S BEEN MINE, BOYS.

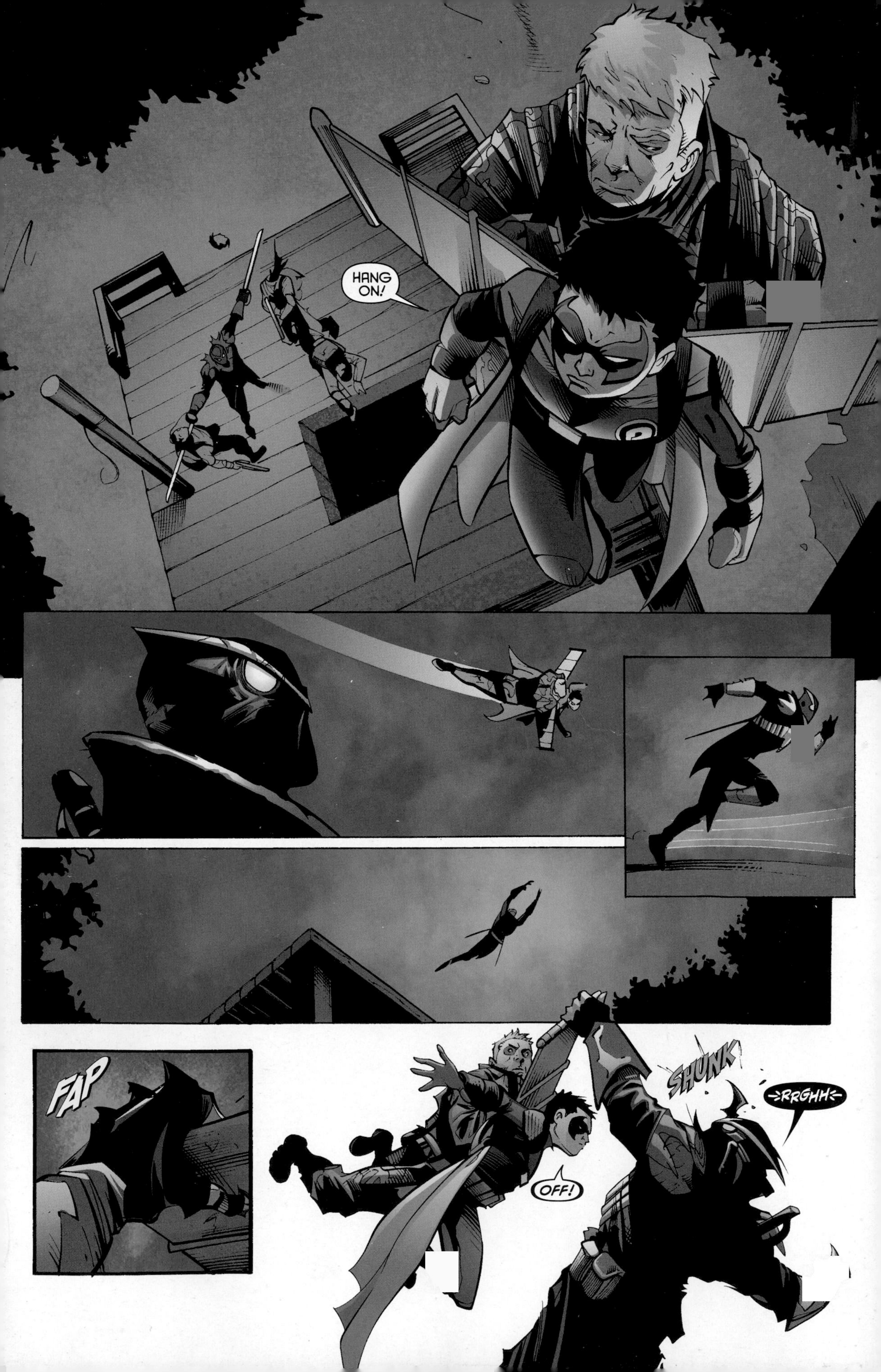
HANG ON!
FAP
SHUNK
RRGHH
OFF!

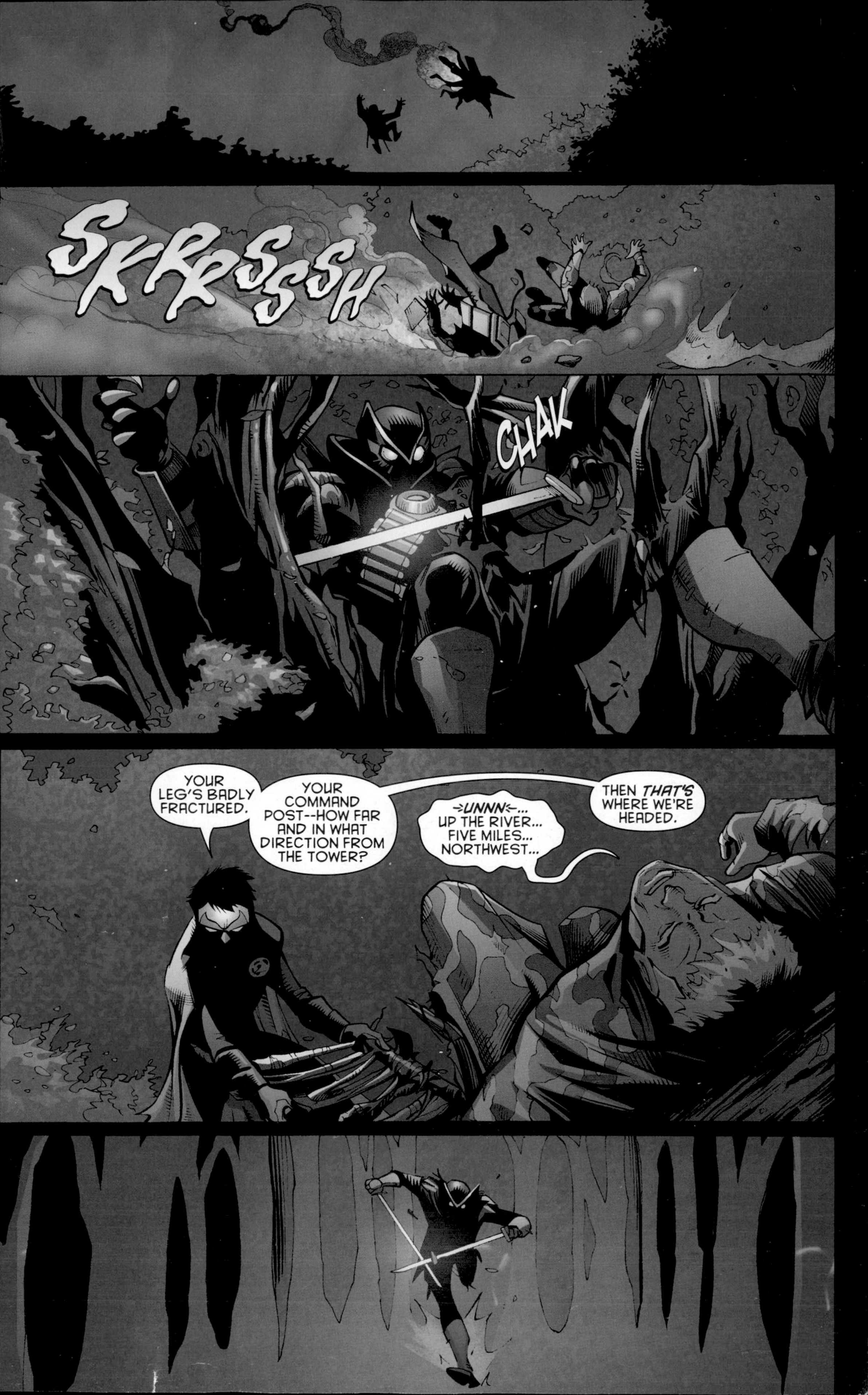
SKRRSSSH
CHAK
YOUR LEG'S BADLY FRACTURED.
YOUR COMMAND POST--HOW FAR AND IN WHAT DIRECTION FROM THE TOWER?
UNNN... UP THE RIVER... FIVE MILES... NORTHWEST...
THEN THAT'S WHERE WE'RE HEADED.

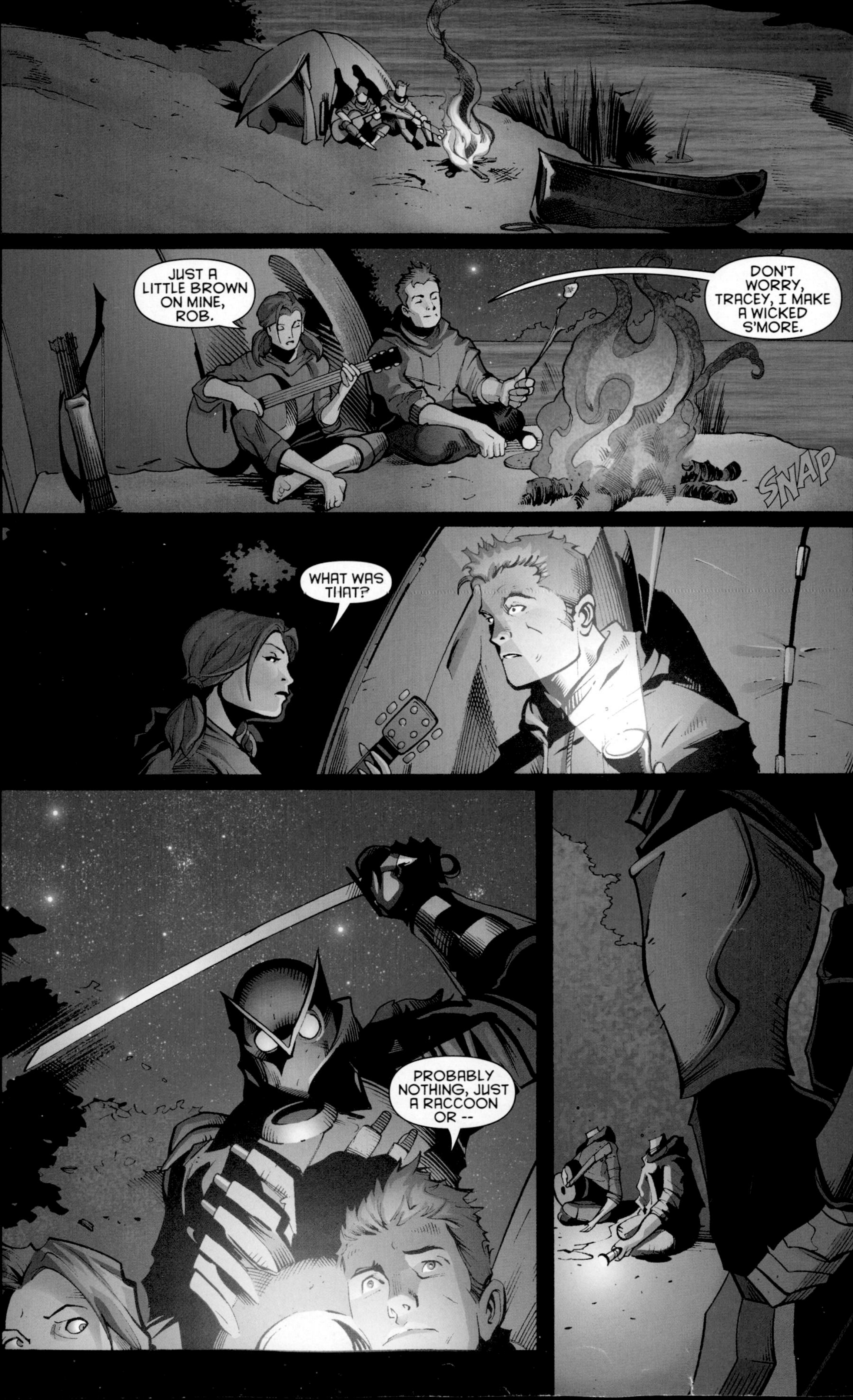
JUST A LITTLE BROWN ON MINE, ROB.
DON'T WORRY, TRACEY, I MAKE A WICKED S'MORE.
SNAP
WHAT WAS THAT?
PROBABLY NOTHING, JUST A RACCOON OR --

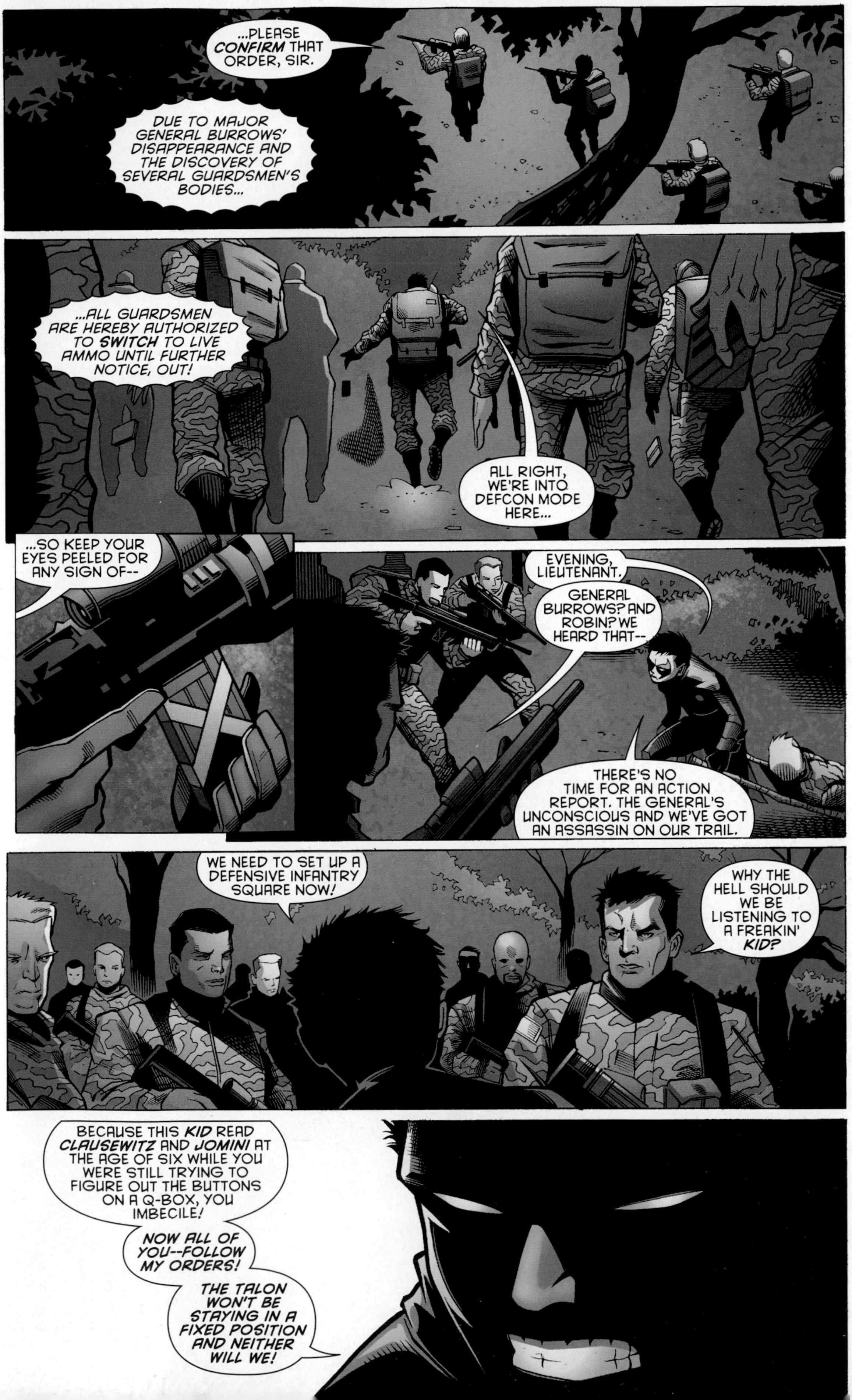
...PLEASE CONFIRM THAT ORDER, SIR.
DUE TO MAJOR GENERAL BURROWS' DISAPPEARANCE AND THE DISCOVERY OF SEVERAL GUARDSMEN'S BODIES...
...ALL GUARDSMEN ARE HEREBY AUTHORIZED TO SWITCH TO LIVE AMMO UNTIL FURTHER NOTICE, OUT!
ALL RIGHT, WE'RE INTO DEFCON MODE HERE...
...SO KEEP YOUR EYES PEELED FOR ANY SIGN OF--
EVENING, LIEUTENANT.
GENERAL BURROWS? AND ROBIN? WE HEARD THAT--
THERE'S NO TIME FOR AN ACTION REPORT. THE GENERAL'S UNCONSCIOUS AND WE'VE GOT AN ASSASSIN ON OUR TRAIL.
WE NEED TO SET UP A DEFENSIVE INFANTRY SQUARE NOW!
WHY THE HELL SHOULD WE BE LISTENING TO A FREAKIN' KID?
BECAUSE THIS KID READ CLAUSEWITZ AND JOMINI AT THE AGE OF SIX WHILE YOU WERE STILL TRYING TO FIGURE OUT THE BUTTONS ON A Q-BOX, YOU IMBECILE!
NOW ALL OF YOU--FOLLOW MY ORDERS!
THE TALON WON'T BE STAYING IN A FIXED POSITION AND NEITHER WILL WE!

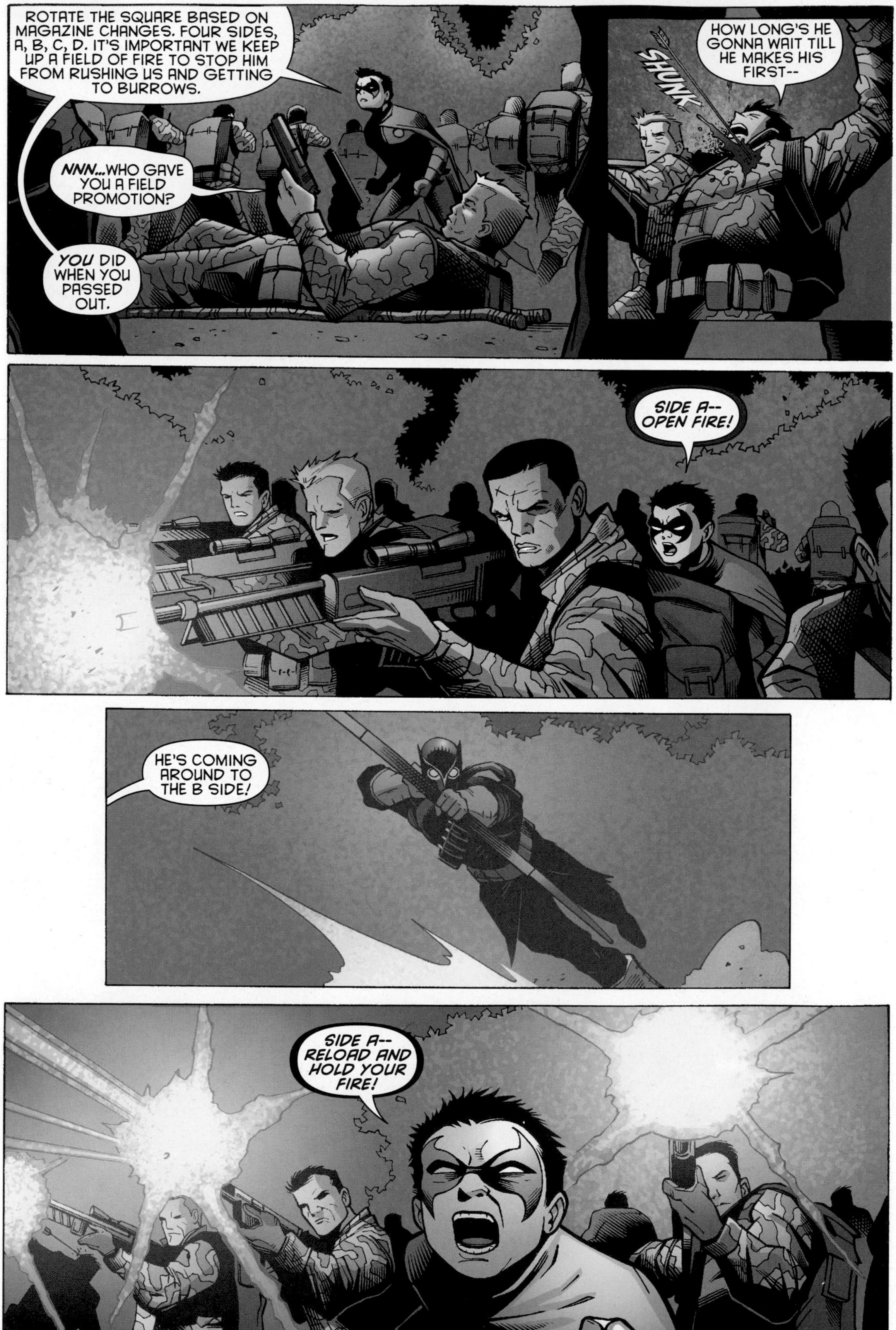
ROTATE THE SQUARE BASED ON MAGAZINE CHANGES. FOUR SIDES, A, B, C, D. IT'S IMPORTANT WE KEEP UP A FIELD OF FIRE TO STOP HIM FROM RUSHING US AND GETTING TO BURROWS.
NNN...WHO GAVE YOU A FIELD PROMOTION?
YOU DID WHEN YOU PASSED OUT.
SHUNK
HOW LONG'S HE GONNA WAIT TILL HE MAKES HIS FIRST--
SIDE A-- OPEN FIRE!
HE'S COMING AROUND TO THE B SIDE!
SIDE A-- RELOAD AND HOLD YOUR FIRE!

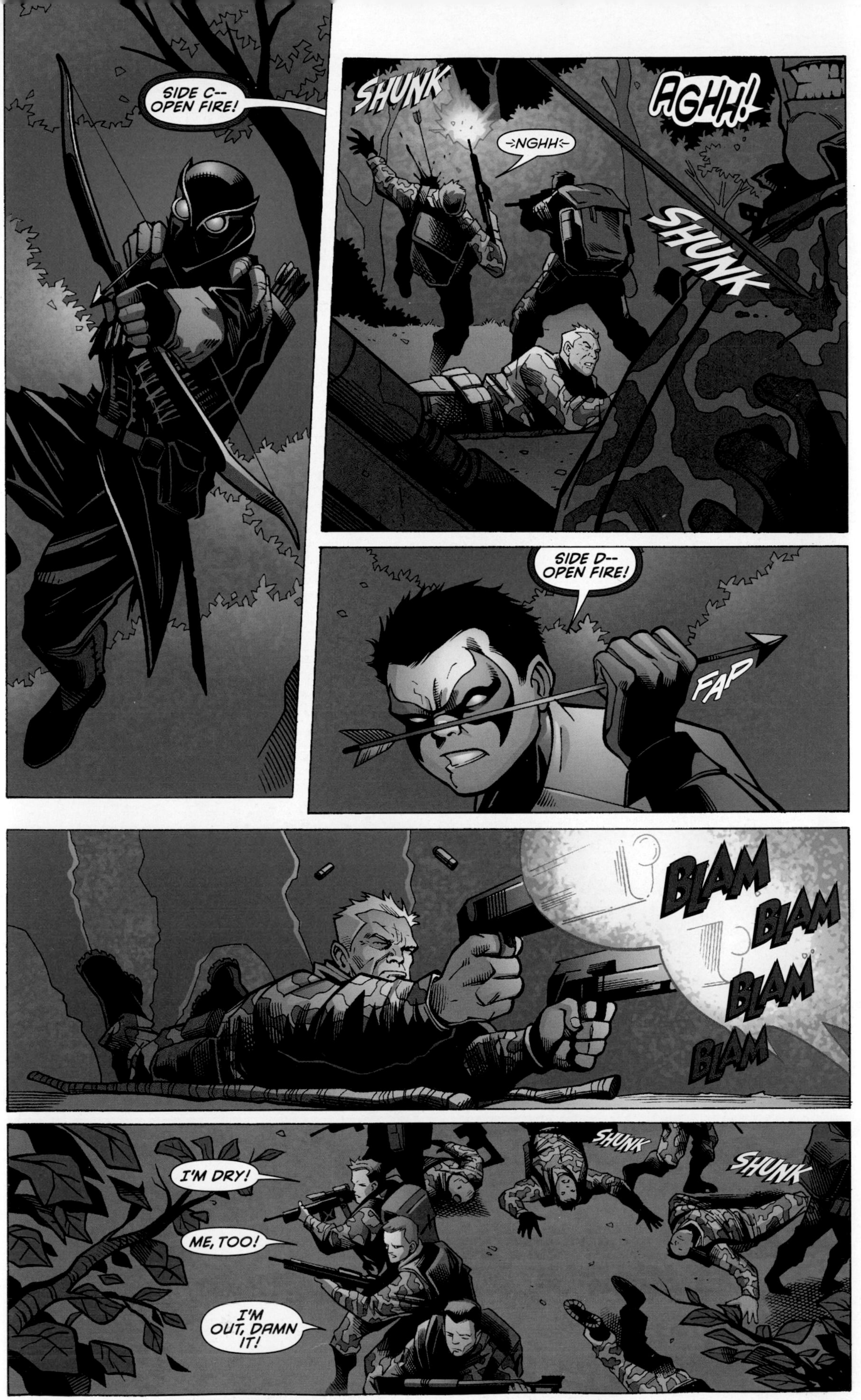
SIDE C--
OPEN FIRE!
SHUNK
-NGHH-
AGHH!
SHUNK
SHUNK
SIDE D--
OPEN FIRE!
FAP
BLAM
BLAM
BLAM
BLAM
SHUNK
SHUNK
I'M DRY!
ME, TOO!
I'M
OUT, DAMN
IT!

THERE'S ONLY ONE THING LEFT WHEN THE AMMO RUNS OUT, KID.

I KNOW.

FIX BAYONETS.

CHARGE!

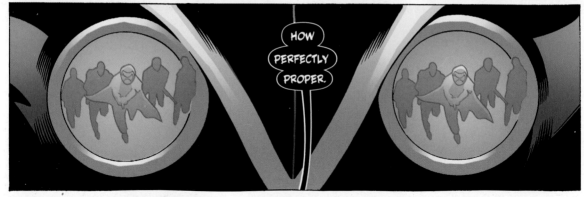

HOW PERFECTLY PROPER.

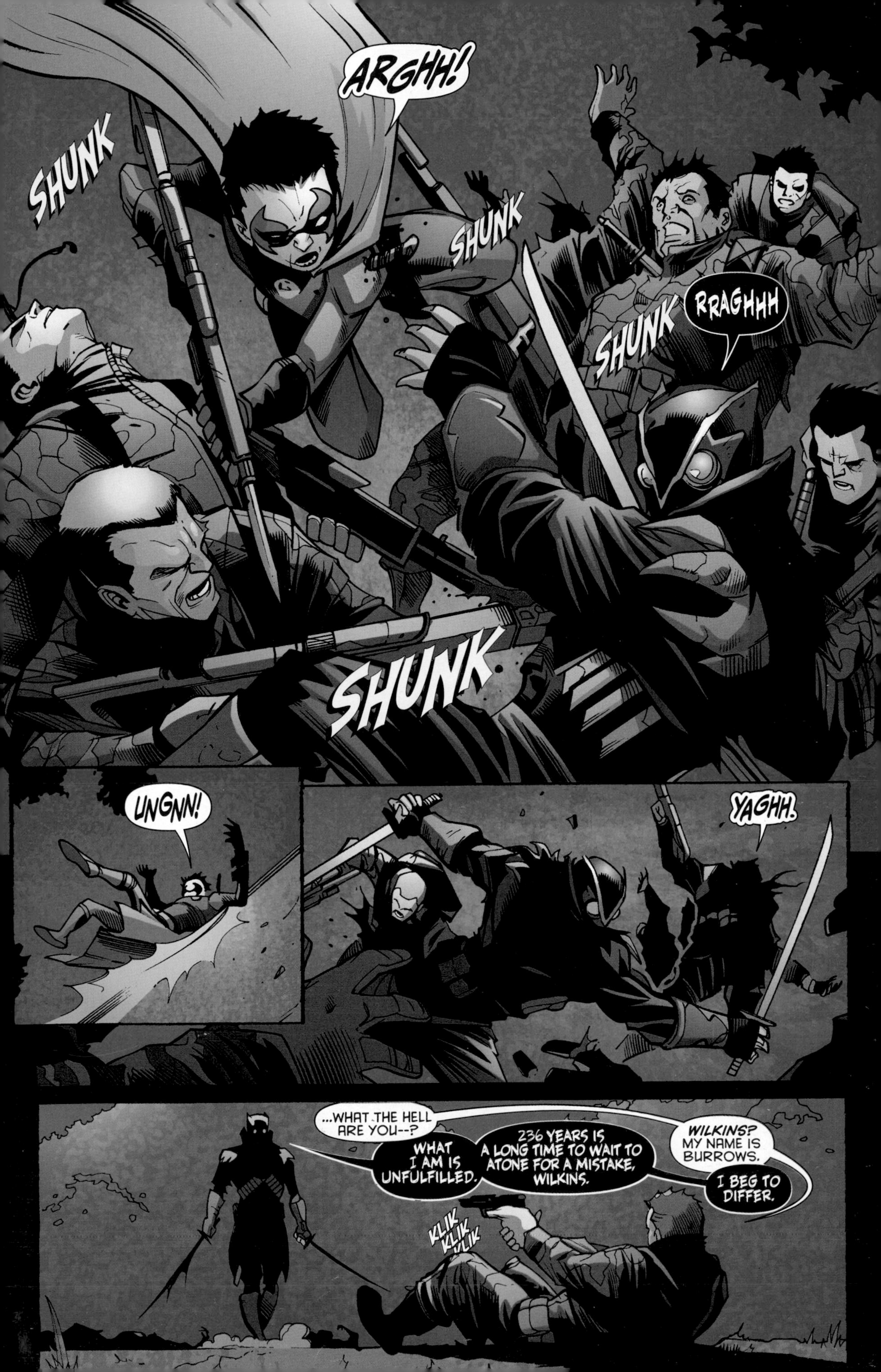
ARGHH!
SHUNK
SHUNK
SHUNK
RRAGHHH
SHUNK
UNGNN!
YAGHH.
...WHAT THE HELL ARE YOU--?
WHAT I AM IS UNFULFILLED.
236 YEARS IS A LONG TIME TO WAIT TO ATONE FOR A MISTAKE, WILKINS.
WILKINS? MY NAME IS BURROWS.
I BEG TO DIFFER.
KLIK KLIK KLIK

"BACK IN 1778, **EDWIN WILKINS**, A CONTINENTAL ARMY SPY, TOOK ON A DANGEROUS MISSION IN GOTHAM BUT ONLY ON THE CONDITION THAT HIS FAMILY BE TAKEN CARE OF IN CASE OF HIS DEATH, WHICH, EVERYONE ASSUMED, WAS LIKELY."

"**GENERAL WASHINGTON** HIMSELF PROMISED WILKINS THAT HIS LOVED ONES WOULD RECEIVE A SIGNIFICANT **LAND GRANT** FOR HIS SERVICE IF THEIR **WAR OF INDEPENDENCE** PROVED TRIUMPHANT."

"I WAS SUMMONED FROM MY NEST AND GIVEN AN ORDER BY THE COURT OF OWLS TO **ERADICATE** WILKINS AND ALL BLOOD RELATIVES..."

"AFTER SWIMMING UNDERWATER THROUGH SENTRY POINTS, I SECRETLY SLIPPED ONTO THE BRITISH PRISON FRIGATE AND **KILLED** EDWIN IN HIS SLEEP."

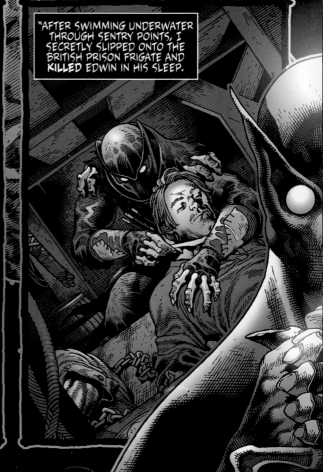

"...SO THE LAND GRANT THAT WOULD PASS TO HIM AND HIS ANCESTORS IN THE UNLIKELY CASE OF A COLONIAL VICTORY COULD LATER BE BOUGHT WITHOUT DIFFICULTY BY A FAVORITE SON OF THE COURT AND DEVELOPED FOR THEIR OWN INTERESTS.

"WILKINS' MISSION WAS SUCCESSFUL AND HE MANAGED TO PASS THE INFORMATION HE HAD GLEANED TO CAPTAIN ALEXANDER HAMILTON ONLY MOMENTS PRIOR TO HIS **CAPTURE** BY THE BRITISH.

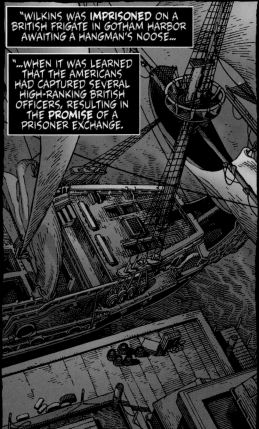

"WILKINS WAS **IMPRISONED** ON A BRITISH FRIGATE IN GOTHAM HARBOR AWAITING A HANGMAN'S NOOSE...

"...WHEN IT WAS LEARNED THAT THE AMERICANS HAD CAPTURED SEVERAL HIGH-RANKING BRITISH OFFICERS, RESULTING IN THE **PROMISE** OF A PRISONER EXCHANGE.

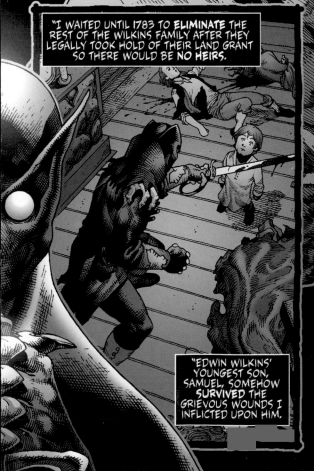

"I WAITED UNTIL 1783 TO **ELIMINATE** THE REST OF THE WILKINS FAMILY AFTER THEY LEGALLY TOOK HOLD OF THEIR LAND GRANT SO THERE WOULD BE **NO HEIRS.**

"EDWIN WILKINS' YOUNGEST SON, SAMUEL, SOMEHOW **SURVIVED** THE GRIEVOUS WOUNDS I INFLICTED UPON HIM.

"SAMUEL WAS APPARENTLY HIDDEN AWAY AND RAISED BY FRIENDS OF THE WILKINS FAMILY WHILE THE COURT OF OWLS EVENTUALLY TOOK CONTROL OF THE LAND.

"THIS FAMILY'S SURNAME WAS BURROW

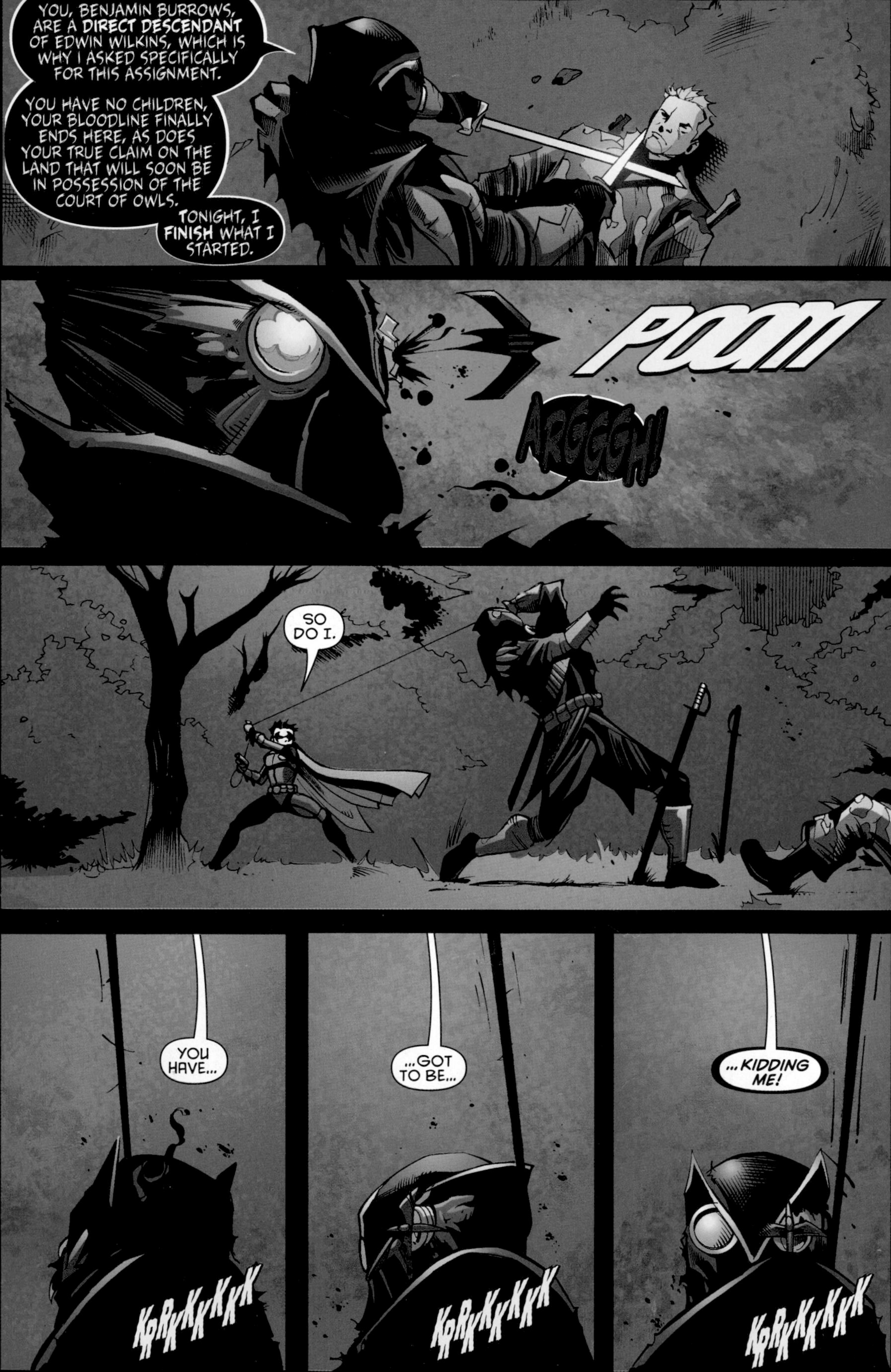
YOU, BENJAMIN BURROWS, ARE A DIRECT DESCENDANT OF EDWIN WILKINS, WHICH IS WHY I ASKED SPECIFICALLY FOR THIS ASSIGNMENT.
YOU HAVE NO CHILDREN, YOUR BLOODLINE FINALLY ENDS HERE, AS DOES YOUR TRUE CLAIM ON THE LAND THAT WILL SOON BE IN POSSESSION OF THE COURT OF OWLS.
TONIGHT, I FINISH WHAT I STARTED.
POOM
ARGGGH!
SO DO I.
YOU HAVE...
...GOT TO BE...
...KIDDING ME!
KRRKKKKKK
KRRKKKKKK
KRRKKKKKK

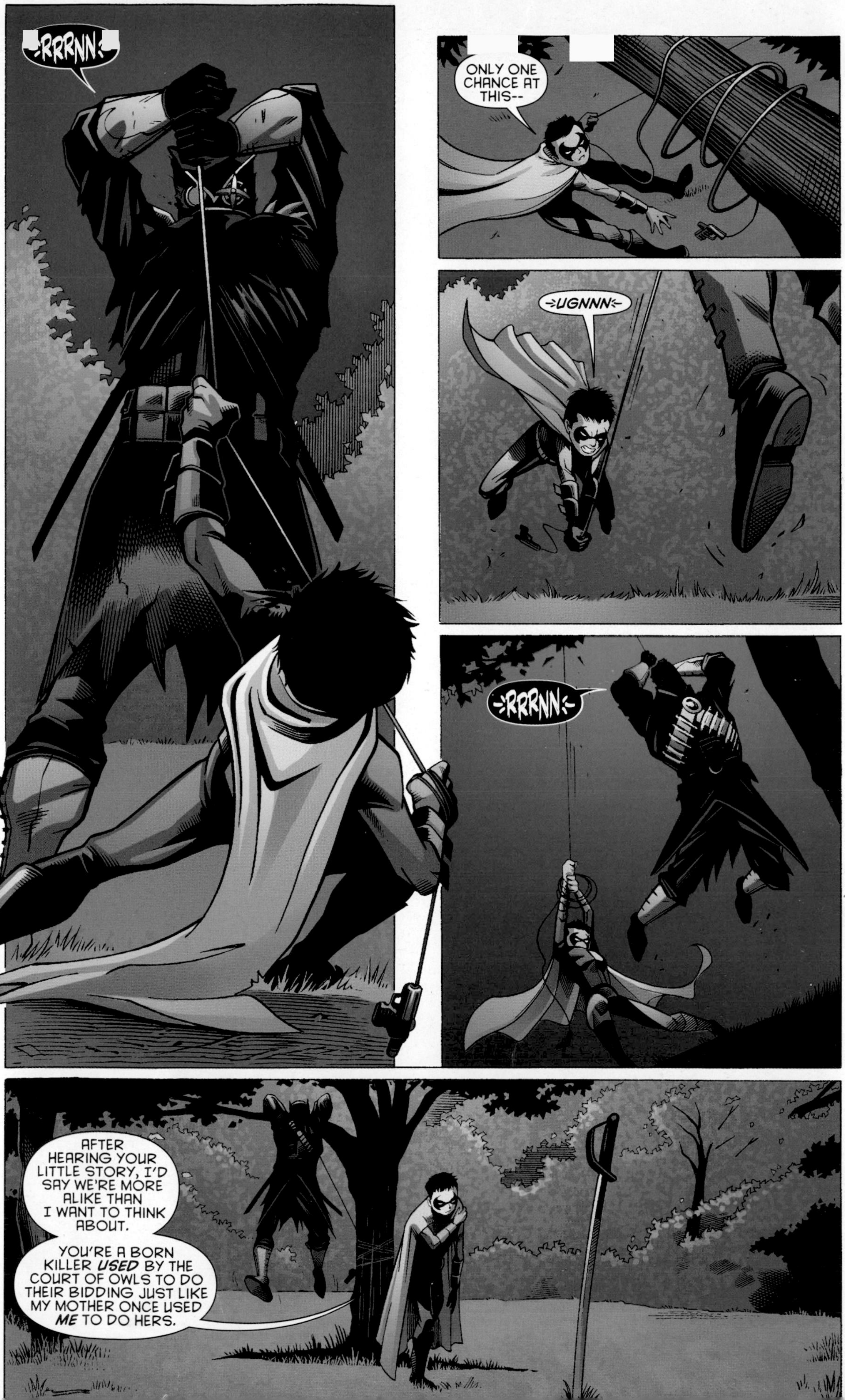
RRRNN
ONLY ONE CHANCE AT THIS--
UGNNN
RRRNN
AFTER HEARING YOUR LITTLE STORY, I'D SAY WE'RE MORE ALIKE THAN I WANT TO THINK ABOUT.
YOU'RE A BORN KILLER USED BY THE COURT OF OWLS TO DO THEIR BIDDING JUST LIKE MY MOTHER ONCE USED ME TO DO HERS.

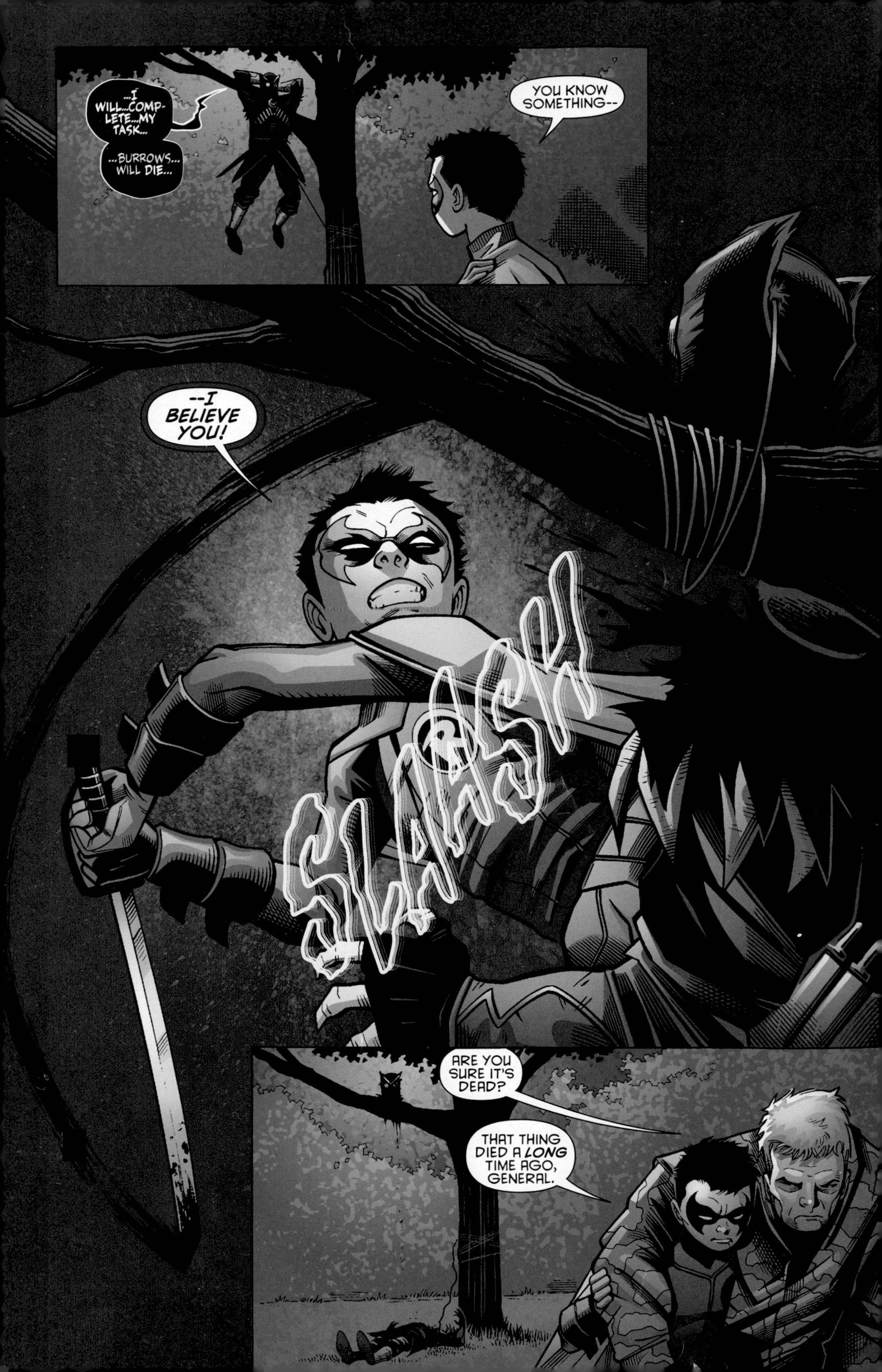
...I WILL...COMPLETE...MY TASK...
...BURROWS... WILL DIE...
YOU KNOW SOMETHING--
--I BELIEVE YOU!
SLASH
ARE YOU SURE IT'S DEAD?
THAT THING DIED A LONG TIME AGO, GENERAL.

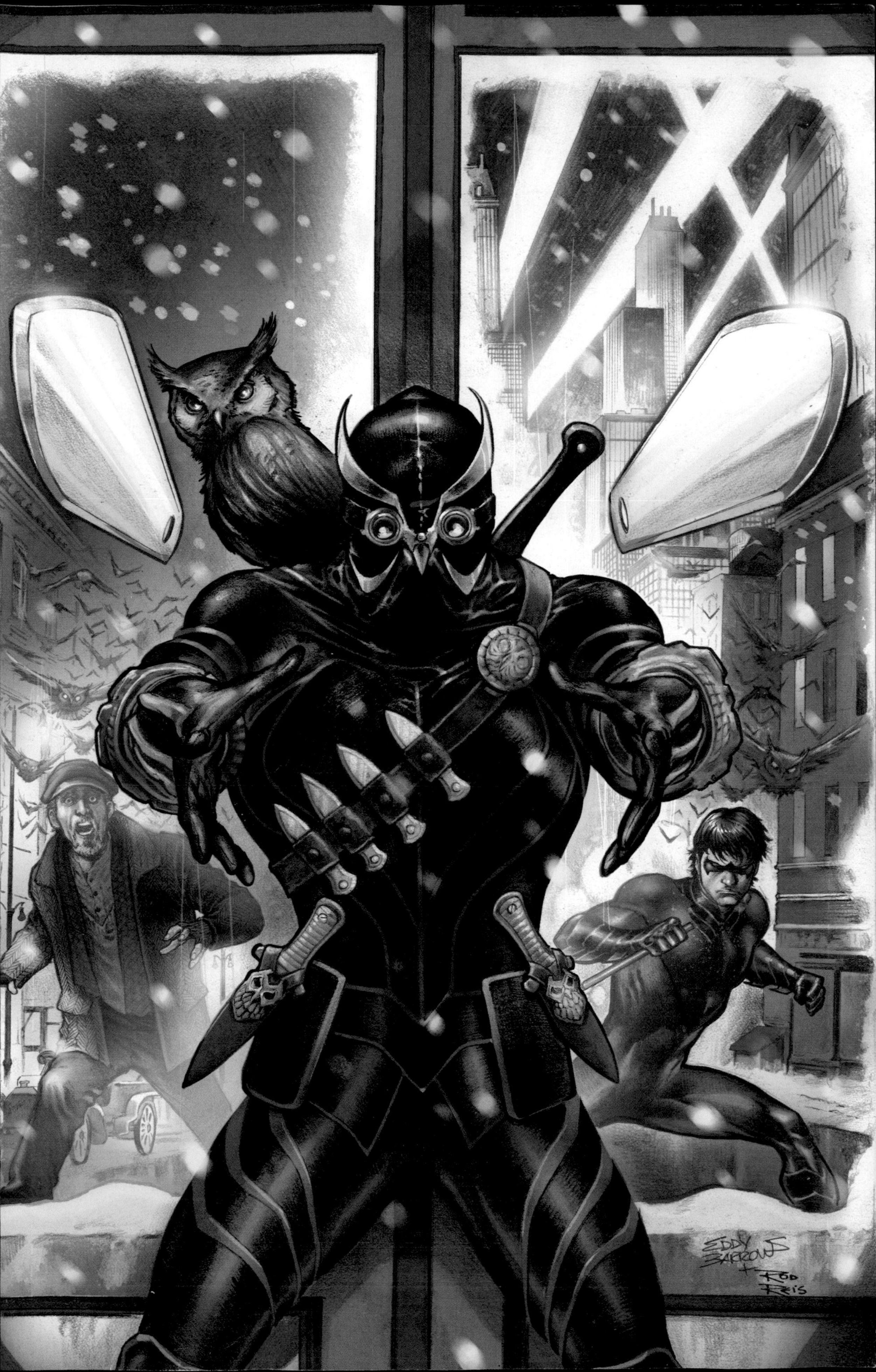
EDDY BARROWS
+
ROD REIS

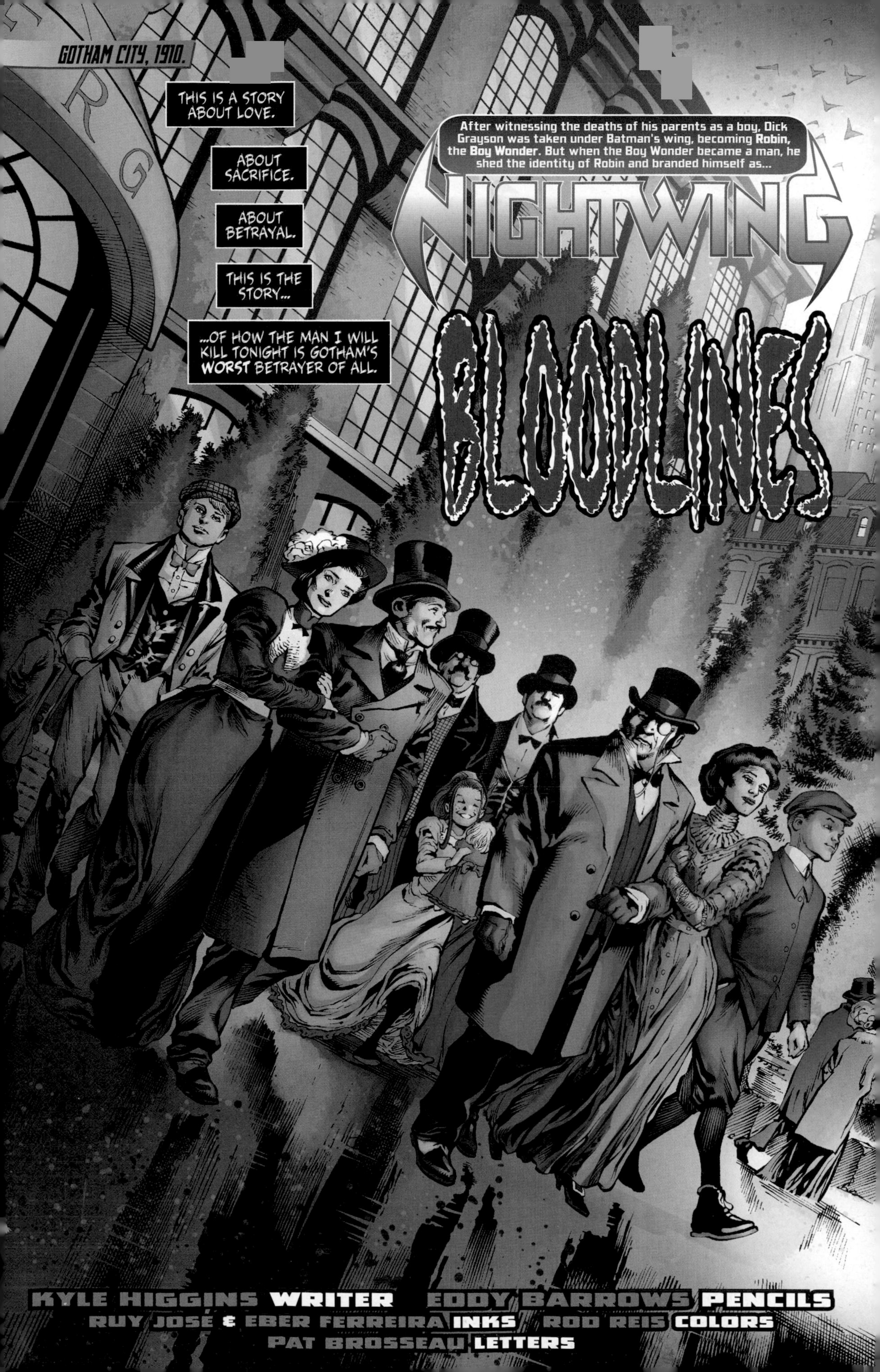

GOTHAM CITY, 1910.
THIS IS A STORY ABOUT LOVE.
ABOUT SACRIFICE.
ABOUT BETRAYAL.
THIS IS THE STORY...
...OF HOW THE MAN I WILL KILL TONIGHT IS GOTHAM'S WORST BETRAYER OF ALL.
After witnessing the deaths of his parents as a boy, Dick Grayson was taken under Batman's wing, becoming Robin, the Boy Wonder. But when the Boy Wonder became a man, he shed the identity of Robin and branded himself as...
NIGHTWING
BLOODLINES
KYLE HIGGINS WRITER EDDY BARROWS PENCILS
RUY JOSÉ & EBER FERREIRA INKS ROD REIS COLORS
PAT BROSSEAU LETTERS

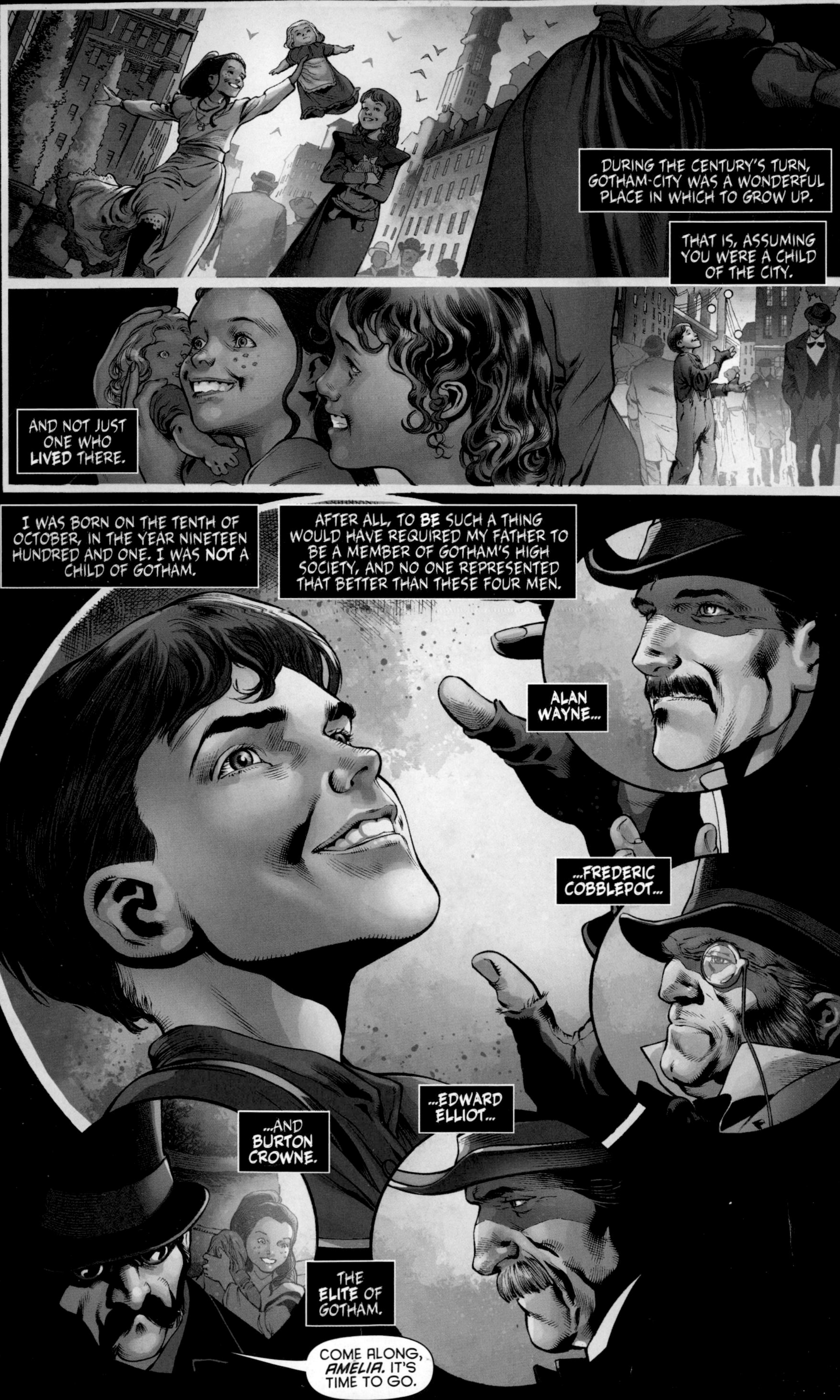
DURING THE CENTURY'S TURN, GOTHAM-CITY WAS A WONDERFUL PLACE IN WHICH TO GROW UP.
THAT IS, ASSUMING YOU WERE A CHILD OF THE CITY.
AND NOT JUST ONE WHO LIVED THERE.
I WAS BORN ON THE TENTH OF OCTOBER, IN THE YEAR NINETEEN HUNDRED AND ONE. I WAS NOT A CHILD OF GOTHAM.
AFTER ALL, TO BE SUCH A THING WOULD HAVE REQUIRED MY FATHER TO BE A MEMBER OF GOTHAM'S HIGH SOCIETY, AND NO ONE REPRESENTED THAT BETTER THAN THESE FOUR MEN.
ALAN WAYNE...
...FREDERIC COBBLEPOT...
...EDWARD ELLIOT...
...AND BURTON CROWNE.
THE ELITE OF GOTHAM.
COME ALONG, AMELIA. IT'S TIME TO GO.

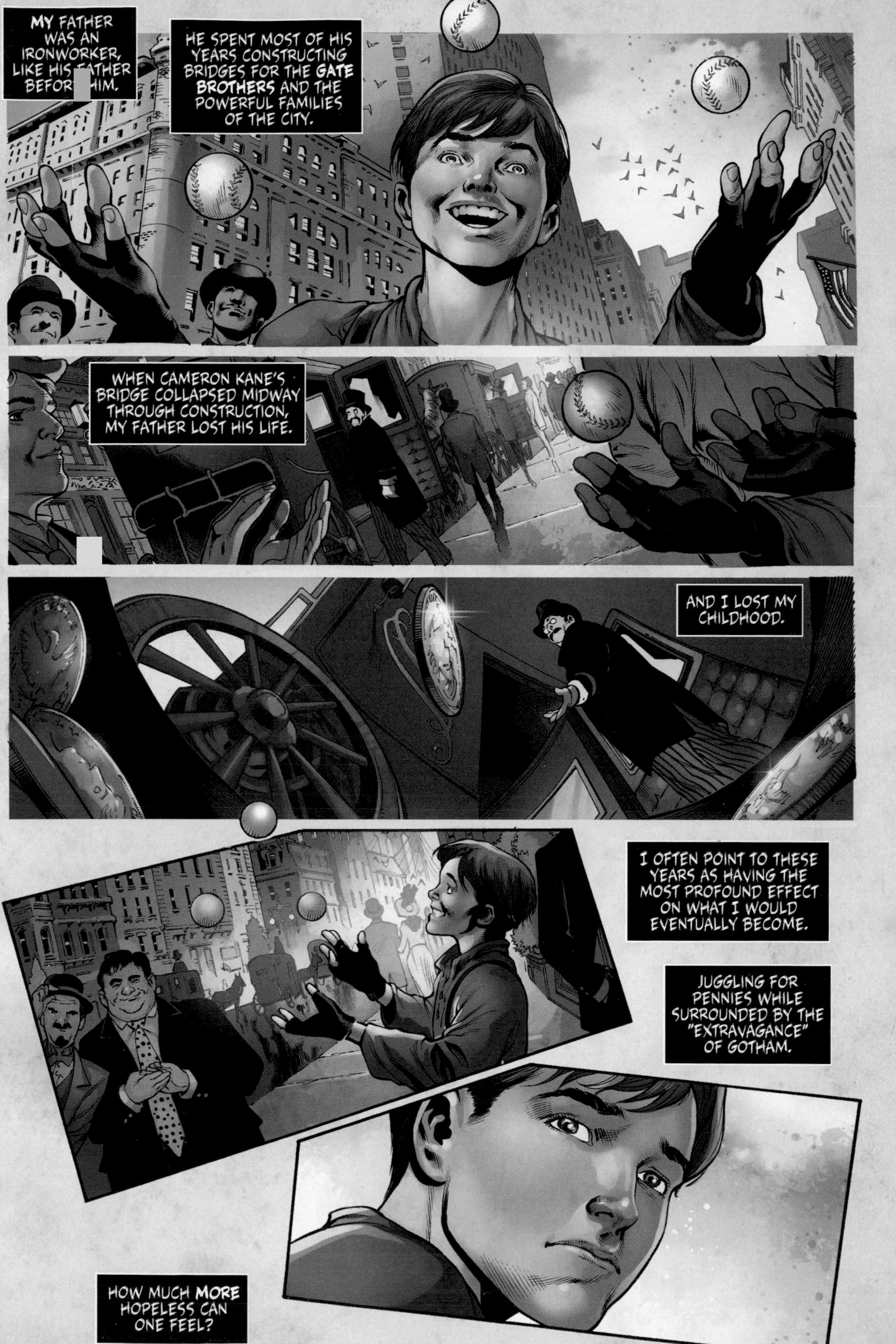
MY FATHER WAS AN IRONWORKER, LIKE HIS FATHER BEFORE HIM.
HE SPENT MOST OF HIS YEARS CONSTRUCTING BRIDGES FOR THE GATE BROTHERS AND THE POWERFUL FAMILIES OF THE CITY.
WHEN CAMERON KANE'S BRIDGE COLLAPSED MIDWAY THROUGH CONSTRUCTION, MY FATHER LOST HIS LIFE.
AND I LOST MY CHILDHOOD.
I OFTEN POINT TO THESE YEARS AS HAVING THE MOST PROFOUND EFFECT ON WHAT I WOULD EVENTUALLY BECOME.
JUGGLING FOR PENNIES WHILE SURROUNDED BY THE "EXTRAVAGANCE" OF GOTHAM.
HOW MUCH MORE HOPELESS CAN ONE FEEL?

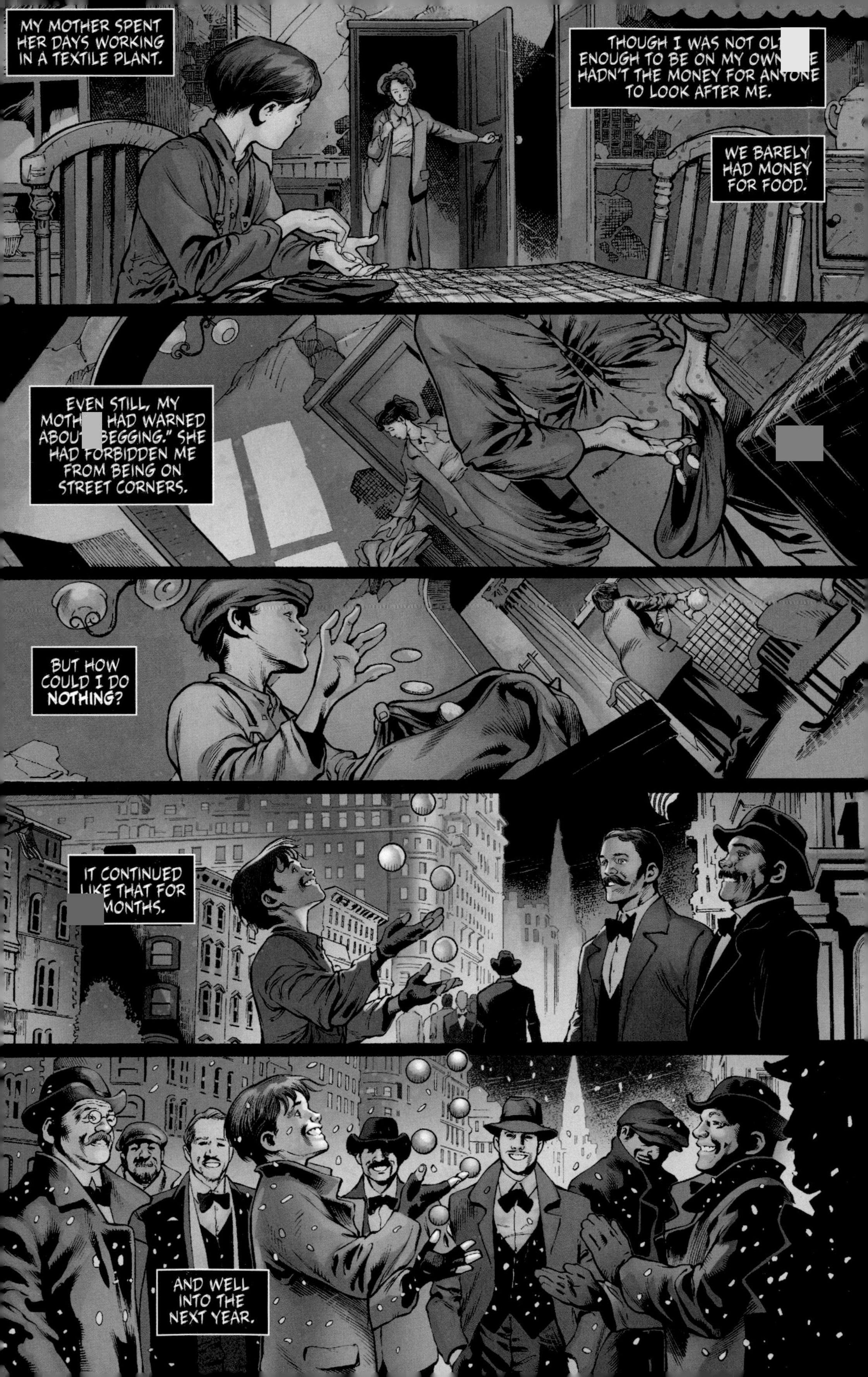
MY MOTHER SPENT HER DAYS WORKING IN A TEXTILE PLANT.
THOUGH I WAS NOT OL ENOUGH TO BE ON MY OWN E HADN'T THE MONEY FOR ANYONE TO LOOK AFTER ME.
WE BARELY HAD MONEY FOR FOOD.
EVEN STILL, MY MOTH HAD WARNED ABOU EGGING." SHE HAD FORBIDDEN ME FROM BEING ON STREET CORNERS.
BUT HOW COULD I DO **NOTHING?**
IT CONTINUED KE THAT FOR MONTHS.
AND WELL INTO THE NEXT YEAR.

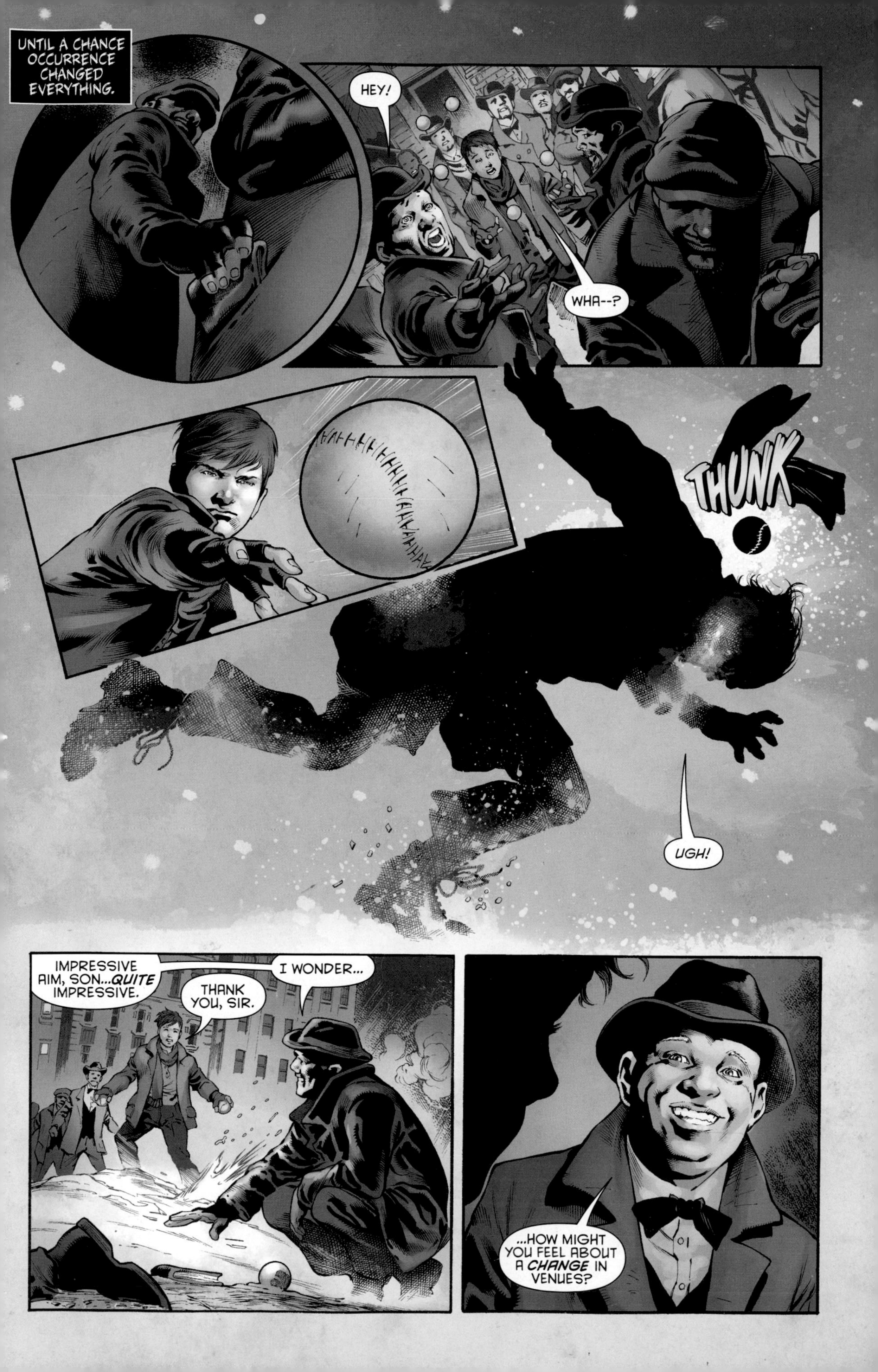
UNTIL A CHANCE OCCURRENCE CHANGED EVERYTHING.
HEY!
WHA--?
THUNK
UGH!
IMPRESSIVE AIM, SON...QUITE IMPRESSIVE.
THANK YOU, SIR.
I WONDER...
...HOW MIGHT YOU FEEL ABOUT A CHANGE IN VENUES?

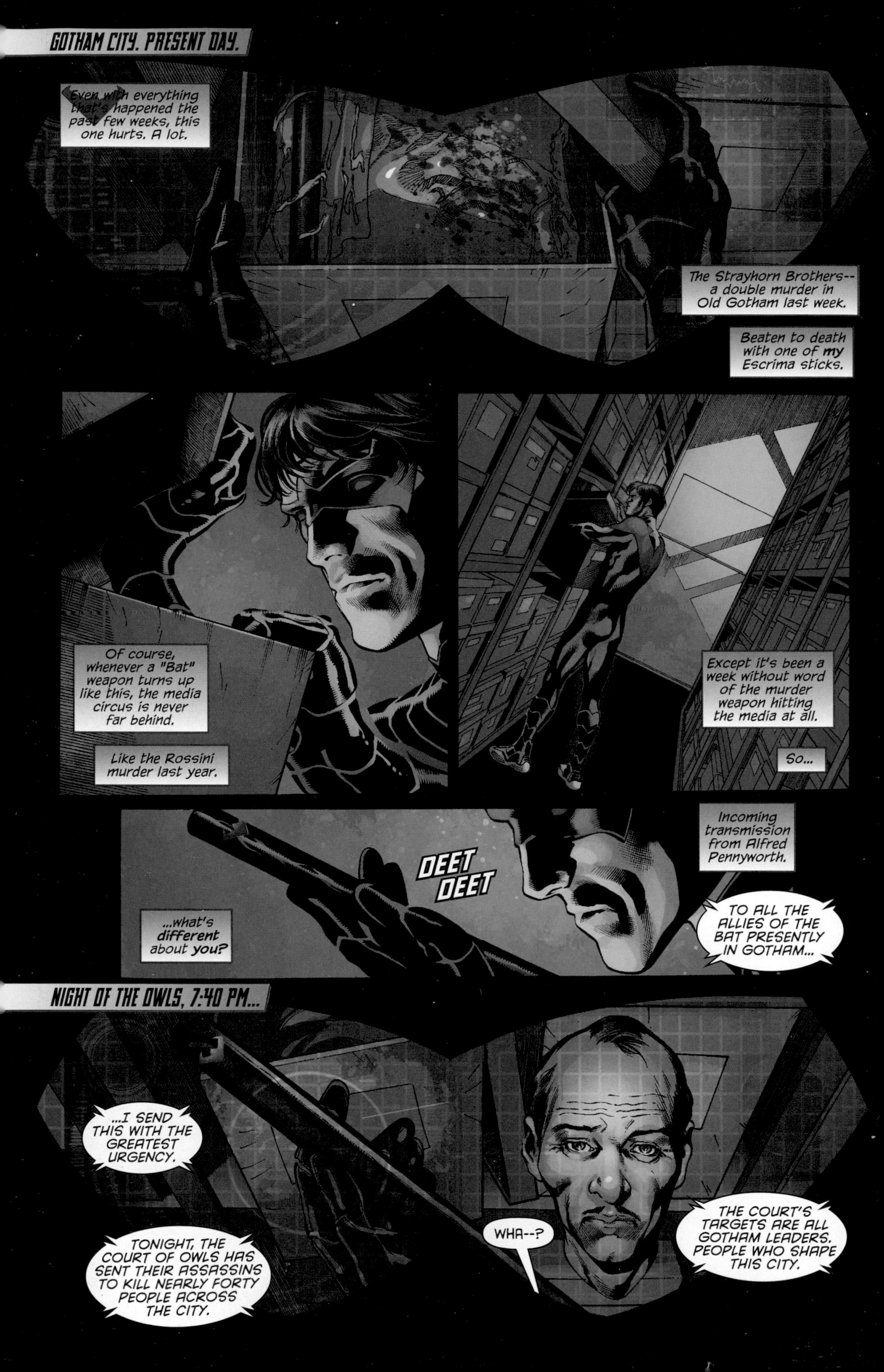
GOTHAM CITY. PRESENT DAY.
Even with everything that's happened the past few weeks, this one hurts. A lot.
The Strayhorn Brothers-- a double murder in Old Gotham last week.
Beaten to death with one of my Escrima sticks.
Of course, whenever a "Bat" weapon turns up like this, the media circus is never far behind.
Like the Rossini murder last year.
Except it's been a week without word of the murder weapon hitting the media at all.
So...
...what's different about you?
DEET DEET
Incoming transmission from Alfred Pennyworth.
TO ALL THE ALLIES OF THE BAT PRESENTLY IN GOTHAM...
NIGHT OF THE OWLS, 7:40 PM...
...I SEND THIS WITH THE GREATEST URGENCY.
TONIGHT, THE COURT OF OWLS HAS SENT THEIR ASSASSINS TO KILL NEARLY FORTY PEOPLE ACROSS THE CITY.
WHA--?
THE COURT'S TARGETS ARE ALL GOTHAM LEADERS. PEOPLE WHO SHAPE THIS CITY.

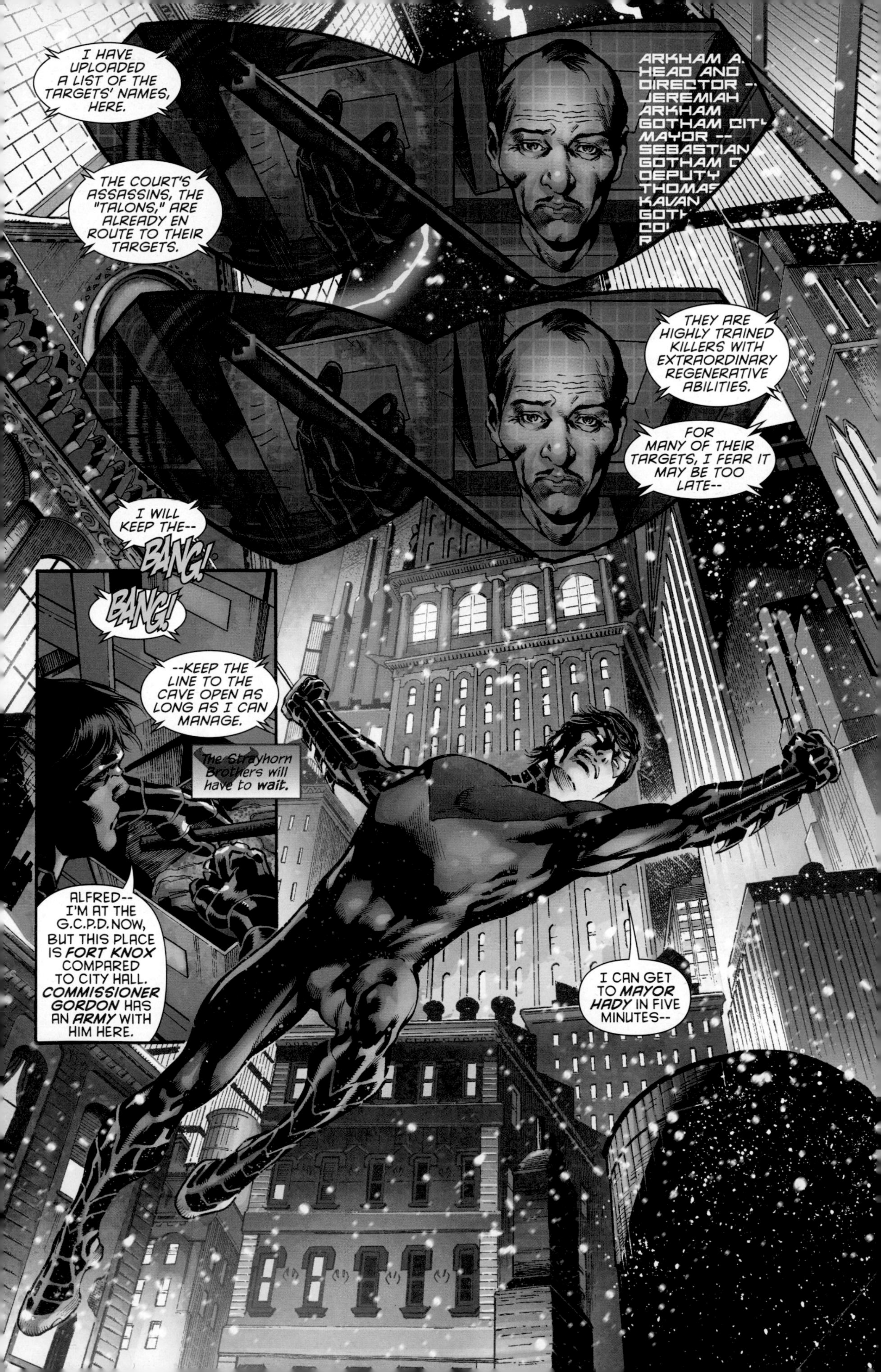
I HAVE UPLOADED A LIST OF THE TARGETS' NAMES, HERE.
ARKHAM A. HEAD AND DIRECTOR -- JEREMIAH ARKHAM
GOTHAM CITY MAYOR -- SEBASTIAN
GOTHAM C DEPUTY THOMAS KAVAN
THE COURT'S ASSASSINS, THE "TALONS," ARE ALREADY EN ROUTE TO THEIR TARGETS.
THEY ARE HIGHLY TRAINED KILLERS WITH EXTRAORDINARY REGENERATIVE ABILITIES.
FOR MANY OF THEIR TARGETS, I FEAR IT MAY BE TOO LATE--
I WILL KEEP THE--
BANG!
BANG!
--KEEP THE LINE TO THE CAVE OPEN AS LONG AS I CAN MANAGE.
The Strayhorn Brothers will have to wait.
ALFRED-- I'M AT THE G.C.P.D. NOW, BUT THIS PLACE IS FORT KNOX COMPARED TO CITY HALL. COMMISSIONER GORDON HAS AN ARMY WITH HIM HERE.
I CAN GET TO MAYOR HADY IN FIVE MINUTES--

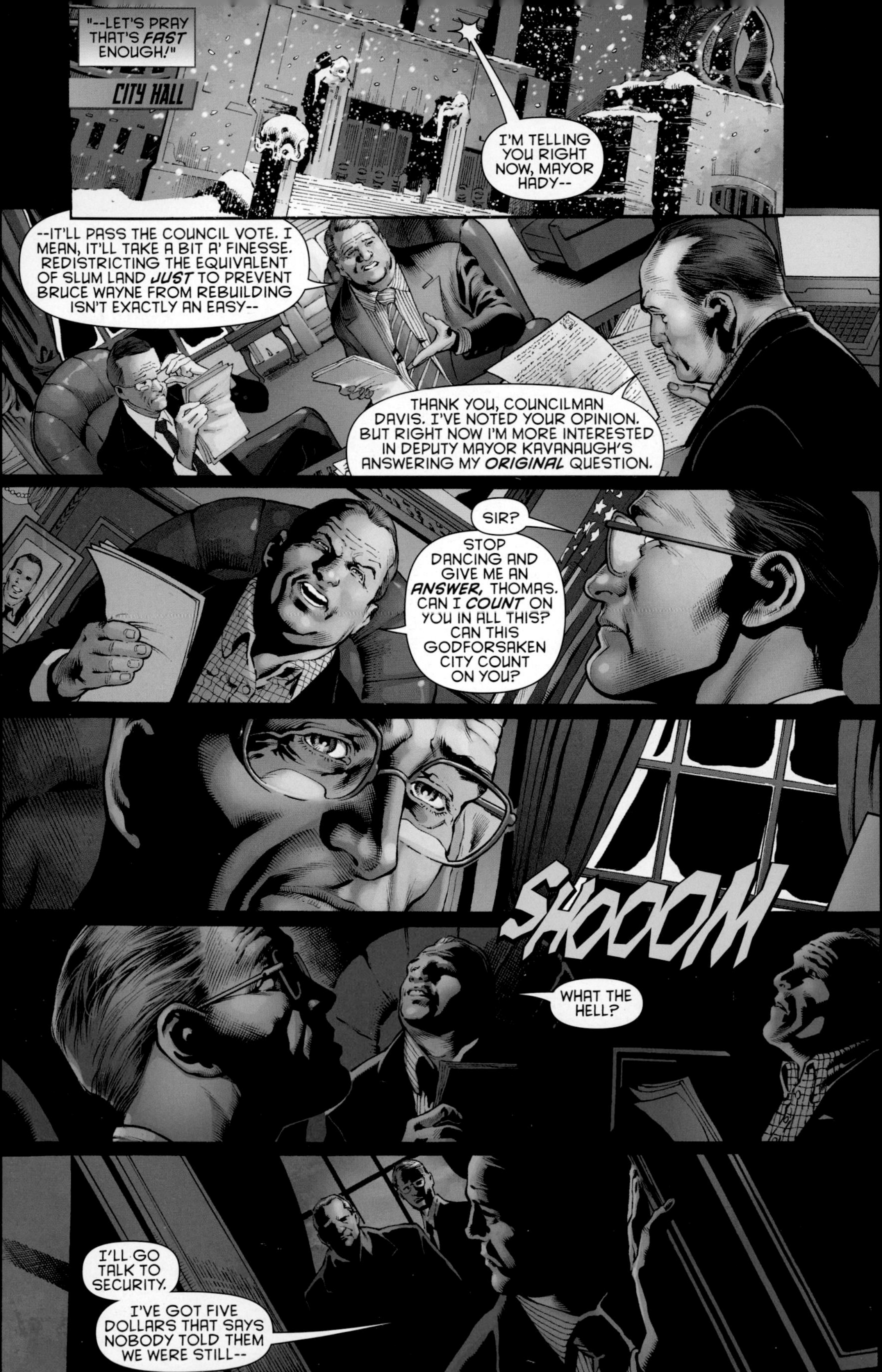
"--LET'S PRAY THAT'S FAST ENOUGH!"
CITY HALL
I'M TELLING YOU RIGHT NOW, MAYOR HADY--
--IT'LL PASS THE COUNCIL VOTE. I MEAN, IT'LL TAKE A BIT A' FINESSE. REDISTRICTING THE EQUIVALENT OF SLUM LAND JUST TO PREVENT BRUCE WAYNE FROM REBUILDING ISN'T EXACTLY AN EASY--
THANK YOU, COUNCILMAN DAVIS. I'VE NOTED YOUR OPINION. BUT RIGHT NOW I'M MORE INTERESTED IN DEPUTY MAYOR KAVANAUGH'S ANSWERING MY ORIGINAL QUESTION.
SIR?
STOP DANCING AND GIVE ME AN ANSWER, THOMAS. CAN I COUNT ON YOU IN ALL THIS? CAN THIS GODFORSAKEN CITY COUNT ON YOU?
SHOOOM
WHAT THE HELL?
I'LL GO TALK TO SECURITY.
I'VE GOT FIVE DOLLARS THAT SAYS NOBODY TOLD THEM WE WERE STILL--

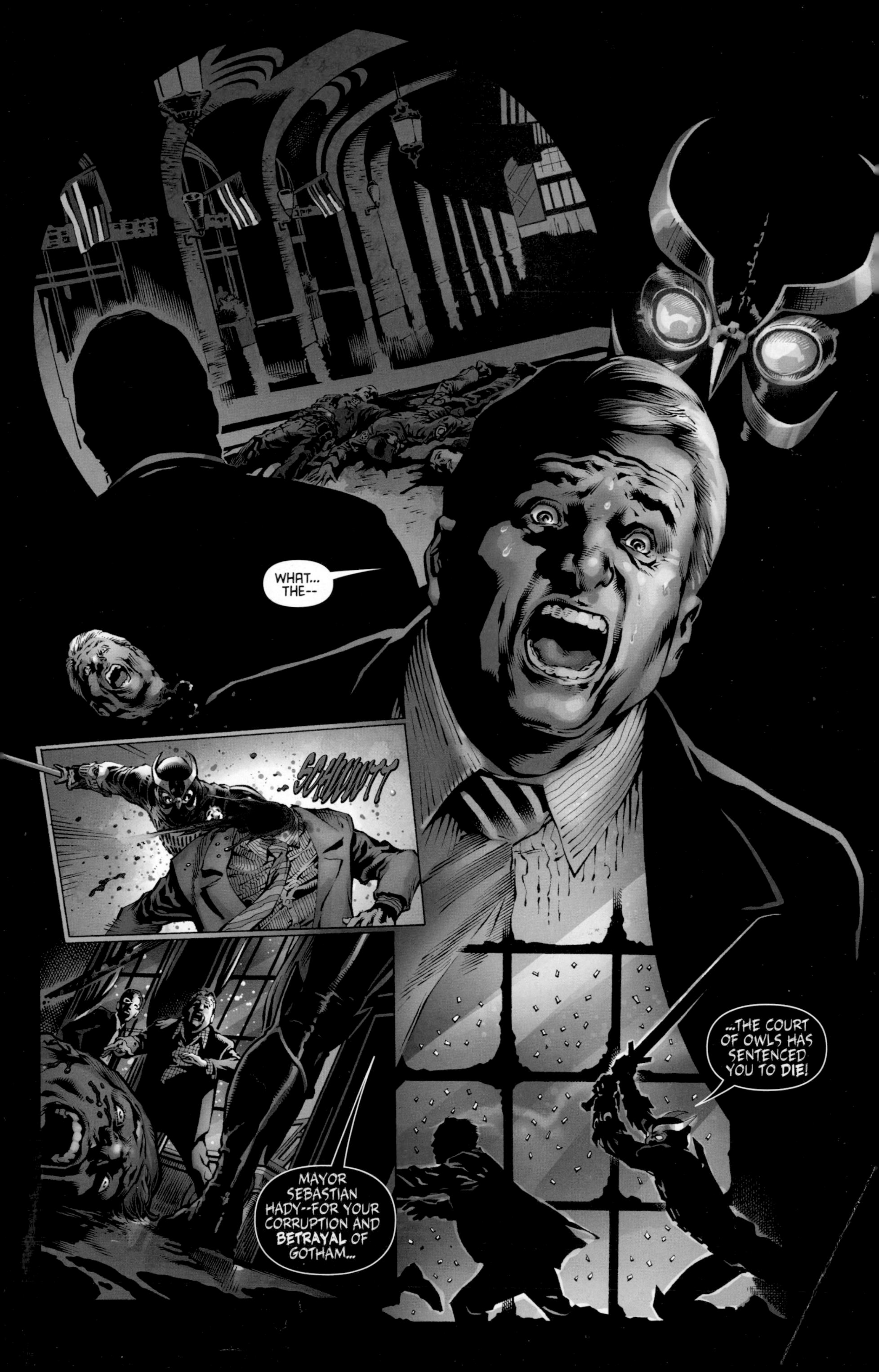

WHAT... THE--
SCHWWTT
MAYOR SEBASTIAN HADY--FOR YOUR CORRUPTION AND BETRAYAL OF GOTHAM...
...THE COURT OF OWLS HAS SENTENCED YOU TO DIE!

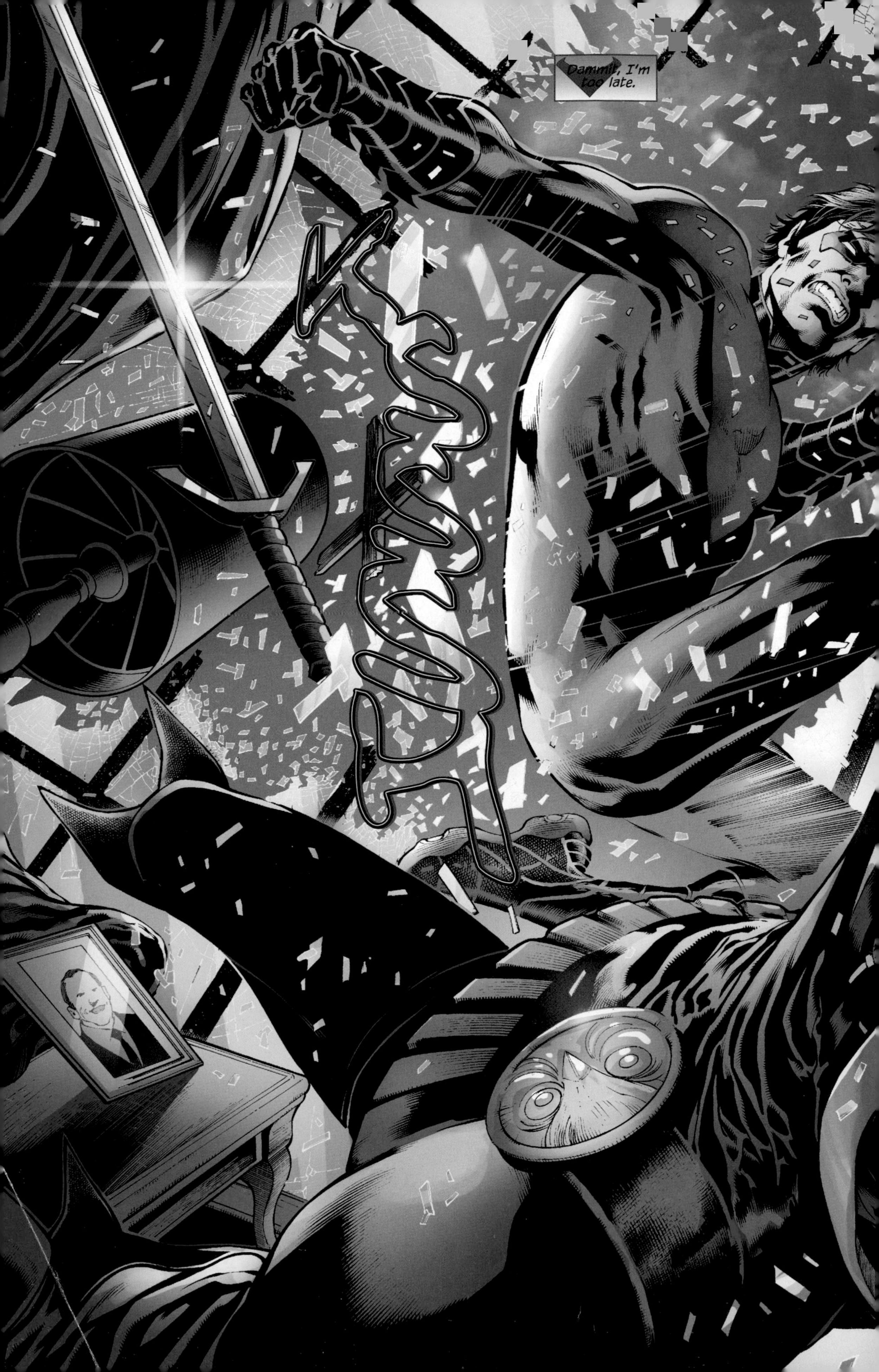
Dammit, I'm too late.

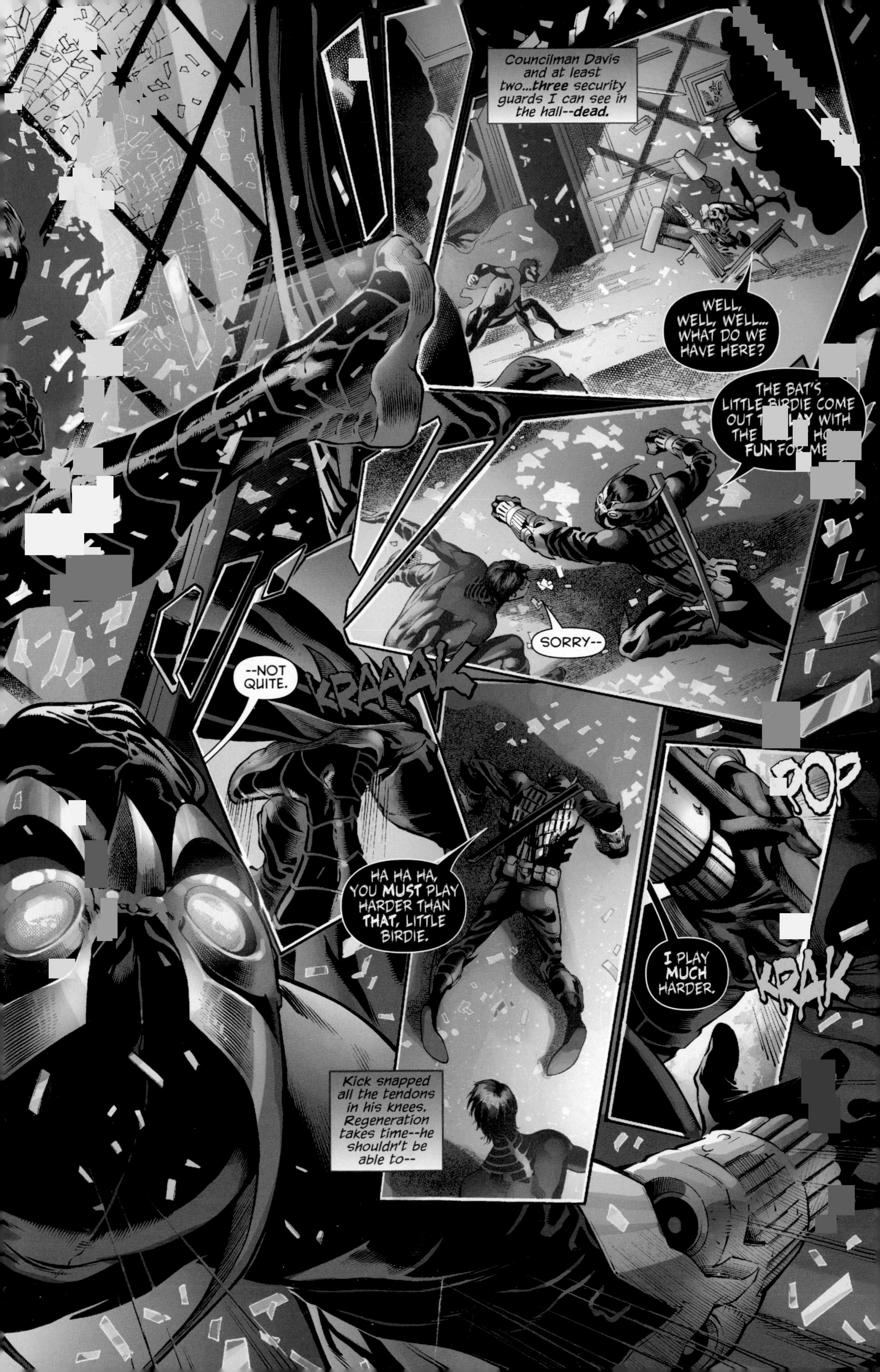
Councilman Davis and at least two...three security guards I can see in the hall--dead.
WELL, WELL, WELL... WHAT DO WE HAVE HERE?
THE BAT'S LITTLE BIRDIE COME
SORRY--
--NOT QUITE.
KRAAAK
HA HA HA, YOU MUST PLAY HARDER THAN THAT, LITTLE BIRDIE.
POP
I PLAY MUCH HARDER.
KRAK
Kick snapped all the tendons in his knees. Regeneration takes time--he shouldn't be able to--

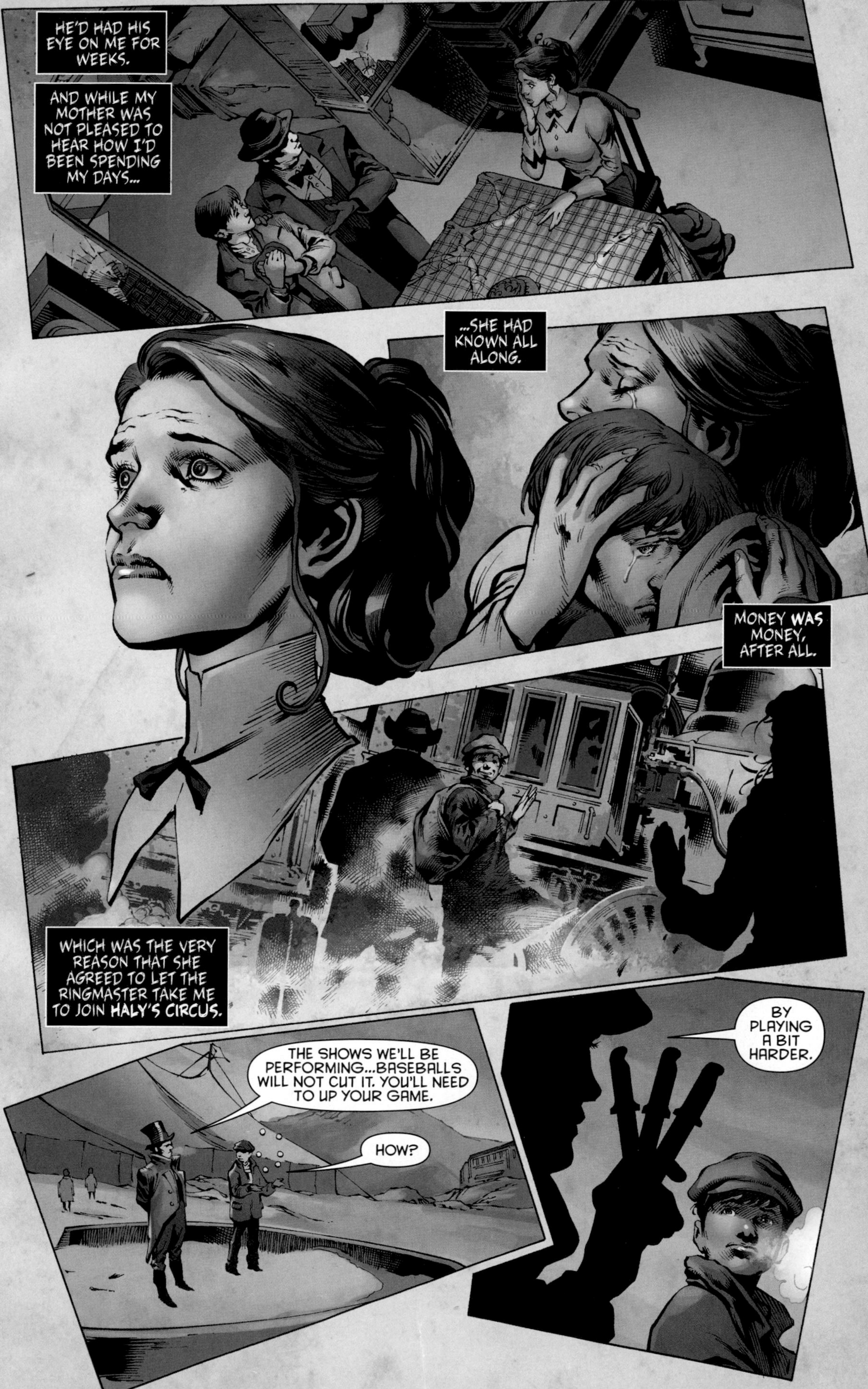

HE'D HAD HIS EYE ON ME FOR WEEKS.
AND WHILE MY MOTHER WAS NOT PLEASED TO HEAR HOW I'D BEEN SPENDING MY DAYS...
...SHE HAD KNOWN ALL ALONG.
MONEY WAS MONEY, AFTER ALL.
WHICH WAS THE VERY REASON THAT SHE AGREED TO LET THE RINGMASTER TAKE ME TO JOIN HALY'S CIRCUS.
THE SHOWS WE'LL BE PERFORMING...BASEBALLS WILL NOT CUT IT. YOU'LL NEED TO UP YOUR GAME.
HOW?
BY PLAYING A BIT HARDER.

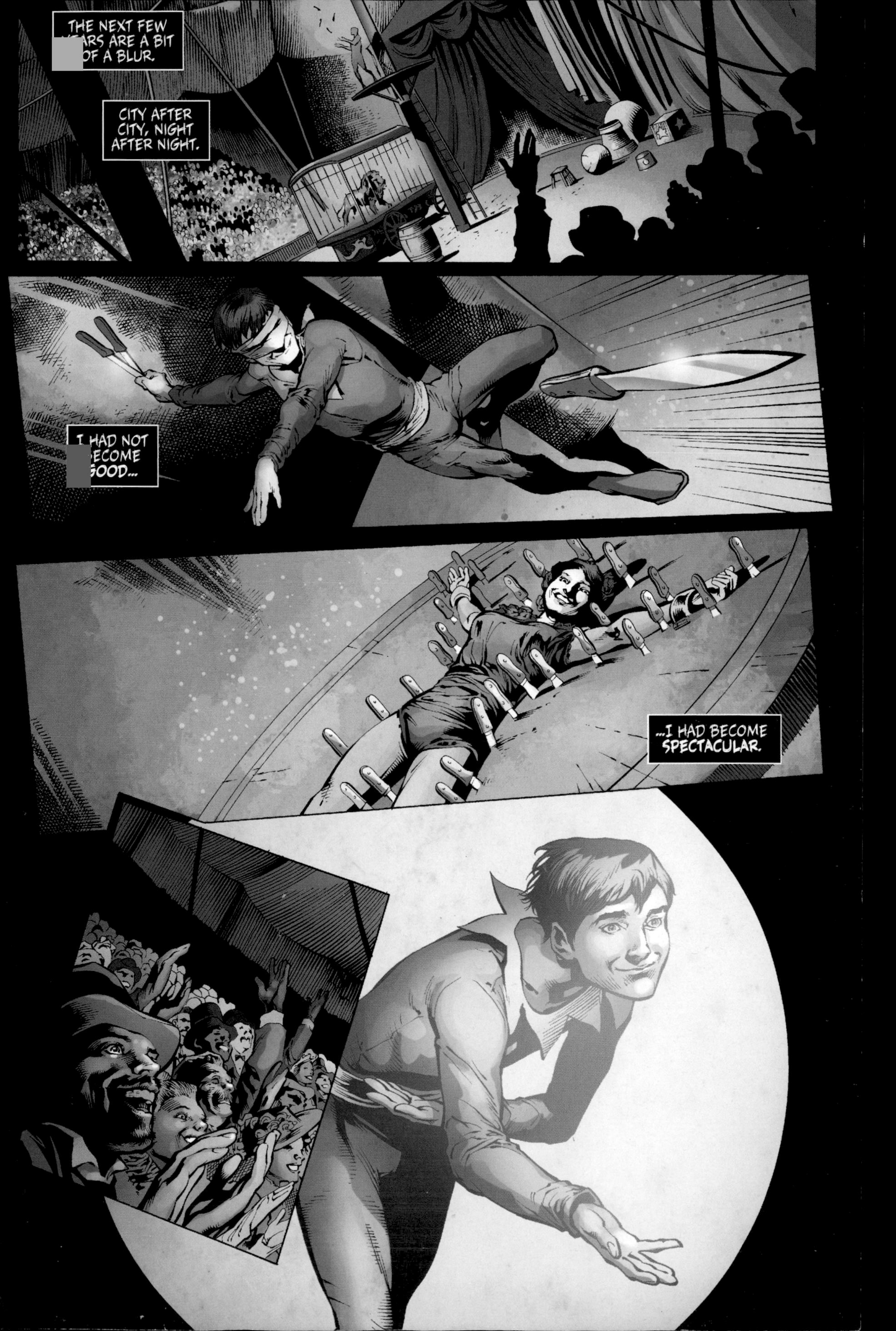
THE NEXT FEW [redacted]EARS ARE A BIT OF A BLUR.
CITY AFTER CITY, NIGHT AFTER NIGHT.
I HAD NOT [redacted]ECOME GOOD...
...I HAD BECOME SPECTACULAR.

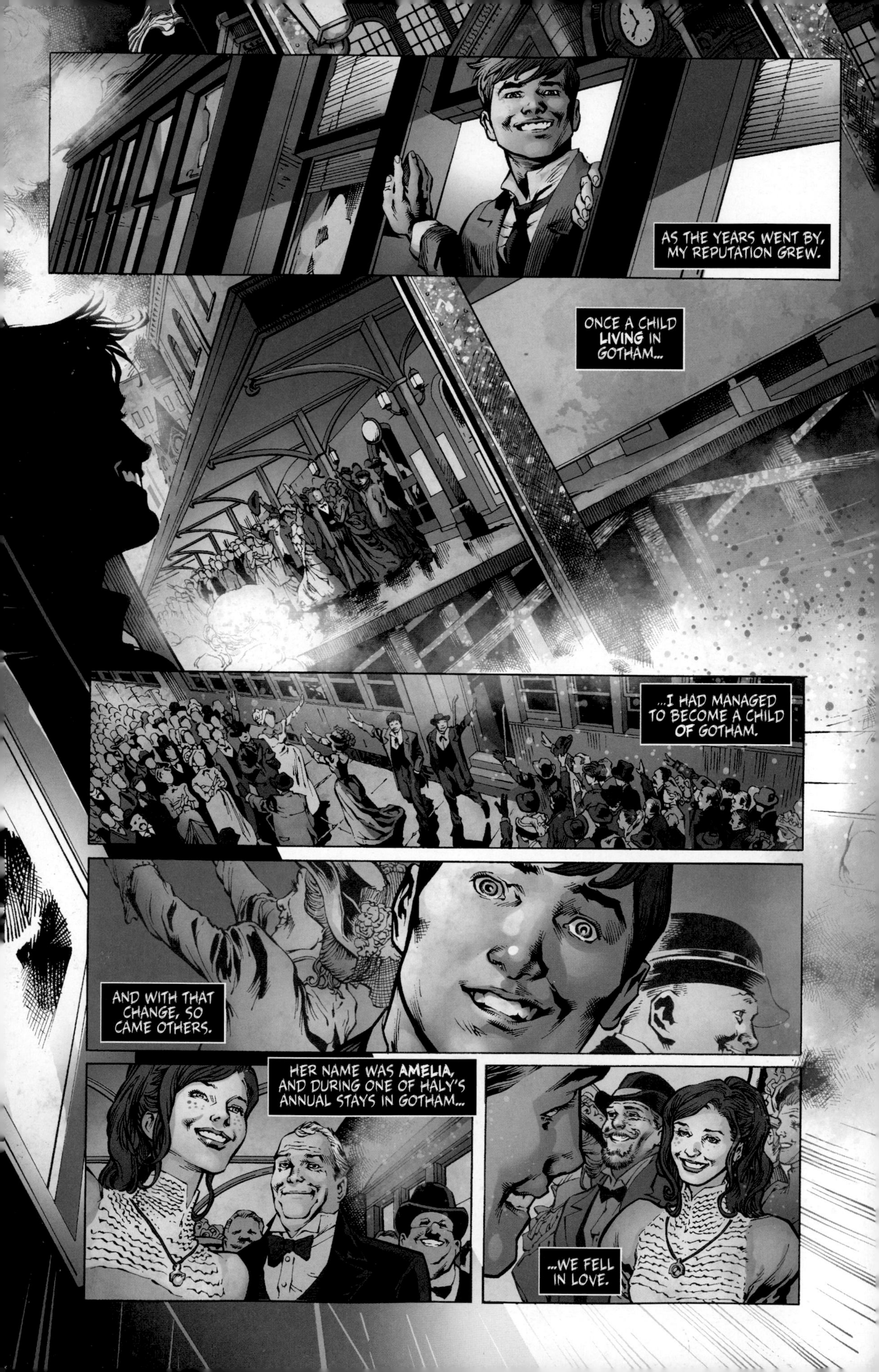
AS THE YEARS WENT BY, MY REPUTATION GREW.
ONCE A CHILD LIVING IN GOTHAM...
...I HAD MANAGED TO BECOME A CHILD OF GOTHAM.
AND WITH THAT CHANGE, SO CAME OTHERS.
HER NAME WAS AMELIA, AND DURING ONE OF HALY'S ANNUAL STAYS IN GOTHAM...
...WE FELL IN LOVE.

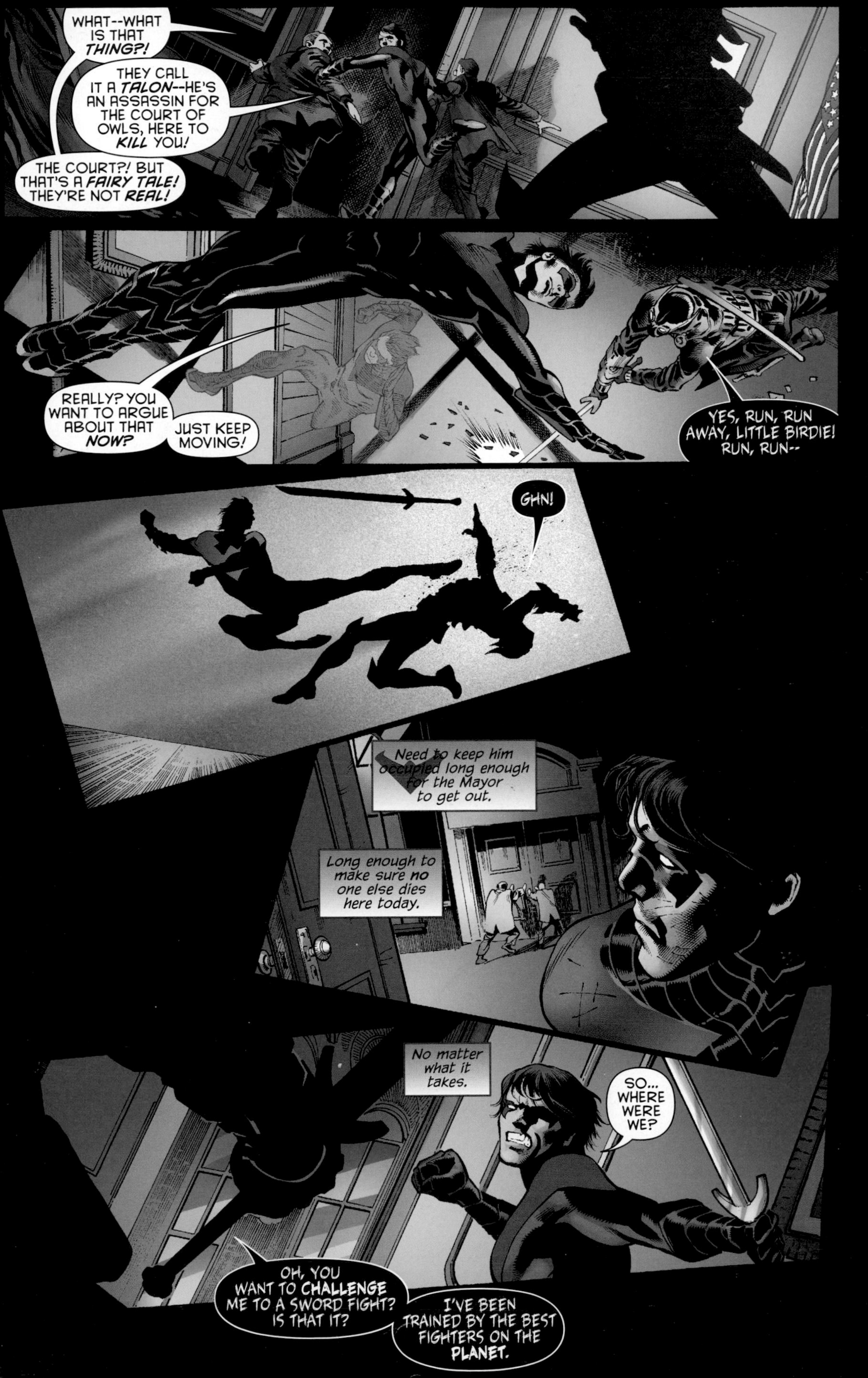
WHAT--WHAT IS THAT THING?!
THEY CALL IT A TALON--HE'S AN ASSASSIN FOR THE COURT OF OWLS, HERE TO KILL YOU!
THE COURT?! BUT THAT'S A FAIRY TALE! THEY'RE NOT REAL!
REALLY? YOU WANT TO ARGUE ABOUT THAT NOW?
JUST KEEP MOVING!
YES, RUN, RUN AWAY, LITTLE BIRDIE! RUN, RUN--
GHN!
Need to keep him occupied long enough for the Mayor to get out.
Long enough to make sure no one else dies here today.
No matter what it takes.
SO... WHERE WERE WE?
OH, YOU WANT TO CHALLENGE ME TO A SWORD FIGHT? IS THAT IT?
I'VE BEEN TRAINED BY THE BEST FIGHTERS ON THE PLANET.

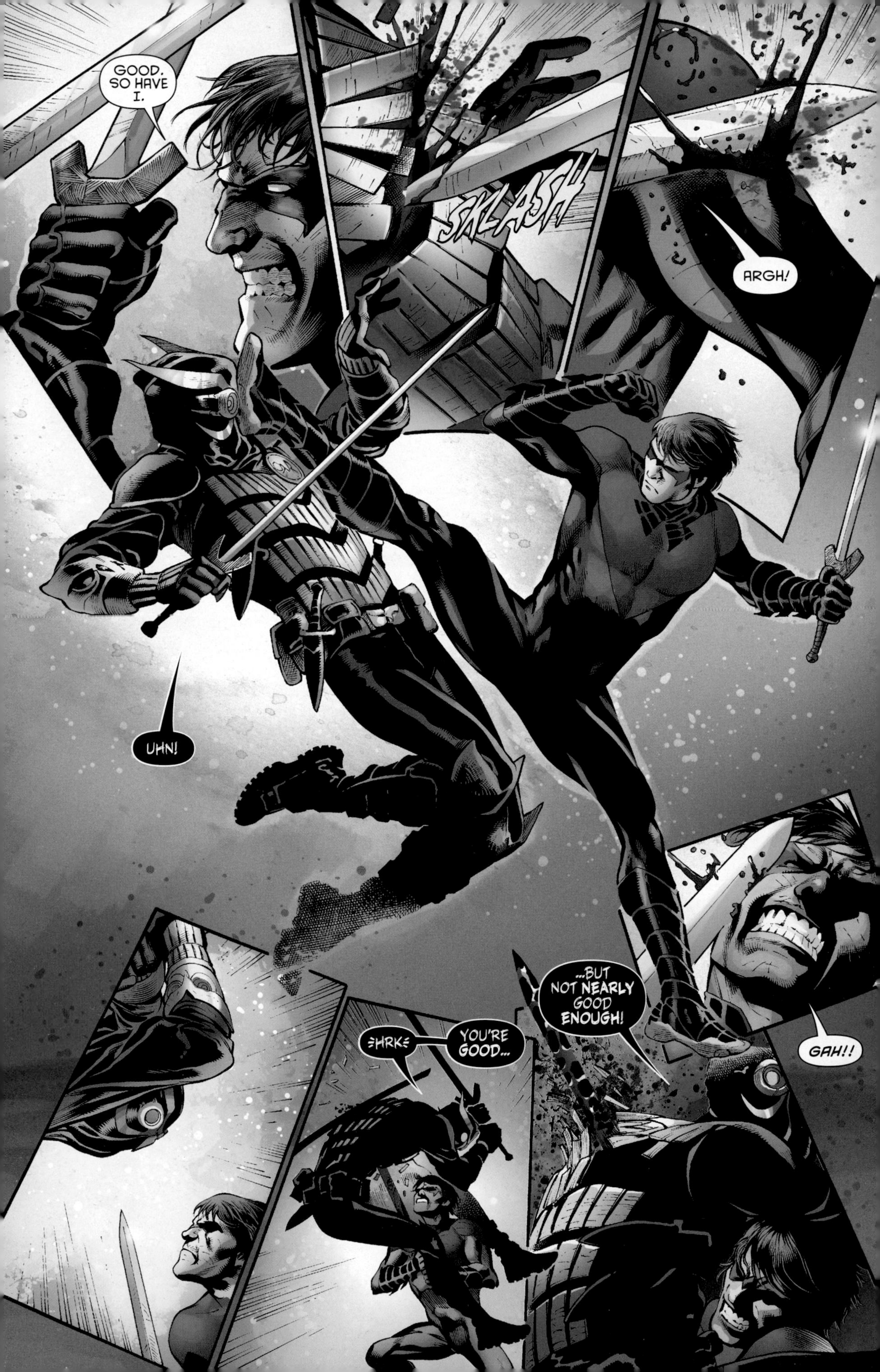
GOOD. SO HAVE I.
SKLASH
ARGH!
UHN!
HRK
YOU'RE GOOD...
...BUT NOT NEARLY GOOD ENOUGH!
GAH!!

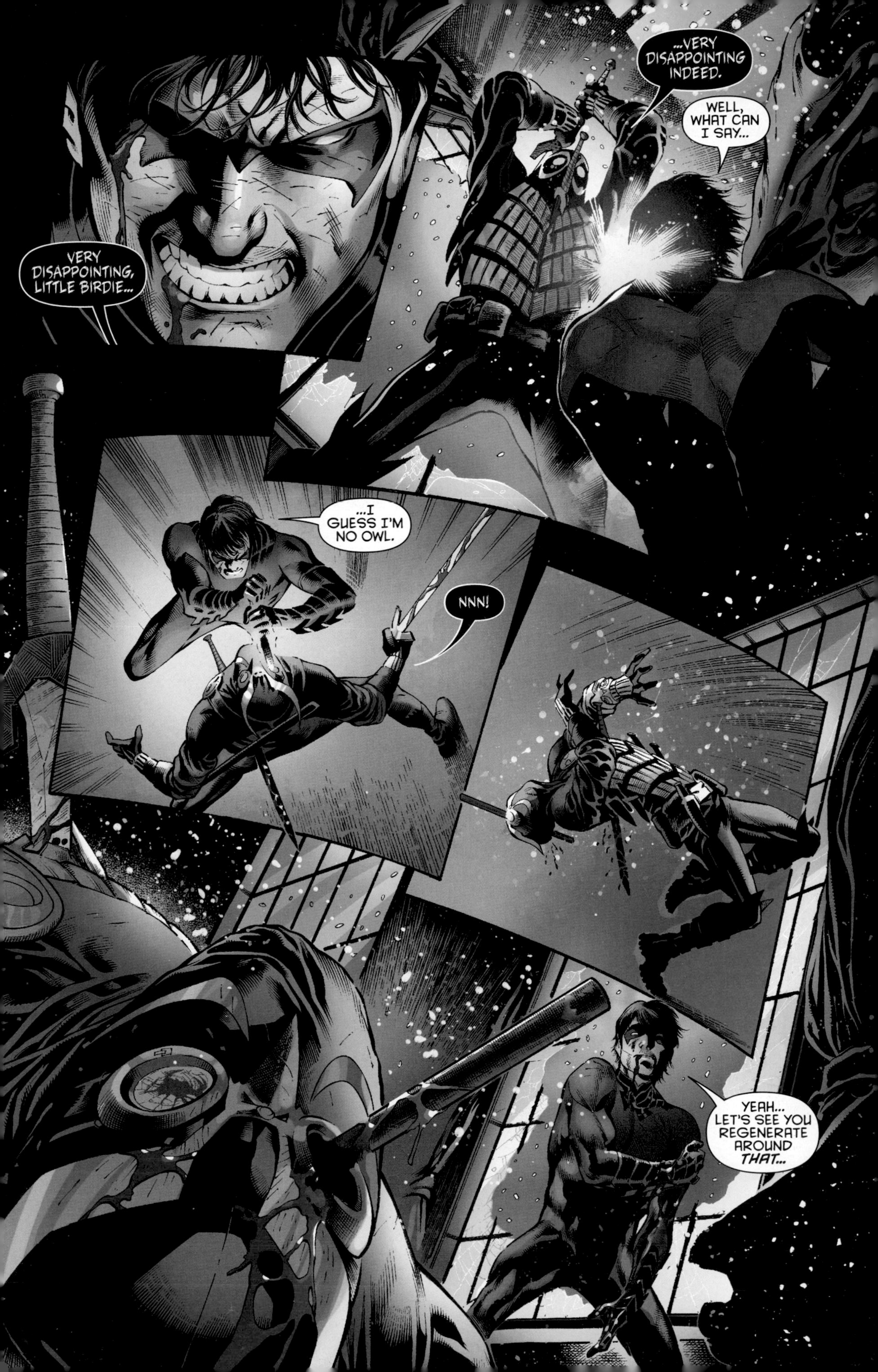
VERY DISAPPOINTING, LITTLE BIRDIE...
...VERY DISAPPOINTING INDEED.
WELL, WHAT CAN I SAY...
...I GUESS I'M NO OWL.
NNN!
YEAH... LET'S SEE YOU REGENERATE AROUND *THAT*...

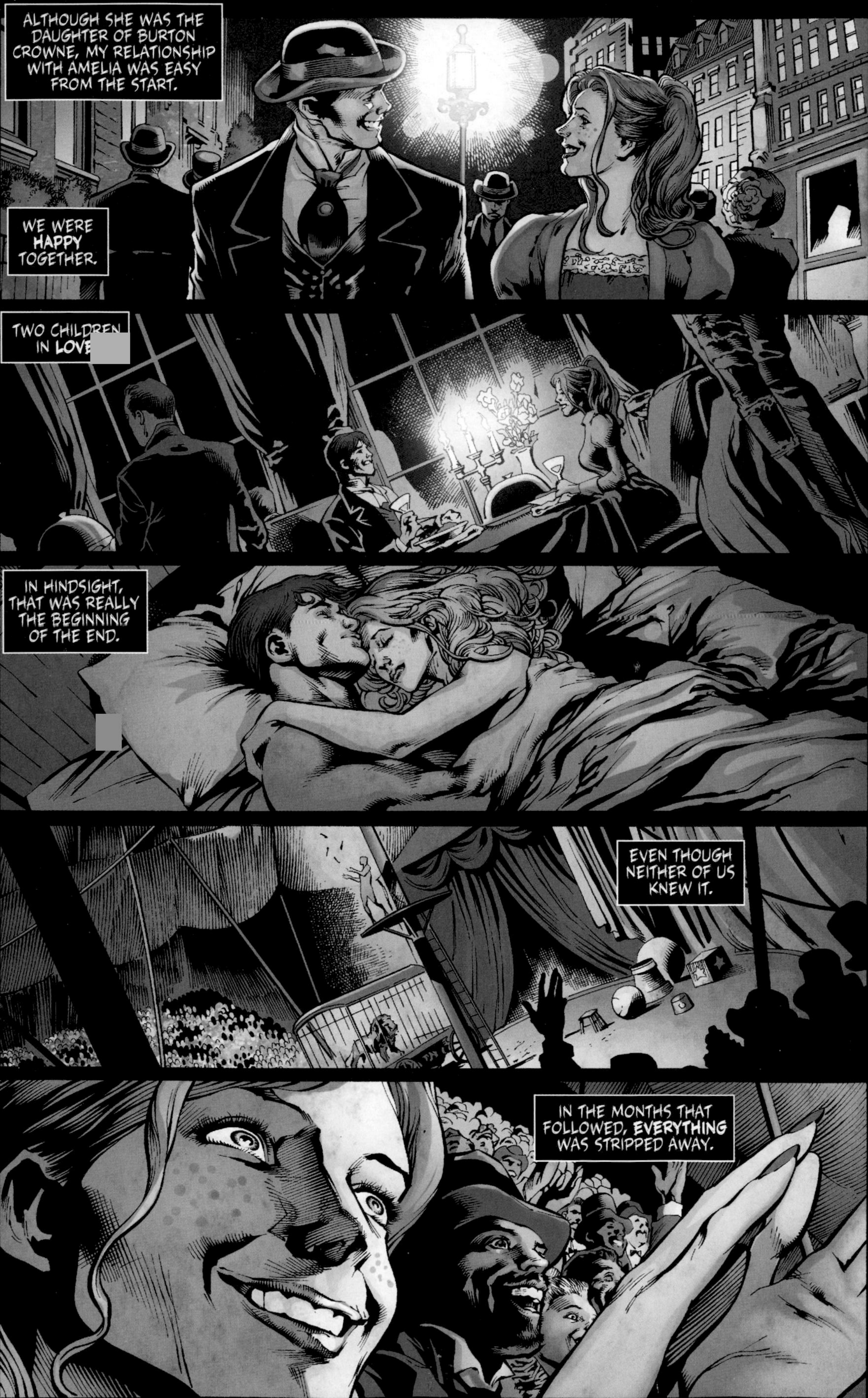
ALTHOUGH SHE WAS THE DAUGHTER OF BURTON CROWNE, MY RELATIONSHIP WITH AMELIA WAS EASY FROM THE START.
WE WERE **HAPPY** TOGETHER.
TWO CHILDREN IN **LOVE**
IN HINDSIGHT, THAT WAS REALLY THE BEGINNING OF THE END.
EVEN THOUGH NEITHER OF US KNEW IT.
IN THE MONTHS THAT FOLLOWED, **EVERYTHING** WAS STRIPPED AWAY.

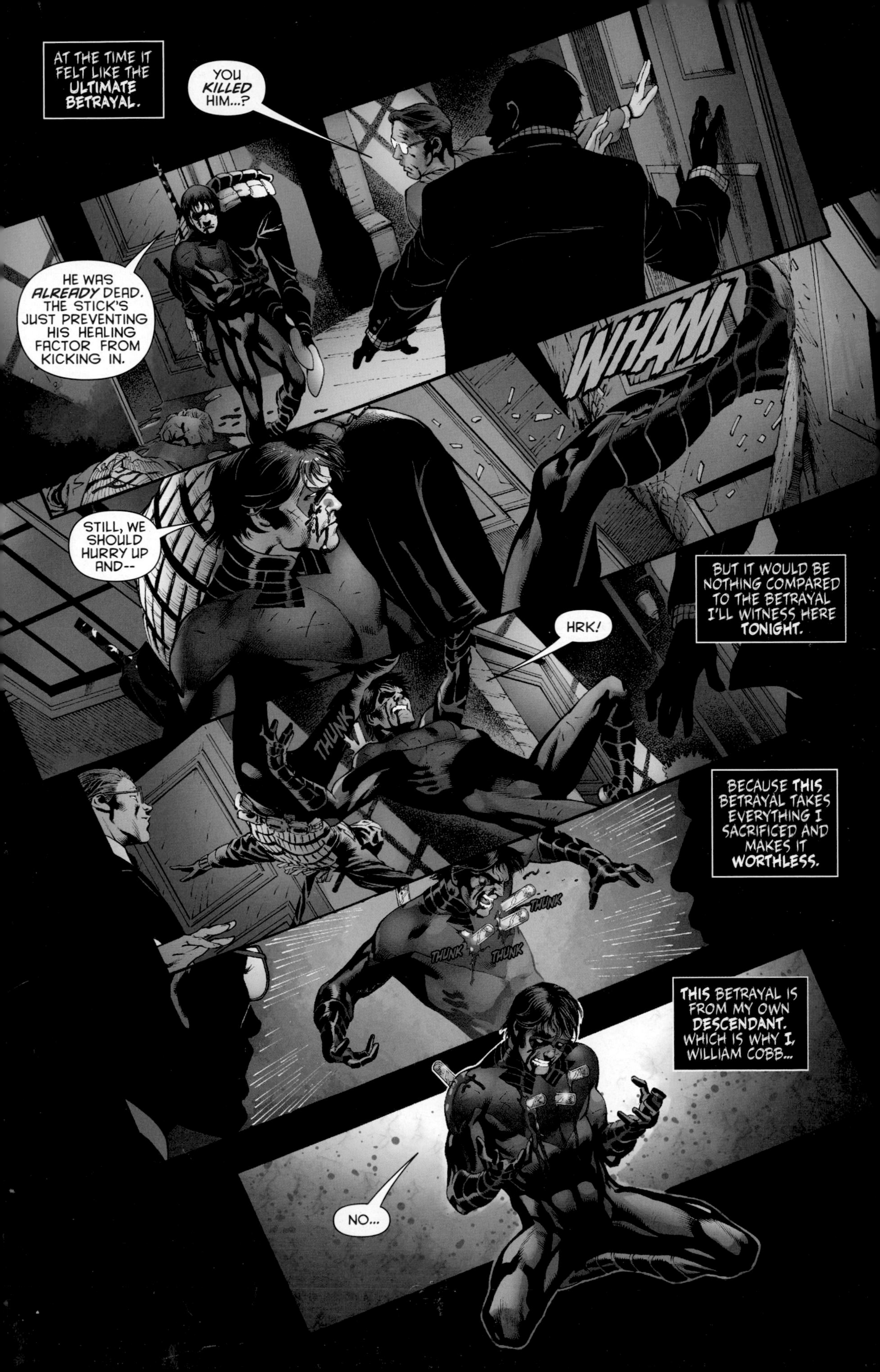
AT THE TIME IT FELT LIKE THE ULTIMATE BETRAYAL.
YOU KILLED HIM...?
HE WAS ALREADY DEAD. THE STICK'S JUST PREVENTING HIS HEALING FACTOR FROM KICKING IN.
WHAM
STILL, WE SHOULD HURRY UP AND--
BUT IT WOULD BE NOTHING COMPARED TO THE BETRAYAL I'LL WITNESS HERE TONIGHT.
HRK!
THUNK
BECAUSE THIS BETRAYAL TAKES EVERYTHING I SACRIFICED AND MAKES IT WORTHLESS.
THUNK
THUNK
THUNK
THIS BETRAYAL IS FROM MY OWN DESCENDANT. WHICH IS WHY I, WILLIAM COBB...
NO...

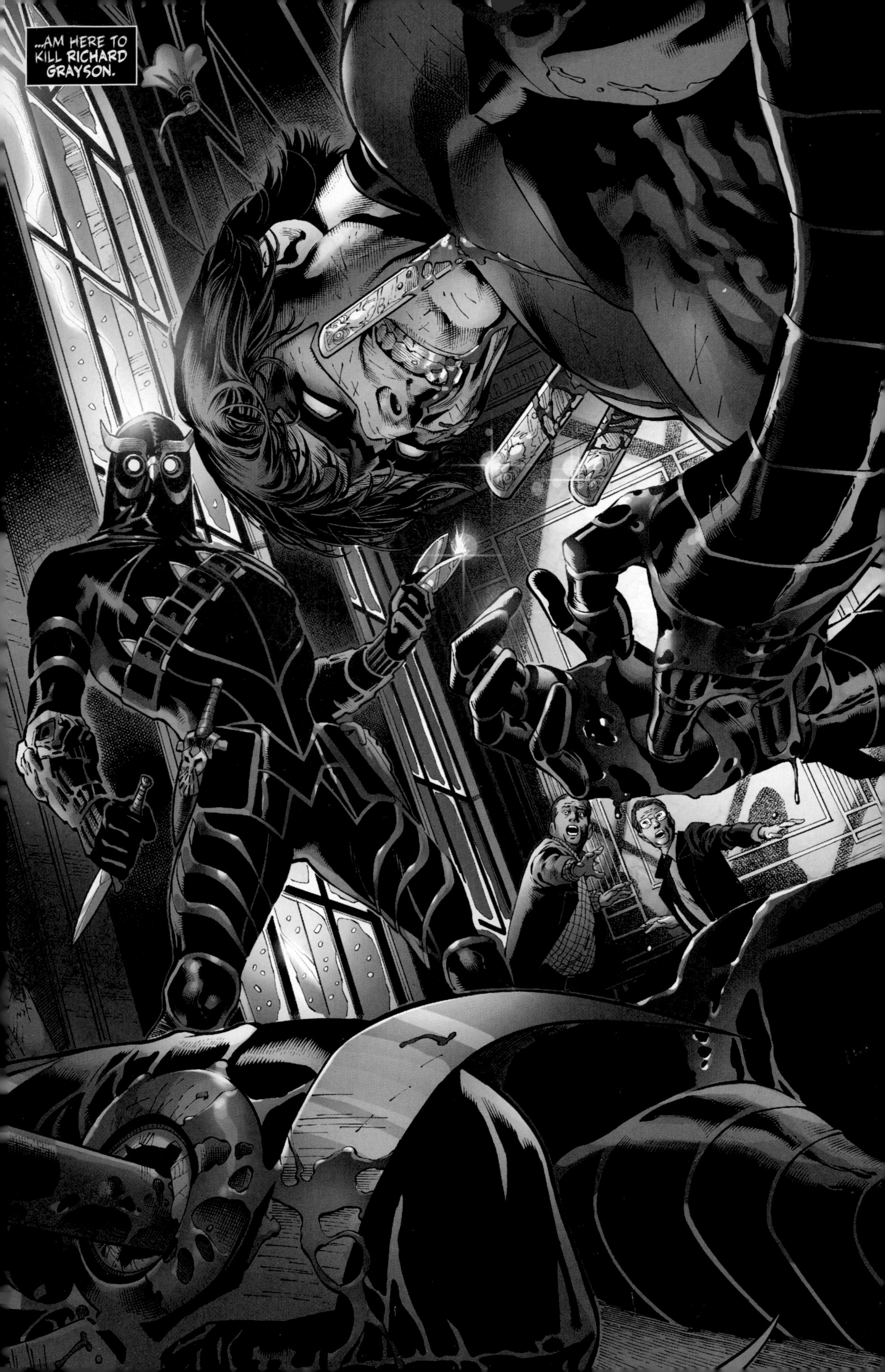
...AM HERE TO KILL RICHARD GRAYSON.

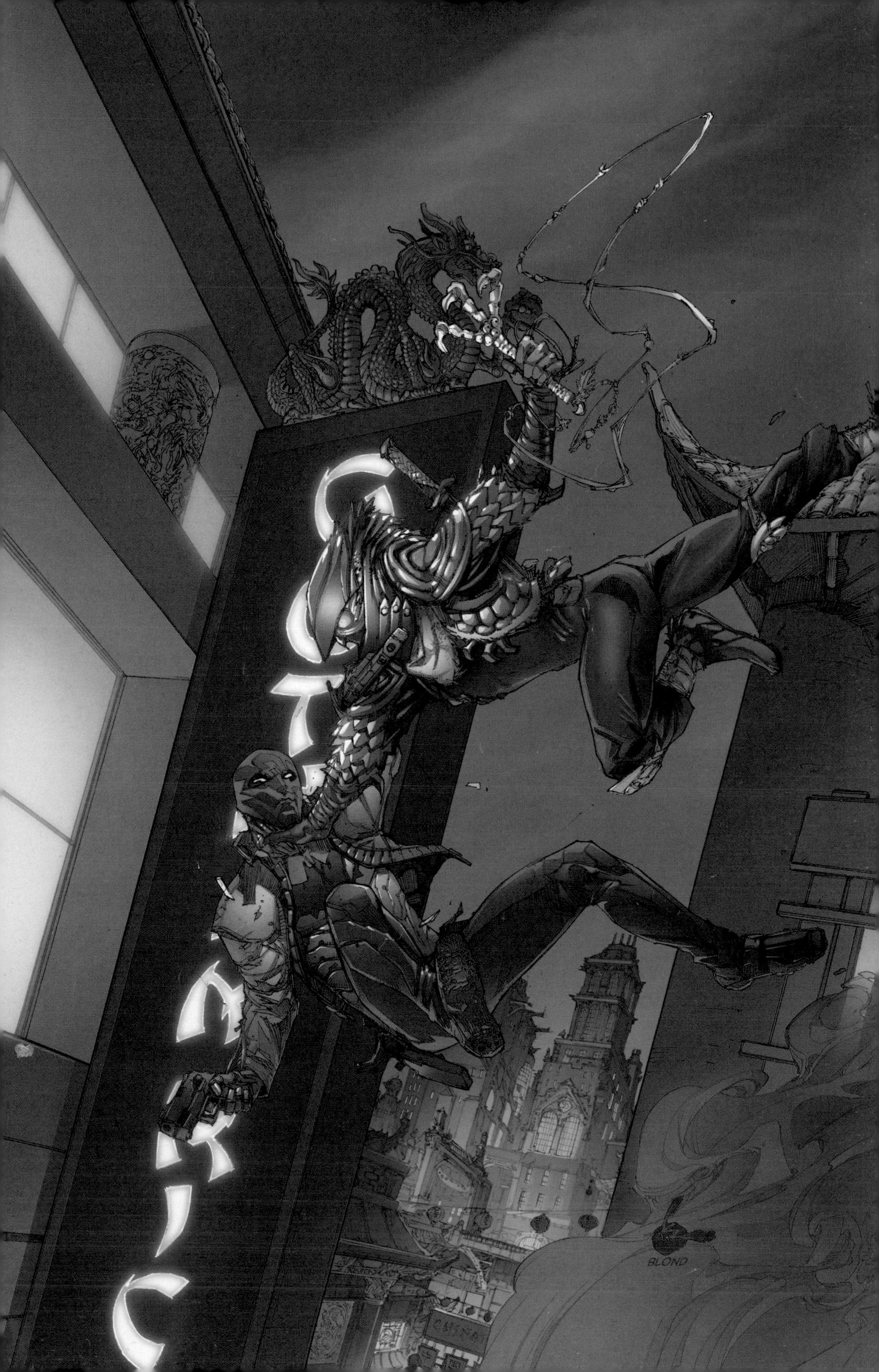
BLOND

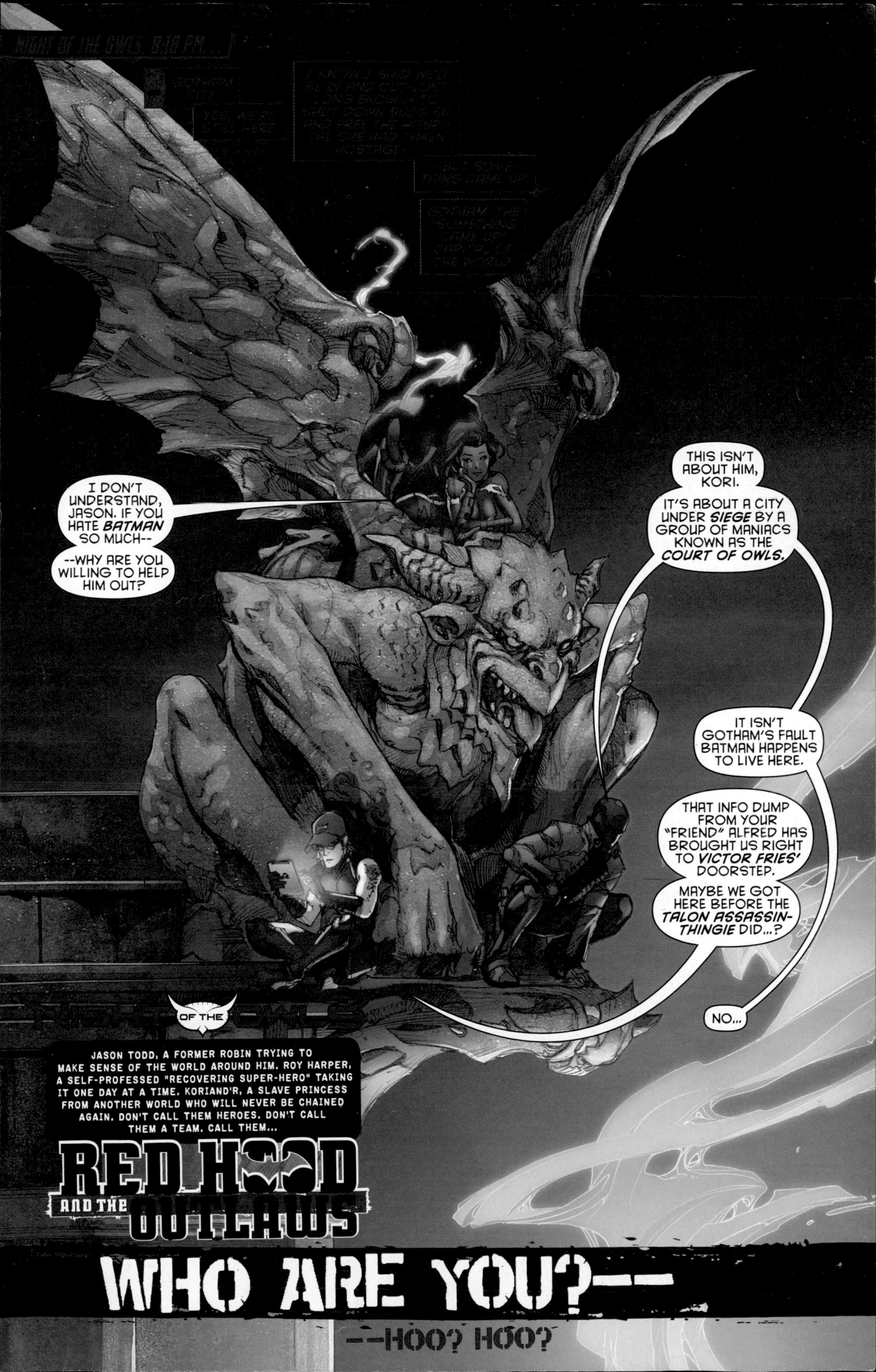
I DON'T UNDERSTAND, JASON. IF YOU HATE BATMAN SO MUCH--
--WHY ARE YOU WILLING TO HELP HIM OUT?
THIS ISN'T ABOUT HIM, KORI.
IT'S ABOUT A CITY UNDER SIEGE BY A GROUP OF MANIACS KNOWN AS THE COURT OF OWLS.
IT ISN'T GOTHAM'S FAULT BATMAN HAPPENS TO LIVE HERE.
THAT INFO DUMP FROM YOUR "FRIEND" ALFRED HAS BROUGHT US RIGHT TO VICTOR FRIES' DOORSTEP.
MAYBE WE GOT HERE BEFORE THE TALON ASSASSIN-THINGIE DID...?
NO...
NIGHT OF THE OWLS
JASON TODD, A FORMER ROBIN TRYING TO MAKE SENSE OF THE WORLD AROUND HIM. ROY HARPER, A SELF-PROFESSED "RECOVERING SUPER-HERO" TAKING IT ONE DAY AT A TIME. KORIAND'R, A SLAVE PRINCESS FROM ANOTHER WORLD WHO WILL NEVER BE CHAINED AGAIN. DON'T CALL THEM HEROES. DON'T CALL THEM A TEAM. CALL THEM...
RED HOOD AND THE OUTLAWS
WHO ARE YOU?--
--HOO? HOO?

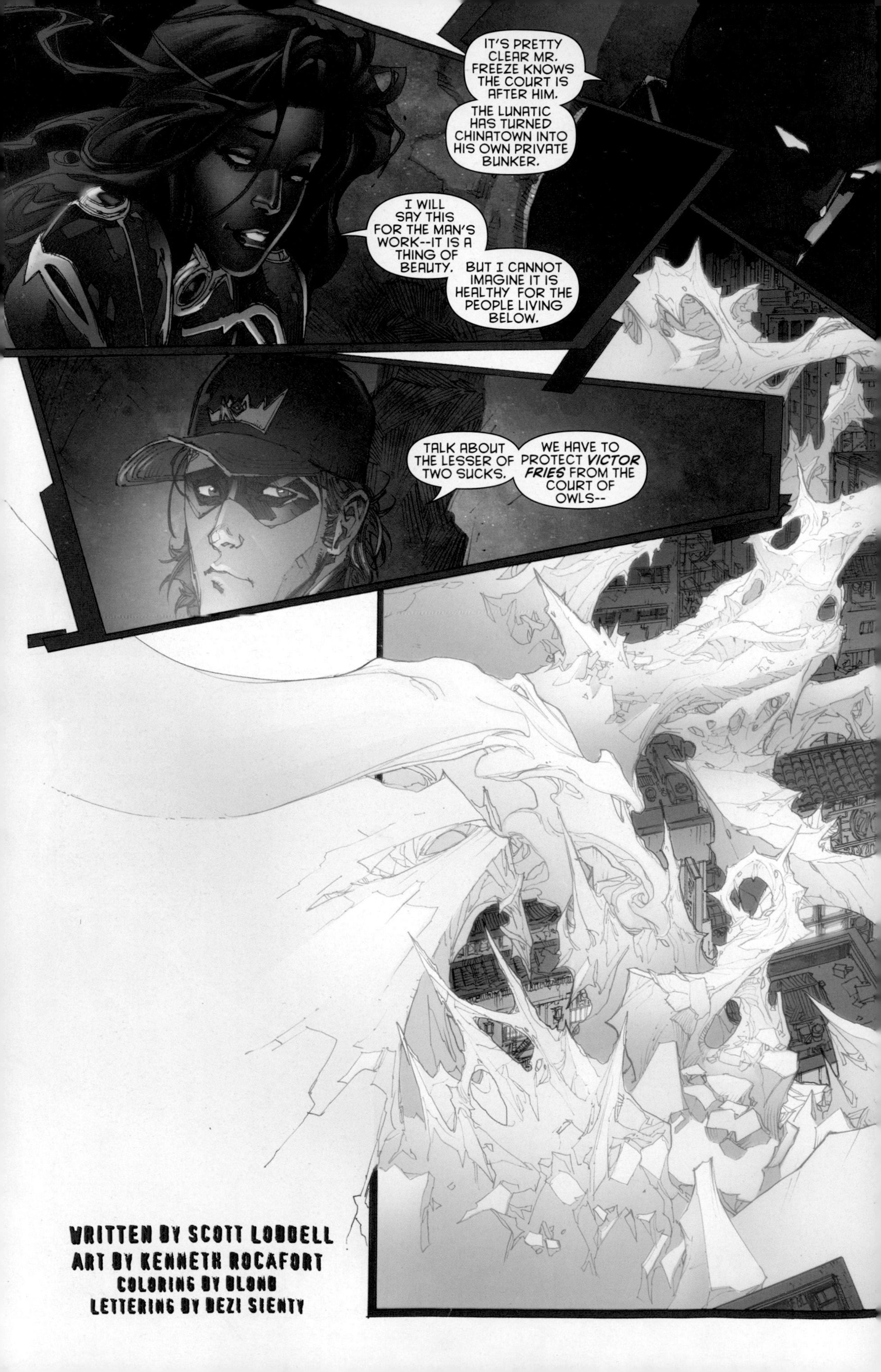
IT'S PRETTY CLEAR MR. FREEZE KNOWS THE COURT IS AFTER HIM.
THE LUNATIC HAS TURNED CHINATOWN INTO HIS OWN PRIVATE BUNKER.
I WILL SAY THIS FOR THE MAN'S WORK--IT IS A THING OF BEAUTY.
BUT I CANNOT IMAGINE IT IS HEALTHY FOR THE PEOPLE LIVING BELOW.
TALK ABOUT THE LESSER OF TWO SUCKS.
WE HAVE TO PROTECT *VICTOR FRIES* FROM THE COURT OF OWLS--
WRITTEN BY SCOTT LOBDELL
ART BY KENNETH ROCAFORT
COLORING BY BLOND
LETTERING BY DEZI SIENTY

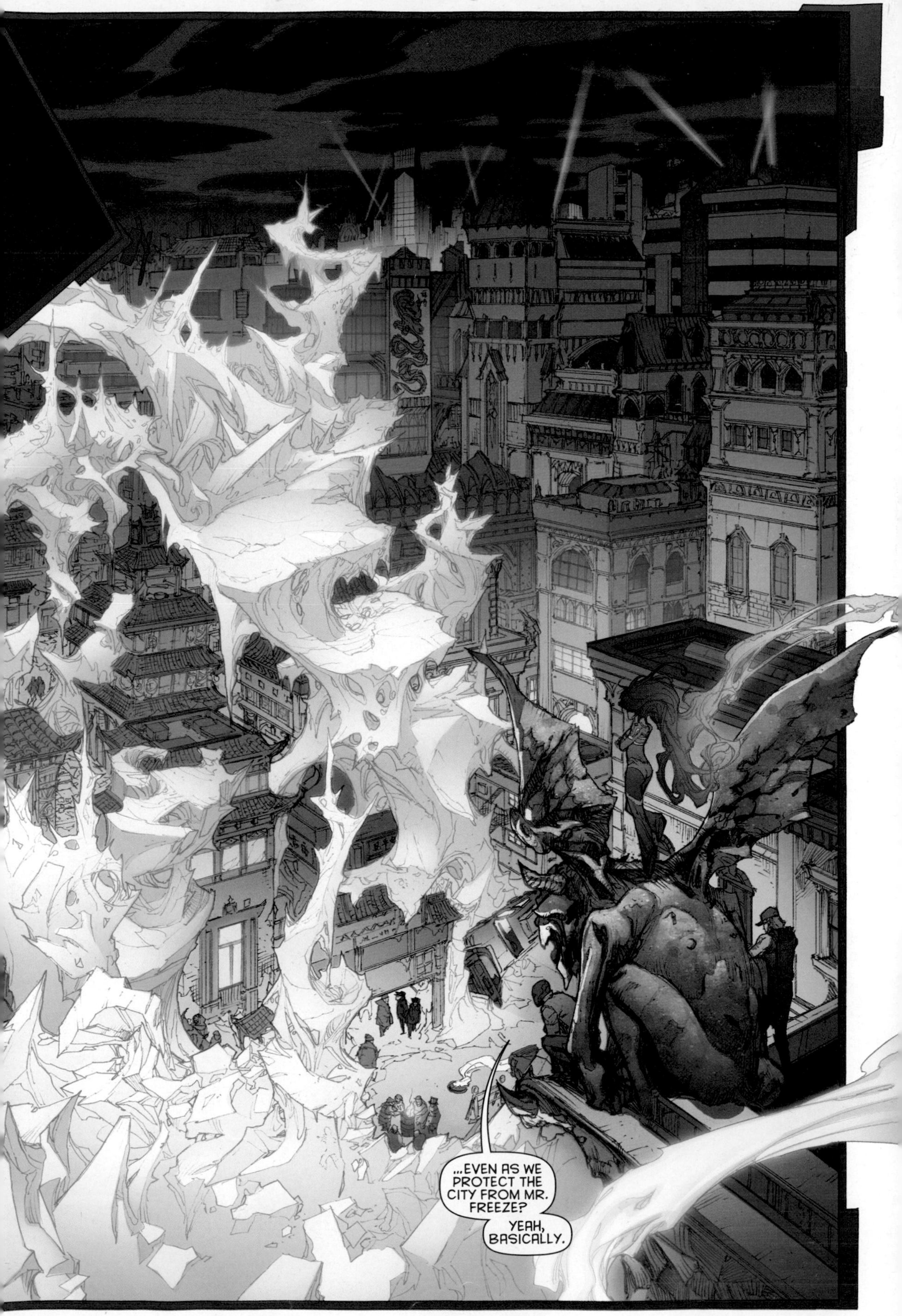
...EVEN AS WE PROTECT THE CITY FROM MR. FREEZE?
YEAH, BASICALLY.

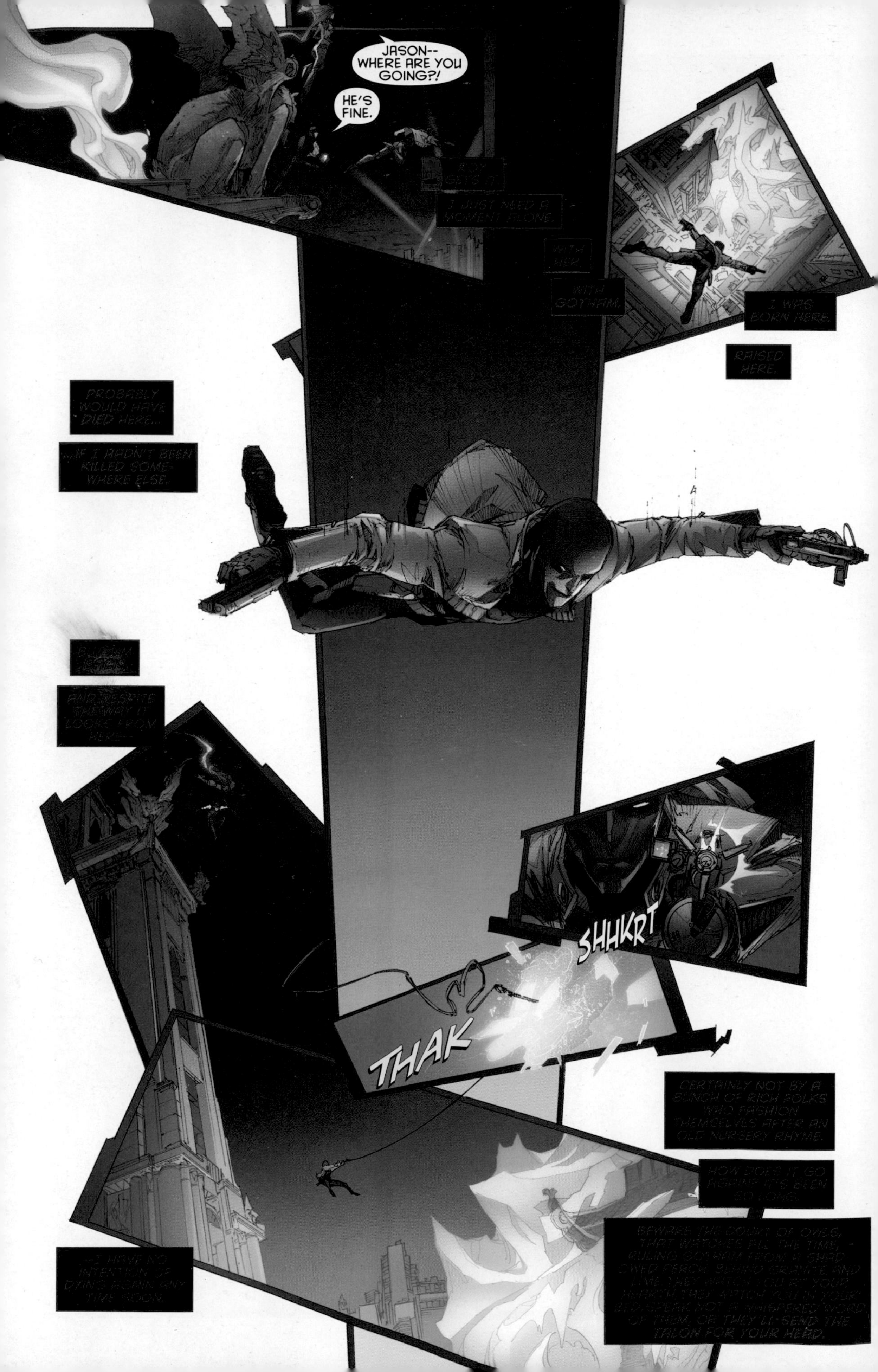
JASON-- WHERE ARE YOU GOING?!
HE'S FINE.
ROY GETS IT.
I JUST NEED A MOMENT ALONE.
WITH HER.
WITH GOTHAM.
I WAS BORN HERE.
RAISED HERE.
PROBABLY WOULD HAVE DIED HERE...
...IF I HADN'T BEEN KILLED SOMEWHERE ELSE.
AND DESPITE THE WAY IT LOOKS FROM HERE--
SHHKRT
THAK
CERTAINLY NOT BY A BUNCH OF RICH FOLKS WHO FASHION THEMSELVES AFTER AN OLD NURSERY RHYME.
HOW DOES IT GO AGAIN? IT'S BEEN SO LONG.
BEWARE THE COURT OF OWLS, THAT WATCHES ALL THE TIME, RULING GOTHAM FROM A SHADOWED PERCH, BEHIND GRANITE AND LIME. THEY WATCH YOU AT YOUR HEARTH, THEY WATCH YOU IN YOUR BED. SPEAK NOT A WHISPERED WORD OF THEM, OR THEY'LL SEND THE TALON FOR YOUR HEAD.
--I HAVE NO INTENTION OF DYING AGAIN ANY TIME SOON.

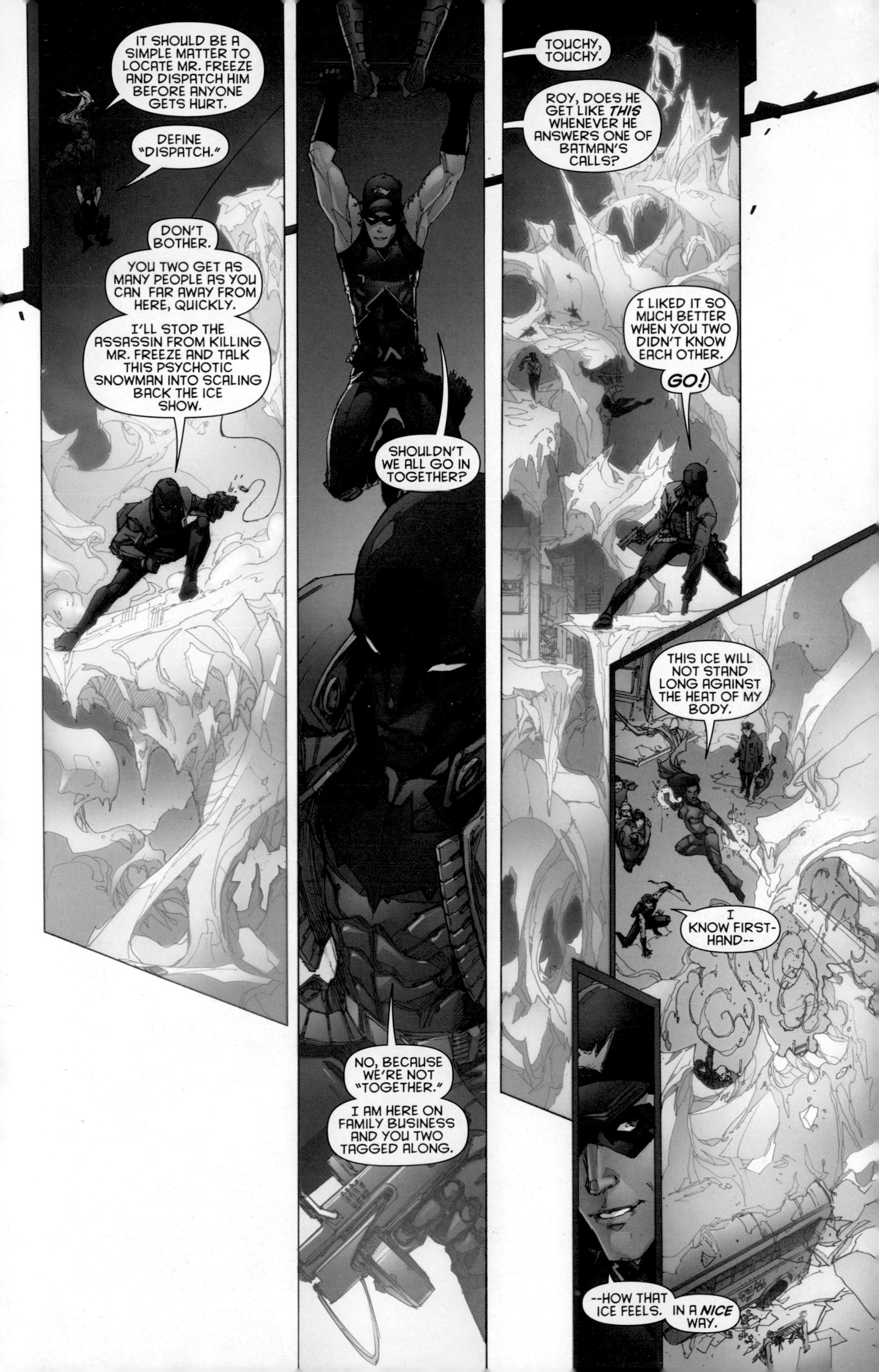
IT SHOULD BE A SIMPLE MATTER TO LOCATE MR. FREEZE AND DISPATCH HIM BEFORE ANYONE GETS HURT.
DEFINE "DISPATCH."
DON'T BOTHER.
YOU TWO GET AS MANY PEOPLE AS YOU CAN FAR AWAY FROM HERE, QUICKLY.
I'LL STOP THE ASSASSIN FROM KILLING MR. FREEZE AND TALK THIS PSYCHOTIC SNOWMAN INTO SCALING BACK THE ICE SHOW.
SHOULDN'T WE ALL GO IN TOGETHER?
NO, BECAUSE WE'RE NOT "TOGETHER."
I AM HERE ON FAMILY BUSINESS AND YOU TWO TAGGED ALONG.
TOUCHY, TOUCHY.
ROY, DOES HE GET LIKE *THIS* WHENEVER HE ANSWERS ONE OF BATMAN'S CALLS?
I LIKED IT SO MUCH BETTER WHEN YOU TWO DIDN'T KNOW EACH OTHER.
GO!
THIS ICE WILL NOT STAND LONG AGAINST THE HEAT OF MY BODY.
I KNOW FIRST-HAND--
--HOW THAT ICE FEELS.
IN A *NICE* WAY.

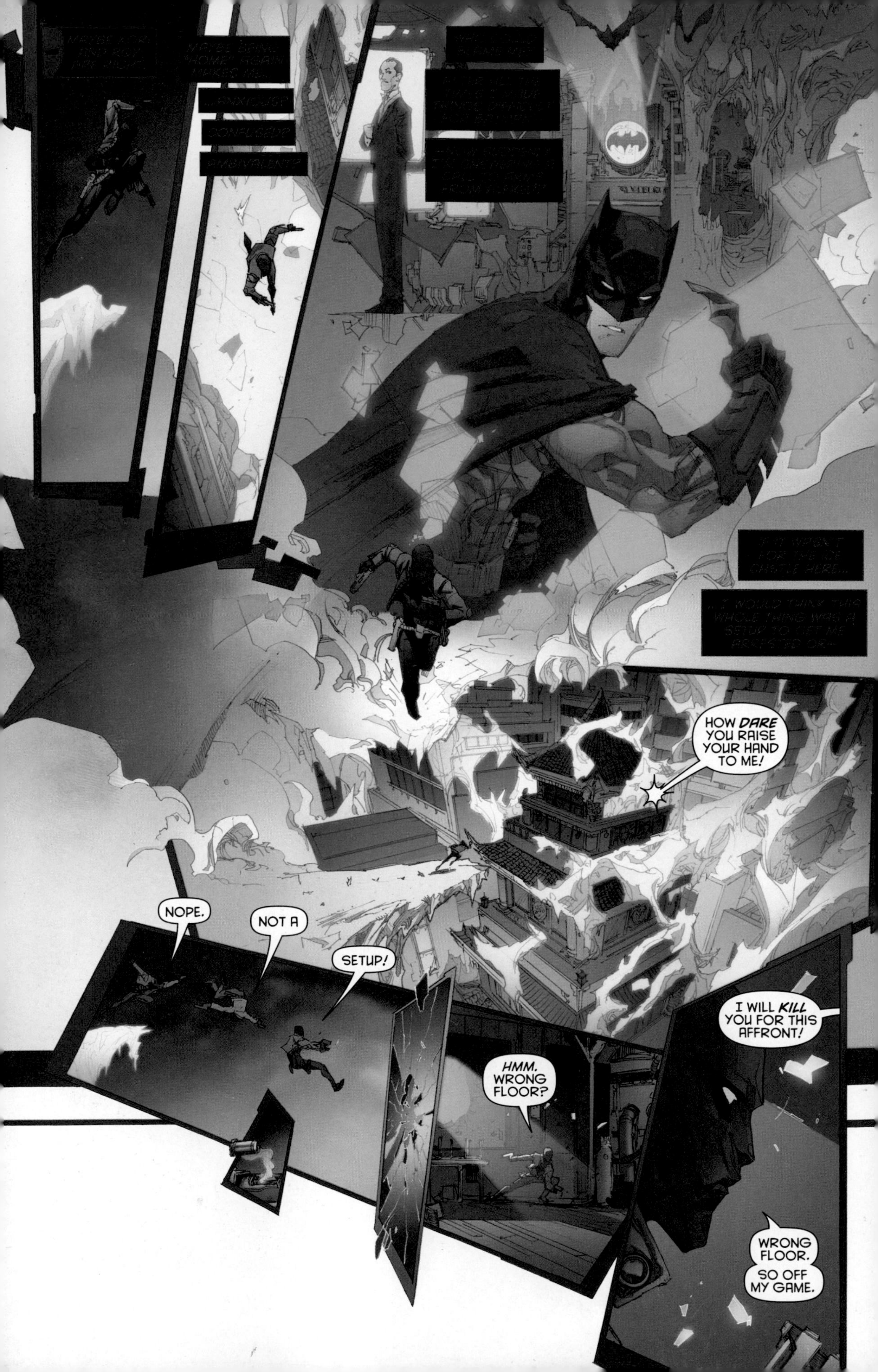

MAYBE BEING "HOME" AGAIN MAKES ME...
...ANXIOUS?
CONFUSED?
AMBIVALENT?
IF IT WASN'T FOR THE ICE CASTLE HERE...
...I WOULD THINK THIS WHOLE THING WAS A SETUP TO GET ME ARRESTED OR--
HOW DARE YOU RAISE YOUR HAND TO ME!
NOPE.
NOT A
SETUP!
HMM. WRONG FLOOR?
I WILL KILL YOU FOR THIS AFFRONT!
WRONG FLOOR.
SO OFF MY GAME.

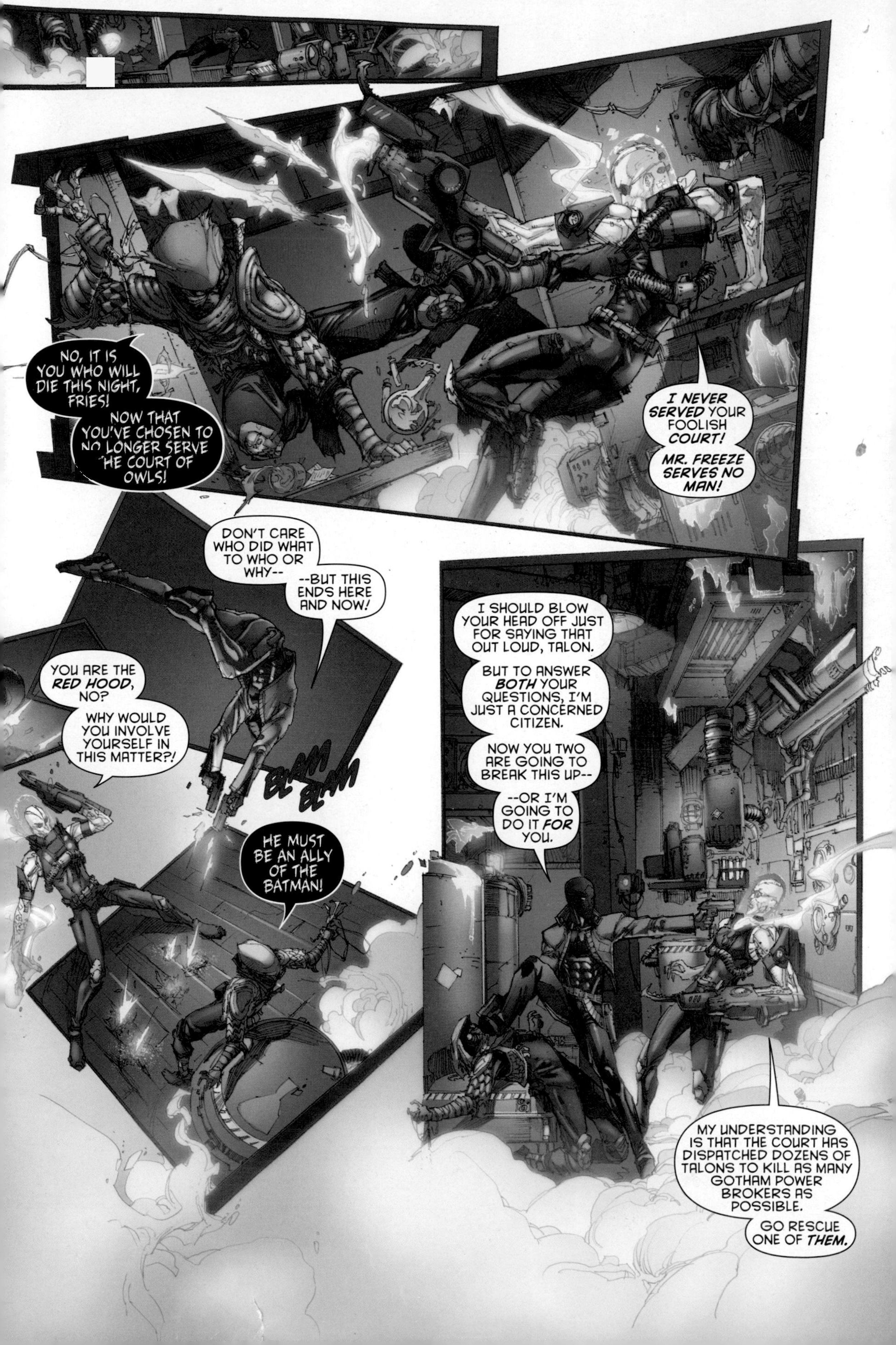

NO, IT IS YOU WHO WILL DIE THIS NIGHT, FRIES!
NOW THAT YOU'VE CHOSEN TO NO LONGER SERVE THE COURT OF OWLS!
I NEVER SERVED YOUR FOOLISH COURT!
MR. FREEZE SERVES NO MAN!
DON'T CARE WHO DID WHAT TO WHO OR WHY--
--BUT THIS ENDS HERE AND NOW!
YOU ARE THE RED HOOD, NO?
WHY WOULD YOU INVOLVE YOURSELF IN THIS MATTER?!
BLAM BLAM
HE MUST BE AN ALLY OF THE BATMAN!
I SHOULD BLOW YOUR HEAD OFF JUST FOR SAYING THAT OUT LOUD, TALON.
BUT TO ANSWER BOTH YOUR QUESTIONS, I'M JUST A CONCERNED CITIZEN.
NOW YOU TWO ARE GOING TO BREAK THIS UP--
--OR I'M GOING TO DO IT FOR YOU.
MY UNDERSTANDING IS THAT THE COURT HAS DISPATCHED DOZENS OF TALONS TO KILL AS MANY GOTHAM POWER BROKERS AS POSSIBLE.
GO RESCUE ONE OF THEM.

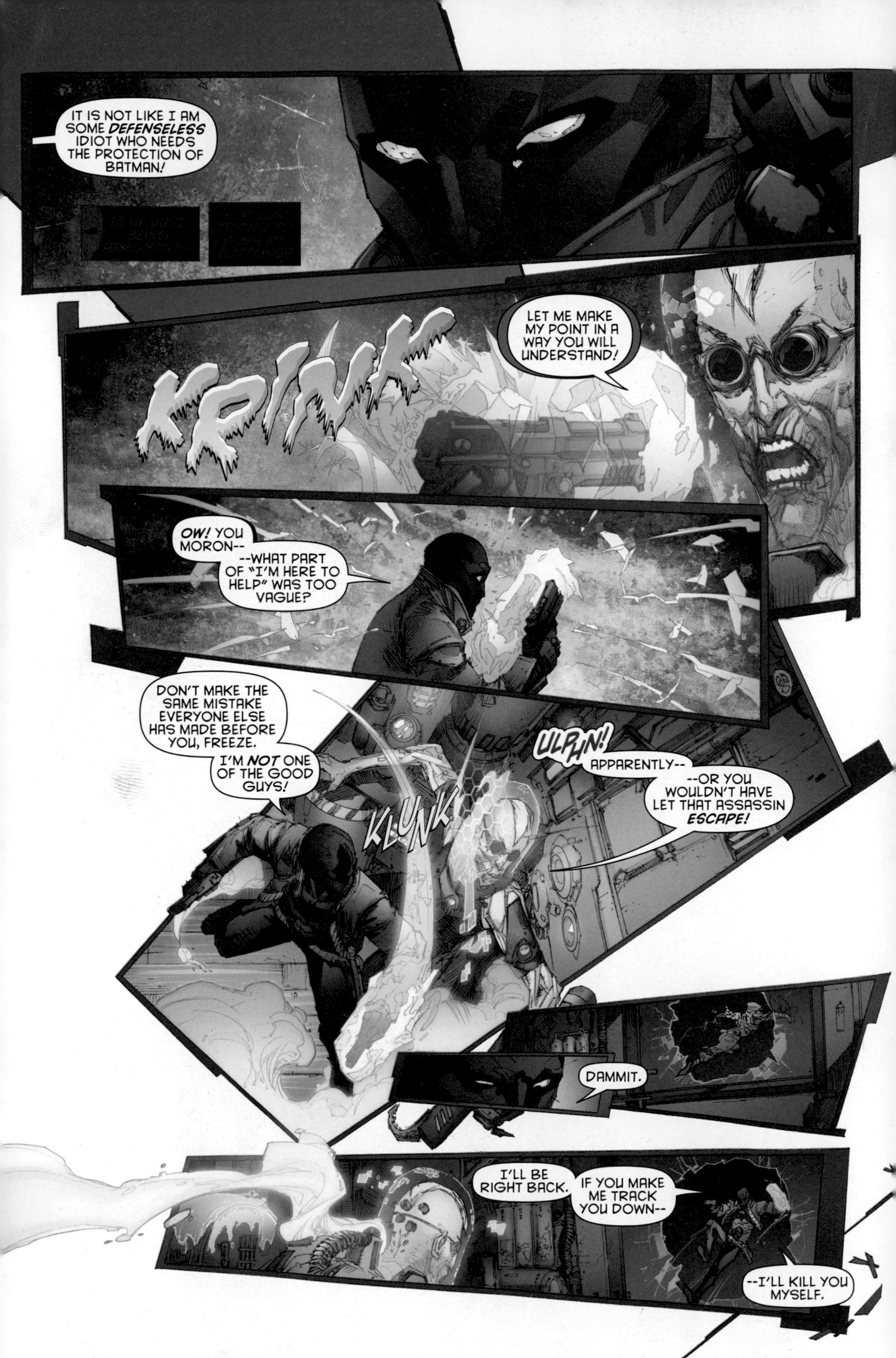

IT IS NOT LIKE I AM SOME DEFENSELESS IDIOT WHO NEEDS THE PROTECTION OF BATMAN!
[redacted]
[redacted]
KRINK
LET ME MAKE MY POINT IN A WAY YOU WILL UNDERSTAND!
OW! YOU MORON--
--WHAT PART OF "I'M HERE TO HELP" WAS TOO VAGUE?
DON'T MAKE THE SAME MISTAKE EVERYONE ELSE HAS MADE BEFORE YOU, FREEZE.
I'M NOT ONE OF THE GOOD GUYS!
KLUNK
ULPHN!
APPARENTLY--
--OR YOU WOULDN'T HAVE LET THAT ASSASSIN ESCAPE!
DAMMIT.
I'LL BE RIGHT BACK.
IF YOU MAKE ME TRACK YOU DOWN--
--I'LL KILL YOU MYSELF.

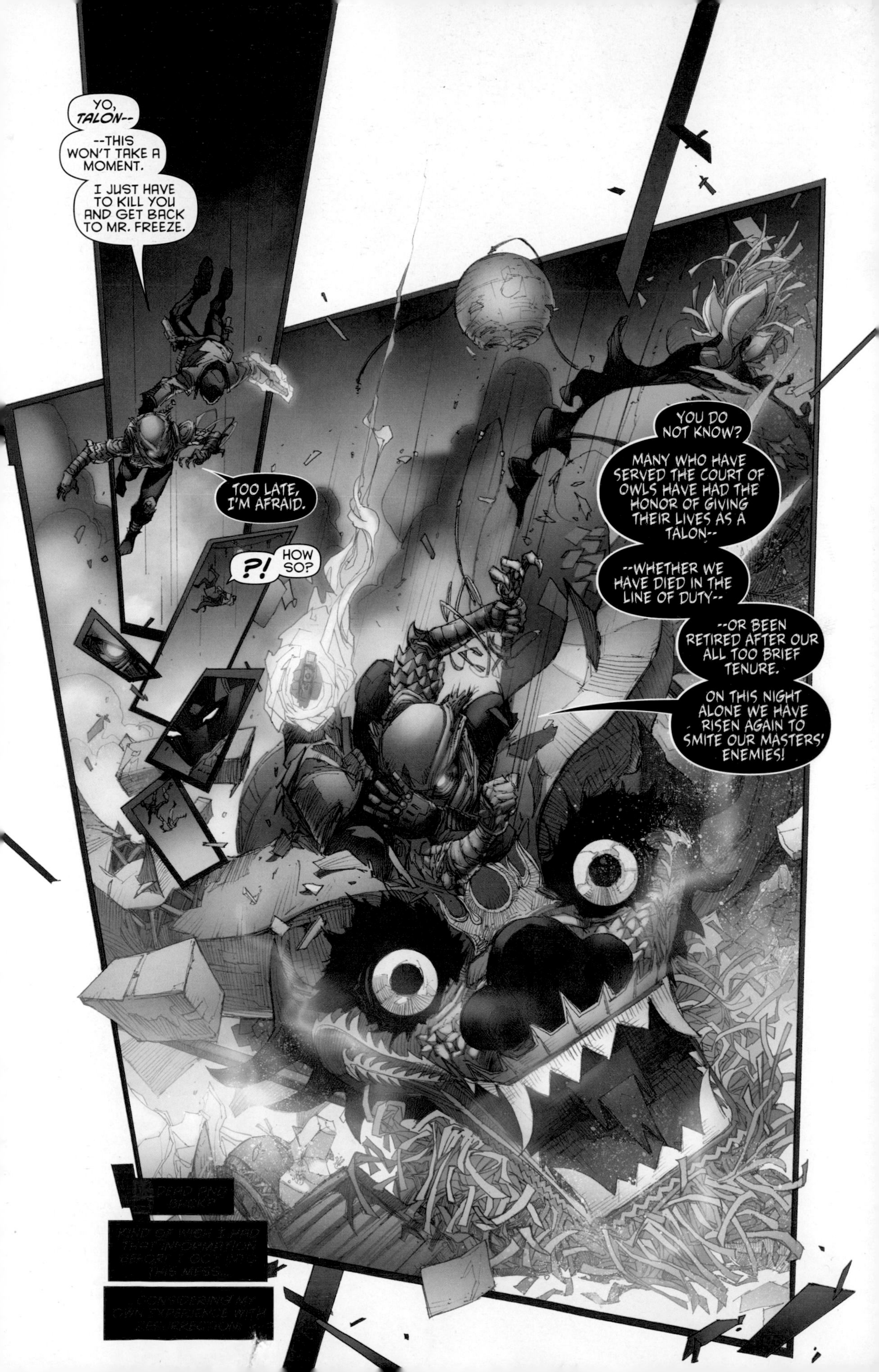
YO, TALON--
--THIS WON'T TAKE A MOMENT.
I JUST HAVE TO KILL YOU AND GET BACK TO MR. FREEZE.
TOO LATE, I'M AFRAID.
?!
HOW SO?
YOU DO NOT KNOW?
MANY WHO HAVE SERVED THE COURT OF OWLS HAVE HAD THE HONOR OF GIVING THEIR LIVES AS A TALON--
--WHETHER WE HAVE DIED IN THE LINE OF DUTY--
--OR BEEN RETIRED AFTER OUR ALL TOO BRIEF TENURE.
ON THIS NIGHT ALONE WE HAVE RISEN AGAIN TO SMITE OUR MASTERS' ENEMIES!
DEAD AND BACK?
KIND OF WISH I HAD THAT INFORMATION BEFORE I GOT INTO THIS MESS...
CONSIDERING MY OWN EXPERIENCE WITH RESURRECTION.

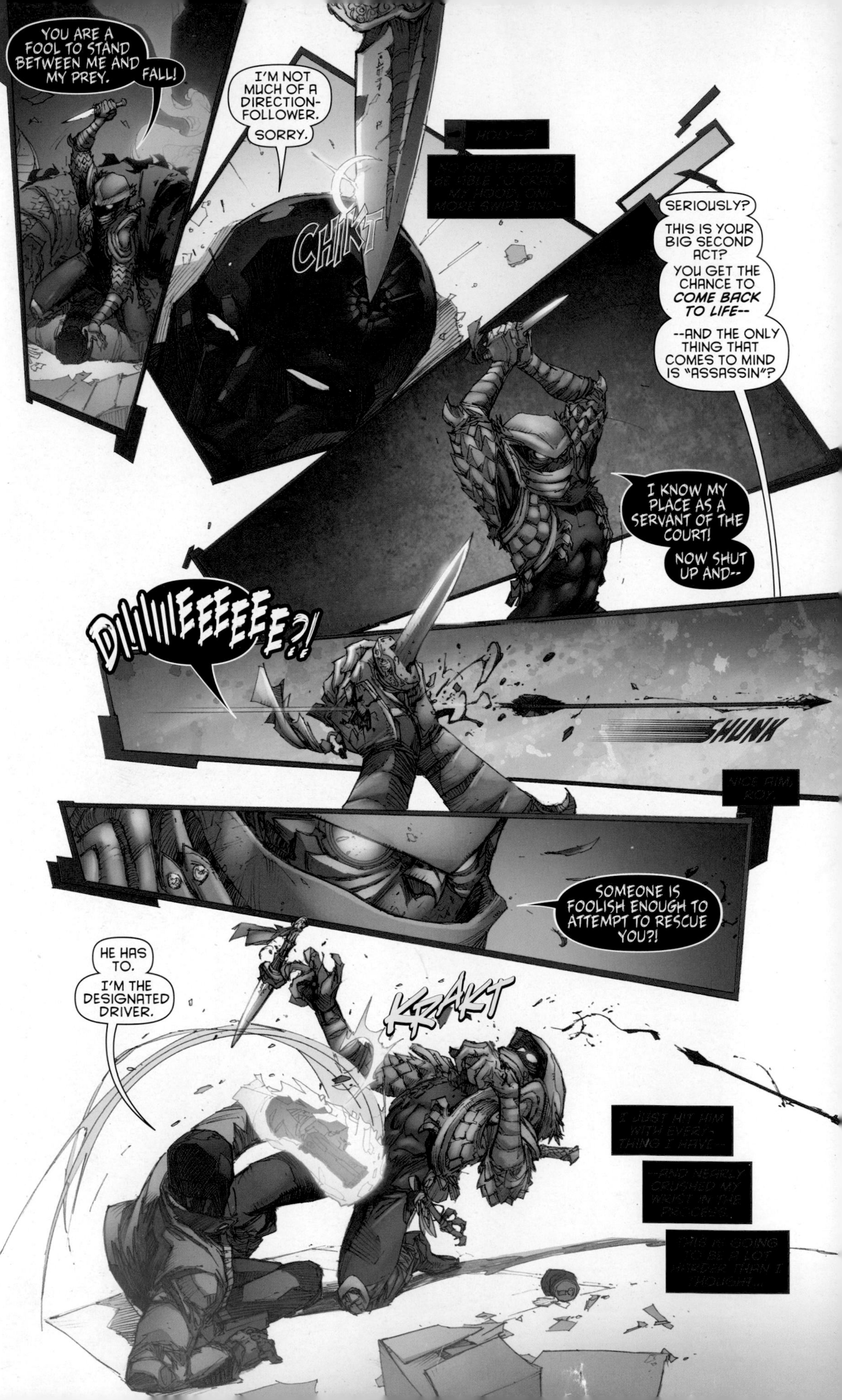

YOU ARE A FOOL TO STAND BETWEEN ME AND MY PREY.
FALL!
I'M NOT MUCH OF A DIRECTION-FOLLOWER.
SORRY.
CHIKT
HOLY--?!
NO KNIFE SHOULD BE ABLE TO CRACK MY HOOD. ONE MORE SWIPE AND--
SERIOUSLY?
THIS IS YOUR BIG SECOND ACT?
YOU GET THE CHANCE TO ***COME BACK TO LIFE***--
--AND THE ONLY THING THAT COMES TO MIND IS "ASSASSIN"?
I KNOW MY PLACE AS A SERVANT OF THE COURT!
NOW SHUT UP AND--
DIIIIIEEEEEE?!
SHUNK
NICE AIM, ROY.
SOMEONE IS FOOLISH ENOUGH TO ATTEMPT TO RESCUE YOU?!
HE HAS TO.
I'M THE DESIGNATED DRIVER.
KRAKT
I JUST HIT HIM WITH EVERY-THING I HAVE--
--AND NEARLY CRUSHED MY WRIST IN THE PROCESS.
THIS IS GOING TO BE A LOT HARDER THAN I THOUGHT...

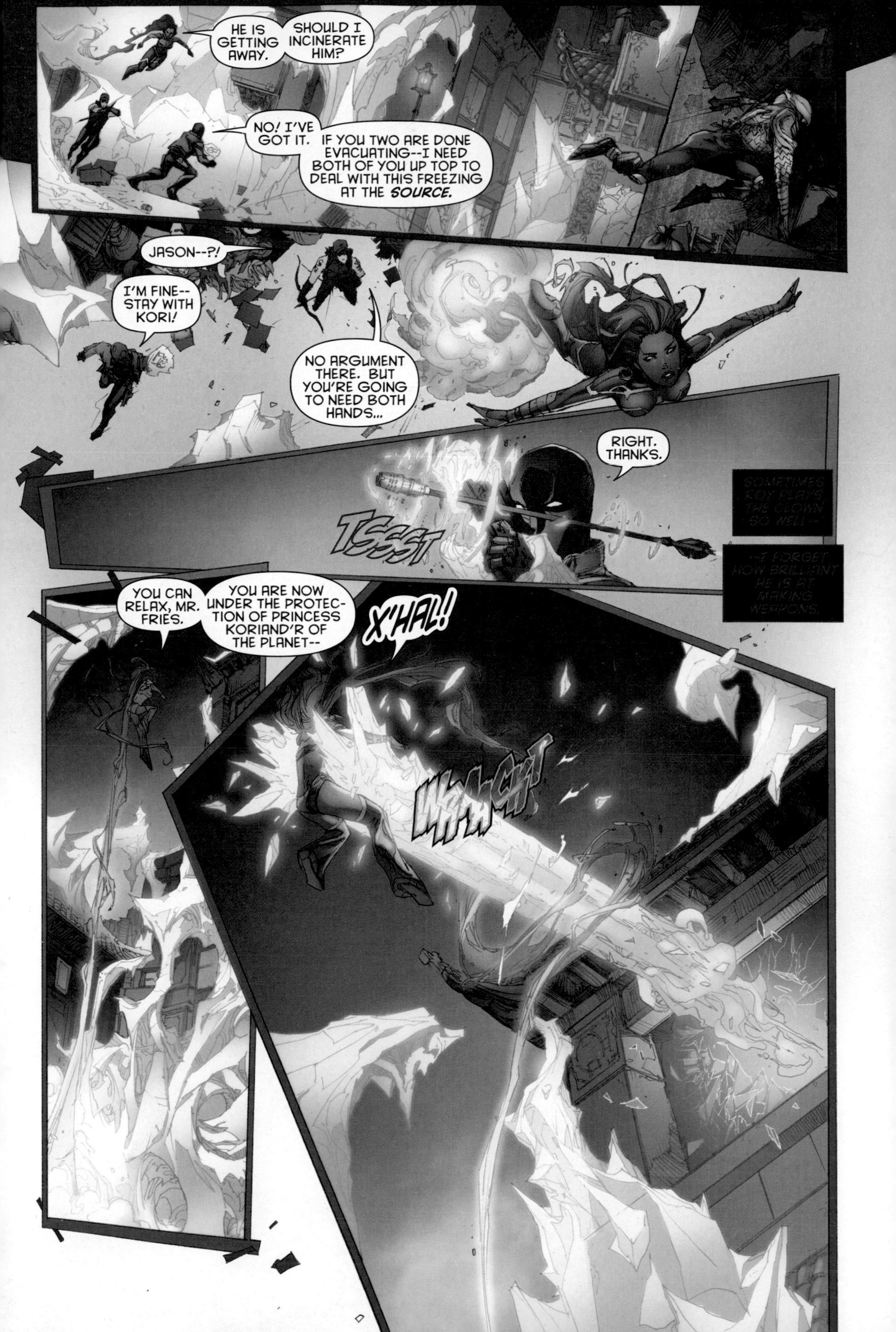
HE IS GETTING AWAY.
SHOULD I INCINERATE HIM?
NO! I'VE GOT IT.
IF YOU TWO ARE DONE EVACUATING--I NEED BOTH OF YOU UP TOP TO DEAL WITH THIS FREEZING AT THE *SOURCE.*
JASON--?!
I'M FINE--STAY WITH KORI!
NO ARGUMENT THERE. BUT YOU'RE GOING TO NEED BOTH HANDS...
RIGHT. THANKS.
TSSST
SOMETIMES ROY PLAYS THE CLOWN SO WELL--
--I FORGET HOW BRILLIANT HE IS AT MAKING WEAPONS.
YOU CAN RELAX, MR. FRIES.
YOU ARE NOW UNDER THE PROTECTION OF PRINCESS KORIAND'R OF THE PLANET--
X'HAL!
WHAACKT!

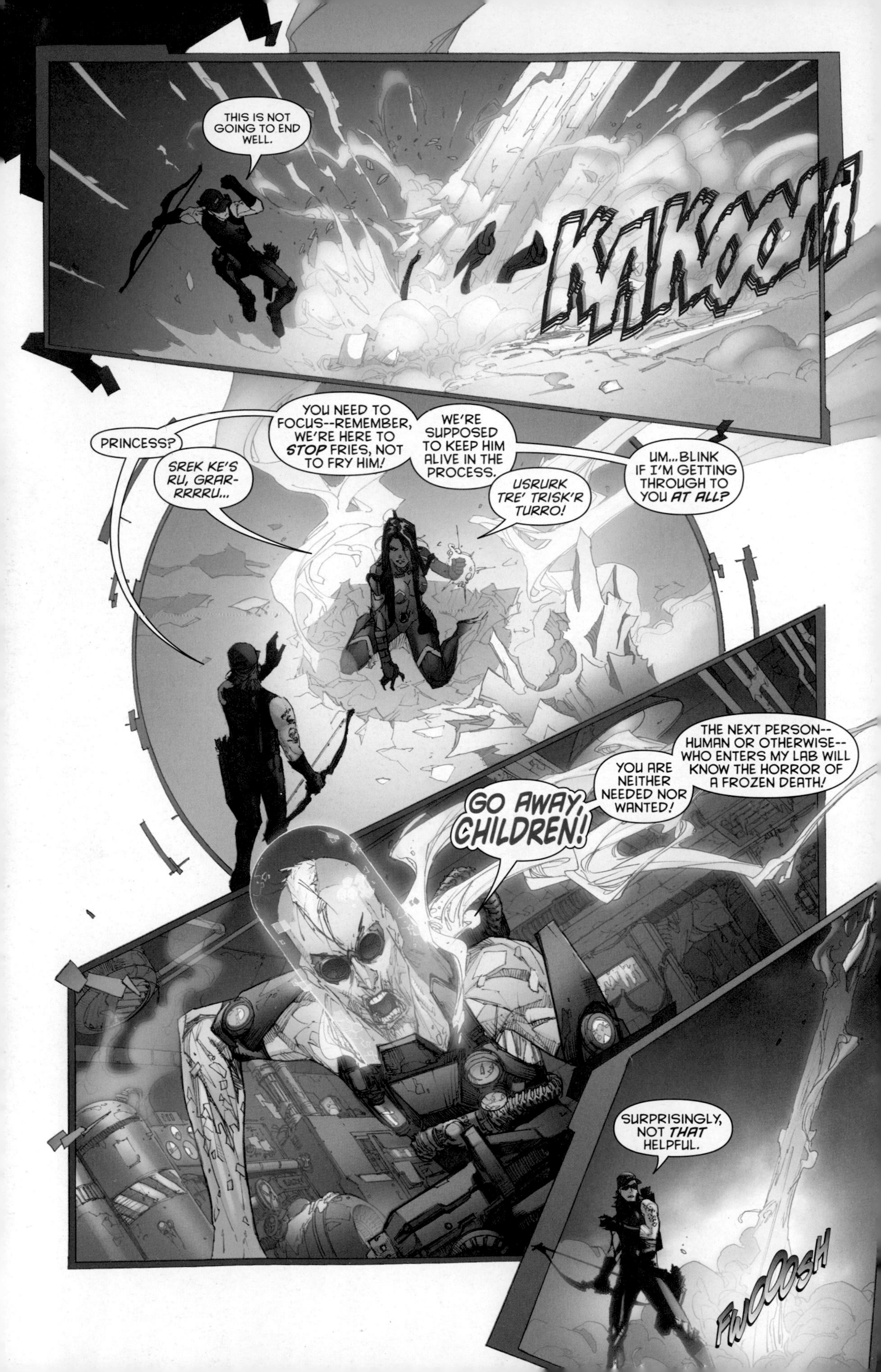
THIS IS NOT GOING TO END WELL.
KA-KRAKOOM
PRINCESS?
YOU NEED TO FOCUS--REMEMBER, WE'RE HERE TO STOP FRIES, NOT TO FRY HIM!
WE'RE SUPPOSED TO KEEP HIM ALIVE IN THE PROCESS.
UM...BLINK IF I'M GETTING THROUGH TO YOU AT ALL?
SREK KE'S RU, GRAR-RRRRU...
USRURK TRE' TRISK'R TURRO!
GO AWAY, CHILDREN!
YOU ARE NEITHER NEEDED NOR WANTED!
THE NEXT PERSON--HUMAN OR OTHERWISE--WHO ENTERS MY LAB WILL KNOW THE HORROR OF A FROZEN DEATH!
SURPRISINGLY, NOT THAT HELPFUL.
FWOOOSH

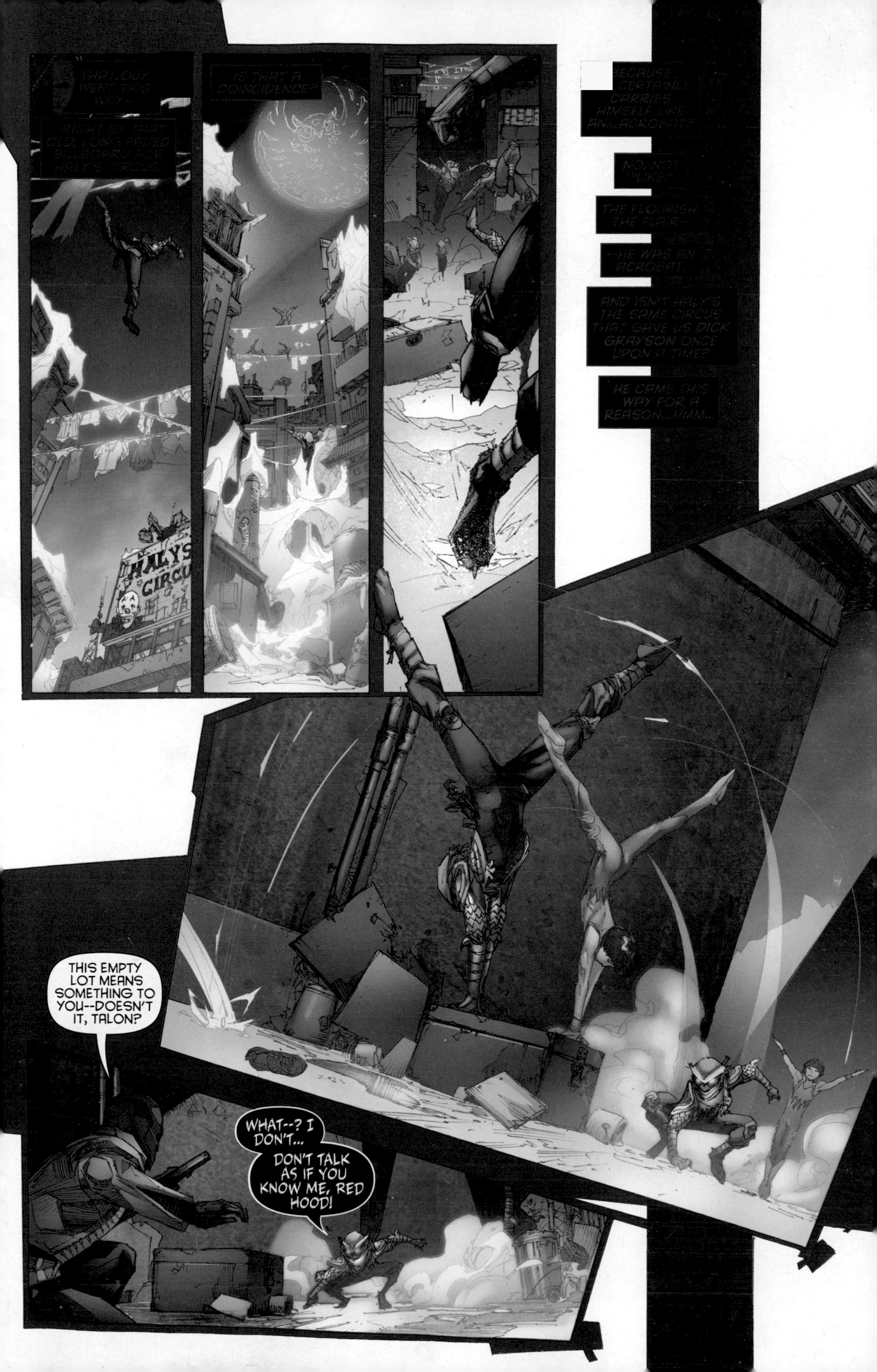
THAT GUY WENT THIS WAY--
--RIGHT BY THAT OLD, LONG FADED BILLBOARD FOR HALY'S CIRCUS.
HALY'S CIRCUS
IS THAT A COINCIDENCE?
BECAUSE, CERTAINLY CARRIES HIMSELF LIKE AN...ACROBAT?
NO, NOT "LIKE."
THE FLOURISH, THE FLAIR--
--HE WAS AN ACROBAT.
AND ISN'T HALY'S THE SAME CIRCUS THAT GAVE US DICK GRAYSON ONCE UPON A TIME?
HE CAME THIS WAY FOR A REASON...HMM...
THIS EMPTY LOT MEANS SOMETHING TO YOU--DOESN'T IT, TALON?
WHAT--? I DON'T...
DON'T TALK AS IF YOU KNOW ME, RED HOOD!

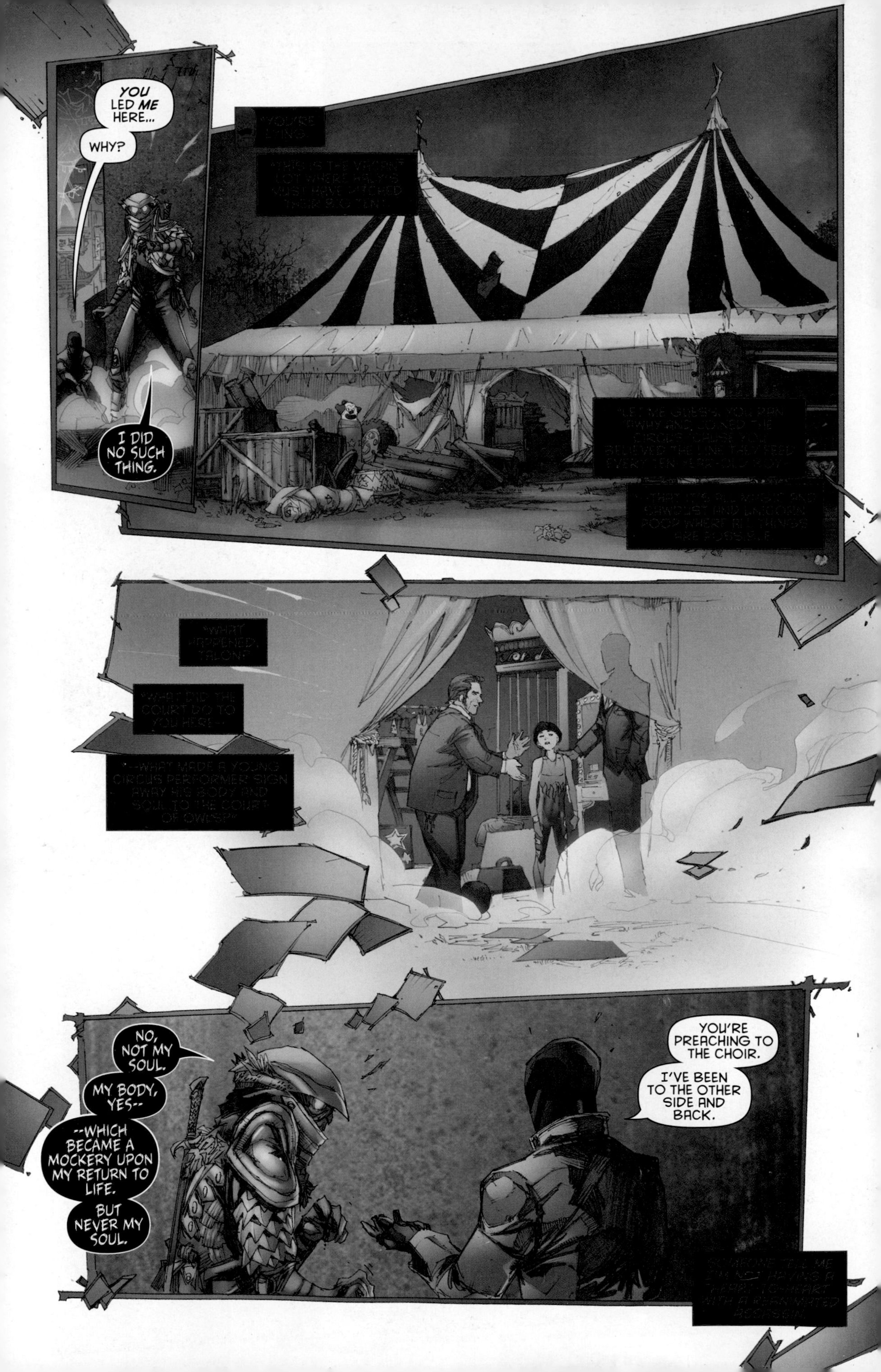
YOU LED ME HERE...
WHY?
"YOU'RE LYING.
"THIS IS THE VACANT LOT WHERE HALY'S MUST HAVE PITCHED THEIR BIG TENT.
"LET ME GUESS. YOU RAN AWAY AND JOINED THE CIRCUS 'CAUSE YOU BELIEVED THE LINE THEY FEED EVERY TEN-YEAR-OLD BOY--
"--THAT IT'S ALL MAGIC AND SAWDUST AND UNICORN POOP WHERE ALL THINGS ARE POSSIBLE.
I DID NO SUCH THING.
"WHAT HAPPENED, TALON?
"WHAT DID THE COURT DO TO YOU HERE--
"--WHAT MADE A YOUNG CIRCUS PERFORMER SIGN AWAY HIS BODY AND SOUL TO THE COURT OF OWLS?"
NO, NOT MY SOUL.
MY BODY, YES--
--WHICH BECAME A MOCKERY UPON MY RETURN TO LIFE.
BUT NEVER MY SOUL.
YOU'RE PREACHING TO THE CHOIR.
I'VE BEEN TO THE OTHER SIDE AND BACK.
SOMEONE TELL ME I'M NOT HAVING A HEART-TO-HEART WITH A REANIMATED ASSASSIN.

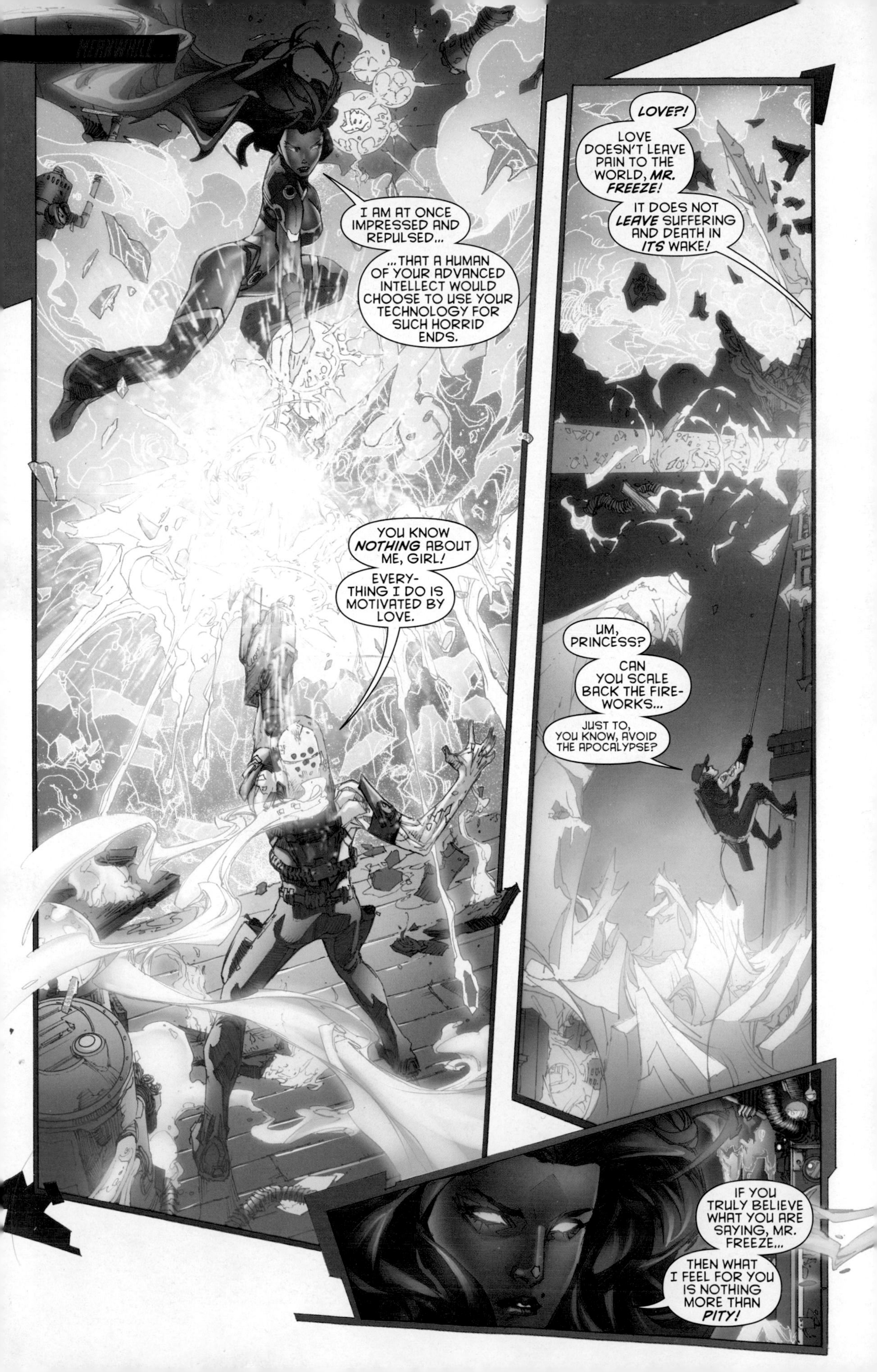
MEANWHILE...
I AM AT ONCE IMPRESSED AND REPULSED...
...THAT A HUMAN OF YOUR ADVANCED INTELLECT WOULD CHOOSE TO USE YOUR TECHNOLOGY FOR SUCH HORRID ENDS.
YOU KNOW *NOTHING* ABOUT ME, GIRL!
EVERY-THING I DO IS MOTIVATED BY LOVE.
LOVE?!
LOVE DOESN'T LEAVE PAIN TO THE WORLD, *MR. FREEZE!*
IT DOES NOT *LEAVE* SUFFERING AND DEATH IN *ITS* WAKE!
UM, PRINCESS?
CAN YOU SCALE BACK THE FIRE-WORKS...
JUST TO, YOU KNOW, AVOID THE APOCALYPSE?
IF YOU TRULY BELIEVE WHAT YOU ARE SAYING, MR. FREEZE...
THEN WHAT I FEEL FOR YOU IS NOTHING MORE THAN *PITY!*

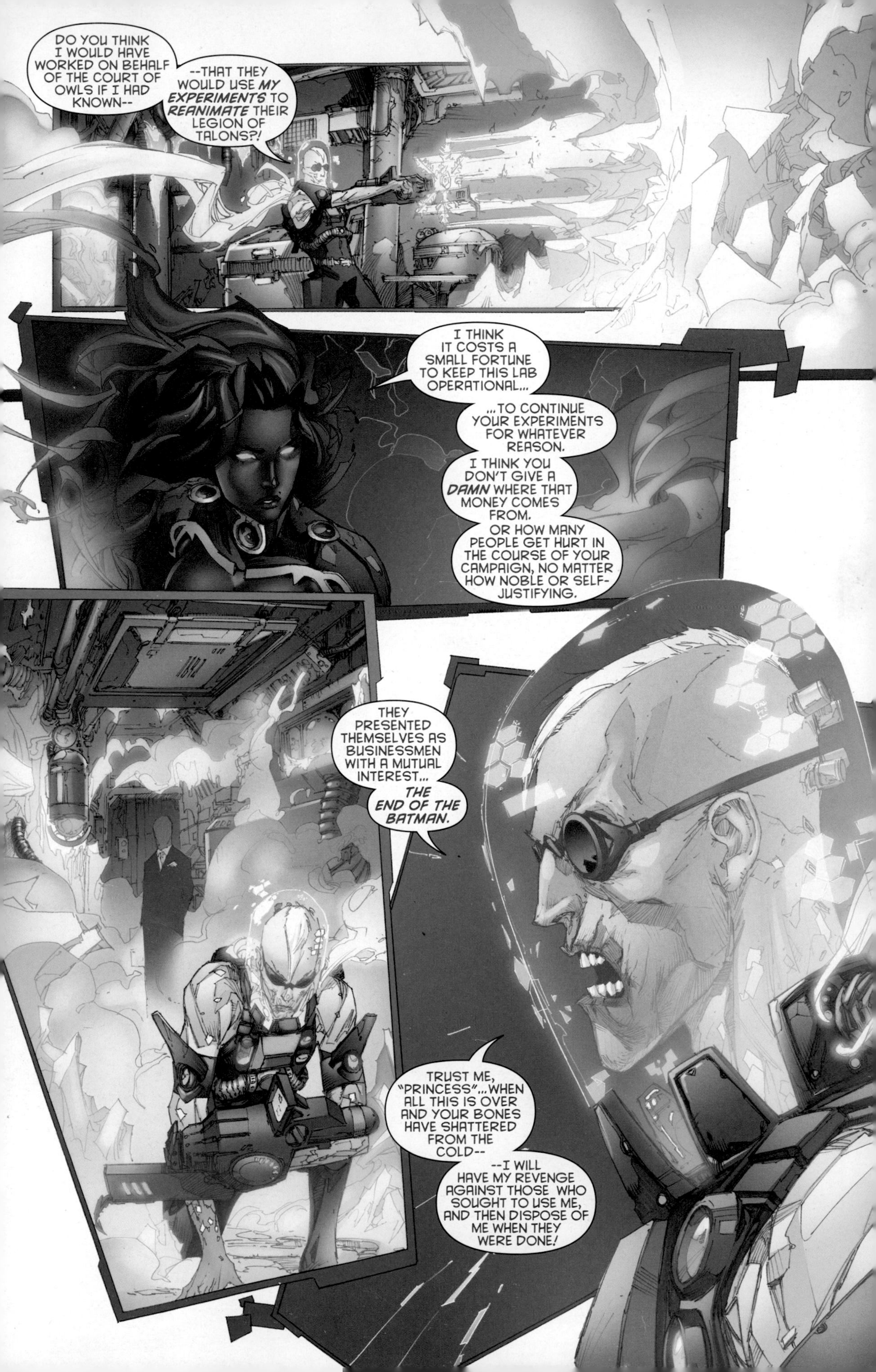
DO YOU THINK I WOULD HAVE WORKED ON BEHALF OF THE COURT OF OWLS IF I HAD KNOWN--
--THAT THEY WOULD USE MY EXPERIMENTS TO REANIMATE THEIR LEGION OF TALONS?!
I THINK IT COSTS A SMALL FORTUNE TO KEEP THIS LAB OPERATIONAL...
...TO CONTINUE YOUR EXPERIMENTS FOR WHATEVER REASON.
I THINK YOU DON'T GIVE A DAMN WHERE THAT MONEY COMES FROM.
OR HOW MANY PEOPLE GET HURT IN THE COURSE OF YOUR CAMPAIGN, NO MATTER HOW NOBLE OR SELF-JUSTIFYING.
THEY PRESENTED THEMSELVES AS BUSINESSMEN WITH A MUTUAL INTEREST... THE END OF THE BATMAN.
TRUST ME, "PRINCESS"...WHEN ALL THIS IS OVER AND YOUR BONES HAVE SHATTERED FROM THE COLD--
--I WILL HAVE MY REVENGE AGAINST THOSE WHO SOUGHT TO USE ME, AND THEN DISPOSE OF ME WHEN THEY WERE DONE!

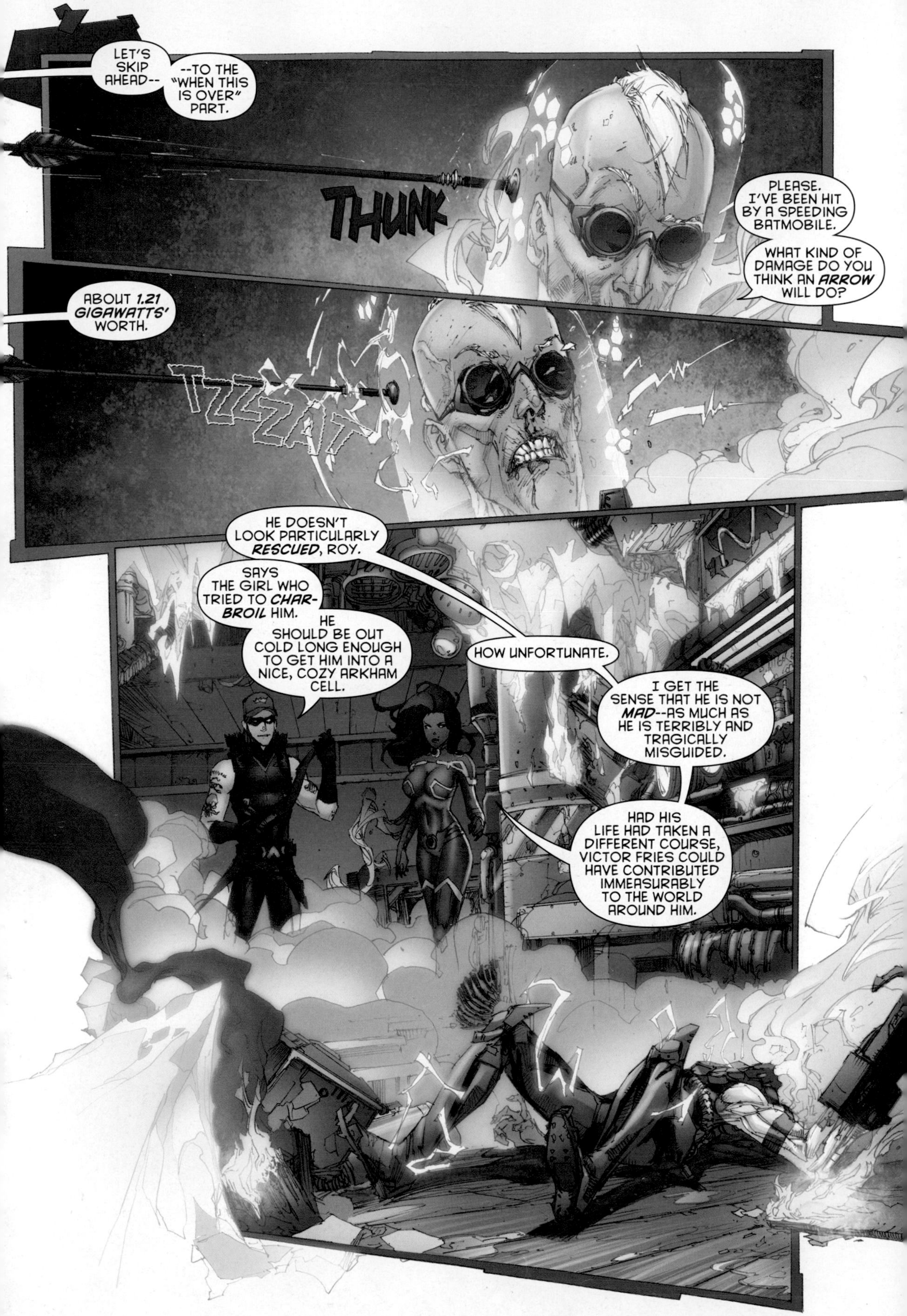
LET'S SKIP AHEAD--
--TO THE "WHEN THIS IS OVER" PART.
THUNK
PLEASE. I'VE BEEN HIT BY A SPEEDING BATMOBILE.
WHAT KIND OF DAMAGE DO YOU THINK AN ARROW WILL DO?
ABOUT 1.21 GIGAWATTS' WORTH.
TZZZAT
HE DOESN'T LOOK PARTICULARLY RESCUED, ROY.
SAYS THE GIRL WHO TRIED TO CHAR-BROIL HIM.
HE SHOULD BE OUT COLD LONG ENOUGH TO GET HIM INTO A NICE, COZY ARKHAM CELL.
HOW UNFORTUNATE.
I GET THE SENSE THAT HE IS NOT MAD--AS MUCH AS HE IS TERRIBLY AND TRAGICALLY MISGUIDED.
HAD HIS LIFE HAD TAKEN A DIFFERENT COURSE, VICTOR FRIES COULD HAVE CONTRIBUTED IMMEASURABLY TO THE WORLD AROUND HIM.

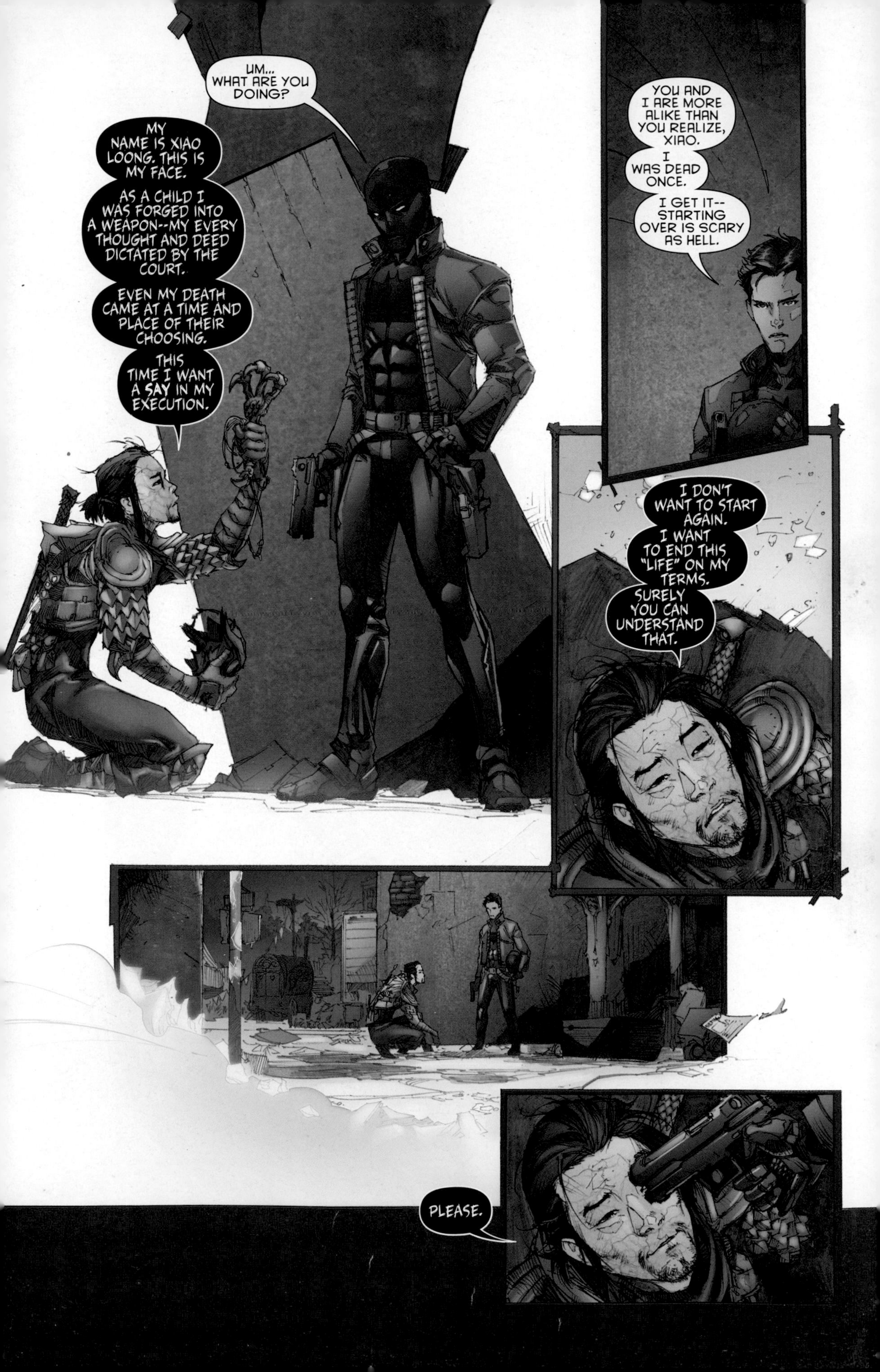
UM... WHAT ARE YOU DOING?
MY NAME IS XIAO LOONG. THIS IS MY FACE.
AS A CHILD I WAS FORGED INTO A WEAPON--MY EVERY THOUGHT AND DEED DICTATED BY THE COURT.
EVEN MY DEATH CAME AT A TIME AND PLACE OF THEIR CHOOSING.
THIS TIME I WANT A SAY IN MY EXECUTION.
YOU AND I ARE MORE ALIKE THAN YOU REALIZE, XIAO.
I WAS DEAD ONCE.
I GET IT--STARTING OVER IS SCARY AS HELL.
I DON'T WANT TO START AGAIN.
I WANT TO END THIS "LIFE" ON MY TERMS.
SURELY YOU CAN UNDERSTAND THAT.
PLEASE.

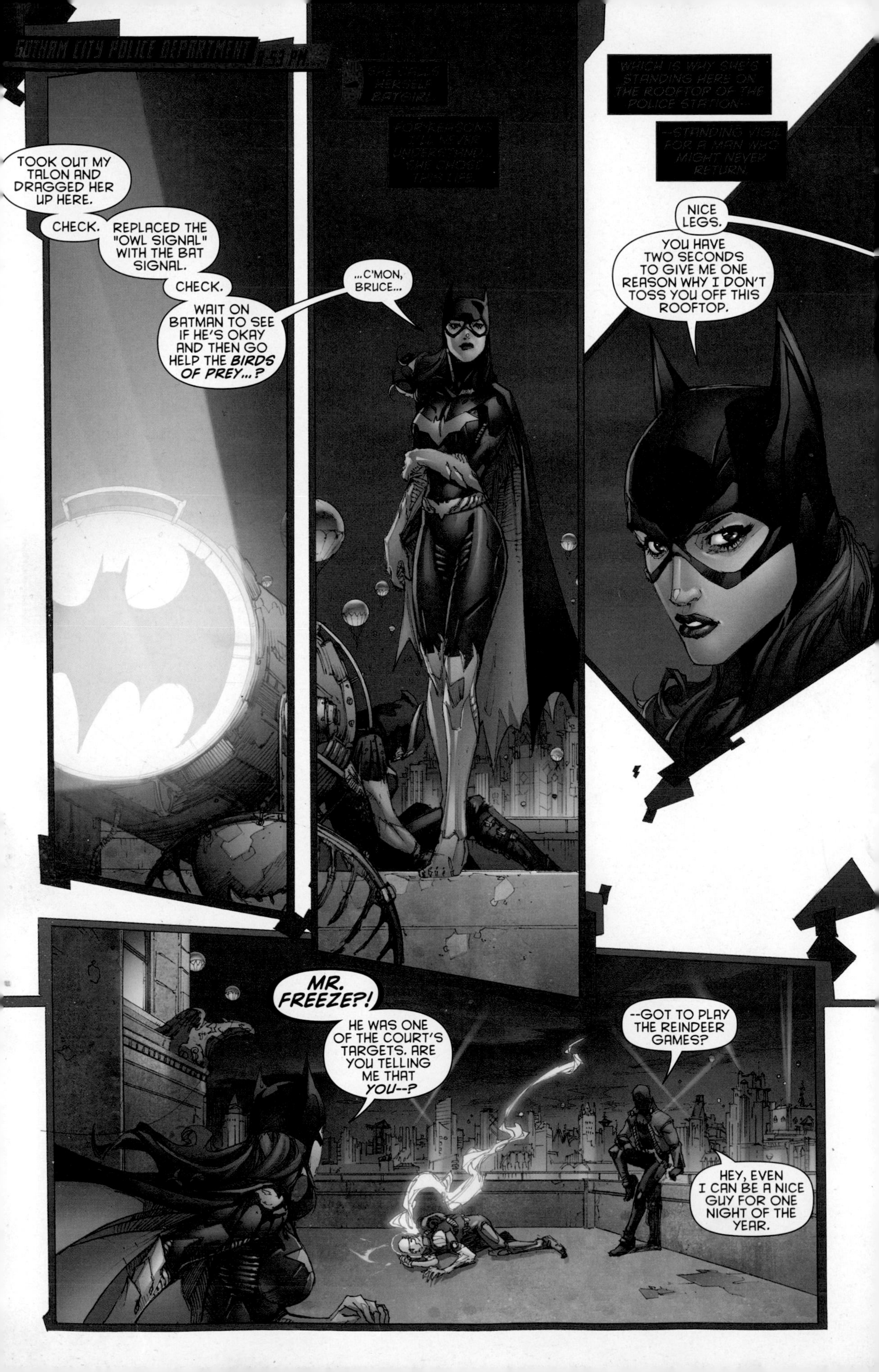
GOTHAM CITY POLICE DEPARTMENT
TOOK OUT MY TALON AND DRAGGED HER UP HERE.
CHECK.
REPLACED THE "OWL SIGNAL" WITH THE BAT SIGNAL.
CHECK.
WAIT ON BATMAN TO SEE IF HE'S OKAY AND THEN GO HELP THE BIRDS OF PREY...?
SHE CALLS HERSELF BATGIRL.
FOR REASONS I'LL NEVER UNDERSTAND... SHE CHOSE THIS LIFE.
...C'MON, BRUCE...
WHICH IS WHY SHE'S STANDING HERE ON THE ROOFTOP OF THE POLICE STATION--
--STANDING VIGIL FOR A MAN WHO MIGHT NEVER RETURN.
NICE LEGS.
YOU HAVE TWO SECONDS TO GIVE ME ONE REASON WHY I DON'T TOSS YOU OFF THIS ROOFTOP.
MR. FREEZE?!
HE WAS ONE OF THE COURT'S TARGETS. ARE YOU TELLING ME THAT YOU--?
--GOT TO PLAY THE REINDEER GAMES?
HEY, EVEN I CAN BE A NICE GUY FOR ONE NIGHT OF THE YEAR.

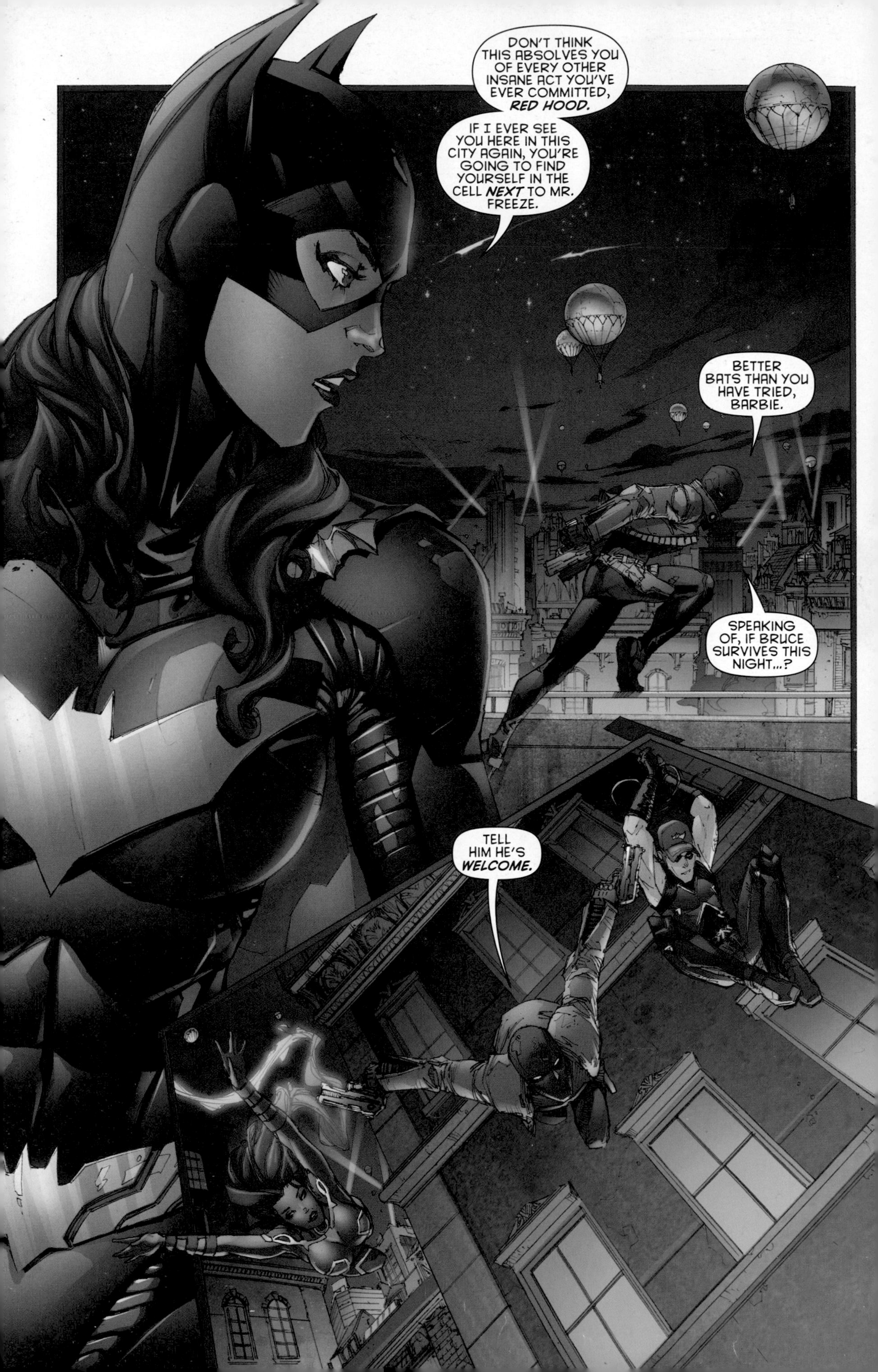
DON'T THINK THIS ABSOLVES YOU OF EVERY OTHER INSANE ACT YOU'VE EVER COMMITTED, RED HOOD.
IF I EVER SEE YOU HERE IN THIS CITY AGAIN, YOU'RE GOING TO FIND YOURSELF IN THE CELL NEXT TO MR. FREEZE.
BETTER BATS THAN YOU HAVE TRIED, BARBIE.
SPEAKING OF, IF BRUCE SURVIVES THIS NIGHT...?
TELL HIM HE'S WELCOME.

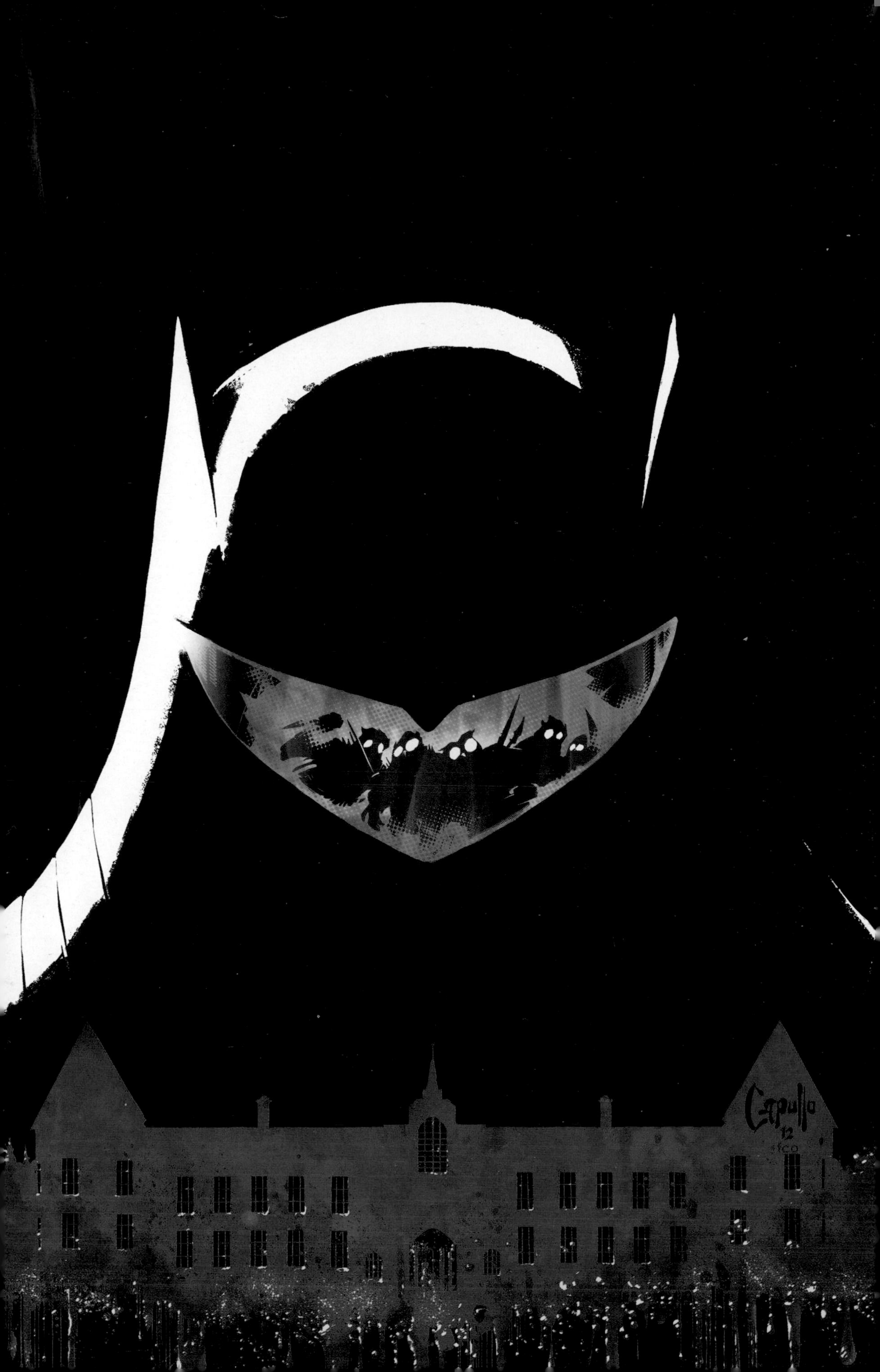

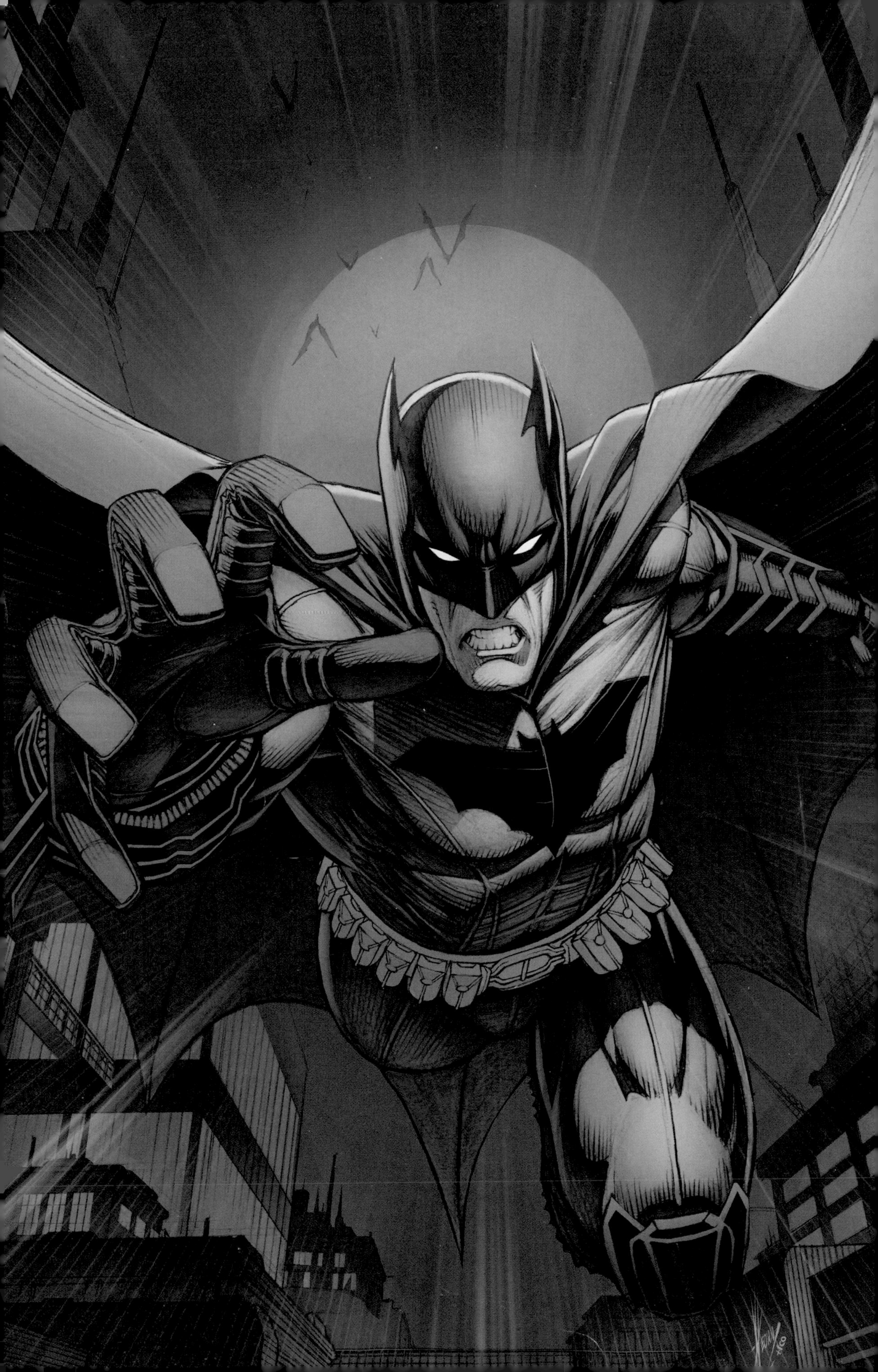

The first members
of my family to live
in the manor were
Solomon and Joshua
Wayne--brothers.
They bought the
house in 1855.

But they didn't
move in until two
years later.

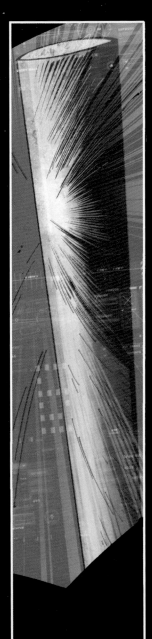

The reason was **bats.**

A massive infestation
of bats in the cave
system beneath the land.

They brought in a chiroptologist
from Gotham University, and
according to him, to get rid of
the bats, they'd have to introduce
a **predator** into the cave.

So the Wayne brothers did.

They carted in all sorts of birds,
from Peregrine Falcons to kestrels,
and unleashed them in different
sections of the cave.

The most effective killers of bats,
though, were the **tiger owls.**

My ancestors let owls loose in the cave...

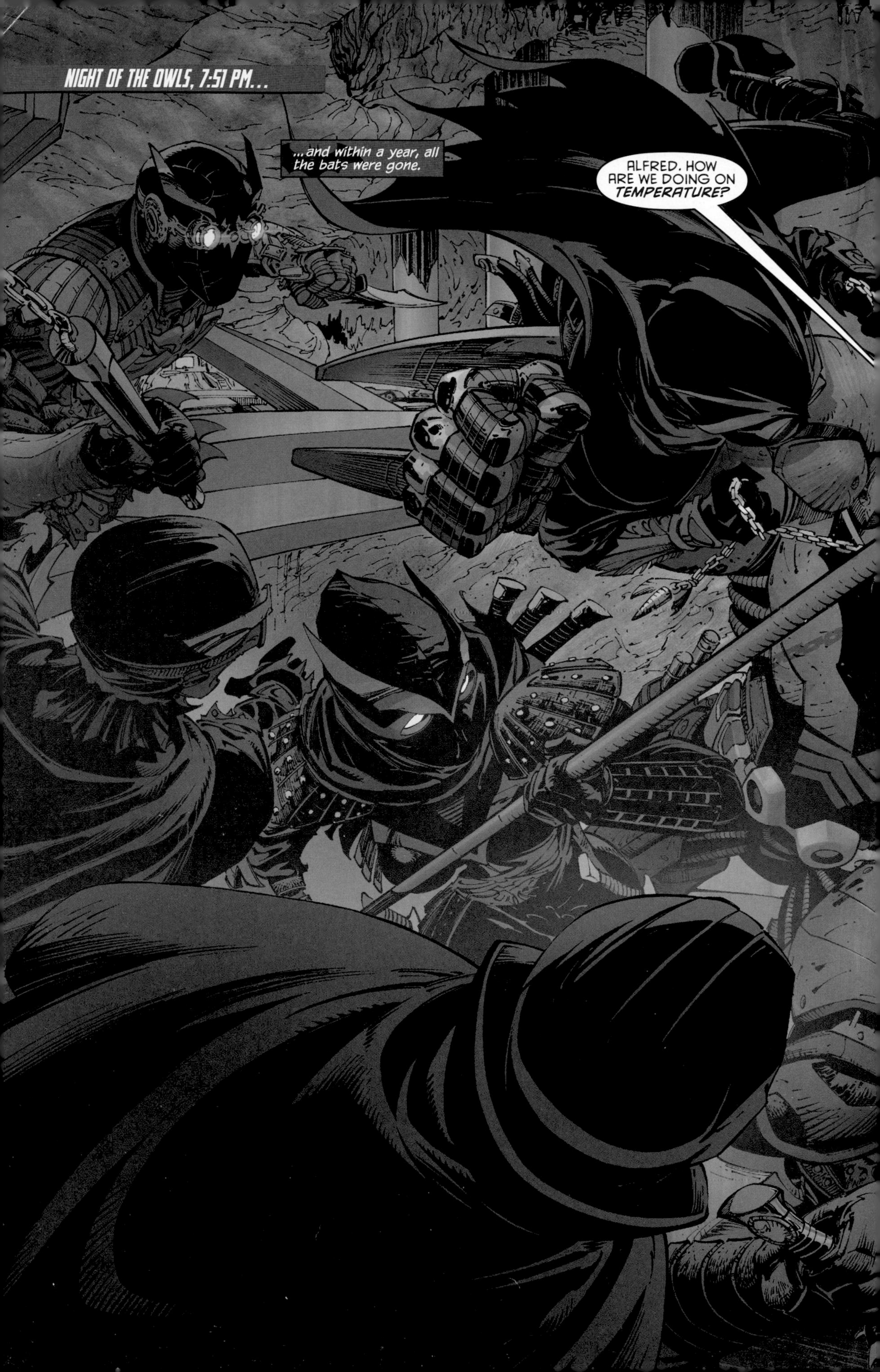
NIGHT OF THE OWLS, 7:51 PM...
...and within a year, all the bats were gone.
ALFRED. HOW ARE WE DOING ON TEMPERATURE?

DC COMICS presents BATMAN in

NIGHT of the OWLS

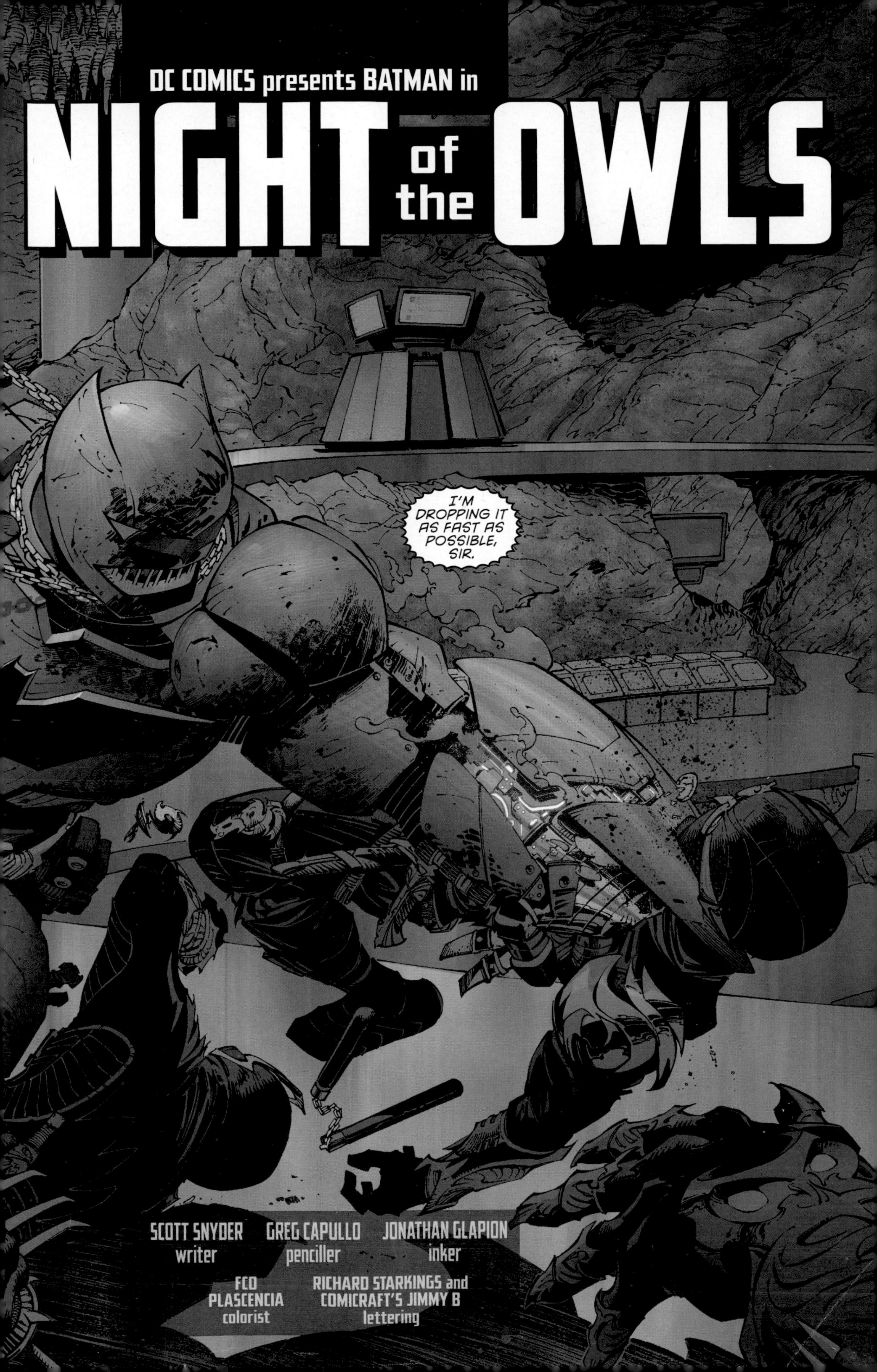
I'M DROPPING IT AS FAST AS POSSIBLE, SIR.

SCOTT SNYDER writer
GREG CAPULLO penciller
JONATHAN GLAPION inker
FCO PLASCENCIA colorist
RICHARD STARKINGS and COMICRAFT'S JIMMY B lettering

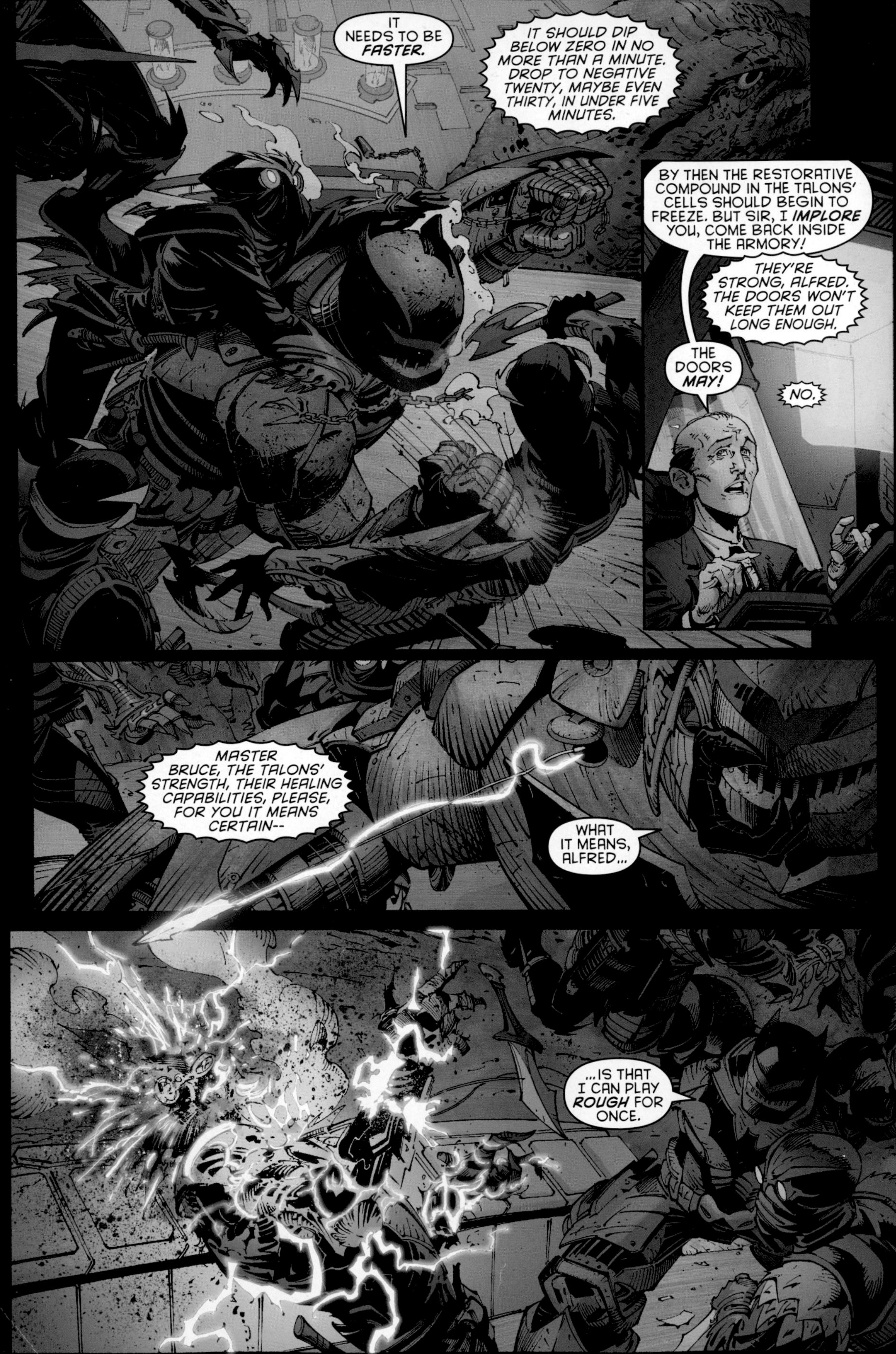

IT NEEDS TO BE FASTER.
IT SHOULD DIP BELOW ZERO IN NO MORE THAN A MINUTE. DROP TO NEGATIVE TWENTY, MAYBE EVEN THIRTY, IN UNDER FIVE MINUTES.
BY THEN THE RESTORATIVE COMPOUND IN THE TALONS' CELLS SHOULD BEGIN TO FREEZE. BUT SIR, I IMPLORE YOU, COME BACK INSIDE THE ARMORY!
THEY'RE STRONG, ALFRED. THE DOORS WON'T KEEP THEM OUT LONG ENOUGH.
THE DOORS MAY!
NO.
MASTER BRUCE, THE TALONS' STRENGTH, THEIR HEALING CAPABILITIES, PLEASE, FOR YOU IT MEANS CERTAIN--
WHAT IT MEANS, ALFRED...
...IS THAT I CAN PLAY ROUGH FOR ONCE.

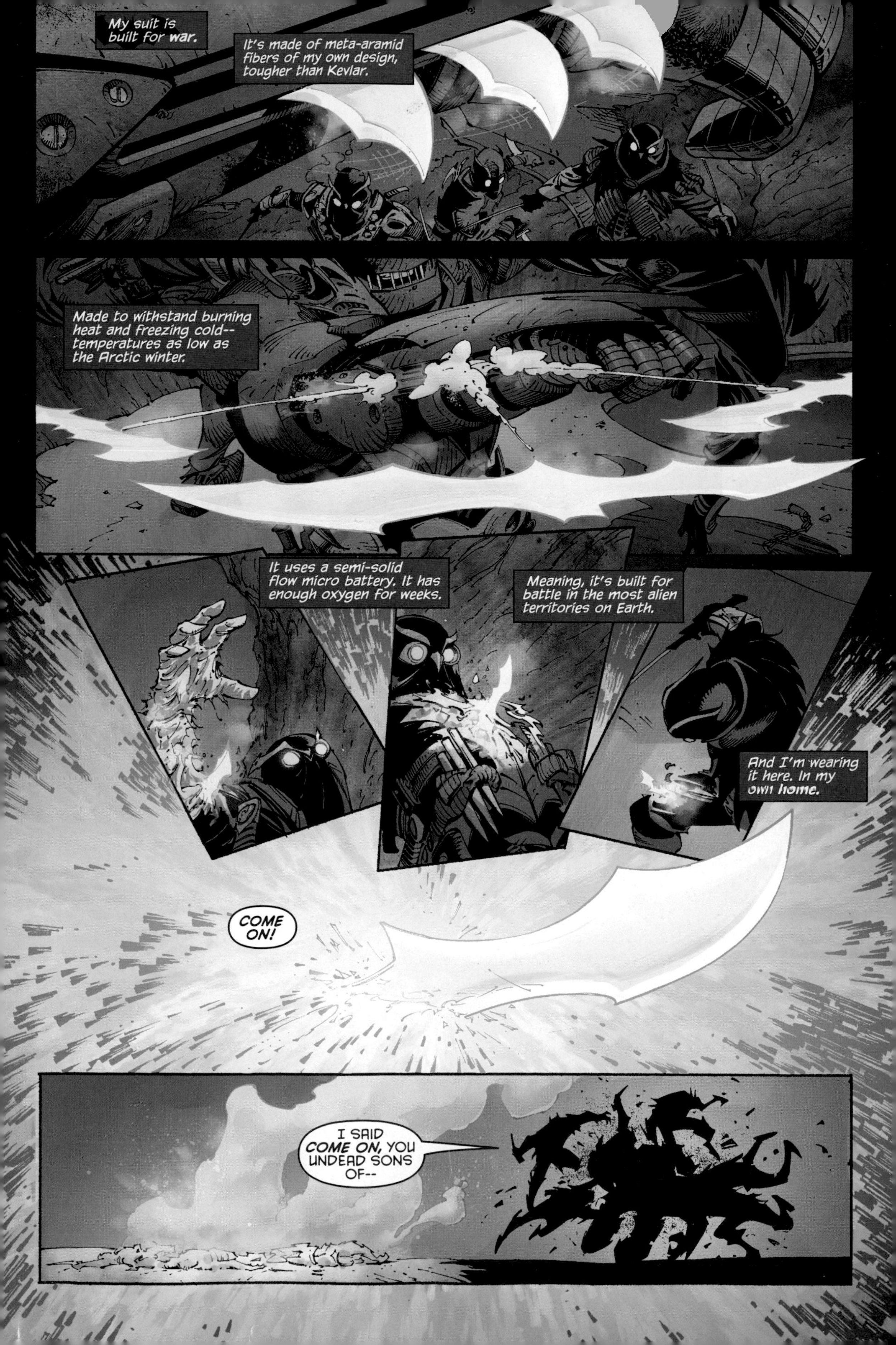
My suit is built for war.
It's made of meta-aramid fibers of my own design, tougher than Kevlar.
Made to withstand burning heat and freezing cold-- temperatures as low as the Arctic winter.
It uses a semi-solid flow micro battery. It has enough oxygen for weeks.
Meaning, it's built for battle in the most alien territories on Earth.
And I'm wearing it here. In my own home.
COME ON!
I SAID COME ON, YOU UNDEAD SONS OF--

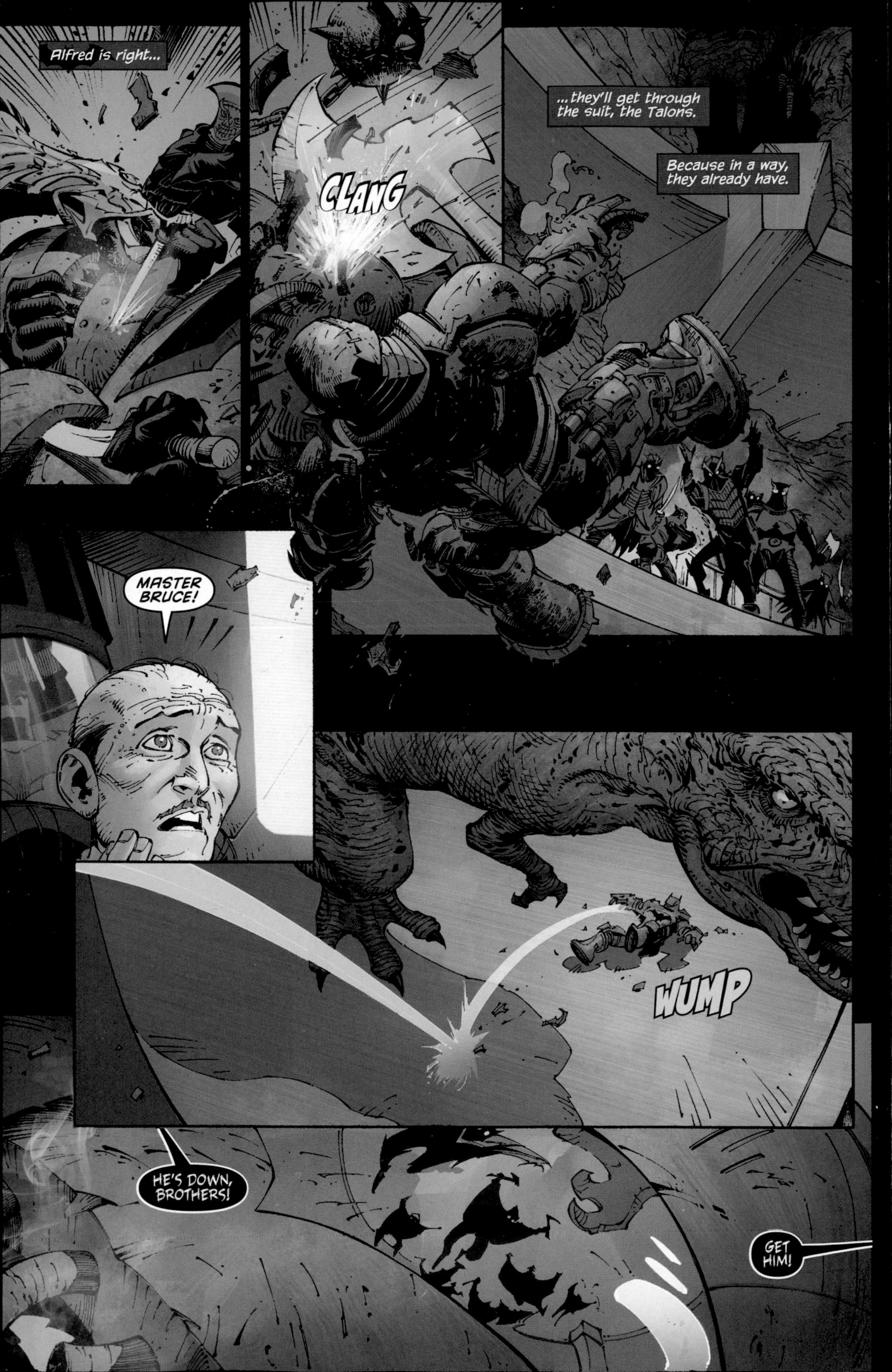
Alfred is right...
CLANG
...they'll get through the suit, the Talons.
Because in a way, they already have.
MASTER BRUCE!
WUMP
HE'S DOWN, BROTHERS!
GET HIM!

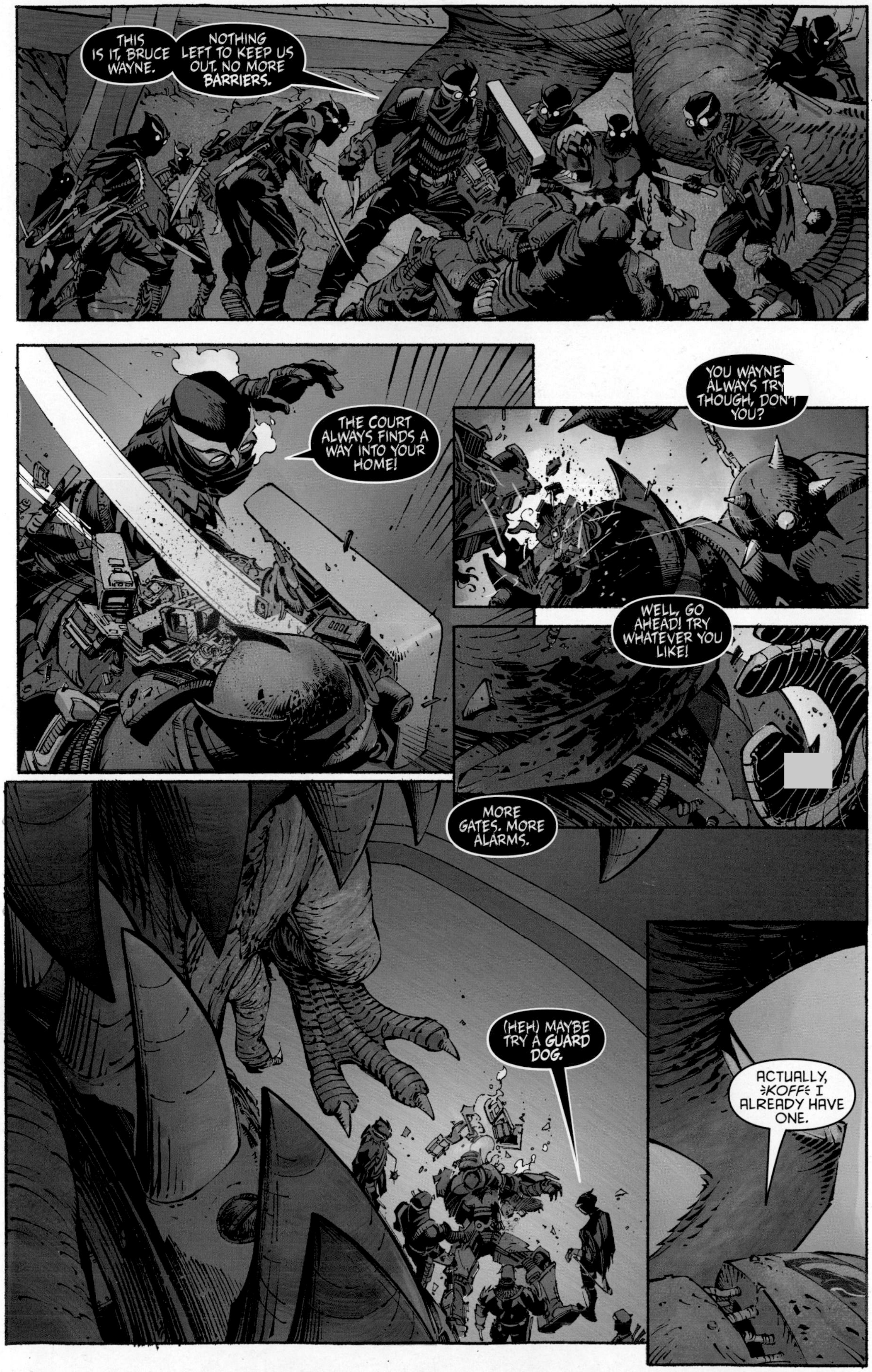
THIS IS IT, BRUCE WAYNE.
NOTHING LEFT TO KEEP US OUT. NO MORE BARRIERS.
THE COURT ALWAYS FINDS A WAY INTO YOUR HOME!
YOU WAYNE ALWAYS TRY THOUGH, DON'T YOU?
WELL, GO AHEAD! TRY WHATEVER YOU LIKE!
MORE GATES. MORE ALARMS.
(HEH) MAYBE TRY A GUARD DOG.
ACTUALLY, *KOFF* I ALREADY HAVE ONE.

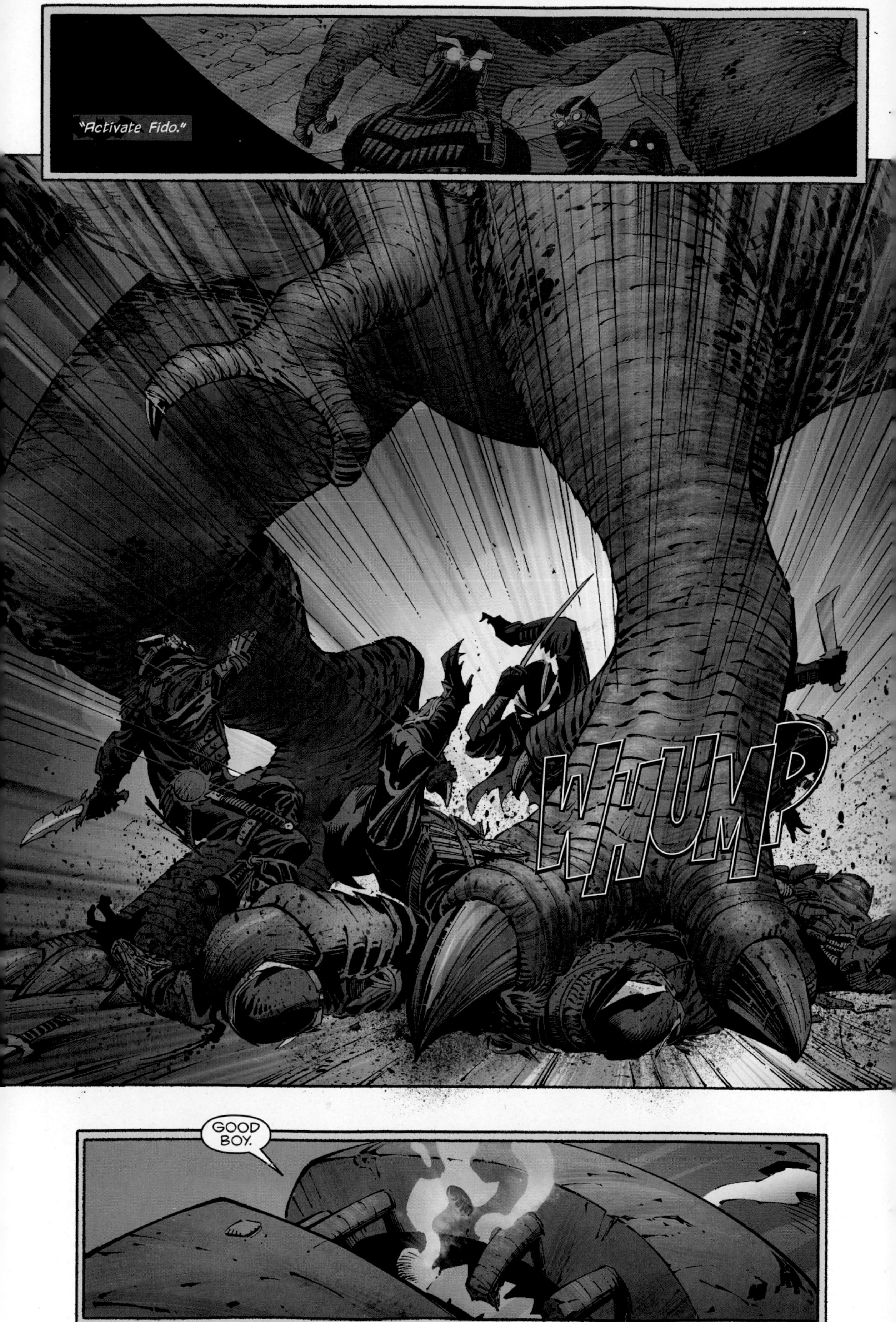
"Activate Fido."
WHUMP
GOOD BOY.

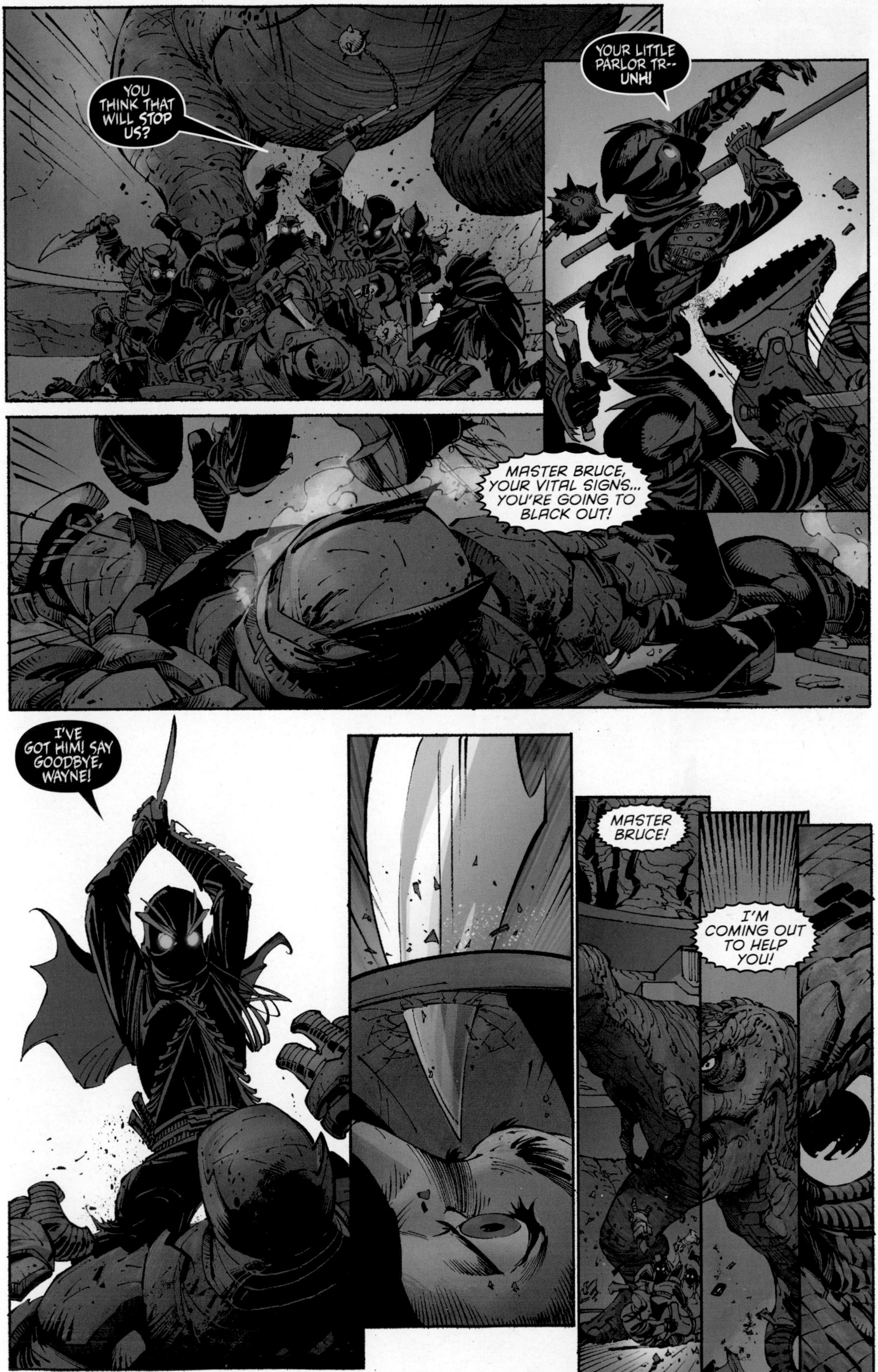
YOU THINK THAT WILL STOP US?
YOUR LITTLE PARLOR TR-- UNH!
MASTER BRUCE, YOUR VITAL SIGNS... YOU'RE GOING TO BLACK OUT!
I'VE GOT HIM! SAY GOODBYE, WAYNE!
MASTER BRUCE!
I'M COMING OUT TO HELP YOU!

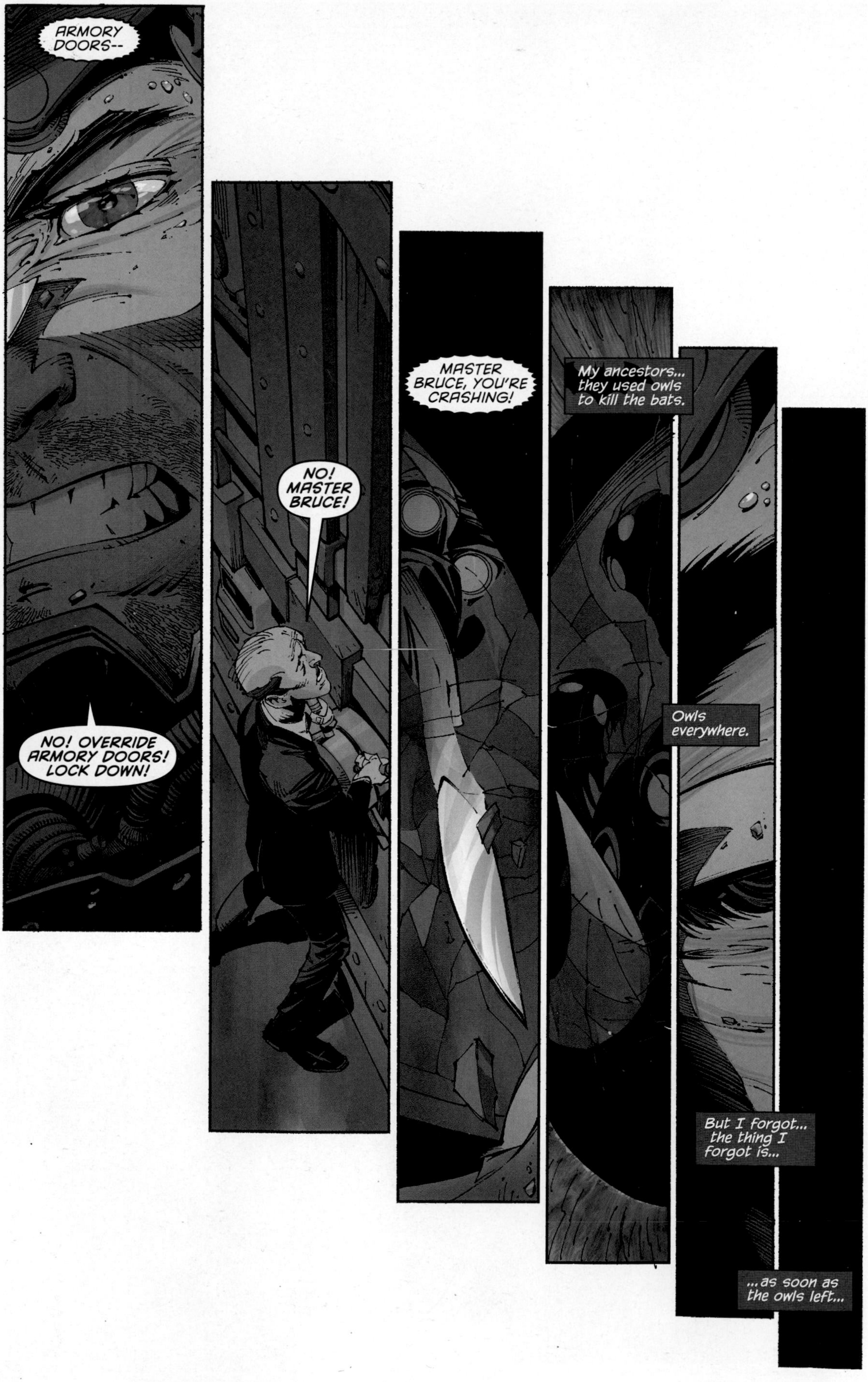
ARMORY DOORS--
NO! OVERRIDE ARMORY DOORS! LOCK DOWN!
NO! MASTER BRUCE!
MASTER BRUCE, YOU'RE CRASHING!
My ancestors... they used owls to kill the bats.
Owls everywhere.
But I forgot... the thing I forgot is...
...as soon as the owls left...

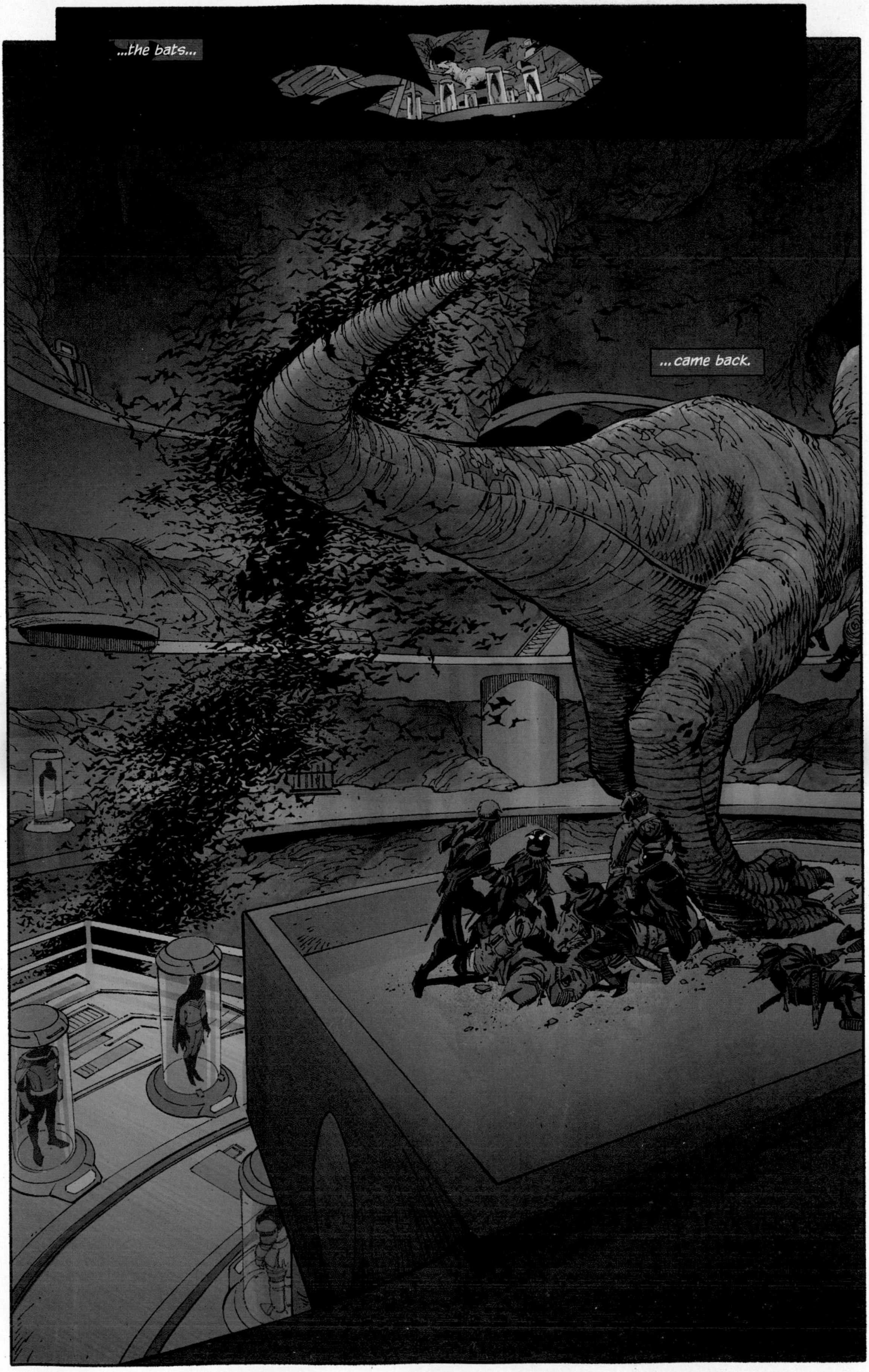
...the bats...
...came back.

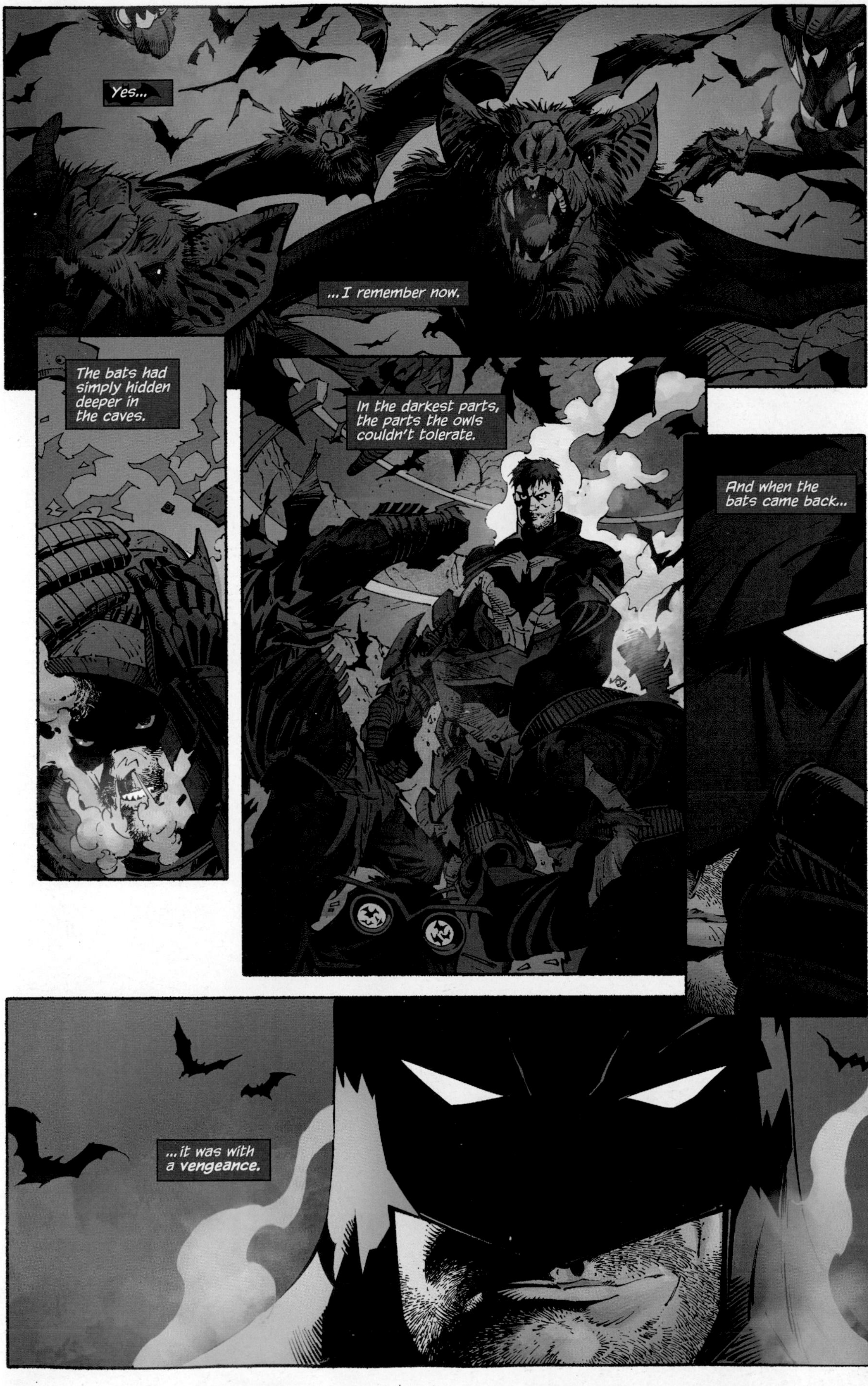
Yes...
...I remember now.
The bats had simply hidden deeper in the caves.
In the darkest parts, the parts the owls couldn't tolerate.
And when the bats came back...
...it was with a vengeance.

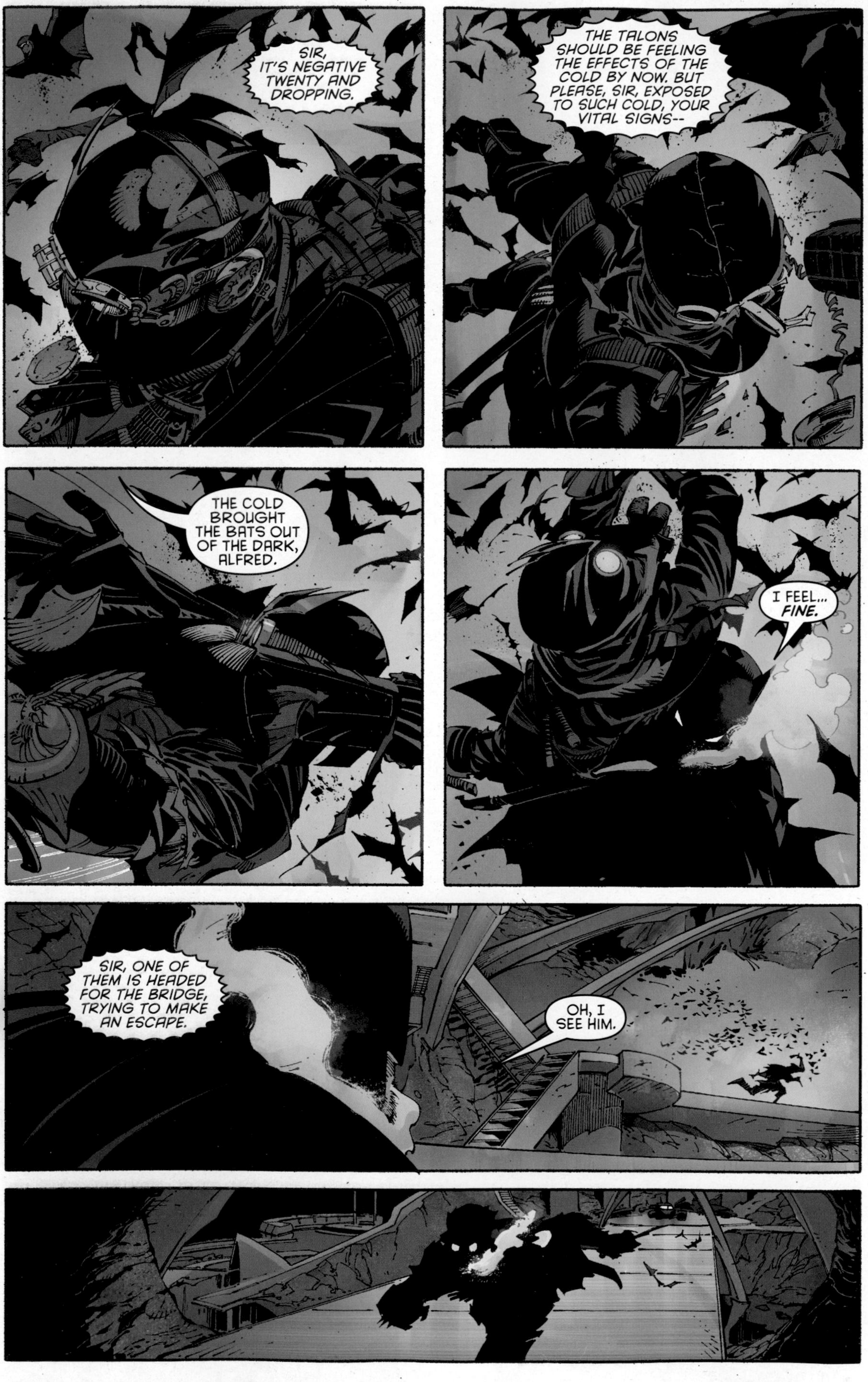
SIR, IT'S NEGATIVE TWENTY AND DROPPING.
THE TALONS SHOULD BE FEELING THE EFFECTS OF THE COLD BY NOW. BUT PLEASE, SIR, EXPOSED TO SUCH COLD, YOUR VITAL SIGNS--
THE COLD BROUGHT THE BATS OUT OF THE DARK, ALFRED.
I FEEL... FINE.
SIR, ONE OF THEM IS HEADED FOR THE BRIDGE, TRYING TO MAKE AN ESCAPE.
OH, I SEE HIM.

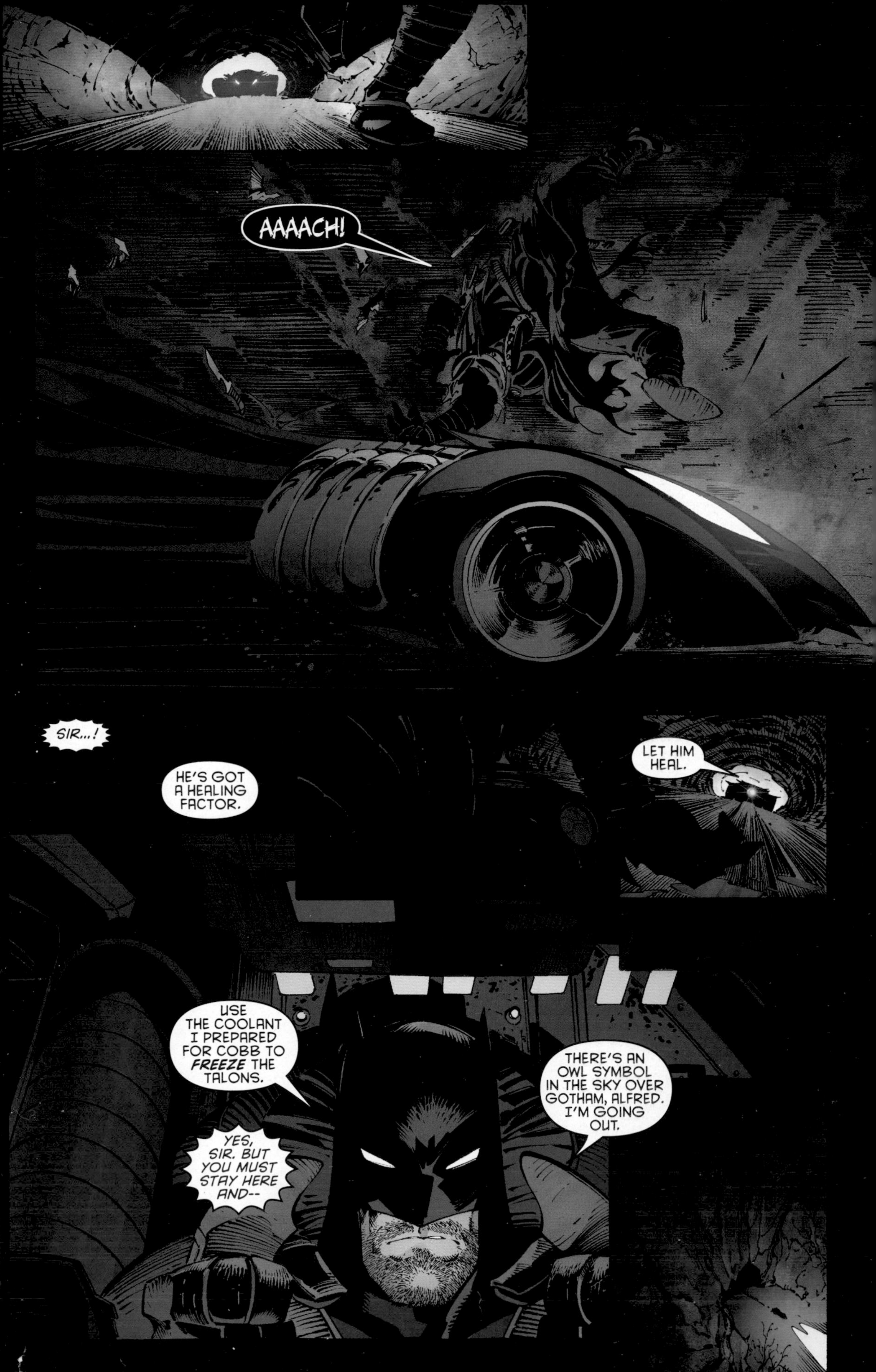
AAAACH!
SIR...!
HE'S GOT A HEALING FACTOR.
LET HIM HEAL.
USE THE COOLANT I PREPARED FOR COBB TO *FREEZE* THE TALONS.
YES, SIR. BUT YOU MUST STAY HERE AND--
THERE'S AN OWL SYMBOL IN THE SKY OVER GOTHAM, ALFRED. I'M GOING OUT.

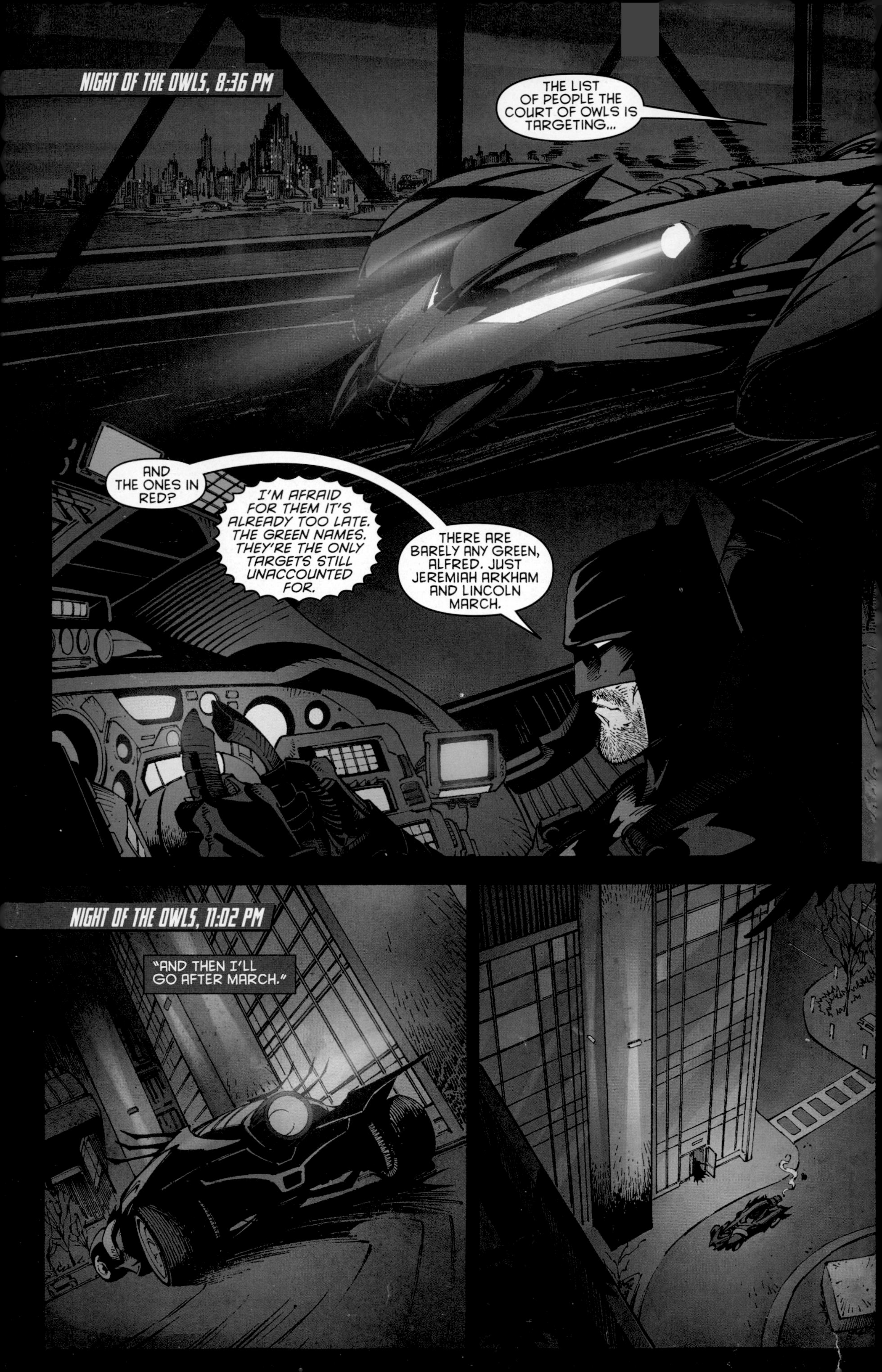
NIGHT OF THE OWLS, 8:36 PM
THE LIST OF PEOPLE THE COURT OF OWLS IS TARGETING...
AND THE ONES IN RED?
I'M AFRAID FOR THEM IT'S ALREADY TOO LATE. THE GREEN NAMES. THEY'RE THE ONLY TARGETS STILL UNACCOUNTED FOR.
THERE ARE BARELY ANY GREEN, ALFRED. JUST JEREMIAH ARKHAM AND LINCOLN MARCH.
NIGHT OF THE OWLS, 11:02 PM
"AND THEN I'LL GO AFTER MARCH."

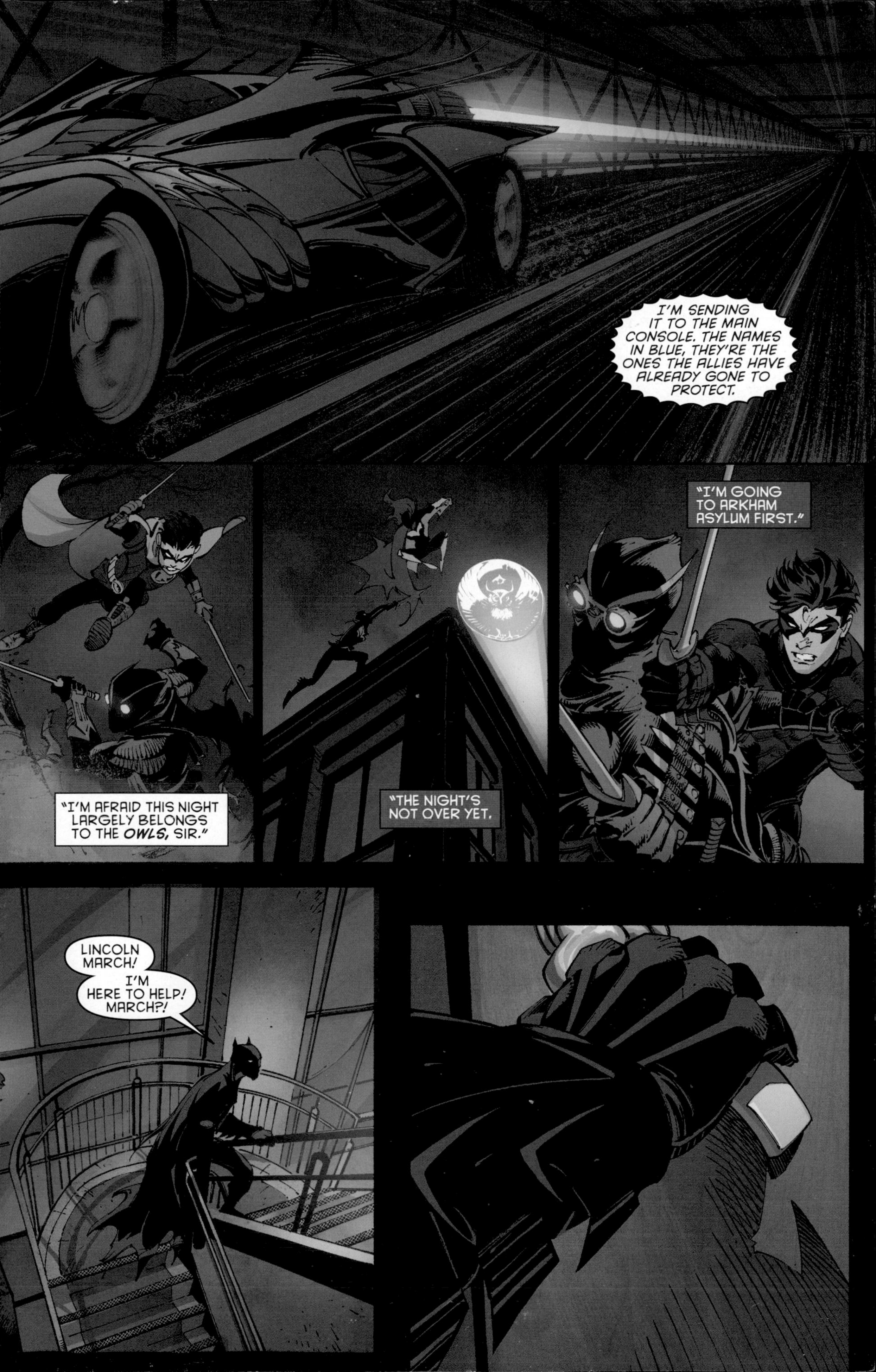
I'M SENDING IT TO THE MAIN CONSOLE. THE NAMES IN BLUE, THEY'RE THE ONES THE ALLIES HAVE ALREADY GONE TO PROTECT.
"I'M AFRAID THIS NIGHT LARGELY BELONGS TO THE OWLS, SIR."
"THE NIGHT'S NOT OVER YET.
"I'M GOING TO ARKHAM ASYLUM FIRST."
LINCOLN MARCH!
I'M HERE TO HELP! MARCH?!

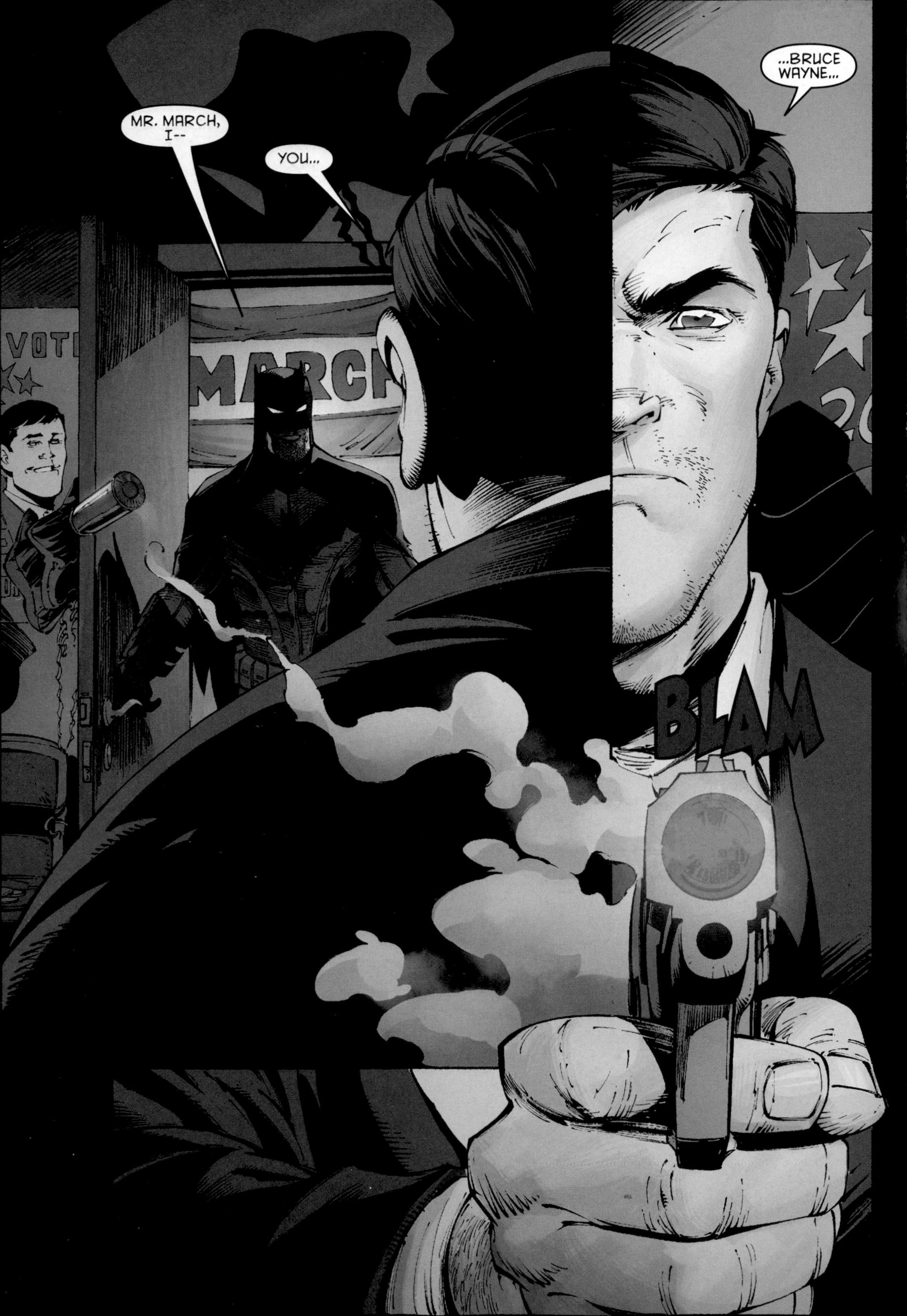
MR. MARCH, I--
YOU...
...BRUCE WAYNE...
MARCH
VOTE
BLAM

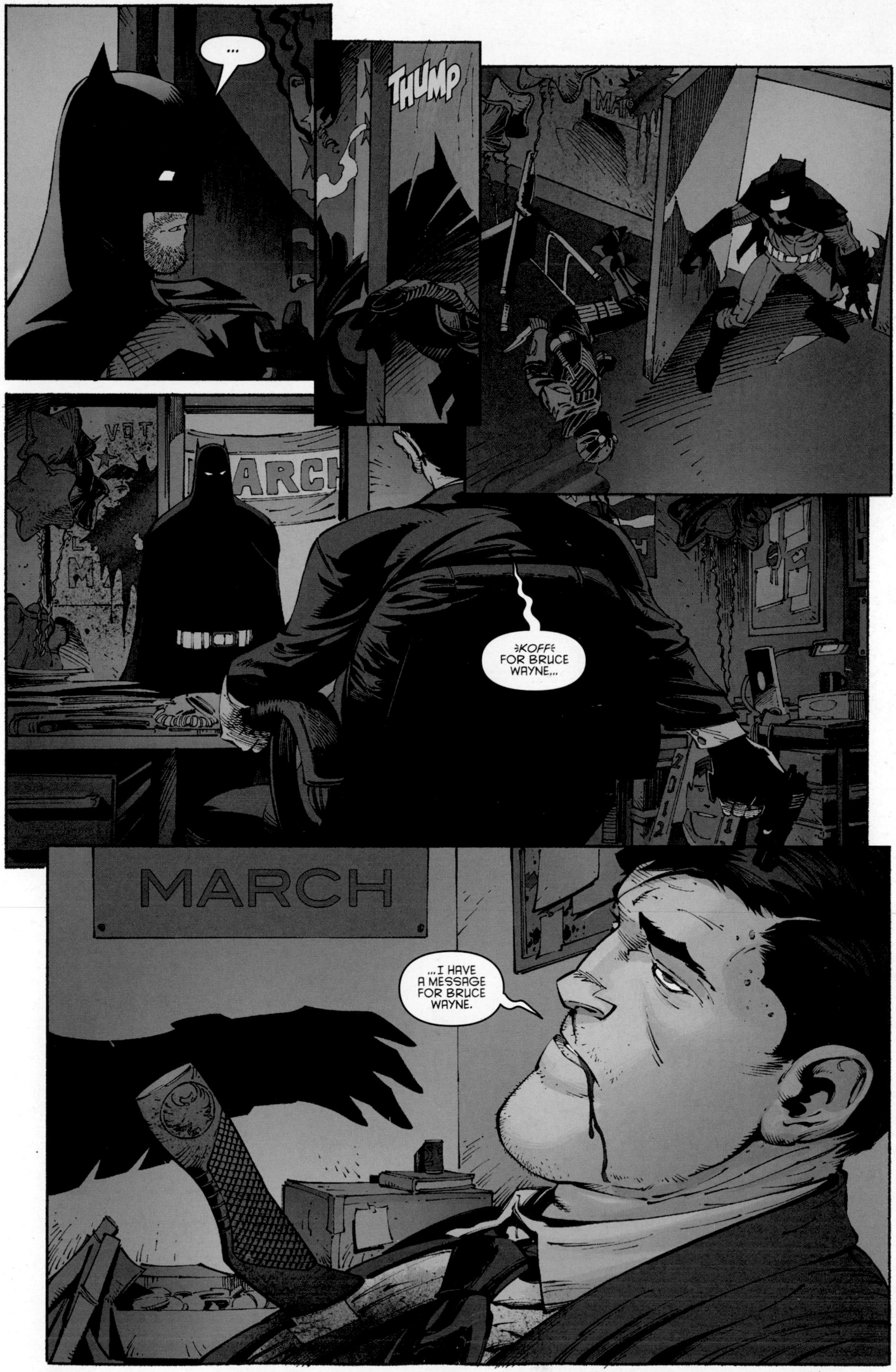
...
THUMP
MARCH
KOFF FOR BRUCE WAYNE...
MARCH
...I HAVE A MESSAGE FOR BRUCE WAYNE.

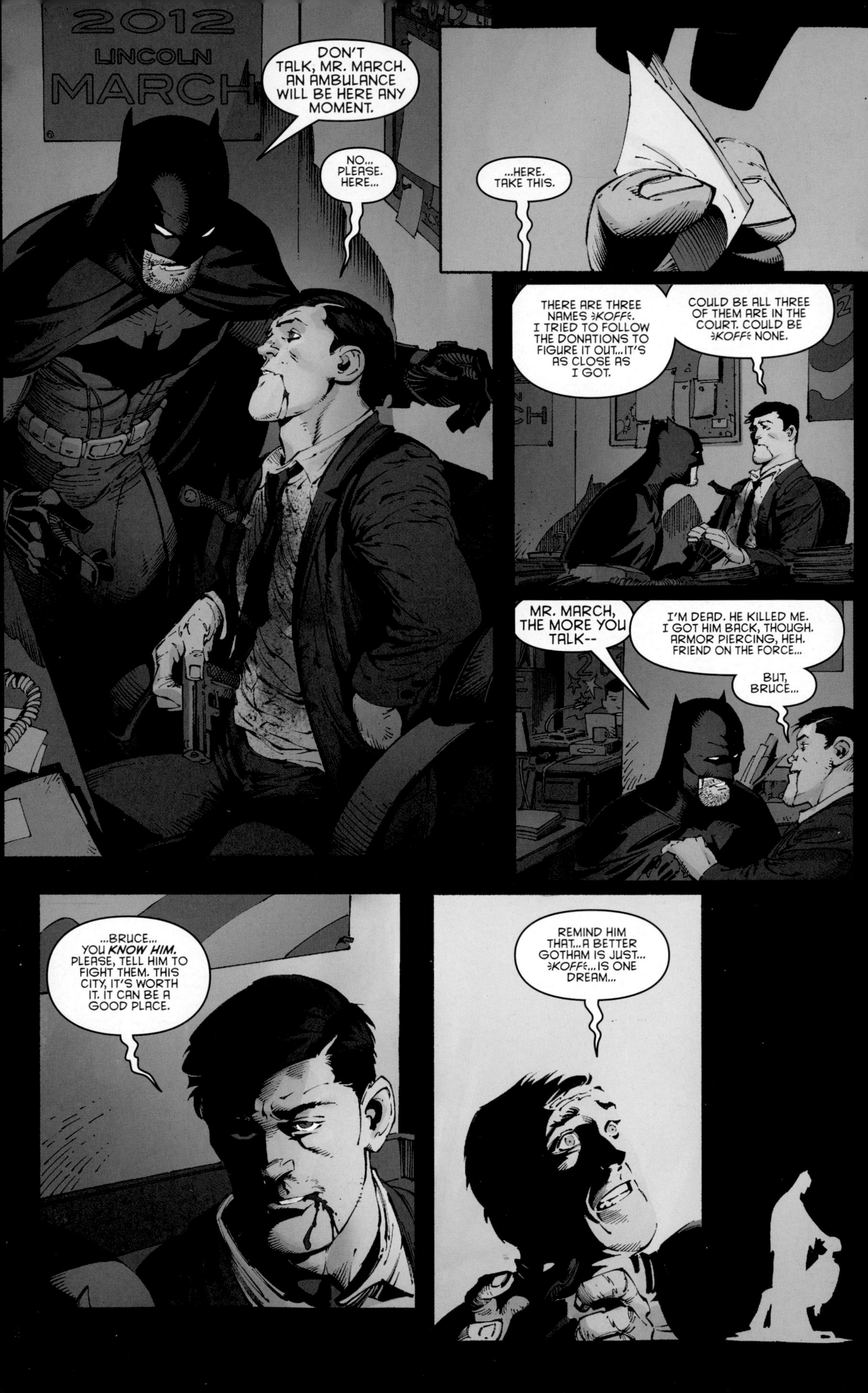
2012
LINCOLN
MARCH
DON'T TALK, MR. MARCH. AN AMBULANCE WILL BE HERE ANY MOMENT.
NO... PLEASE. HERE...
...HERE. TAKE THIS.
THERE ARE THREE NAMES *KOFF*. I TRIED TO FOLLOW THE DONATIONS TO FIGURE IT OUT...IT'S AS CLOSE AS I GOT.
COULD BE ALL THREE OF THEM ARE IN THE COURT. COULD BE *KOFF* NONE.
MR. MARCH, THE MORE YOU TALK--
I'M DEAD. HE KILLED ME. I GOT HIM BACK, THOUGH. ARMOR PIERCING, HEH. FRIEND ON THE FORCE...
BUT, BRUCE...
...BRUCE... YOU **KNOW HIM.** PLEASE, TELL HIM TO FIGHT THEM. THIS CITY, IT'S WORTH IT. IT CAN BE A GOOD PLACE.
REMIND HIM THAT...A BETTER GOTHAM IS JUST... *KOFF*...IS ONE DREAM...

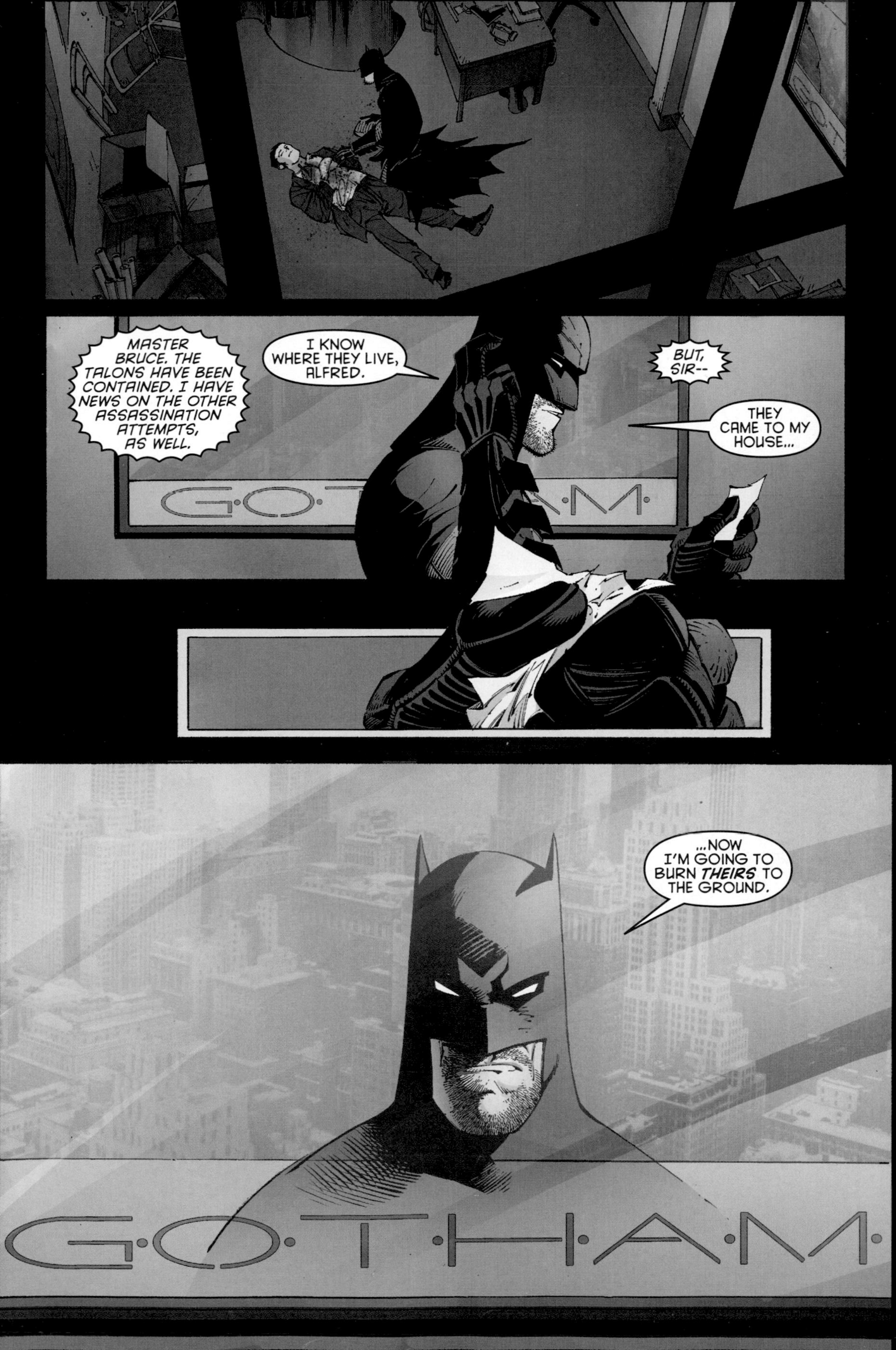
MASTER BRUCE. THE TALONS HAVE BEEN CONTAINED. I HAVE NEWS ON THE OTHER ASSASSINATION ATTEMPTS, AS WELL.
I KNOW WHERE THEY LIVE, ALFRED.
BUT, SIR--
THEY CAME TO MY HOUSE...
G·O·T·H·A·M
...NOW I'M GOING TO BURN *THEIRS* TO THE GROUND.
G·O·T·H·A·M

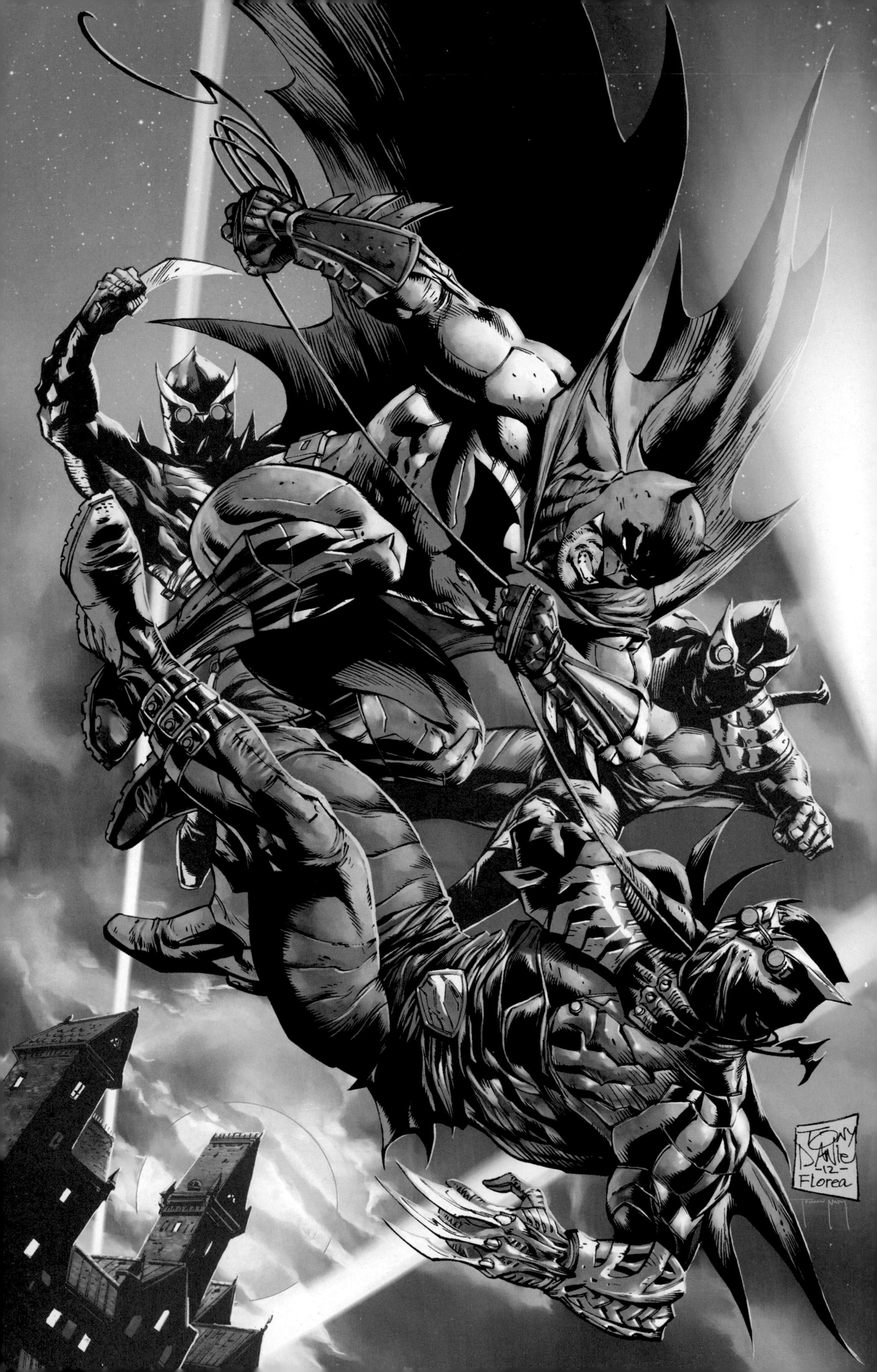

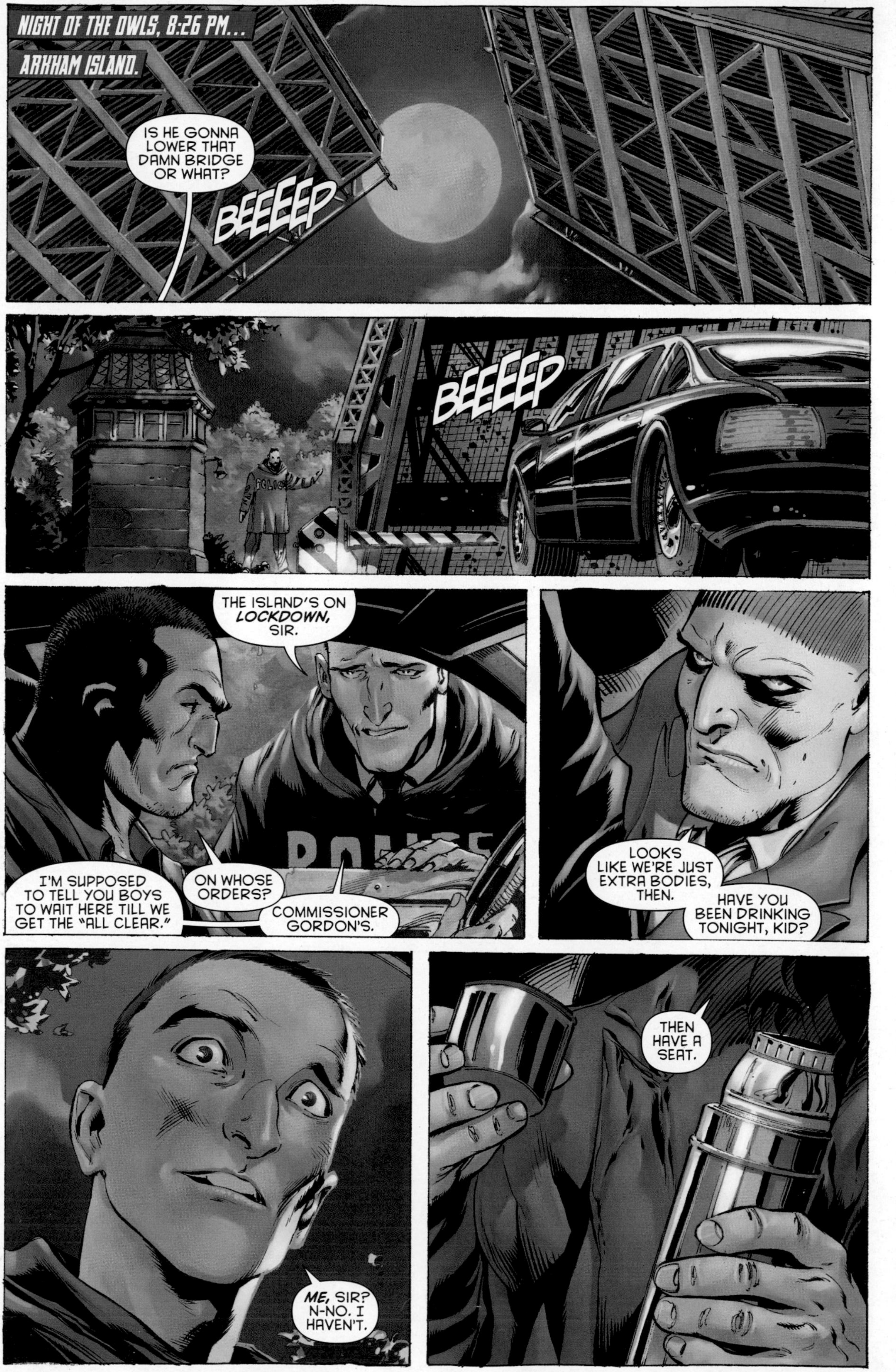
NIGHT OF THE OWLS, 8:26 PM...
ARKHAM ISLAND.
IS HE GONNA LOWER THAT DAMN BRIDGE OR WHAT?
BEEEEP
BEEEEP
THE ISLAND'S ON *LOCKDOWN,* SIR.
I'M SUPPOSED TO TELL YOU BOYS TO WAIT HERE TILL WE GET THE "ALL CLEAR."
ON WHOSE ORDERS?
COMMISSIONER GORDON'S.
LOOKS LIKE WE'RE JUST EXTRA BODIES, THEN.
HAVE YOU BEEN DRINKING TONIGHT, KID?
ME, SIR? N-NO. I HAVEN'T.
THEN HAVE A SEAT.

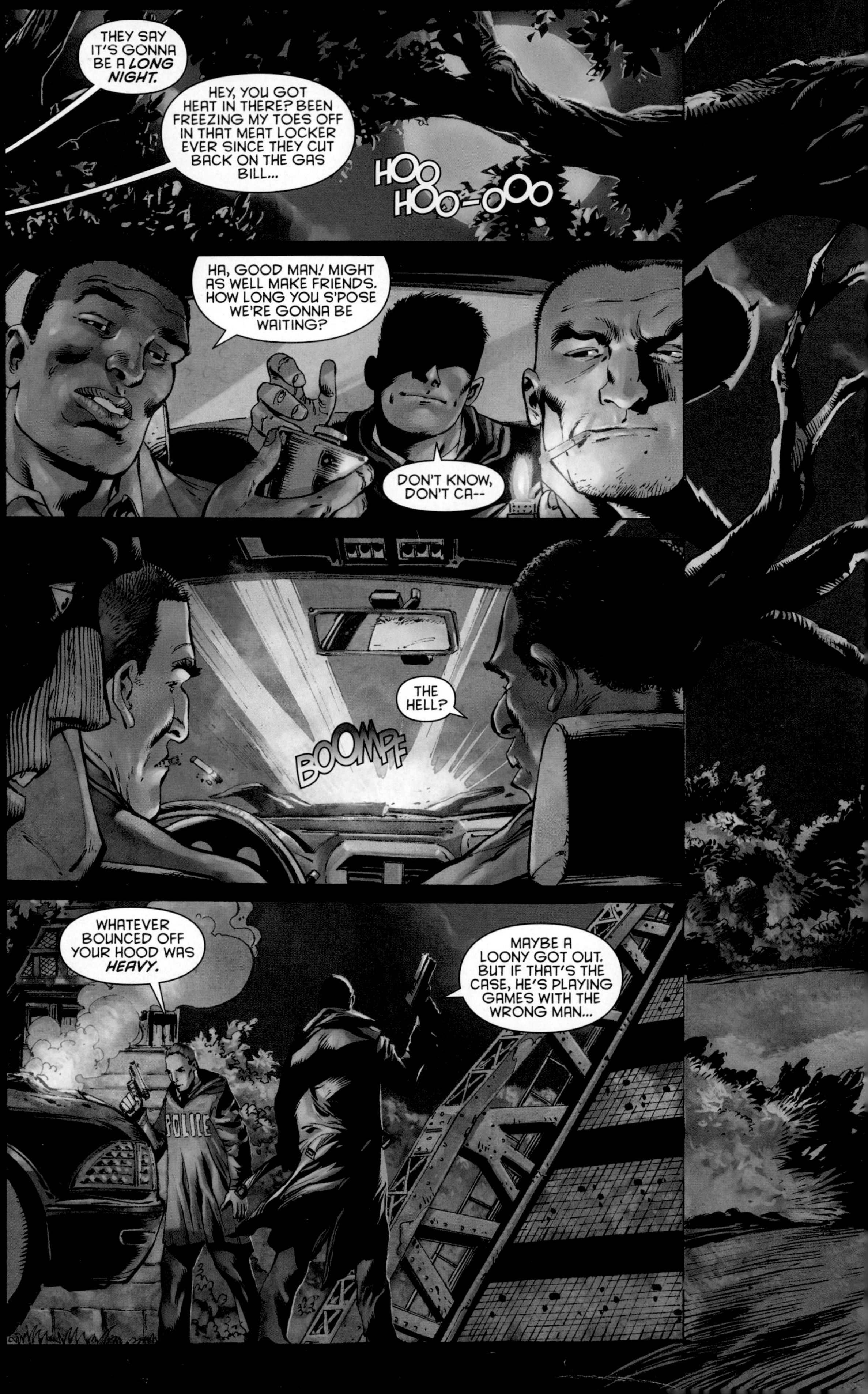
THEY SAY IT'S GONNA BE A LONG NIGHT.
HEY, YOU GOT HEAT IN THERE? BEEN FREEZING MY TOES OFF IN THAT MEAT LOCKER EVER SINCE THEY CUT BACK ON THE GAS BILL...
HOO HOO-OOO
HA, GOOD MAN! MIGHT AS WELL MAKE FRIENDS. HOW LONG YOU S'POSE WE'RE GONNA BE WAITING?
DON'T KNOW, DON'T CA--
THE HELL?
BOOMPF
WHATEVER BOUNCED OFF YOUR HOOD WAS HEAVY.
MAYBE A LOONY GOT OUT. BUT IF THAT'S THE CASE, HE'S PLAYING GAMES WITH THE WRONG MAN...
POLICE

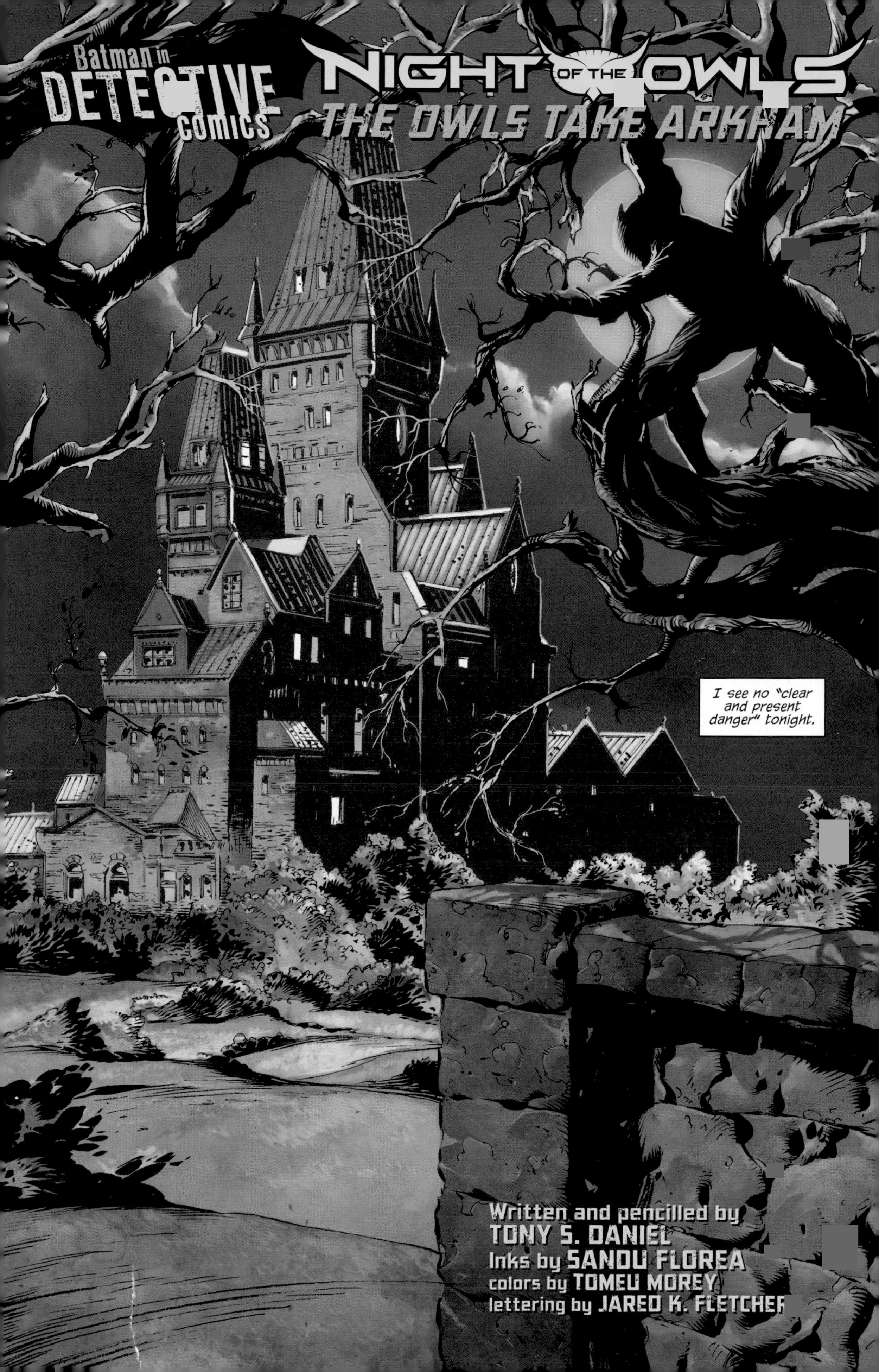
Batman in DETECTIVE COMICS
NIGHT OF THE OWLS
THE OWLS TAKE ARKHAM
I see no "clear and present danger" tonight.
Written and pencilled by TONY S. DANIEL
Inks by SANDU FLOREA
colors by TOMEU MOREY
lettering by JARED K. FLETCHER

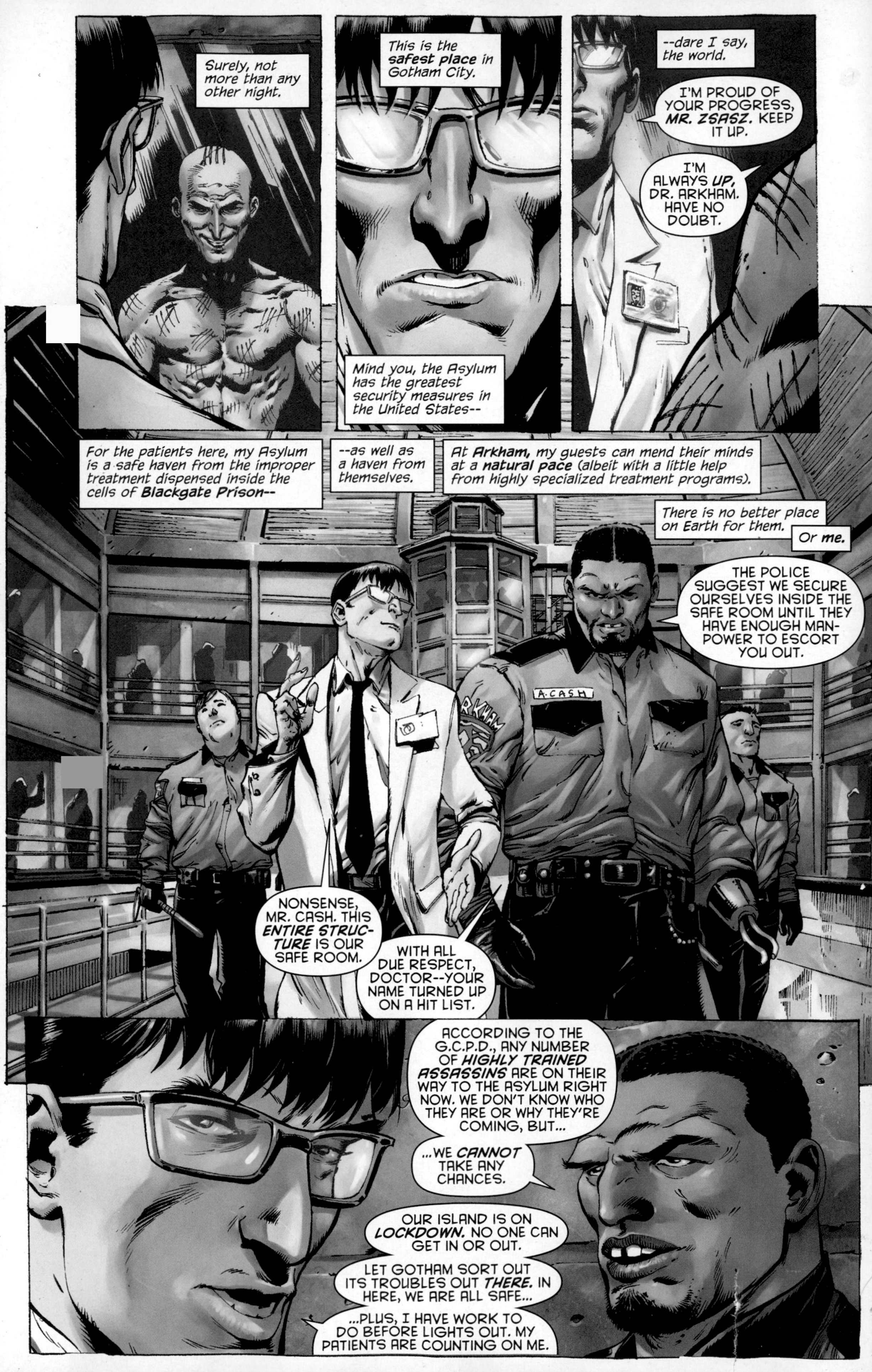
Surely, not more than any other night.
This is the safest place in Gotham City.
Mind you, the Asylum has the greatest security measures in the United States--
--dare I say, the world.
I'M PROUD OF YOUR PROGRESS, MR. ZSASZ. KEEP IT UP.
I'M ALWAYS UP, DR. ARKHAM. HAVE NO DOUBT.
For the patients here, my Asylum is a safe haven from the improper treatment dispensed inside the cells of Blackgate Prison--
--as well as a haven from themselves.
At Arkham, my guests can mend their minds at a natural pace (albeit with a little help from highly specialized treatment programs).
There is no better place on Earth for them.
Or me.
A. CASH
THE POLICE SUGGEST WE SECURE OURSELVES INSIDE THE SAFE ROOM UNTIL THEY HAVE ENOUGH MAN-POWER TO ESCORT YOU OUT.
NONSENSE, MR. CASH. THIS ENTIRE STRUCTURE IS OUR SAFE ROOM.
WITH ALL DUE RESPECT, DOCTOR--YOUR NAME TURNED UP ON A HIT LIST.
ACCORDING TO THE G.C.P.D., ANY NUMBER OF HIGHLY TRAINED ASSASSINS ARE ON THEIR WAY TO THE ASYLUM RIGHT NOW. WE DON'T KNOW WHO THEY ARE OR WHY THEY'RE COMING, BUT...
...WE CANNOT TAKE ANY CHANCES.
OUR ISLAND IS ON LOCKDOWN. NO ONE CAN GET IN OR OUT.
LET GOTHAM SORT OUT ITS TROUBLES OUT THERE. IN HERE, WE ARE ALL SAFE...
...PLUS, I HAVE WORK TO DO BEFORE LIGHTS OUT. MY PATIENTS ARE COUNTING ON ME.

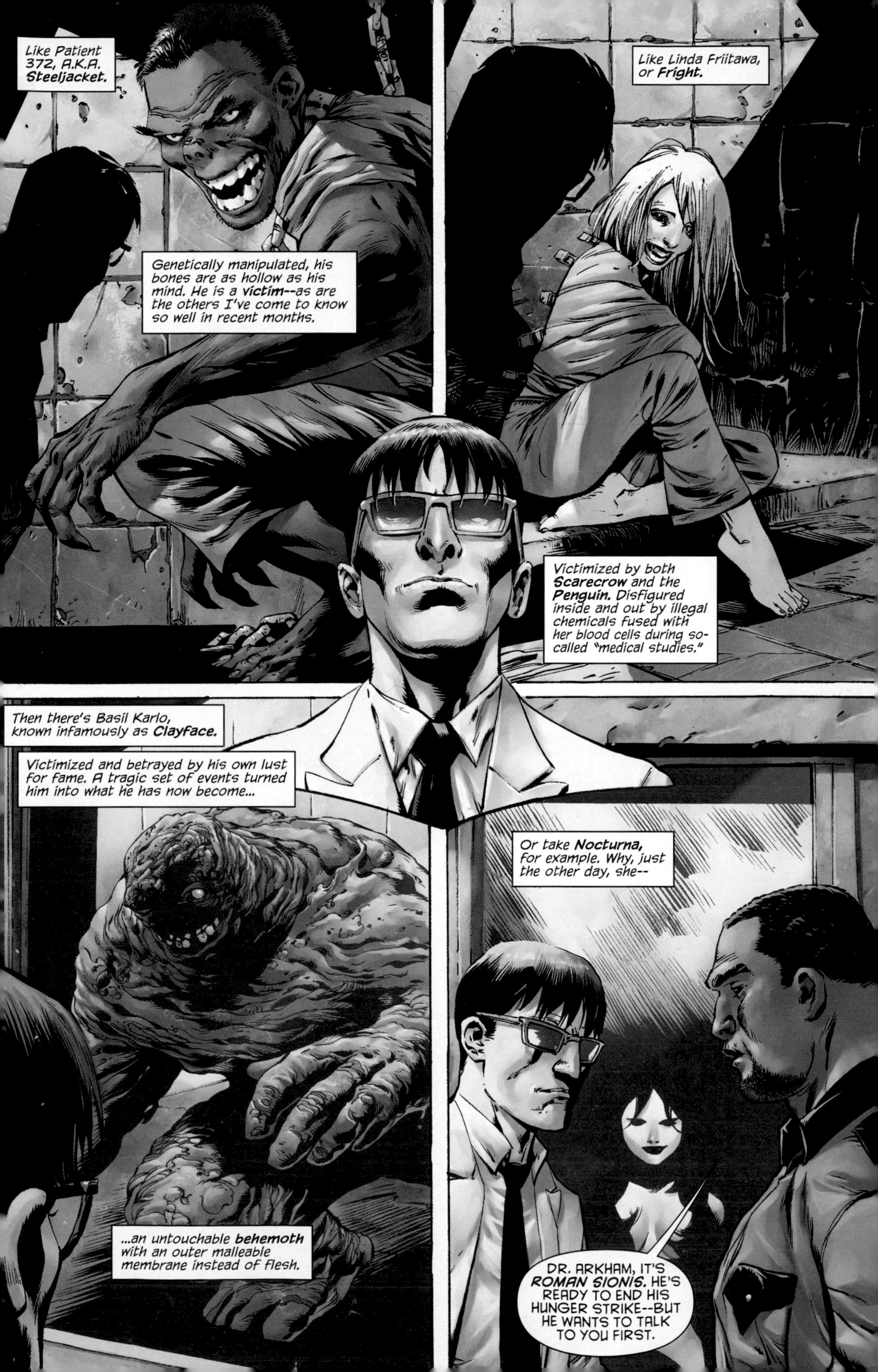
Like Patient 372, A.K.A. Steeljacket.
Genetically manipulated, his bones are as hollow as his mind. He is a victim--as are the others I've come to know so well in recent months.
Like Linda Friitawa, or Fright.
Victimized by both Scarecrow and the Penguin. Disfigured inside and out by illegal chemicals fused with her blood cells during so-called "medical studies."
Then there's Basil Karlo, known infamously as Clayface.
Victimized and betrayed by his own lust for fame. A tragic set of events turned him into what he has now become...
...an untouchable behemoth with an outer malleable membrane instead of flesh.
Or take Nocturna, for example. Why, just the other day, she--
DR. ARKHAM, IT'S ROMAN SIONIS. HE'S READY TO END HIS HUNGER STRIKE--BUT HE WANTS TO TALK TO YOU FIRST.

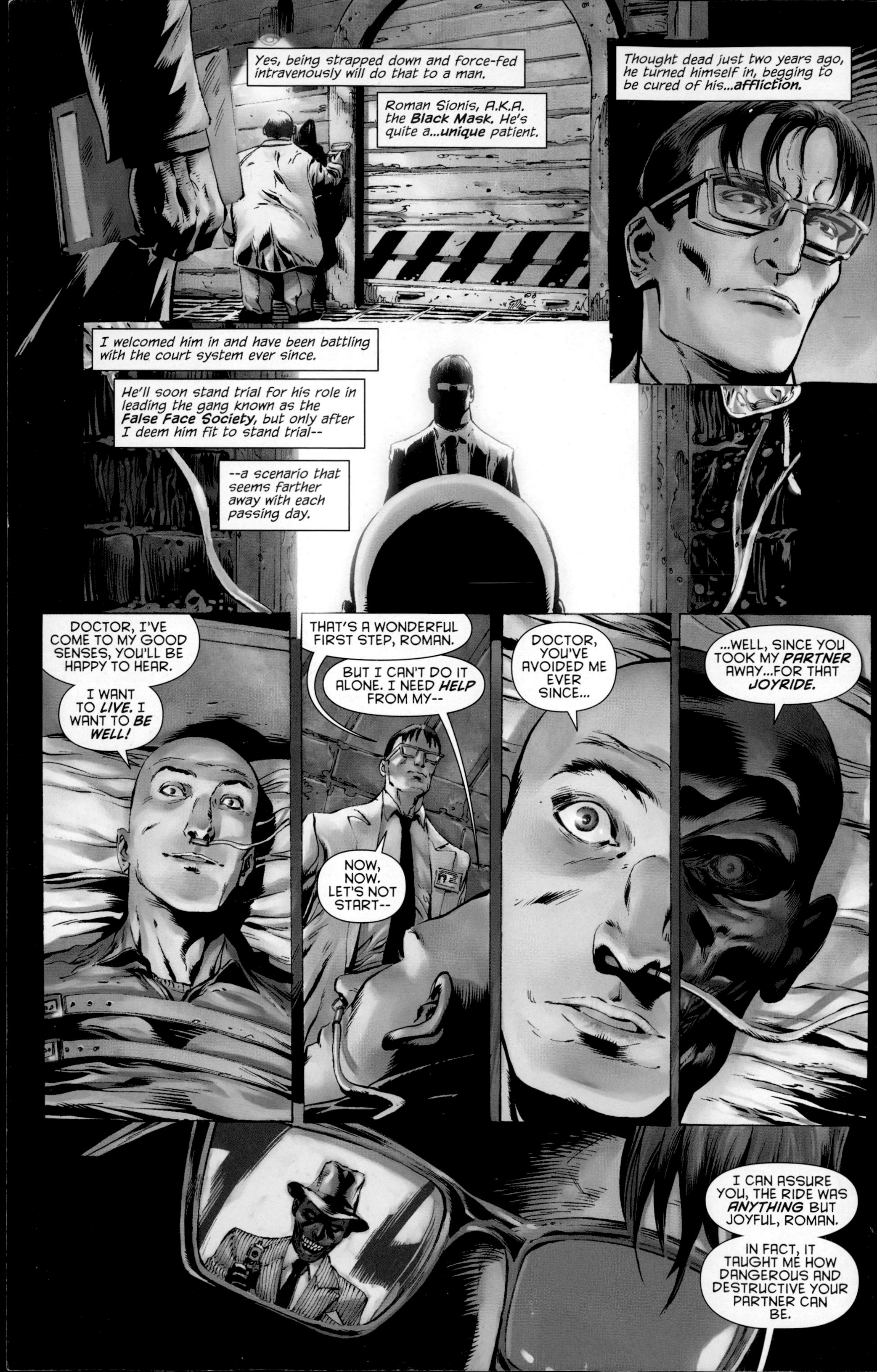
Yes, being strapped down and force-fed intravenously will do that to a man.
Roman Sionis, A.K.A. the **Black Mask.** He's quite a...**unique** patient.
Thought dead just two years ago, he turned himself in, begging to be cured of his...**affliction.**
I welcomed him in and have been battling with the court system ever since.
He'll soon stand trial for his role in leading the gang known as the **False Face Society,** but only after I deem him fit to stand trial--
--a scenario that seems farther away with each passing day.
DOCTOR, I'VE COME TO MY GOOD SENSES, YOU'LL BE HAPPY TO HEAR.
I WANT TO ***LIVE.*** I WANT TO ***BE WELL!***
THAT'S A WONDERFUL FIRST STEP, ROMAN.
BUT I CAN'T DO IT ALONE. I NEED ***HELP*** FROM MY--
NOW, NOW. LET'S NOT START--
DOCTOR, YOU'VE AVOIDED ME EVER SINCE...
...WELL, SINCE YOU TOOK MY ***PARTNER*** AWAY...FOR THAT ***JOYRIDE.***
I CAN ASSURE YOU, THE RIDE WAS ***ANYTHING*** BUT JOYFUL, ROMAN.
IN FACT, IT TAUGHT ME HOW DANGEROUS AND DESTRUCTIVE YOUR PARTNER CAN BE.

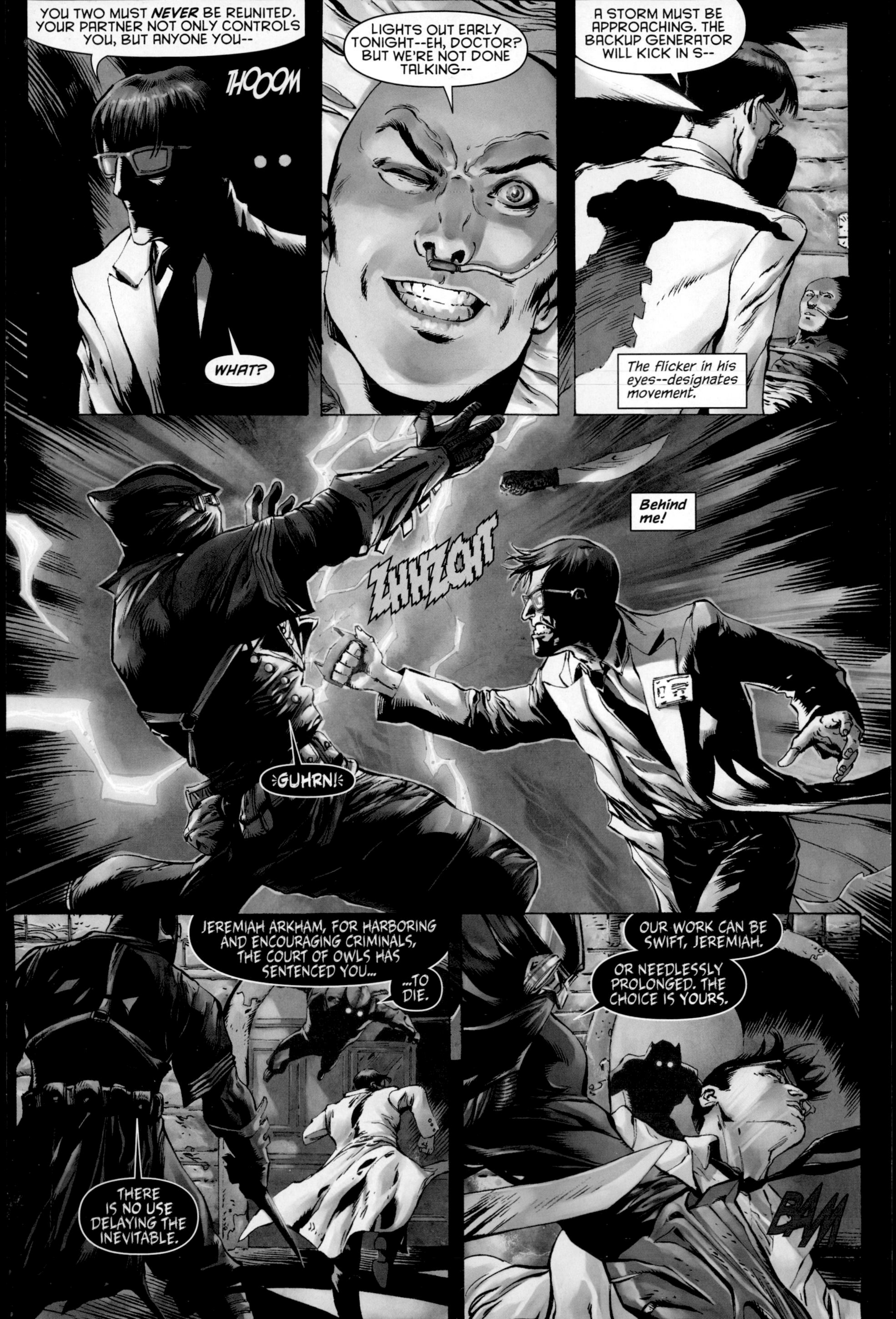
YOU TWO MUST NEVER BE REUNITED. YOUR PARTNER NOT ONLY CONTROLS YOU, BUT ANYONE YOU--
THOOOM
WHAT?
LIGHTS OUT EARLY TONIGHT--EH, DOCTOR? BUT WE'RE NOT DONE TALKING--
A STORM MUST BE APPROACHING. THE BACKUP GENERATOR WILL KICK IN S--
The flicker in his eyes--designates movement.
Behind me!
ZHHZCHT
GUHRN!
JEREMIAH ARKHAM, FOR HARBORING AND ENCOURAGING CRIMINALS, THE COURT OF OWLS HAS SENTENCED YOU...
...TO DIE.
THERE IS NO USE DELAYING THE INEVITABLE.
OUR WORK CAN BE SWIFT, JEREMIAH.
OR NEEDLESSLY PROLONGED. THE CHOICE IS YOURS.
BAM

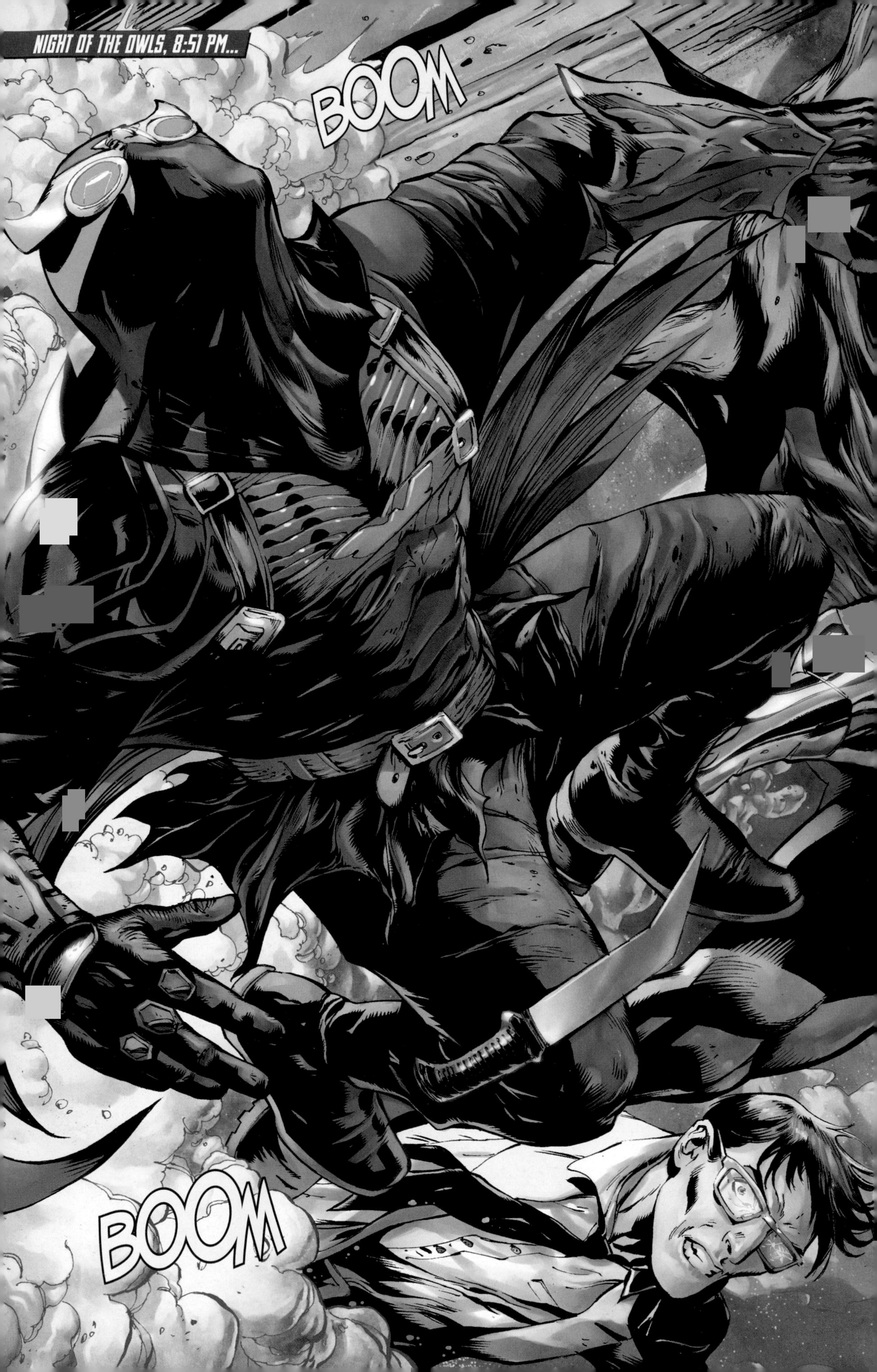
NIGHT OF THE OWLS, 8:51 PM...
BOOM
BOOM

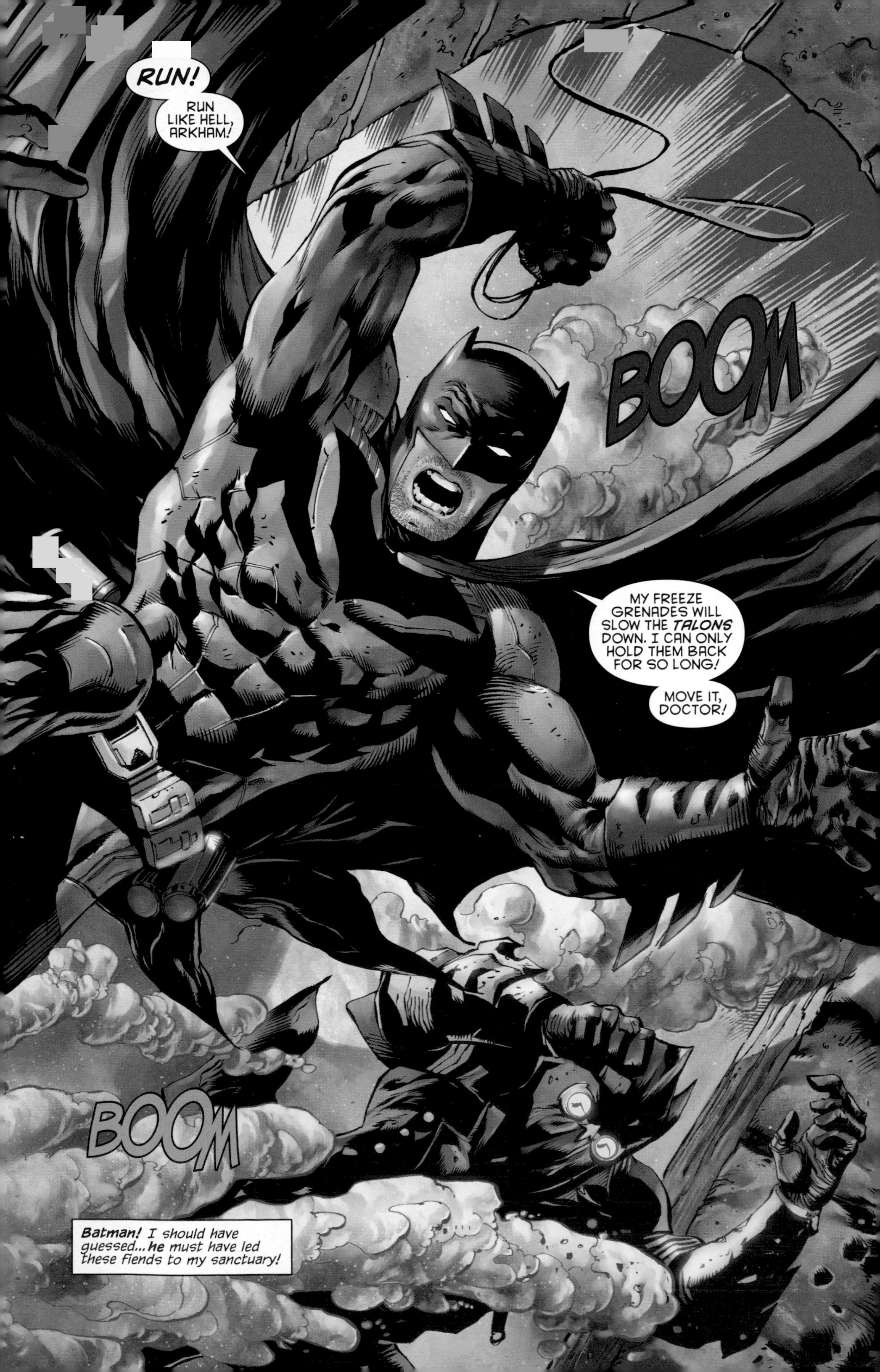
RUN!
RUN LIKE HELL, ARKHAM!
BOOM
MY FREEZE GRENADES WILL SLOW THE TALONS DOWN. I CAN ONLY HOLD THEM BACK FOR SO LONG!
MOVE IT, DOCTOR!
BOOM
Batman! I should have guessed...he must have led these fiends to my sanctuary!

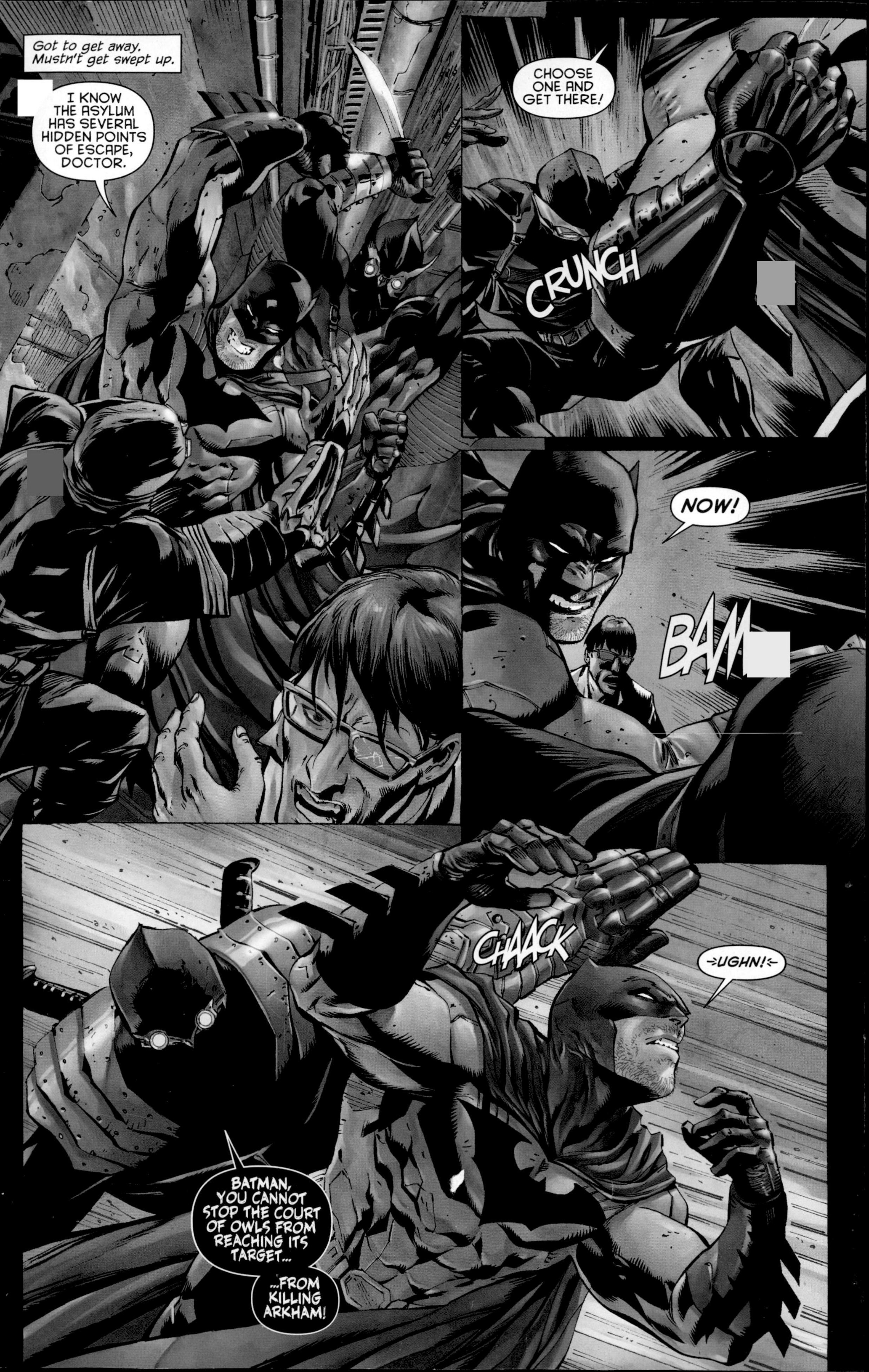
Got to get away. Mustn't get swept up.
I KNOW THE ASYLUM HAS SEVERAL HIDDEN POINTS OF ESCAPE, DOCTOR.
CHOOSE ONE AND GET THERE!
CRUNCH
NOW!
BAM
CHAACK
UGHN!
BATMAN, YOU CANNOT STOP THE COURT OF OWLS FROM REACHING ITS TARGET...
...FROM KILLING ARKHAM!

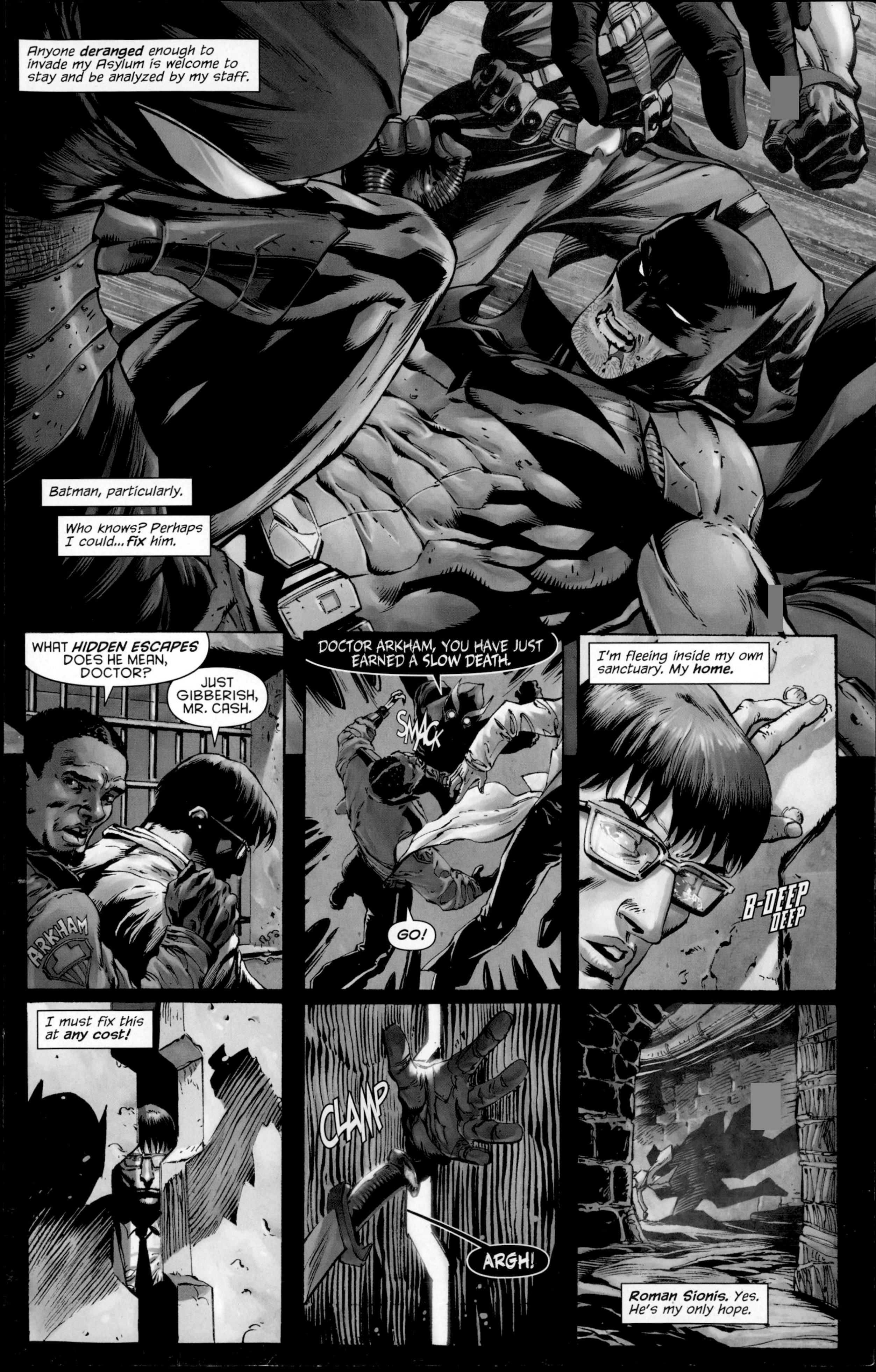
Anyone deranged enough to invade my Asylum is welcome to stay and be analyzed by my staff.
Batman, particularly.
Who knows? Perhaps I could... fix him.
WHAT HIDDEN ESCAPES DOES HE MEAN, DOCTOR?
JUST GIBBERISH, MR. CASH.
ARKHAM
DOCTOR ARKHAM, YOU HAVE JUST EARNED A SLOW DEATH.
SMACK
GO!
I'm fleeing inside my own sanctuary. My home.
B-DEEP DEEP
I must fix this at any cost!
CLAMP
ARGH!
Roman Sionis. Yes. He's my only hope.

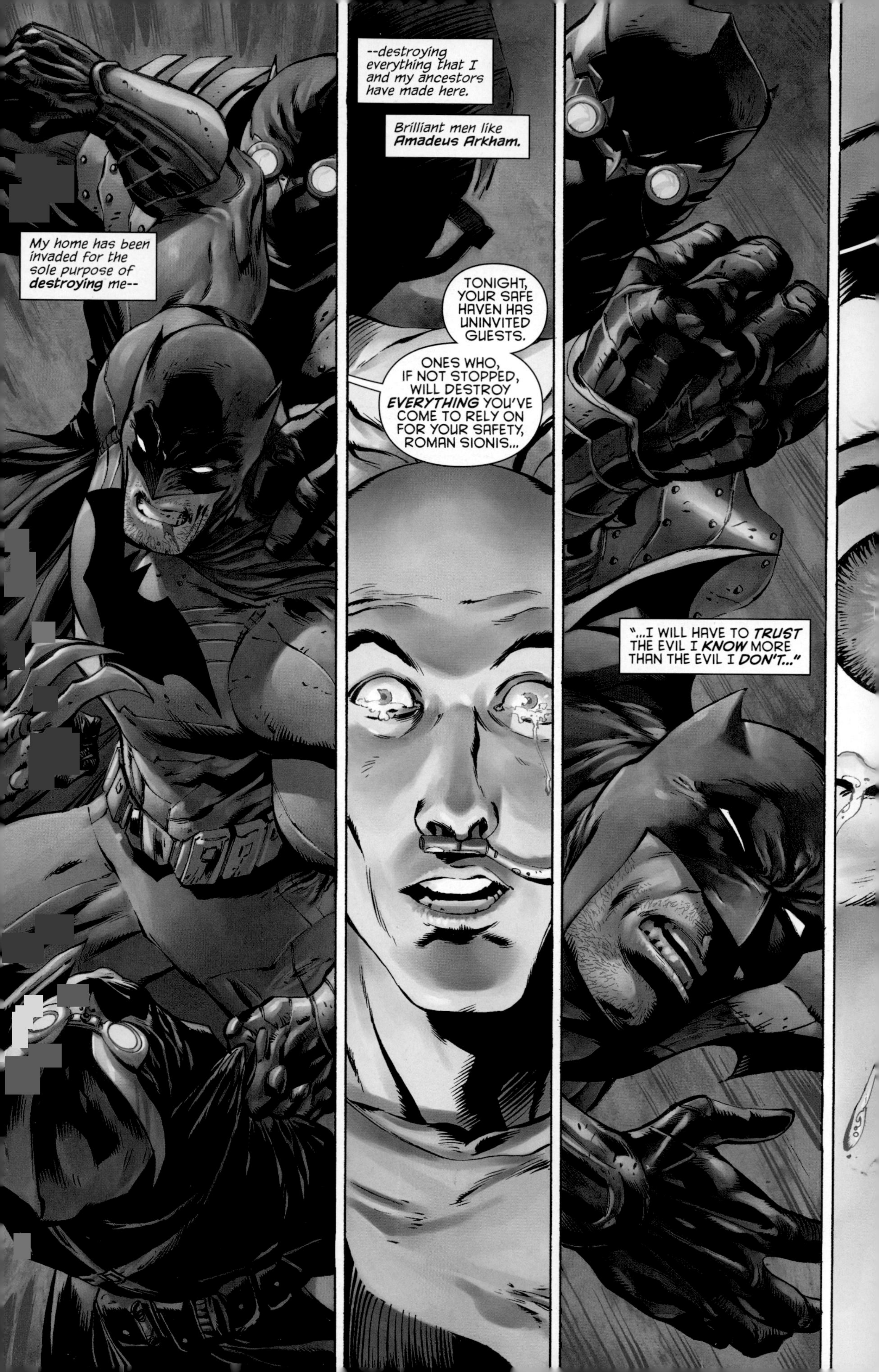
My home has been invaded for the sole purpose of *destroying* me--
--destroying everything that I and my ancestors have made here.
Brilliant men like *Amadeus Arkham.*
TONIGHT, YOUR SAFE HAVEN HAS UNINVITED GUESTS.
ONES WHO, IF NOT STOPPED, WILL DESTROY *EVERYTHING* YOU'VE COME TO RELY ON FOR YOUR SAFETY, ROMAN SIONIS...
"...I WILL HAVE TO *TRUST* THE EVIL I *KNOW* MORE THAN THE EVIL I *DON'T*..."

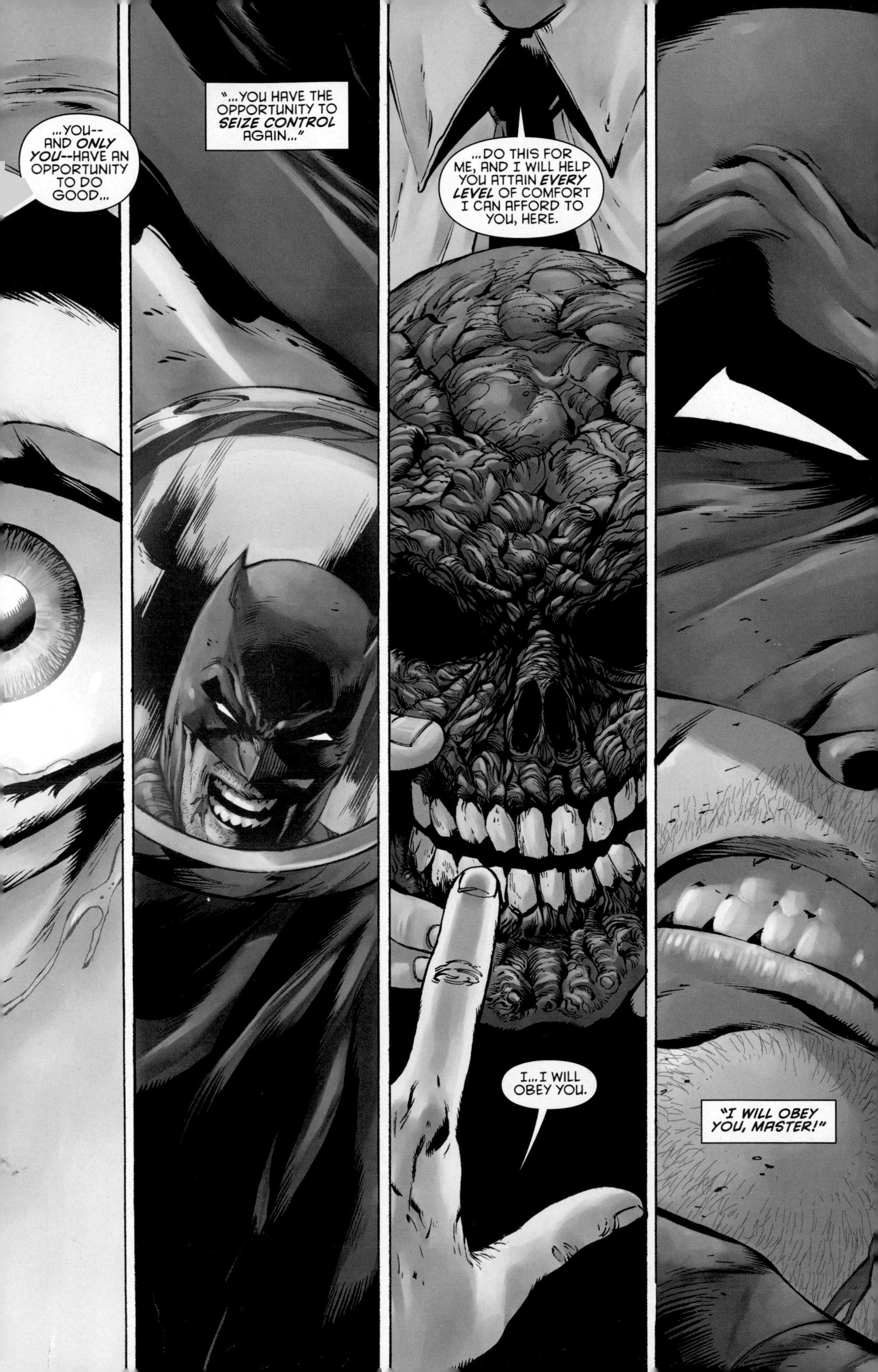
...YOU--
AND ONLY YOU--HAVE AN OPPORTUNITY TO DO GOOD...
"...YOU HAVE THE OPPORTUNITY TO SEIZE CONTROL AGAIN..."
...DO THIS FOR ME, AND I WILL HELP YOU ATTAIN EVERY LEVEL OF COMFORT I CAN AFFORD TO YOU, HERE.
I...I WILL OBEY YOU.
"I WILL OBEY YOU, MASTER!"

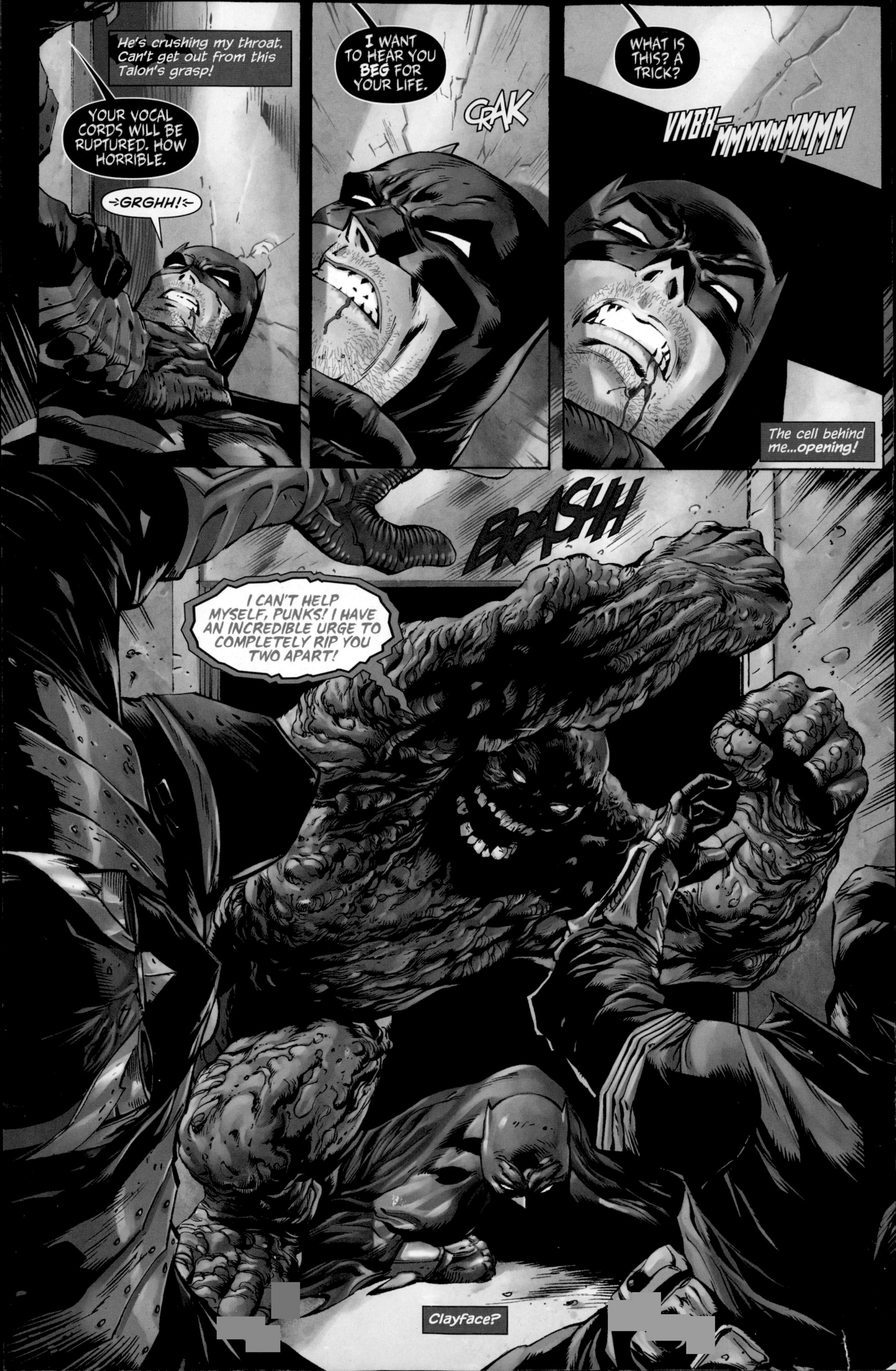
He's crushing my throat. Can't get out from this Talon's grasp!
YOUR VOCAL CORDS WILL BE RUPTURED. HOW HORRIBLE.
GRGHH!
I WANT TO HEAR YOU BEG FOR YOUR LIFE.
CRAK
WHAT IS THIS? A TRICK?
VMBK—MMMMMMMMM
The cell behind me...opening!
BRASHH
I CAN'T HELP MYSELF, PUNKS! I HAVE AN INCREDIBLE URGE TO COMPLETELY RIP YOU TWO APART!
Clayface?

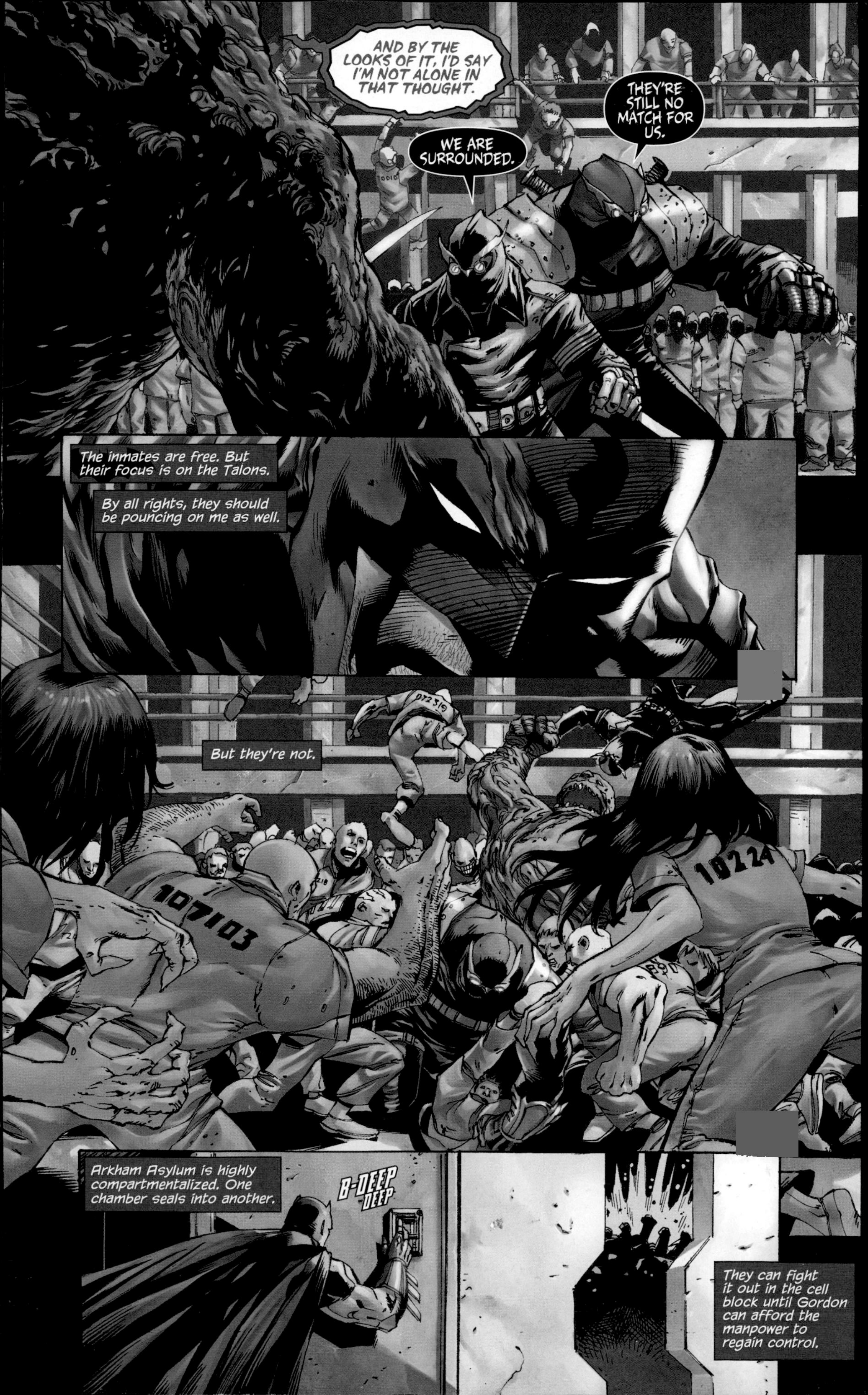
AND BY THE LOOKS OF IT, I'D SAY I'M NOT ALONE IN THAT THOUGHT.
WE ARE SURROUNDED.
THEY'RE STILL NO MATCH FOR US.
The inmates are free. But their focus is on the Talons.
By all rights, they should be pouncing on me as well.
But they're not.
Arkham Asylum is highly compartmentalized. One chamber seals into another.
B-DEEP DEEP
They can fight it out in the cell block until Gordon can afford the manpower to regain control.

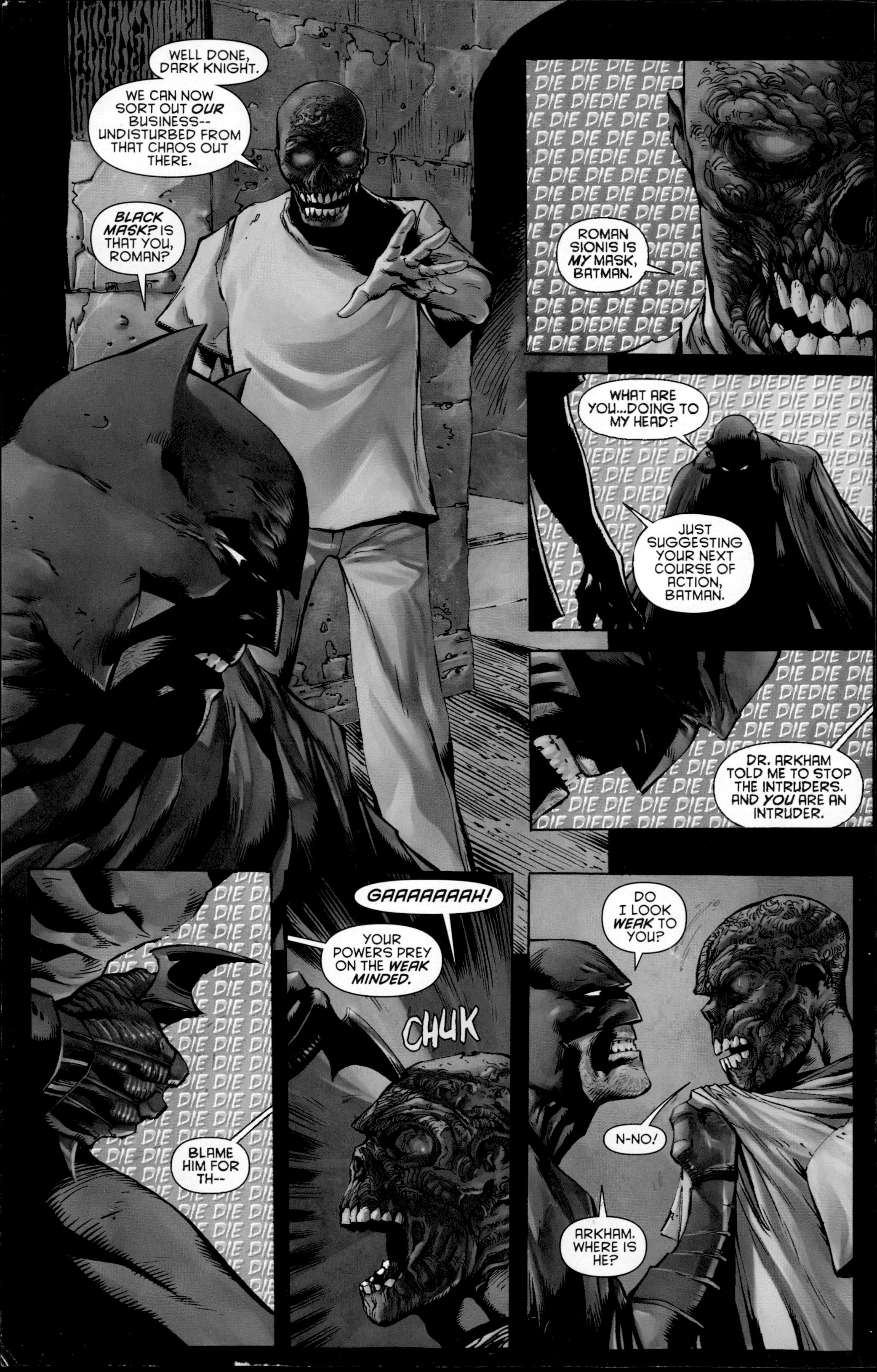
WELL DONE, DARK KNIGHT.
WE CAN NOW SORT OUT *OUR* BUSINESS-- UNDISTURBED FROM THAT CHAOS OUT THERE.
BLACK MASK? IS THAT YOU, ROMAN?
ROMAN SIONIS IS *MY* MASK, BATMAN.
WHAT ARE YOU...DOING TO MY HEAD?
JUST SUGGESTING YOUR NEXT COURSE OF ACTION, BATMAN.
DR. ARKHAM TOLD ME TO STOP THE INTRUDERS. AND *YOU* ARE AN INTRUDER.
BLAME HIM FOR TH--
GAAAAAAAH!
YOUR POWERS PREY ON THE *WEAK MINDED.*
CHUK
DO I LOOK *WEAK* TO YOU?
N-NO!
ARKHAM. WHERE IS HE?

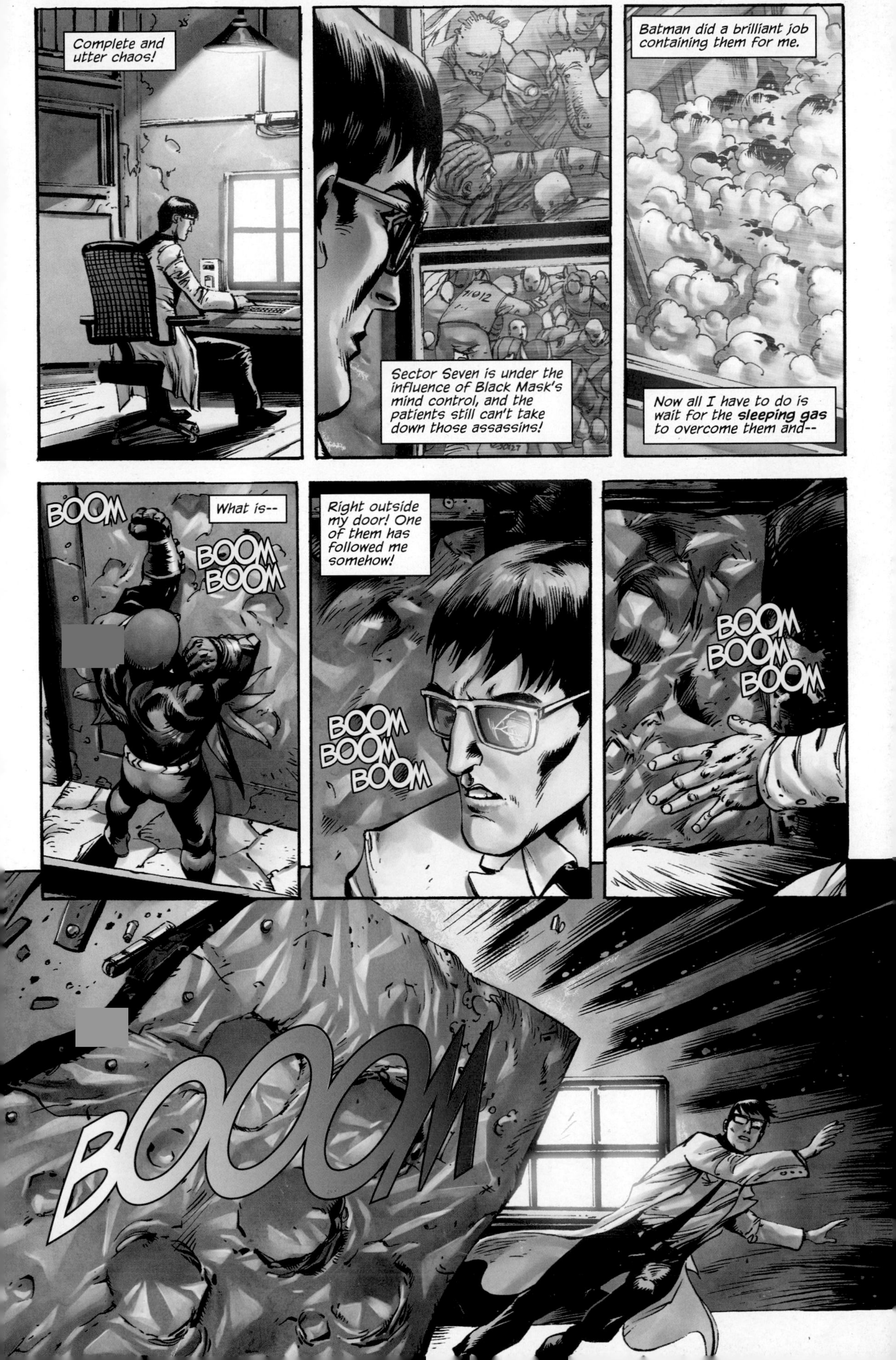
Complete and utter chaos!
Sector Seven is under the influence of Black Mask's mind control, and the patients still can't take down those assassins!
Batman did a brilliant job containing them for me.
Now all I have to do is wait for the **sleeping gas** to overcome them and--
BOOM
What is--
BOOM BOOM
Right outside my door! One of them has followed me somehow!
BOOM BOOM BOOM
BOOM BOOM BOOM
BOOOM

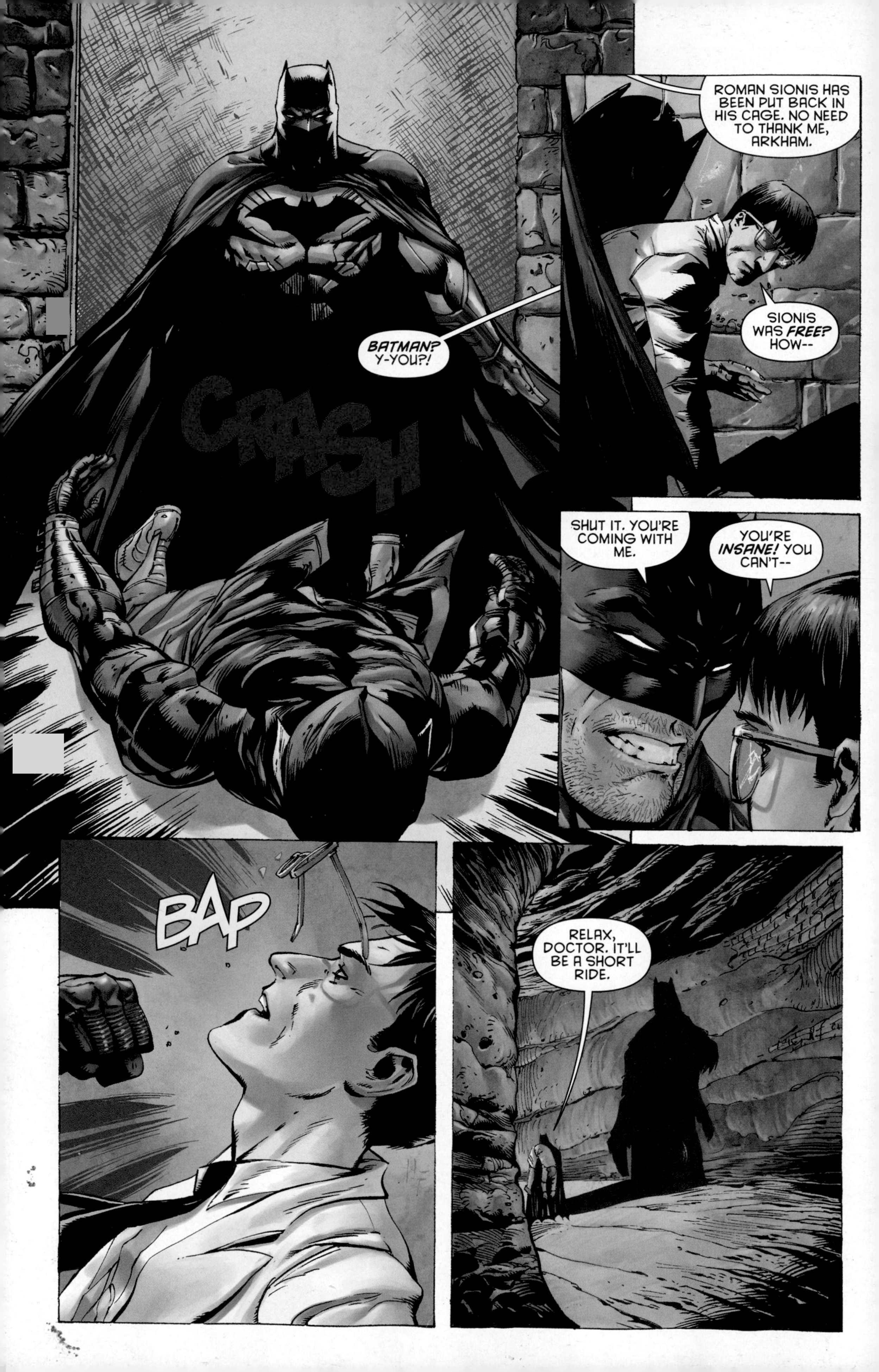
ROMAN SIONIS HAS BEEN PUT BACK IN HIS CAGE. NO NEED TO THANK ME, ARKHAM.
BATMAN? Y-YOU?!
CRASH
SIONIS WAS *FREE?* HOW--
SHUT IT. YOU'RE COMING WITH ME.
YOU'RE *INSANE!* YOU CAN'T--
BAP
RELAX, DOCTOR. IT'LL BE A SHORT RIDE.

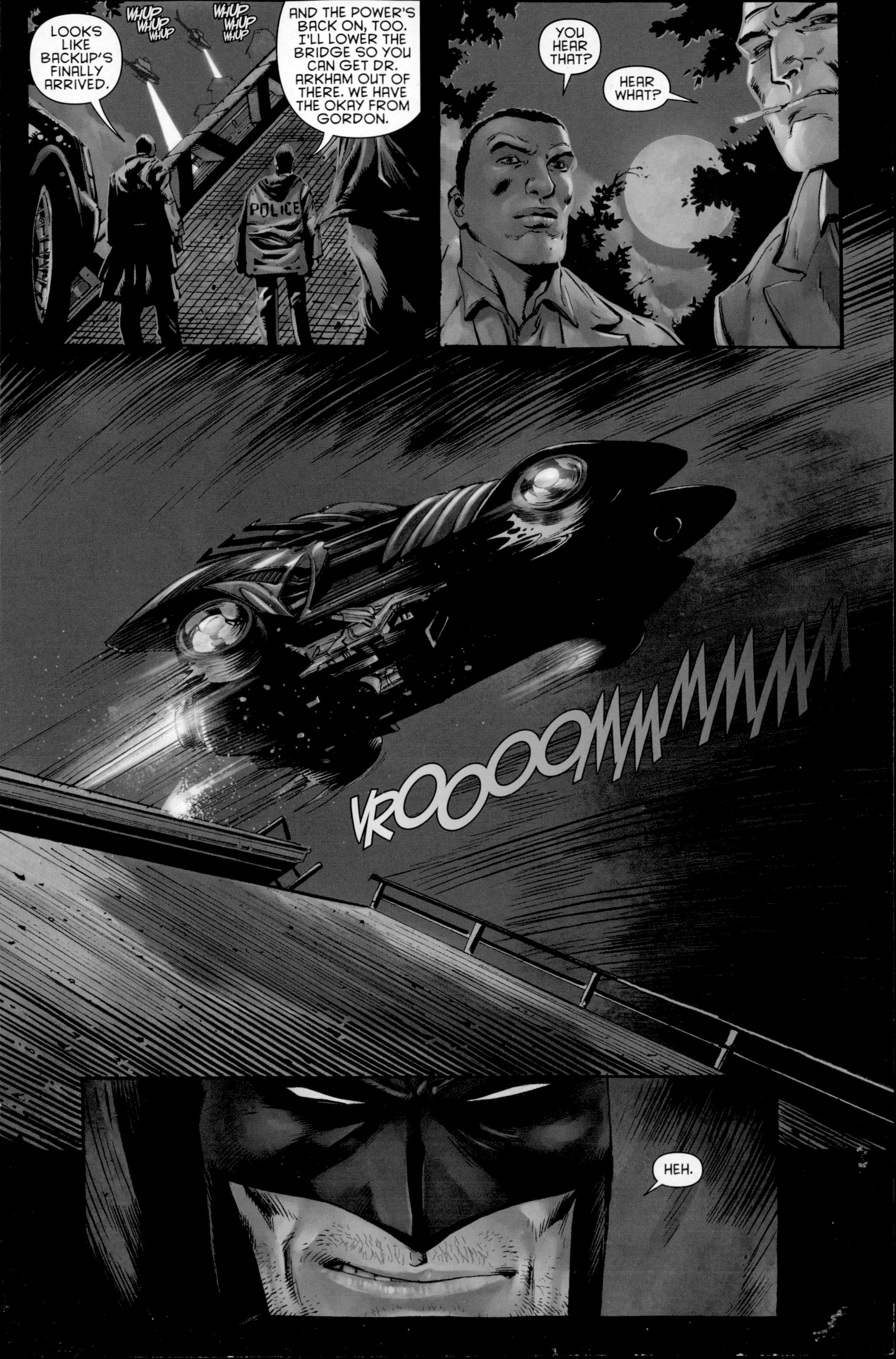

WHUP WHUP WHUP
WHUP WHUP WHUP
LOOKS LIKE BACKUP'S FINALLY ARRIVED.
AND THE POWER'S BACK ON, TOO. I'LL LOWER THE BRIDGE SO YOU CAN GET DR. ARKHAM OUT OF THERE. WE HAVE THE OKAY FROM GORDON.
POLICE
YOU HEAR THAT?
HEAR WHAT?
VROOOOMMMMMMMM
HEH.

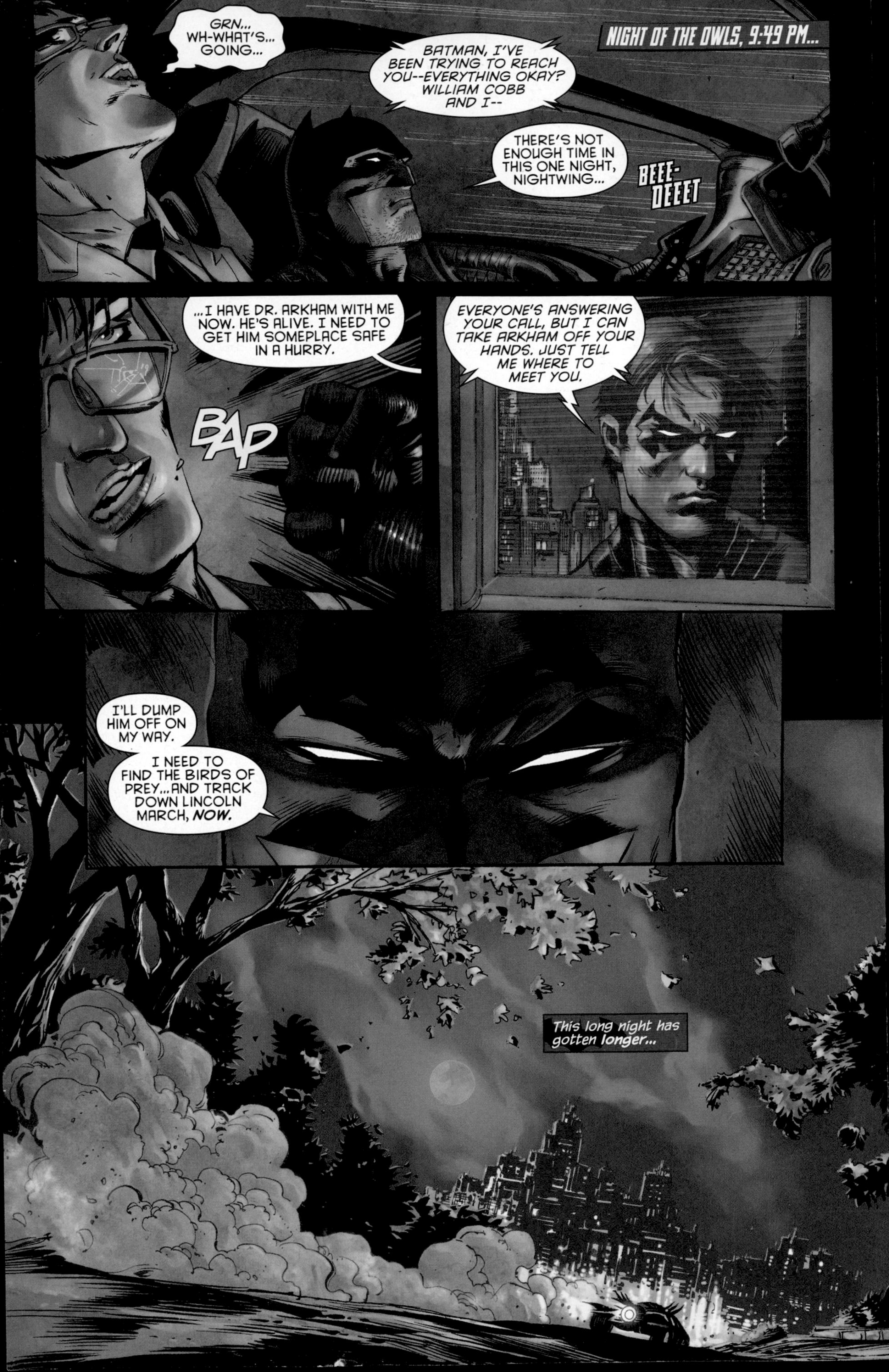
NIGHT OF THE OWLS, 9:49 PM...
GRN... WH-WHAT'S... GOING...
BATMAN, I'VE BEEN TRYING TO REACH YOU--EVERYTHING OKAY? WILLIAM COBB AND I--
THERE'S NOT ENOUGH TIME IN THIS ONE NIGHT, NIGHTWING...
BEEE-DEEET
...I HAVE DR. ARKHAM WITH ME NOW. HE'S ALIVE. I NEED TO GET HIM SOMEPLACE SAFE IN A HURRY.
BAP
EVERYONE'S ANSWERING YOUR CALL, BUT I CAN TAKE ARKHAM OFF YOUR HANDS. JUST TELL ME WHERE TO MEET YOU.
I'LL DUMP HIM OFF ON MY WAY.
I NEED TO FIND THE BIRDS OF PREY...AND TRACK DOWN LINCOLN MARCH, NOW.
This long night has gotten longer...

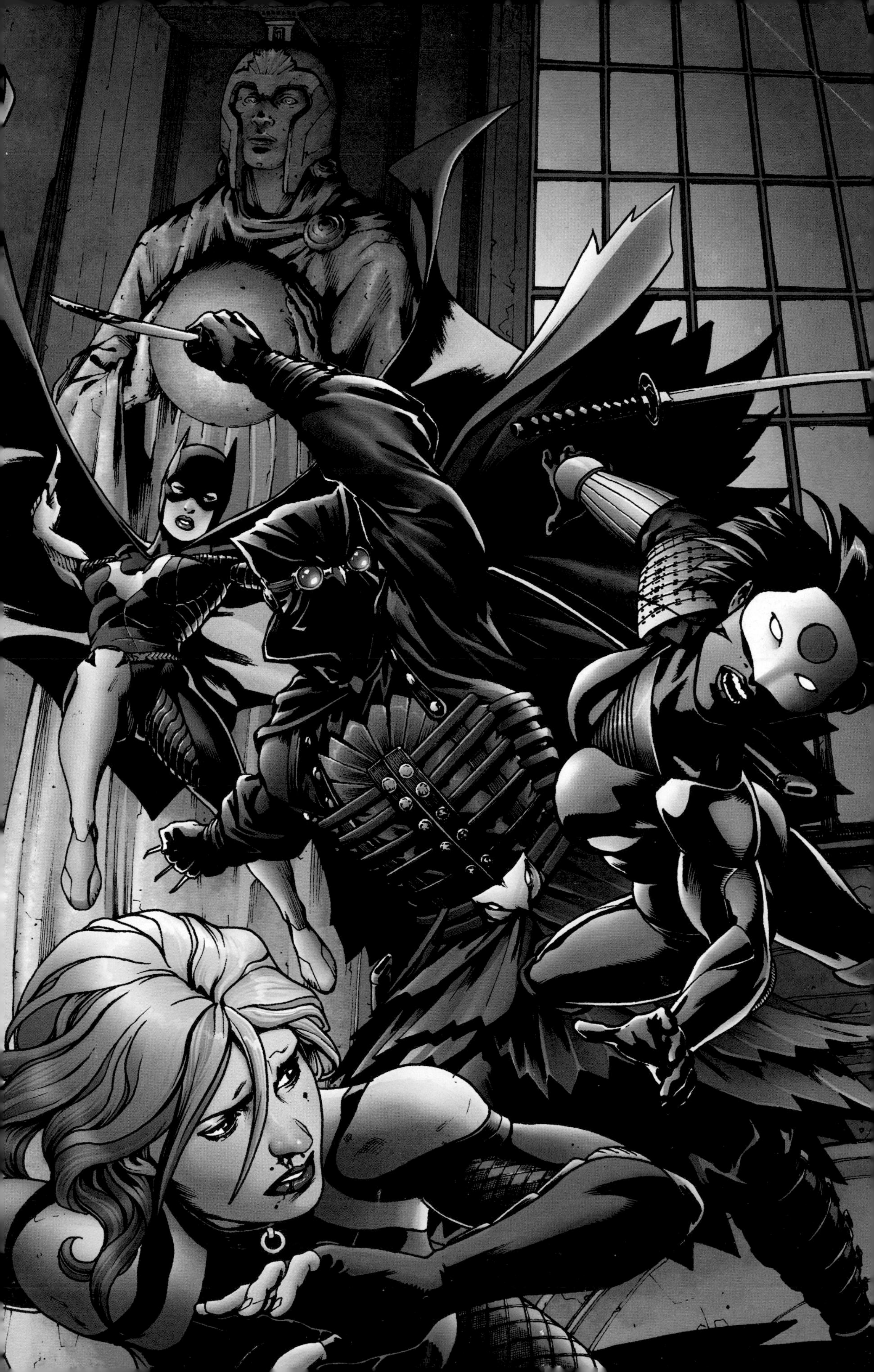

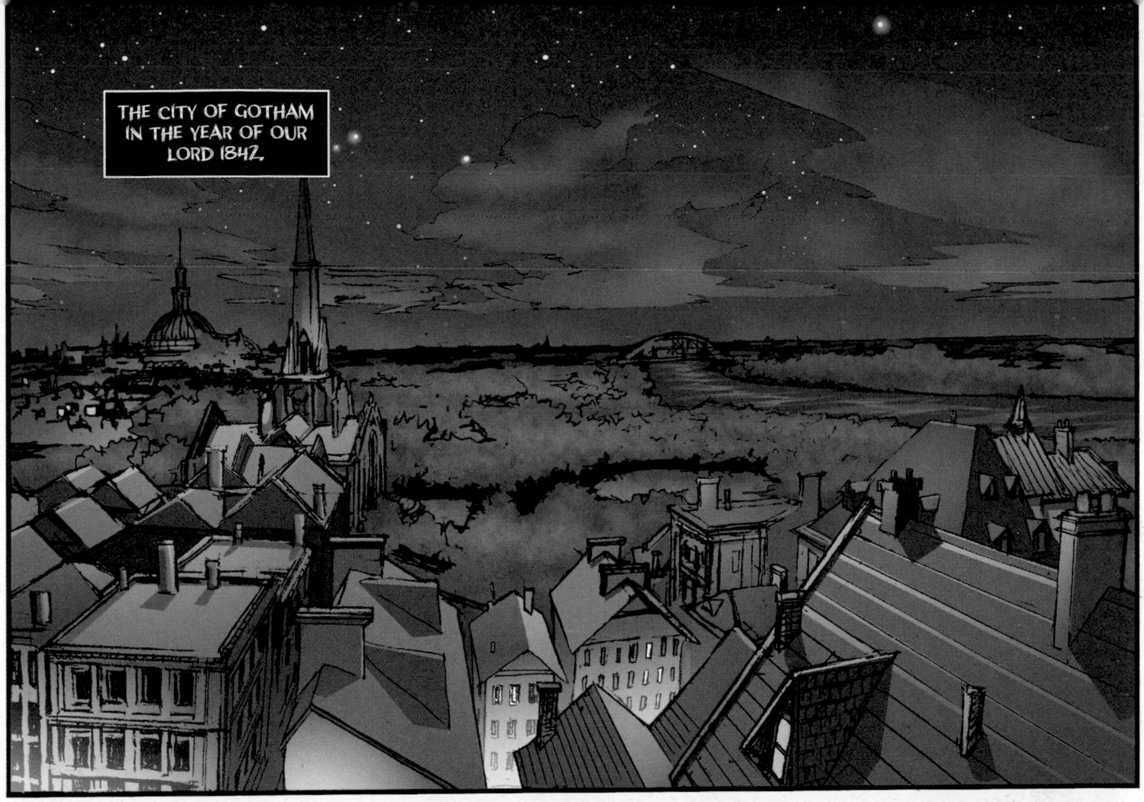
THE CITY OF GOTHAM IN THE YEAR OF OUR LORD 1842.

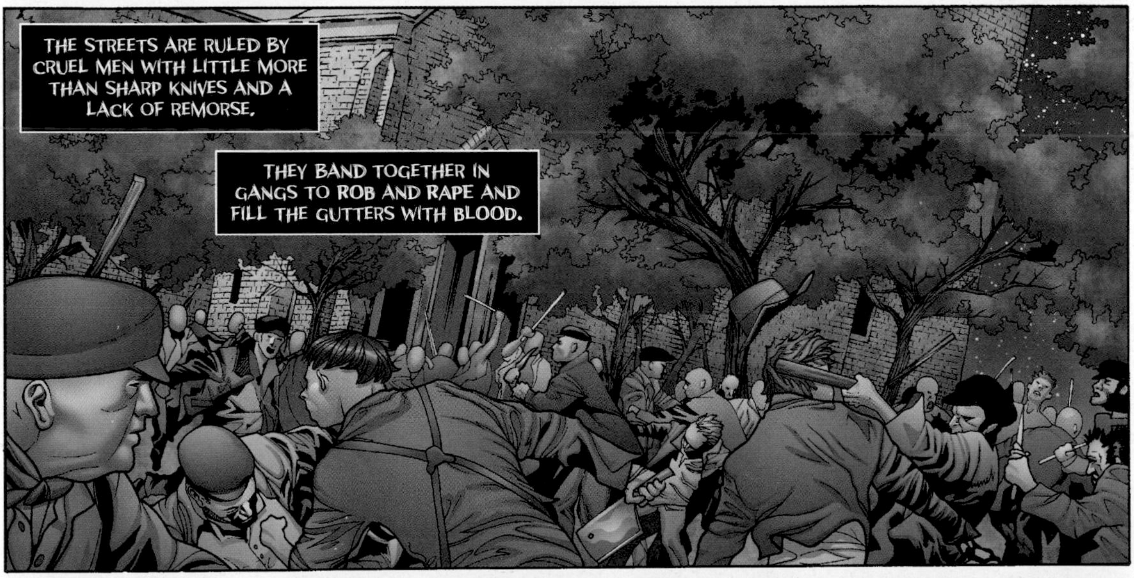
THE STREETS ARE RULED BY CRUEL MEN WITH LITTLE MORE THAN SHARP KNIVES AND A LACK OF REMORSE.
THEY BAND TOGETHER IN GANGS TO ROB AND RAPE AND FILL THE GUTTERS WITH BLOOD.

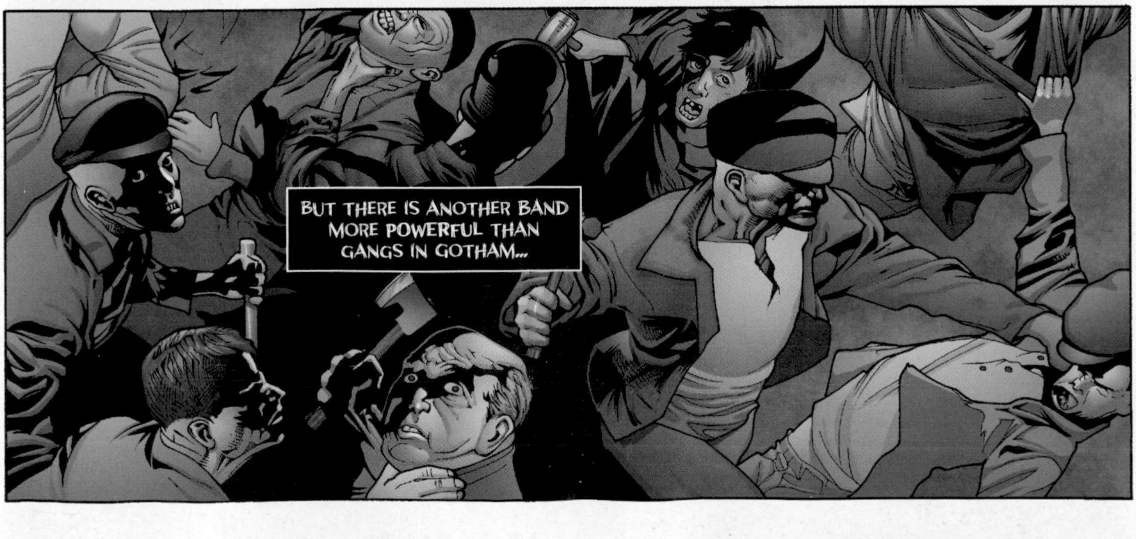
BUT THERE IS ANOTHER BAND MORE POWERFUL THAN GANGS IN GOTHAM...

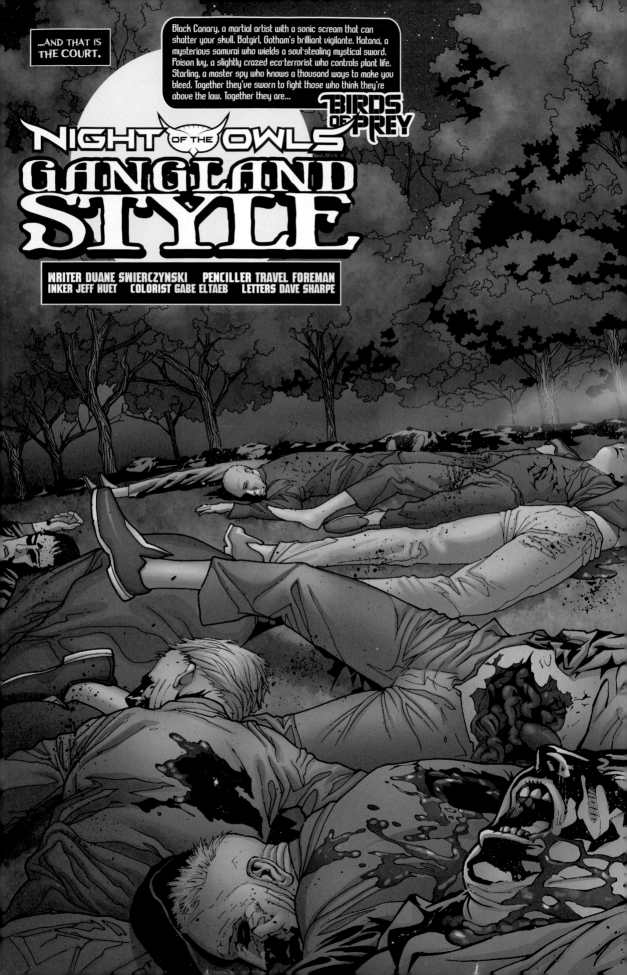

...AND THAT IS THE COURT.

Black Canary, a martial artist with a sonic scream that can shatter your skull. Batgirl, Gotham's brilliant vigilante. Katana, a mysterious samurai who wields a soul-stealing mystical sword. Poison Ivy, a slightly crazed eco-terrorist who controls plant life. Starling, a master spy who knows a thousand ways to make you bleed. Together they've sworn to fight those who think they're above the law. Together they are...

BIRDS OF PREY

NIGHT OF THE OWLS
GANGLAND STYLE

WRITER DUANE SWIERCZYNSKI   PENCILLER TRAVEL FOREMAN
INKER JEFF HUET   COLORIST GABE ELTAEB   LETTERS DAVE SHARPE

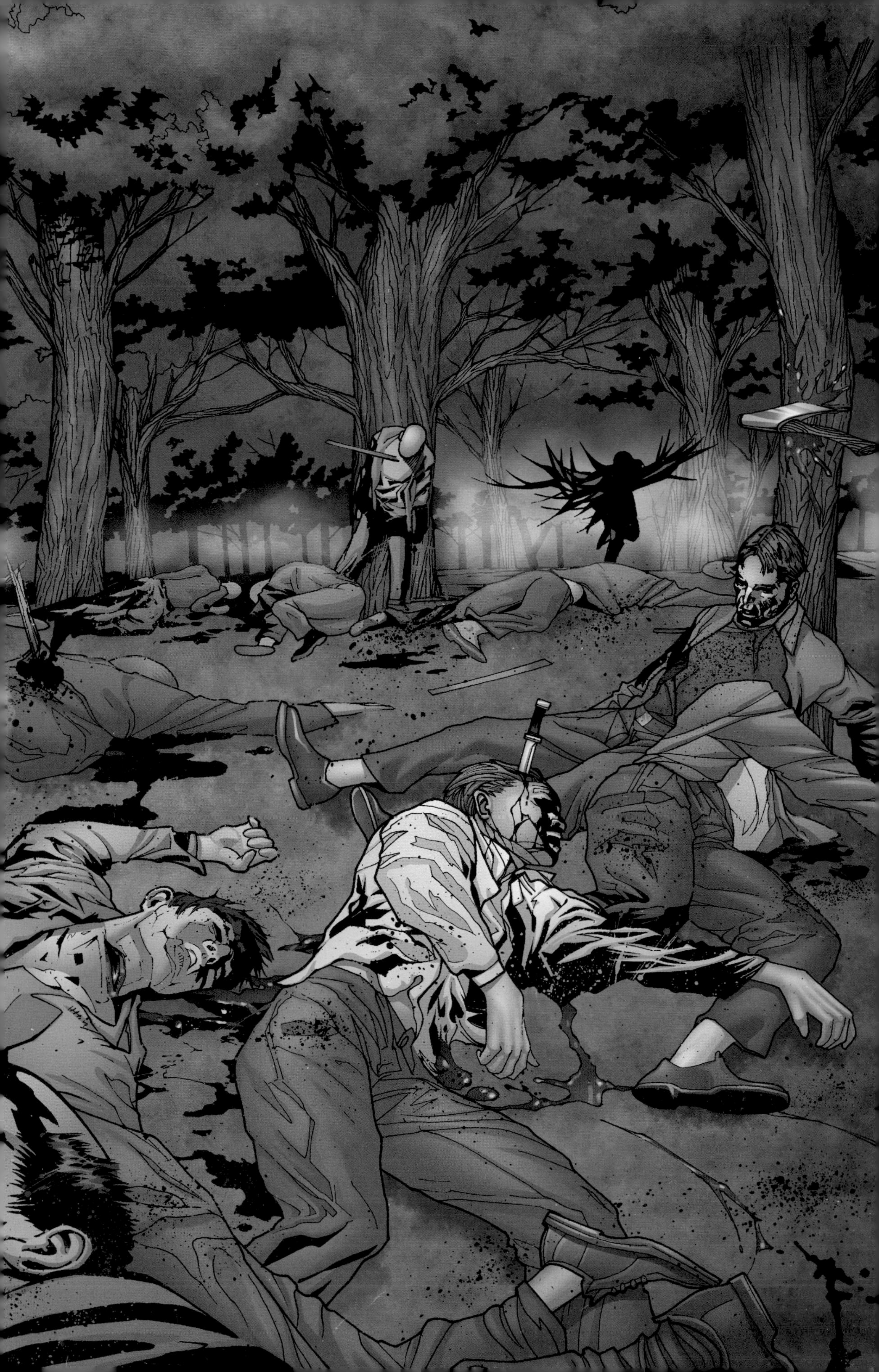

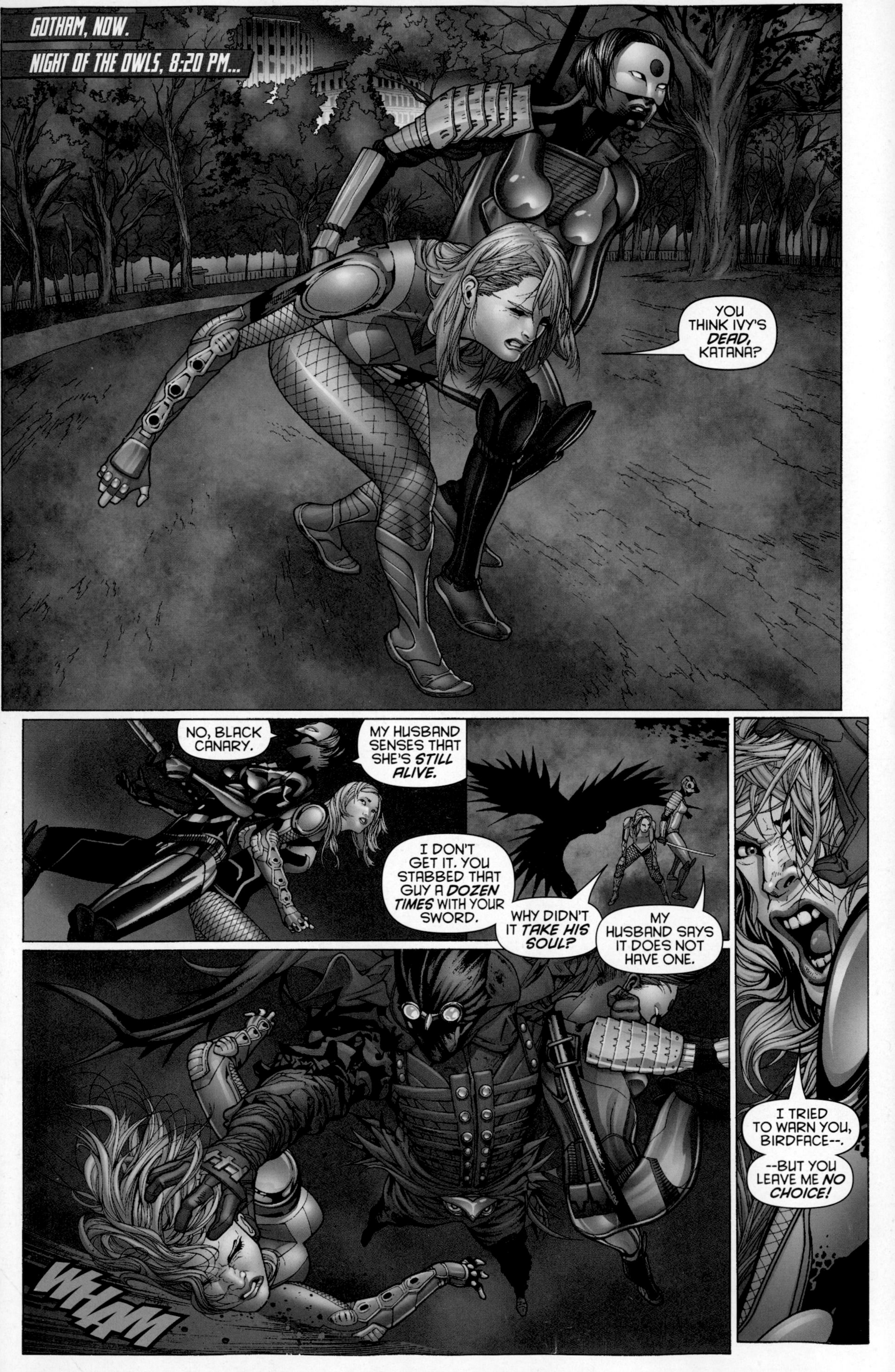
GOTHAM, NOW.
NIGHT OF THE OWLS, 8:20 PM...
YOU THINK IVY'S DEAD, KATANA?
NO, BLACK CANARY.
MY HUSBAND SENSES THAT SHE'S STILL ALIVE.
I DON'T GET IT. YOU STABBED THAT GUY A DOZEN TIMES WITH YOUR SWORD.
WHY DIDN'T IT TAKE HIS SOUL?
MY HUSBAND SAYS IT DOES NOT HAVE ONE.
I TRIED TO WARN YOU, BIRDFACE--.
--BUT YOU LEAVE ME NO CHOICE!
WHAM

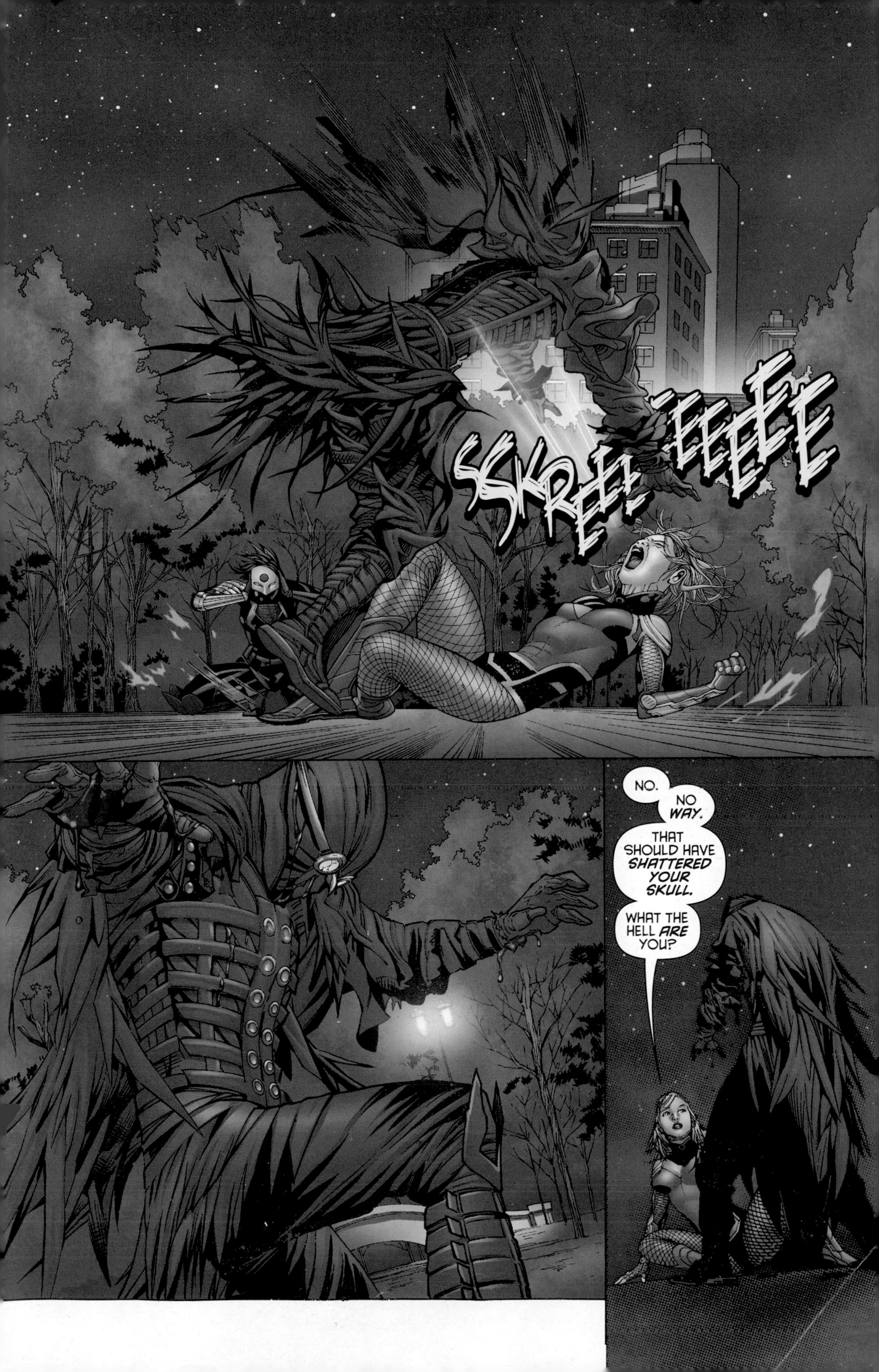

SKREEEEEEEEEEE
NO.
NO WAY.
THAT SHOULD HAVE SHATTERED YOUR SKULL.
WHAT THE HELL ARE YOU?

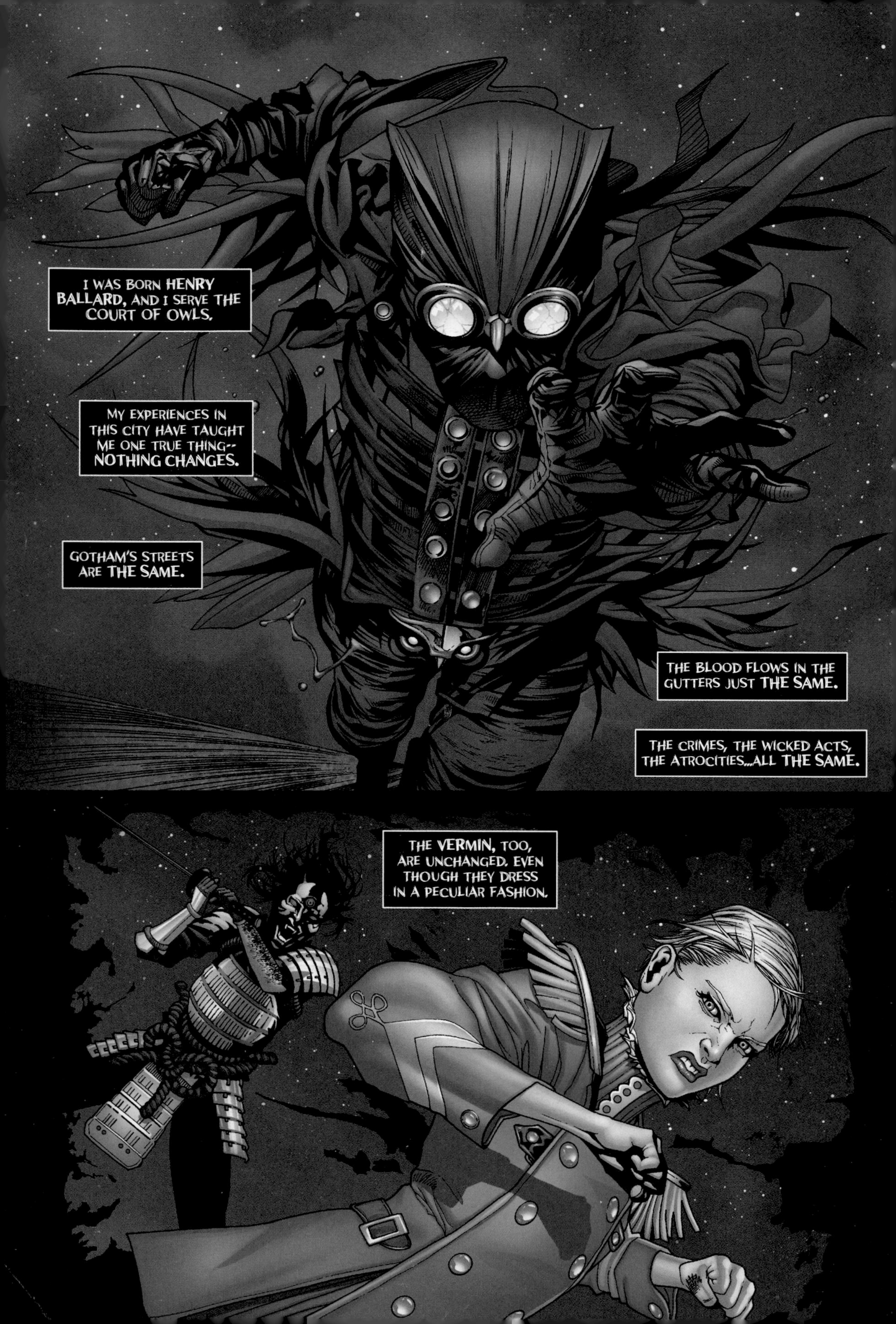
I WAS BORN HENRY BALLARD, AND I SERVE THE COURT OF OWLS.
MY EXPERIENCES IN THIS CITY HAVE TAUGHT ME ONE TRUE THING--NOTHING CHANGES.
GOTHAM'S STREETS ARE THE SAME.
THE BLOOD FLOWS IN THE GUTTERS JUST THE SAME.
THE CRIMES, THE WICKED ACTS, THE ATROCITIES...ALL THE SAME.
THE VERMIN, TOO, ARE UNCHANGED. EVEN THOUGH THEY DRESS IN A PECULIAR FASHION.

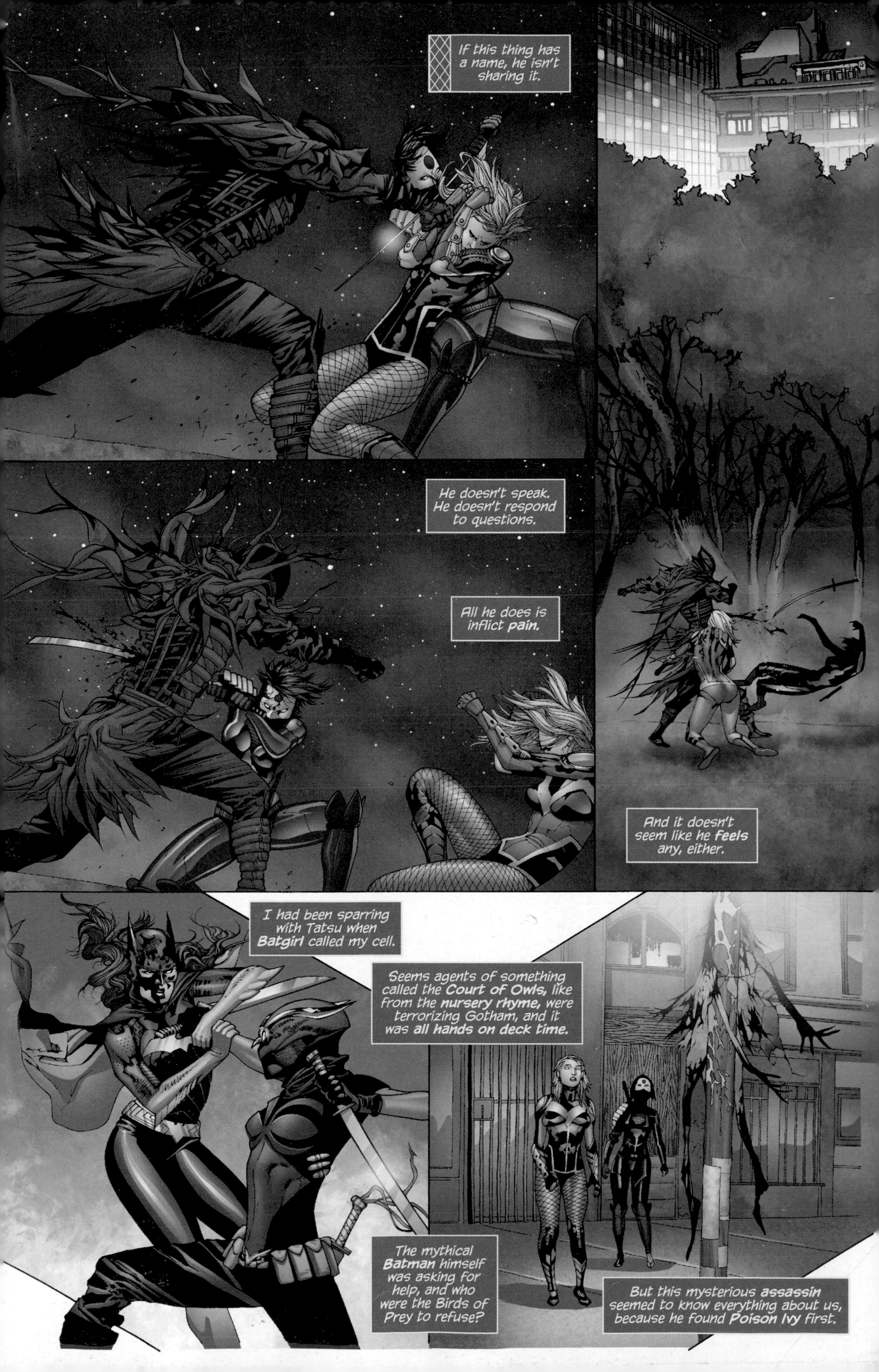
If this thing has a name, he isn't sharing it.
He doesn't speak. He doesn't respond to questions.
All he does is inflict pain.
And it doesn't seem like he feels any, either.
I had been sparring with Tatsu when Batgirl called my cell.
Seems agents of something called the Court of Owls, like from the nursery rhyme, were terrorizing Gotham, and it was all hands on deck time.
The mythical Batman himself was asking for help, and who were the Birds of Prey to refuse?
But this mysterious assassin seemed to know everything about us, because he found Poison Ivy first.

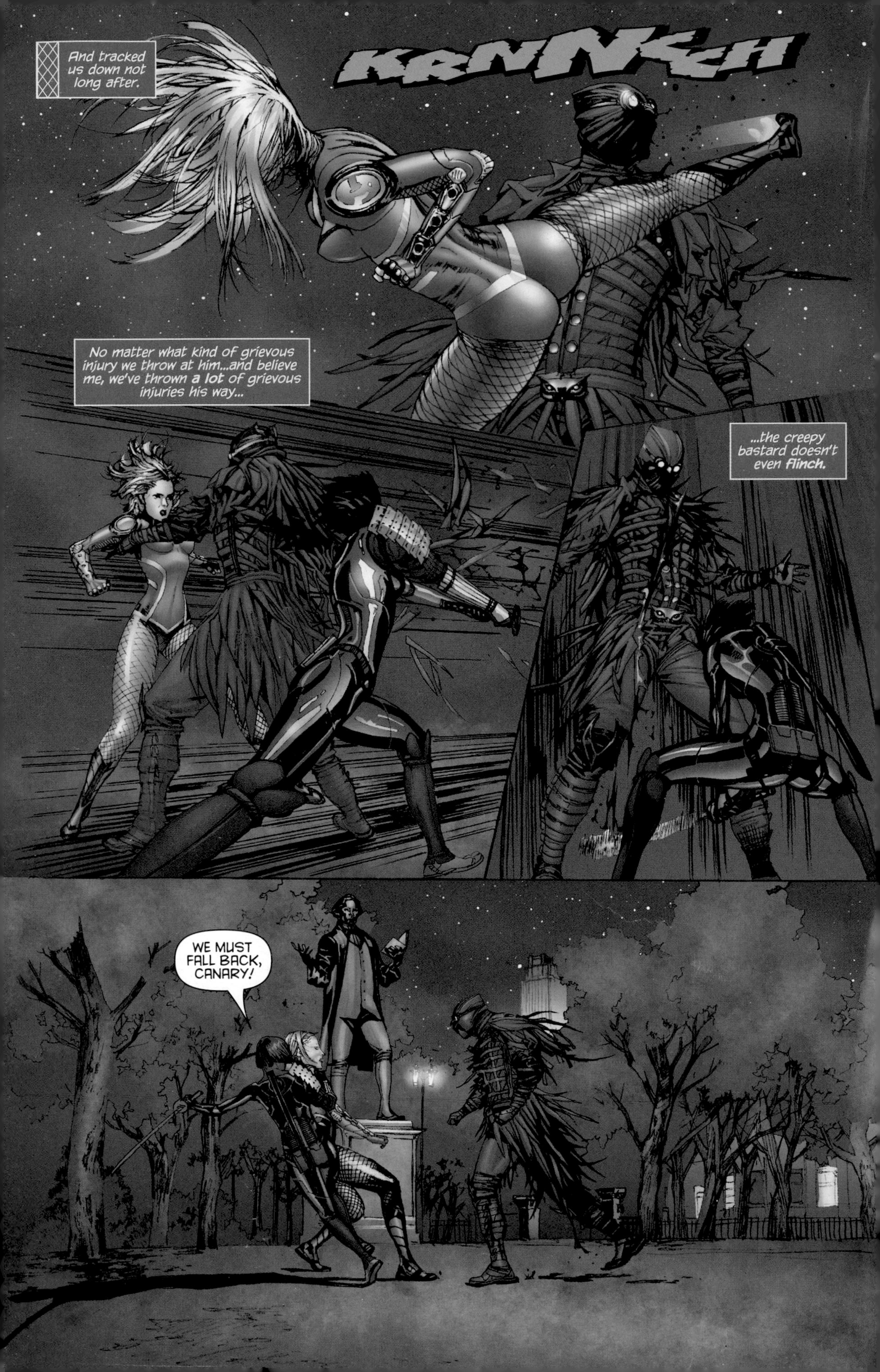
And tracked us down not long after.
KRNNKCH
No matter what kind of grievous injury we throw at him...and believe me, we've thrown a lot of grievous injuries his way...
...the creepy bastard doesn't even flinch.
WE MUST FALL BACK, CANARY!

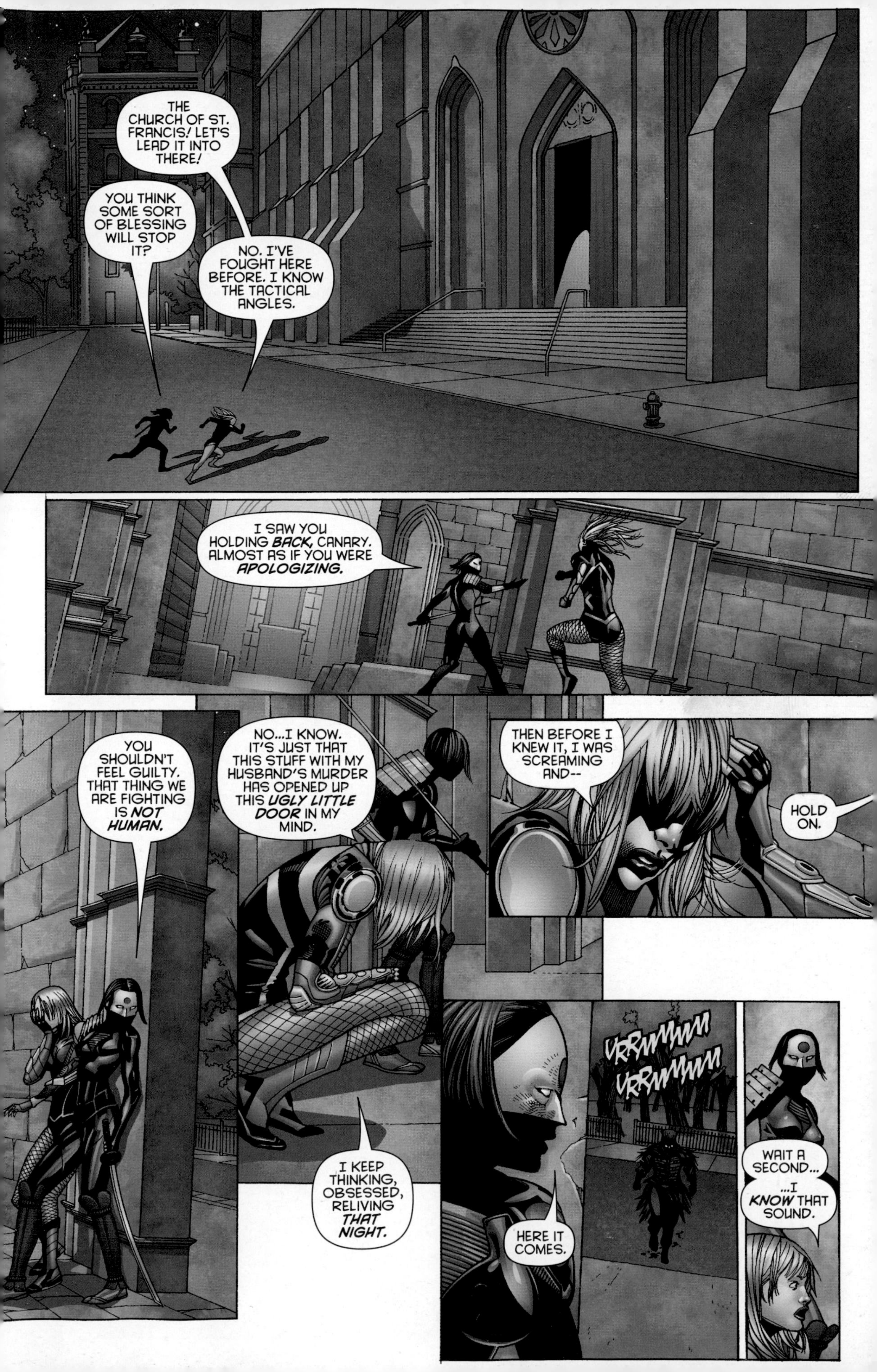
THE CHURCH OF ST. FRANCIS! LET'S LEAD IT INTO THERE!
YOU THINK SOME SORT OF BLESSING WILL STOP IT?
NO. I'VE FOUGHT HERE BEFORE. I KNOW THE TACTICAL ANGLES.
I SAW YOU HOLDING BACK, CANARY. ALMOST AS IF YOU WERE APOLOGIZING.
YOU SHOULDN'T FEEL GUILTY. THAT THING WE ARE FIGHTING IS NOT HUMAN.
NO...I KNOW. IT'S JUST THAT THIS STUFF WITH MY HUSBAND'S MURDER HAS OPENED UP THIS UGLY LITTLE DOOR IN MY MIND.
I KEEP THINKING, OBSESSED, RELIVING THAT NIGHT.
THEN BEFORE I KNEW IT, I WAS SCREAMING AND--
HOLD ON.
HERE IT COMES.
VRRMMMM
VRRMMMM
WAIT A SECOND...
...I KNOW THAT SOUND.

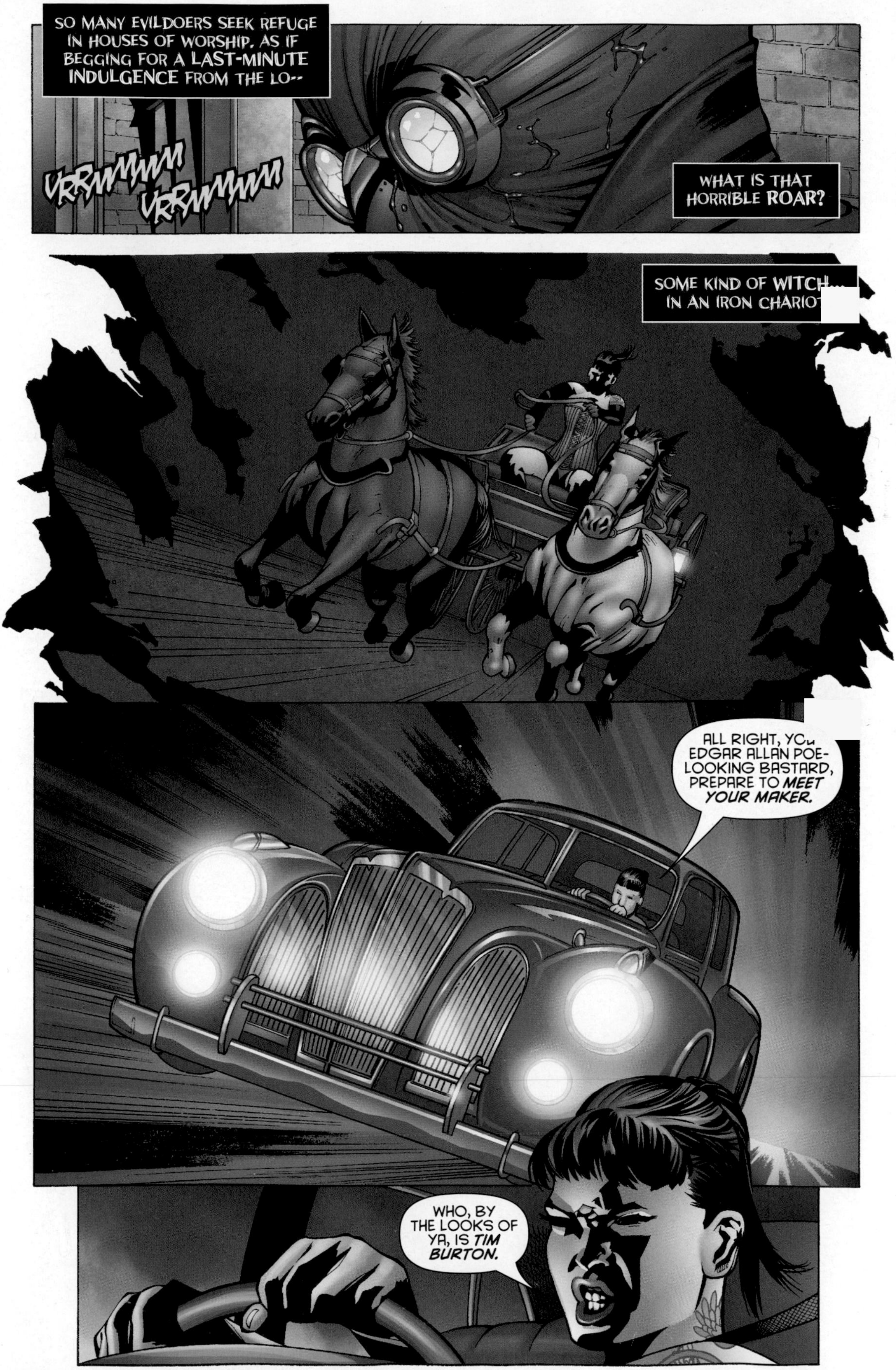
SO MANY EVILDOERS SEEK REFUGE IN HOUSES OF WORSHIP, AS IF BEGGING FOR A LAST-MINUTE INDULGENCE FROM THE LO--
VRRMMMM
VRRMMMM
WHAT IS THAT HORRIBLE ROAR?
SOME KIND OF WITCH
IN AN IRON CHARIO
ALL RIGHT, YO
EDGAR ALLAN POE-LOOKING BASTARD, PREPARE TO *MEET YOUR MAKER.*
WHO, BY THE LOOKS OF YA, IS *TIM BURTON.*

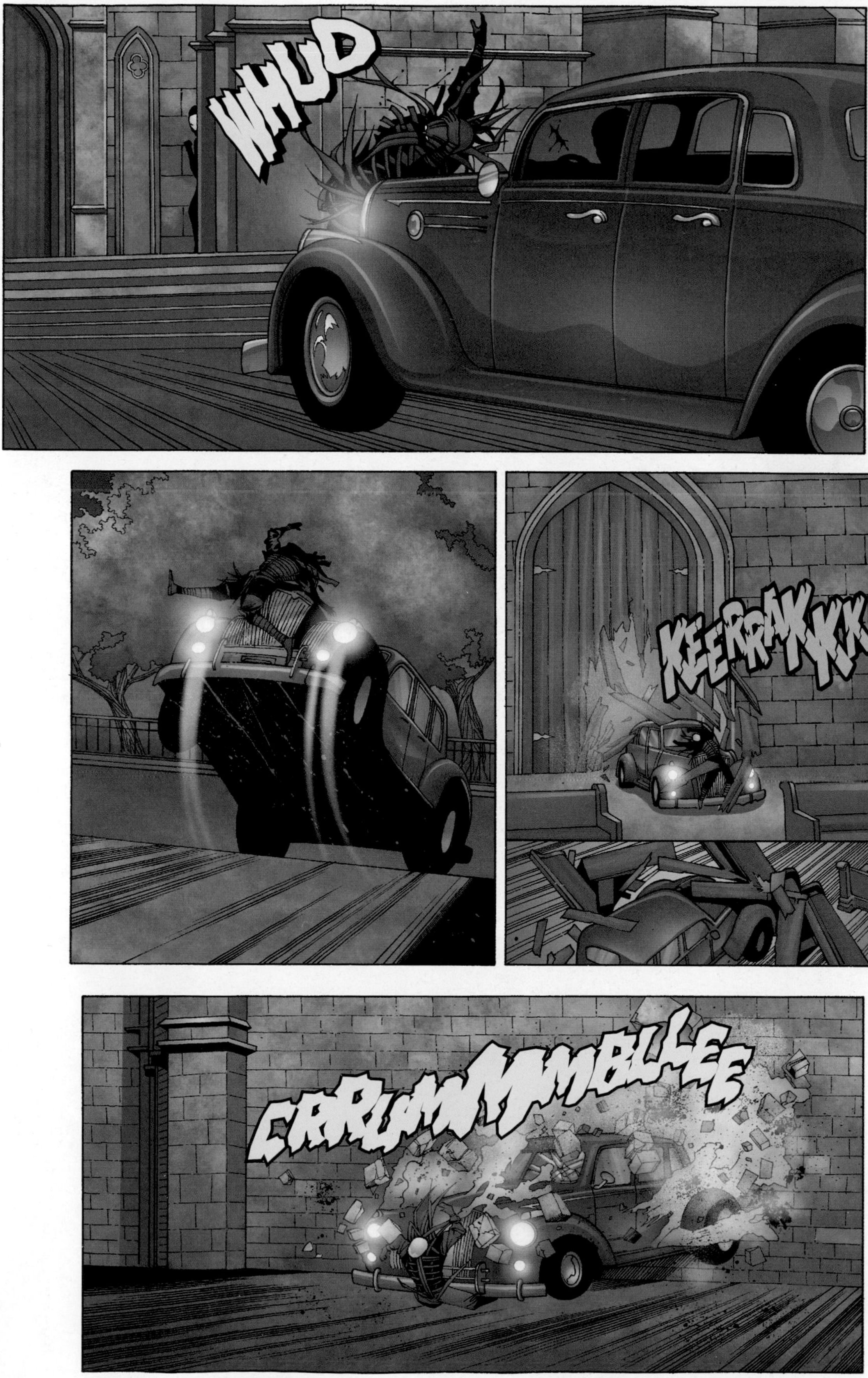
WHUD
KEERRAKKKK
CRRUMMMMBLLEE

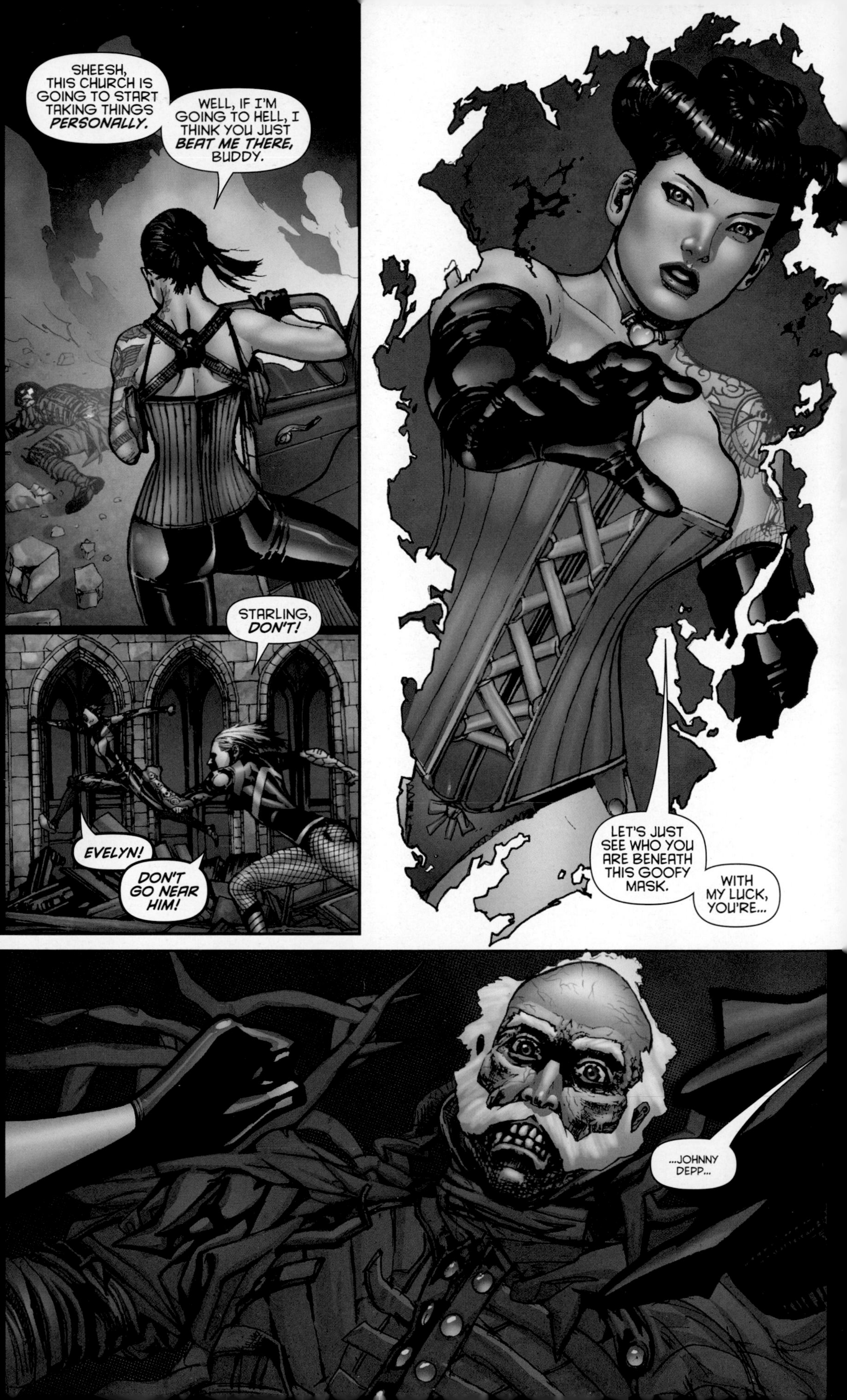
SHEESH, THIS CHURCH IS GOING TO START TAKING THINGS PERSONALLY.
WELL, IF I'M GOING TO HELL, I THINK YOU JUST BEAT ME THERE, BUDDY.
STARLING, DON'T!
EVELYN!
DON'T GO NEAR HIM!
LET'S JUST SEE WHO YOU ARE BENEATH THIS GOOFY MASK.
WITH MY LUCK, YOU'RE...
...JOHNNY DEPP...

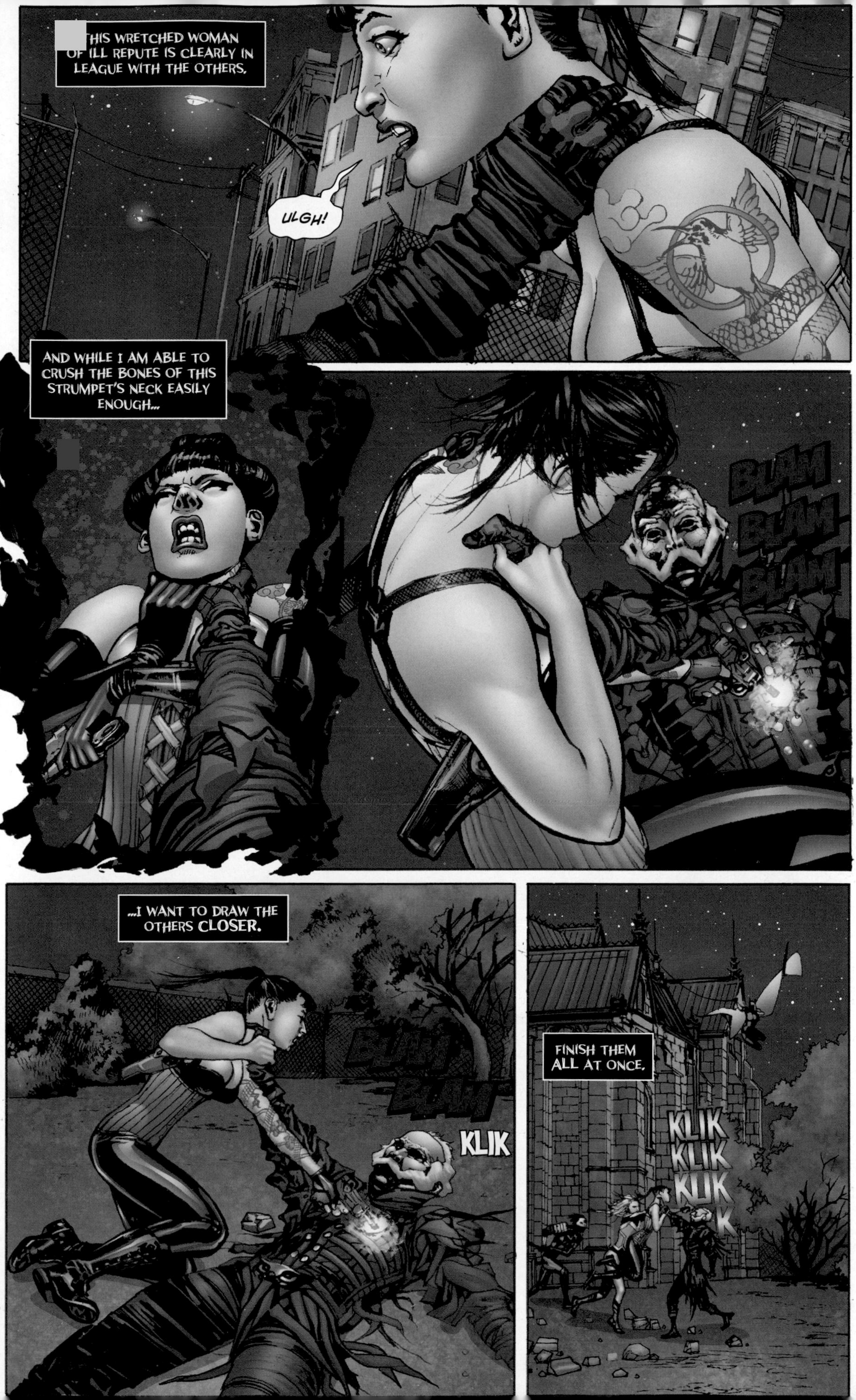
THIS WRETCHED WOMAN OF ILL REPUTE IS CLEARLY IN LEAGUE WITH THE OTHERS.
ULGH!
AND WHILE I AM ABLE TO CRUSH THE BONES OF THIS STRUMPET'S NECK EASILY ENOUGH...
BLAM BLAM BLAM
...I WANT TO DRAW THE OTHERS CLOSER.
KLIK
FINISH THEM ALL AT ONCE.
KLIK KLIK KLIK K

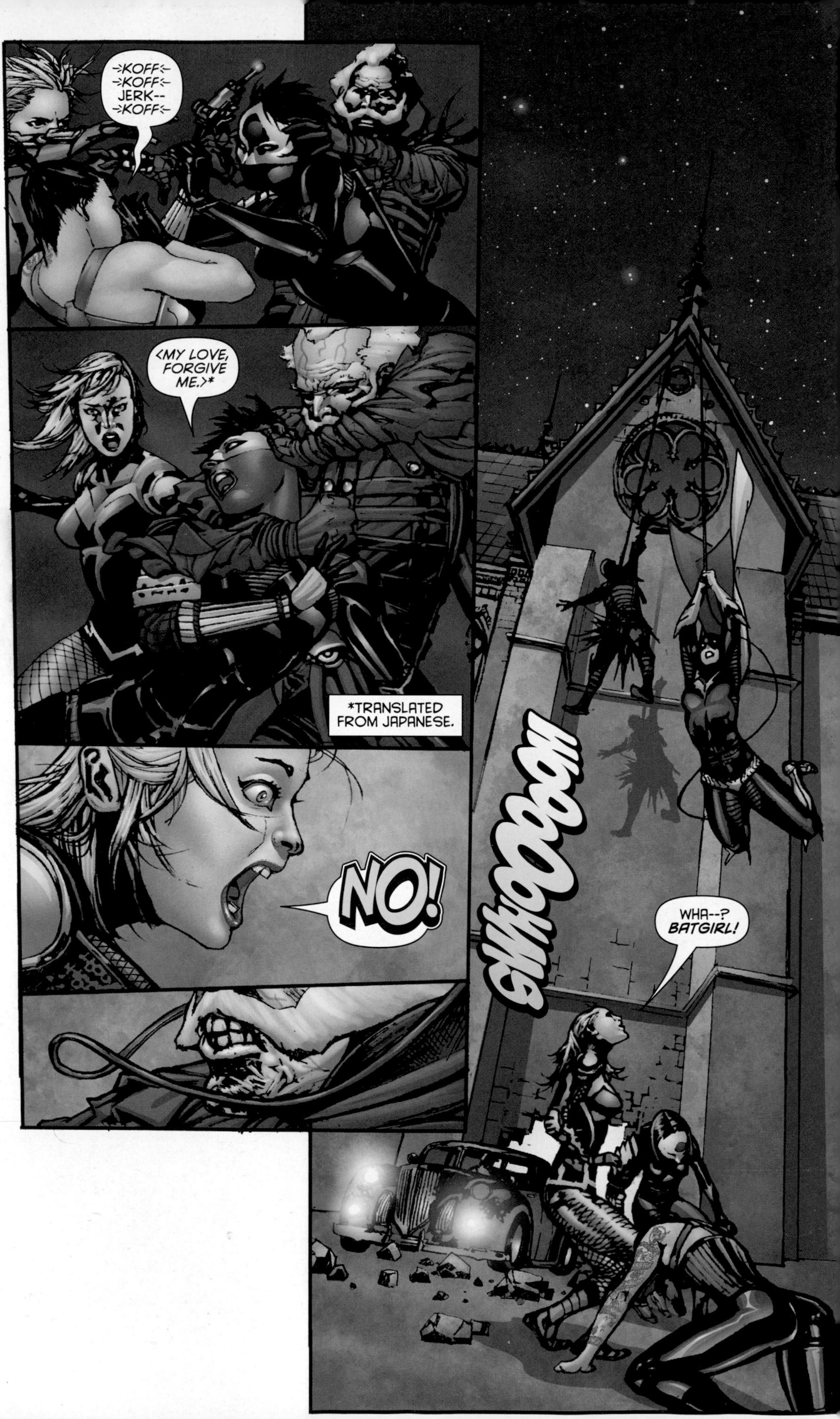

-KOFF- -KOFF- JERK-- -KOFF-
<MY LOVE, FORGIVE ME.>*
*TRANSLATED FROM JAPANESE.
NO!
SHWOOOOM
WHA--? BATGIRL!

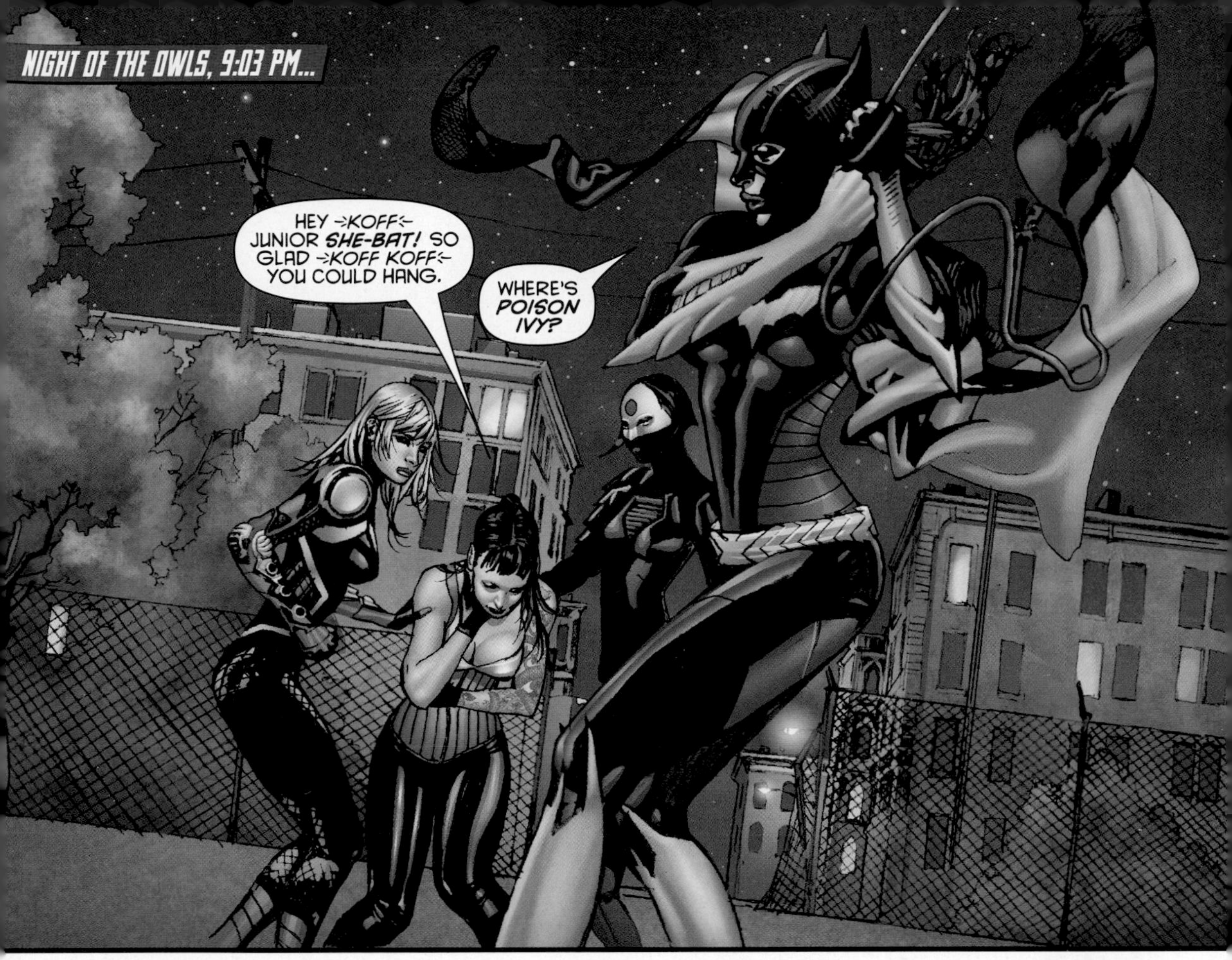
NIGHT OF THE OWLS, 9:03 PM...
HEY ⇒KOFF⇐ JUNIOR SHE-BAT! SO GLAD ⇒KOFF KOFF⇐ YOU COULD HANG.
WHERE'S POISON IVY?

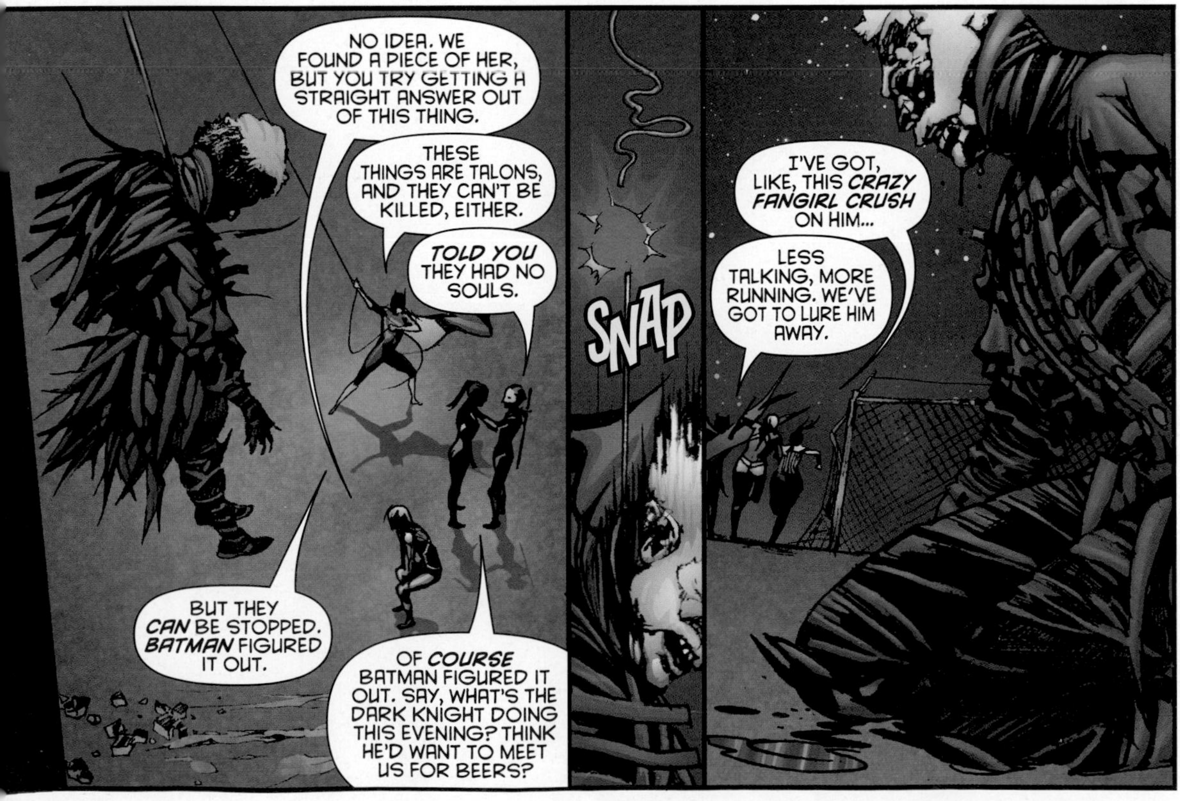
NO IDEA. WE FOUND A PIECE OF HER, BUT YOU TRY GETTING A STRAIGHT ANSWER OUT OF THIS THING.
THESE THINGS ARE TALONS, AND THEY CAN'T BE KILLED, EITHER.
TOLD YOU THEY HAD NO SOULS.
BUT THEY CAN BE STOPPED. BATMAN FIGURED IT OUT.
OF COURSE BATMAN FIGURED IT OUT. SAY, WHAT'S THE DARK KNIGHT DOING THIS EVENING? THINK HE'D WANT TO MEET US FOR BEERS?
SNAP
I'VE GOT, LIKE, THIS CRAZY FANGIRL CRUSH ON HIM...
LESS TALKING, MORE RUNNING. WE'VE GOT TO LURE HIM AWAY.

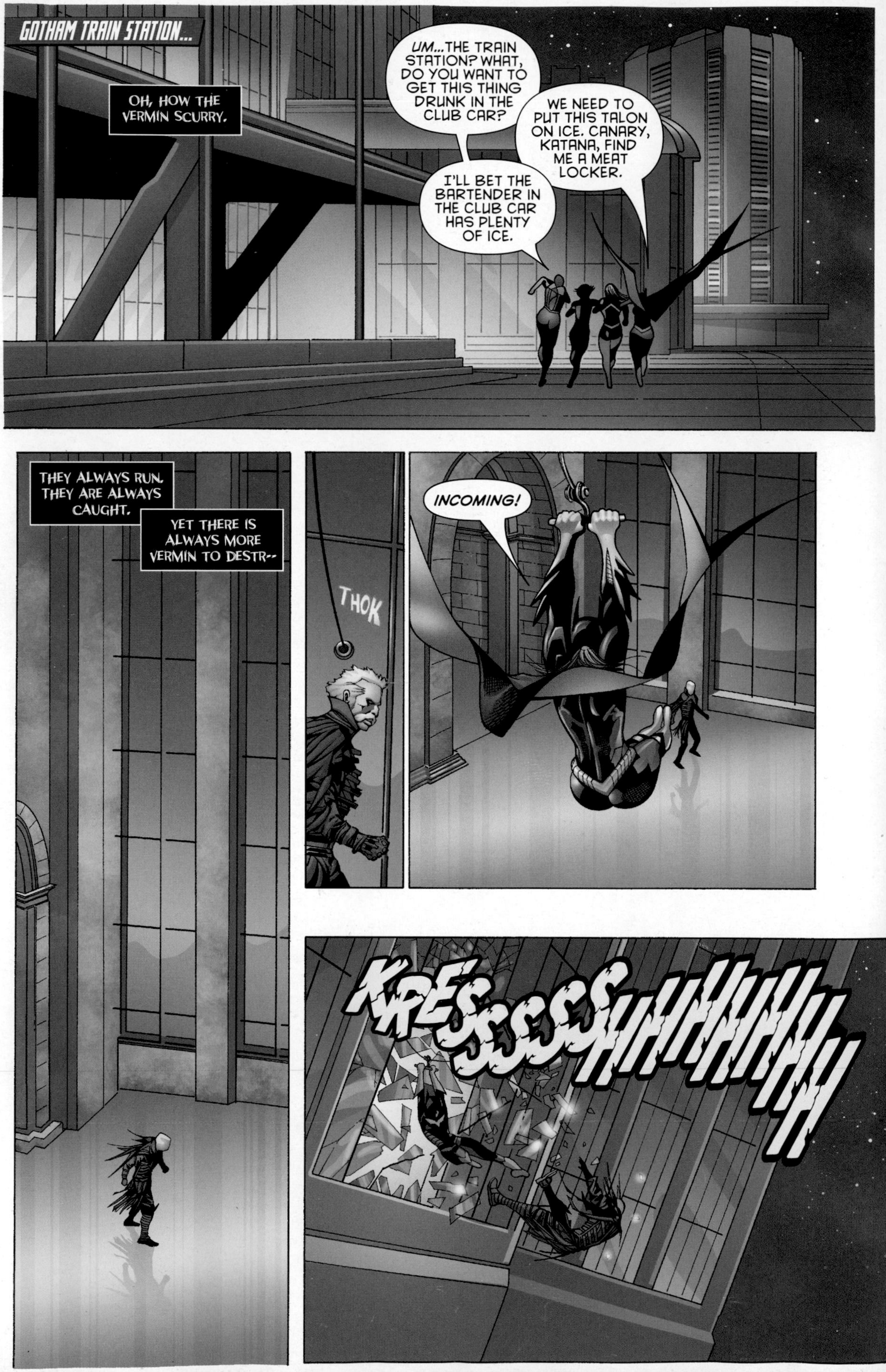
GOTHAM TRAIN STATION...
OH, HOW THE VERMIN SCURRY.
UM...THE TRAIN STATION? WHAT, DO YOU WANT TO GET THIS THING DRUNK IN THE CLUB CAR?
WE NEED TO PUT THIS TALON ON ICE. CANARY, KATANA, FIND ME A MEAT LOCKER.
I'LL BET THE BARTENDER IN THE CLUB CAR HAS PLENTY OF ICE.
THEY ALWAYS RUN. THEY ARE ALWAYS CAUGHT.
YET THERE IS ALWAYS MORE VERMIN TO DESTR--
THOK
INCOMING!
KRESSSSSSHHHHHHHH

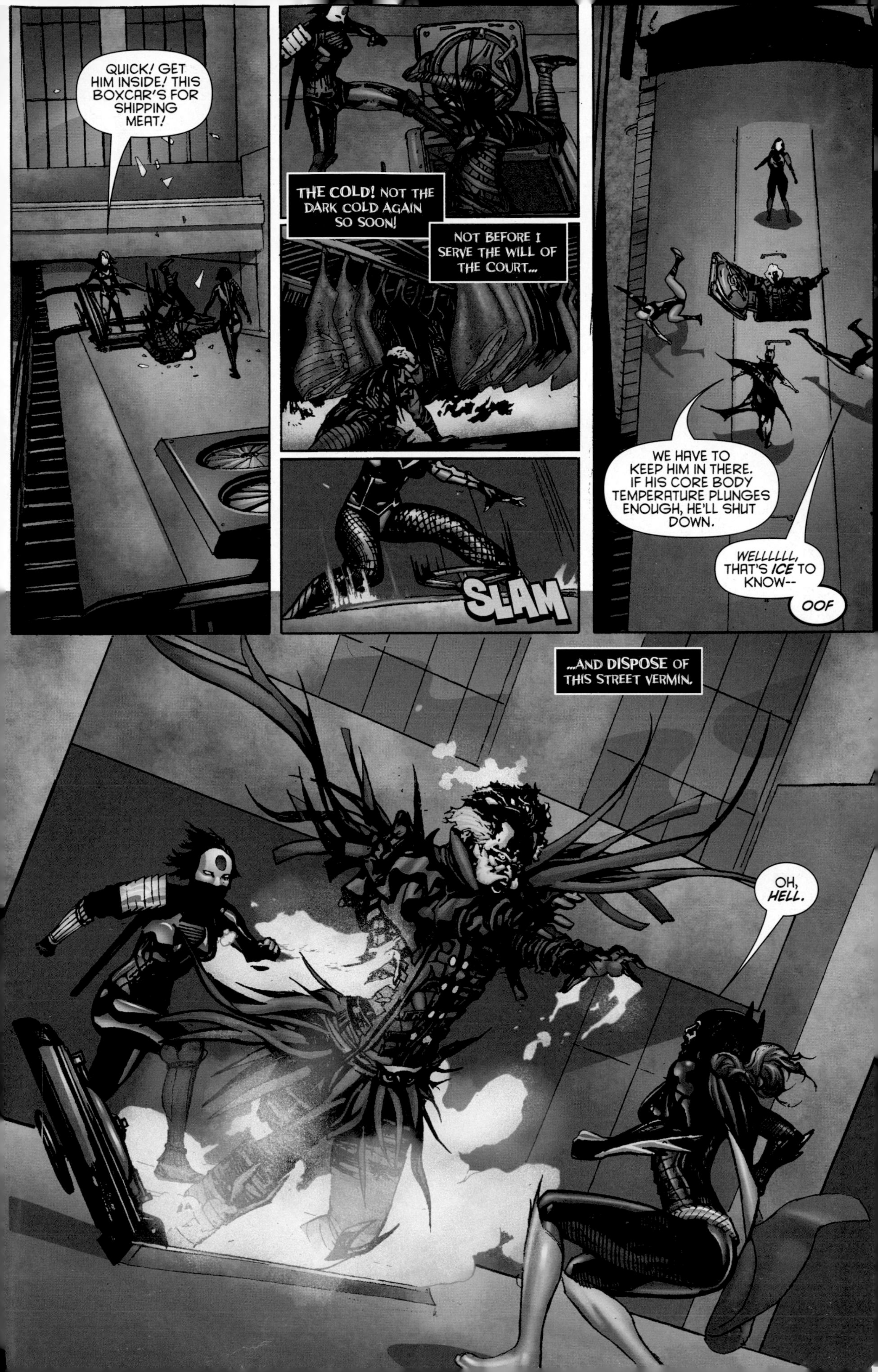
QUICK! GET HIM INSIDE! THIS BOXCAR'S FOR SHIPPING MEAT!
THE COLD! NOT THE DARK COLD AGAIN SO SOON!
NOT BEFORE I SERVE THE WILL OF THE COURT...
SLAM
WE HAVE TO KEEP HIM IN THERE. IF HIS CORE BODY TEMPERATURE PLUNGES ENOUGH, HE'LL SHUT DOWN.
WELLLLLLL, THAT'S ICE TO KNOW--
OOF
...AND DISPOSE OF THIS STREET VERMIN.
OH, HELL.

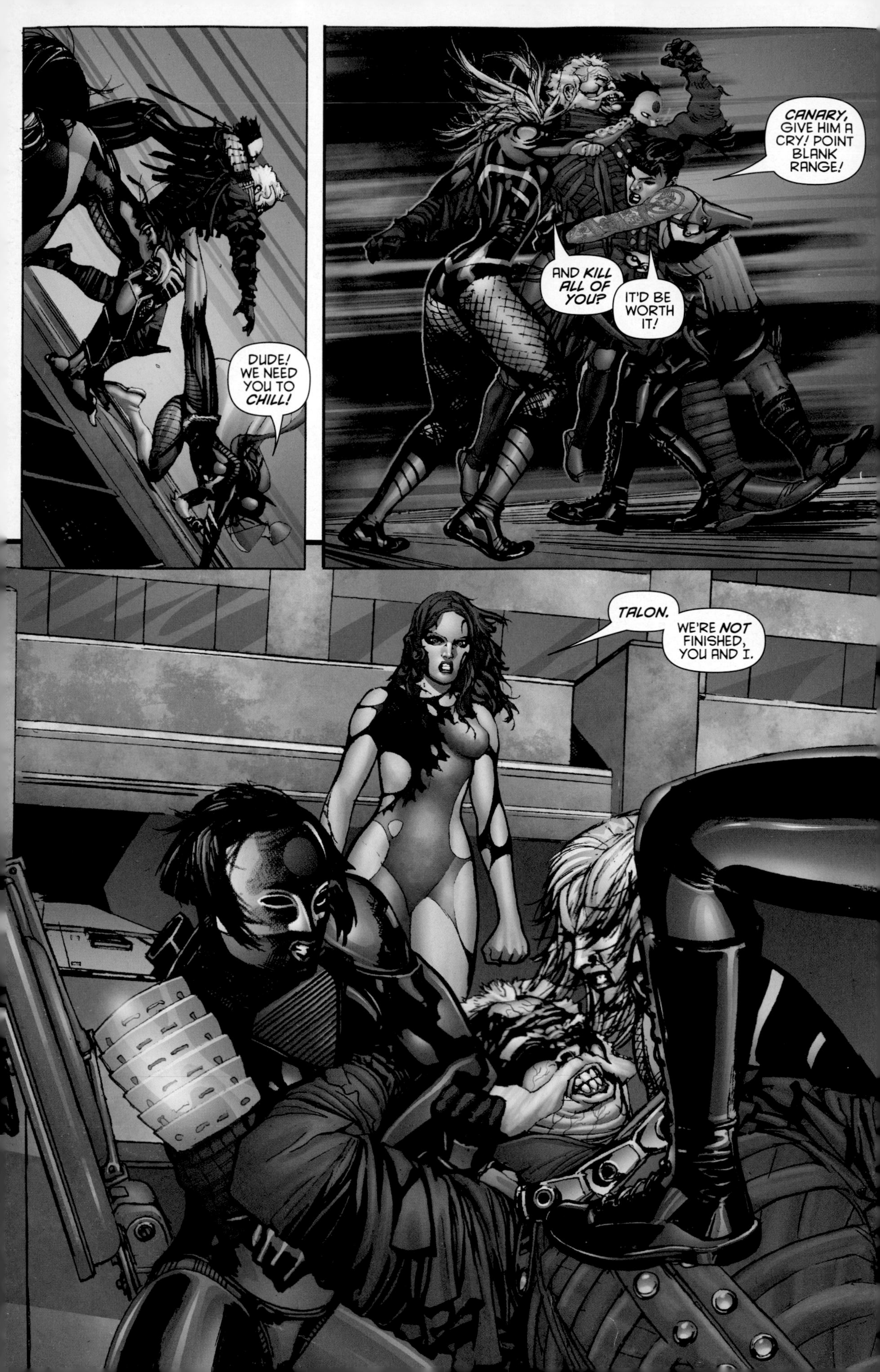
DUDE! WE NEED YOU TO CHILL!
CANARY, GIVE HIM A CRY! POINT BLANK RANGE!
AND KILL ALL OF YOU?
IT'D BE WORTH IT!
TALON.
WE'RE NOT FINISHED, YOU AND I.

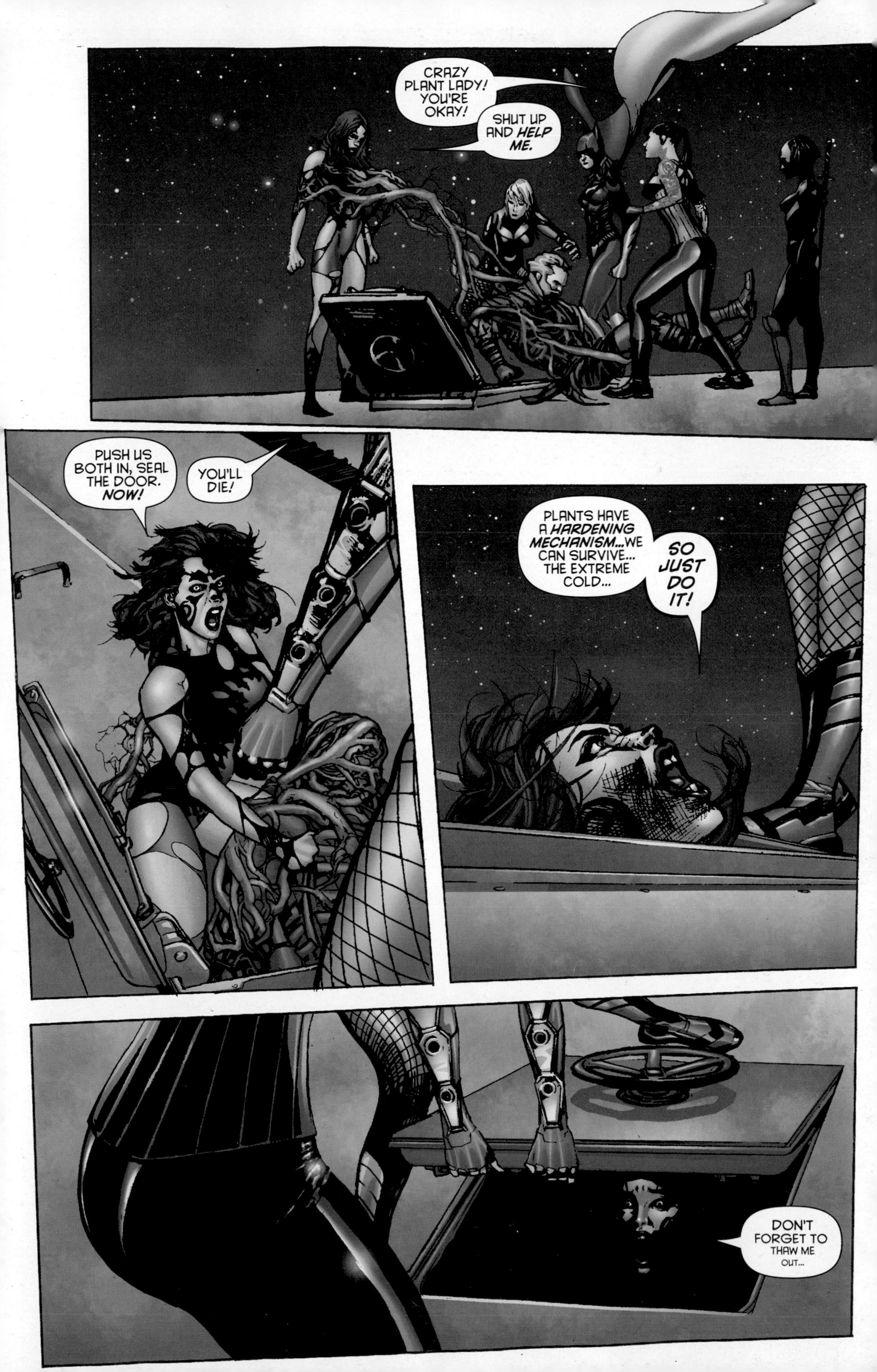
CRAZY PLANT LADY! YOU'RE OKAY!
SHUT UP AND *HELP ME.*
PUSH US BOTH IN, SEAL THE DOOR. *NOW!*
YOU'LL DIE!
PLANTS HAVE A *HARDENING MECHANISM*...WE CAN SURVIVE... THE EXTREME COLD...
SO JUST DO IT!
DON'T FORGET TO THAW ME OUT...

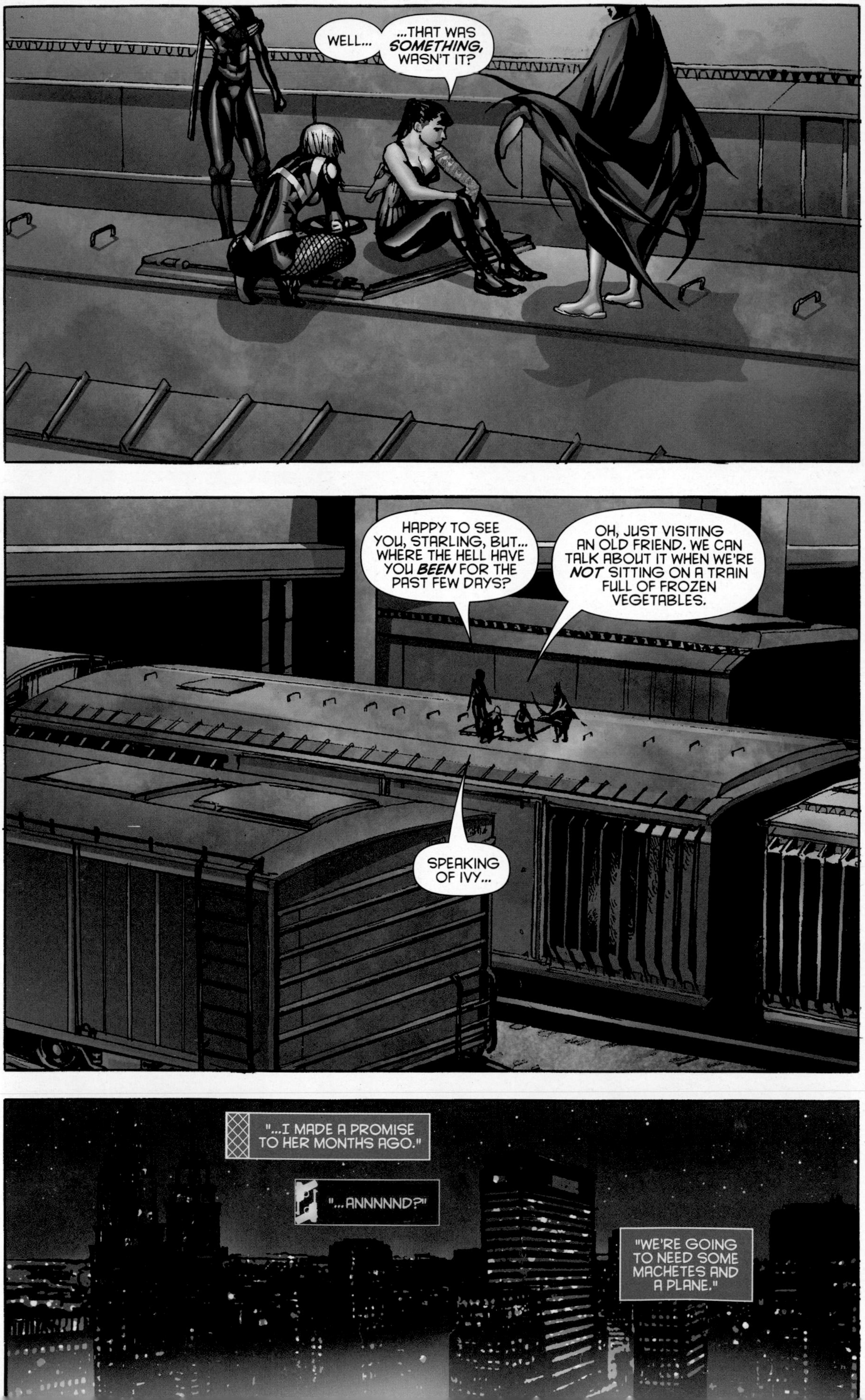
WELL...
...THAT WAS SOMETHING, WASN'T IT?
HAPPY TO SEE YOU, STARLING, BUT... WHERE THE HELL HAVE YOU BEEN FOR THE PAST FEW DAYS?
OH, JUST VISITING AN OLD FRIEND. WE CAN TALK ABOUT IT WHEN WE'RE NOT SITTING ON A TRAIN FULL OF FROZEN VEGETABLES.
SPEAKING OF IVY...
"...I MADE A PROMISE TO HER MONTHS AGO."
"...ANNNNND?"
"WE'RE GOING TO NEED SOME MACHETES AND A PLANE."

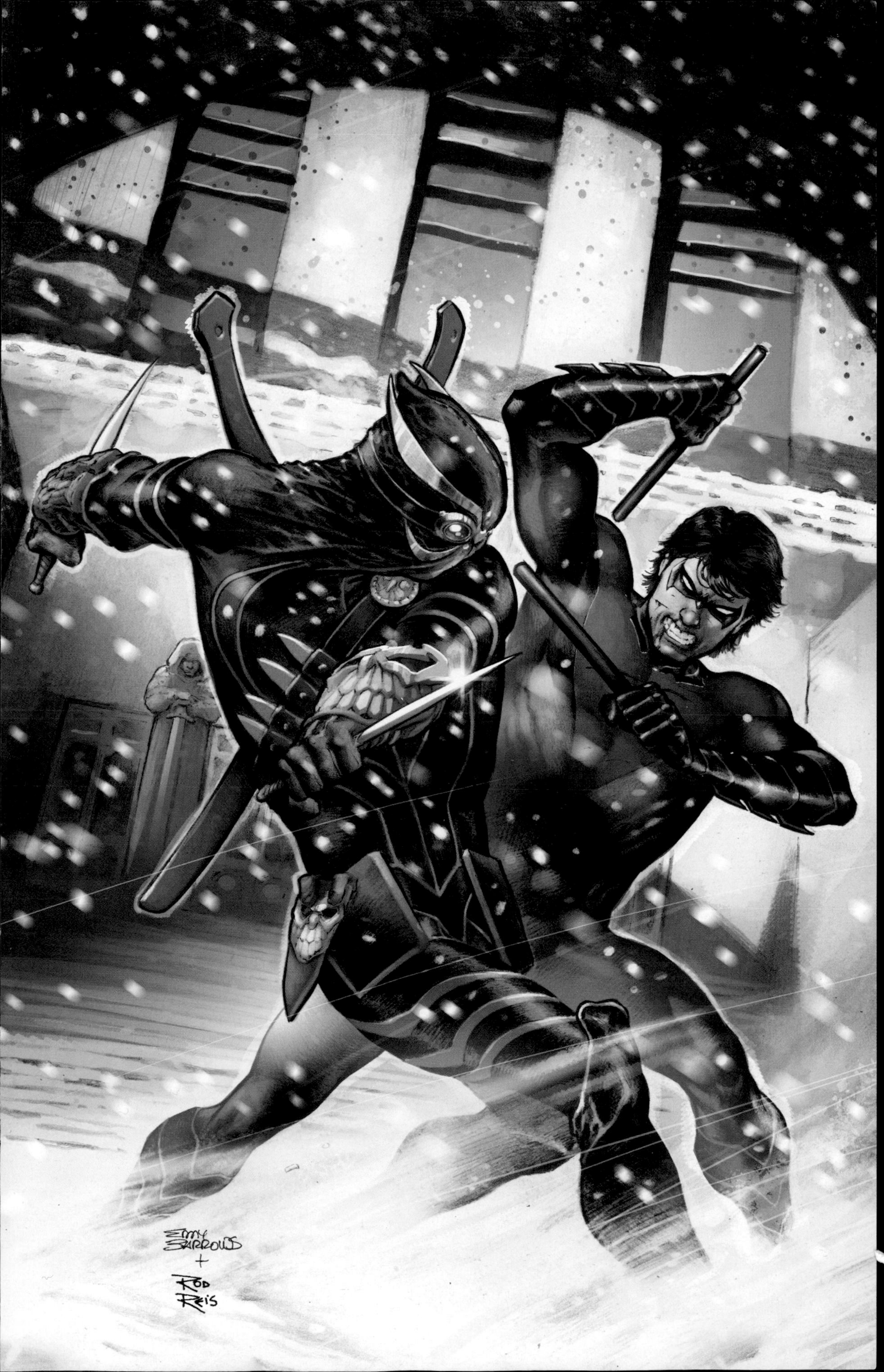
EDDY BARROWS
+
ROD REIS

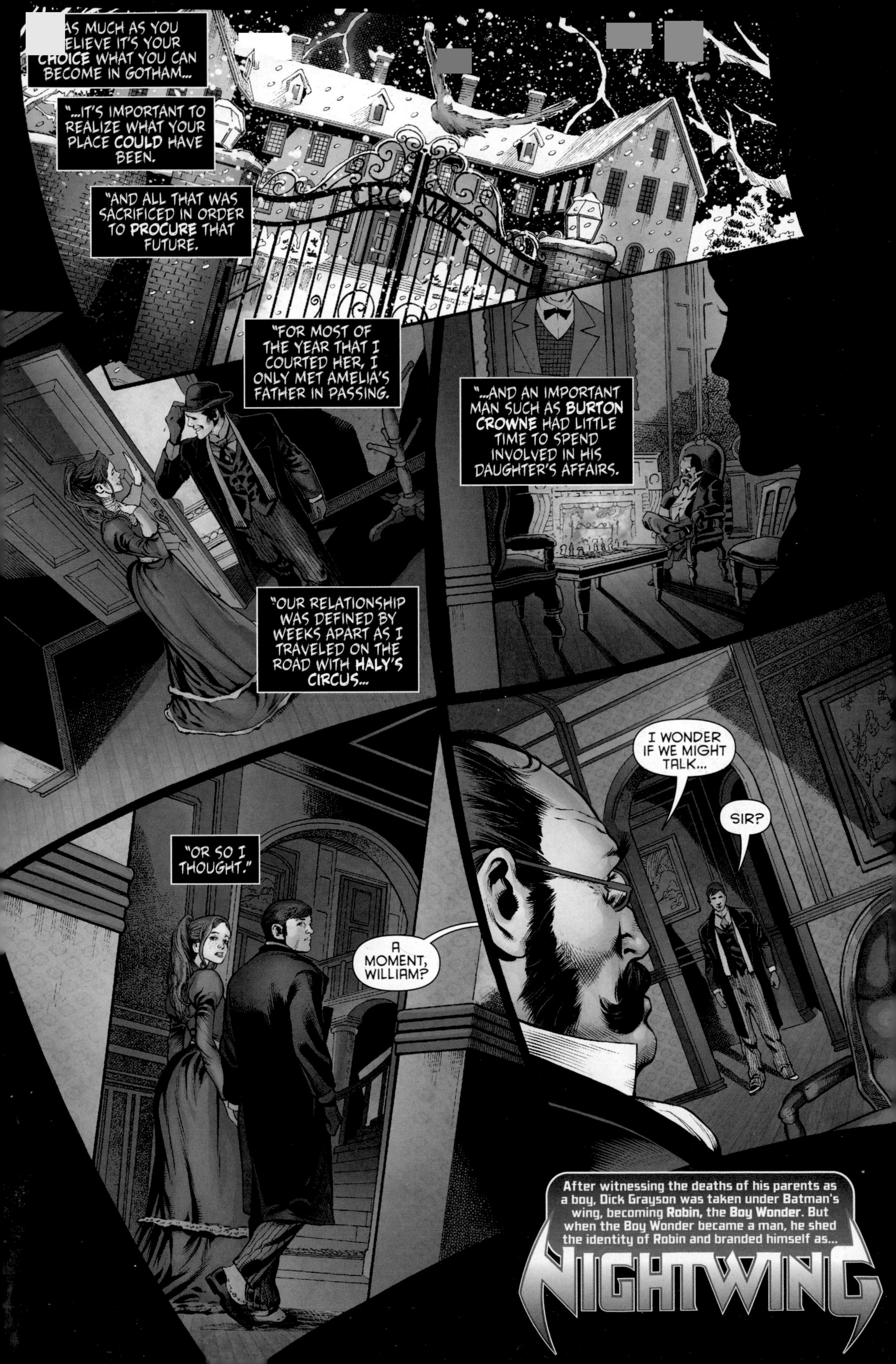
AS MUCH AS YOU ELIEVE IT'S YOUR CHOICE WHAT YOU CAN BECOME IN GOTHAM...
"...IT'S IMPORTANT TO REALIZE WHAT YOUR PLACE COULD HAVE BEEN.
"AND ALL THAT WAS SACRIFICED IN ORDER TO PROCURE THAT FUTURE.
CROWNE
"FOR MOST OF THE YEAR THAT I COURTED HER, I ONLY MET AMELIA'S FATHER IN PASSING.
"...AND AN IMPORTANT MAN SUCH AS BURTON CROWNE HAD LITTLE TIME TO SPEND INVOLVED IN HIS DAUGHTER'S AFFAIRS.
"OUR RELATIONSHIP WAS DEFINED BY WEEKS APART AS I TRAVELED ON THE ROAD WITH HALY'S CIRCUS...
"OR SO I THOUGHT."
A MOMENT, WILLIAM?
I WONDER IF WE MIGHT TALK...
SIR?
After witnessing the deaths of his parents as a boy, Dick Grayson was taken under Batman's wing, becoming Robin, the Boy Wonder. But when the Boy Wonder became a man, he shed the identity of Robin and branded himself as...
NIGHTWING

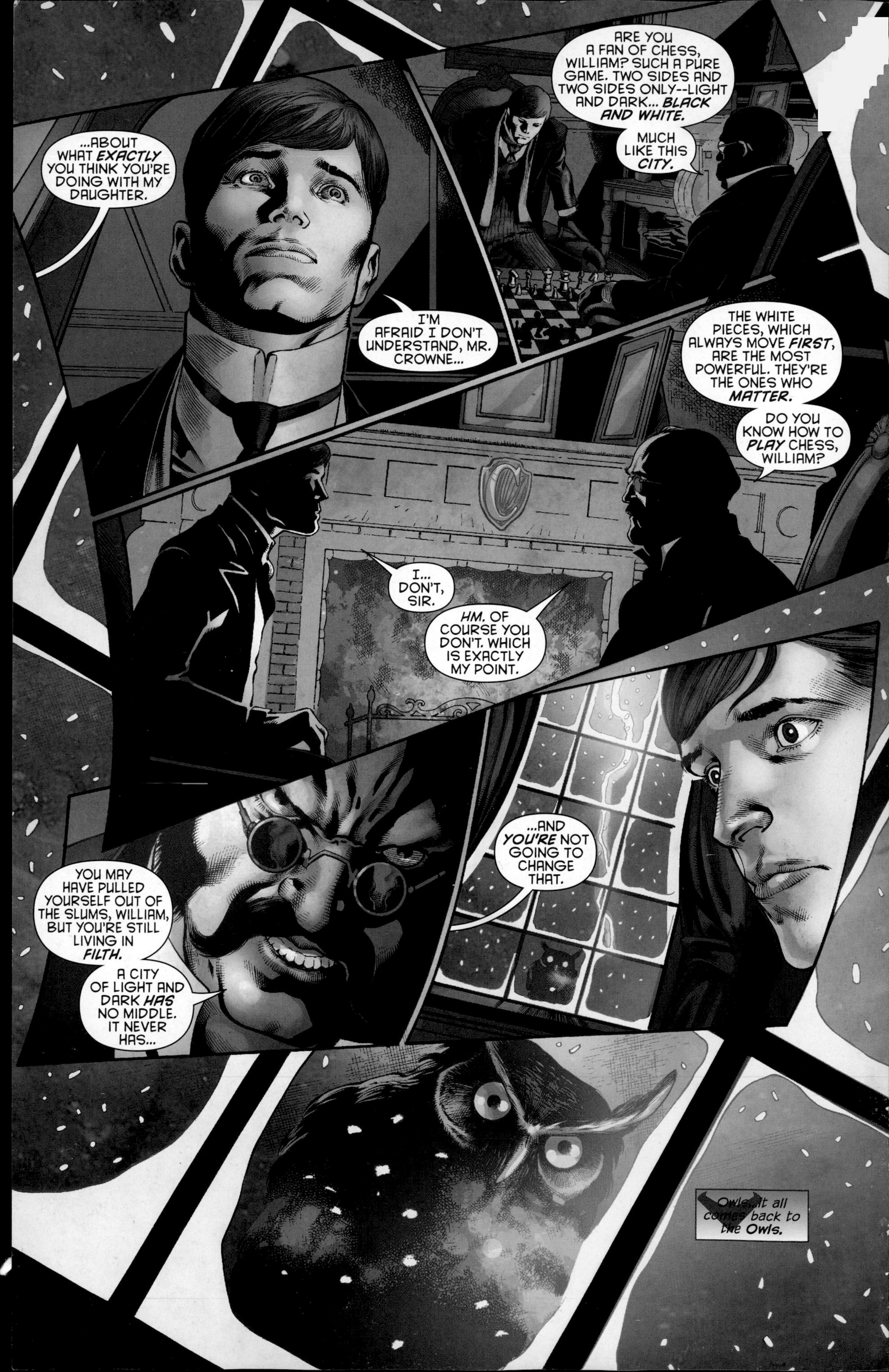
...ABOUT WHAT *EXACTLY* YOU THINK YOU'RE DOING WITH MY DAUGHTER.
ARE YOU A FAN OF CHESS, WILLIAM? SUCH A PURE GAME. TWO SIDES AND TWO SIDES ONLY--LIGHT AND DARK... *BLACK AND WHITE.*
MUCH LIKE THIS *CITY.*
I'M AFRAID I DON'T UNDERSTAND, MR. CROWNE...
THE WHITE PIECES, WHICH ALWAYS MOVE *FIRST*, ARE THE MOST POWERFUL. THEY'RE THE ONES WHO *MATTER.*
DO YOU KNOW HOW TO *PLAY* CHESS, WILLIAM?
I... DON'T, SIR.
HM. OF COURSE YOU DON'T. WHICH IS EXACTLY MY POINT.
YOU MAY HAVE PULLED YOURSELF OUT OF THE SLUMS, WILLIAM, BUT YOU'RE STILL LIVING IN *FILTH.*
A CITY OF LIGHT AND DARK *HAS* NO MIDDLE. IT NEVER HAS...
...AND *YOU'RE* NOT GOING TO CHANGE THAT.
Owls...it all comes back to the *Owls.*

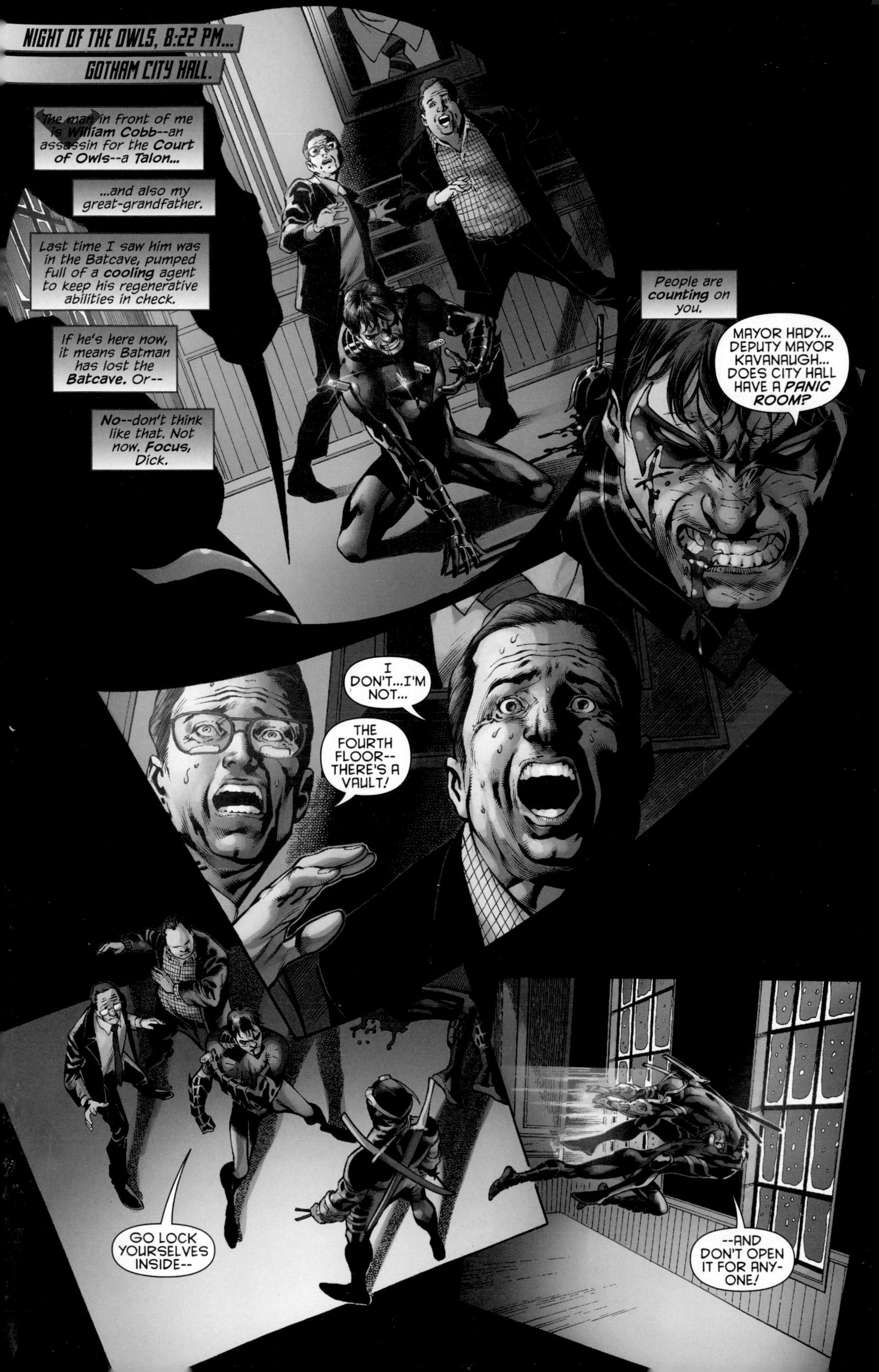
NIGHT OF THE OWLS, 8:22 PM...
GOTHAM CITY HALL.
The man in front of me is William Cobb--an assassin for the Court of Owls--a Talon...
...and also my great-grandfather.
Last time I saw him was in the Batcave, pumped full of a cooling agent to keep his regenerative abilities in check.
If he's here now, it means Batman has lost the Batcave. Or--
No--don't think like that. Not now. Focus, Dick.
People are counting on you.
MAYOR HADY... DEPUTY MAYOR KAVANAUGH... DOES CITY HALL HAVE A PANIC ROOM?
I DON'T...I'M NOT...
THE FOURTH FLOOR-- THERE'S A VAULT!
GO LOCK YOURSELVES INSIDE--
--AND DON'T OPEN IT FOR ANYONE!

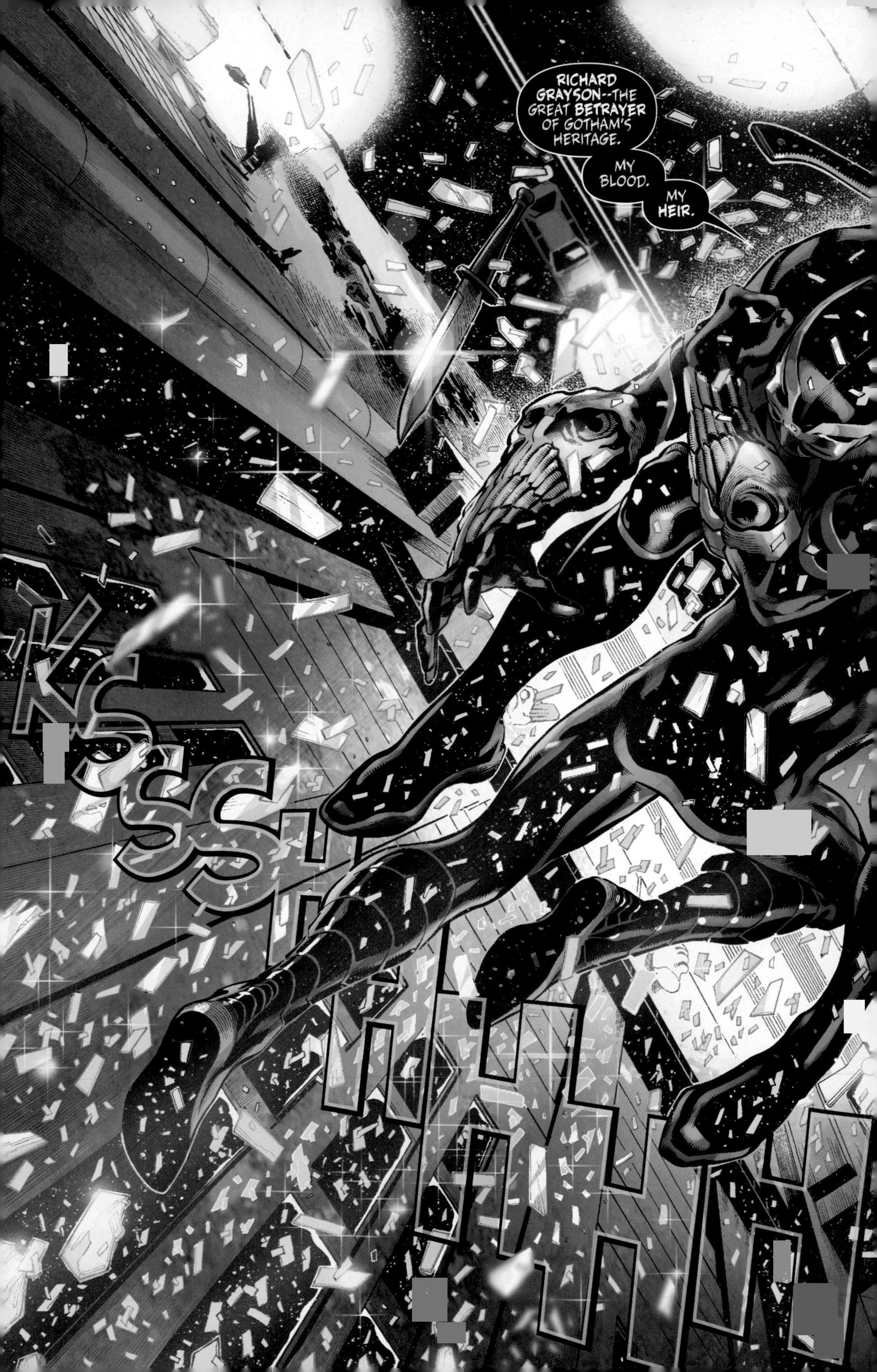
RICHARD GRAYSON--THE GREAT BETRAYER OF GOTHAM'S HERITAGE.
MY BLOOD.
MY HEIR.

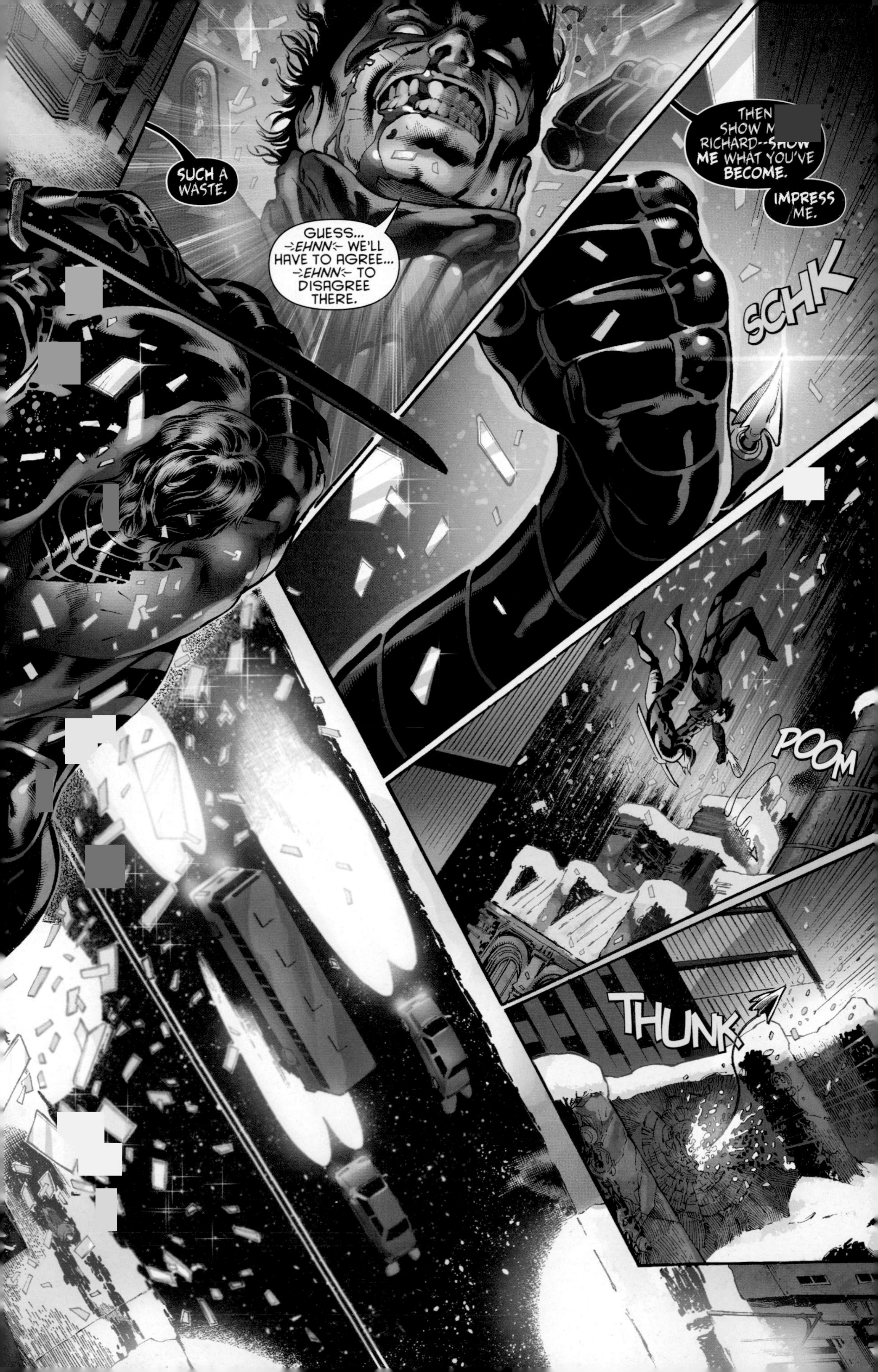
SUCH A WASTE.
GUESS... -EHNN- WE'LL HAVE TO AGREE... -EHNN- TO DISAGREE THERE.
THEN SHOW M RICHARD--SHOW ME WHAT YOU'VE BECOME.
IMPRESS ME.
SCHK
POOM
THUNK

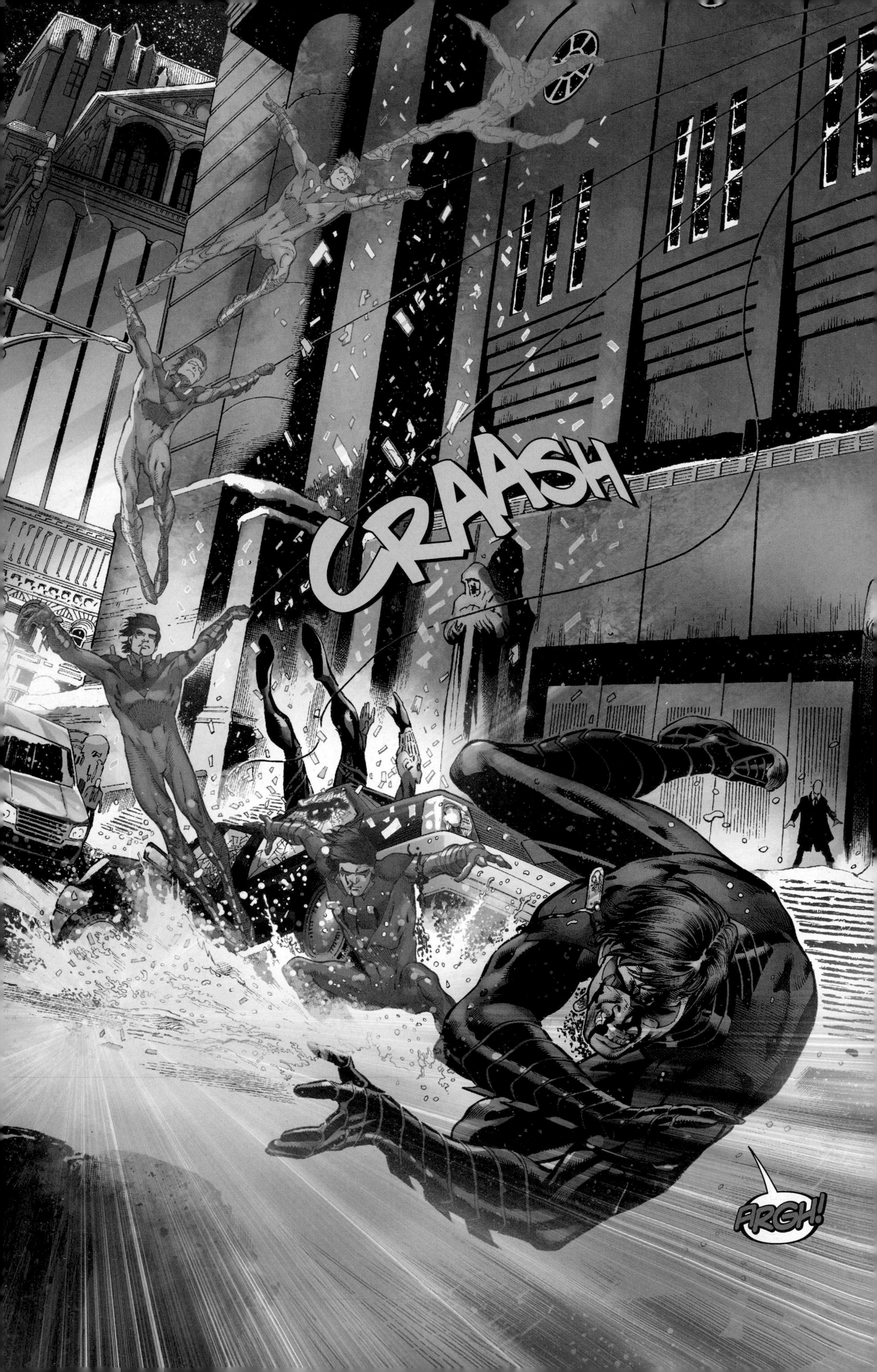
CRAASH
ARGH!

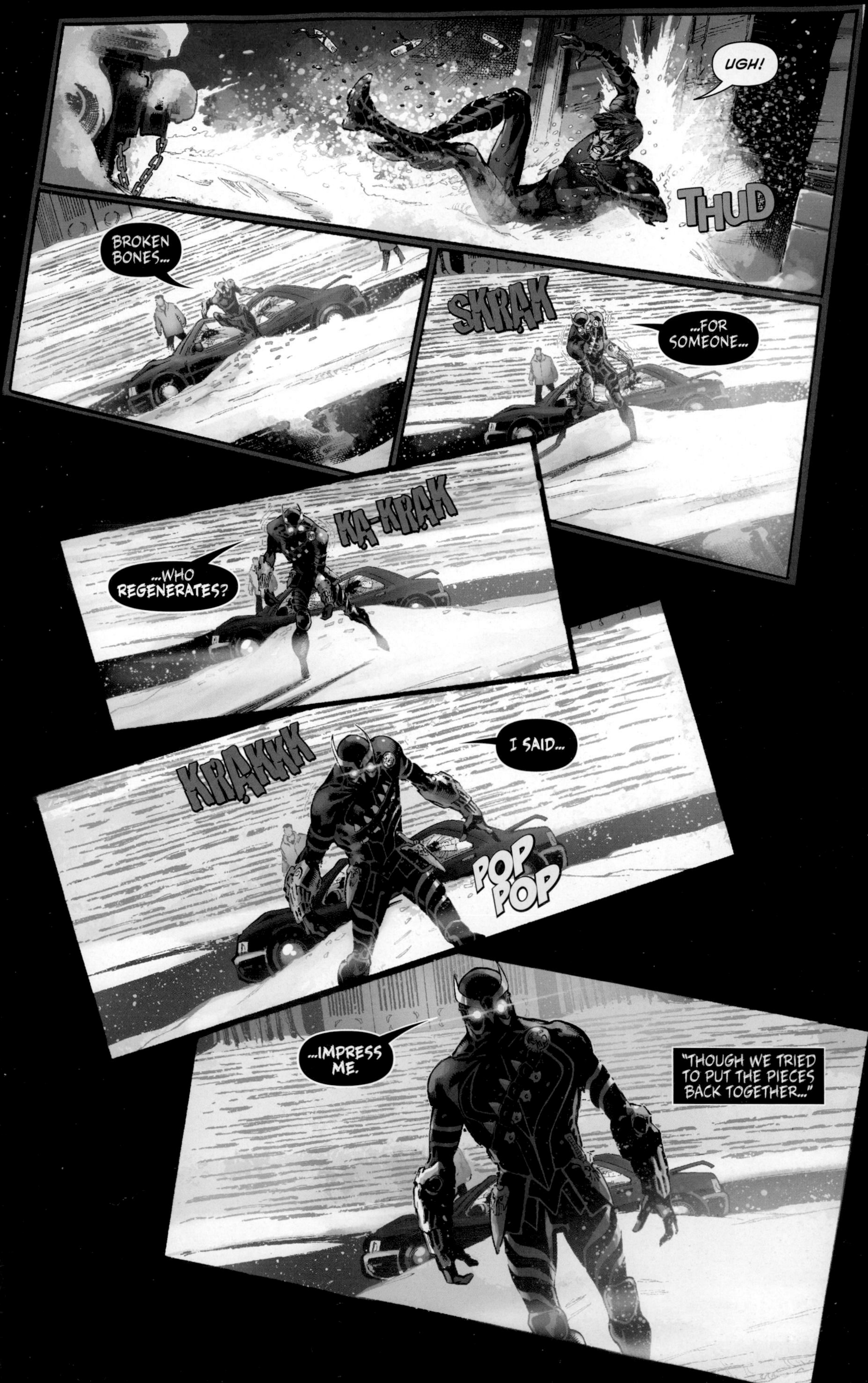
UGH!
THUD
BROKEN BONES...
SKRAK
...FOR SOMEONE...
KA-KRAK
...WHO REGENERATES?
KRAKKK
I SAID...
POP POP
...IMPRESS ME.
"THOUGH WE TRIED TO PUT THE PIECES BACK TOGETHER..."

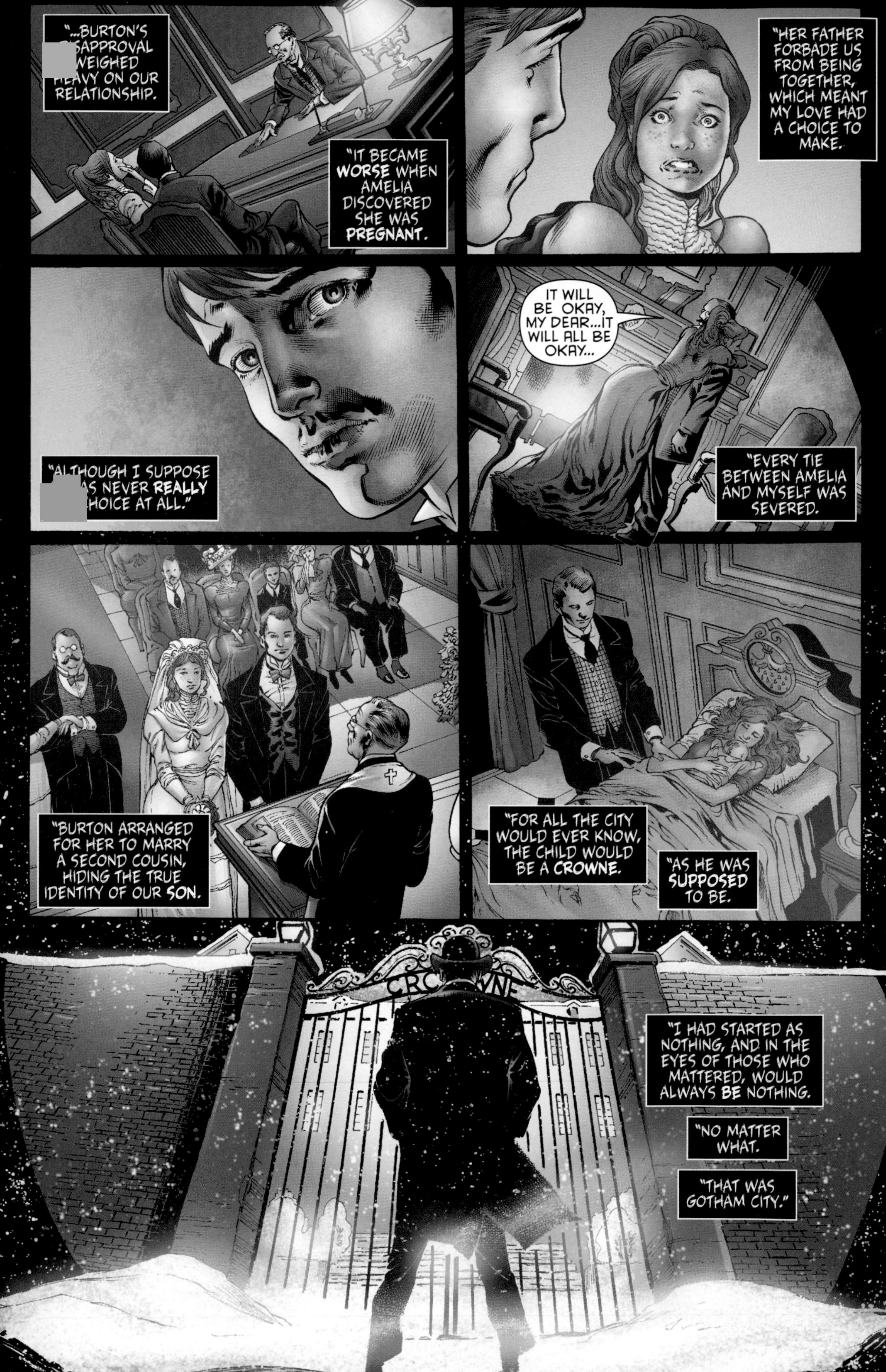
"...BURTON'S ISAPPROVAL WEIGHED EAVY ON OUR RELATIONSHIP.
"IT BECAME WORSE WHEN AMELIA DISCOVERED SHE WAS PREGNANT.
"HER FATHER FORBADE US FROM BEING TOGETHER, WHICH MEANT MY LOVE HAD A CHOICE TO MAKE.
"ALTHOUGH I SUPPOSE AS NEVER REALLY HOICE AT ALL."
IT WILL BE OKAY, MY DEAR...IT WILL ALL BE OKAY...
"EVERY TIE BETWEEN AMELIA AND MYSELF WAS SEVERED.
"BURTON ARRANGED FOR HER TO MARRY A SECOND COUSIN, HIDING THE TRUE IDENTITY OF OUR SON.
"FOR ALL THE CITY WOULD EVER KNOW, THE CHILD WOULD BE A CROWNE.
"AS HE WAS SUPPOSED TO BE.
"I HAD STARTED AS NOTHING, AND IN THE EYES OF THOSE WHO MATTERED, WOULD ALWAYS BE NOTHING.
"NO MATTER WHAT.
"THAT WAS GOTHAM CITY."

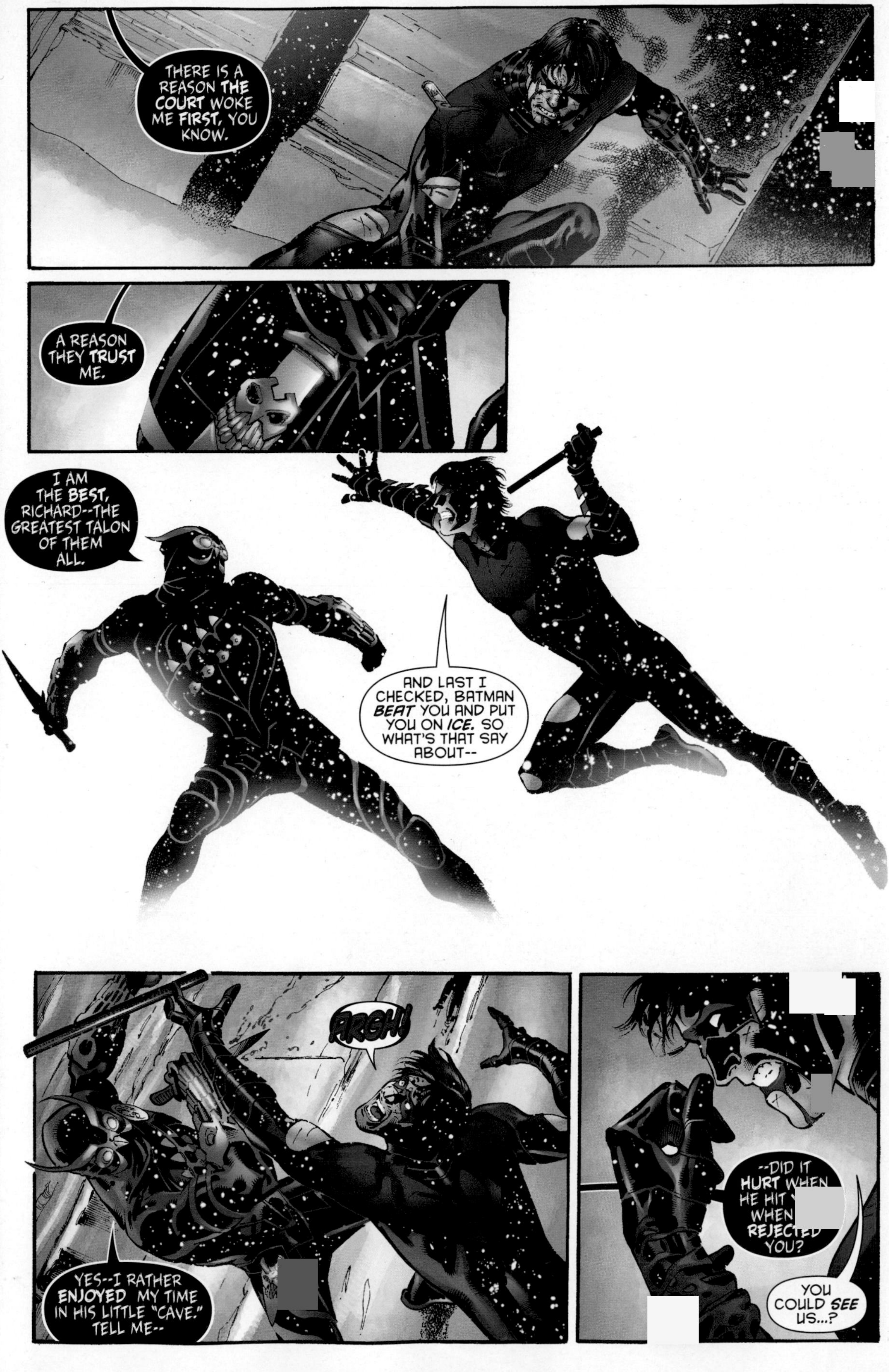
THERE IS A REASON THE COURT WOKE ME FIRST, YOU KNOW.
A REASON THEY TRUST ME.
I AM THE BEST, RICHARD--THE GREATEST TALON OF THEM ALL.
AND LAST I CHECKED, BATMAN BEAT YOU AND PUT YOU ON ICE. SO WHAT'S THAT SAY ABOUT--
ARGH!
YES--I RATHER ENJOYED MY TIME IN HIS LITTLE "CAVE." TELL ME--
--DID IT HURT WHEN HE HIT WHEN REJECTED YOU?
YOU COULD SEE US...?

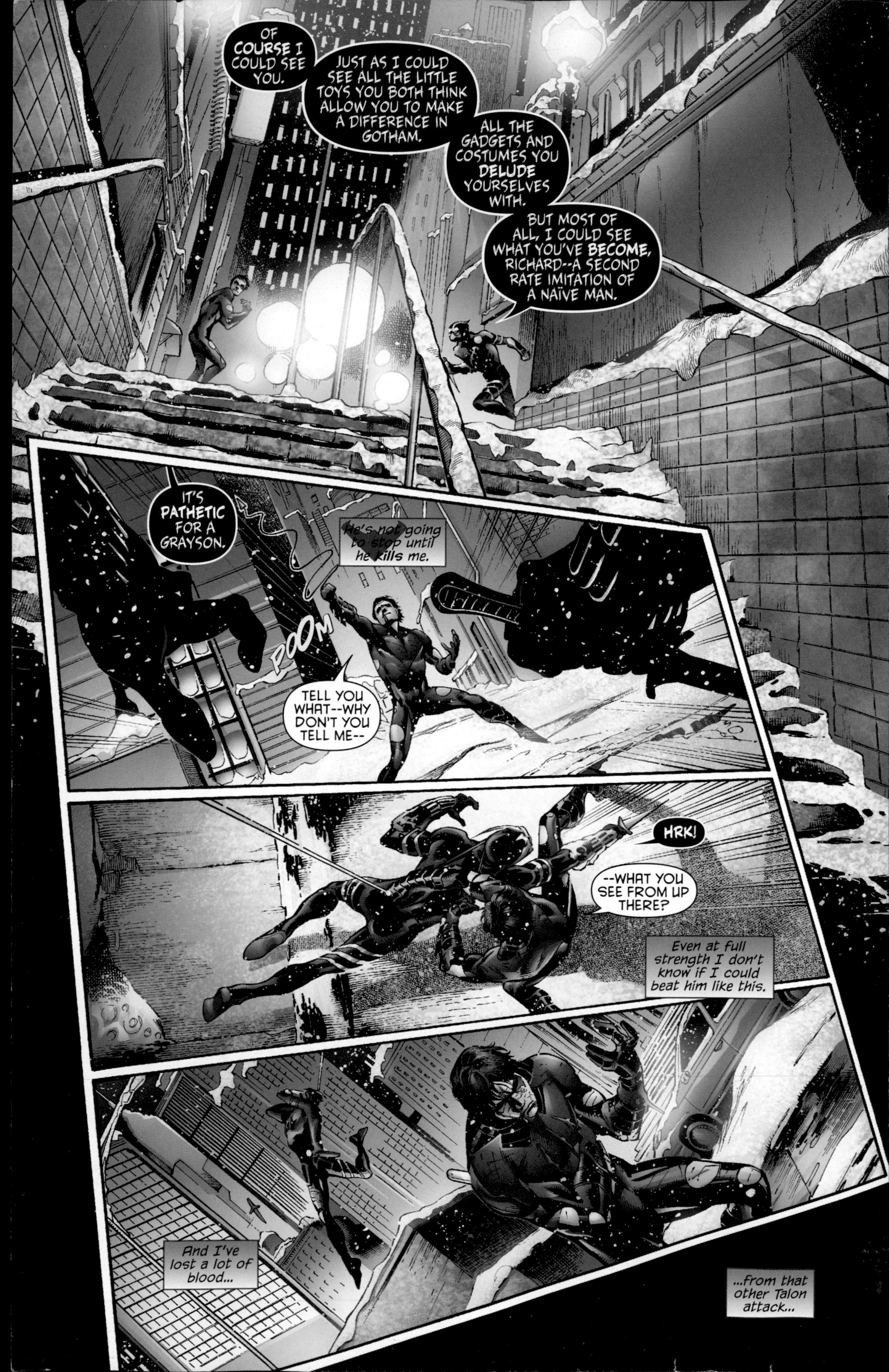

OF **COURSE** I COULD SEE YOU.
JUST AS I COULD SEE ALL THE LITTLE TOYS YOU BOTH THINK ALLOW YOU TO MAKE A DIFFERENCE IN GOTHAM.
ALL THE GADGETS AND COSTUMES YOU **DELUDE** YOURSELVES WITH.
BUT MOST OF ALL, I COULD SEE WHAT YOU'VE **BECOME,** RICHARD--A SECOND RATE IMITATION OF A NAÏVE MAN.
IT'S **PATHETIC** FOR A GRAYSON.
*He's not going to stop until he **kills** me.*
POOM
TELL YOU WHAT--WHY DON'T YOU TELL ME--
HRK!
--WHAT YOU SEE FROM UP THERE?
Even at full strength I don't know if I could beat him like this.
And I've lost a lot of blood...
...from that other Talon attack...

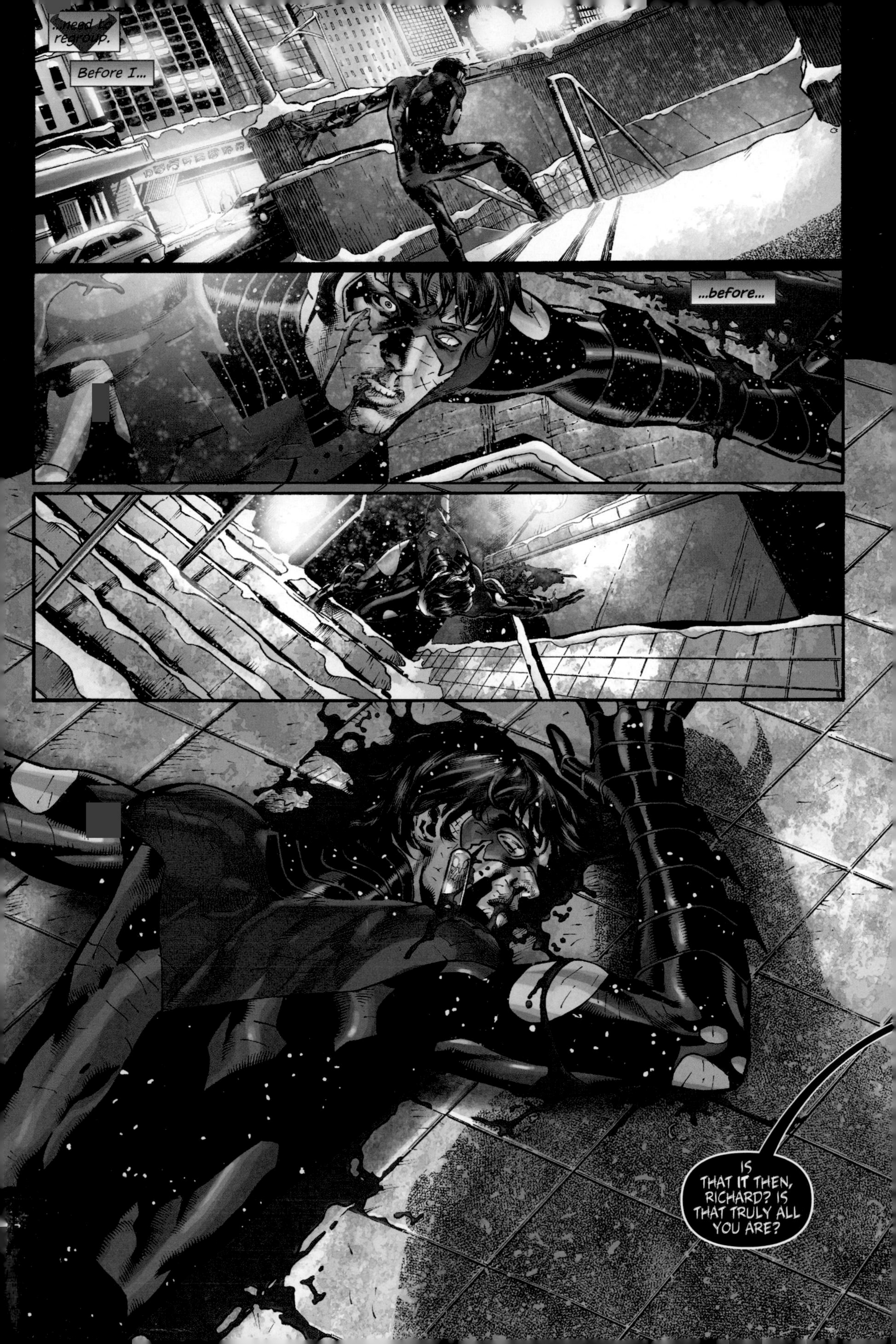
...need to regroup.
Before I...
...before...
IS THAT IT THEN, RICHARD? IS THAT TRULY ALL YOU ARE?

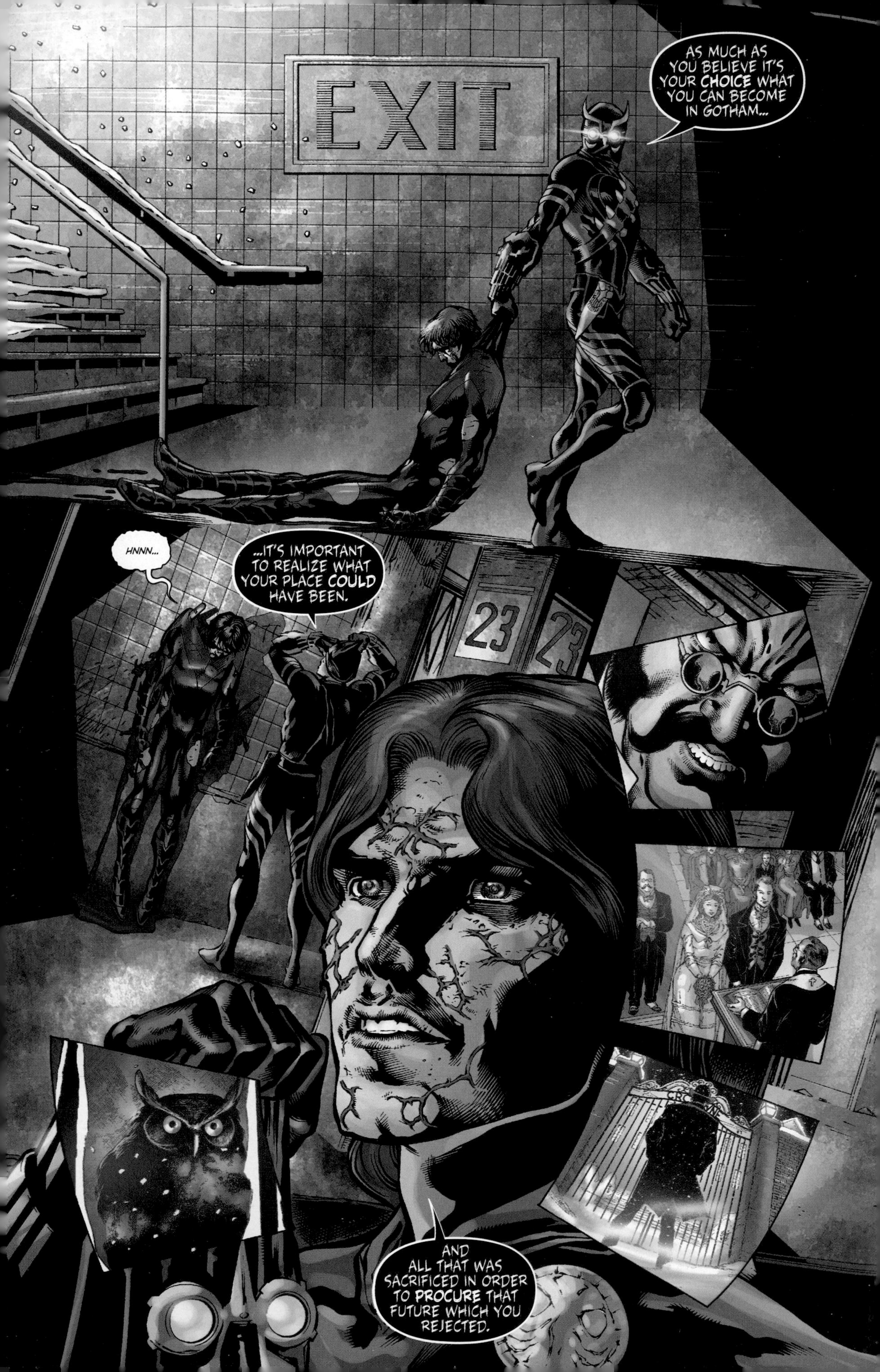
EXIT
AS MUCH AS YOU BELIEVE IT'S YOUR CHOICE WHAT YOU CAN BECOME IN GOTHAM...
HNNN...
...IT'S IMPORTANT TO REALIZE WHAT YOUR PLACE COULD HAVE BEEN.
23
23
AND ALL THAT WAS SACRIFICED IN ORDER TO PROCURE THAT FUTURE WHICH YOU REJECTED.

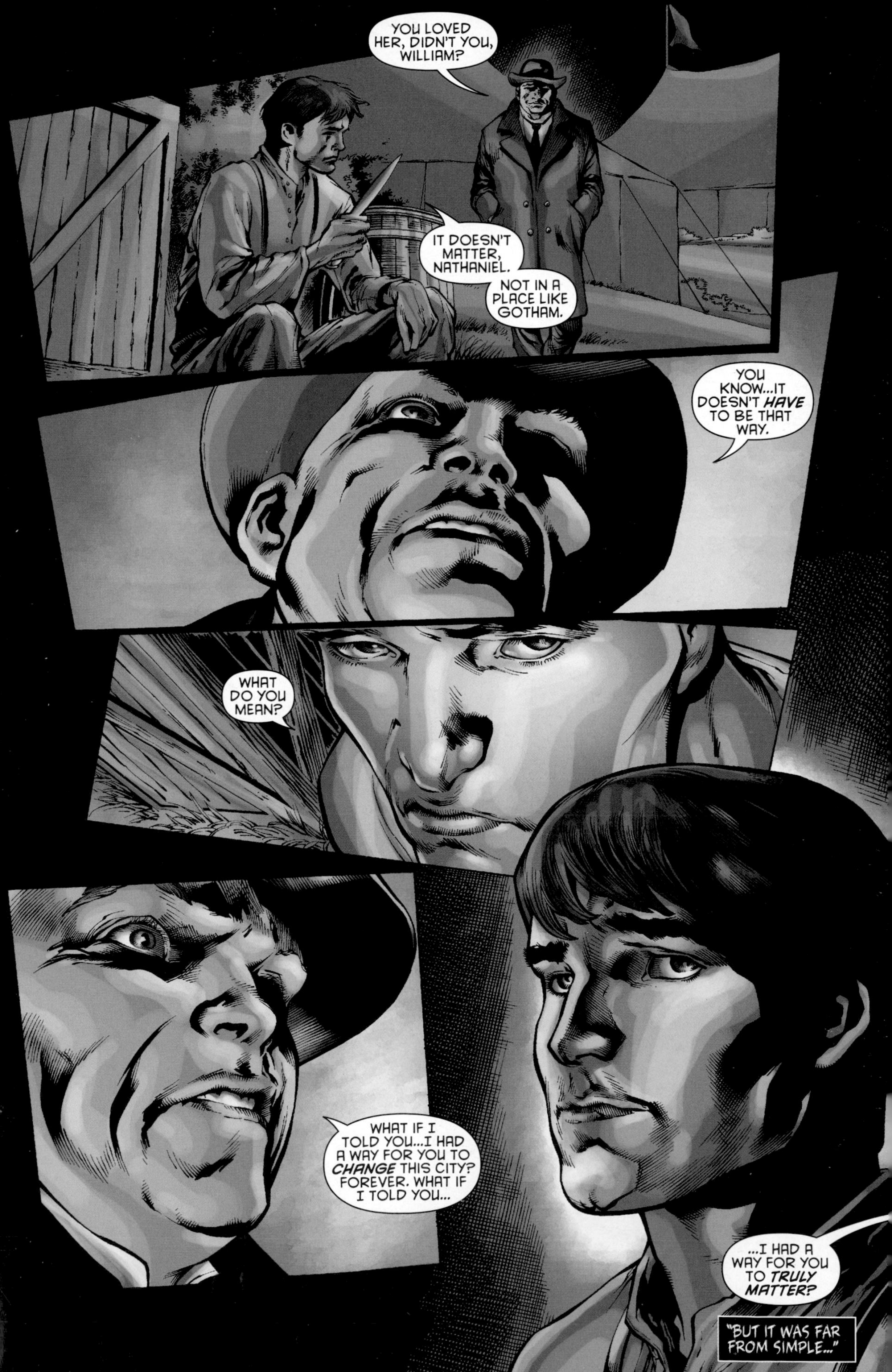
YOU LOVED HER, DIDN'T YOU, WILLIAM?
IT DOESN'T MATTER, NATHANIEL.
NOT IN A PLACE LIKE GOTHAM.
YOU KNOW...IT DOESN'T HAVE TO BE THAT WAY.
WHAT DO YOU MEAN?
WHAT IF I TOLD YOU...I HAD A WAY FOR YOU TO CHANGE THIS CITY? FOREVER. WHAT IF I TOLD YOU...
...I HAD A WAY FOR YOU TO TRULY MATTER?
"BUT IT WAS FAR FROM SIMPLE..."

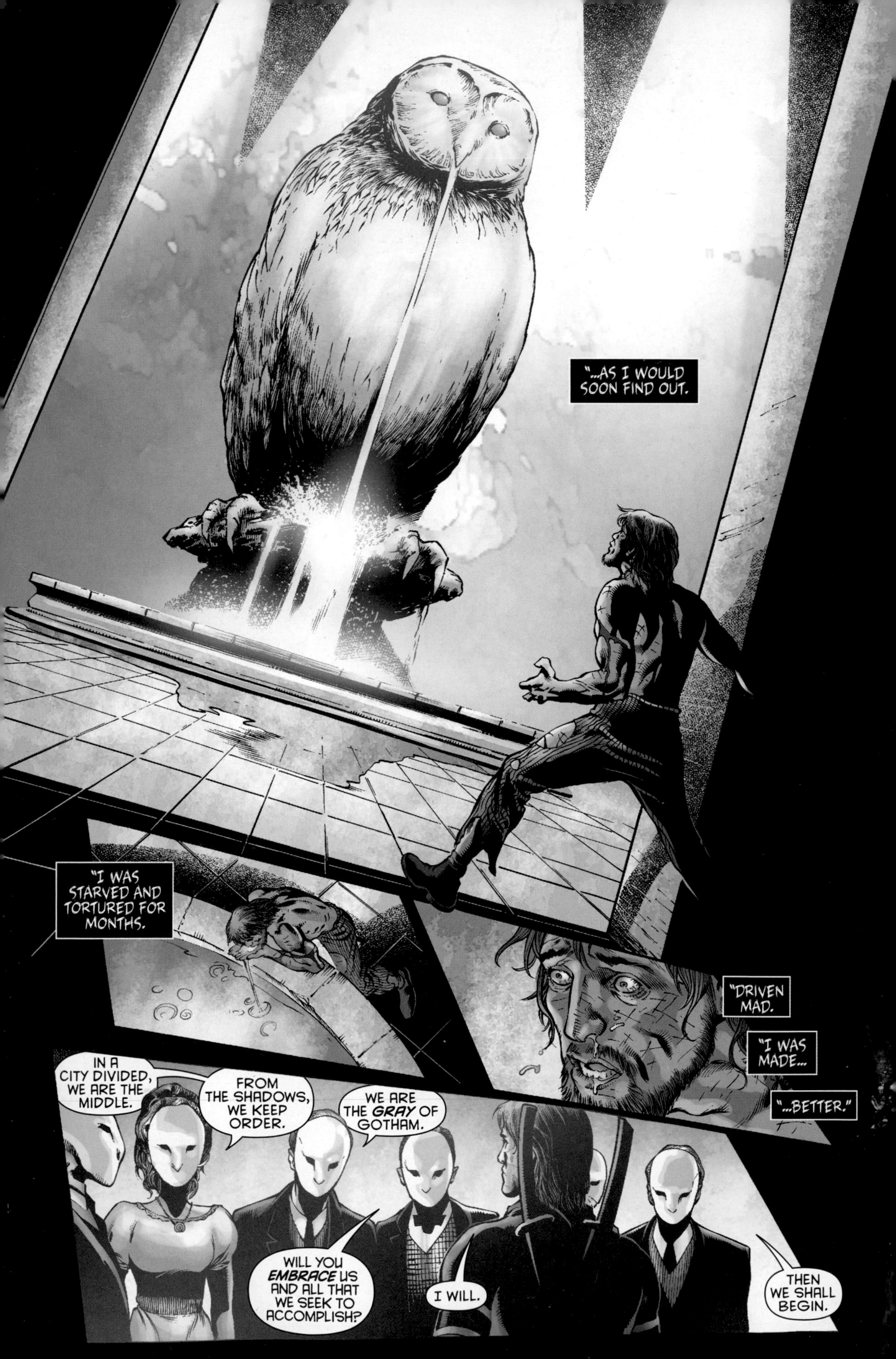
"...AS I WOULD SOON FIND OUT.
"I WAS STARVED AND TORTURED FOR MONTHS.
"DRIVEN MAD.
"I WAS MADE...
"...BETTER."
IN A CITY DIVIDED, WE ARE THE MIDDLE.
FROM THE SHADOWS, WE KEEP ORDER.
WE ARE THE GRAY OF GOTHAM.
WILL YOU EMBRACE US AND ALL THAT WE SEEK TO ACCOMPLISH?
I WILL.
THEN WE SHALL BEGIN.

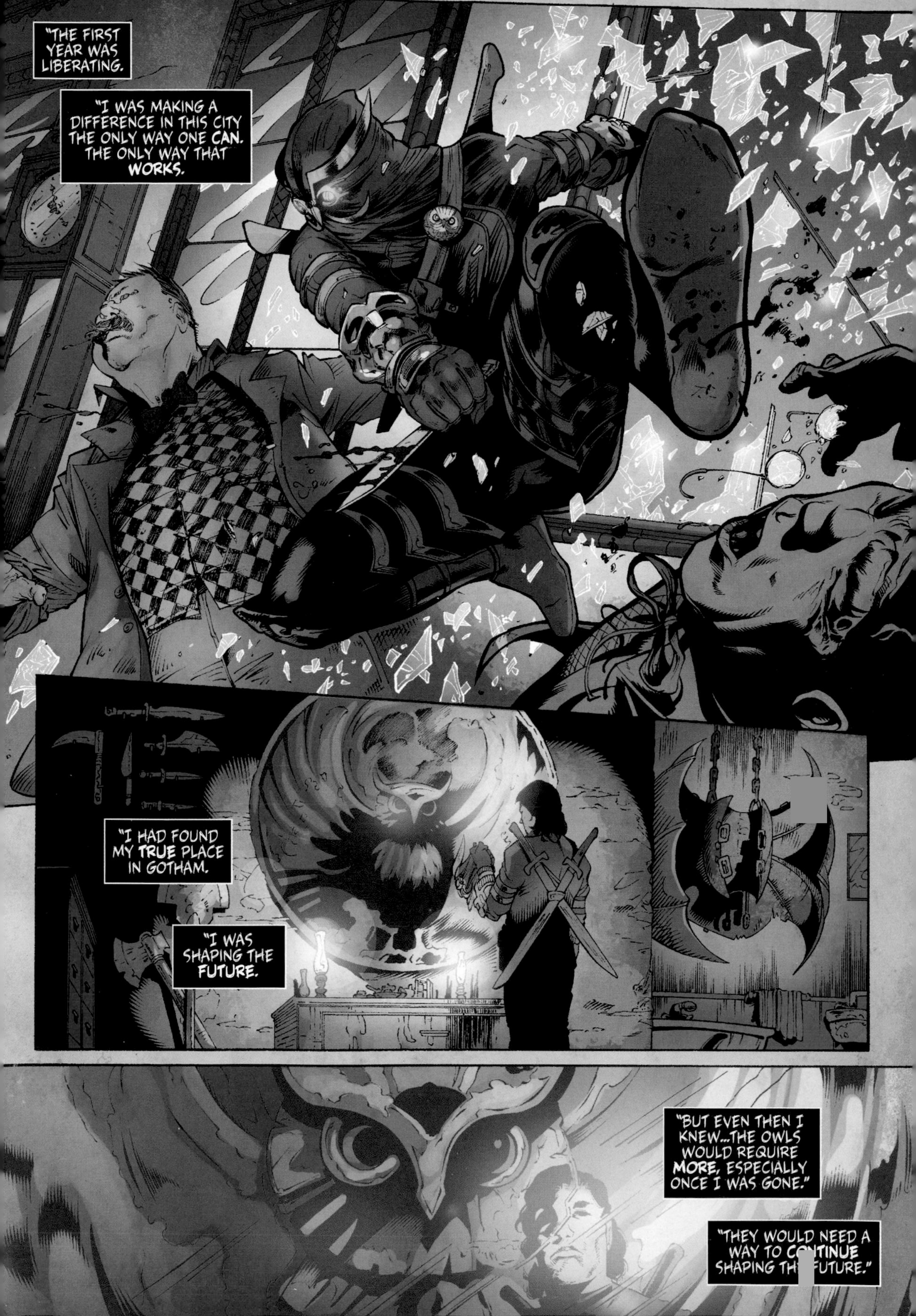
"THE FIRST YEAR WAS LIBERATING.
"I WAS MAKING A DIFFERENCE IN THIS CITY THE ONLY WAY ONE **CAN**. THE ONLY WAY THAT **WORKS**.
"I HAD FOUND MY **TRUE** PLACE IN GOTHAM.
"I WAS SHAPING THE **FUTURE**.
"BUT EVEN THEN I KNEW...THE OWLS WOULD REQUIRE **MORE**, ESPECIALLY ONCE I WAS GONE."
"THEY WOULD NEED A WAY TO **CONTINUE** SHAPING TH FUTURE."

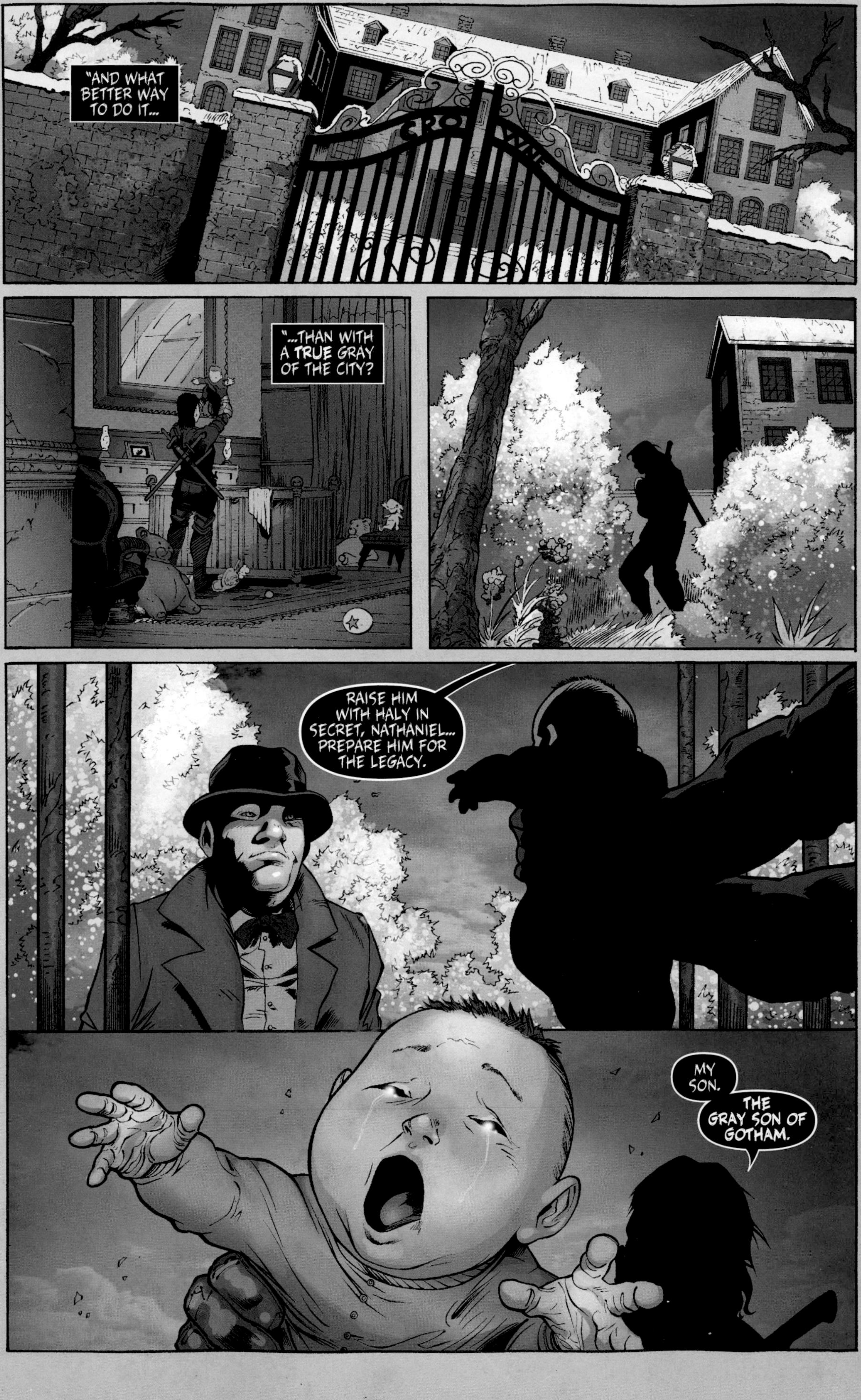
"AND WHAT BETTER WAY TO DO IT...
"...THAN WITH A TRUE GRAY OF THE CITY?
RAISE HIM WITH HALY IN SECRET, NATHANIEL... PREPARE HIM FOR THE LEGACY.
MY SON.
THE GRAY SON OF GOTHAM.

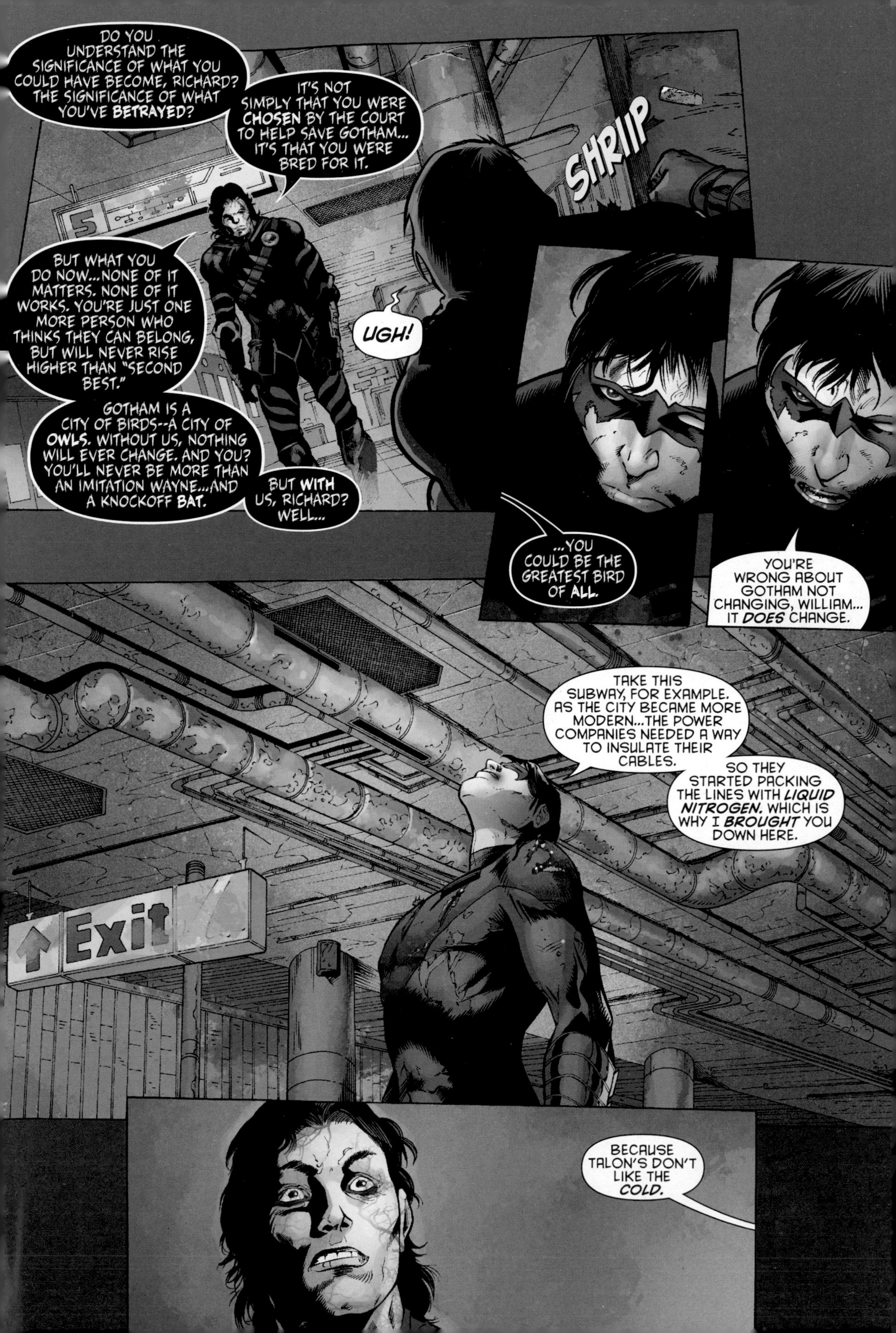
DO YOU UNDERSTAND THE SIGNIFICANCE OF WHAT YOU COULD HAVE BECOME, RICHARD? THE SIGNIFICANCE OF WHAT YOU'VE BETRAYED?
IT'S NOT SIMPLY THAT YOU WERE CHOSEN BY THE COURT TO HELP SAVE GOTHAM... IT'S THAT YOU WERE BRED FOR IT.
SHRIIP
BUT WHAT YOU DO NOW...NONE OF IT MATTERS. NONE OF IT WORKS. YOU'RE JUST ONE MORE PERSON WHO THINKS THEY CAN BELONG, BUT WILL NEVER RISE HIGHER THAN "SECOND BEST."
UGH!
GOTHAM IS A CITY OF BIRDS--A CITY OF OWLS. WITHOUT US, NOTHING WILL EVER CHANGE. AND YOU? YOU'LL NEVER BE MORE THAN AN IMITATION WAYNE...AND A KNOCKOFF BAT.
BUT WITH US, RICHARD? WELL...
...YOU COULD BE THE GREATEST BIRD OF ALL.
YOU'RE WRONG ABOUT GOTHAM NOT CHANGING, WILLIAM... IT DOES CHANGE.
TAKE THIS SUBWAY, FOR EXAMPLE. AS THE CITY BECAME MORE MODERN...THE POWER COMPANIES NEEDED A WAY TO INSULATE THEIR CABLES.
SO THEY STARTED PACKING THE LINES WITH LIQUID NITROGEN. WHICH IS WHY I BROUGHT YOU DOWN HERE.
Exit
BECAUSE TALON'S DON'T LIKE THE COLD.

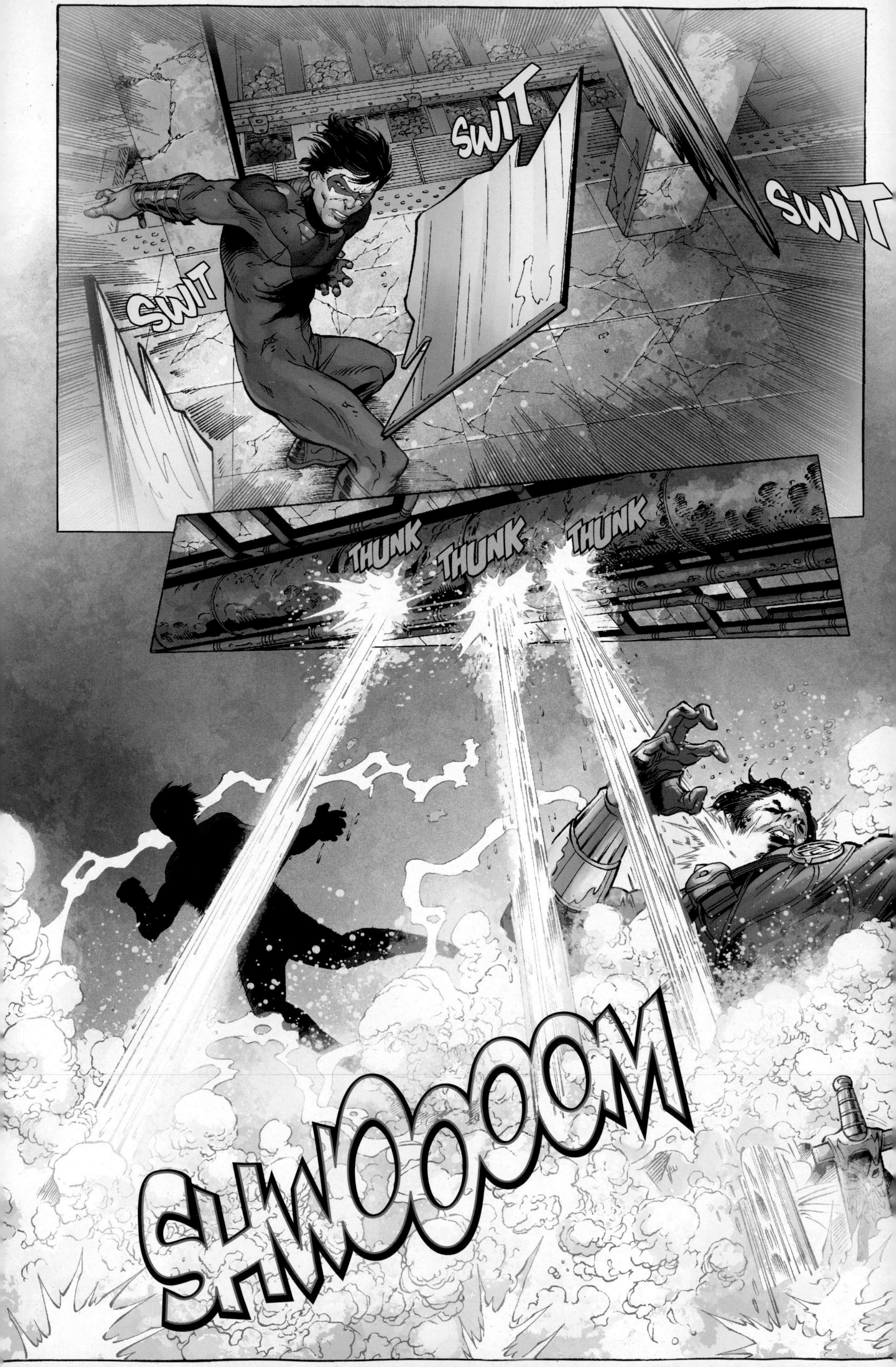

SWIT
SWIT
SWIT
THUNK
THUNK
THUNK
SHWOOOOOM

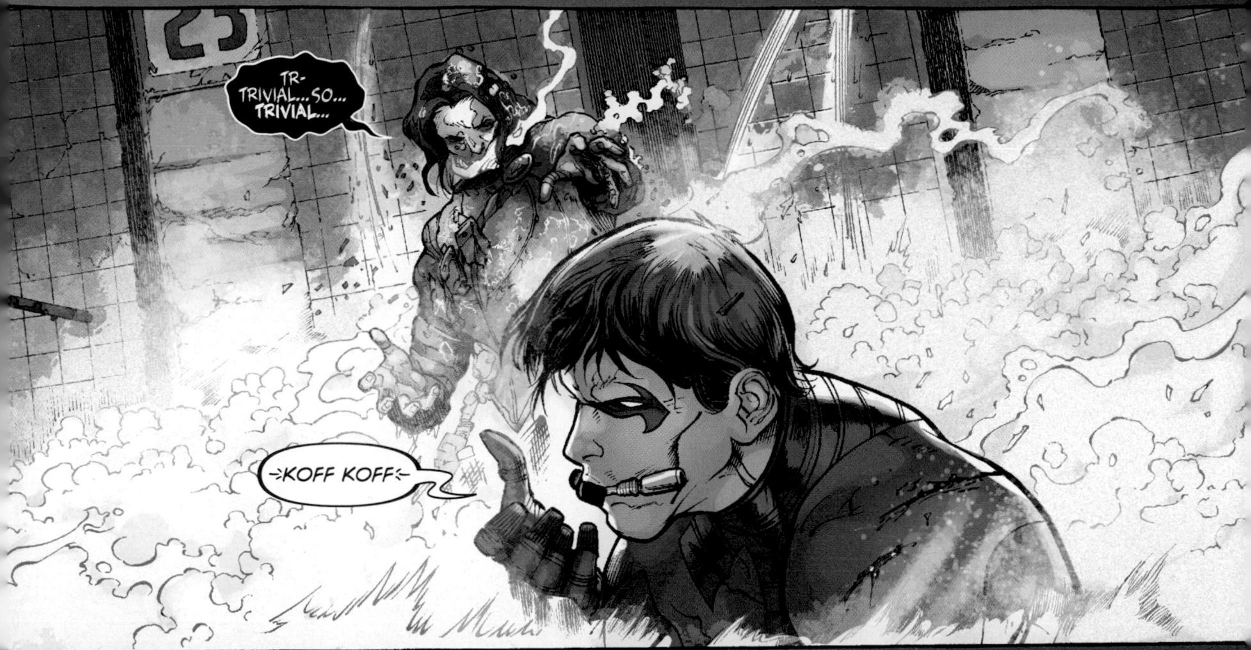
TR-TRIVIAL...SO... TRIVIAL...
KOFF KOFF

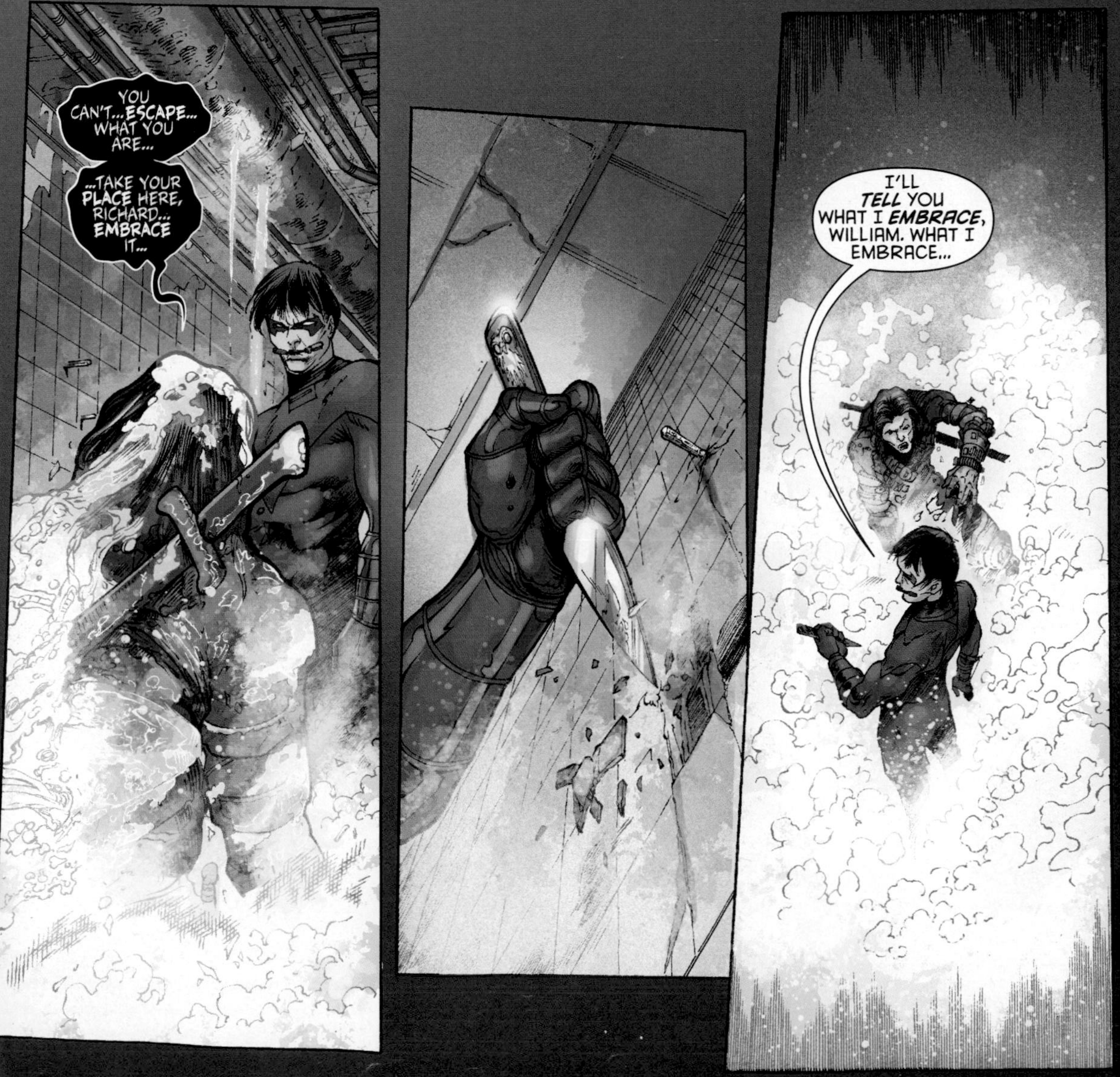
YOU CAN'T...ESCAPE... WHAT YOU ARE...
...TAKE YOUR PLACE HERE, RICHARD... EMBRACE IT...
I'LL TELL YOU WHAT I EMBRACE, WILLIAM. WHAT I EMBRACE...

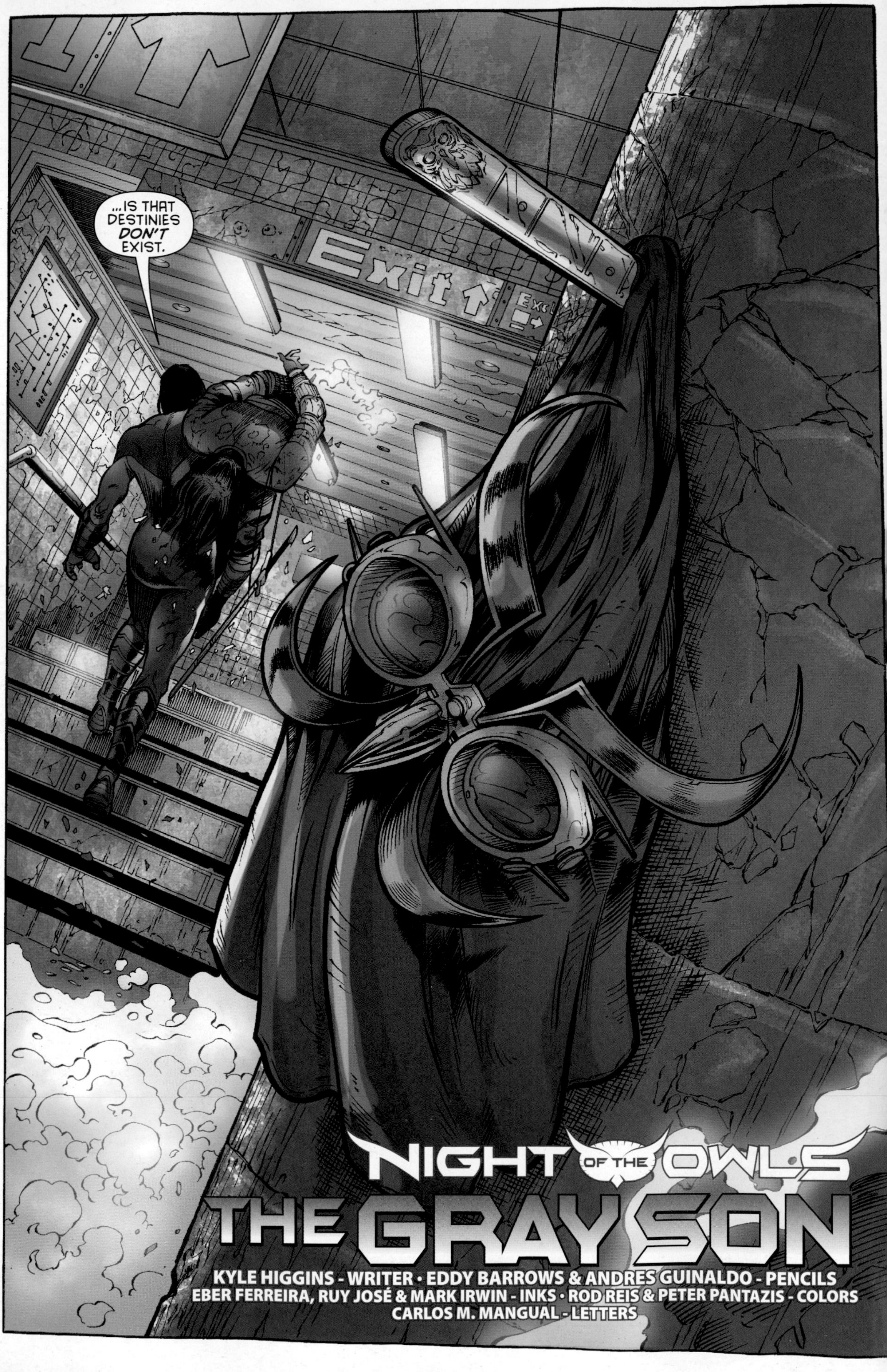

...IS THAT DESTINIES DON'T EXIST.
Exit
NIGHT OF THE OWLS
THE GRAYSON
KYLE HIGGINS - WRITER · EDDY BARROWS & ANDRES GUINALDO - PENCILS
EBER FERREIRA, RUY JOSÉ & MARK IRWIN - INKS · ROD REIS & PETER PANTAZIS - COLORS
CARLOS M. MANGUAL - LETTERS

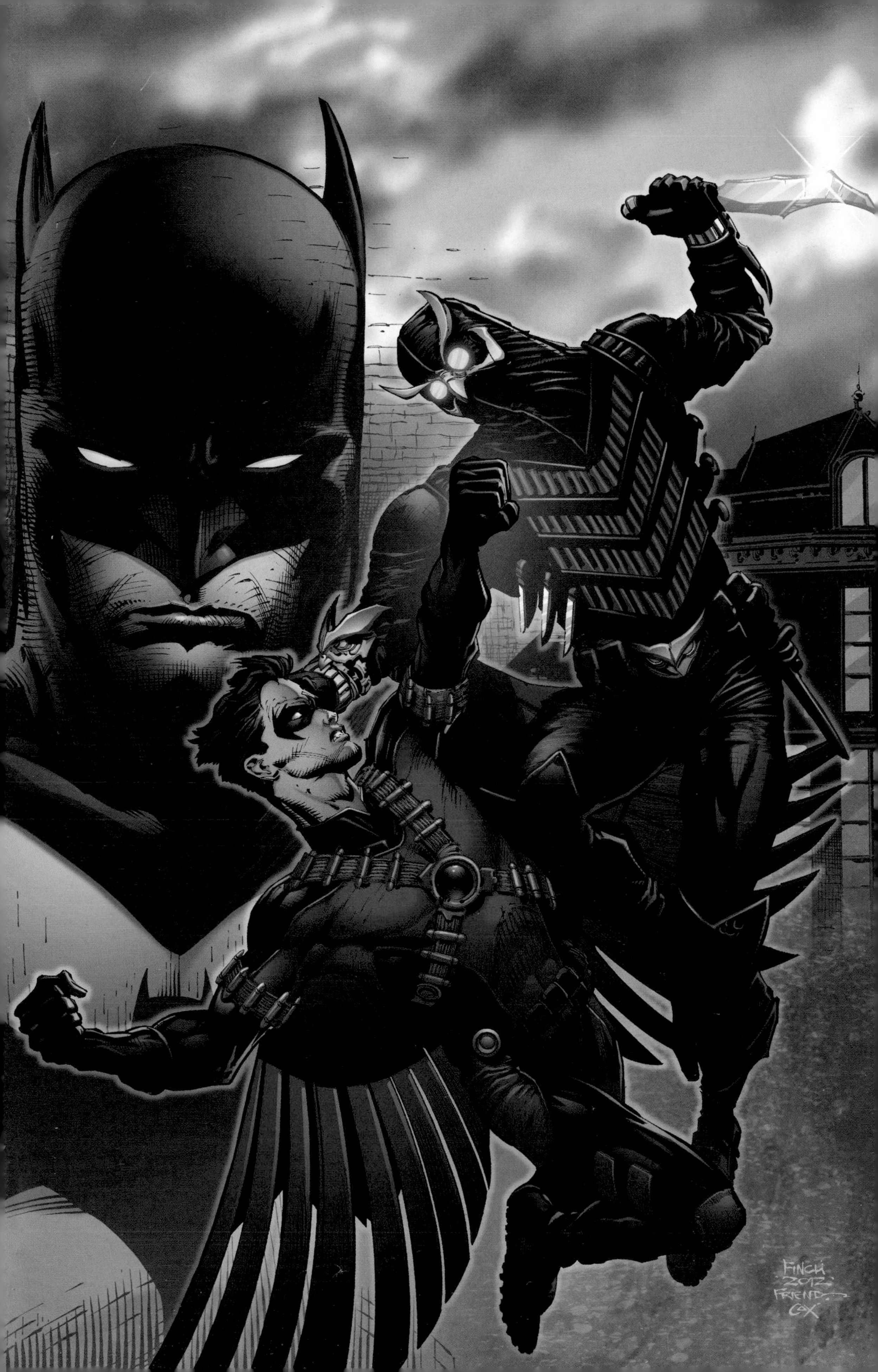
FINCH
2012
FRIEND
COX

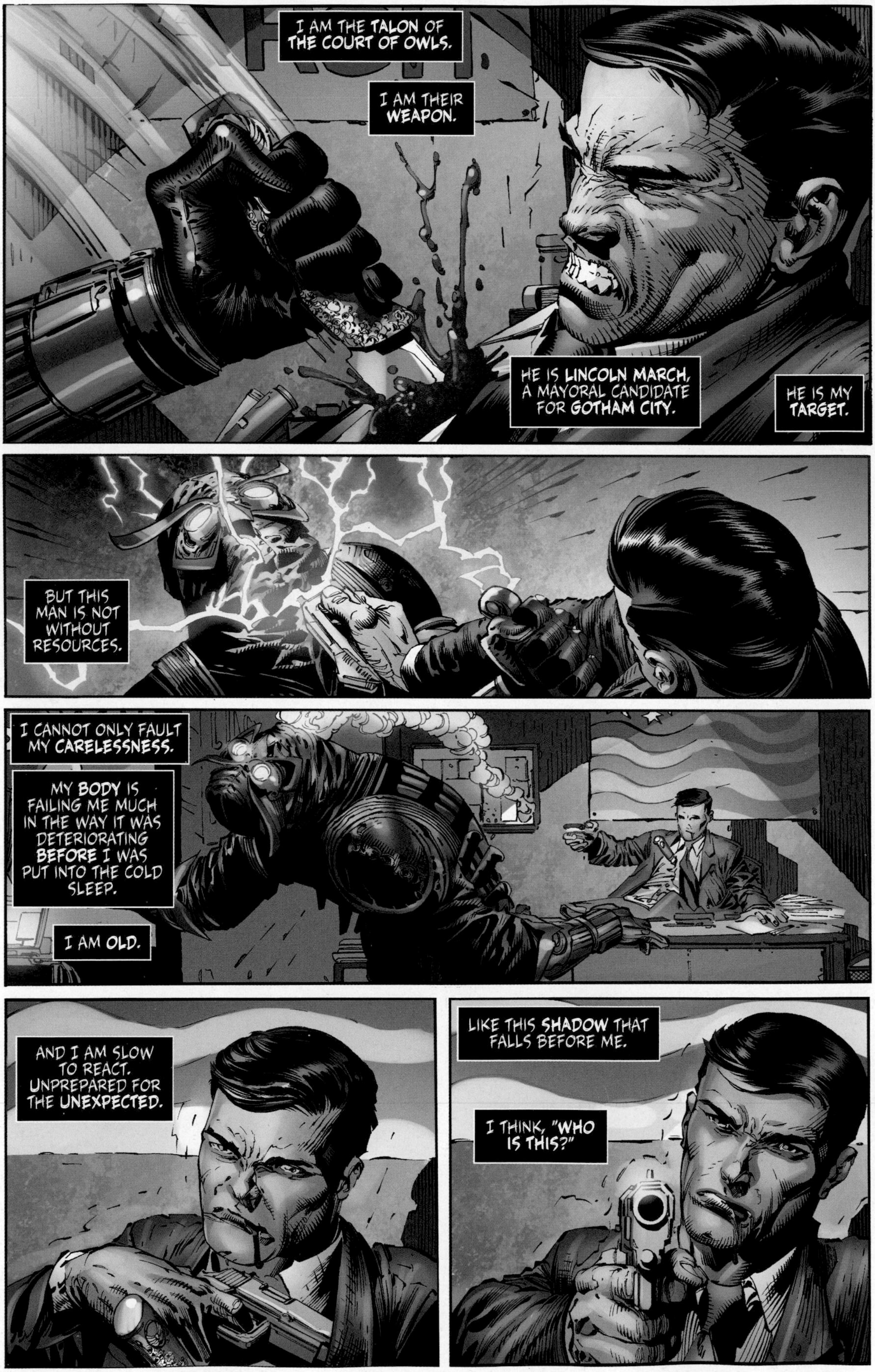
I AM THE TALON OF THE COURT OF OWLS.
I AM THEIR WEAPON.
HE IS LINCOLN MARCH, A MAYORAL CANDIDATE FOR GOTHAM CITY.
HE IS MY TARGET.
BUT THIS MAN IS NOT WITHOUT RESOURCES.
I CANNOT ONLY FAULT MY CARELESSNESS.
MY BODY IS FAILING ME MUCH IN THE WAY IT WAS DETERIORATING BEFORE I WAS PUT INTO THE COLD SLEEP.
I AM OLD.
AND I AM SLOW TO REACT. UNPREPARED FOR THE UNEXPECTED.
LIKE THIS SHADOW THAT FALLS BEFORE ME.
I THINK, "WHO IS THIS?"

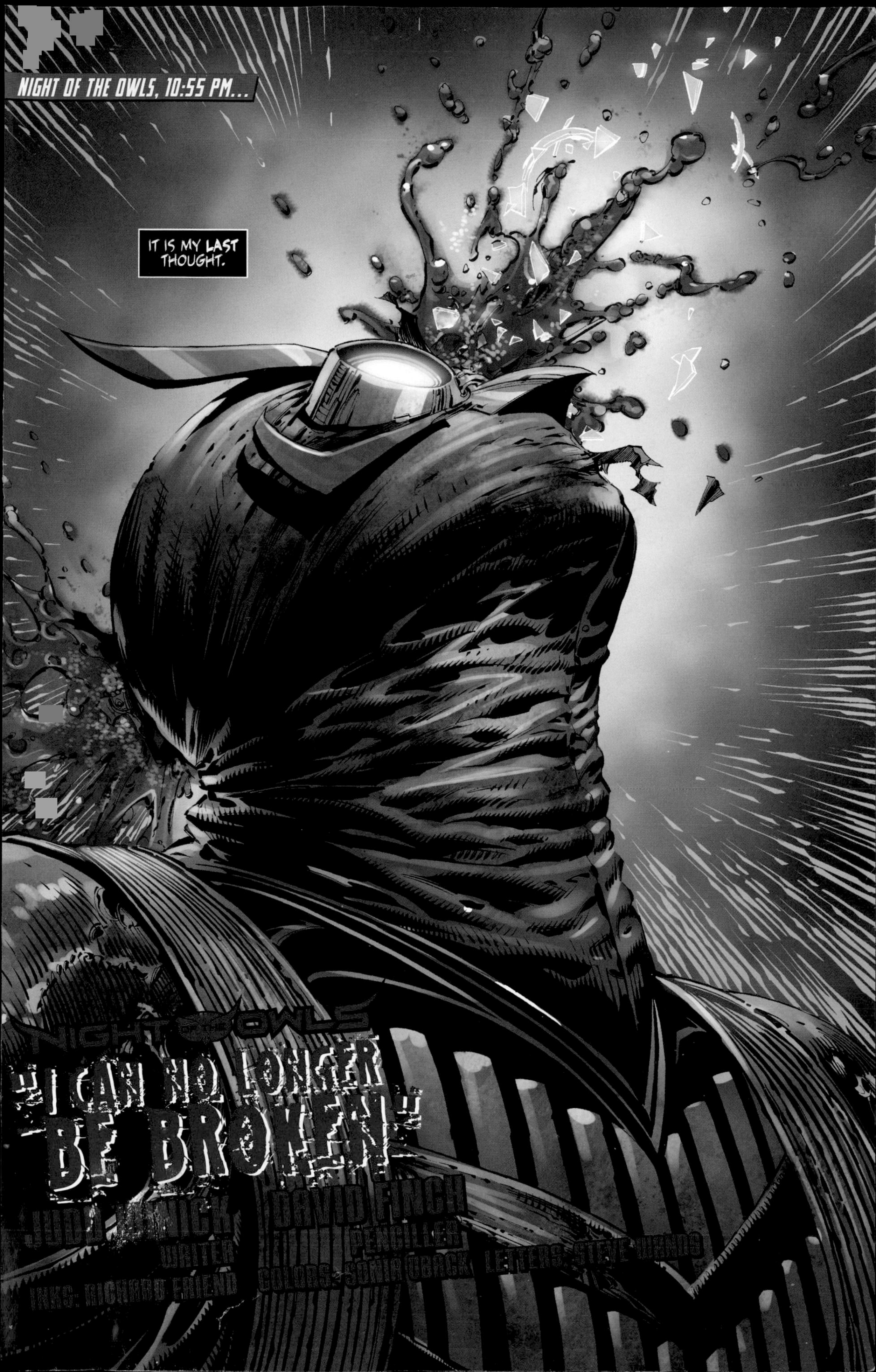
NIGHT OF THE OWLS, 10:55 PM...
IT IS MY LAST THOUGHT.
NIGHT OF THE OWLS
"I CAN NO LONGER BE BROKEN"
DAVID FINCH
WRITER
PENCILLER
INKS: RICHARD FRIEND
COLORS: SONIA OBACK
LETTERS: STEVE WANDS

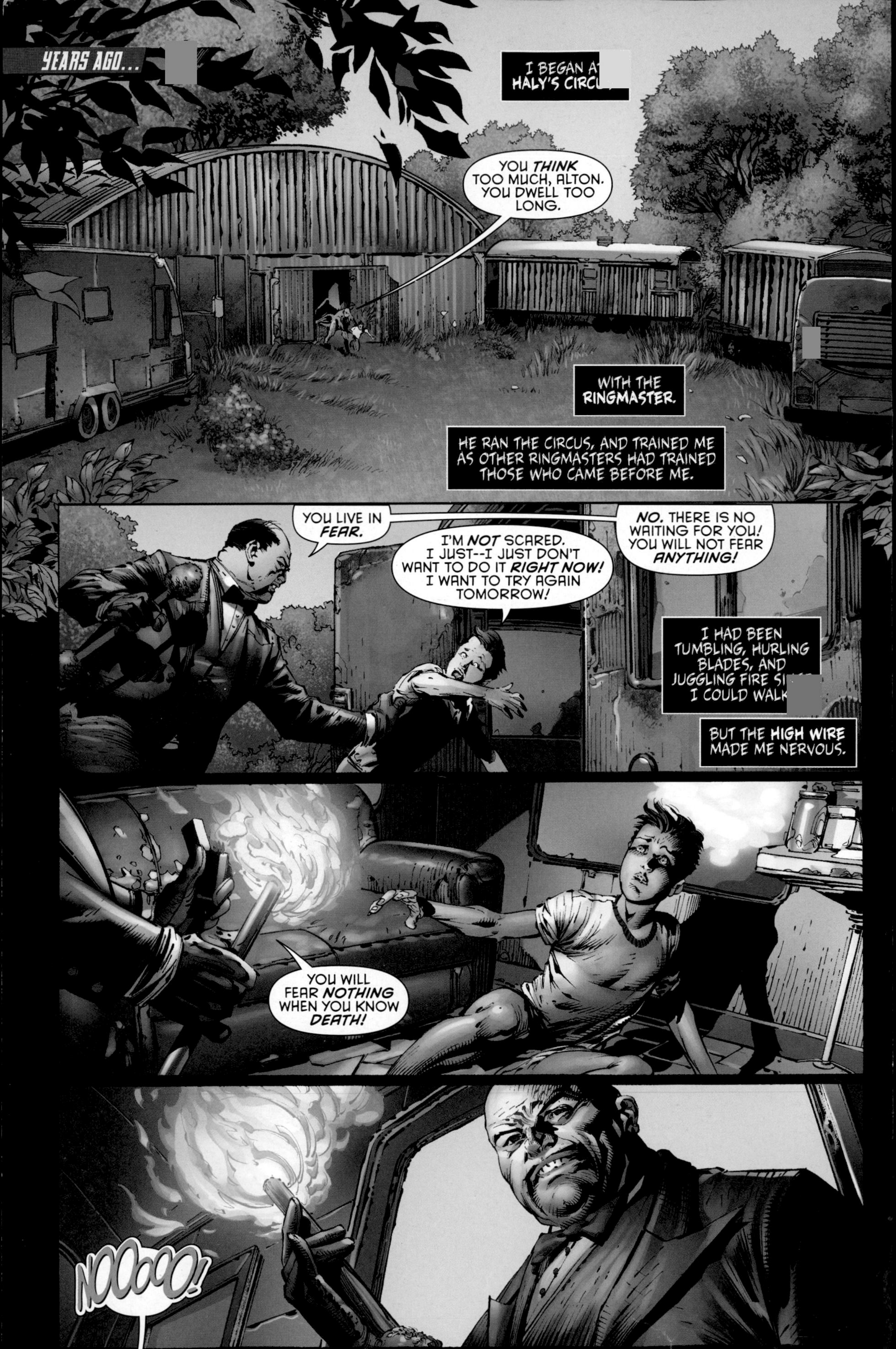
YEARS AGO...
I BEGAN AT HALY'S CIRCU
YOU THINK TOO MUCH, ALTON. YOU DWELL TOO LONG.
WITH THE RINGMASTER.
HE RAN THE CIRCUS, AND TRAINED ME AS OTHER RINGMASTERS HAD TRAINED THOSE WHO CAME BEFORE ME.
YOU LIVE IN FEAR.
I'M NOT SCARED. I JUST--I JUST DON'T WANT TO DO IT RIGHT NOW! I WANT TO TRY AGAIN TOMORROW!
NO. THERE IS NO WAITING FOR YOU! YOU WILL NOT FEAR ANYTHING!
I HAD BEEN TUMBLING, HURLING BLADES, AND JUGGLING FIRE SI I COULD WALK
BUT THE HIGH WIRE MADE ME NERVOUS.
YOU WILL FEAR NOTHING WHEN YOU KNOW DEATH!
NOOOOO!

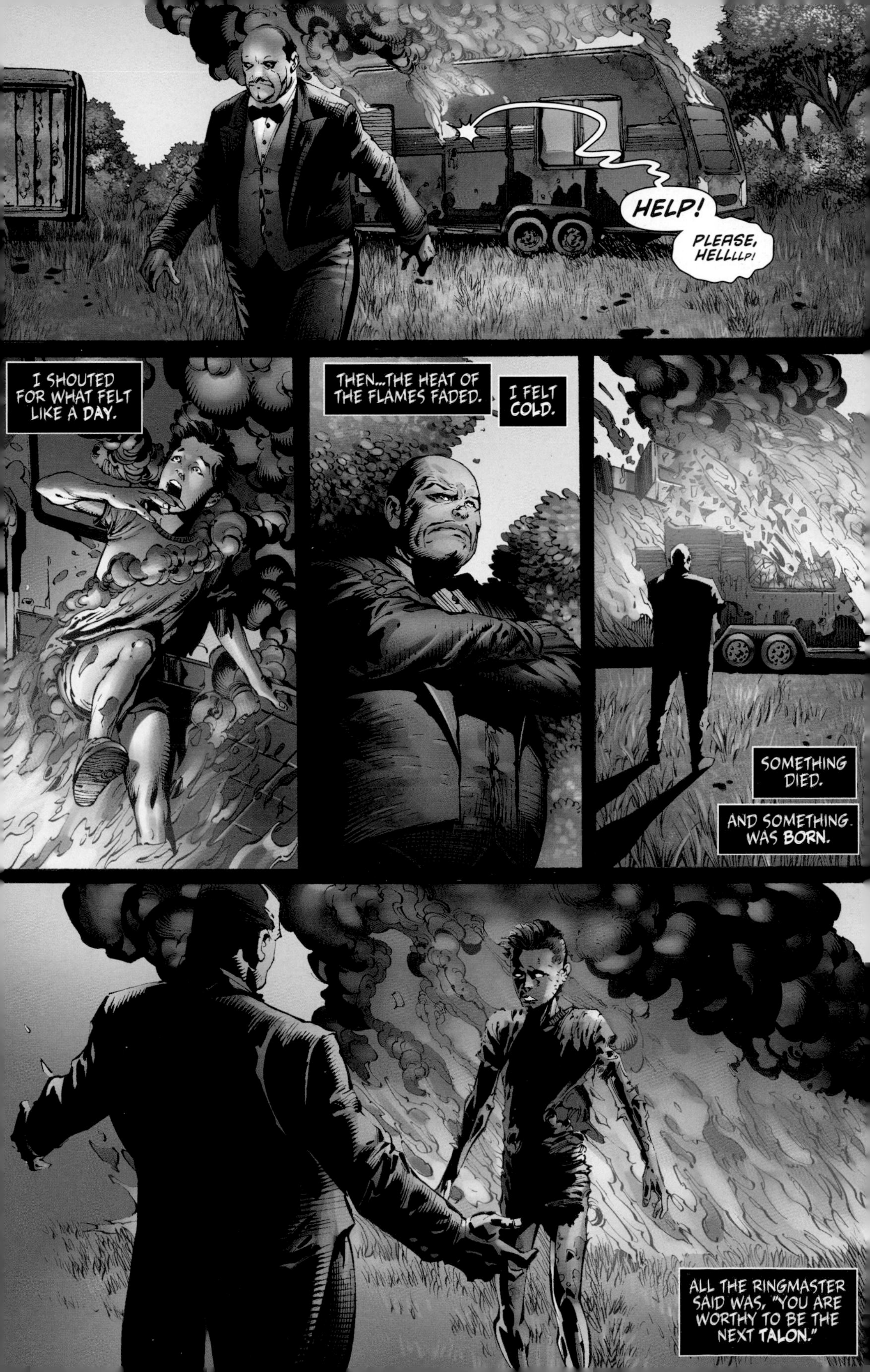

HELP!
PLEASE, HELLLLP!
I SHOUTED FOR WHAT FELT LIKE A DAY.
THEN...THE HEAT OF THE FLAMES FADED.
I FELT COLD.
SOMETHING DIED.
AND SOMETHING WAS BORN.
ALL THE RINGMASTER SAID WAS, "YOU ARE WORTHY TO BE THE NEXT TALON."

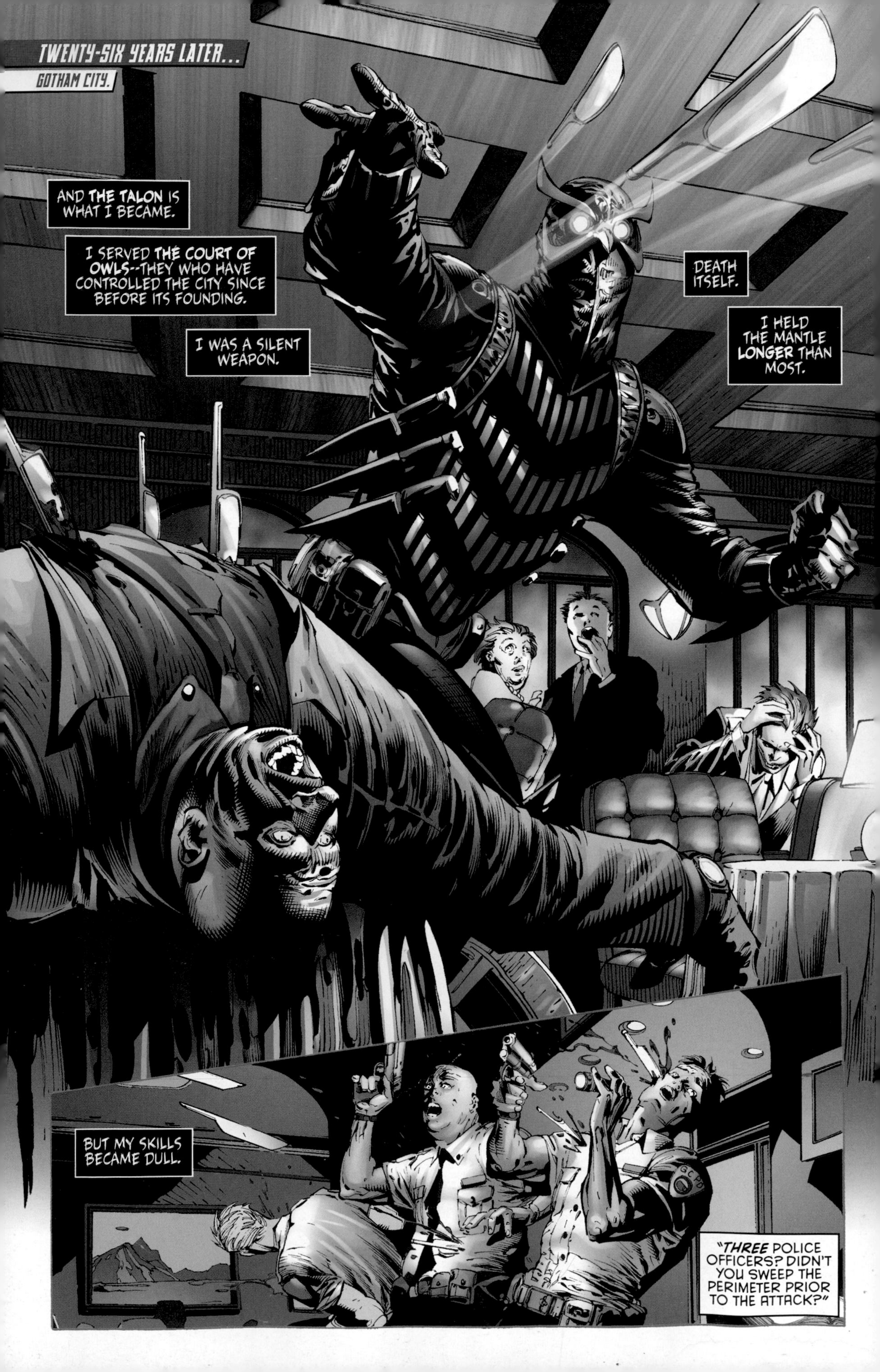
TWENTY-SIX YEARS LATER...
GOTHAM CITY.
AND THE TALON IS WHAT I BECAME.
I SERVED THE COURT OF OWLS--THEY WHO HAVE CONTROLLED THE CITY SINCE BEFORE ITS FOUNDING.
I WAS A SILENT WEAPON.
DEATH ITSELF.
I HELD THE MANTLE LONGER THAN MOST.
BUT MY SKILLS BECAME DULL.
"THREE POLICE OFFICERS? DIDN'T YOU SWEEP THE PERIMETER PRIOR TO THE ATTACK?"

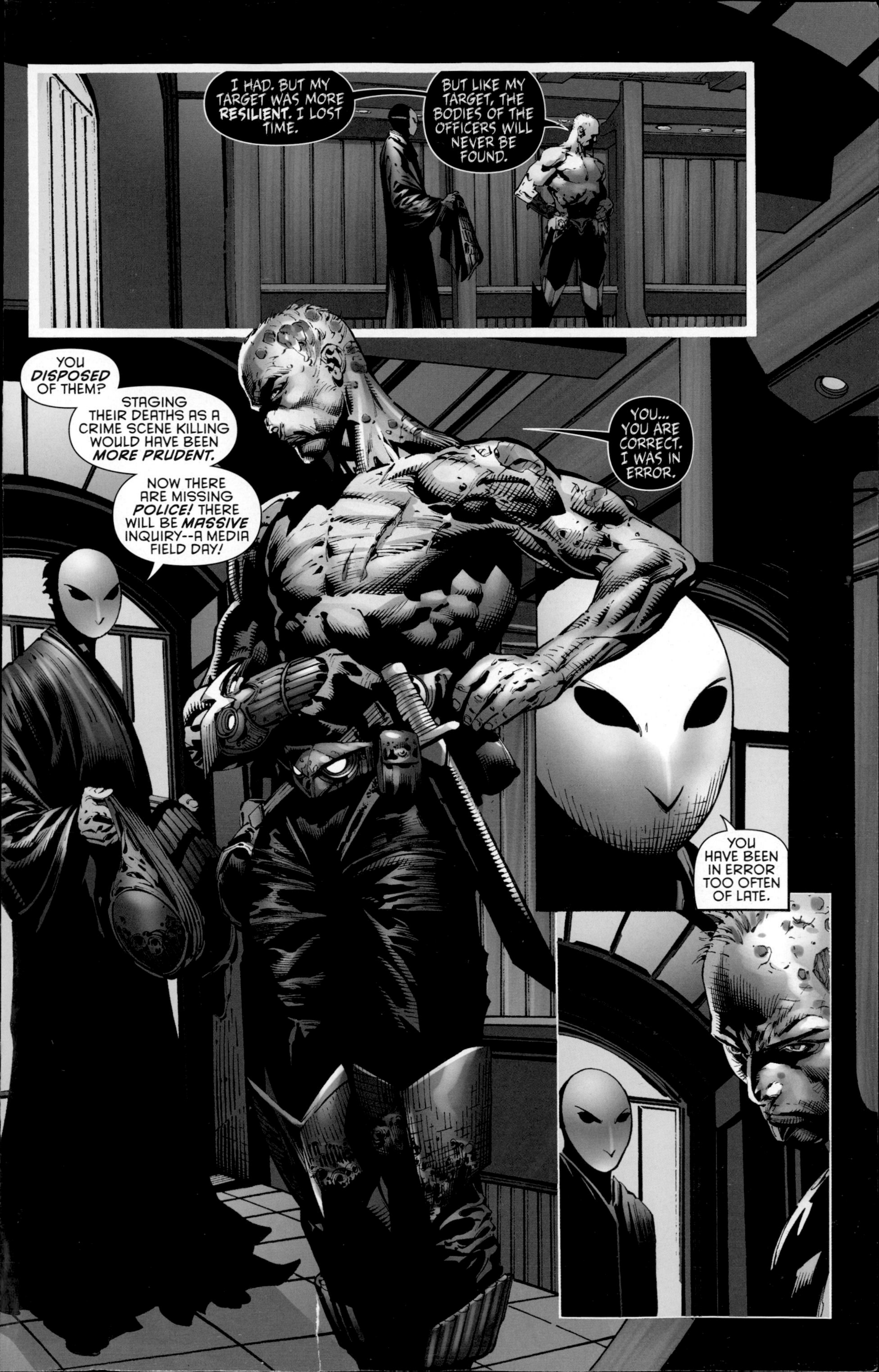
I HAD. BUT MY TARGET WAS MORE **RESILIENT**. I LOST TIME.
BUT LIKE MY TARGET, THE BODIES OF THE OFFICERS WILL NEVER BE FOUND.
YOU ***DISPOSED*** OF THEM?
STAGING THEIR DEATHS AS A CRIME SCENE KILLING WOULD HAVE BEEN ***MORE PRUDENT.***
NOW THERE ARE MISSING ***POLICE!*** THERE WILL BE ***MASSIVE*** INQUIRY--A MEDIA FIELD DAY!
YOU... YOU ARE CORRECT. I WAS IN ERROR.
YOU HAVE BEEN IN ERROR TOO OFTEN OF LATE.

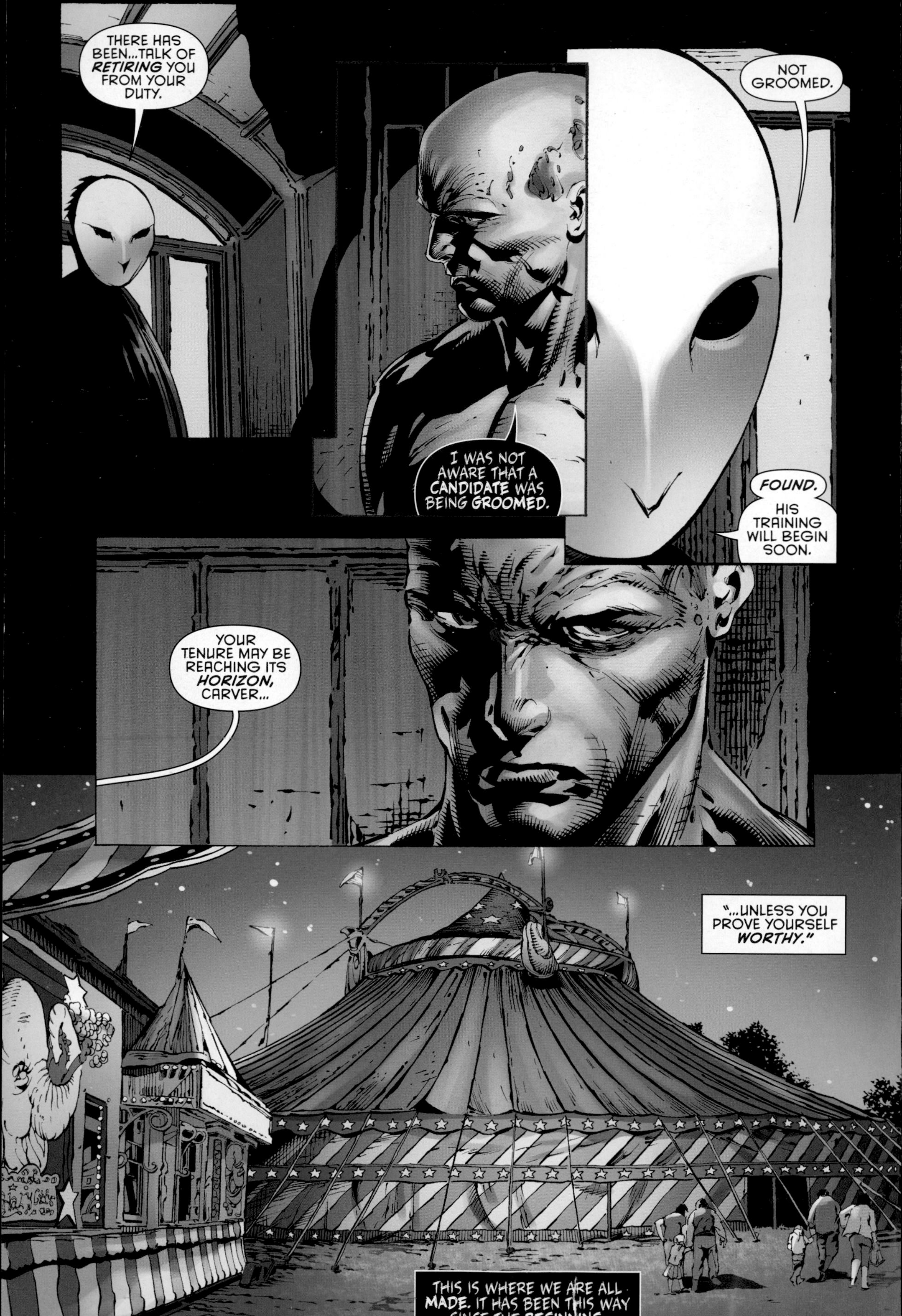
THERE HAS BEEN...TALK OF RETIRING YOU FROM YOUR DUTY.
I WAS NOT AWARE THAT A CANDIDATE WAS BEING GROOMED.
NOT GROOMED.
FOUND.
HIS TRAINING WILL BEGIN SOON.
YOUR TENURE MAY BE REACHING ITS HORIZON, CARVER...
"...UNLESS YOU PROVE YOURSELF WORTHY."
THIS IS WHERE WE ARE ALL MADE. IT HAS BEEN THIS WAY SINCE THE BEGINNING.

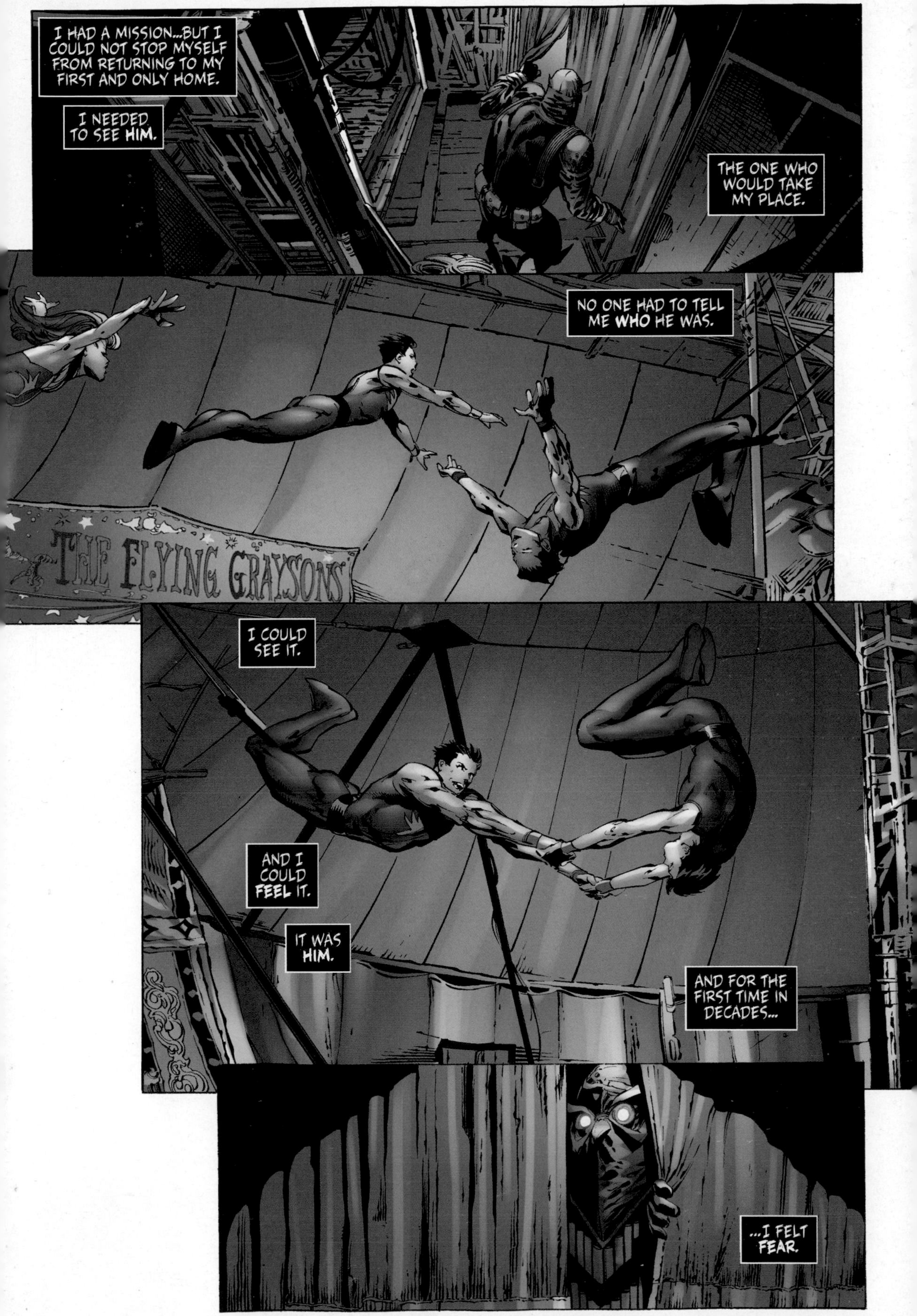
I HAD A MISSION...BUT I COULD NOT STOP MYSELF FROM RETURNING TO MY FIRST AND ONLY HOME.
I NEEDED TO SEE HIM.
THE ONE WHO WOULD TAKE MY PLACE.
NO ONE HAD TO TELL ME WHO HE WAS.
THE FLYING GRAYSONS
I COULD SEE IT.
AND I COULD FEEL IT.
IT WAS HIM.
AND FOR THE FIRST TIME IN DECADES...
...I FELT FEAR.

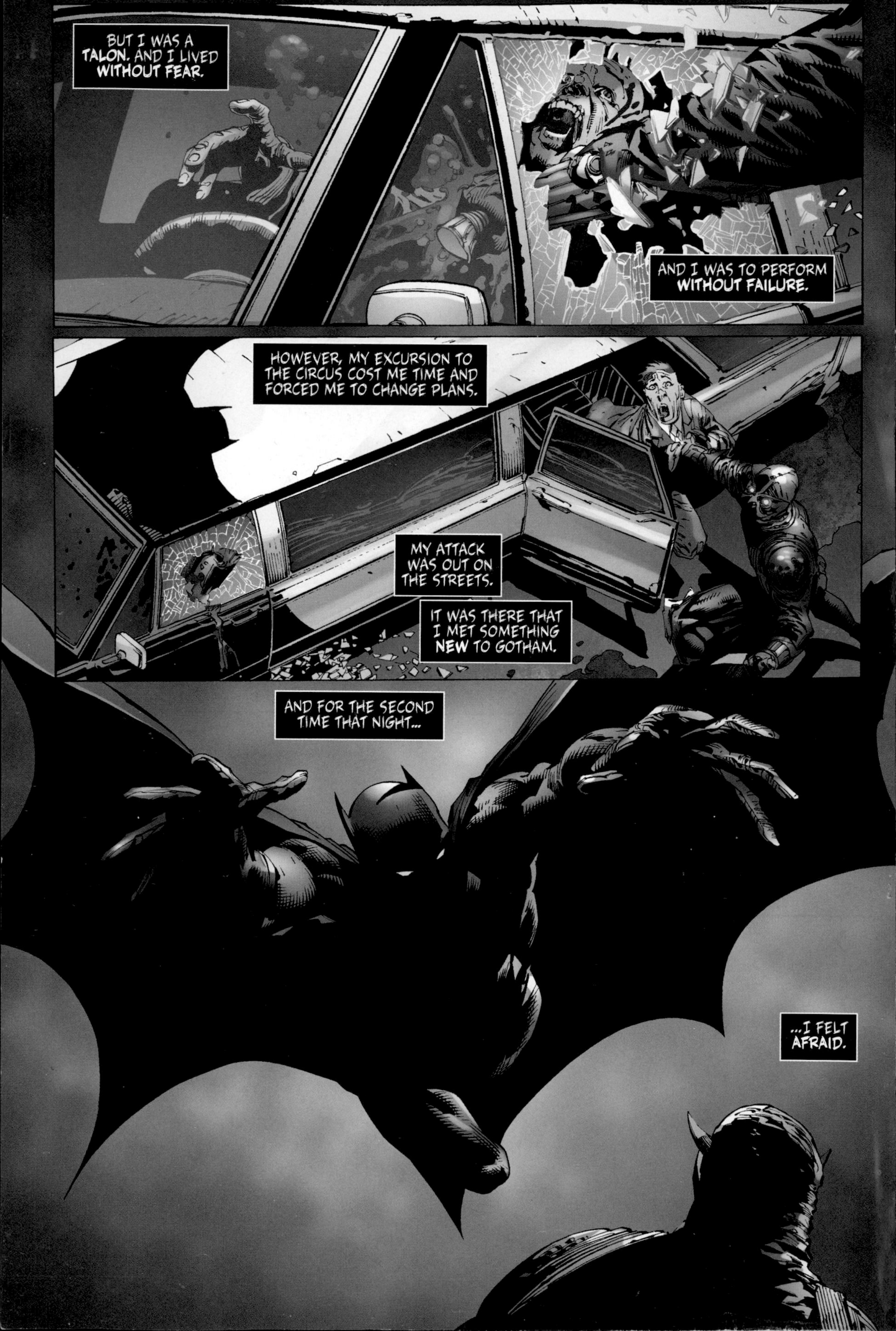

BUT I WAS A TALON. AND I LIVED WITHOUT FEAR.
AND I WAS TO PERFORM WITHOUT FAILURE.
HOWEVER, MY EXCURSION TO THE CIRCUS COST ME TIME AND FORCED ME TO CHANGE PLANS.
MY ATTACK WAS OUT ON THE STREETS.
IT WAS THERE THAT I MET SOMETHING NEW TO GOTHAM.
AND FOR THE SECOND TIME THAT NIGHT...
...I FELT AFRAID.

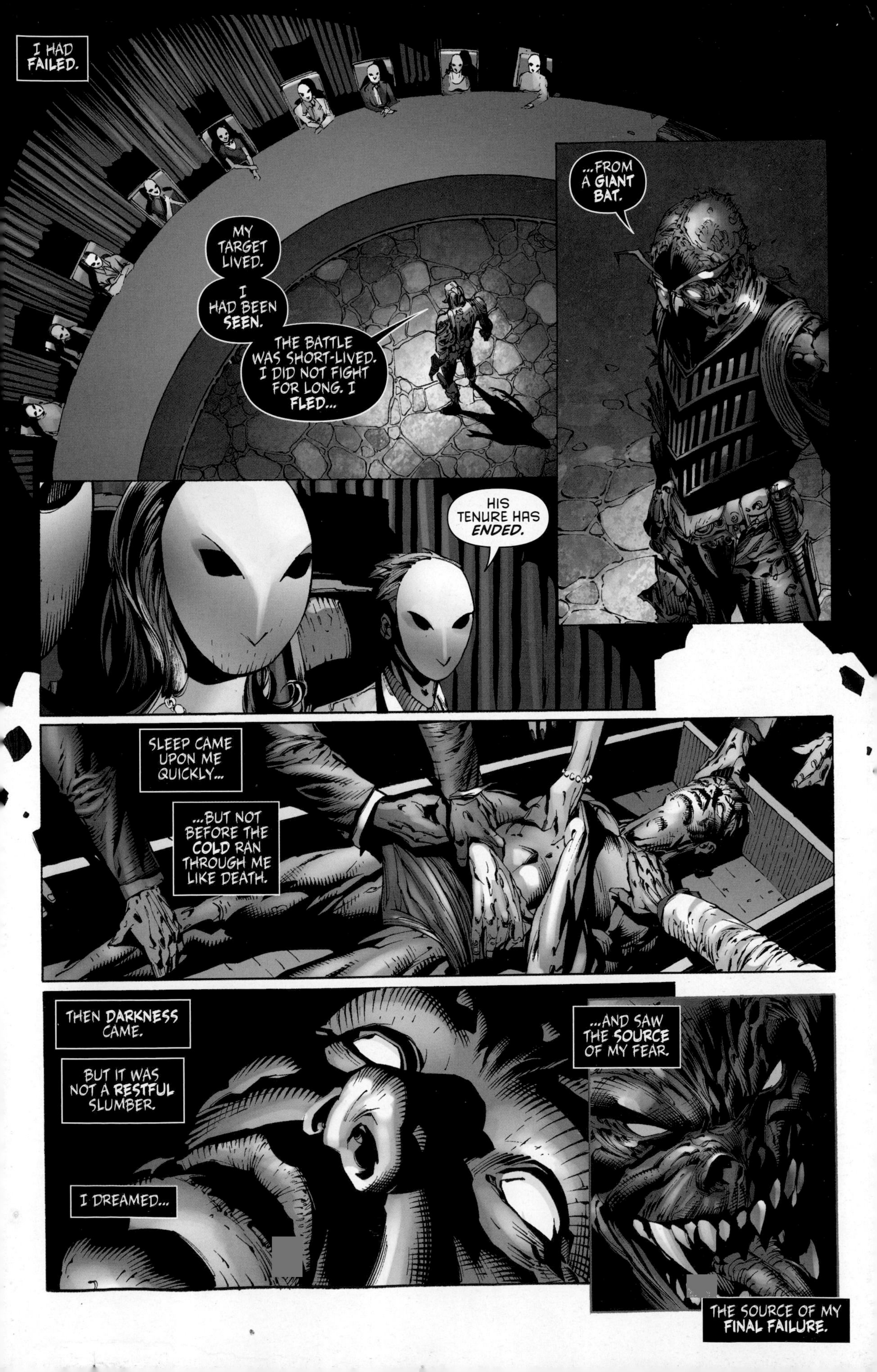
I HAD FAILED.
MY TARGET LIVED.
I HAD BEEN SEEN.
THE BATTLE WAS SHORT-LIVED. I DID NOT FIGHT FOR LONG. I FLED...
...FROM A GIANT BAT.
HIS TENURE HAS ENDED.
SLEEP CAME UPON ME QUICKLY...
...BUT NOT BEFORE THE COLD RAN THROUGH ME LIKE DEATH.
THEN DARKNESS CAME.
BUT IT WAS NOT A RESTFUL SLUMBER.
I DREAMED...
...AND SAW THE SOURCE OF MY FEAR.
THE SOURCE OF MY FINAL FAILURE.

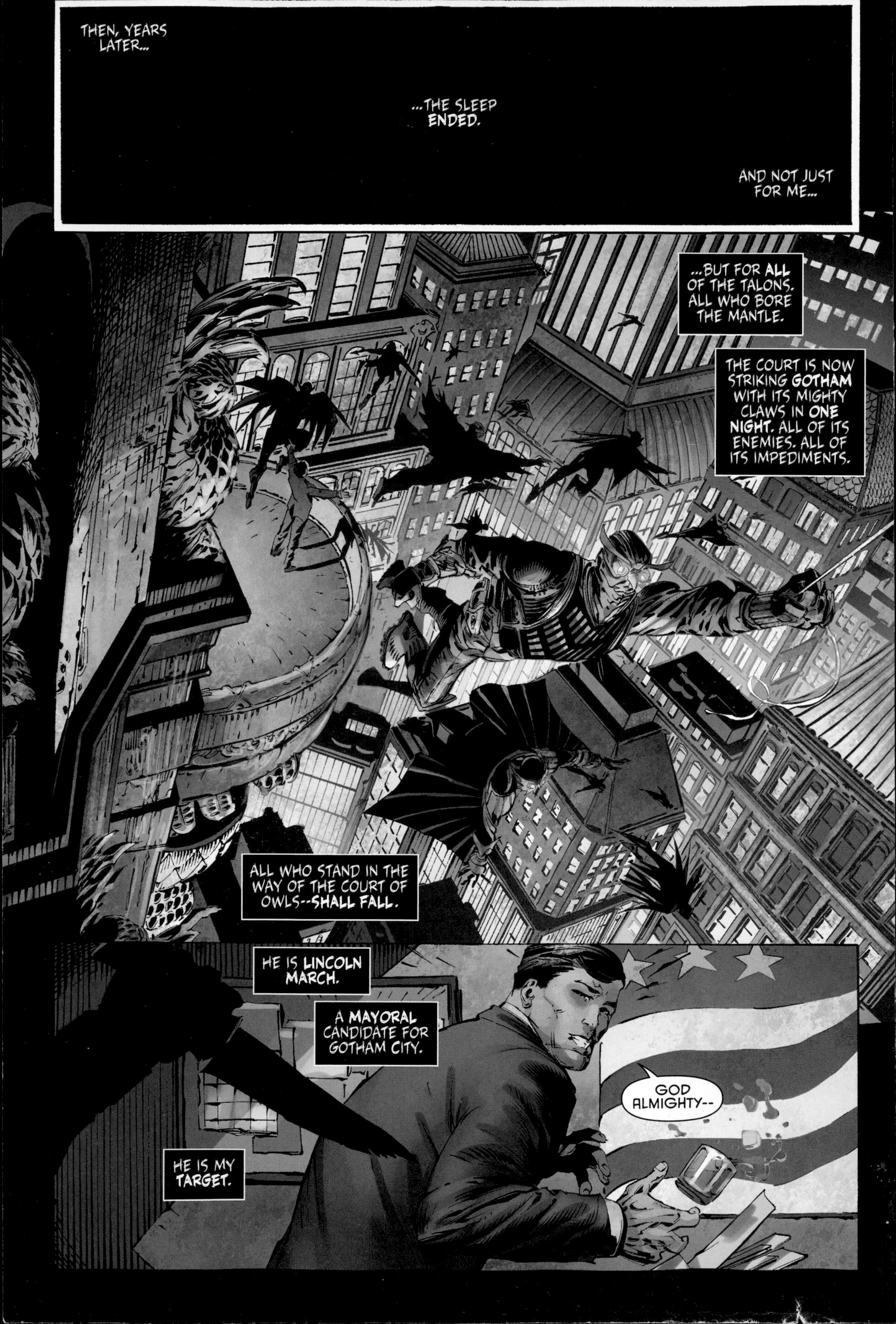
THEN, YEARS LATER...
...THE SLEEP ENDED.
AND NOT JUST FOR ME...
...BUT FOR ALL OF THE TALONS. ALL WHO BORE THE MANTLE.
THE COURT IS NOW STRIKING GOTHAM WITH ITS MIGHTY CLAWS IN ONE NIGHT. ALL OF ITS ENEMIES. ALL OF ITS IMPEDIMENTS.
ALL WHO STAND IN THE WAY OF THE COURT OF OWLS--SHALL FALL.
HE IS LINCOLN MARCH.
A MAYORAL CANDIDATE FOR GOTHAM CITY.
GOD ALMIGHTY--
HE IS MY TARGET.

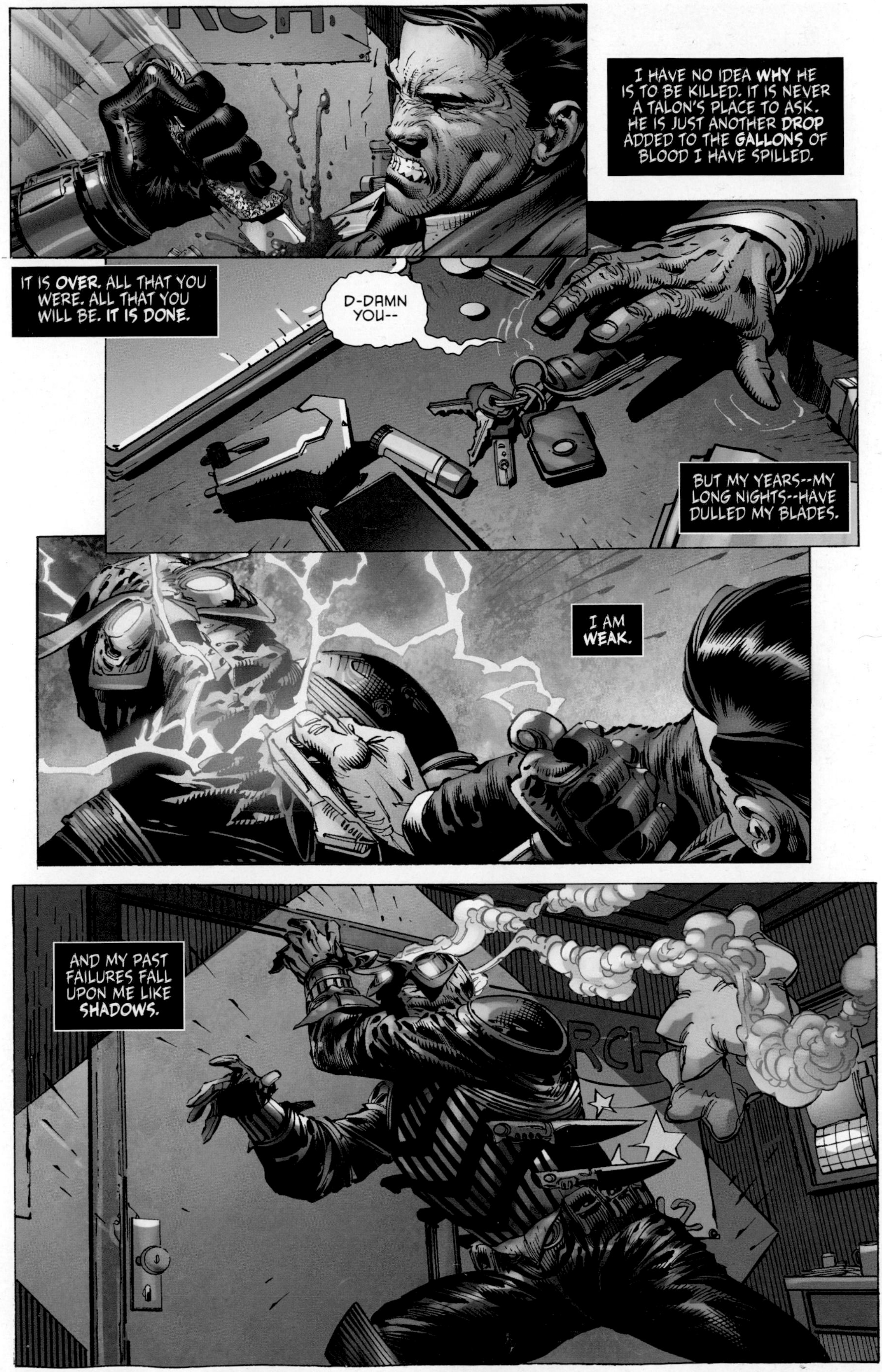
I HAVE NO IDEA WHY HE IS TO BE KILLED. IT IS NEVER A TALON'S PLACE TO ASK. HE IS JUST ANOTHER DROP ADDED TO THE GALLONS OF BLOOD I HAVE SPILLED.
IT IS OVER. ALL THAT YOU WERE. ALL THAT YOU WILL BE. IT IS DONE.
D-DAMN YOU--
BUT MY YEARS--MY LONG NIGHTS--HAVE DULLED MY BLADES.
I AM WEAK.
AND MY PAST FAILURES FALL UPON ME LIKE SHADOWS.

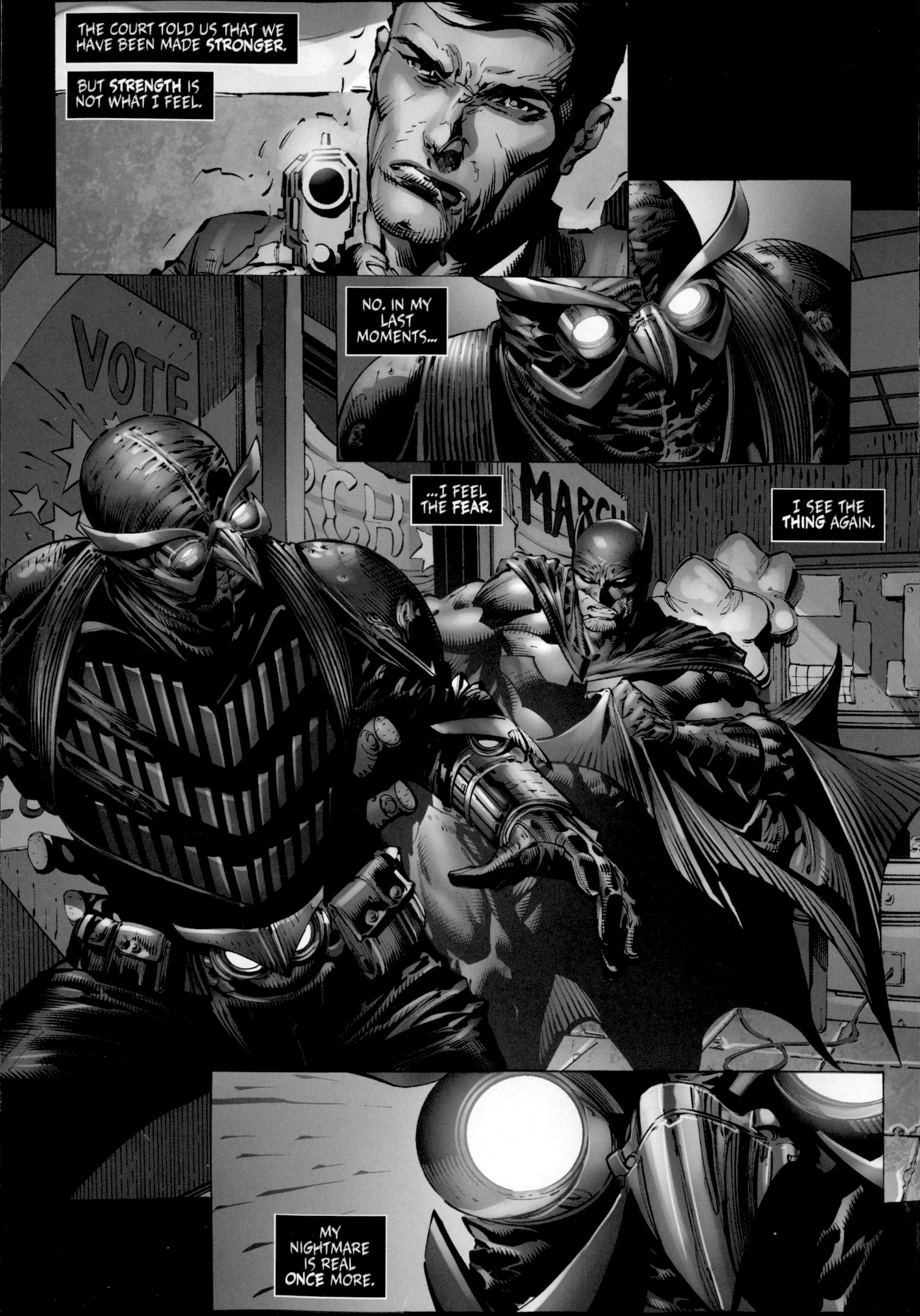
THE COURT TOLD US THAT WE HAVE BEEN MADE STRONGER.
BUT STRENGTH IS NOT WHAT I FEEL.
NO. IN MY LAST MOMENTS...
VOTE
MARCH
...I FEEL THE FEAR.
I SEE THE THING AGAIN.
MY NIGHTMARE IS REAL ONCE MORE.

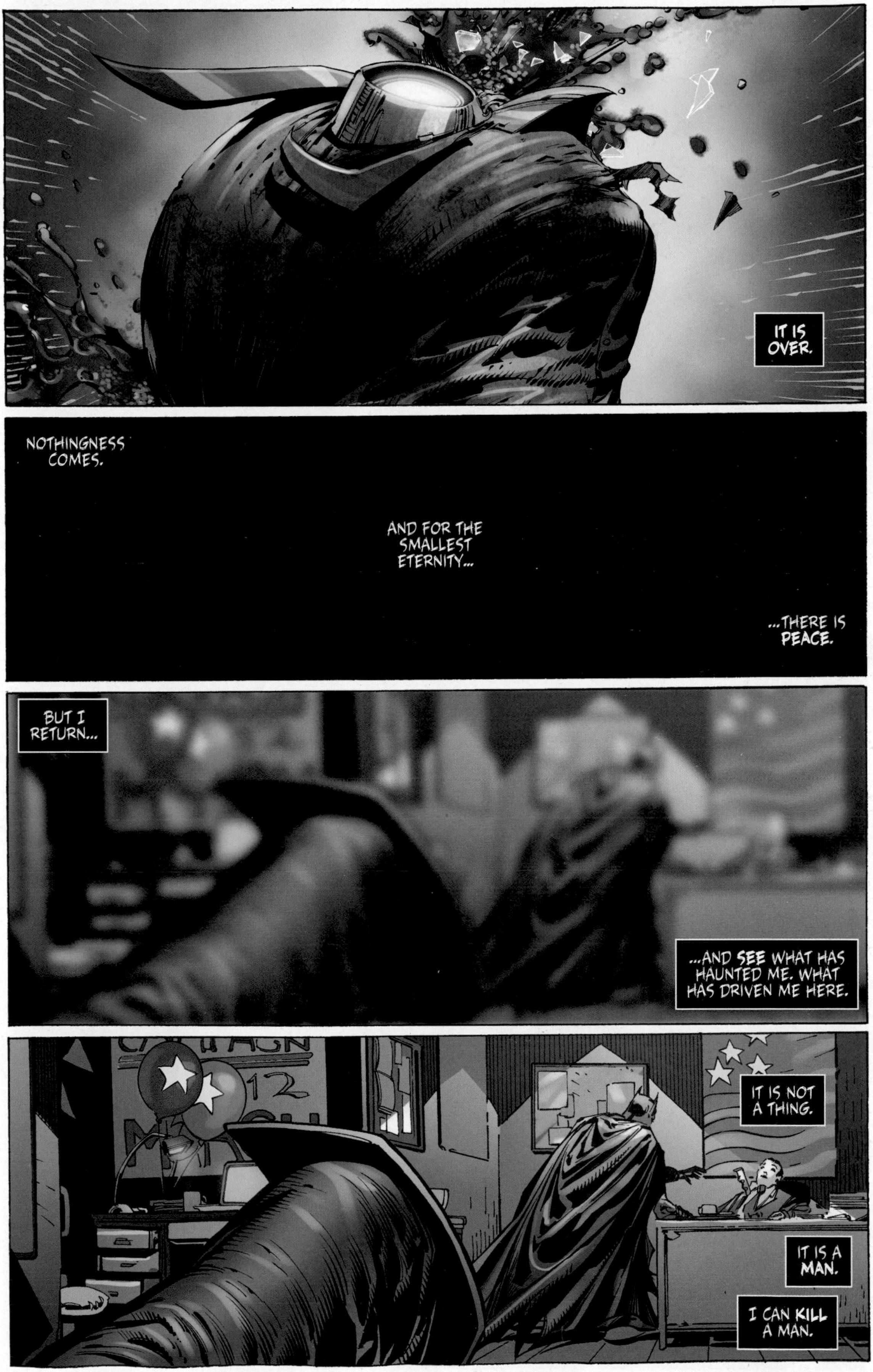
IT IS OVER.
NOTHINGNESS COMES.
AND FOR THE SMALLEST ETERNITY...
...THERE IS PEACE.
BUT I RETURN...
...AND SEE WHAT HAS HAUNTED ME. WHAT HAS DRIVEN ME HERE.
IT IS NOT A THING.
IT IS A MAN.
I CAN KILL A MAN.

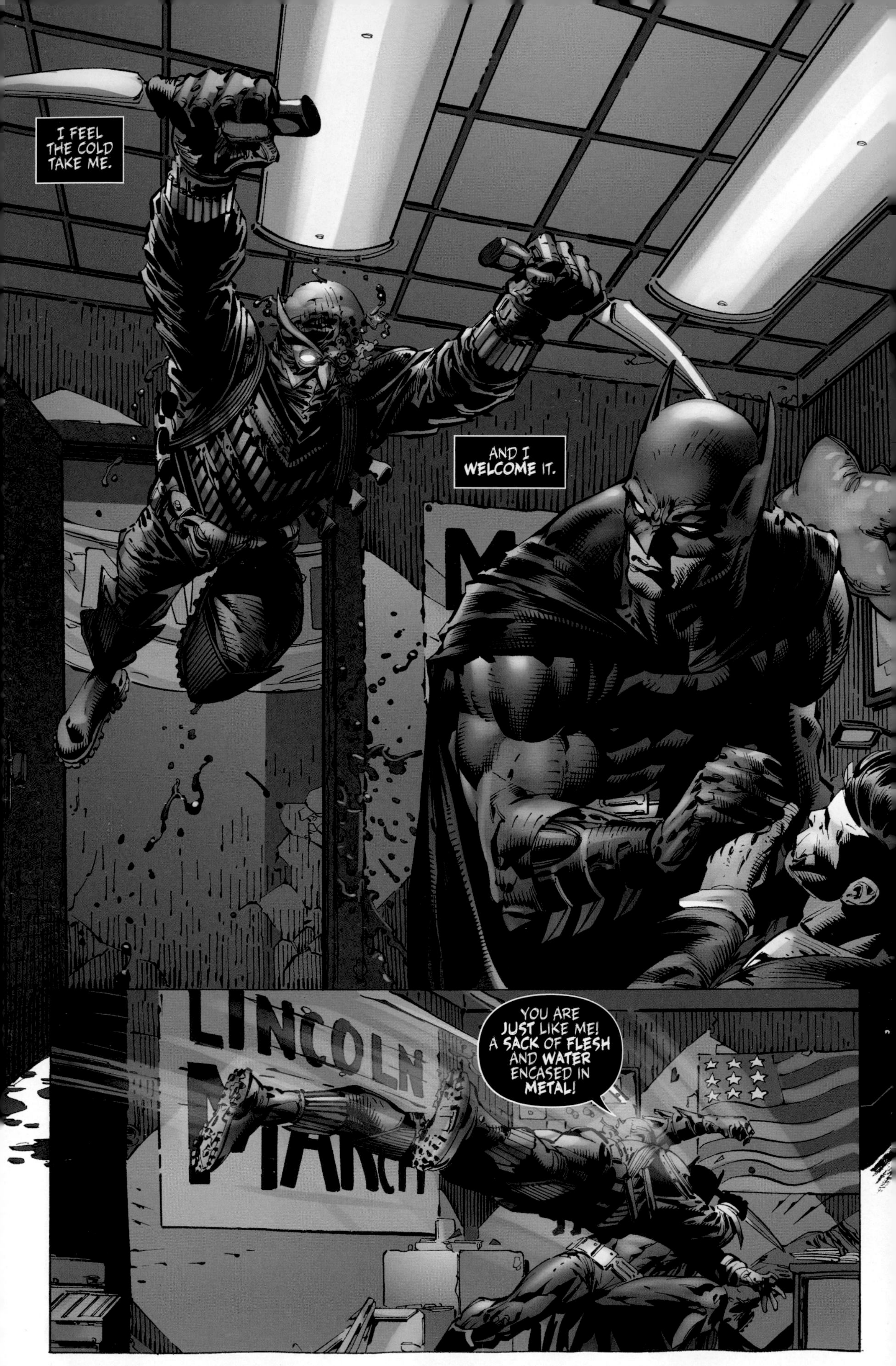
I FEEL THE COLD TAKE ME.
AND I WELCOME IT.
LINCOLN MARCH
YOU ARE JUST LIKE ME! A SACK OF FLESH AND WATER ENCASED IN METAL!

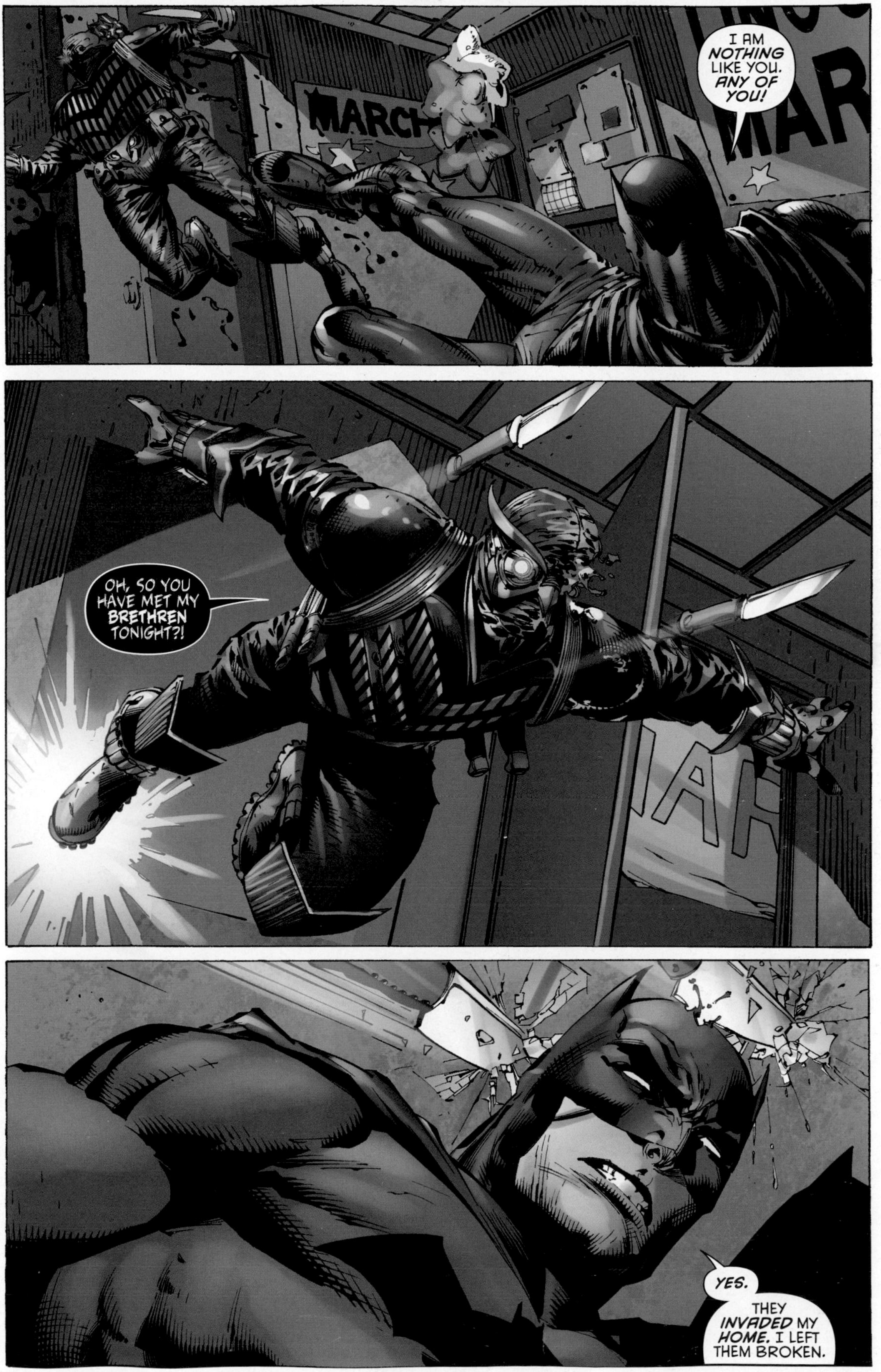
MARCH
I AM NOTHING LIKE YOU. ANY OF YOU!
OH, SO YOU HAVE MET MY BRETHREN TONIGHT?!
YES.
THEY INVADED MY HOME. I LEFT THEM BROKEN.

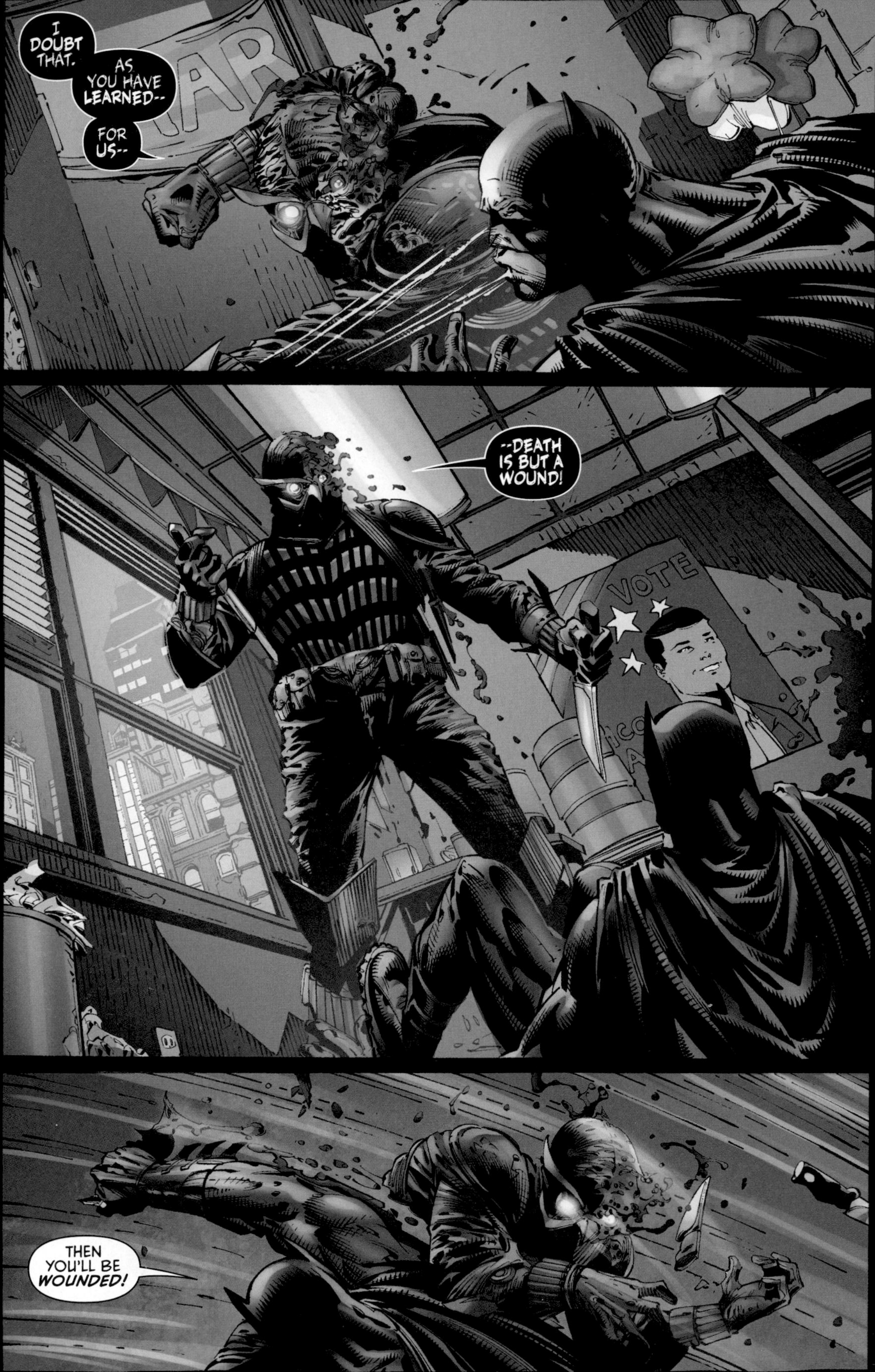
I DOUBT THAT.
AS YOU HAVE LEARNED--
FOR US--
--DEATH IS BUT A WOUND!
VOTE
THEN YOU'LL BE *WOUNDED!*

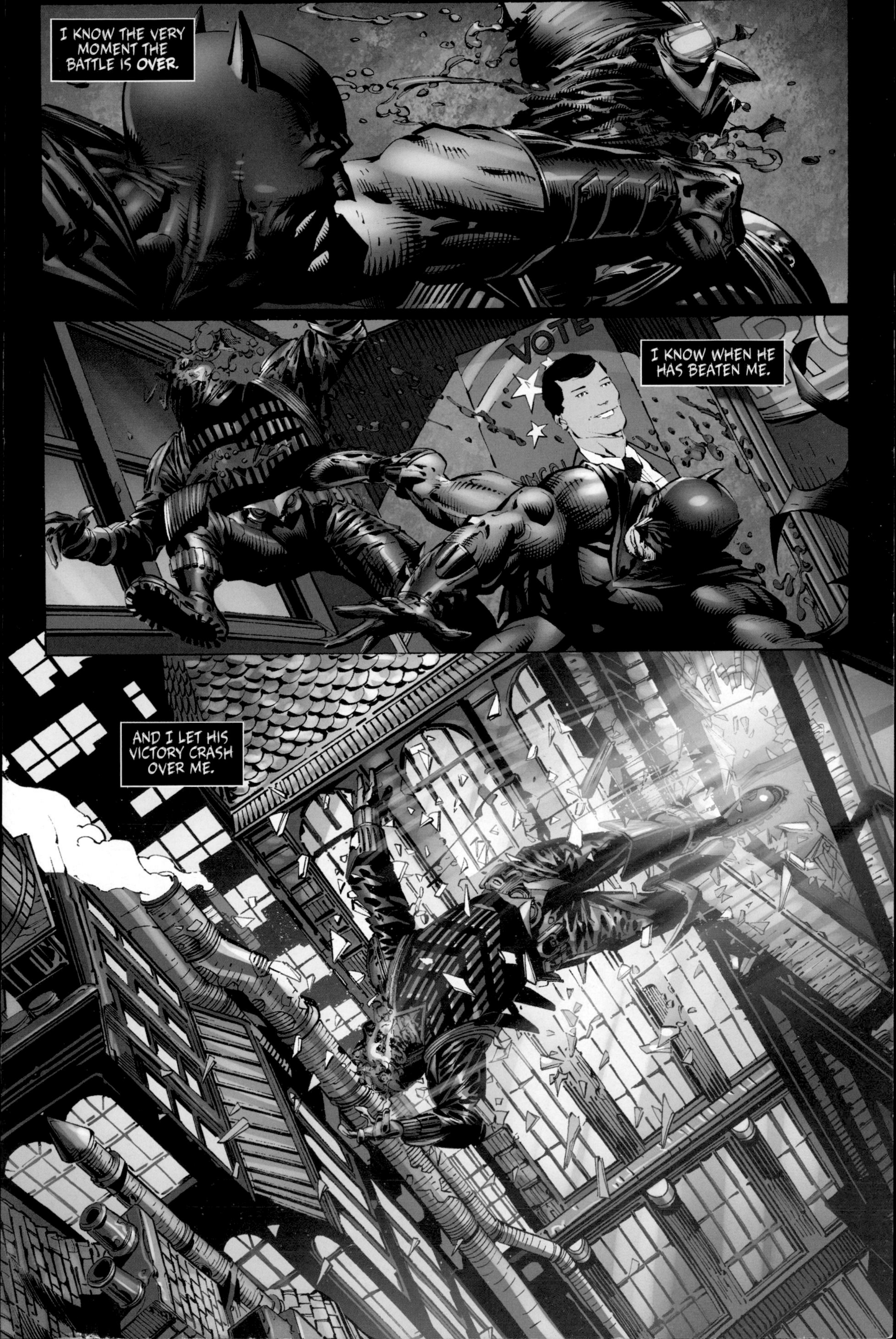
I KNOW THE VERY MOMENT THE BATTLE IS OVER.
VOTE
I KNOW WHEN HE HAS BEATEN ME.
AND I LET HIS VICTORY CRASH OVER ME.

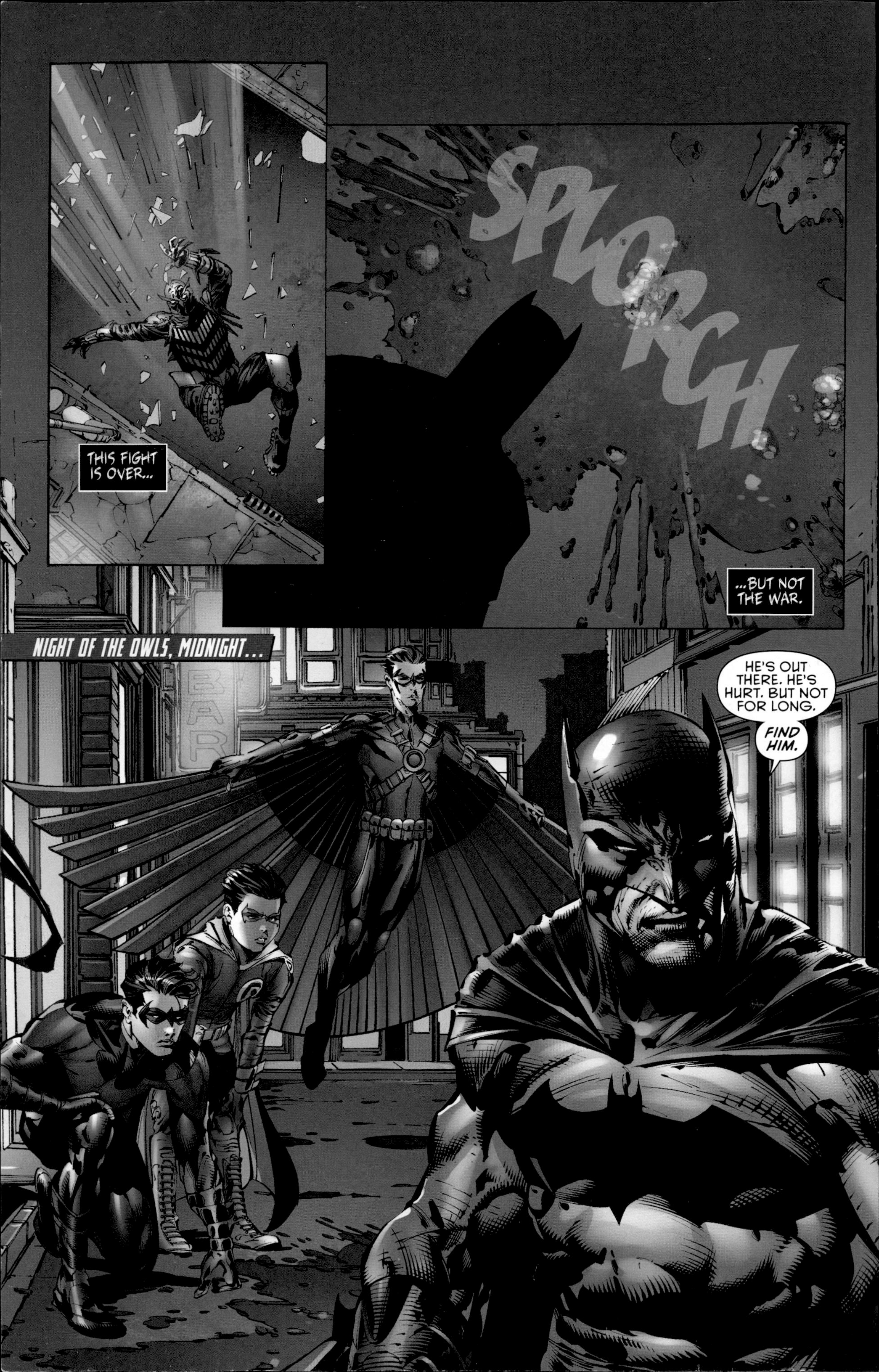
THIS FIGHT IS OVER...
SPLORCH
...BUT NOT THE WAR.
NIGHT OF THE OWLS, MIDNIGHT...
BAR
HE'S OUT THERE. HE'S HURT. BUT NOT FOR LONG.
FIND HIM.

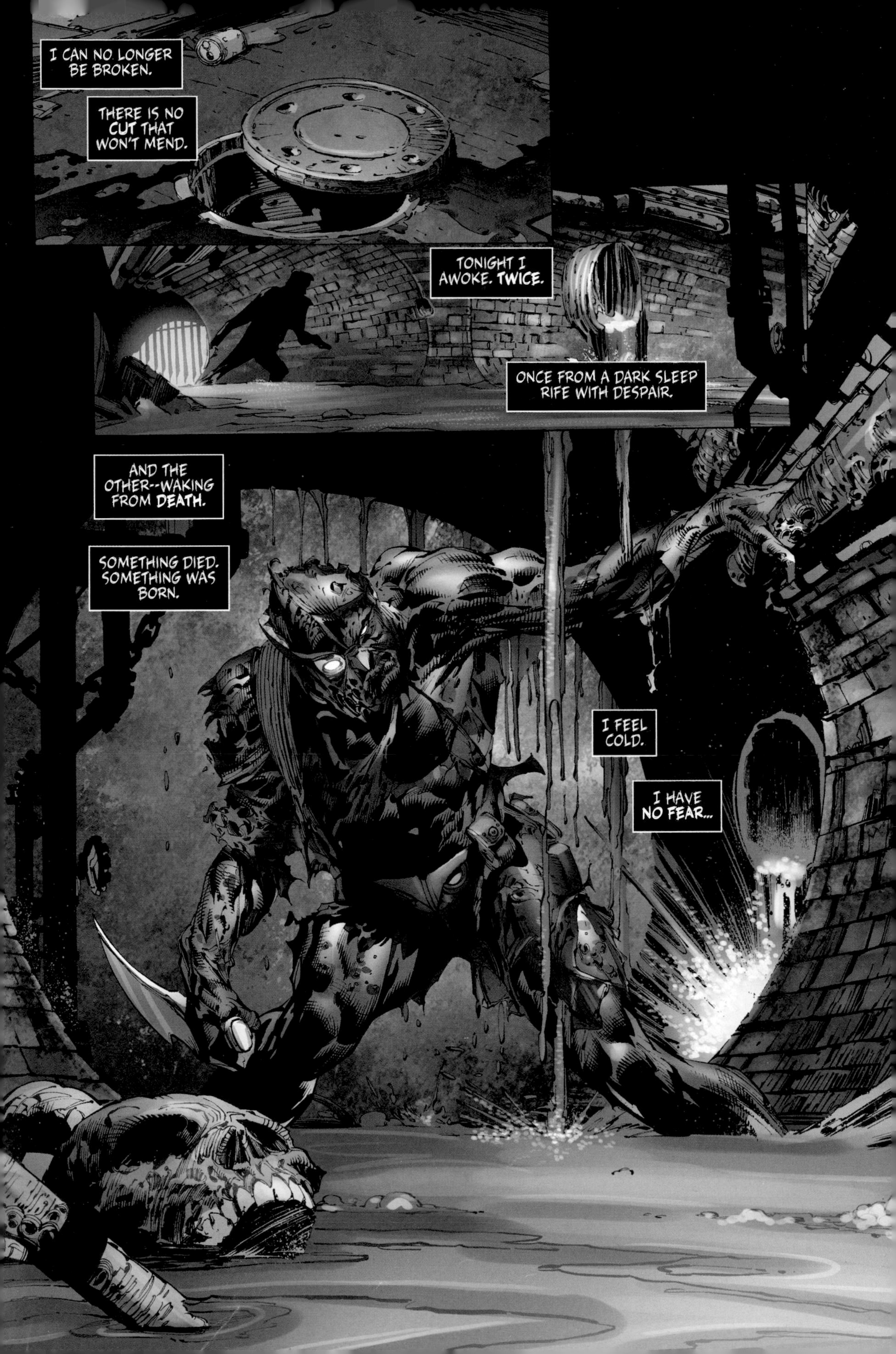
I CAN NO LONGER BE BROKEN.
THERE IS NO CUT THAT WON'T MEND.
TONIGHT I AWOKE. TWICE.
ONCE FROM A DARK SLEEP RIFE WITH DESPAIR.
AND THE OTHER--WAKING FROM DEATH.
SOMETHING DIED. SOMETHING WAS BORN.
I FEEL COLD.
I HAVE NO FEAR...

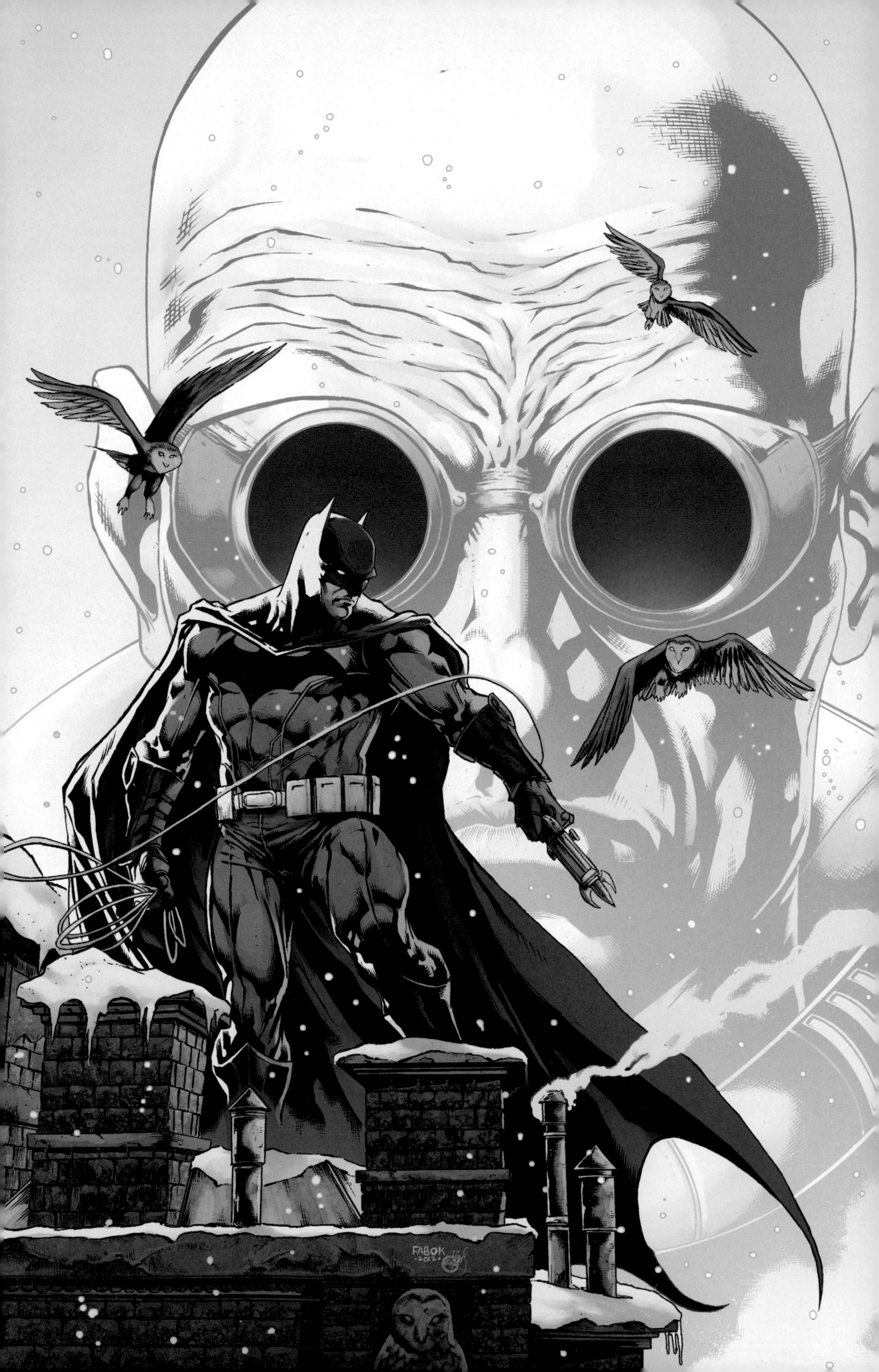
FABOK
•2012•

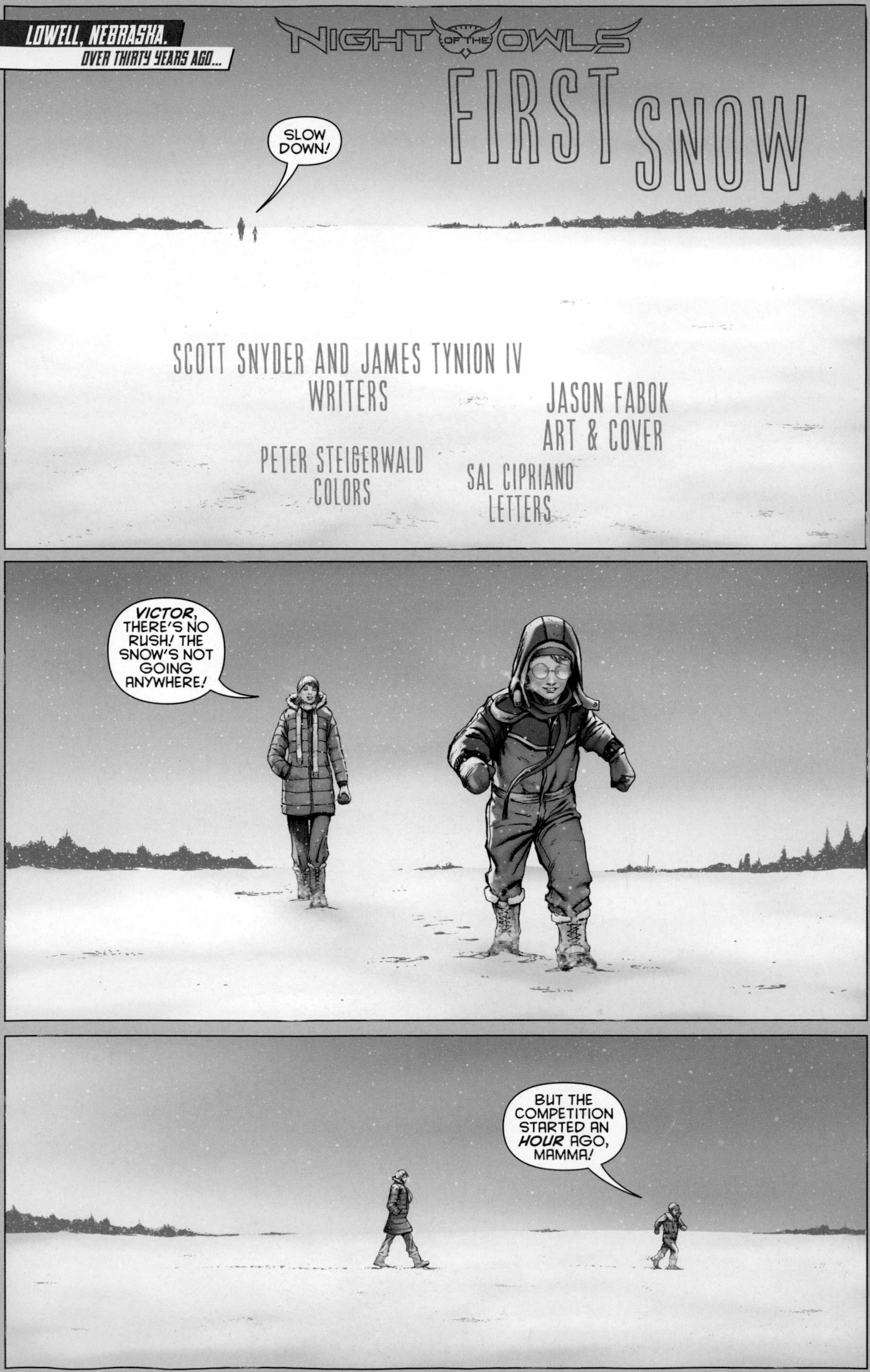

LOWELL, NEBRASKA.
OVER THIRTY YEARS AGO...
NIGHT OF THE OWLS
FIRST SNOW
SLOW DOWN!
SCOTT SNYDER AND JAMES TYNION IV
WRITERS
JASON FABOK
ART & COVER
PETER STEIGERWALD
COLORS
SAL CIPRIANO
LETTERS
VICTOR, THERE'S NO RUSH! THE SNOW'S NOT GOING ANYWHERE!
BUT THE COMPETITION STARTED AN HOUR AGO, MAMMA!

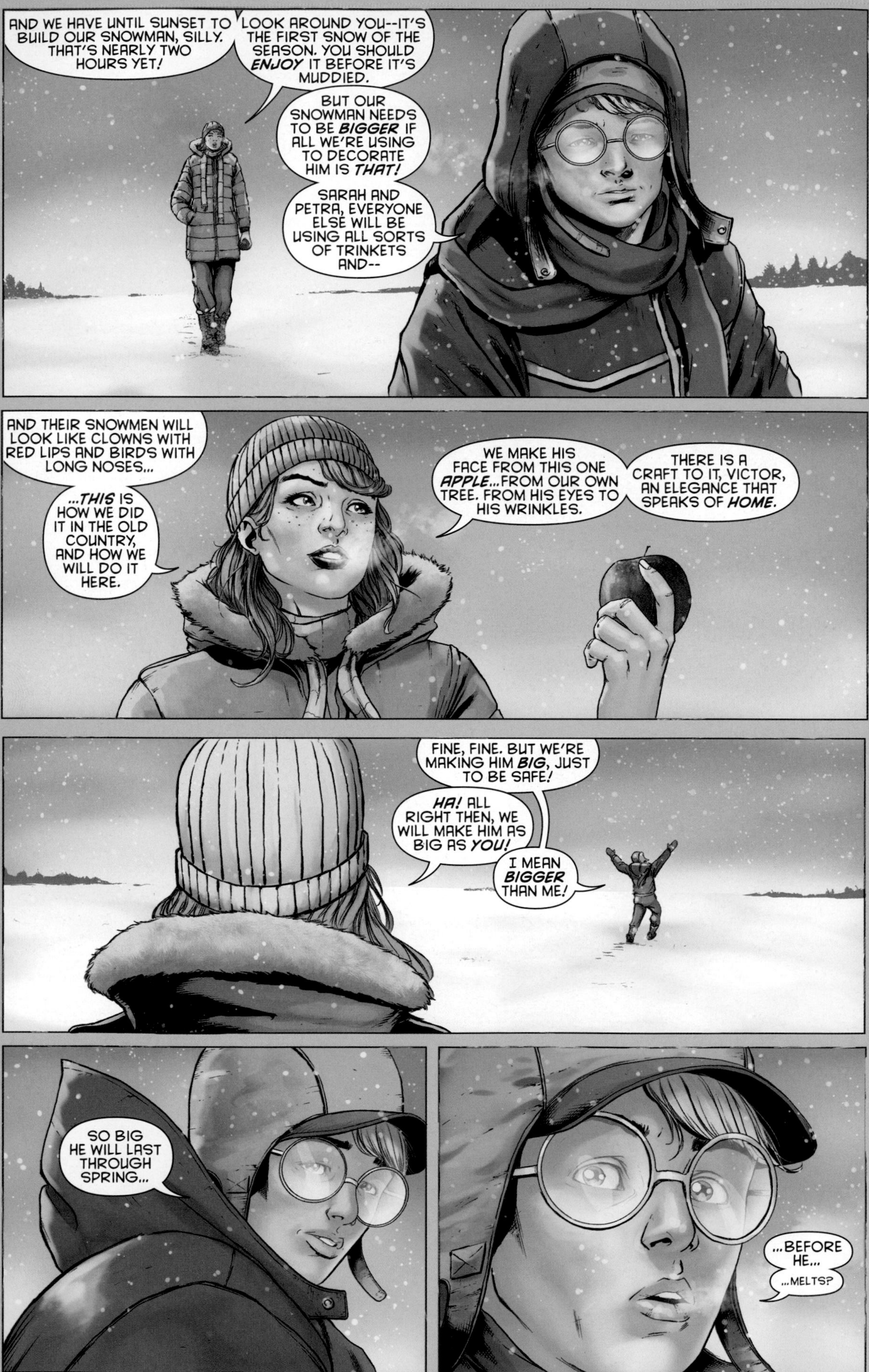
AND WE HAVE UNTIL SUNSET TO BUILD OUR SNOWMAN, SILLY. THAT'S NEARLY TWO HOURS YET!
LOOK AROUND YOU--IT'S THE FIRST SNOW OF THE SEASON. YOU SHOULD ENJOY IT BEFORE IT'S MUDDIED.
BUT OUR SNOWMAN NEEDS TO BE BIGGER IF ALL WE'RE USING TO DECORATE HIM IS THAT!
SARAH AND PETRA, EVERYONE ELSE WILL BE USING ALL SORTS OF TRINKETS AND--
AND THEIR SNOWMEN WILL LOOK LIKE CLOWNS WITH RED LIPS AND BIRDS WITH LONG NOSES...
...THIS IS HOW WE DID IT IN THE OLD COUNTRY, AND HOW WE WILL DO IT HERE.
WE MAKE HIS FACE FROM THIS ONE APPLE...FROM OUR OWN TREE. FROM HIS EYES TO HIS WRINKLES.
THERE IS A CRAFT TO IT, VICTOR, AN ELEGANCE THAT SPEAKS OF HOME.
FINE, FINE. BUT WE'RE MAKING HIM BIG, JUST TO BE SAFE!
HA! ALL RIGHT THEN, WE WILL MAKE HIM AS BIG AS YOU!
I MEAN BIGGER THAN ME!
SO BIG HE WILL LAST THROUGH SPRING...
...BEFORE HE...
...MELTS?

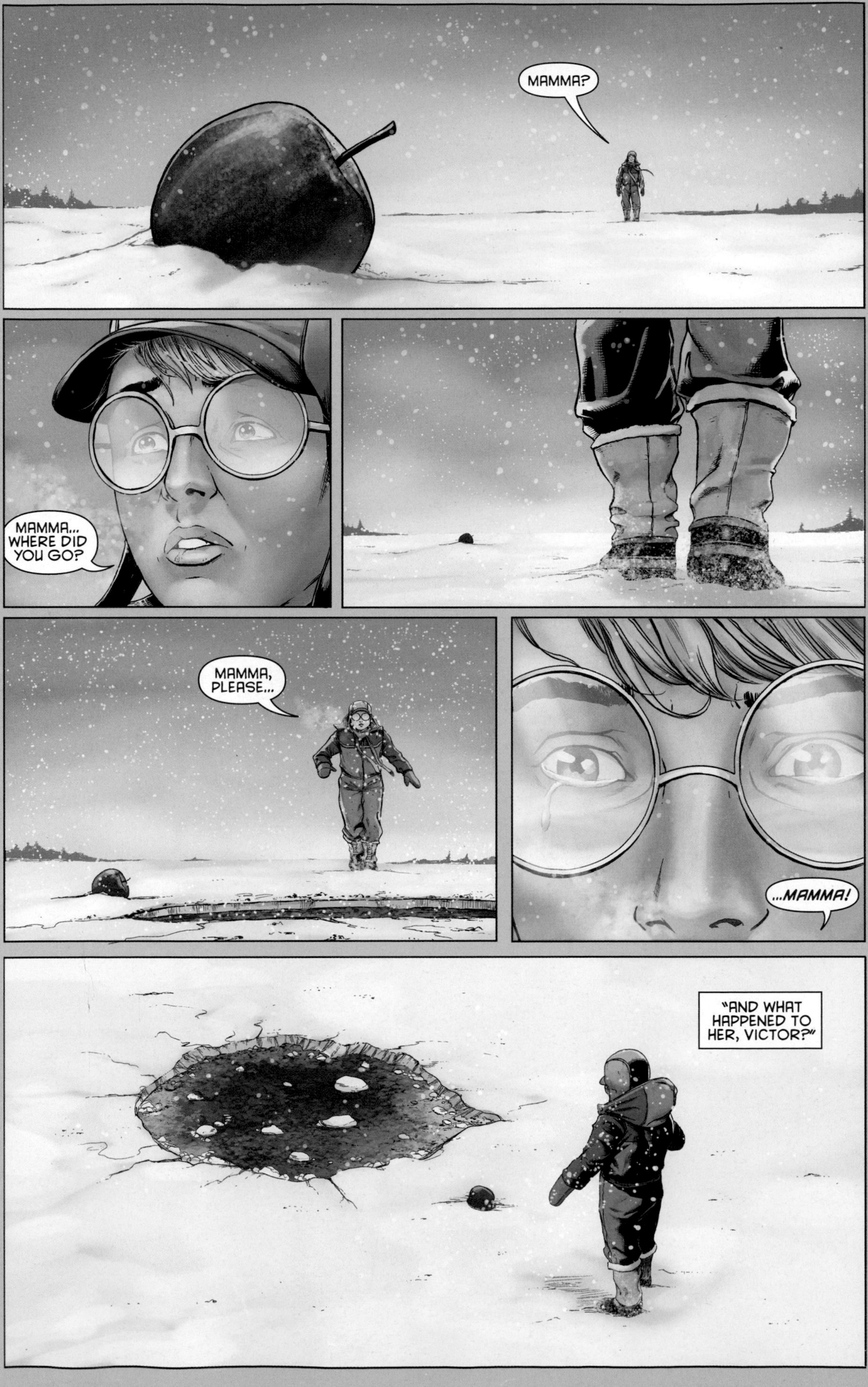
MAMMA?
MAMMA... WHERE DID YOU GO?
MAMMA, PLEASE...
...MAMMA!
"AND WHAT HAPPENED TO HER, VICTOR?"

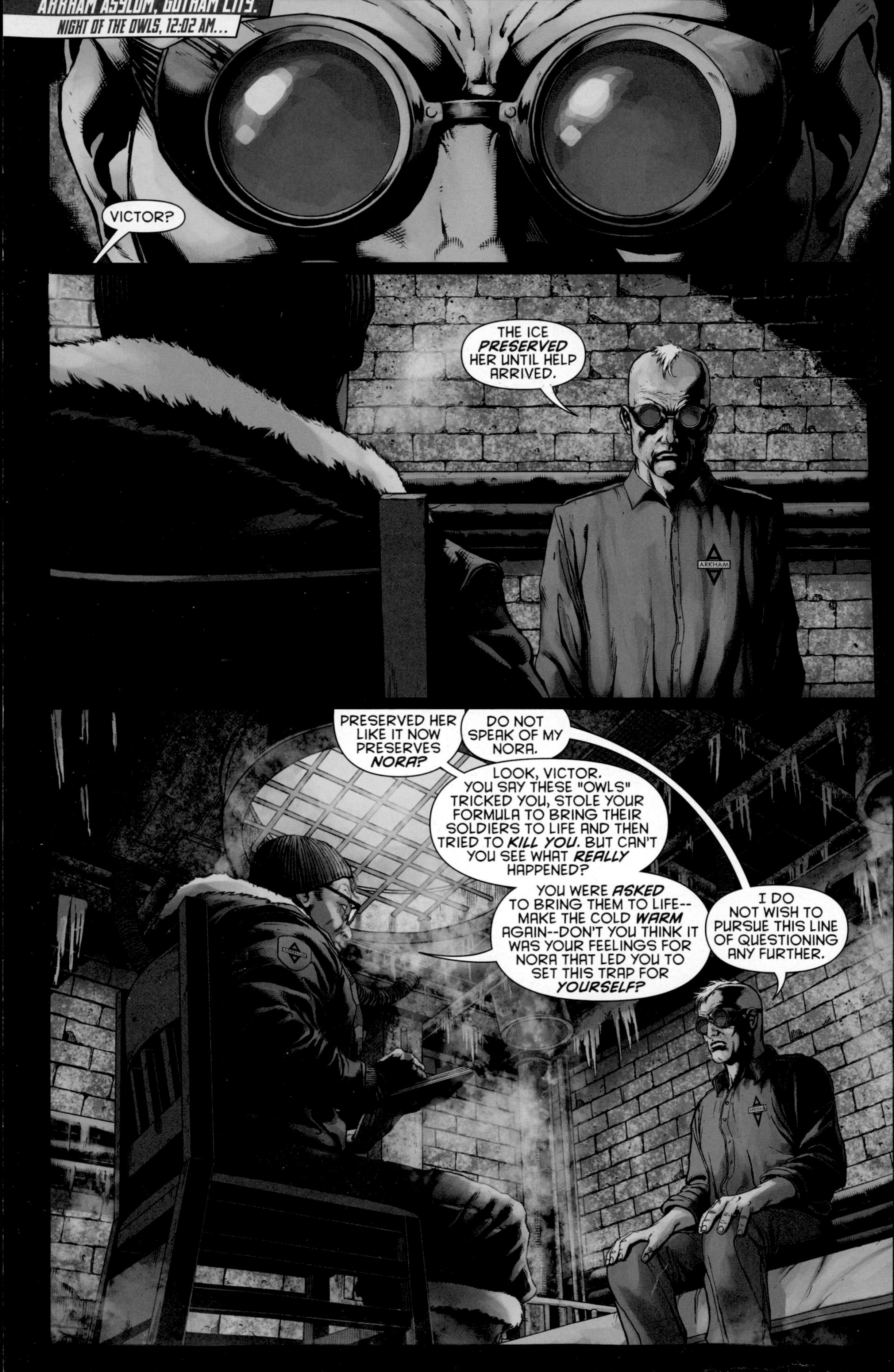

ARKHAM ASYLUM, GOTHAM CITY.
NIGHT OF THE OWLS, 12:02 AM...
VICTOR?
THE ICE *PRESERVED* HER UNTIL HELP ARRIVED.
PRESERVED HER LIKE IT NOW PRESERVES *NORA?*
DO NOT SPEAK OF MY NORA.
LOOK, VICTOR. YOU SAY THESE "OWLS" TRICKED YOU, STOLE YOUR FORMULA TO BRING THEIR SOLDIERS TO LIFE AND THEN TRIED TO *KILL YOU*. BUT CAN'T YOU SEE WHAT *REALLY* HAPPENED?
YOU WERE *ASKED* TO BRING THEM TO LIFE-- MAKE THE COLD *WARM* AGAIN--DON'T YOU THINK IT WAS YOUR FEELINGS FOR NORA THAT LED YOU TO SET THIS TRAP FOR *YOURSELF?*
I DO NOT WISH TO PURSUE THIS LINE OF QUESTIONING ANY FURTHER.
ARKHAM

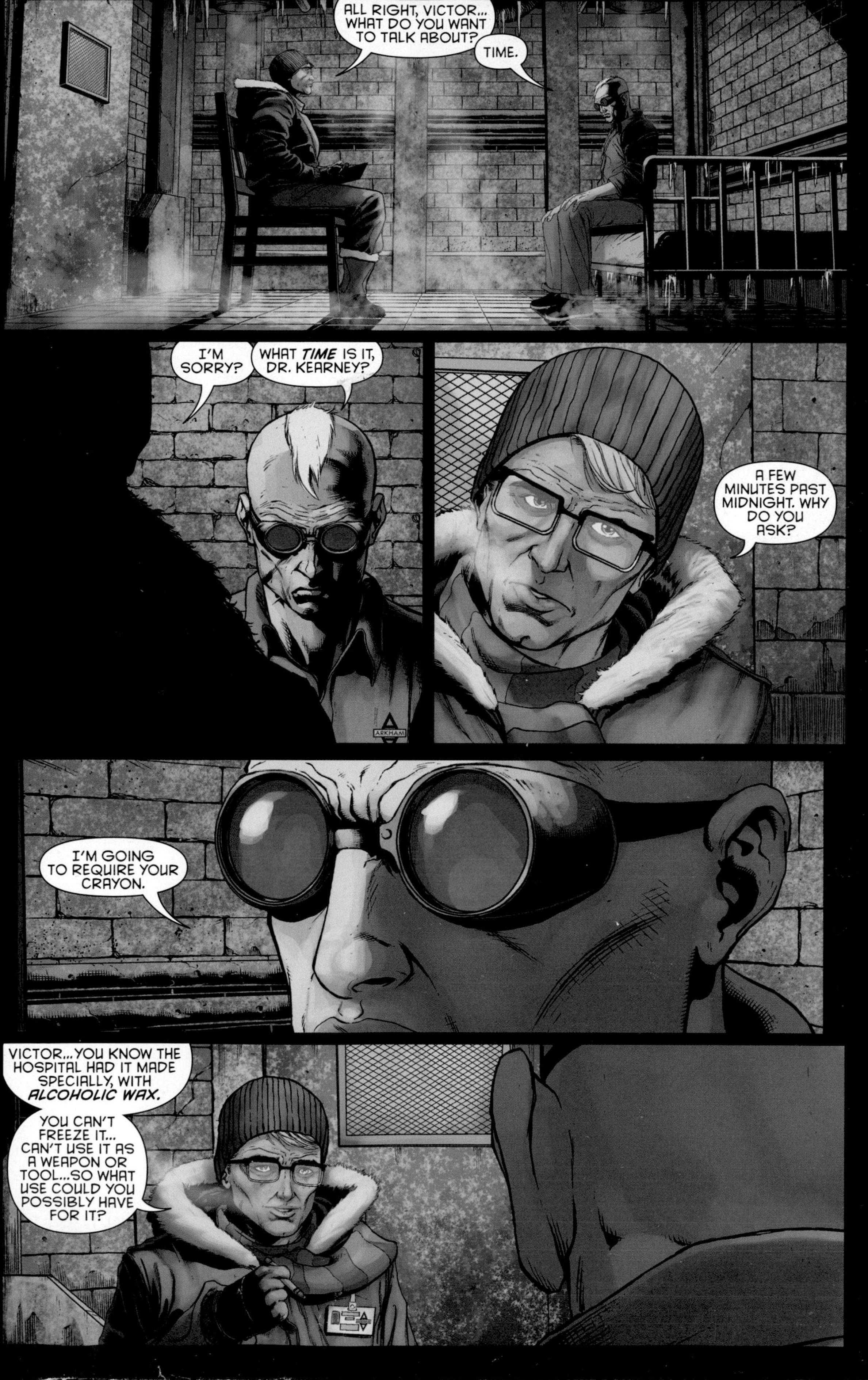

ALL RIGHT, VICTOR... WHAT DO YOU WANT TO TALK ABOUT?
TIME.
I'M SORRY?
WHAT *TIME* IS IT, DR. KEARNEY?
A FEW MINUTES PAST MIDNIGHT. WHY DO YOU ASK?
ARKHAM
I'M GOING TO REQUIRE YOUR CRAYON.
VICTOR...YOU KNOW THE HOSPITAL HAD IT MADE SPECIALLY, WITH ***ALCOHOLIC WAX.***
YOU CAN'T FREEZE IT... CAN'T USE IT AS A WEAPON OR TOOL...SO WHAT USE COULD YOU POSSIBLY HAVE FOR IT?

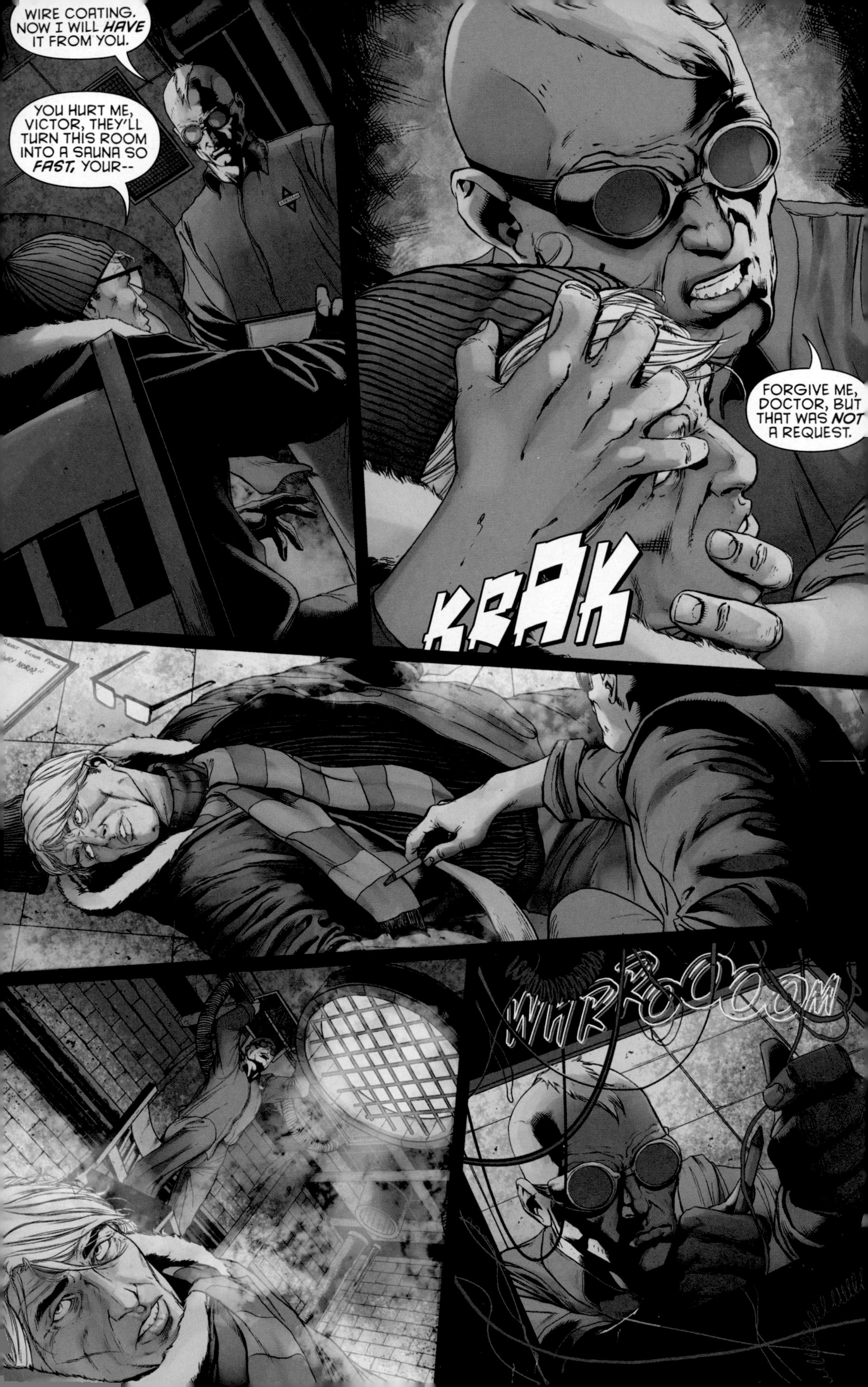
WIRE COATING. NOW I WILL *HAVE* IT FROM YOU.
YOU HURT ME, VICTOR, THEY'LL TURN THIS ROOM INTO A SAUNA SO *FAST,* YOUR--
FORGIVE ME, DOCTOR, BUT THAT WAS *NOT* A REQUEST.
KRAK
WHROOOOOM

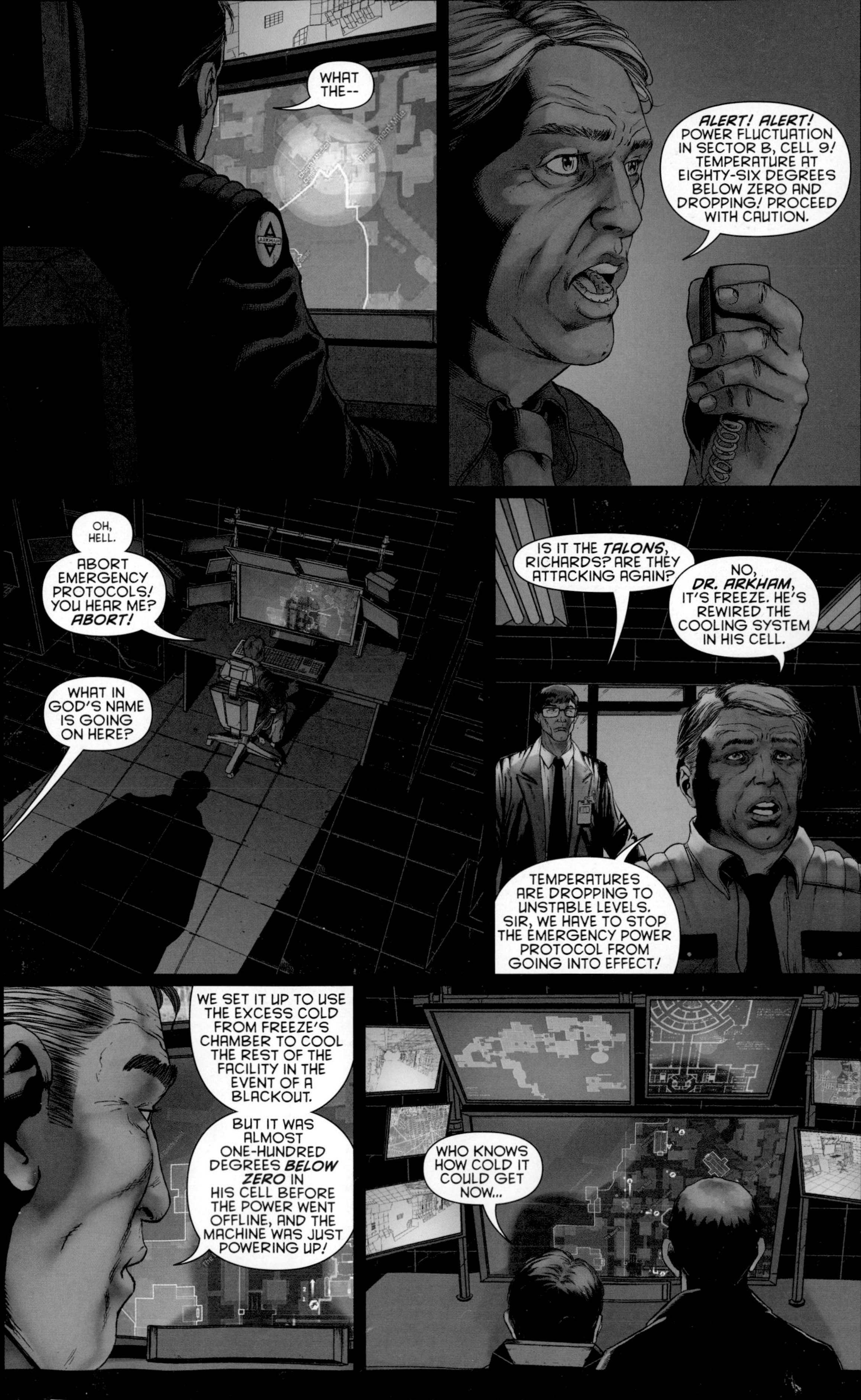

WHAT THE--
ALERT! ALERT! POWER FLUCTUATION IN SECTOR B, CELL 9! TEMPERATURE AT EIGHTY-SIX DEGREES BELOW ZERO AND DROPPING! PROCEED WITH CAUTION.
OH, HELL.
ABORT EMERGENCY PROTOCOLS! YOU HEAR ME? ABORT!
WHAT IN GOD'S NAME IS GOING ON HERE?
IS IT THE TALONS, RICHARDS? ARE THEY ATTACKING AGAIN?
NO, DR. ARKHAM, IT'S FREEZE. HE'S REWIRED THE COOLING SYSTEM IN HIS CELL.
TEMPERATURES ARE DROPPING TO UNSTABLE LEVELS. SIR, WE HAVE TO STOP THE EMERGENCY POWER PROTOCOL FROM GOING INTO EFFECT!
WE SET IT UP TO USE THE EXCESS COLD FROM FREEZE'S CHAMBER TO COOL THE REST OF THE FACILITY IN THE EVENT OF A BLACKOUT.
BUT IT WAS ALMOST ONE-HUNDRED DEGREES BELOW ZERO IN HIS CELL BEFORE THE POWER WENT OFFLINE, AND THE MACHINE WAS JUST POWERING UP!
WHO KNOWS HOW COLD IT COULD GET NOW...

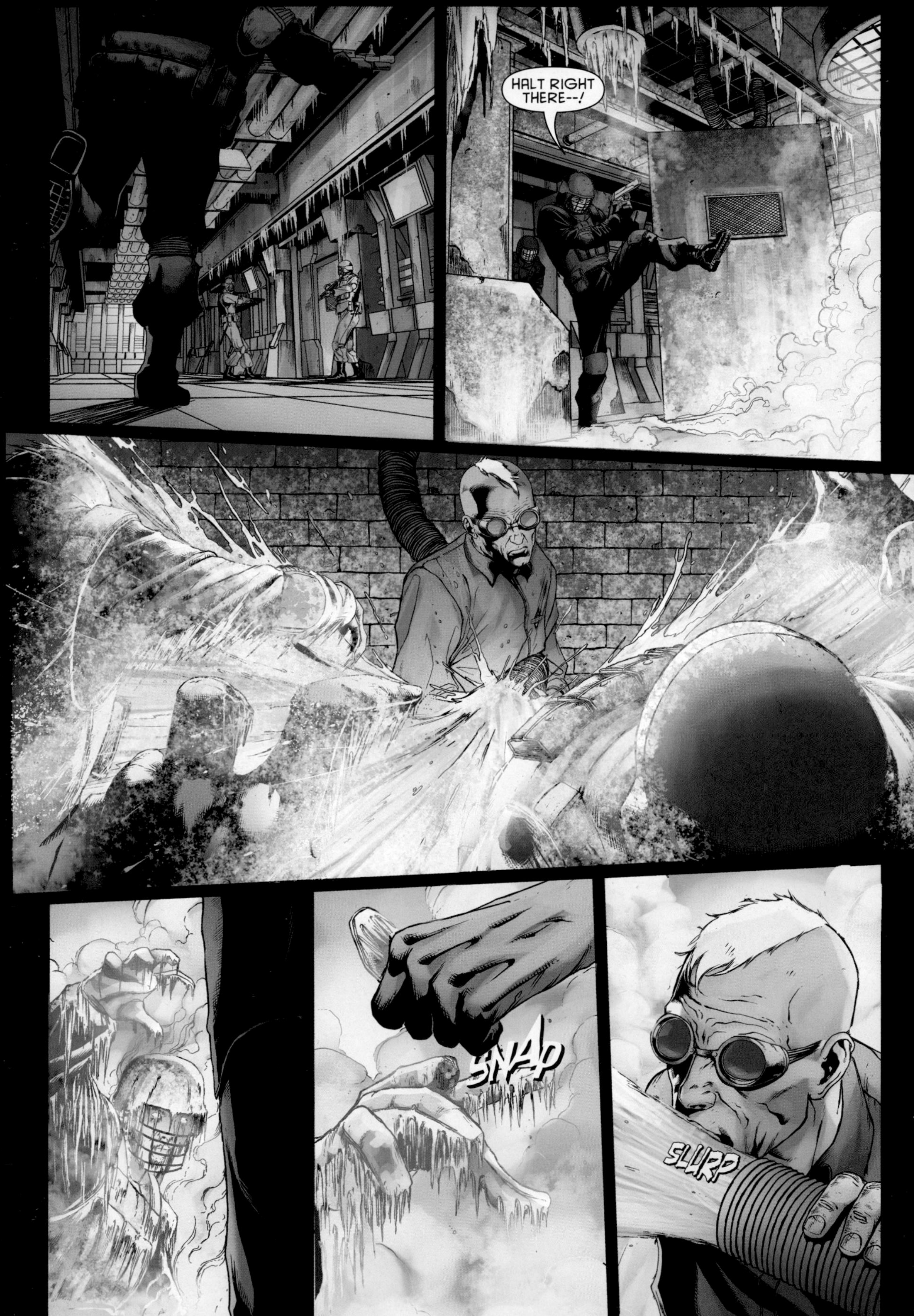
HALT RIGHT THERE--!
SNAP
SLURP

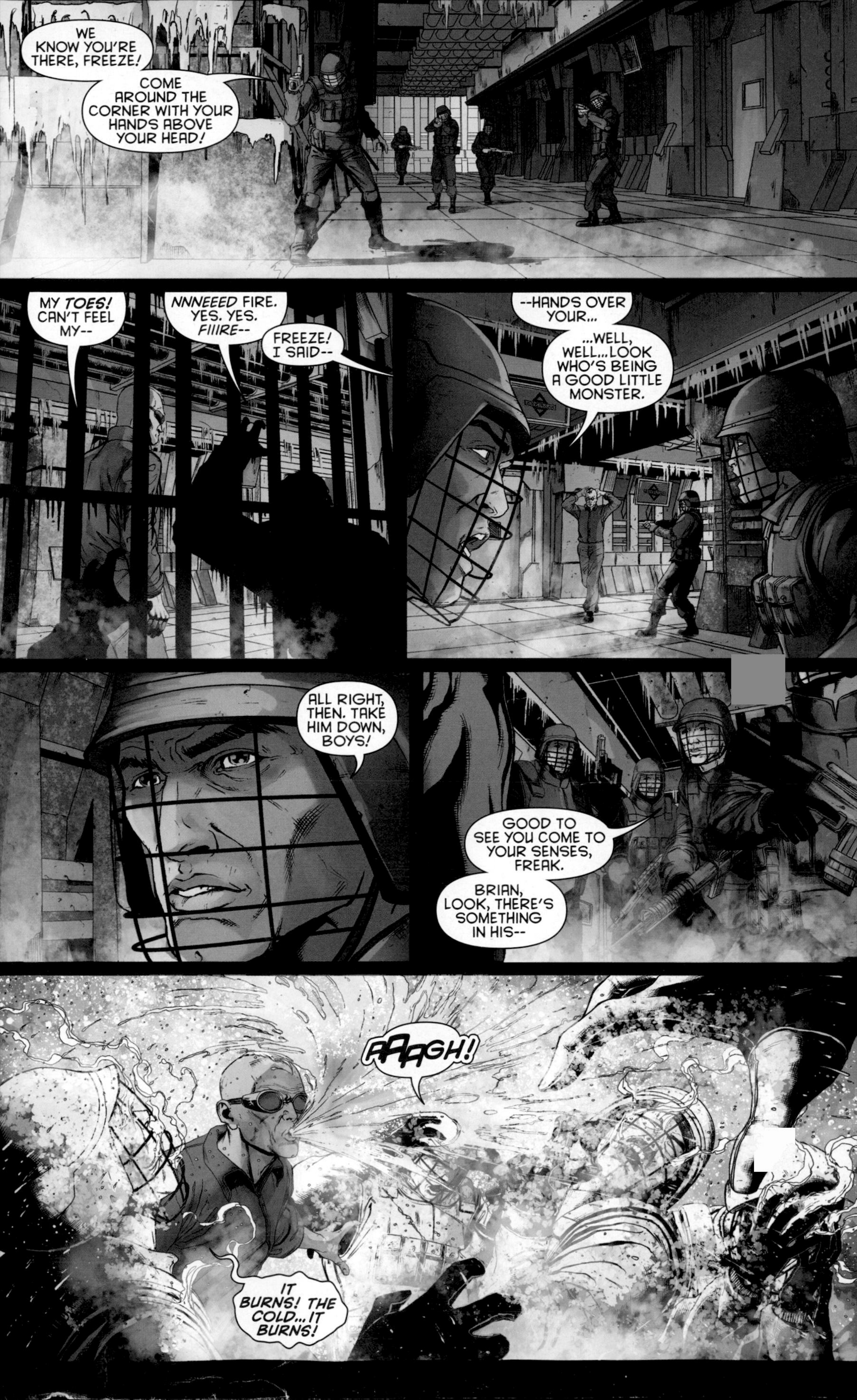
WE KNOW YOU'RE THERE, FREEZE!
COME AROUND THE CORNER WITH YOUR HANDS ABOVE YOUR HEAD!
MY *TOES!* CAN'T FEEL MY--
NNNEEED FIRE. YES. YES. *FIIIRE*--
FREEZE! I SAID--
--HANDS OVER YOUR...
...WELL, WELL...LOOK WHO'S BEING A GOOD LITTLE MONSTER.
ALL RIGHT, THEN. TAKE HIM DOWN, BOYS!
GOOD TO SEE YOU COME TO YOUR SENSES, FREAK.
BRIAN, LOOK, THERE'S SOMETHING IN HIS--
AAAGH!
IT BURNS! THE COLD... IT BURNS!

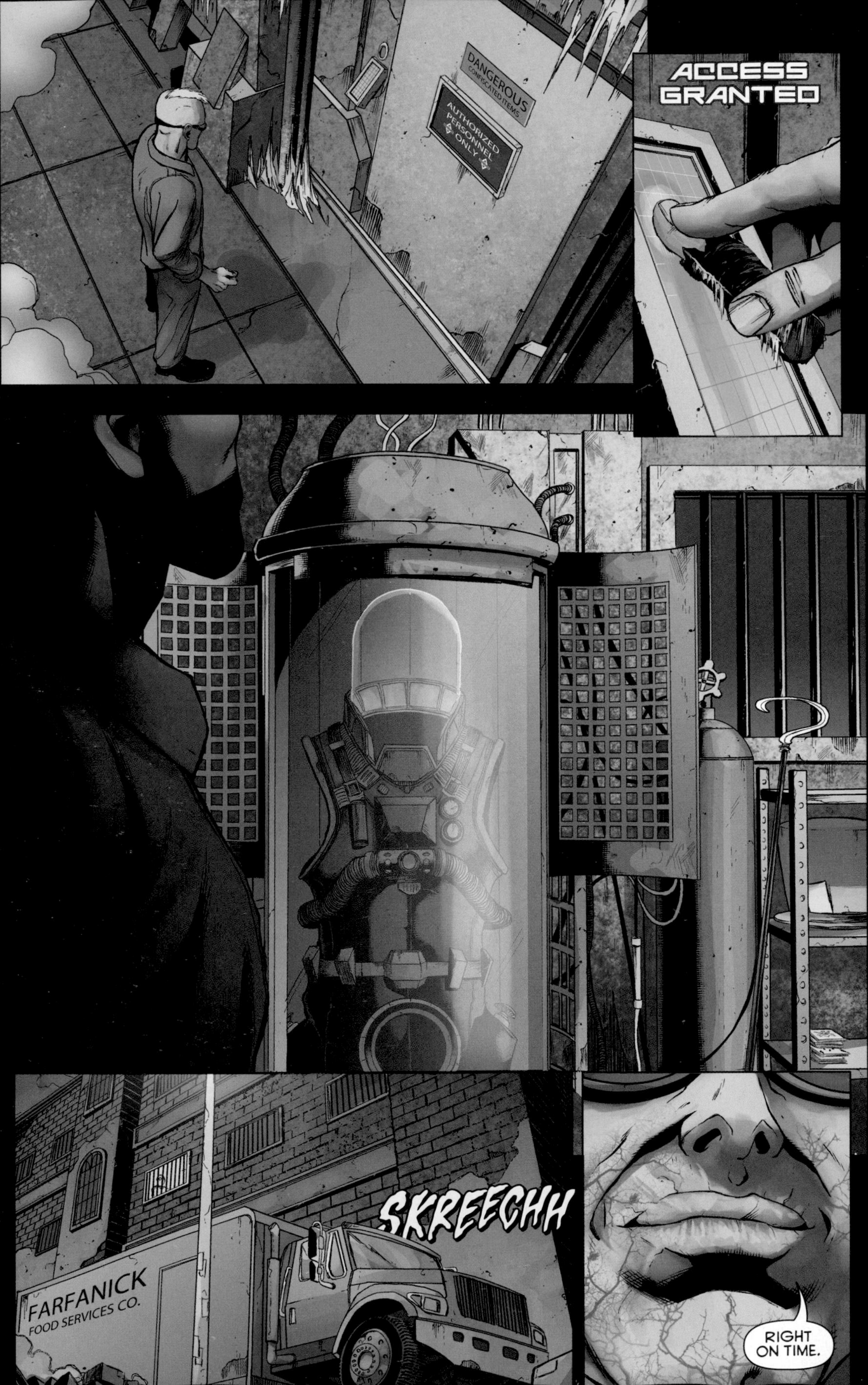
DANGEROUS
CONFISCATED ITEMS
AUTHORIZED PERSONNEL ONLY
ACCESS GRANTED
FARFANICK
FOOD SERVICES CO.
SKREECHH
RIGHT ON TIME.

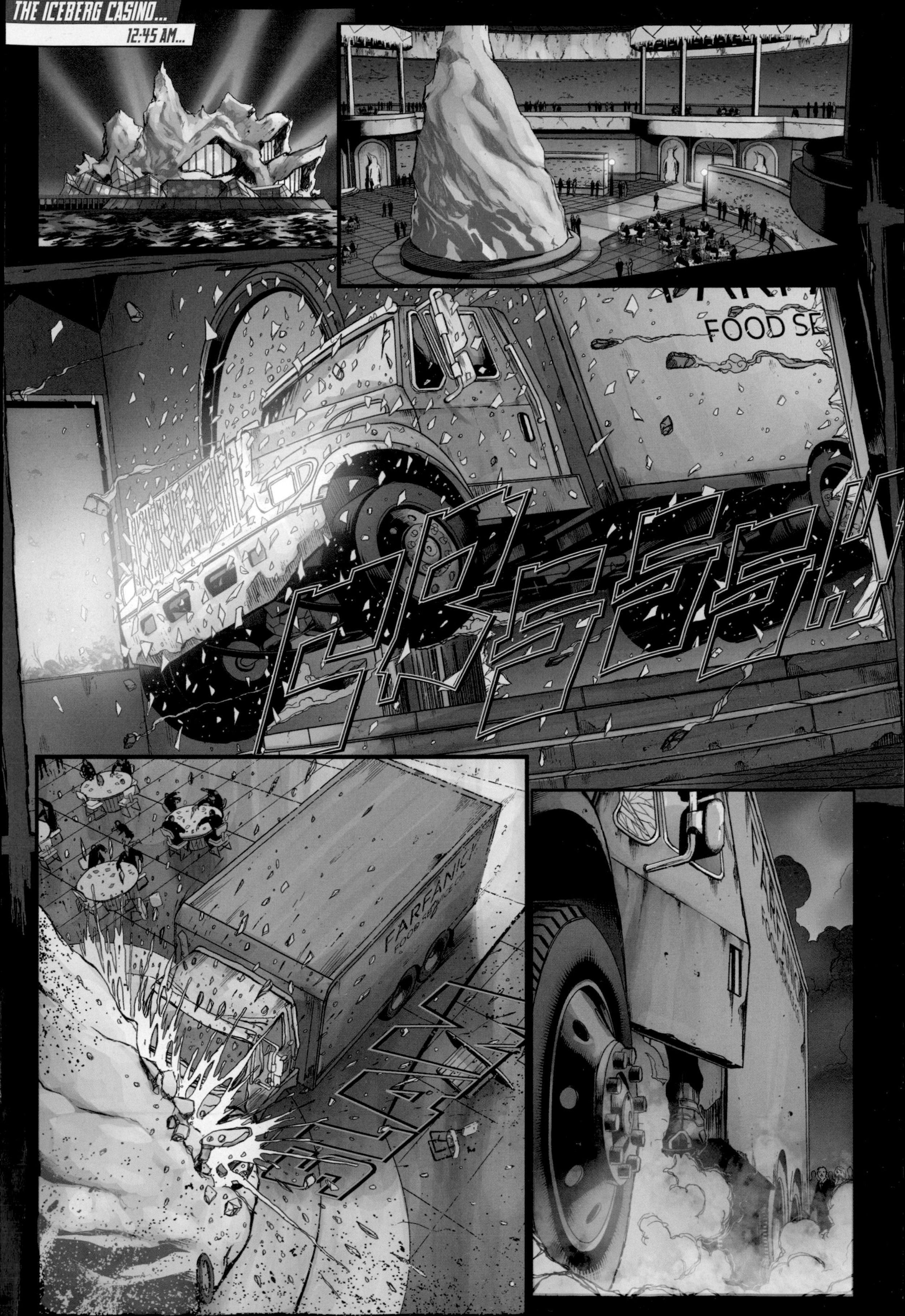
THE ICEBERG CASINO...
12:45 AM...
FOOD SE

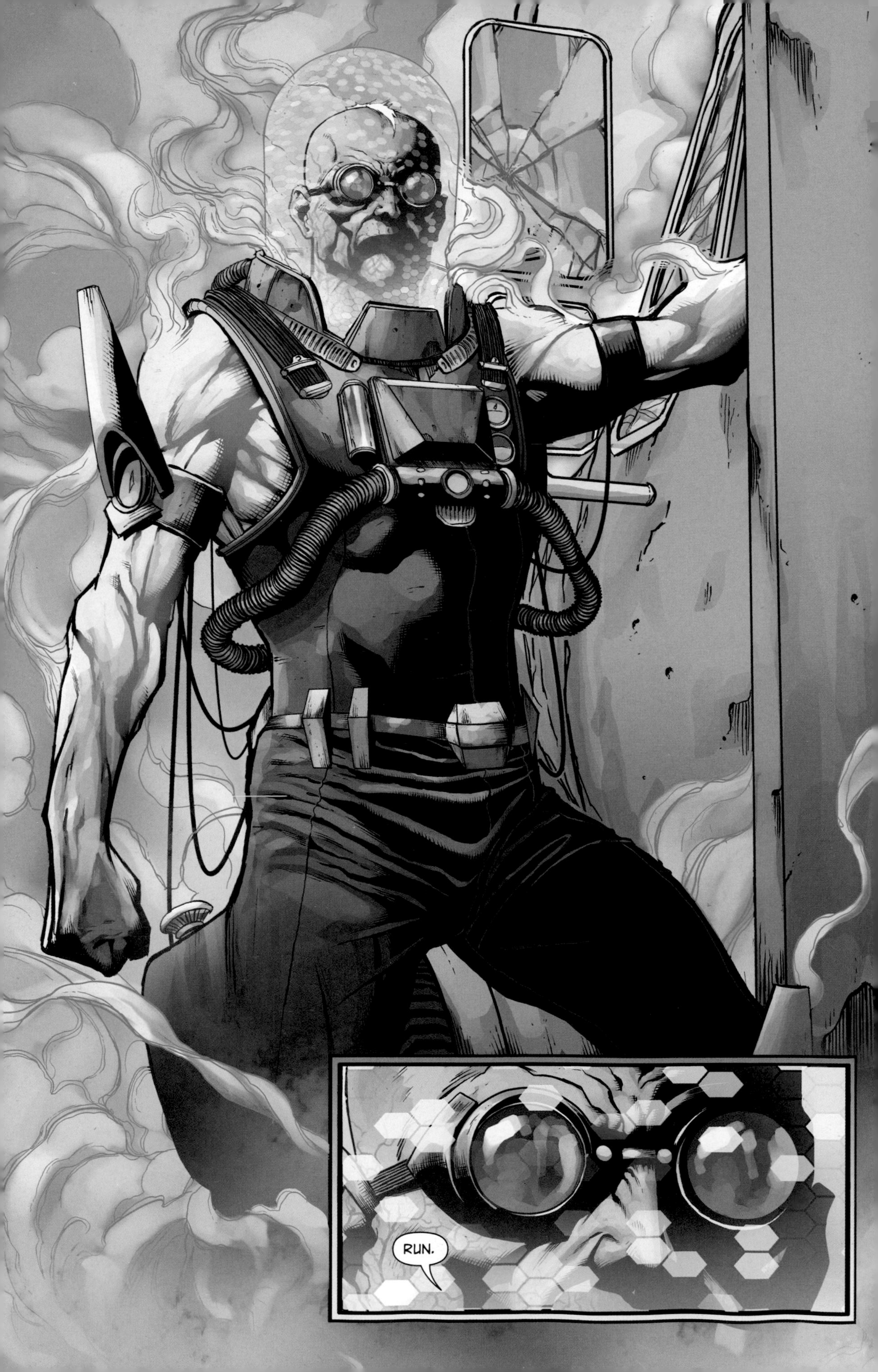
RUN.

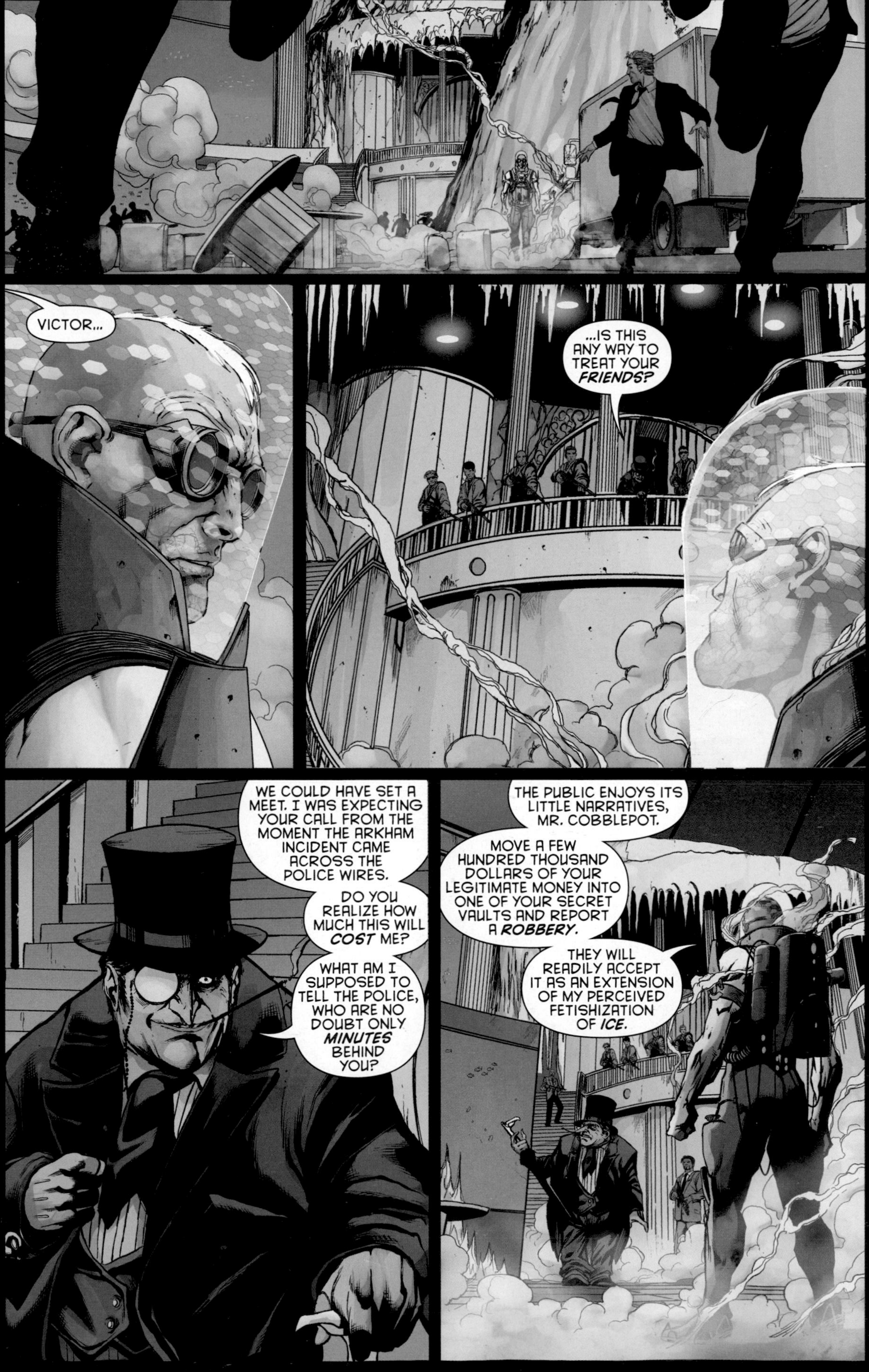
VICTOR...
...IS THIS ANY WAY TO TREAT YOUR FRIENDS?
WE COULD HAVE SET A MEET. I WAS EXPECTING YOUR CALL FROM THE MOMENT THE ARKHAM INCIDENT CAME ACROSS THE POLICE WIRES.
DO YOU REALIZE HOW MUCH THIS WILL COST ME?
WHAT AM I SUPPOSED TO TELL THE POLICE, WHO ARE NO DOUBT ONLY MINUTES BEHIND YOU?
THE PUBLIC ENJOYS ITS LITTLE NARRATIVES, MR. COBBLEPOT.
MOVE A FEW HUNDRED THOUSAND DOLLARS OF YOUR LEGITIMATE MONEY INTO ONE OF YOUR SECRET VAULTS AND REPORT A ROBBERY.
THEY WILL READILY ACCEPT IT AS AN EXTENSION OF MY PERCEIVED FETISHIZATION OF ICE.

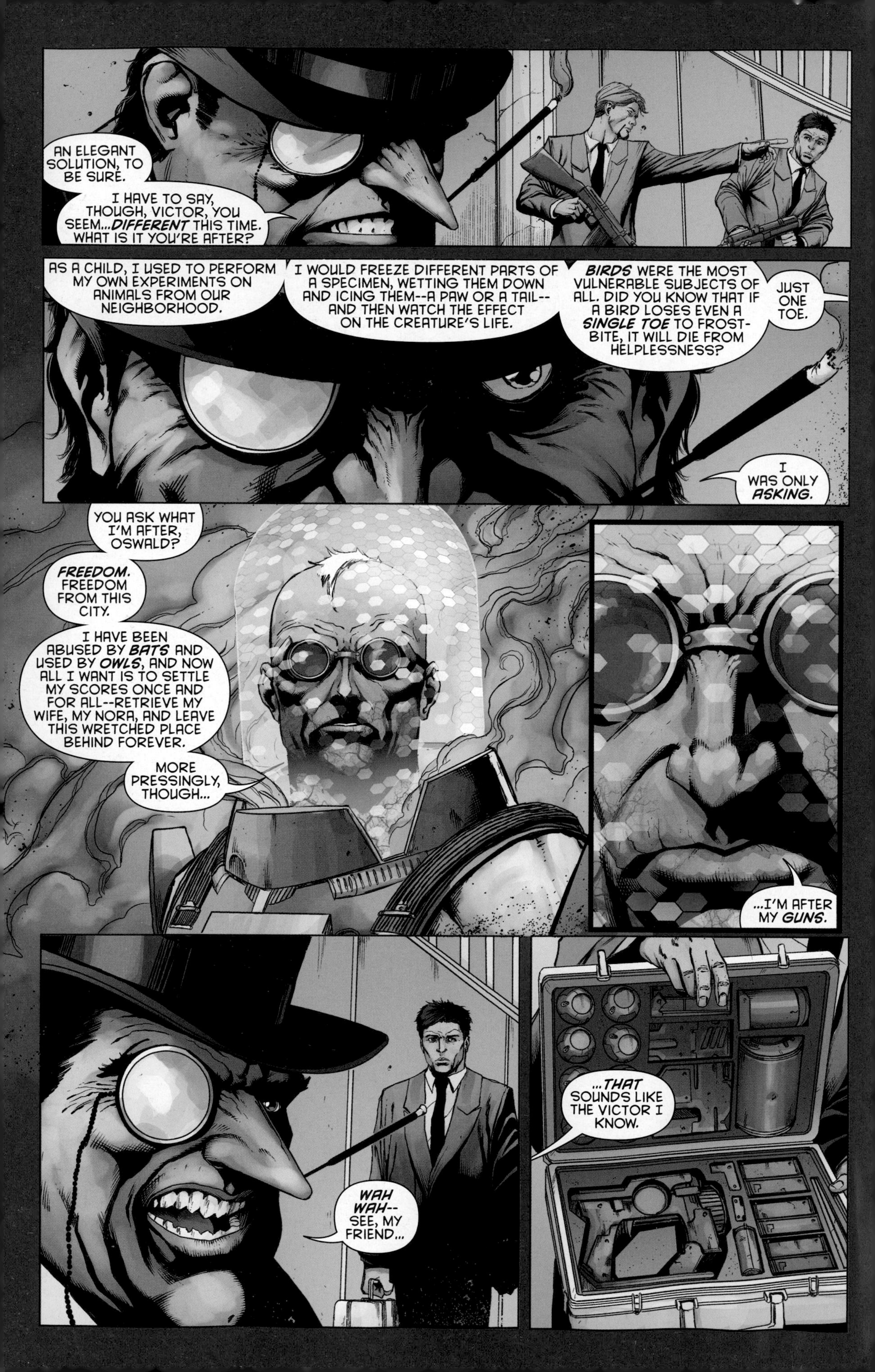
AN ELEGANT SOLUTION, TO BE SURE.
I HAVE TO SAY, THOUGH, VICTOR, YOU SEEM...DIFFERENT THIS TIME. WHAT IS IT YOU'RE AFTER?
AS A CHILD, I USED TO PERFORM MY OWN EXPERIMENTS ON ANIMALS FROM OUR NEIGHBORHOOD.
I WOULD FREEZE DIFFERENT PARTS OF A SPECIMEN, WETTING THEM DOWN AND ICING THEM--A PAW OR A TAIL--AND THEN WATCH THE EFFECT ON THE CREATURE'S LIFE.
BIRDS WERE THE MOST VULNERABLE SUBJECTS OF ALL. DID YOU KNOW THAT IF A BIRD LOSES EVEN A SINGLE TOE TO FROST-BITE, IT WILL DIE FROM HELPLESSNESS?
JUST ONE TOE.
I WAS ONLY ASKING.
YOU ASK WHAT I'M AFTER, OSWALD?
FREEDOM. FREEDOM FROM THIS CITY.
I HAVE BEEN ABUSED BY BATS AND USED BY OWLS, AND NOW ALL I WANT IS TO SETTLE MY SCORES ONCE AND FOR ALL--RETRIEVE MY WIFE, MY NORA, AND LEAVE THIS WRETCHED PLACE BEHIND FOREVER.
MORE PRESSINGLY, THOUGH...
...I'M AFTER MY GUNS.
WAH WAH--SEE, MY FRIEND...
...THAT SOUNDS LIKE THE VICTOR I KNOW.

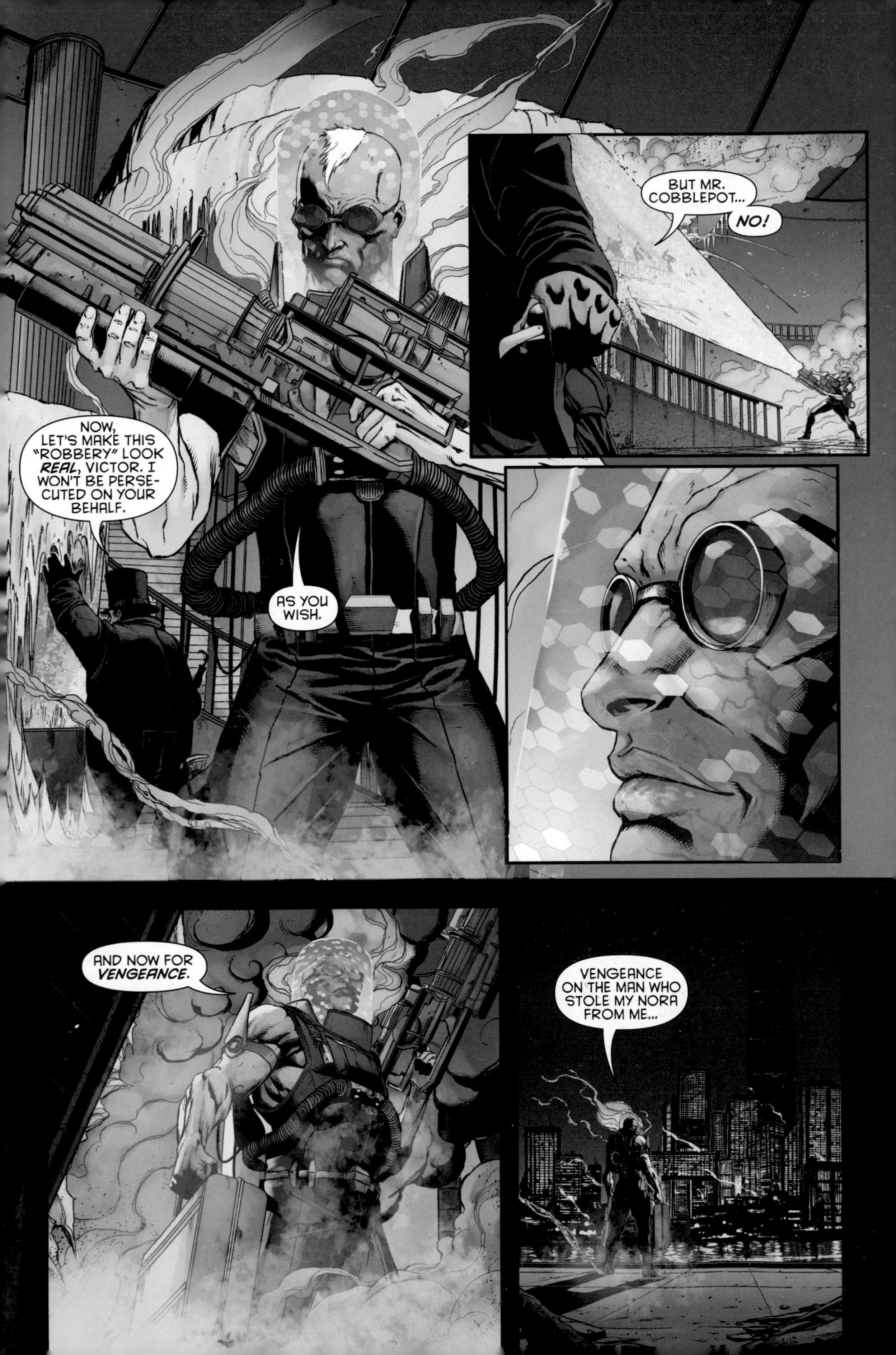
BUT MR. COBBLEPOT...
NO!
NOW, LET'S MAKE THIS "ROBBERY" LOOK REAL, VICTOR. I WON'T BE PERSECUTED ON YOUR BEHALF.
AS YOU WISH.
AND NOW FOR VENGEANCE.
VENGEANCE ON THE MAN WHO STOLE MY NORA FROM ME...

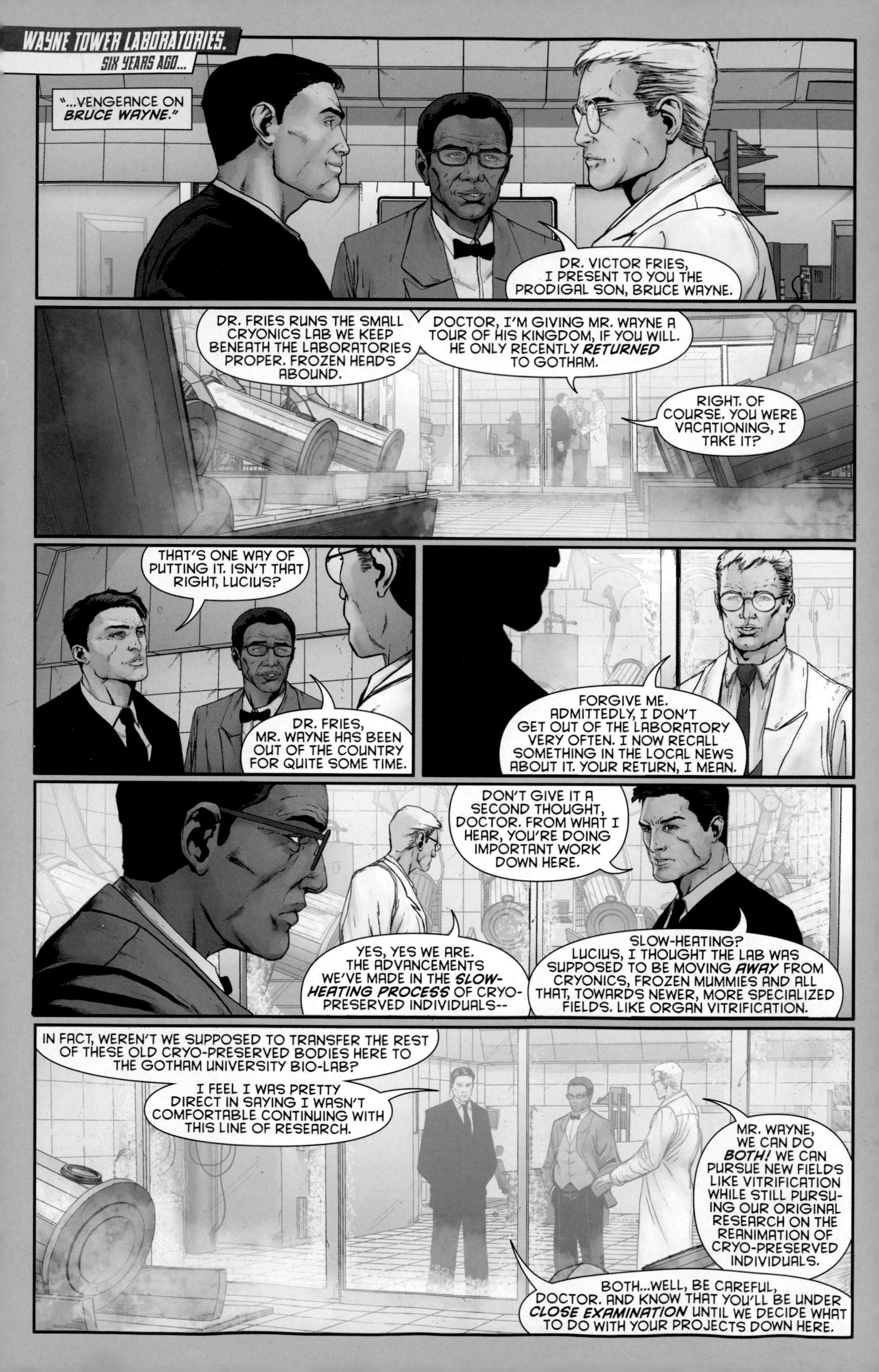
WAYNE TOWER LABORATORIES.
SIX YEARS AGO...
"...VENGEANCE ON BRUCE WAYNE."
DR. VICTOR FRIES, I PRESENT TO YOU THE PRODIGAL SON, BRUCE WAYNE.
DR. FRIES RUNS THE SMALL CRYONICS LAB WE KEEP BENEATH THE LABORATORIES PROPER. FROZEN HEADS ABOUND.
DOCTOR, I'M GIVING MR. WAYNE A TOUR OF HIS KINGDOM, IF YOU WILL. HE ONLY RECENTLY RETURNED TO GOTHAM.
RIGHT. OF COURSE. YOU WERE VACATIONING, I TAKE IT?
THAT'S ONE WAY OF PUTTING IT. ISN'T THAT RIGHT, LUCIUS?
DR. FRIES, MR. WAYNE HAS BEEN OUT OF THE COUNTRY FOR QUITE SOME TIME.
FORGIVE ME. ADMITTEDLY, I DON'T GET OUT OF THE LABORATORY VERY OFTEN. I NOW RECALL SOMETHING IN THE LOCAL NEWS ABOUT IT. YOUR RETURN, I MEAN.
DON'T GIVE IT A SECOND THOUGHT, DOCTOR. FROM WHAT I HEAR, YOU'RE DOING IMPORTANT WORK DOWN HERE.
YES, YES WE ARE. THE ADVANCEMENTS WE'VE MADE IN THE SLOW-HEATING PROCESS OF CRYO-PRESERVED INDIVIDUALS--
SLOW-HEATING? LUCIUS, I THOUGHT THE LAB WAS SUPPOSED TO BE MOVING AWAY FROM CRYONICS, FROZEN MUMMIES AND ALL THAT, TOWARDS NEWER, MORE SPECIALIZED FIELDS. LIKE ORGAN VITRIFICATION.
IN FACT, WEREN'T WE SUPPOSED TO TRANSFER THE REST OF THESE OLD CRYO-PRESERVED BODIES HERE TO THE GOTHAM UNIVERSITY BIO-LAB?
I FEEL I WAS PRETTY DIRECT IN SAYING I WASN'T COMFORTABLE CONTINUING WITH THIS LINE OF RESEARCH.
MR. WAYNE, WE CAN DO BOTH! WE CAN PURSUE NEW FIELDS LIKE VITRIFICATION WHILE STILL PURSUING OUR ORIGINAL RESEARCH ON THE REANIMATION OF CRYO-PRESERVED INDIVIDUALS.
BOTH...WELL, BE CAREFUL, DOCTOR. AND KNOW THAT YOU'LL BE UNDER CLOSE EXAMINATION UNTIL WE DECIDE WHAT TO DO WITH YOUR PROJECTS DOWN HERE.

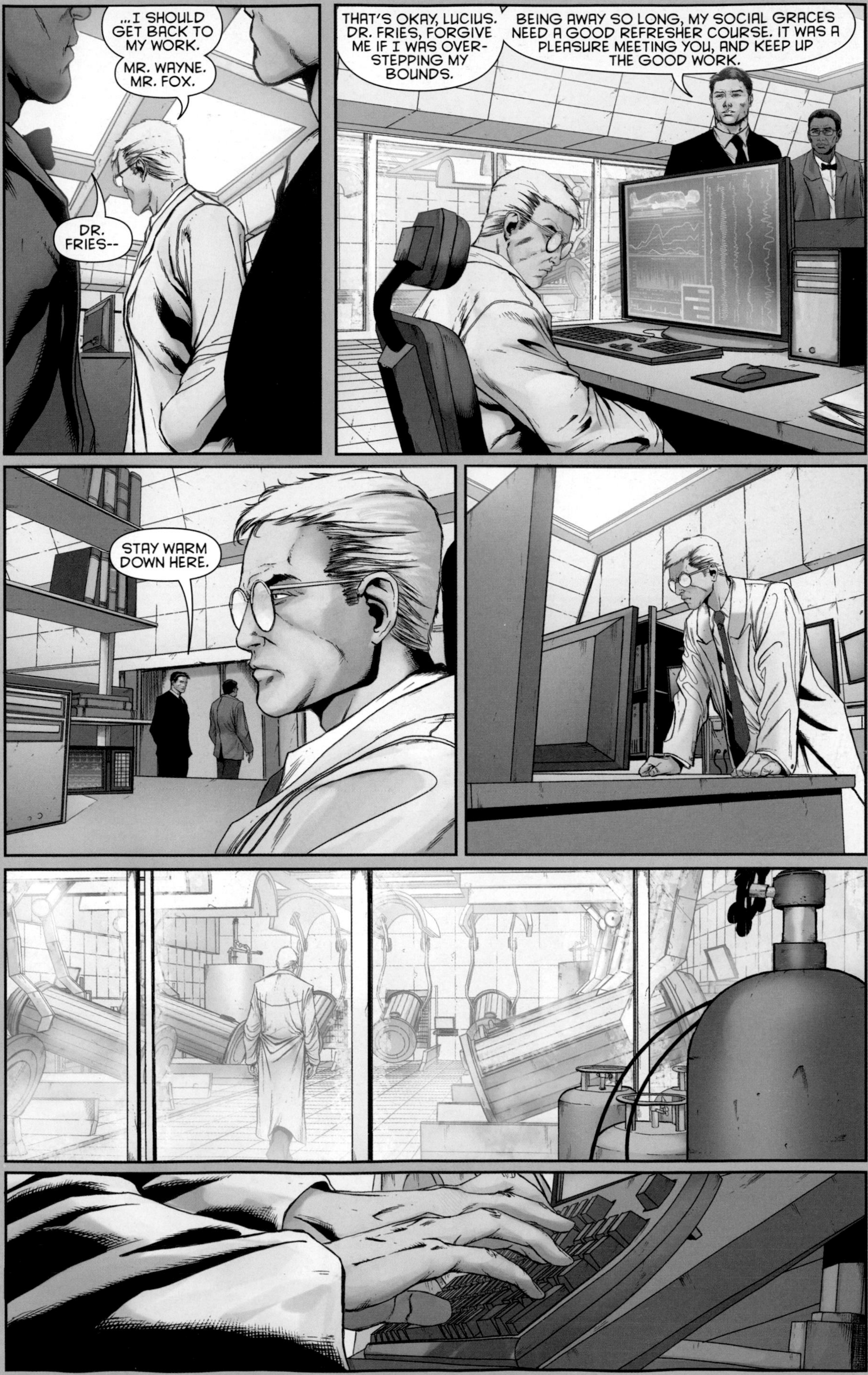
...I SHOULD GET BACK TO MY WORK.
MR. WAYNE. MR. FOX.
DR. FRIES--
THAT'S OKAY, LUCIUS. DR. FRIES, FORGIVE ME IF I WAS OVER-STEPPING MY BOUNDS.
BEING AWAY SO LONG, MY SOCIAL GRACES NEED A GOOD REFRESHER COURSE. IT WAS A PLEASURE MEETING YOU, AND KEEP UP THE GOOD WORK.
STAY WARM DOWN HERE.

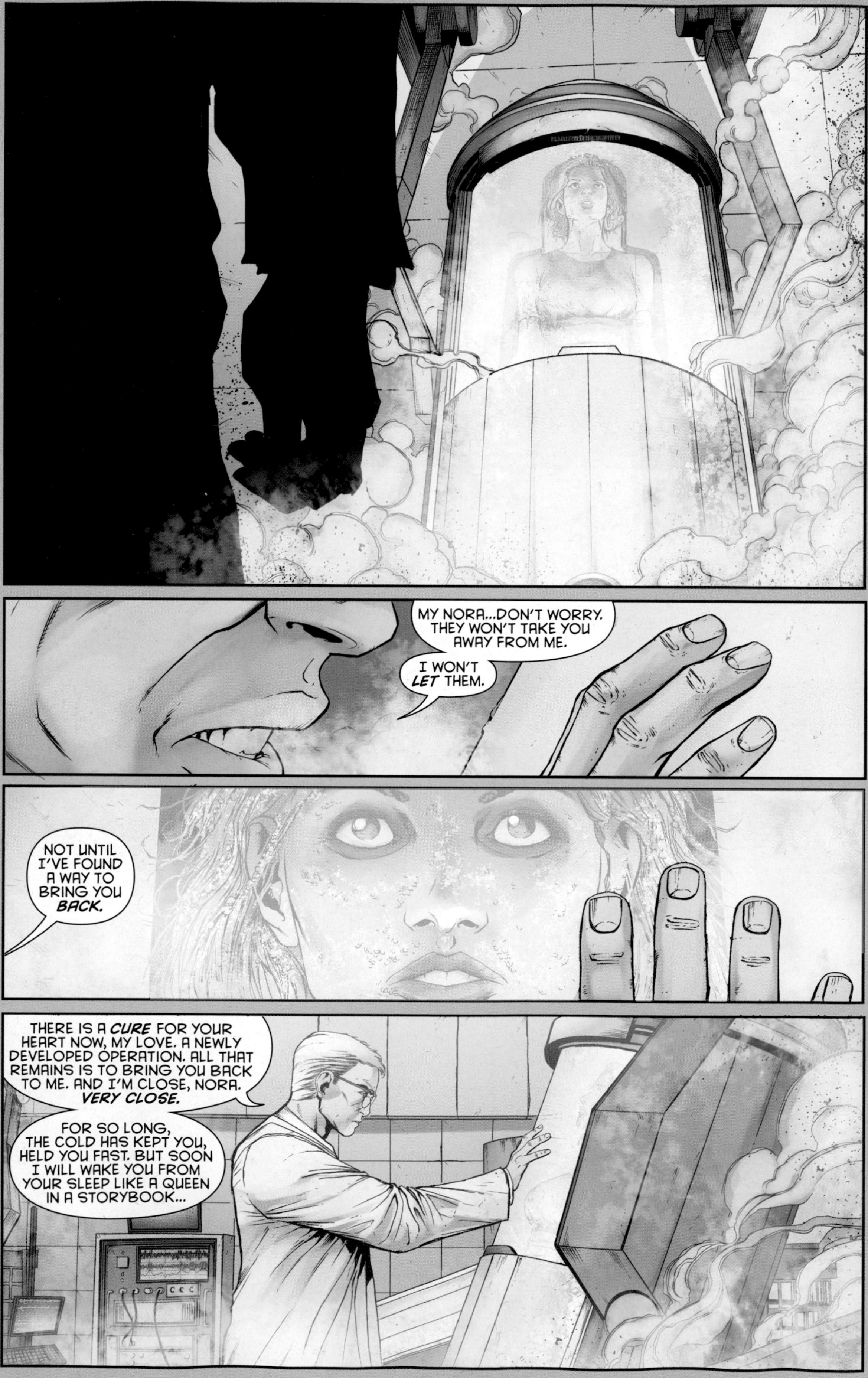
MY NORA...DON'T WORRY. THEY WON'T TAKE YOU AWAY FROM ME.
I WON'T *LET* THEM.
NOT UNTIL I'VE FOUND A WAY TO BRING YOU *BACK.*
THERE IS A *CURE* FOR YOUR HEART NOW, MY LOVE. A NEWLY DEVELOPED OPERATION. ALL THAT REMAINS IS TO BRING YOU BACK TO ME. AND I'M CLOSE, NORA. *VERY CLOSE.*
FOR SO LONG, THE COLD HAS KEPT YOU, HELD YOU FAST. BUT SOON I WILL WAKE YOU FROM YOUR SLEEP LIKE A QUEEN IN A STORYBOOK...

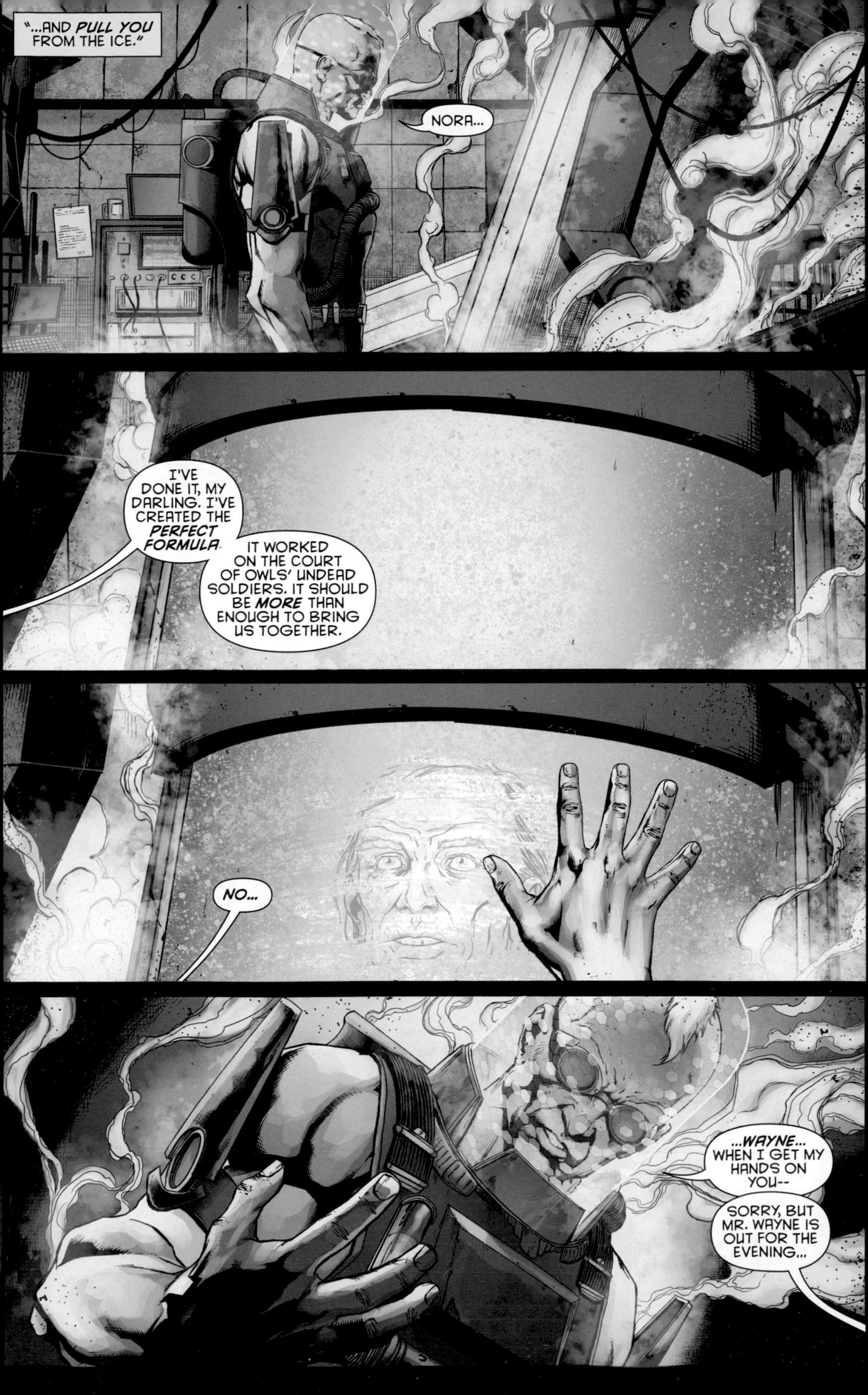
"...AND PULL YOU FROM THE ICE."
NORA...
I'VE DONE IT, MY DARLING. I'VE CREATED THE PERFECT FORMULA.
IT WORKED ON THE COURT OF OWLS' UNDEAD SOLDIERS. IT SHOULD BE MORE THAN ENOUGH TO BRING US TOGETHER.
NO...
...WAYNE... WHEN I GET MY HANDS ON YOU--
SORRY, BUT MR. WAYNE IS OUT FOR THE EVENING...

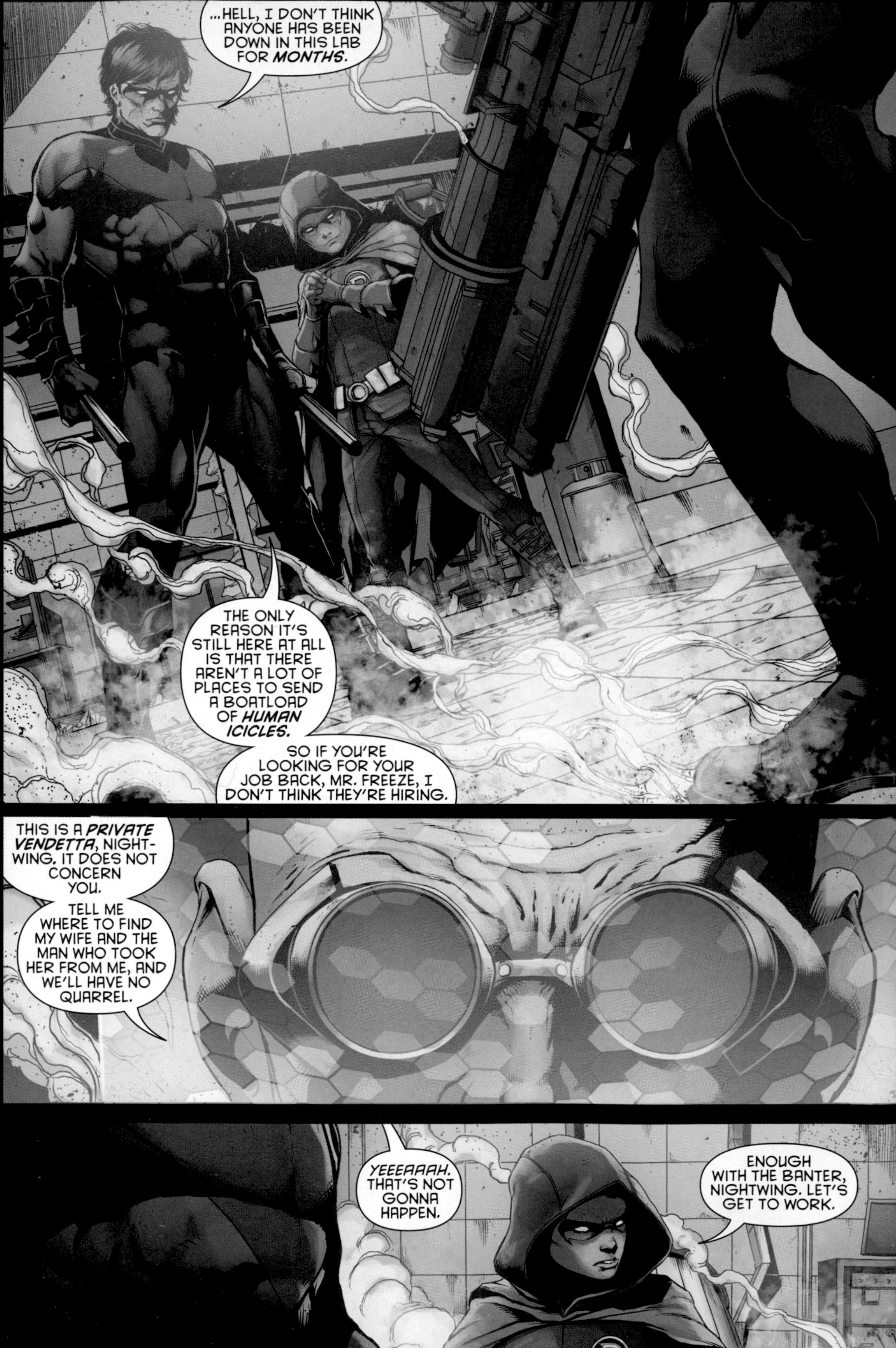
...HELL, I DON'T THINK ANYONE HAS BEEN DOWN IN THIS LAB FOR *MONTHS*.
THE ONLY REASON IT'S STILL HERE AT ALL IS THAT THERE AREN'T A LOT OF PLACES TO SEND A BOATLOAD OF *HUMAN ICICLES*.
SO IF YOU'RE LOOKING FOR YOUR JOB BACK, MR. FREEZE, I DON'T THINK THEY'RE HIRING.
THIS IS A *PRIVATE VENDETTA*, NIGHT-WING. IT DOES NOT CONCERN YOU.
TELL ME WHERE TO FIND MY WIFE AND THE MAN WHO TOOK HER FROM ME, AND WE'LL HAVE NO QUARREL.
YEEEAAAH. THAT'S NOT GONNA HAPPEN.
ENOUGH WITH THE BANTER, NIGHTWING. LET'S GET TO WORK.

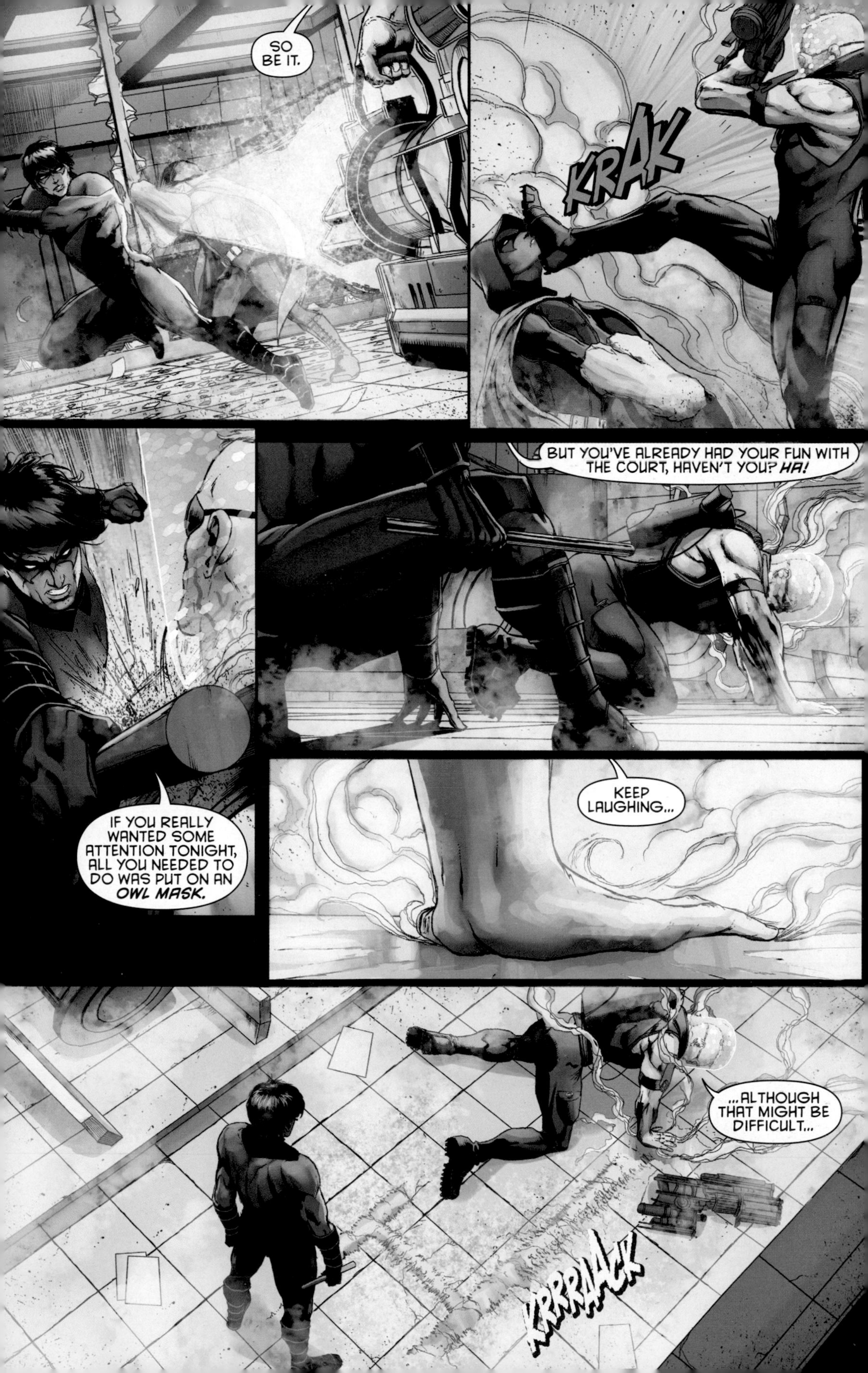
SO BE IT.
KRAK
IF YOU REALLY WANTED SOME ATTENTION TONIGHT, ALL YOU NEEDED TO DO WAS PUT ON AN OWL MASK.
BUT YOU'VE ALREADY HAD YOUR FUN WITH THE COURT, HAVEN'T YOU? HA!
KEEP LAUGHING...
...ALTHOUGH THAT MIGHT BE DIFFICULT...
KRRRAACK

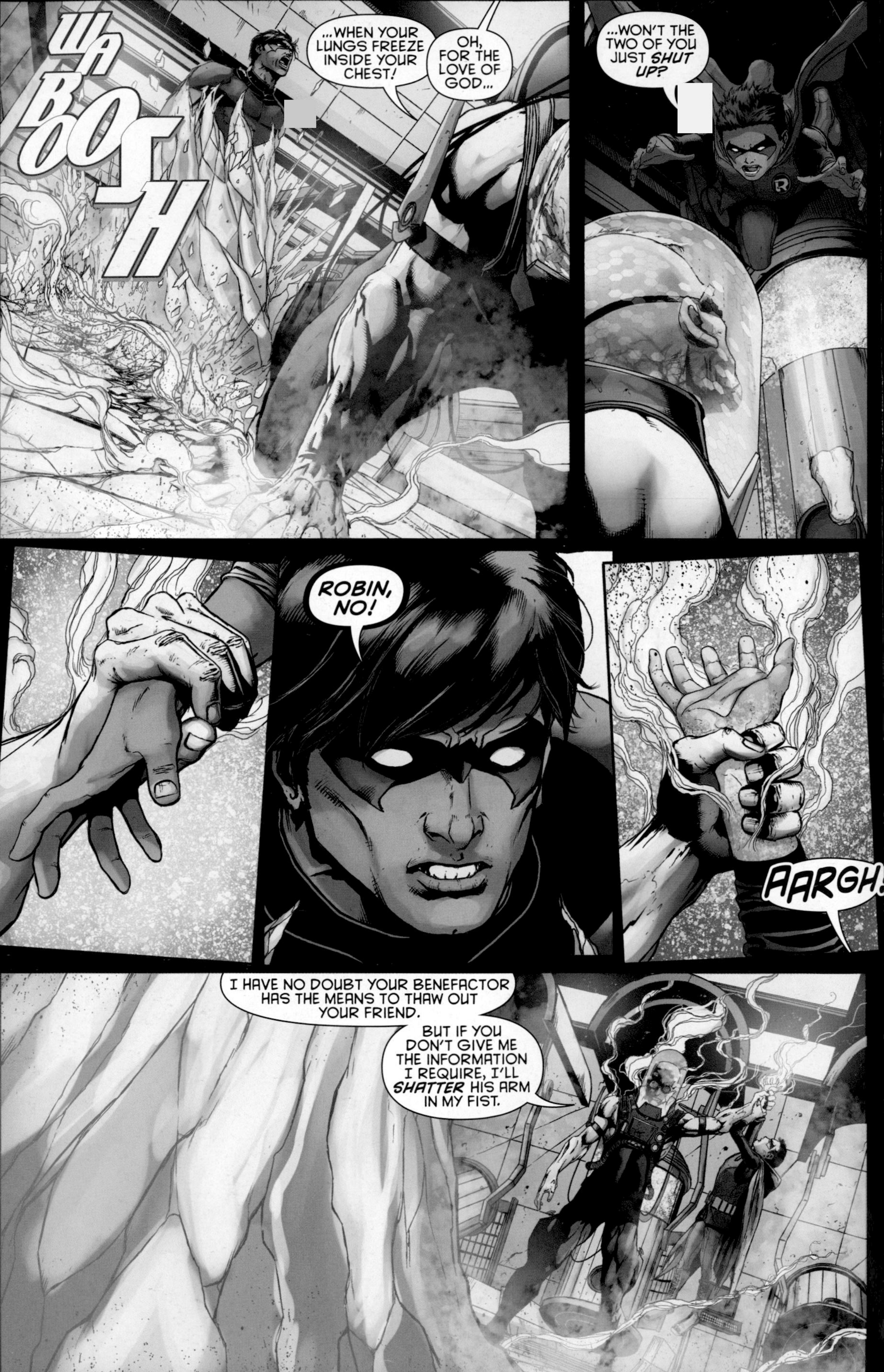
WABOOSH
...WHEN YOUR LUNGS FREEZE INSIDE YOUR CHEST!
OH, FOR THE LOVE OF GOD...
...WON'T THE TWO OF YOU JUST SHUT UP?
ROBIN, NO!
AARGH!
I HAVE NO DOUBT YOUR BENEFACTOR HAS THE MEANS TO THAW OUT YOUR FRIEND.
BUT IF YOU DON'T GIVE ME THE INFORMATION I REQUIRE, I'LL SHATTER HIS ARM IN MY FIST.

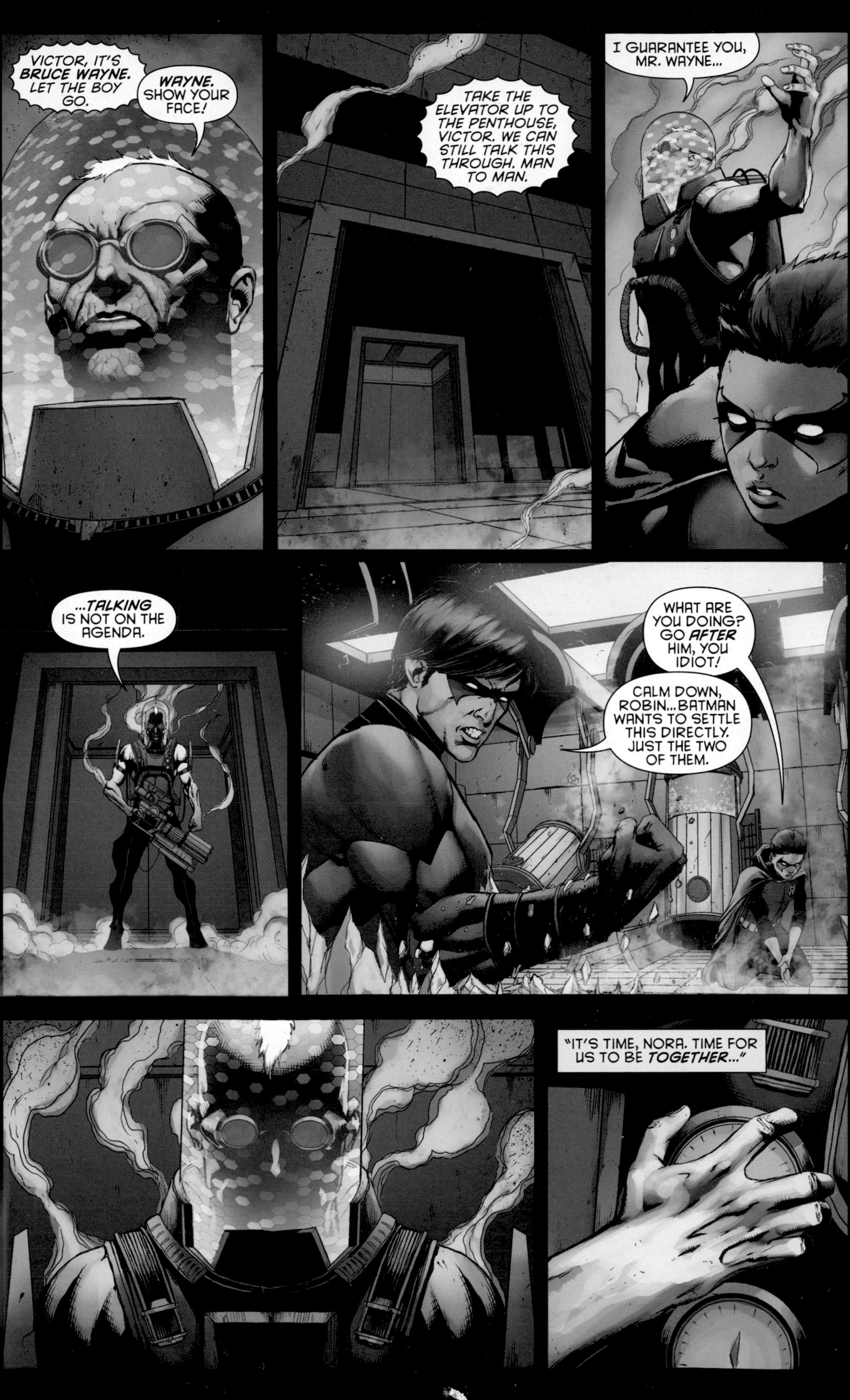

VICTOR, IT'S BRUCE WAYNE. LET THE BOY GO.
WAYNE. SHOW YOUR FACE!
TAKE THE ELEVATOR UP TO THE PENTHOUSE, VICTOR. WE CAN STILL TALK THIS THROUGH. MAN TO MAN.
I GUARANTEE YOU, MR. WAYNE...
...TALKING IS NOT ON THE AGENDA.
WHAT ARE YOU DOING? GO AFTER HIM, YOU IDIOT!
CALM DOWN, ROBIN...BATMAN WANTS TO SETTLE THIS DIRECTLY. JUST THE TWO OF THEM.
"IT'S TIME, NORA. TIME FOR US TO BE TOGETHER..."

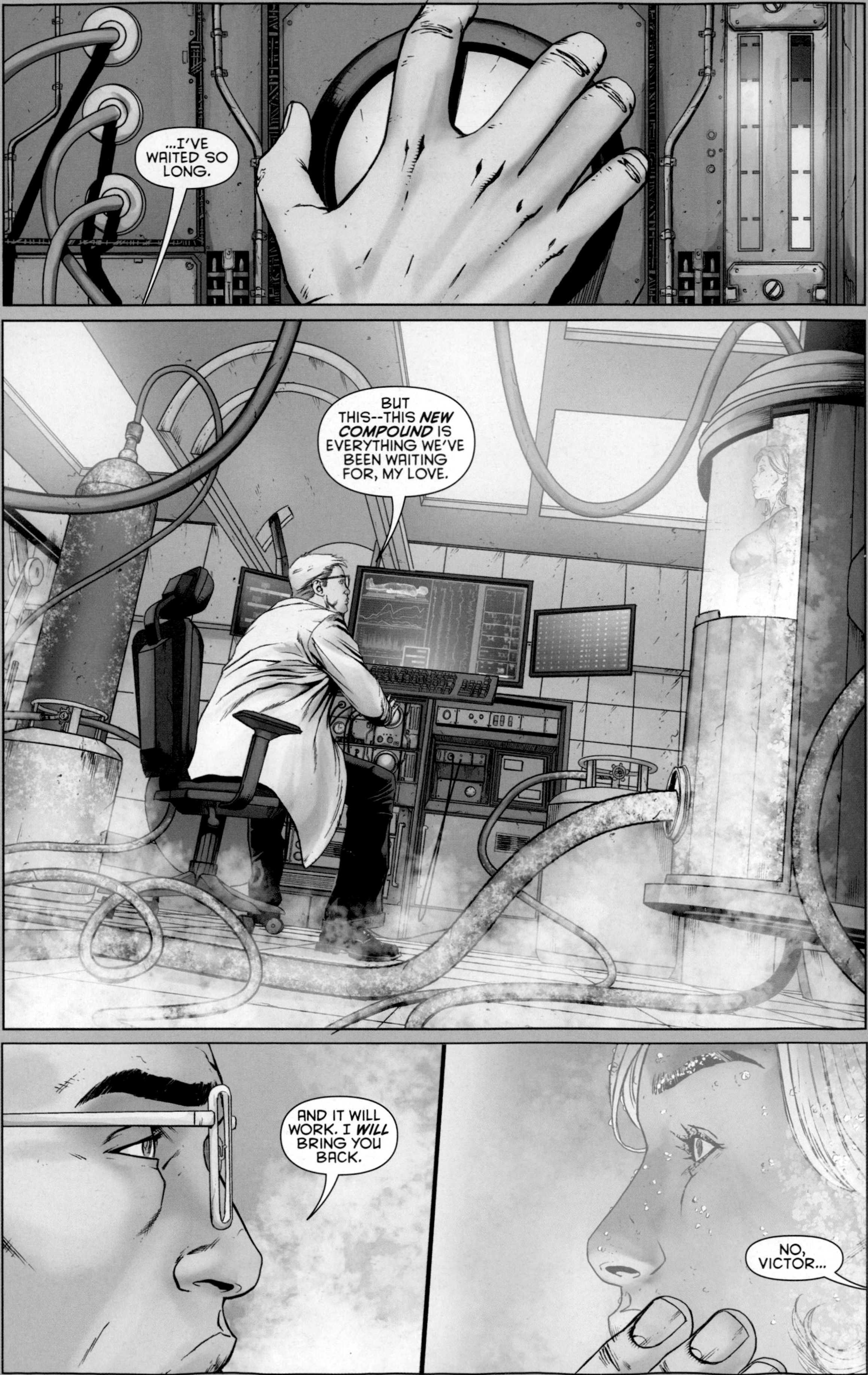
...I'VE WAITED SO LONG.
BUT THIS--THIS *NEW COMPOUND* IS EVERYTHING WE'VE BEEN WAITING FOR, MY LOVE.
AND IT WILL WORK. I *WILL* BRING YOU BACK.
NO, VICTOR...

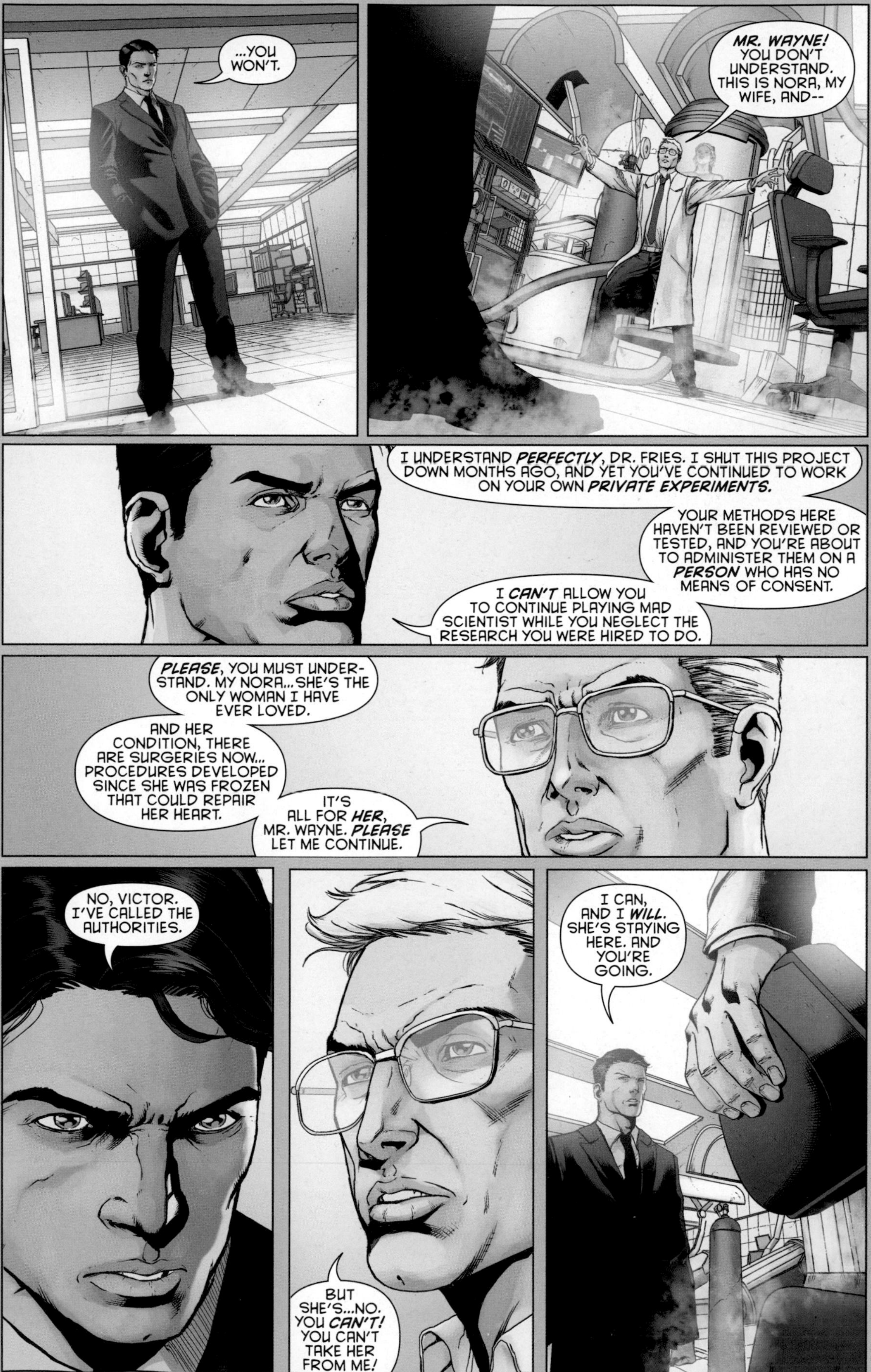
...YOU WON'T.
MR. WAYNE! YOU DON'T UNDERSTAND. THIS IS NORA, MY WIFE, AND--
I UNDERSTAND PERFECTLY, DR. FRIES. I SHUT THIS PROJECT DOWN MONTHS AGO, AND YET YOU'VE CONTINUED TO WORK ON YOUR OWN PRIVATE EXPERIMENTS.
YOUR METHODS HERE HAVEN'T BEEN REVIEWED OR TESTED, AND YOU'RE ABOUT TO ADMINISTER THEM ON A PERSON WHO HAS NO MEANS OF CONSENT.
I CAN'T ALLOW YOU TO CONTINUE PLAYING MAD SCIENTIST WHILE YOU NEGLECT THE RESEARCH YOU WERE HIRED TO DO.
PLEASE, YOU MUST UNDERSTAND. MY NORA...SHE'S THE ONLY WOMAN I HAVE EVER LOVED.
AND HER CONDITION, THERE ARE SURGERIES NOW... PROCEDURES DEVELOPED SINCE SHE WAS FROZEN THAT COULD REPAIR HER HEART.
IT'S ALL FOR HER, MR. WAYNE. PLEASE LET ME CONTINUE.
NO, VICTOR. I'VE CALLED THE AUTHORITIES.
BUT SHE'S...NO. YOU CAN'T! YOU CAN'T TAKE HER FROM ME!
I CAN, AND I WILL. SHE'S STAYING HERE. AND YOU'RE GOING.

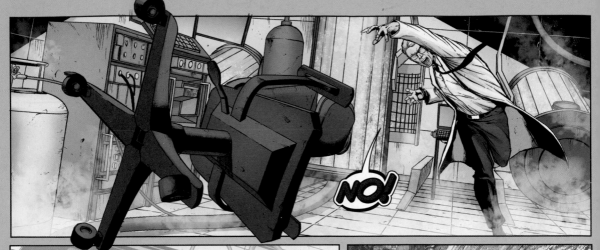

NO!

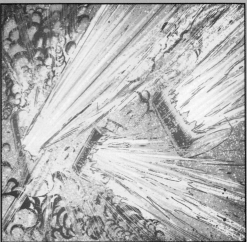

VICTOR, GET OUT OF THE WAY!

AHHHH!

NOOO.... RRRAA. NORA...

"THIS IS *INCREDIBLE*, I'VE NEVER SEEN ANYTHING LIKE IT."

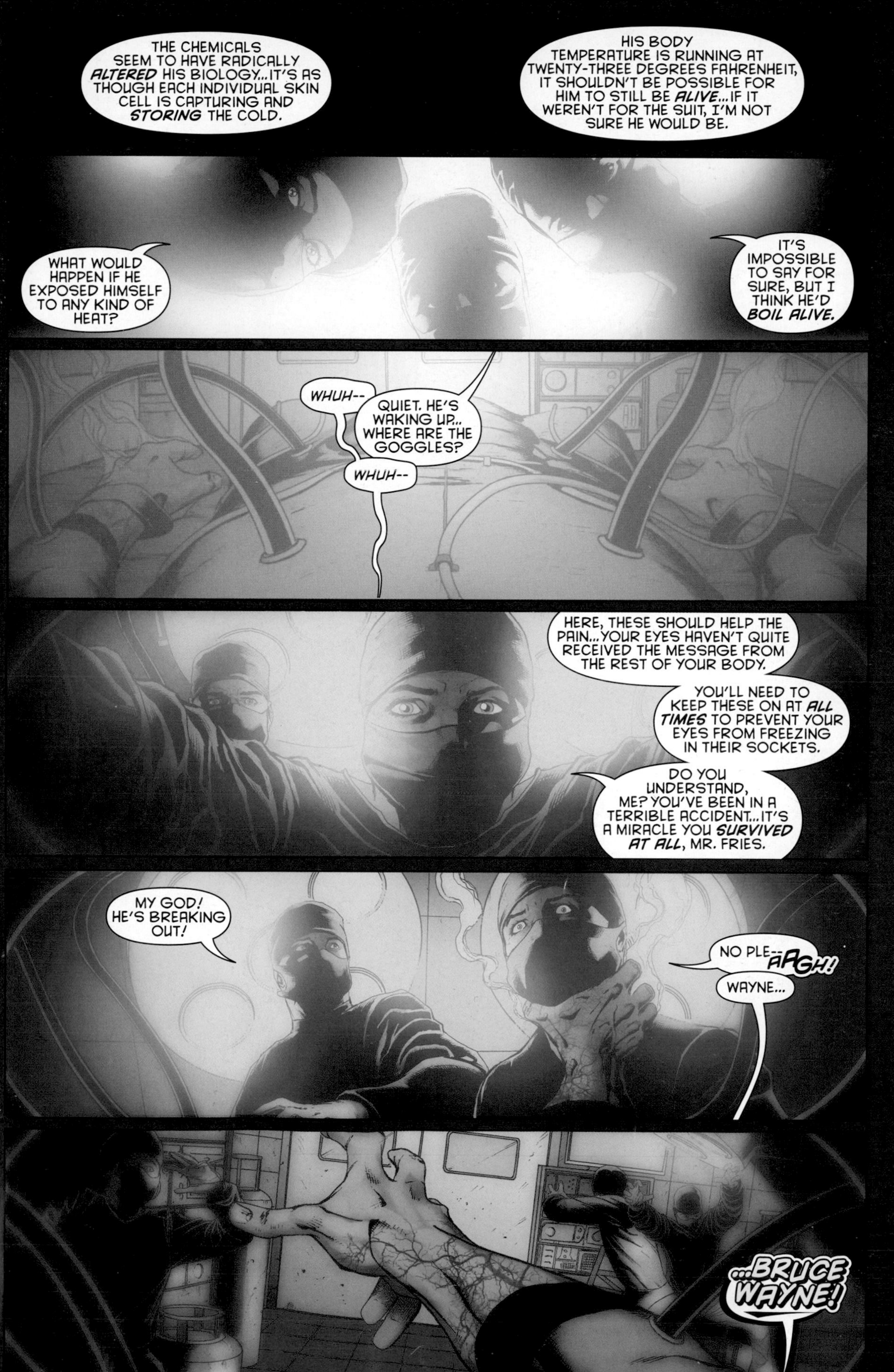
THE CHEMICALS SEEM TO HAVE RADICALLY ALTERED HIS BIOLOGY... IT'S AS THOUGH EACH INDIVIDUAL SKIN CELL IS CAPTURING AND STORING THE COLD.
HIS BODY TEMPERATURE IS RUNNING AT TWENTY-THREE DEGREES FAHRENHEIT, IT SHOULDN'T BE POSSIBLE FOR HIM TO STILL BE ALIVE... IF IT WEREN'T FOR THE SUIT, I'M NOT SURE HE WOULD BE.
WHAT WOULD HAPPEN IF HE EXPOSED HIMSELF TO ANY KIND OF HEAT?
IT'S IMPOSSIBLE TO SAY FOR SURE, BUT I THINK HE'D BOIL ALIVE.
WHUH--
QUIET. HE'S WAKING UP... WHERE ARE THE GOGGLES?
WHUH--
HERE, THESE SHOULD HELP THE PAIN... YOUR EYES HAVEN'T QUITE RECEIVED THE MESSAGE FROM THE REST OF YOUR BODY.
YOU'LL NEED TO KEEP THESE ON AT ALL TIMES TO PREVENT YOUR EYES FROM FREEZING IN THEIR SOCKETS.
DO YOU UNDERSTAND, ME? YOU'VE BEEN IN A TERRIBLE ACCIDENT... IT'S A MIRACLE YOU SURVIVED AT ALL, MR. FRIES.
MY GOD! HE'S BREAKING OUT!
NO PLE-- AAGH!
WAYNE...
...BRUCE WAYNE!

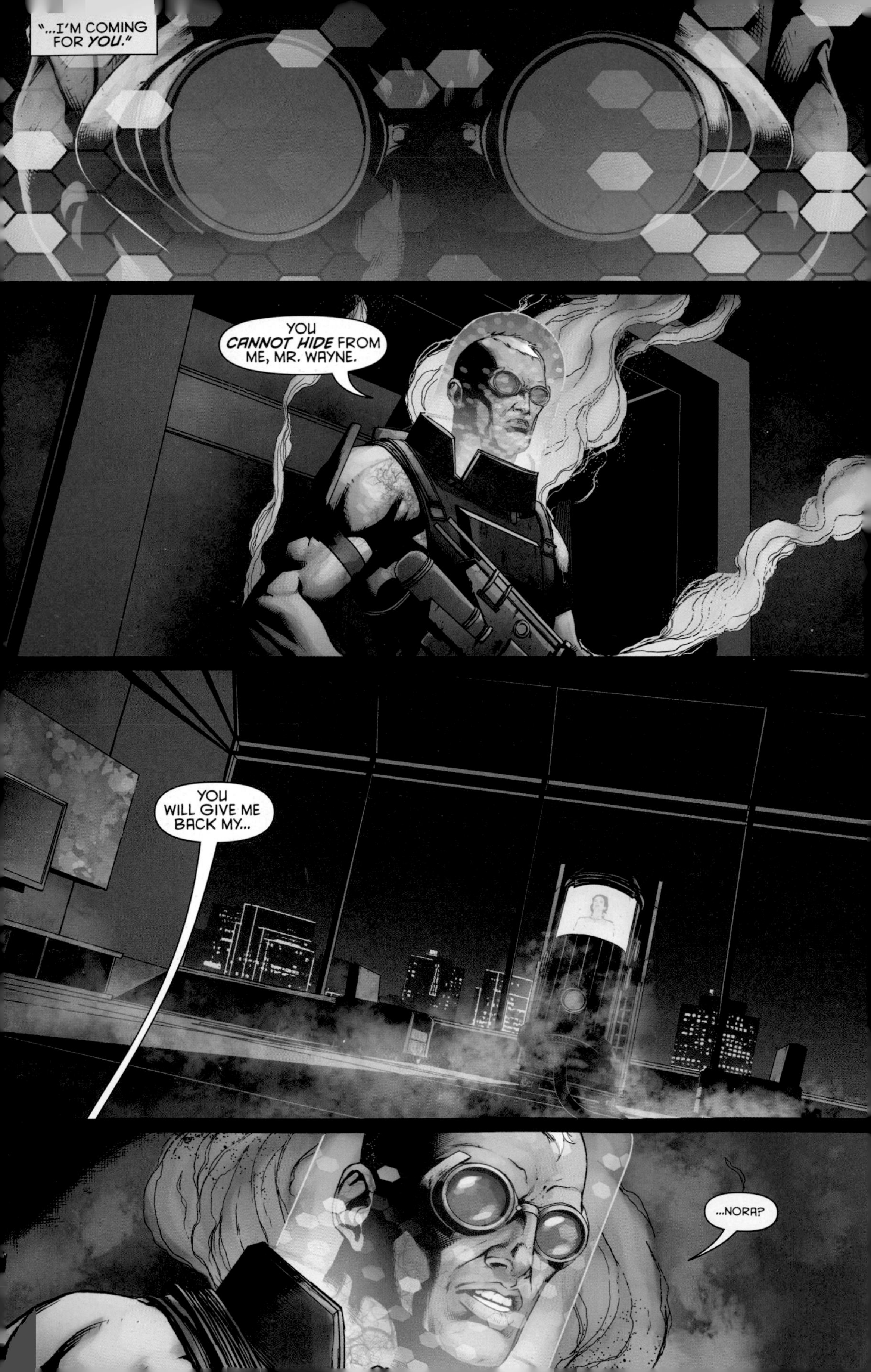
"...I'M COMING FOR *YOU*."
YOU *CANNOT HIDE* FROM ME, MR. WAYNE.
YOU WILL GIVE ME BACK MY...
...NORA?

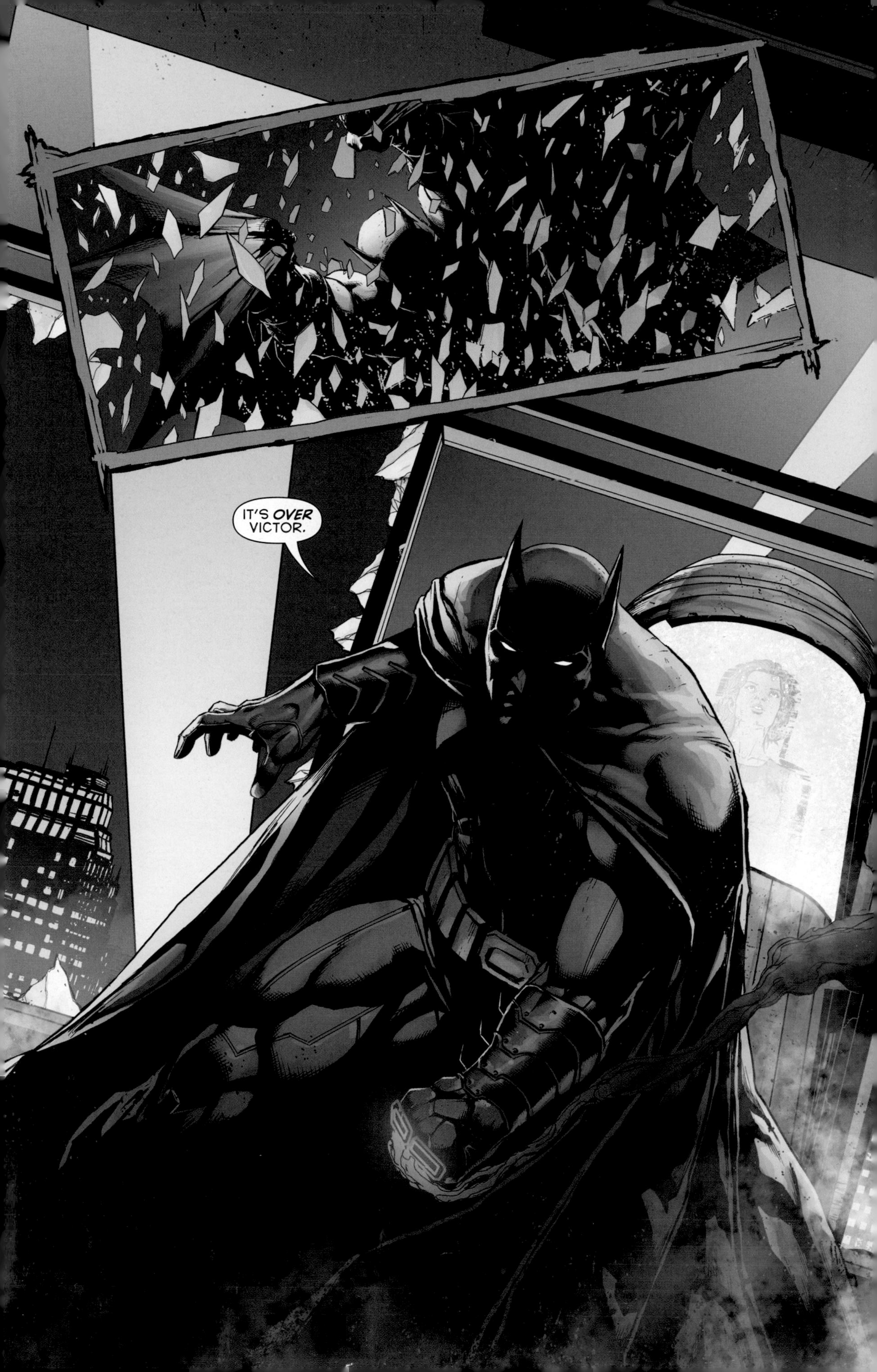
IT'S OVER VICTOR.

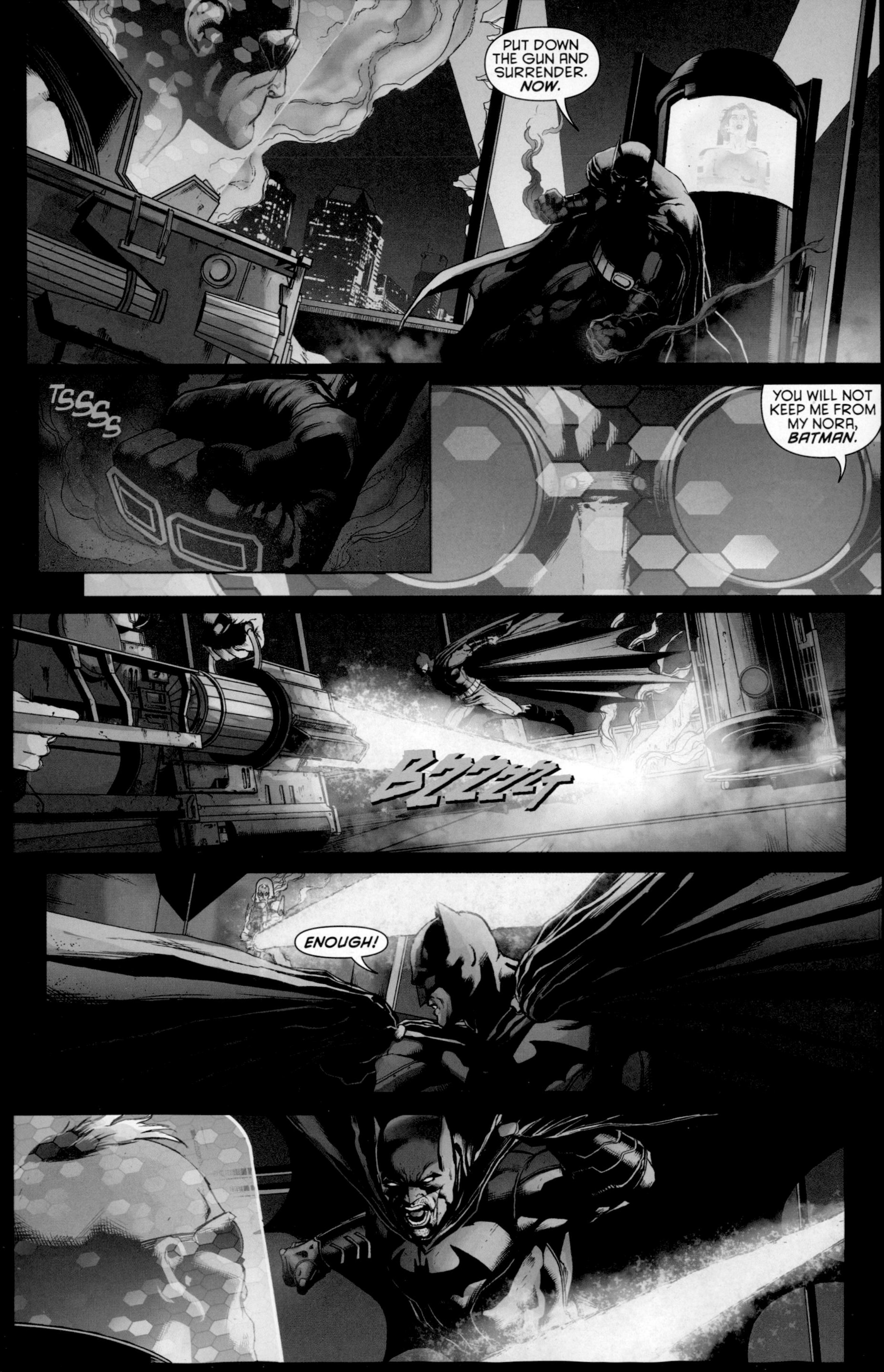
PUT DOWN THE GUN AND SURRENDER. *NOW.*
TSSSSS
YOU WILL NOT KEEP ME FROM MY NORA, *BATMAN.*
BZZZZT
ENOUGH!

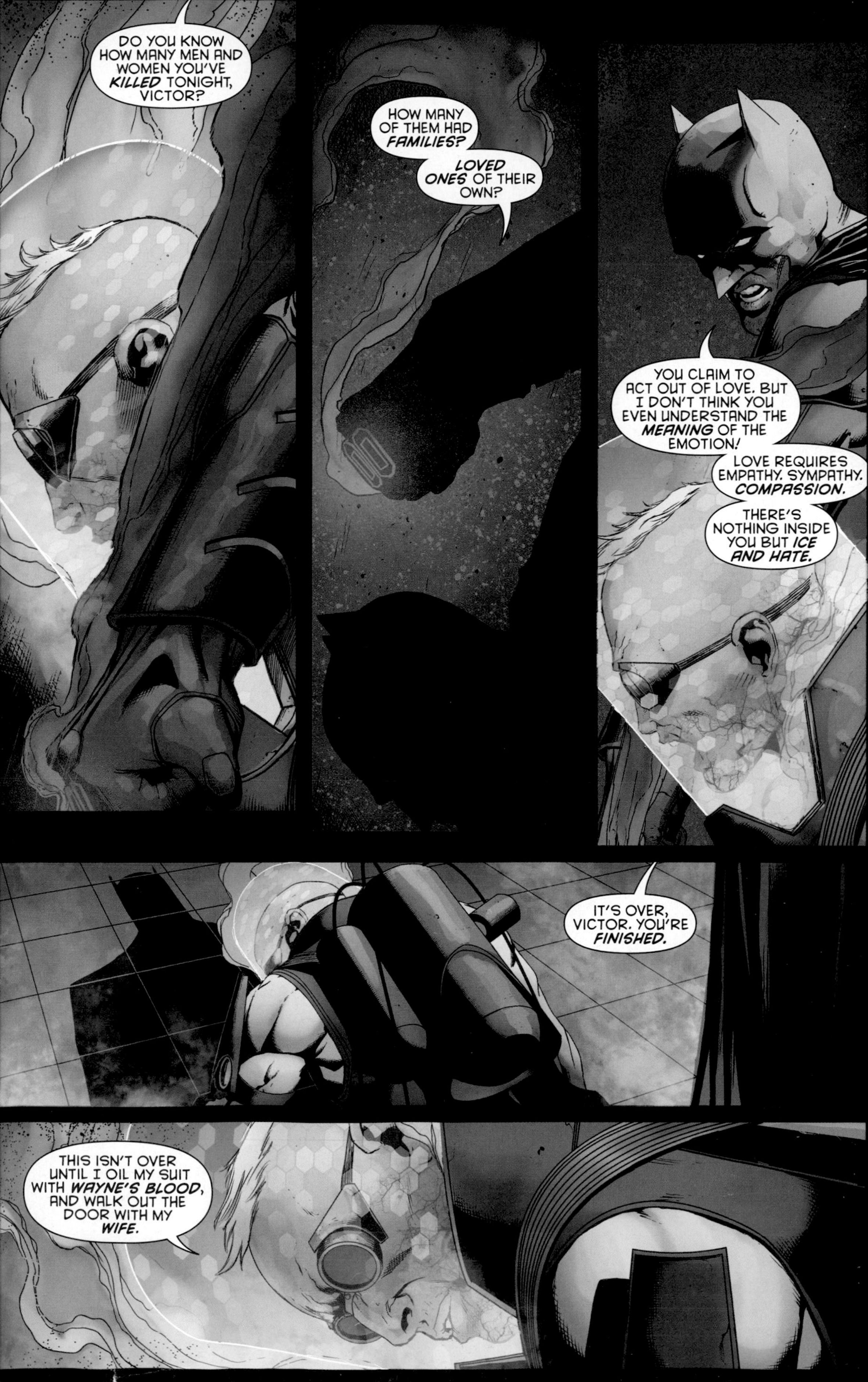
DO YOU KNOW HOW MANY MEN AND WOMEN YOU'VE *KILLED* TONIGHT, VICTOR?
HOW MANY OF THEM HAD *FAMILIES?*
LOVED ONES OF THEIR OWN?
YOU CLAIM TO ACT OUT OF LOVE. BUT I DON'T THINK YOU EVEN UNDERSTAND THE *MEANING* OF THE EMOTION!
LOVE REQUIRES EMPATHY. SYMPATHY. *COMPASSION.*
THERE'S NOTHING INSIDE YOU BUT *ICE AND HATE.*
IT'S OVER, VICTOR. YOU'RE *FINISHED.*
THIS ISN'T OVER UNTIL I OIL MY SUIT WITH *WAYNE'S BLOOD*, AND WALK OUT THE DOOR WITH MY *WIFE.*

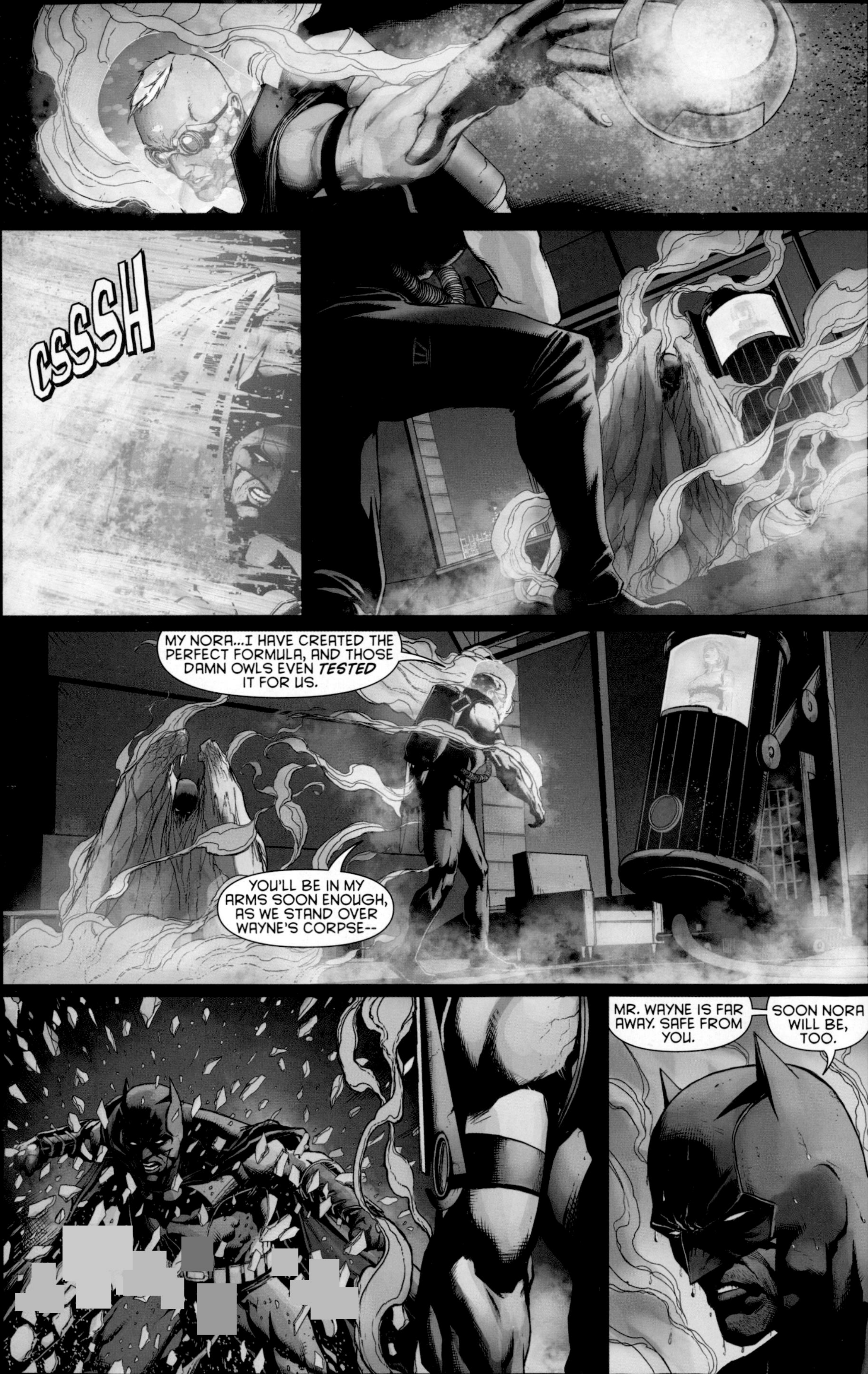
CSSSH
MY NORA...I HAVE CREATED THE PERFECT FORMULA, AND THOSE DAMN OWLS EVEN *TESTED* IT FOR US.
YOU'LL BE IN MY ARMS SOON ENOUGH, AS WE STAND OVER WAYNE'S CORPSE--
MR. WAYNE IS FAR AWAY. SAFE FROM YOU.
SOON NORA WILL BE, TOO.

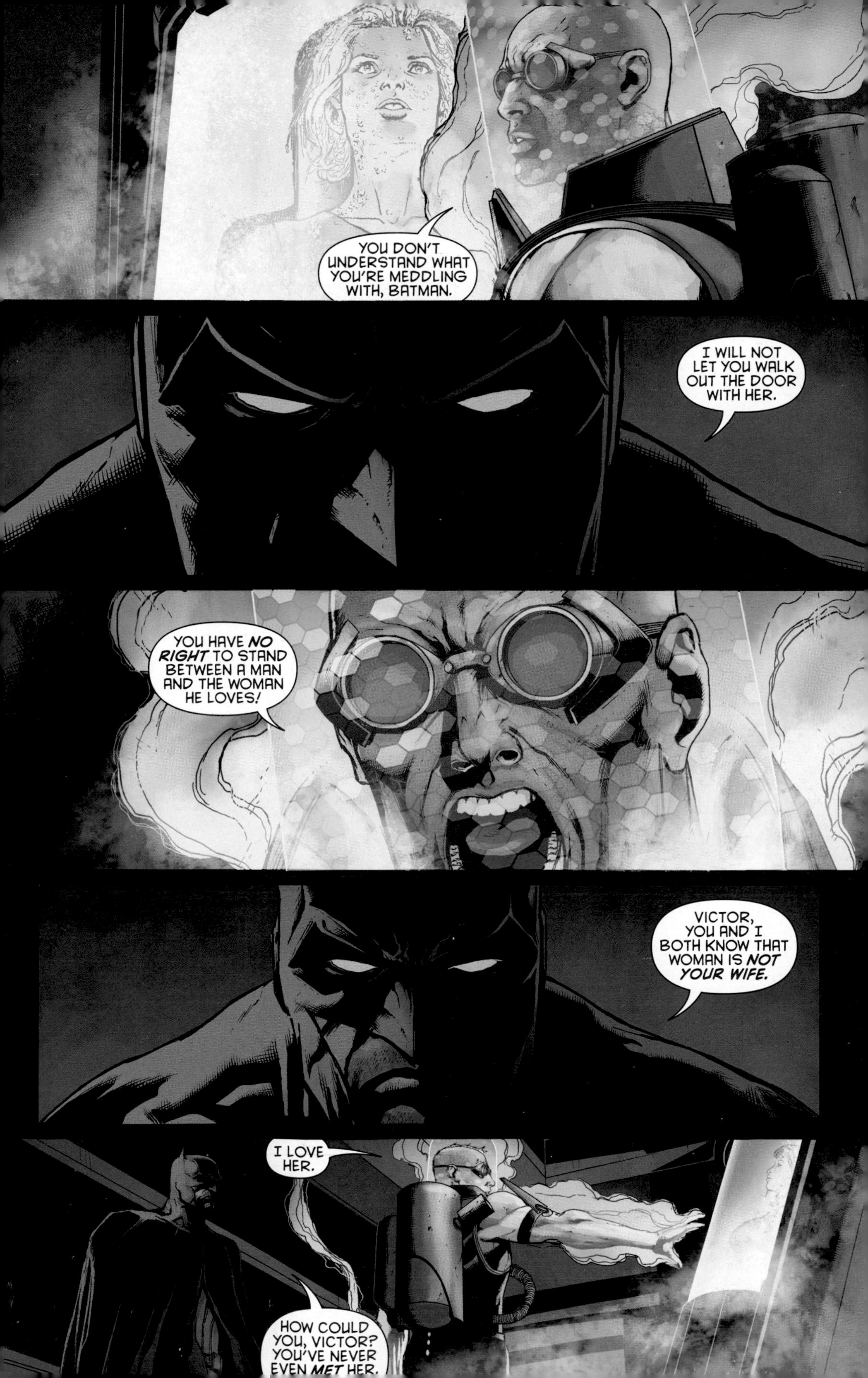
YOU DON'T UNDERSTAND WHAT YOU'RE MEDDLING WITH, BATMAN.
I WILL NOT LET YOU WALK OUT THE DOOR WITH HER.
YOU HAVE *NO RIGHT* TO STAND BETWEEN A MAN AND THE WOMAN HE LOVES!
VICTOR, YOU AND I BOTH KNOW THAT WOMAN IS *NOT YOUR WIFE.*
I LOVE HER.
HOW COULD YOU, VICTOR? YOU'VE NEVER EVEN *MET* HER.

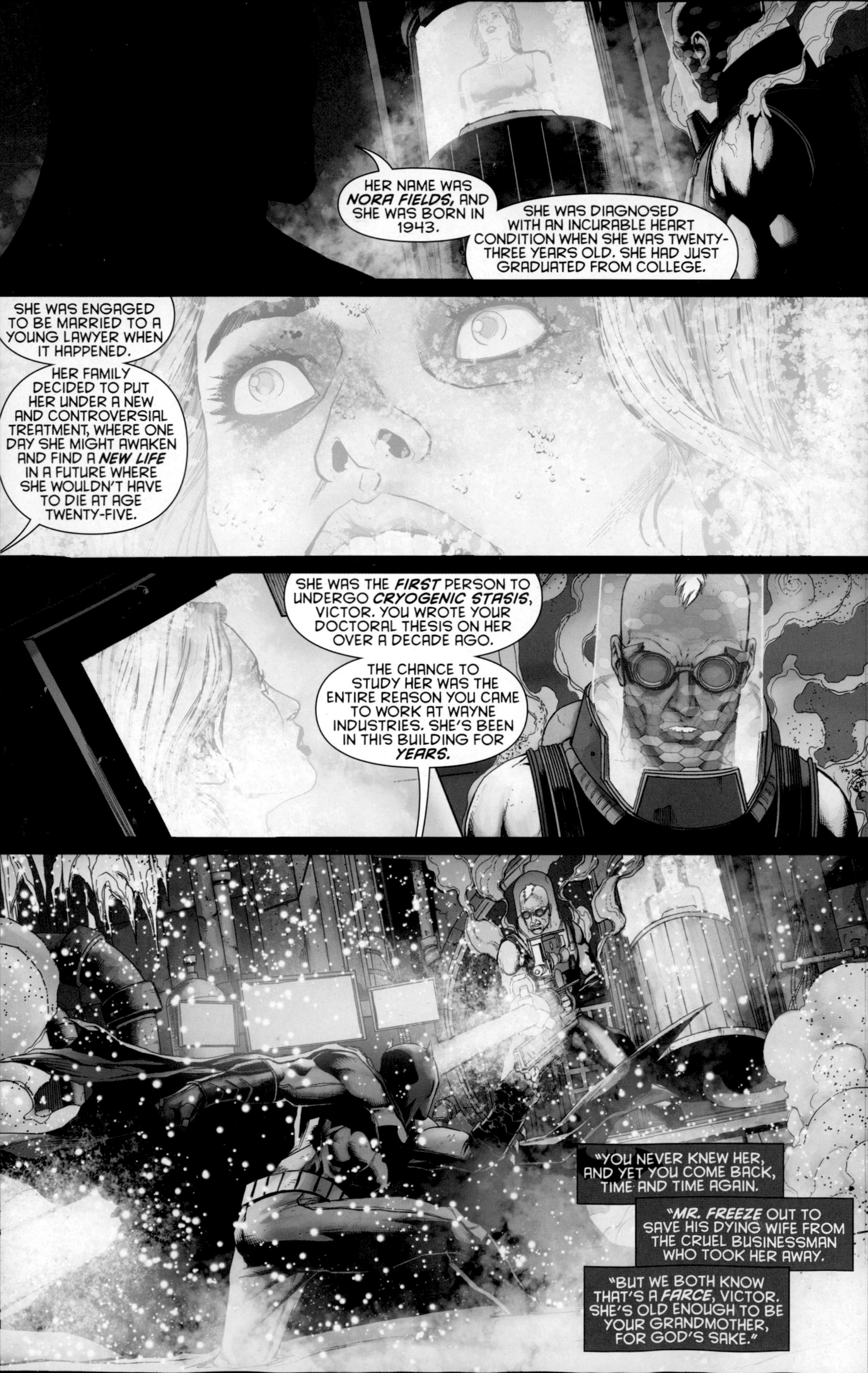

HER NAME WAS *NORA FIELDS,* AND SHE WAS BORN IN 1943.
SHE WAS DIAGNOSED WITH AN INCURABLE HEART CONDITION WHEN SHE WAS TWENTY-THREE YEARS OLD. SHE HAD JUST GRADUATED FROM COLLEGE.
SHE WAS ENGAGED TO BE MARRIED TO A YOUNG LAWYER WHEN IT HAPPENED.
HER FAMILY DECIDED TO PUT HER UNDER A NEW AND CONTROVERSIAL TREATMENT, WHERE ONE DAY SHE MIGHT AWAKEN AND FIND A *NEW LIFE* IN A FUTURE WHERE SHE WOULDN'T HAVE TO DIE AT AGE TWENTY-FIVE.
SHE WAS THE *FIRST* PERSON TO UNDERGO *CRYOGENIC STASIS,* VICTOR. YOU WROTE YOUR DOCTORAL THESIS ON HER OVER A DECADE AGO.
THE CHANCE TO STUDY HER WAS THE ENTIRE REASON YOU CAME TO WORK AT WAYNE INDUSTRIES. SHE'S BEEN IN THIS BUILDING FOR *YEARS.*
"YOU NEVER KNEW HER, AND YET YOU COME BACK, TIME AND TIME AGAIN.
"*MR. FREEZE* OUT TO SAVE HIS DYING WIFE FROM THE CRUEL BUSINESSMAN WHO TOOK HER AWAY.
"BUT WE BOTH KNOW THAT'S A *FARCE,* VICTOR. SHE'S OLD ENOUGH TO BE YOUR GRANDMOTHER, FOR GOD'S SAKE."

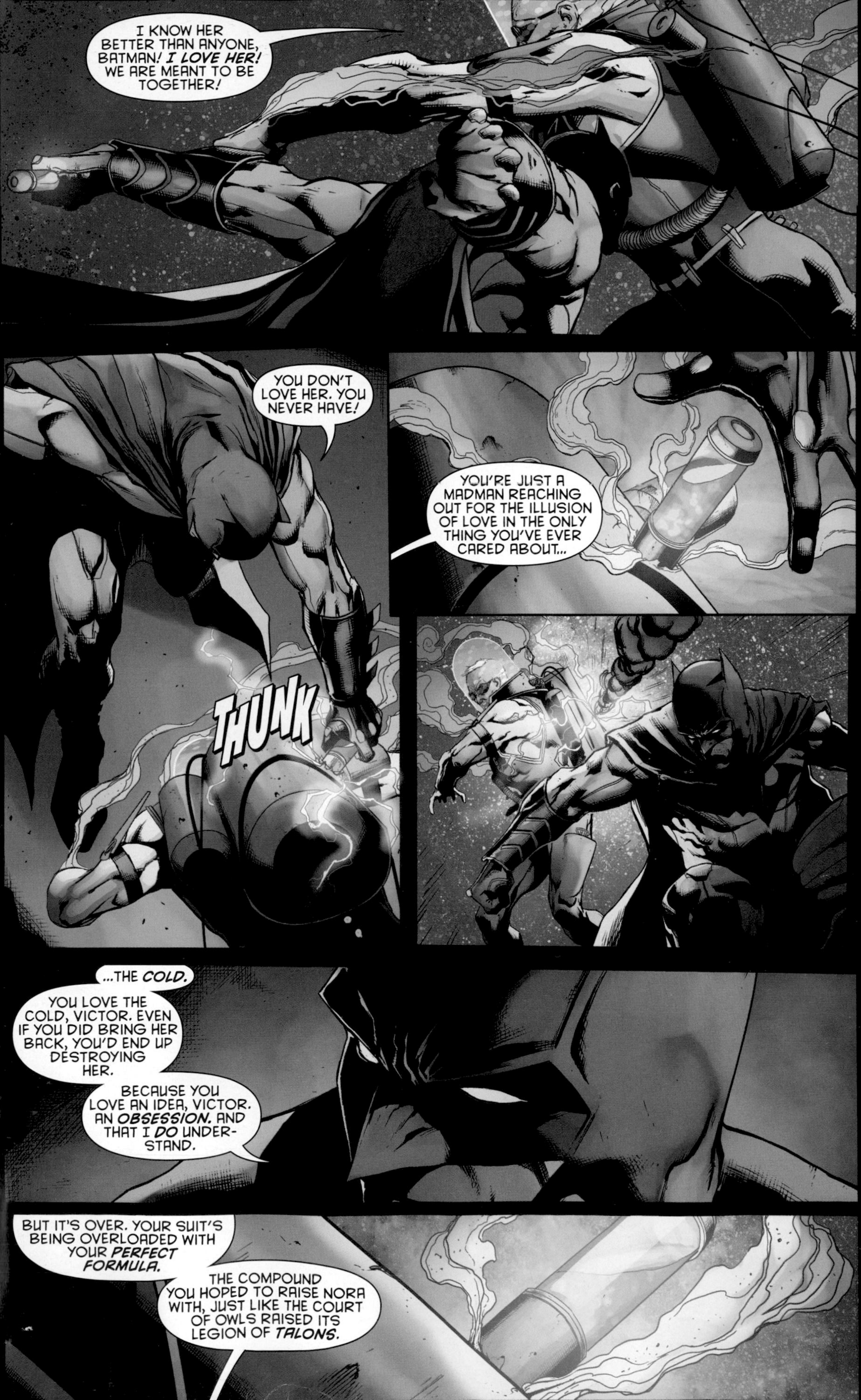
I KNOW HER BETTER THAN ANYONE, BATMAN! I LOVE HER! WE ARE MEANT TO BE TOGETHER!
YOU DON'T LOVE HER. YOU NEVER HAVE!
YOU'RE JUST A MADMAN REACHING OUT FOR THE ILLUSION OF LOVE IN THE ONLY THING YOU'VE EVER CARED ABOUT...
THUNK
...THE COLD.
YOU LOVE THE COLD, VICTOR. EVEN IF YOU DID BRING HER BACK, YOU'D END UP DESTROYING HER.
BECAUSE YOU LOVE AN IDEA, VICTOR. AN OBSESSION. AND THAT I DO UNDER-STAND.
BUT IT'S OVER. YOUR SUIT'S BEING OVERLOADED WITH YOUR PERFECT FORMULA.
THE COMPOUND YOU HOPED TO RAISE NORA WITH, JUST LIKE THE COURT OF OWLS RAISED ITS LEGION OF TALONS.

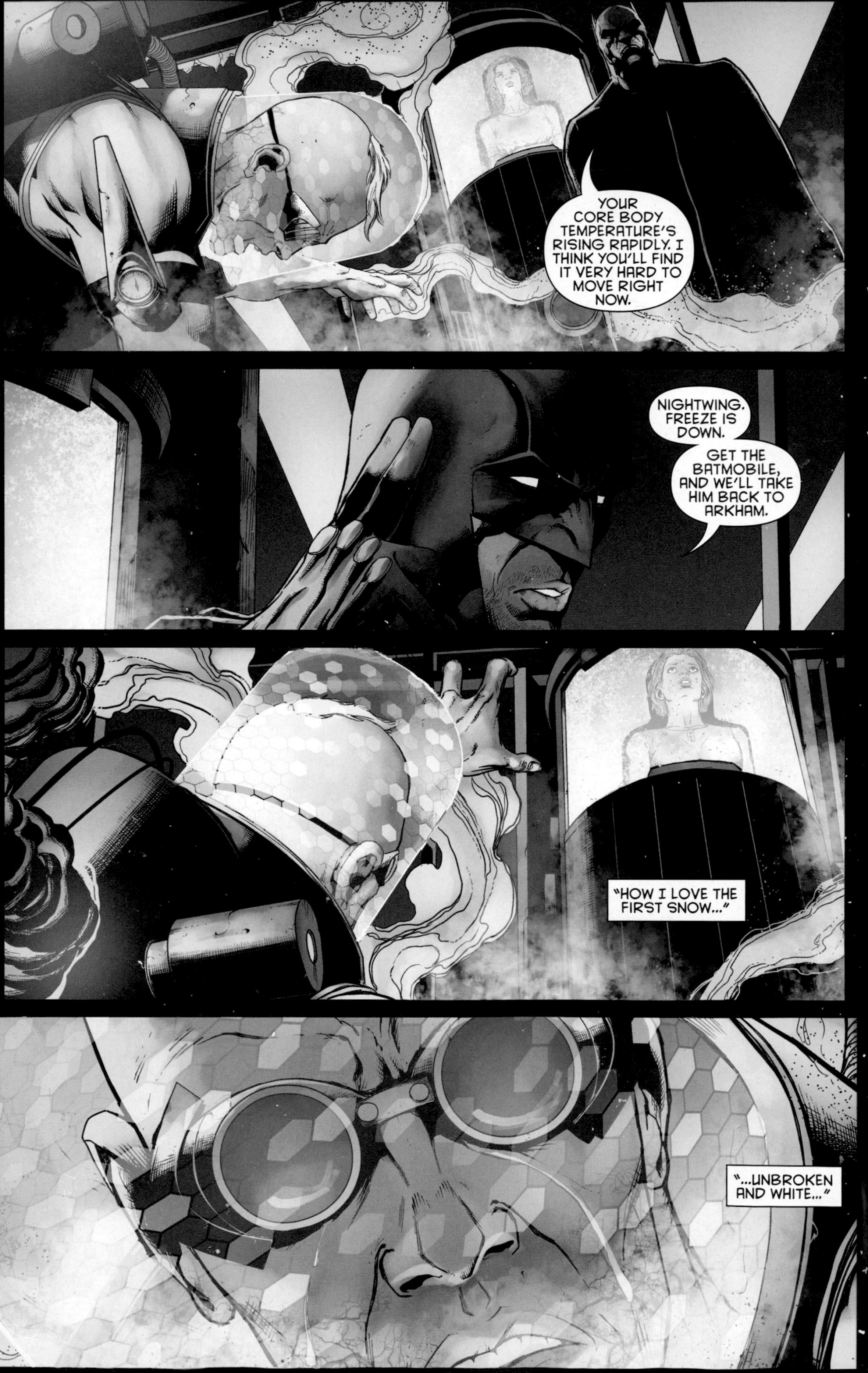
YOUR CORE BODY TEMPERATURE'S RISING RAPIDLY. I THINK YOU'LL FIND IT VERY HARD TO MOVE RIGHT NOW.
NIGHTWING. FREEZE IS DOWN.
GET THE BATMOBILE, AND WE'LL TAKE HIM BACK TO ARKHAM.
"HOW I LOVE THE FIRST SNOW..."
"...UNBROKEN AND WHITE..."

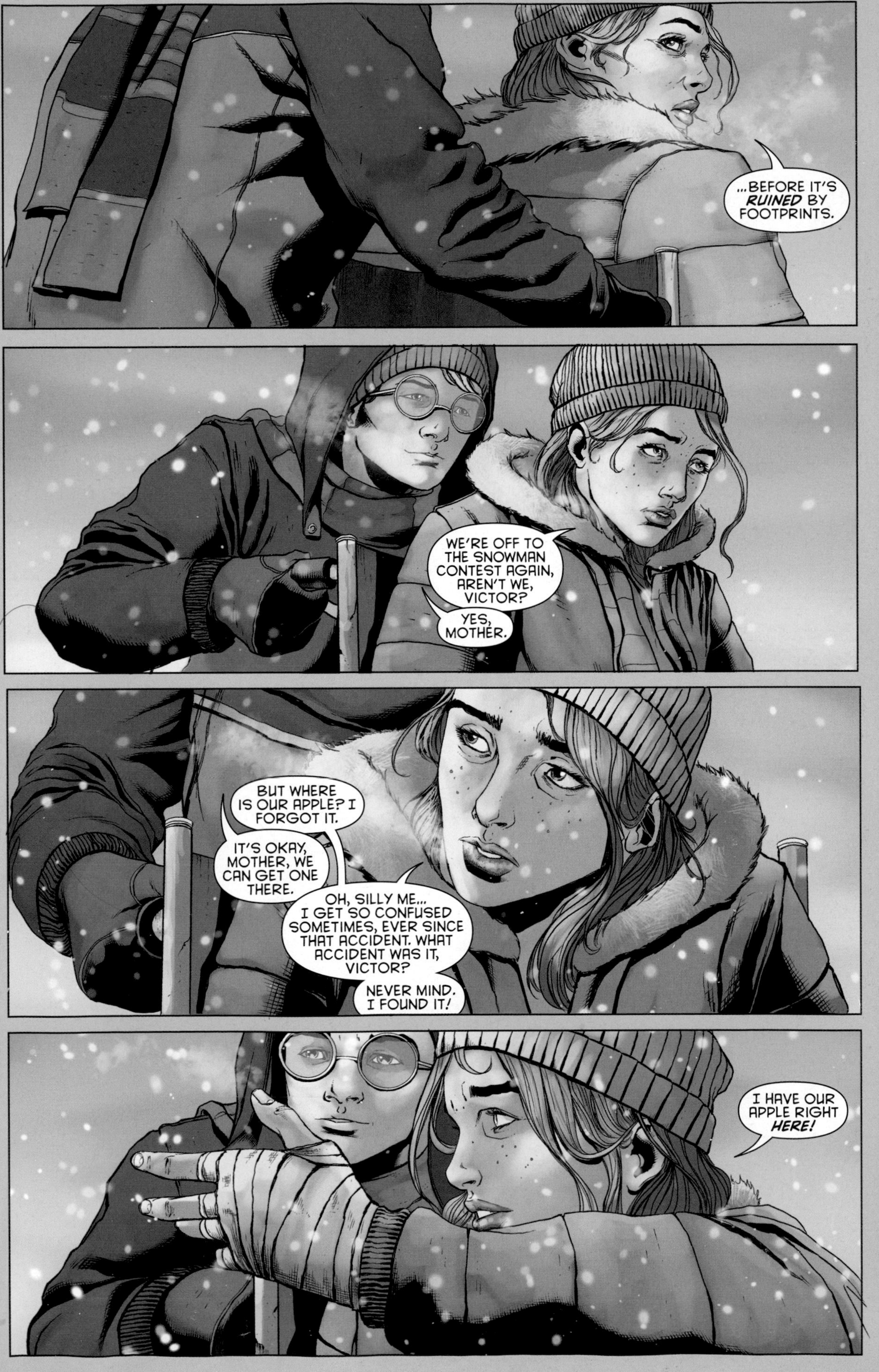
...BEFORE IT'S RUINED BY FOOTPRINTS.
WE'RE OFF TO THE SNOWMAN CONTEST AGAIN, AREN'T WE, VICTOR?
YES, MOTHER.
BUT WHERE IS OUR APPLE? I FORGOT IT.
IT'S OKAY, MOTHER, WE CAN GET ONE THERE.
OH, SILLY ME... I GET SO CONFUSED SOMETIMES, EVER SINCE THAT ACCIDENT. WHAT ACCIDENT WAS IT, VICTOR?
NEVER MIND. I FOUND IT!
I HAVE OUR APPLE RIGHT HERE!

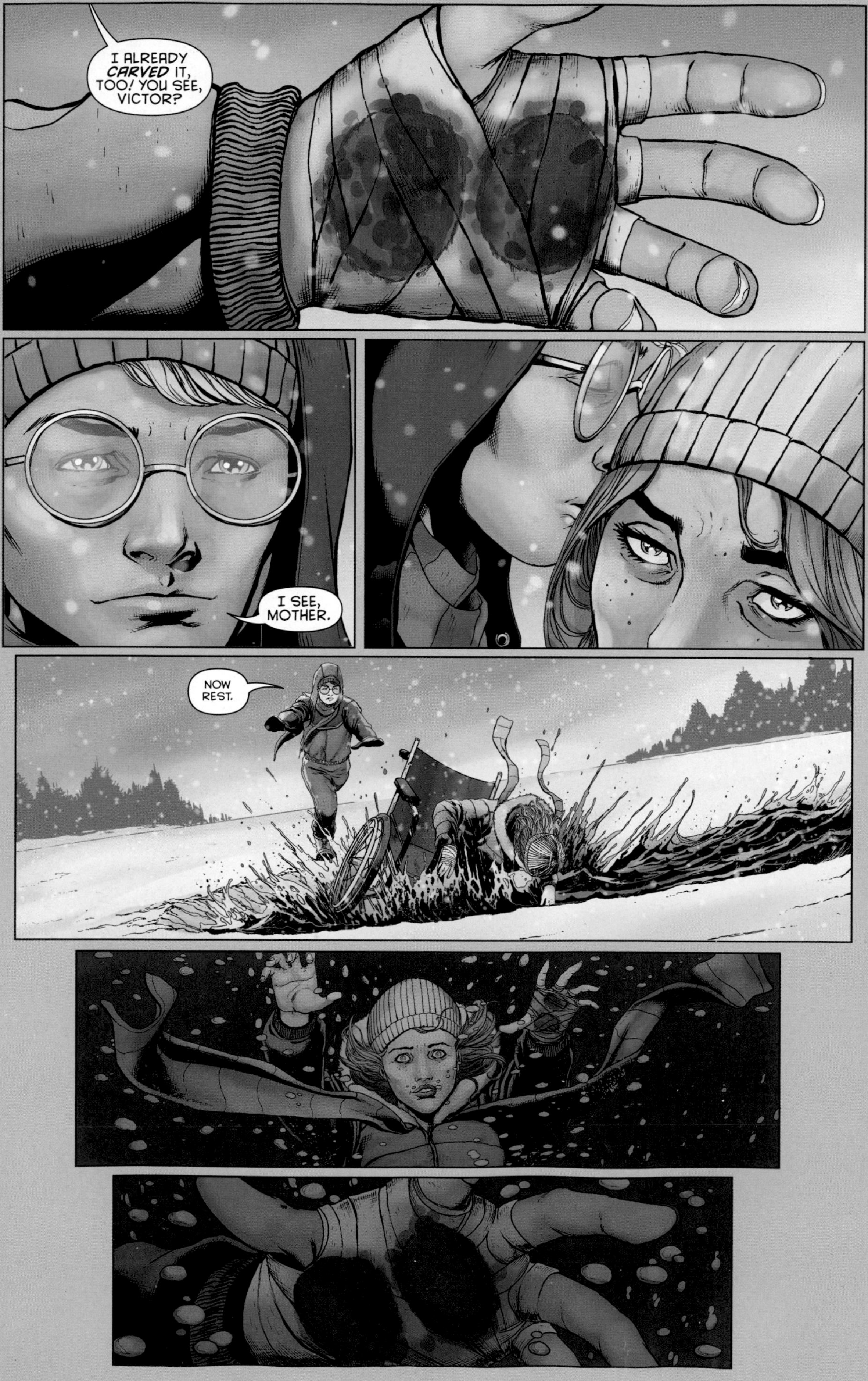
I ALREADY *CARVED* IT, TOO! YOU SEE, VICTOR?
I SEE, MOTHER.
NOW REST.

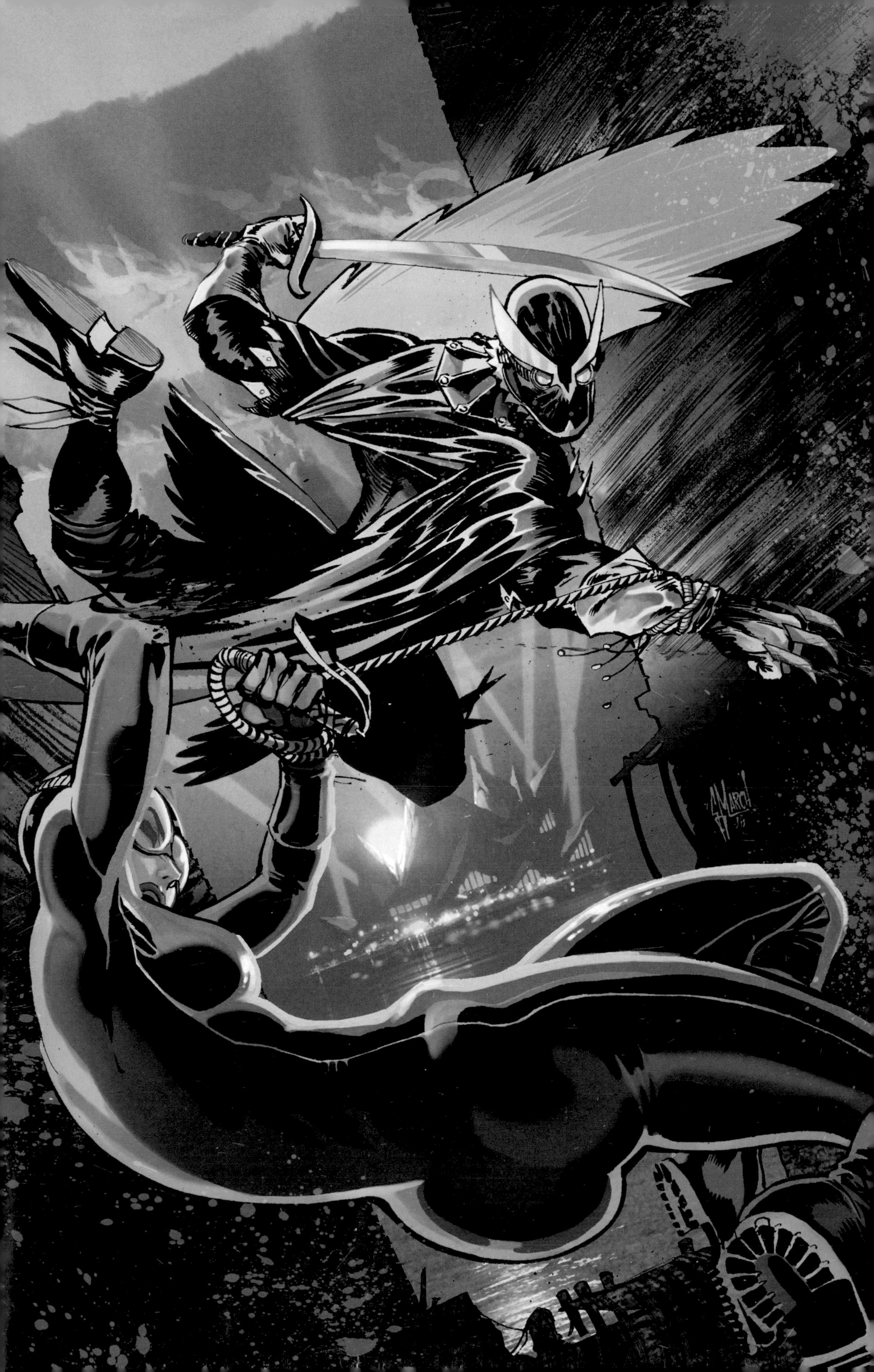

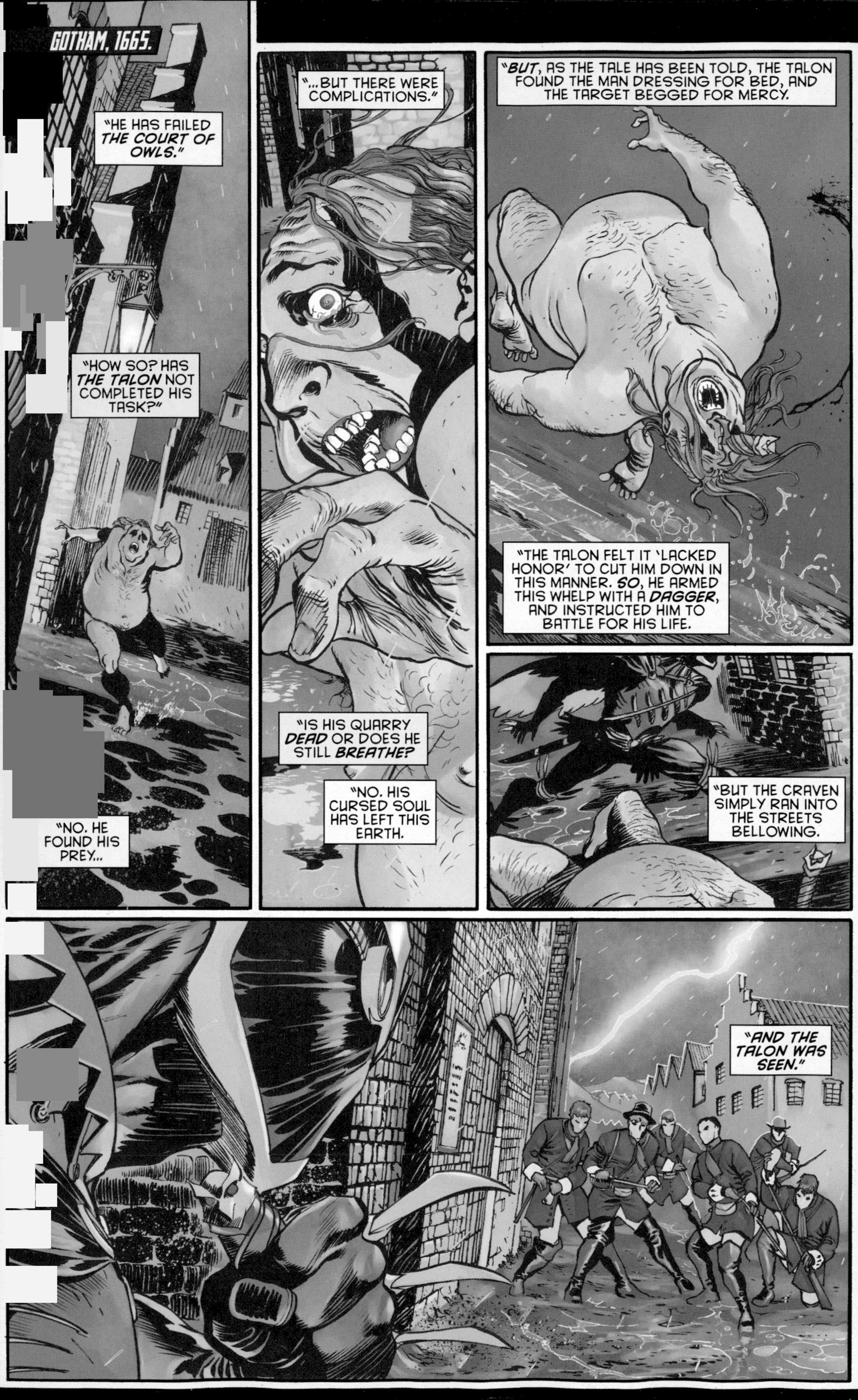
GOTHAM, 1665.
"HE HAS FAILED THE COURT OF OWLS."
"HOW SO? HAS THE TALON NOT COMPLETED HIS TASK?"
"NO. HE FOUND HIS PREY...
"...BUT THERE WERE COMPLICATIONS."
"IS HIS QUARRY DEAD OR DOES HE STILL BREATHE?
"NO. HIS CURSED SOUL HAS LEFT THIS EARTH.
"BUT, AS THE TALE HAS BEEN TOLD, THE TALON FOUND THE MAN DRESSING FOR BED, AND THE TARGET BEGGED FOR MERCY.
"THE TALON FELT IT 'LACKED HONOR' TO CUT HIM DOWN IN THIS MANNER. SO, HE ARMED THIS WHELP WITH A DAGGER, AND INSTRUCTED HIM TO BATTLE FOR HIS LIFE.
"BUT THE CRAVEN SIMPLY RAN INTO THE STREETS BELLOWING.
"AND THE TALON WAS SEEN."

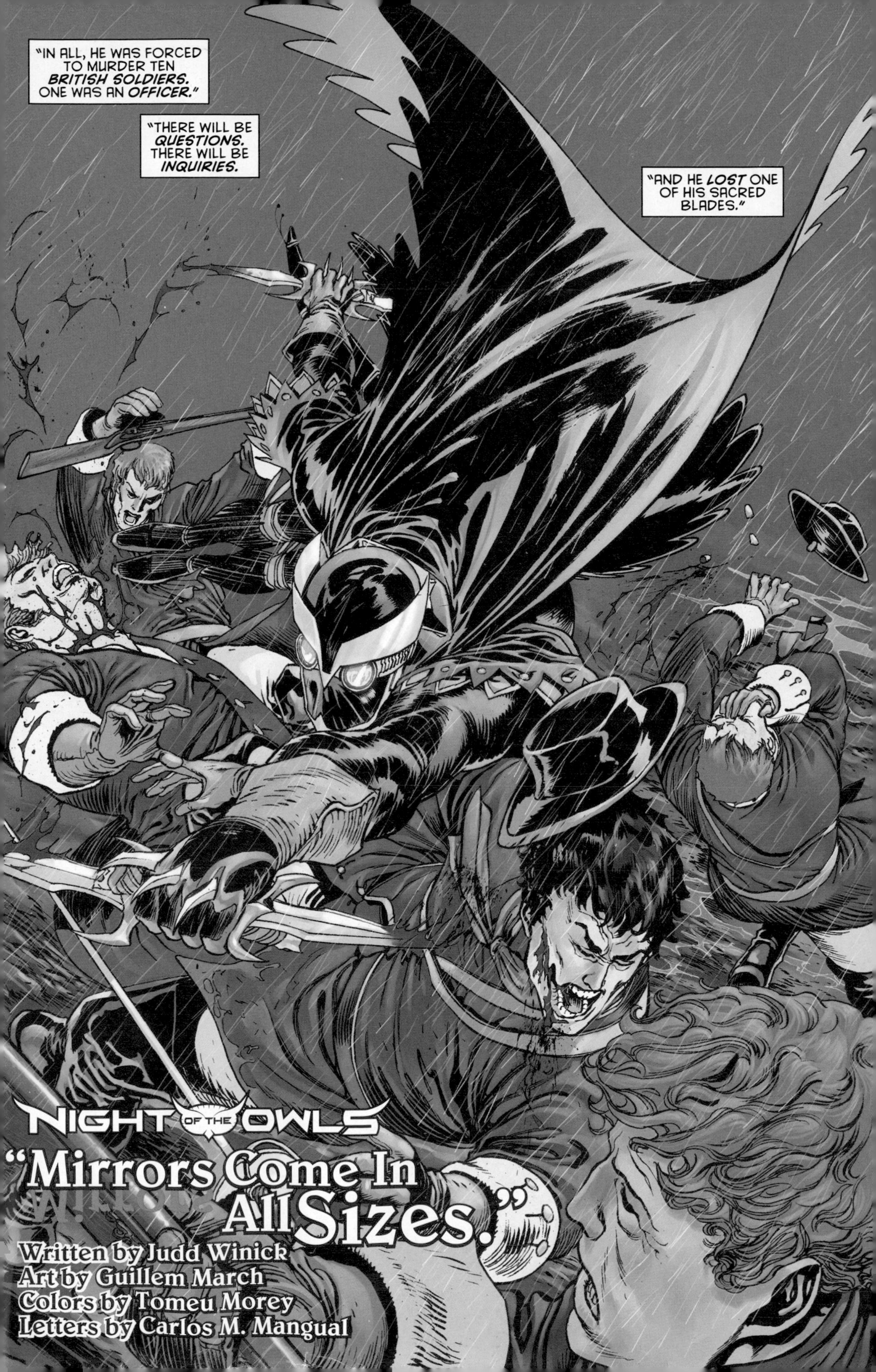
"IN ALL, HE WAS FORCED TO MURDER TEN BRITISH SOLDIERS. ONE WAS AN OFFICER."
"THERE WILL BE QUESTIONS. THERE WILL BE INQUIRIES.
"AND HE LOST ONE OF HIS SACRED BLADES."
NIGHT OF THE OWLS
"Mirrors Come In All Sizes."
Written by Judd Winick
Art by Guillem March
Colors by Tomeu Morey
Letters by Carlos M. Mangual

"AND THIS IS *NOT* THE FIRST TIME THAT HE HAS PROVEN UNRELIABLE DUE TO SOME *MISGUIDED* ATTEMPT AT *HONOR*."

HE HAS NOT PERFORMED AS WELL AS HIS PREDECESSOR. TOO DAMNED *EMOTIONAL*. OUR METHODS IN *BUILDING* THESE MEN INTO THE WEAPONS WE DESIRE THEM TO BE...MAY NOT BE *PERFECTED*.

OUR *NEXT* TALON IS NOT QUITE OF AGE, BUT HE IS *MORE* THAN READY. HIS BLOOD RUNS AS *COLD* AS THE *ICE FLOES*.

AYE, THEN I SUGGEST THAT WE "RETIRE" *EPHRAIM NEWHOUSE*. PREPARE THE ALCHEMY FOR HIS SLEEP.

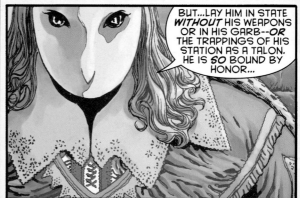

BUT...LAY HIM IN STATE *WITHOUT* HIS WEAPONS OR IN HIS GARB--*OR* THE TRAPPINGS OF HIS STATION AS A TALON. HE IS *SO* BOUND BY HONOR...

"...LET HIM FEEL THE *STING* OF HIS *SHAME*."

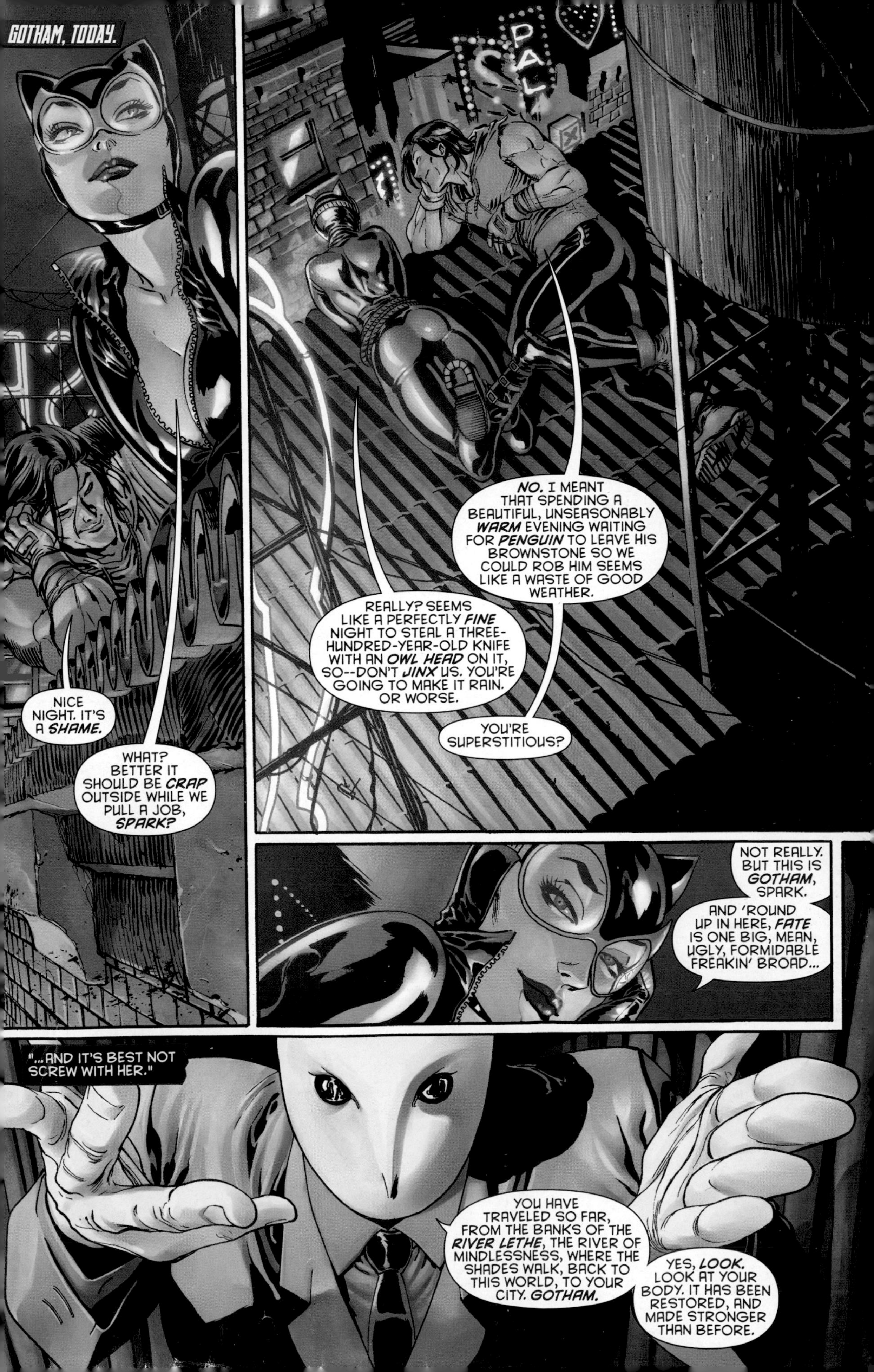
GOTHAM, TODAY.
NICE NIGHT. IT'S A SHAME.
WHAT? BETTER IT SHOULD BE CRAP OUTSIDE WHILE WE PULL A JOB, SPARK?
NO. I MEANT THAT SPENDING A BEAUTIFUL, UNSEASONABLY WARM EVENING WAITING FOR PENGUIN TO LEAVE HIS BROWNSTONE SO WE COULD ROB HIM SEEMS LIKE A WASTE OF GOOD WEATHER.
REALLY? SEEMS LIKE A PERFECTLY FINE NIGHT TO STEAL A THREE-HUNDRED-YEAR-OLD KNIFE WITH AN OWL HEAD ON IT, SO--DON'T JINX US. YOU'RE GOING TO MAKE IT RAIN. OR WORSE.
YOU'RE SUPERSTITIOUS?
NOT REALLY. BUT THIS IS GOTHAM, SPARK.
AND 'ROUND UP IN HERE, FATE IS ONE BIG, MEAN, UGLY, FORMIDABLE FREAKIN' BROAD...
"...AND IT'S BEST NOT SCREW WITH HER."
YOU HAVE TRAVELED SO FAR, FROM THE BANKS OF THE RIVER LETHE, THE RIVER OF MINDLESSNESS, WHERE THE SHADES WALK, BACK TO THIS WORLD, TO YOUR CITY. GOTHAM.
YES, LOOK. LOOK AT YOUR BODY. IT HAS BEEN RESTORED, AND MADE STRONGER THAN BEFORE.

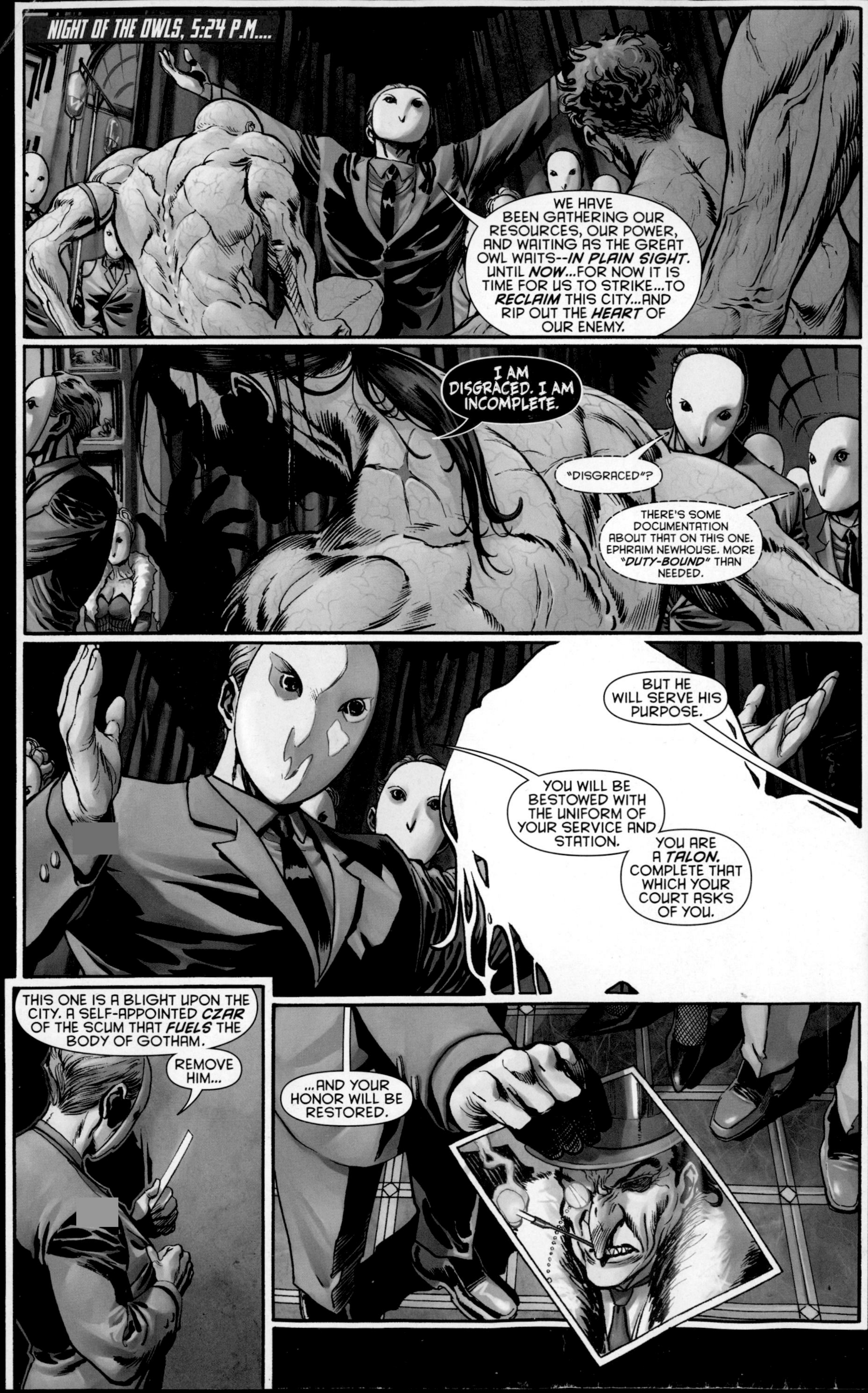
NIGHT OF THE OWLS, 5:24 P.M....
WE HAVE BEEN GATHERING OUR RESOURCES, OUR POWER, AND WAITING AS THE GREAT OWL WAITS--IN PLAIN SIGHT. UNTIL NOW...FOR NOW IT IS TIME FOR US TO STRIKE...TO RECLAIM THIS CITY...AND RIP OUT THE HEART OF OUR ENEMY.
I AM DISGRACED. I AM INCOMPLETE.
"DISGRACED"?
THERE'S SOME DOCUMENTATION ABOUT THAT ON THIS ONE. EPHRAIM NEWHOUSE. MORE "DUTY-BOUND" THAN NEEDED.
BUT HE WILL SERVE HIS PURPOSE.
YOU WILL BE BESTOWED WITH THE UNIFORM OF YOUR SERVICE AND STATION.
YOU ARE A TALON. COMPLETE THAT WHICH YOUR COURT ASKS OF YOU.
THIS ONE IS A BLIGHT UPON THE CITY. A SELF-APPOINTED CZAR OF THE SCUM THAT FUELS THE BODY OF GOTHAM.
REMOVE HIM...
...AND YOUR HONOR WILL BE RESTORED.

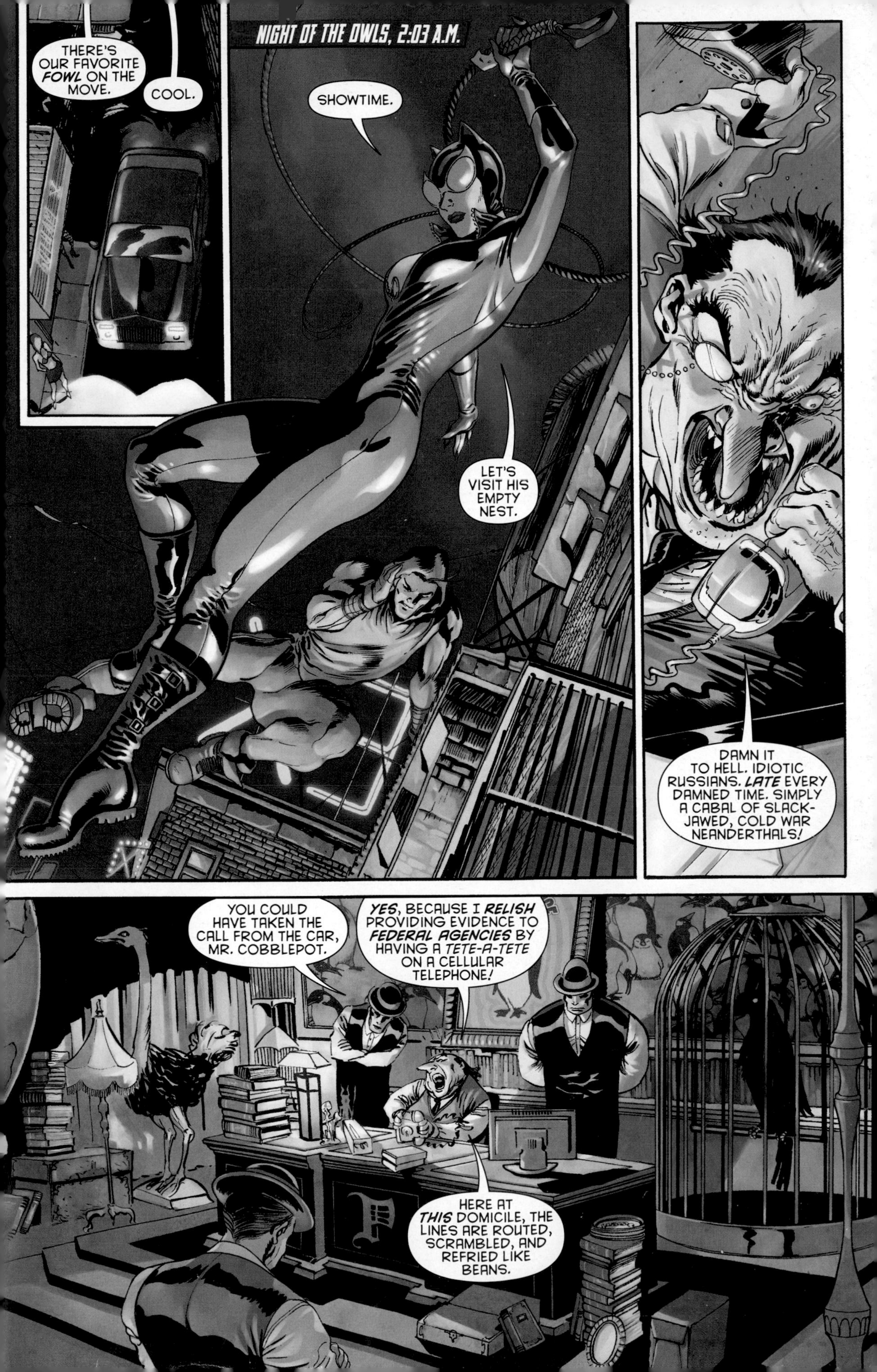
THERE'S OUR FAVORITE FOWL ON THE MOVE.
COOL.
NIGHT OF THE OWLS, 2:03 A.M.
SHOWTIME.
LET'S VISIT HIS EMPTY NEST.
DAMN IT TO HELL. IDIOTIC RUSSIANS. LATE EVERY DAMNED TIME. SIMPLY A CABAL OF SLACK-JAWED, COLD WAR NEANDERTHALS!
YOU COULD HAVE TAKEN THE CALL FROM THE CAR, MR. COBBLEPOT.
YES, BECAUSE I RELISH PROVIDING EVIDENCE TO FEDERAL AGENCIES BY HAVING A TETE-A-TETE ON A CELLULAR TELEPHONE!
HERE AT THIS DOMICILE, THE LINES ARE ROUTED, SCRAMBLED, AND REFRIED LIKE BEANS.

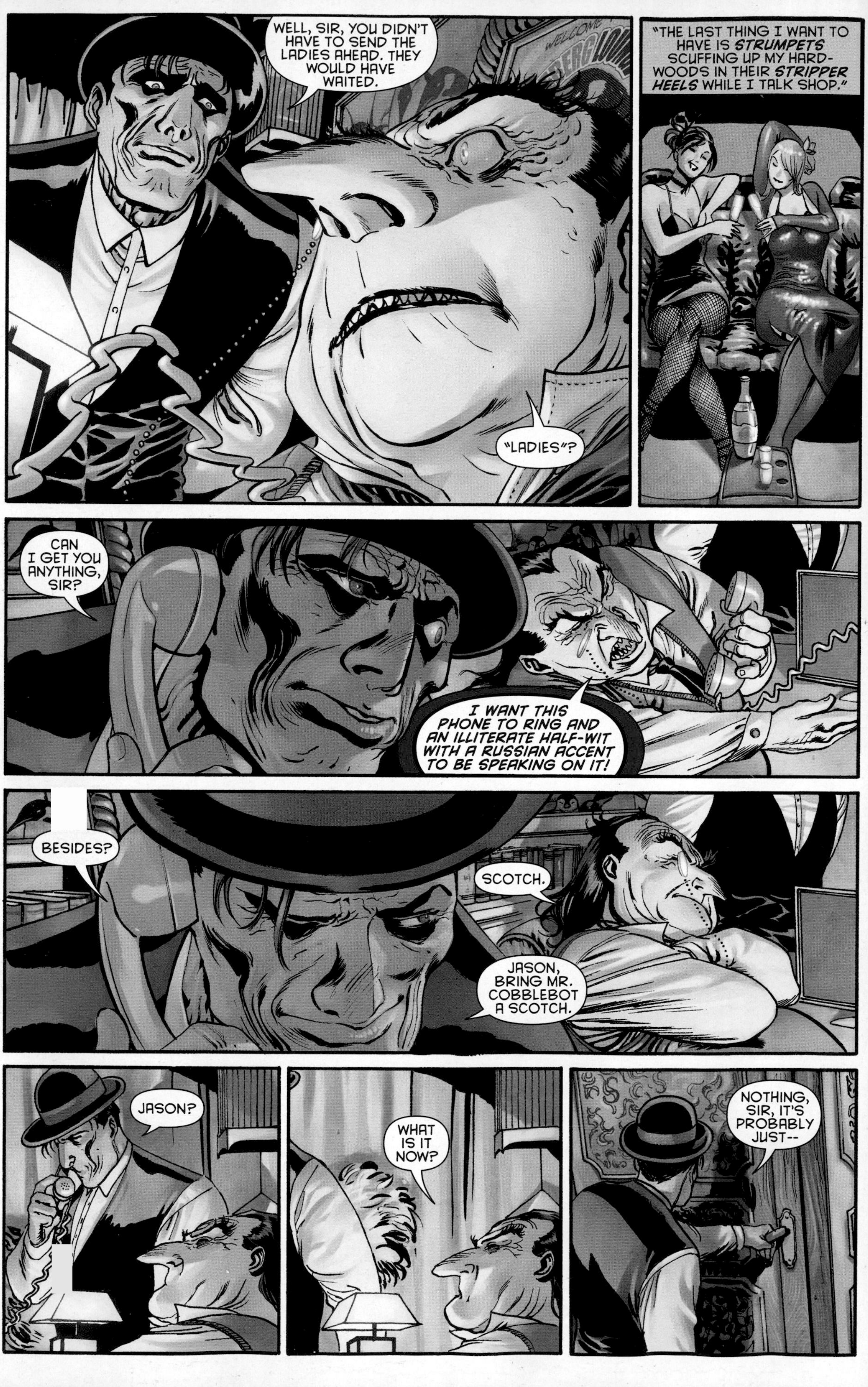

WELL, SIR, YOU DIDN'T HAVE TO SEND THE LADIES AHEAD. THEY WOULD HAVE WAITED.
"LADIES"?
"THE LAST THING I WANT TO HAVE IS STRUMPETS SCUFFING UP MY HARD-WOODS IN THEIR STRIPPER HEELS WHILE I TALK SHOP."
CAN I GET YOU ANYTHING, SIR?
I WANT THIS PHONE TO RING AND AN ILLITERATE HALF-WIT WITH A RUSSIAN ACCENT TO BE SPEAKING ON IT!
BESIDES?
SCOTCH.
JASON, BRING MR. COBBLEBOT A SCOTCH.
JASON?
WHAT IS IT NOW?
NOTHING, SIR, IT'S PROBABLY JUST--

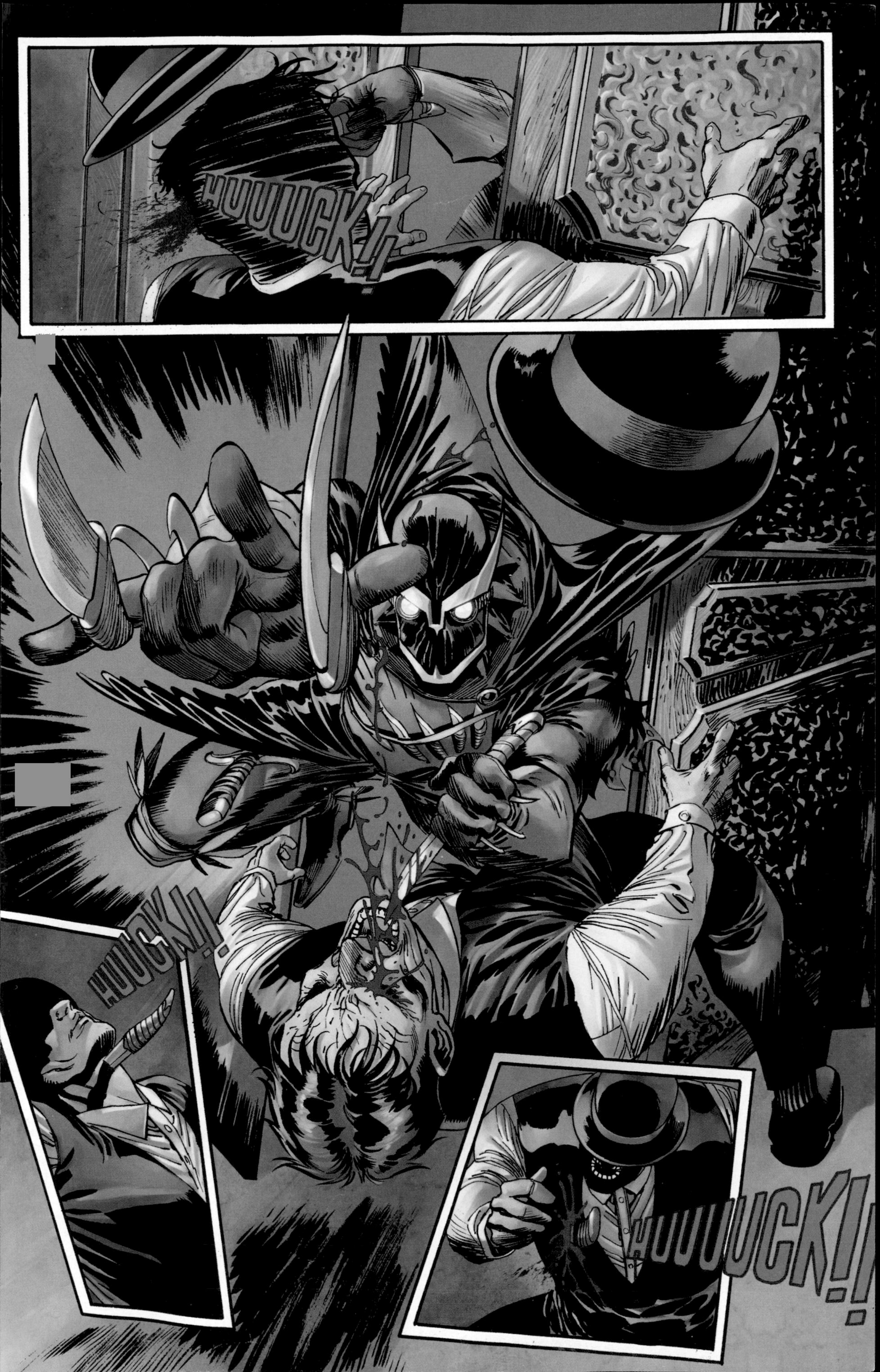
HUUUCK!!
HUUCK!!
HUUUUCK!!

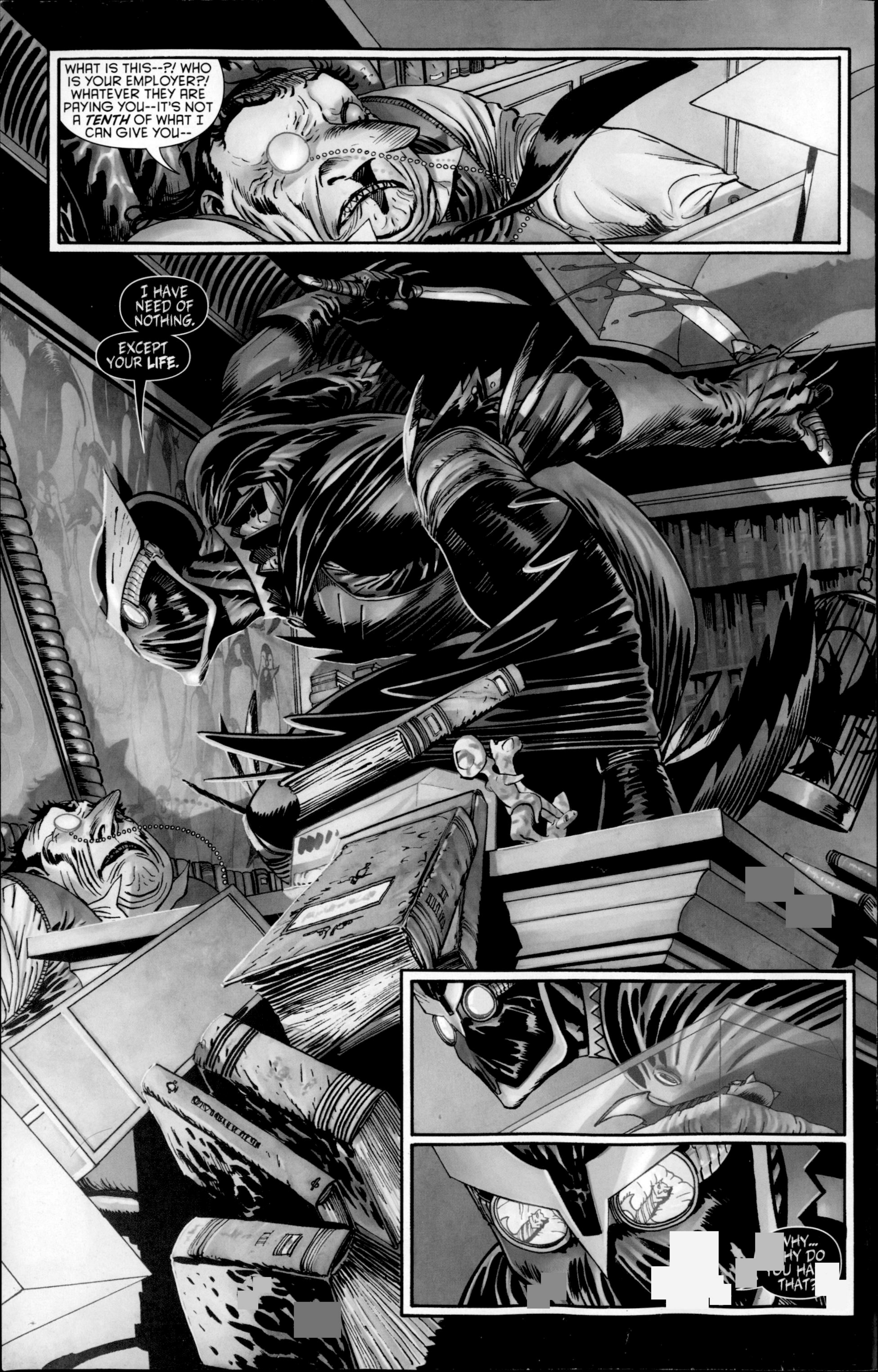
WHAT IS THIS--?! WHO IS YOUR EMPLOYER?! WHATEVER THEY ARE PAYING YOU--IT'S NOT A *TENTH* OF WHAT I CAN GIVE YOU--
I HAVE NEED OF NOTHING.
EXCEPT YOUR **LIFE.**
WHY... HY DO YOU HA THAT?

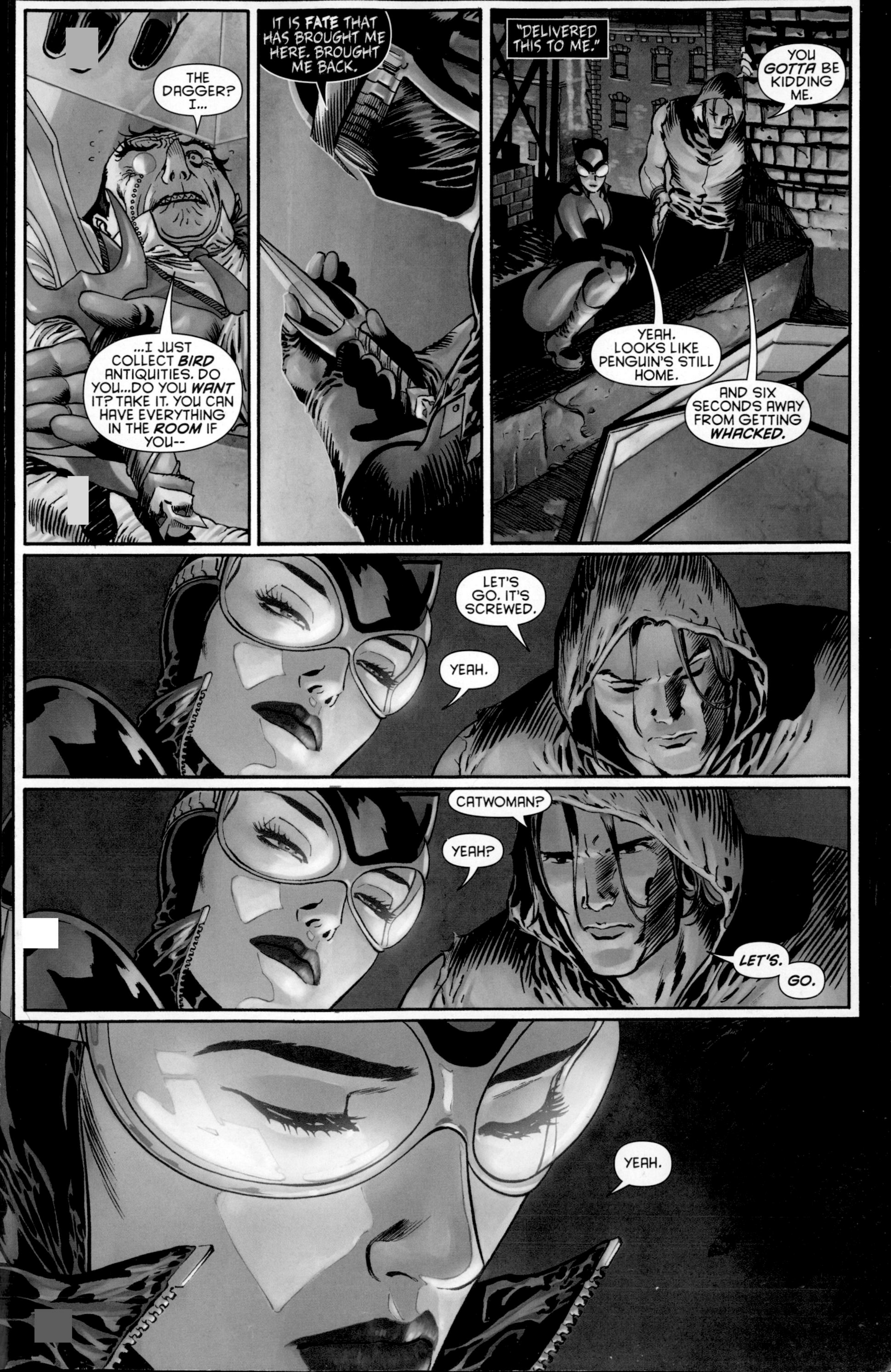
THE DAGGER? I...
...I JUST COLLECT BIRD ANTIQUITIES. DO YOU...DO YOU WANT IT? TAKE IT. YOU CAN HAVE EVERYTHING IN THE ROOM IF YOU--
IT IS FATE THAT HAS BROUGHT ME HERE. BROUGHT ME BACK.
"DELIVERED THIS TO ME."
YOU GOTTA BE KIDDING ME.
YEAH. LOOKS LIKE PENGUIN'S STILL HOME.
AND SIX SECONDS AWAY FROM GETTING WHACKED.
LET'S GO. IT'S SCREWED.
YEAH.
CATWOMAN?
YEAH?
LET'S. GO.
YEAH.

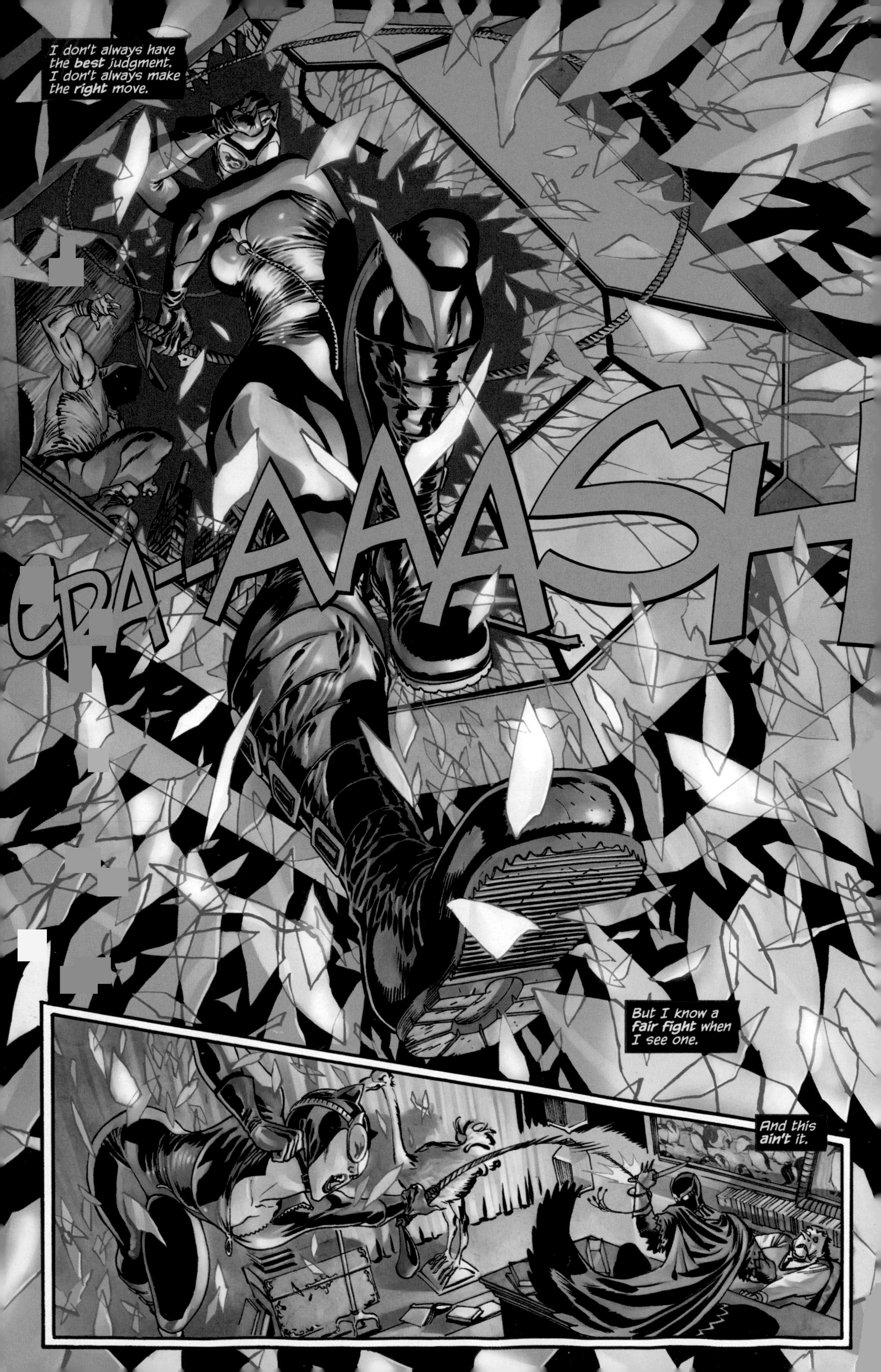
I don't always have the best judgment. I don't always make the right move.
CRA-AAASH
But I know a fair fight when I see one.
And this ain't it.

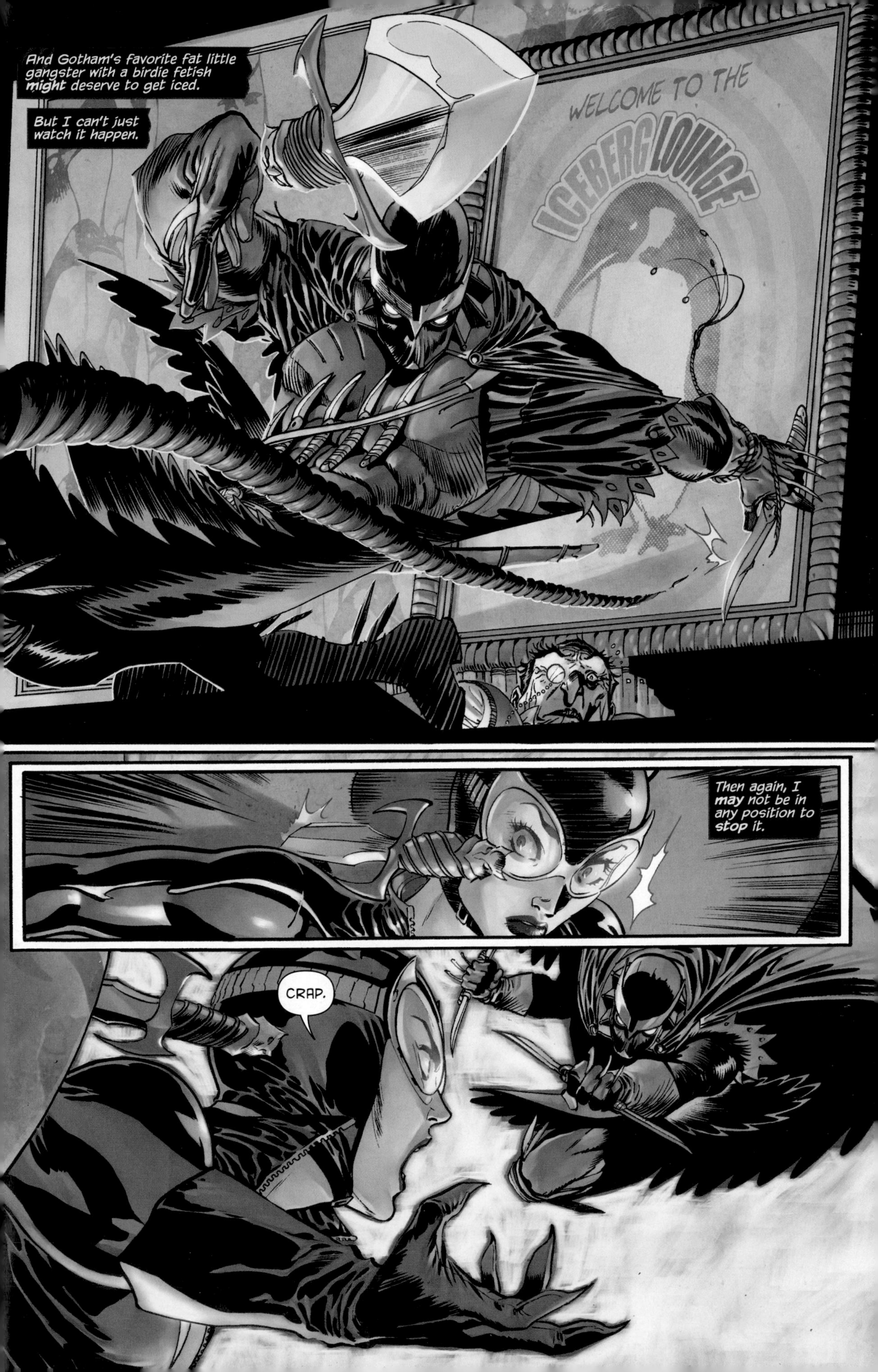

And Gotham's favorite fat little gangster with a birdie fetish might deserve to get iced.
But I can't just watch it happen.
WELCOME TO THE
ICEBERG LOUNGE
Then again, I may not be in any position to stop it.
CRAP.

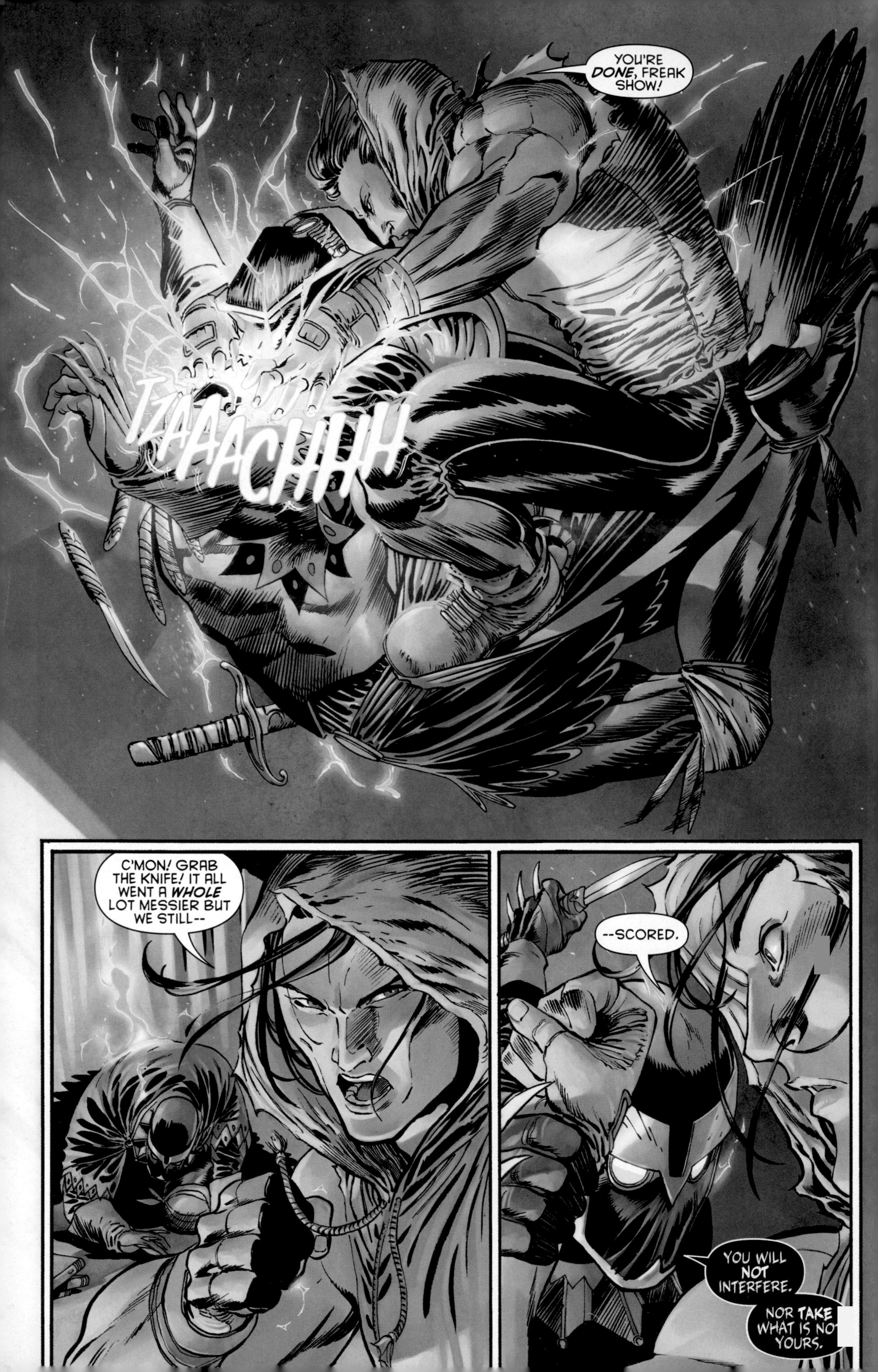
YOU'RE DONE, FREAK SHOW!
TZAAAACHHH
C'MON! GRAB THE KNIFE! IT ALL WENT A WHOLE LOT MESSIER BUT WE STILL--
--SCORED.
YOU WILL NOT INTERFERE.
NOR TAKE WHAT IS NOT YOURS.

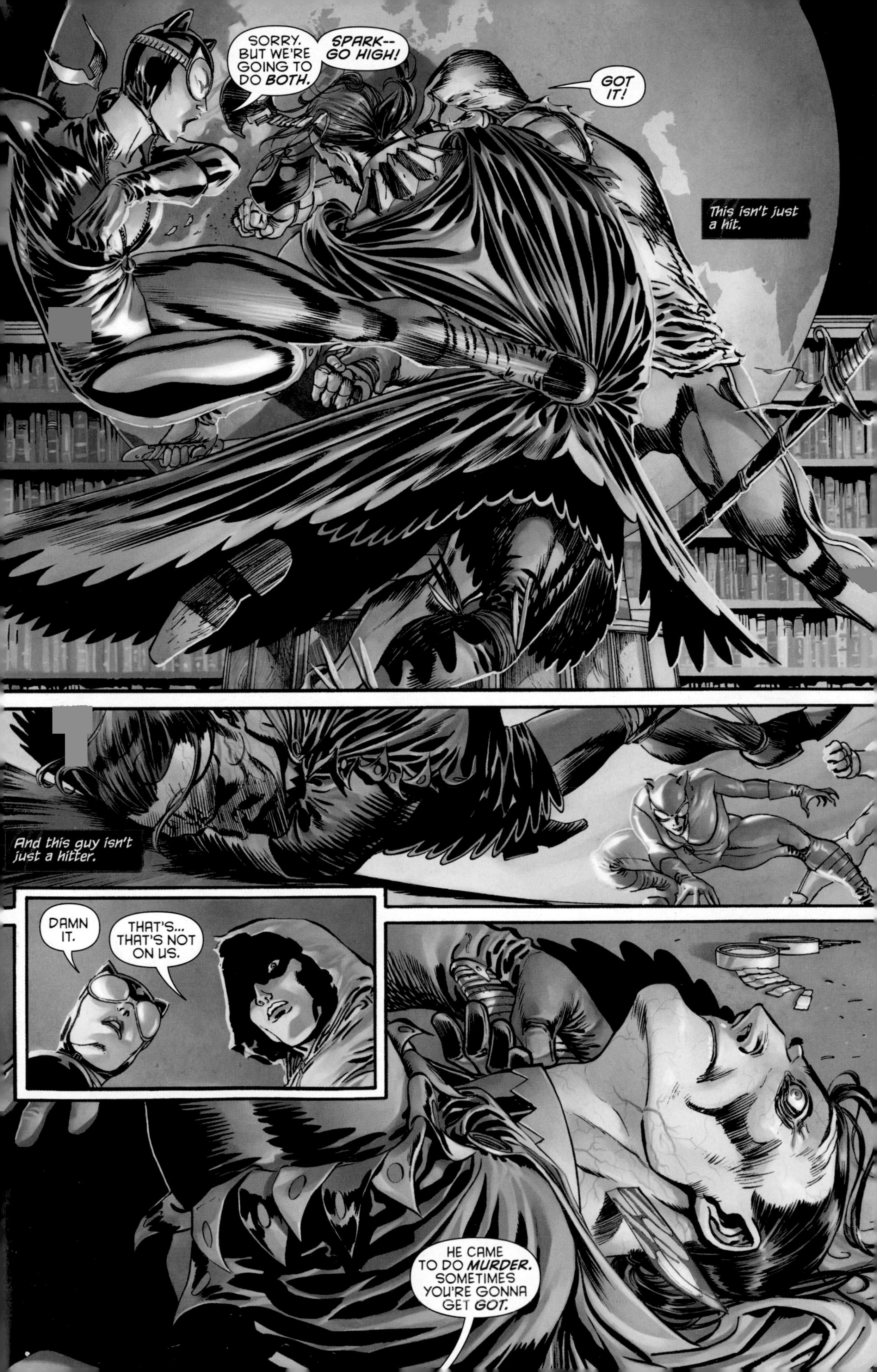
SORRY. BUT WE'RE GOING TO DO *BOTH.*
SPARK-- GO HIGH!
GOT IT!
This isn't just a hit.
And this guy isn't just a hitter.
DAMN IT.
THAT'S... THAT'S NOT ON US.
HE CAME TO DO *MURDER.* SOMETIMES YOU'RE GONNA GET *GOT.*

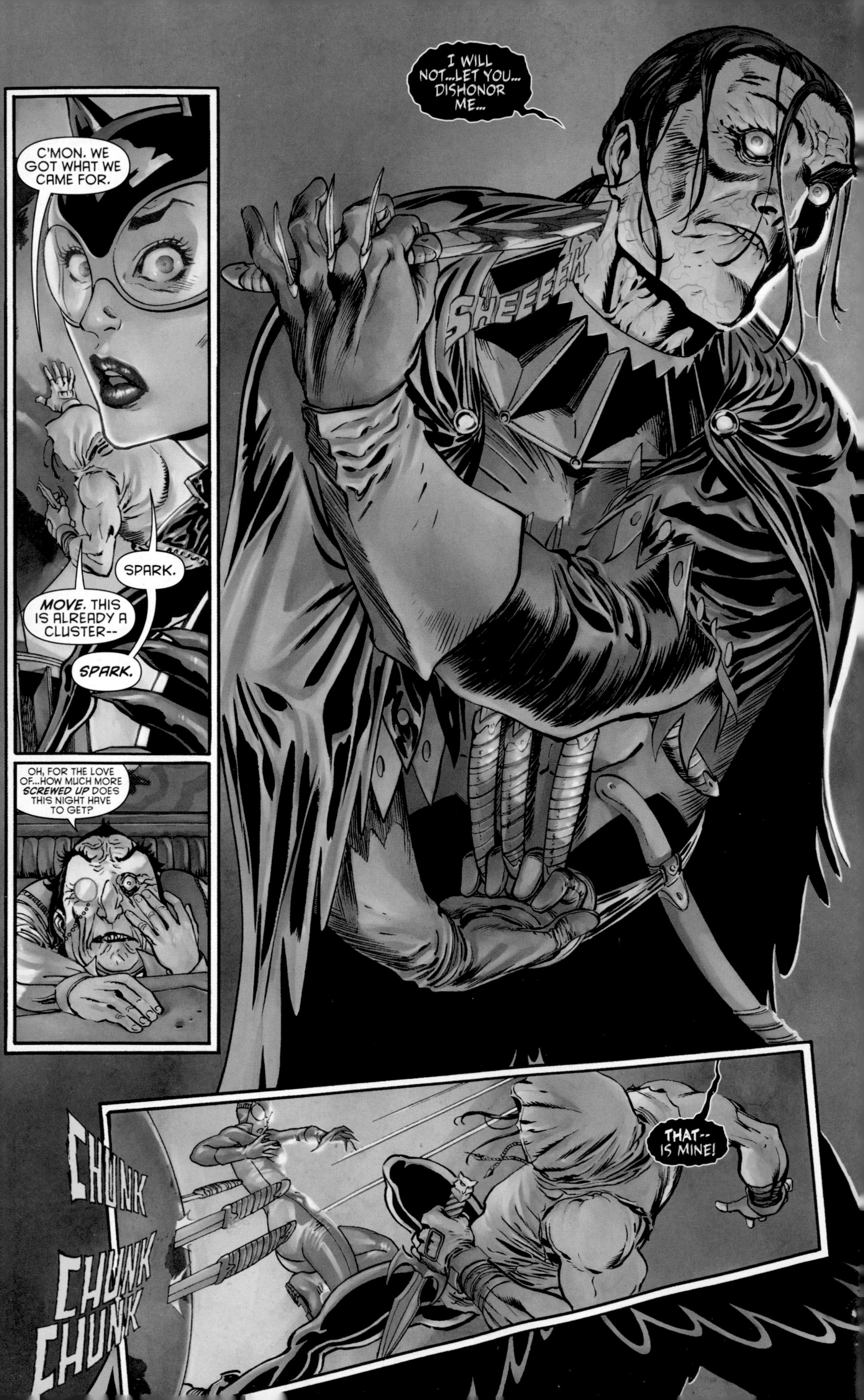
I WILL NOT...LET YOU... DISHONOR ME...
C'MON. WE GOT WHAT WE CAME FOR.
SHEEEEEK
SPARK.
MOVE. THIS IS ALREADY A CLUSTER--
SPARK.
OH, FOR THE LOVE OF...HOW MUCH MORE SCREWED UP DOES THIS NIGHT HAVE TO GET?
CHUNK
CHUNK
CHUNK
THAT-- IS MINE!

HEEROK

MINE!

I HAVE FAILED THE COURT SO MUCH. THEY HAVE BROUGHT ME BACK FROM THE DEPTHS, FROM THE DARK...

...THIS IS MY REDEMPTION. AND FATE HAS BROUGHT ME MY SACRED IMPLEMENT.

I WILL BE WHOLE. I WILL BE WORTHY.

I CAN GET YOU THE REST OF THE KNIVES.

THERE'RE FIVE, RIGHT? I HAVE THE OTHER FOUR. LET HIM GO, AND I'LL GET YOU THE REST.

YOU... YOU CAN BE **WHOLE** AGAIN.

There're things I know. **Really** know.

YOU... YOU HAVE THEM?

I can tell you **exactly** how long it will take to crack a lock just by **looking** at it.

I DO. THEY'RE **YOURS.** JUST LET HIM GO.

I can tell you the best high-heeled shoes to **run** in.

...I WANT THEM BACK.

And I know when I'm facing someone who's been **damaged** by those who raised him.

Mirrors come in **all** sizes.

YOU'LL **HAVE** THEM.

THAT WILL **PLEASE** THEM. I WILL RETURN TO THEM IN **HONOR.**

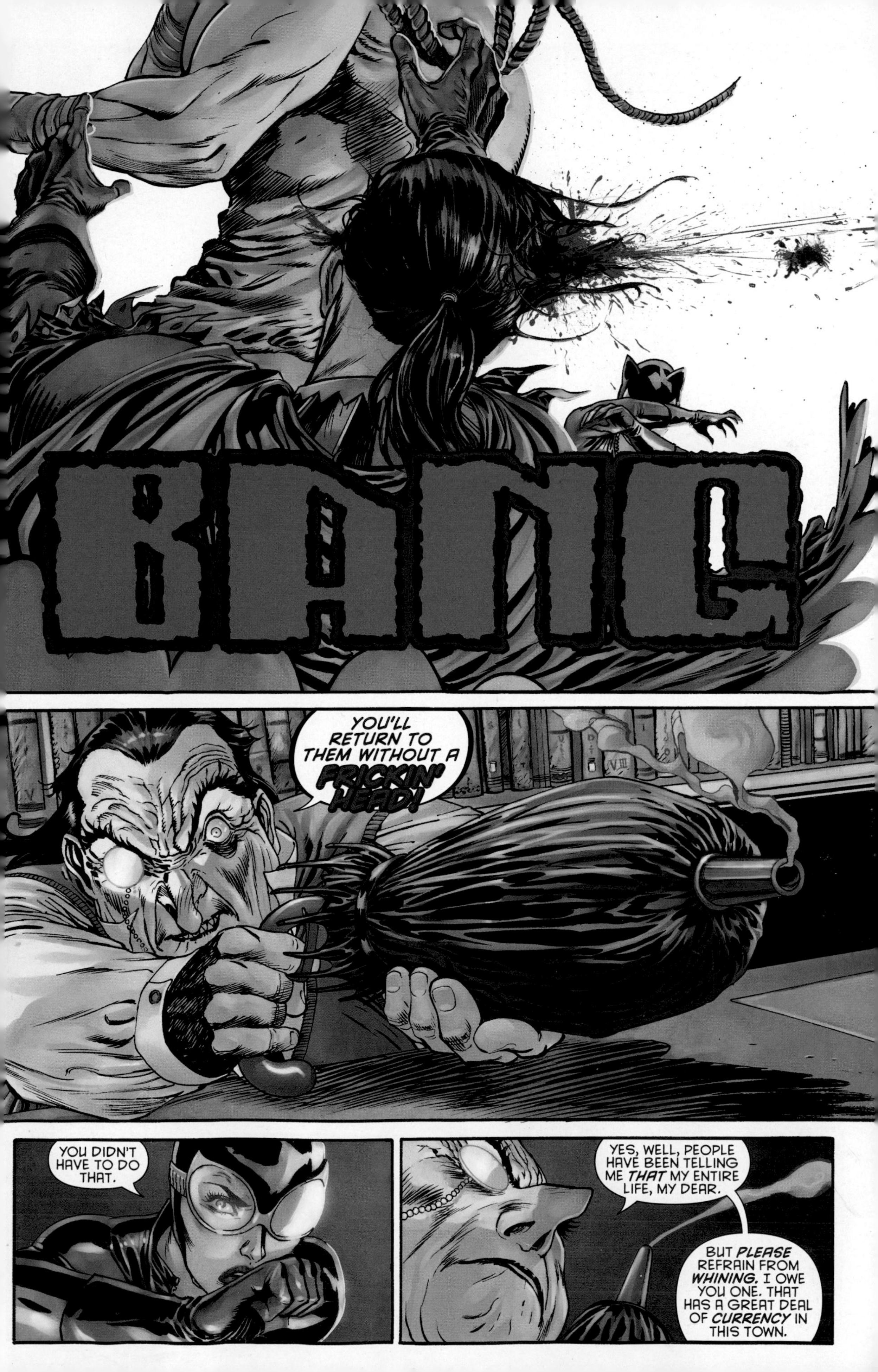
BANG
YOU'LL RETURN TO THEM WITHOUT A FRICKIN' HEAD!
YOU DIDN'T HAVE TO DO THAT.
YES, WELL, PEOPLE HAVE BEEN TELLING ME THAT MY ENTIRE LIFE, MY DEAR.
BUT PLEASE REFRAIN FROM WHINING. I OWE YOU ONE. THAT HAS A GREAT DEAL OF CURRENCY IN THIS TOWN.

GODALMIGHTY... LET'S JUST GET THE HELL *OUT* OF HERE. WE'VE *GOT* THE *BLADE*--LET'S JUST *GO.*

CATWOMAN?

SPARK... I'M GOING TO NEED THAT *BACK.*

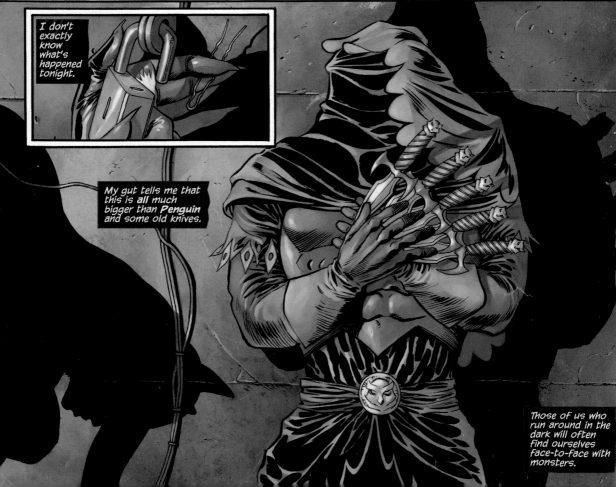

I don't exactly know what's happened tonight.

My gut tells me that this is all much bigger than Penguin and some old knives.

Those of us who run around in the dark will often find ourselves face-to-face with monsters.

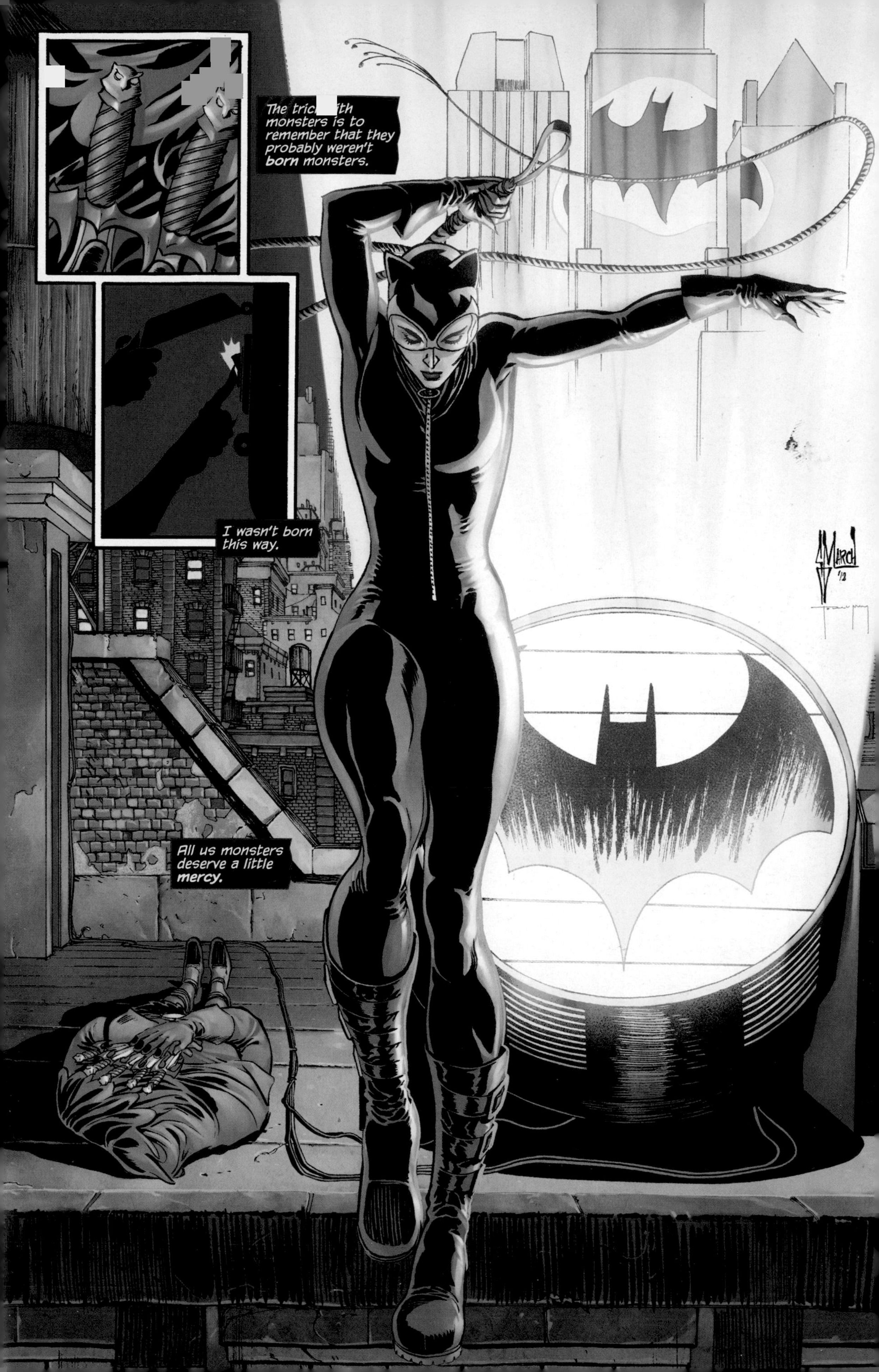

The tric ith monsters is to remember that they probably weren't **born** monsters.
I wasn't born this way.
All us monsters deserve a little **mercy.**

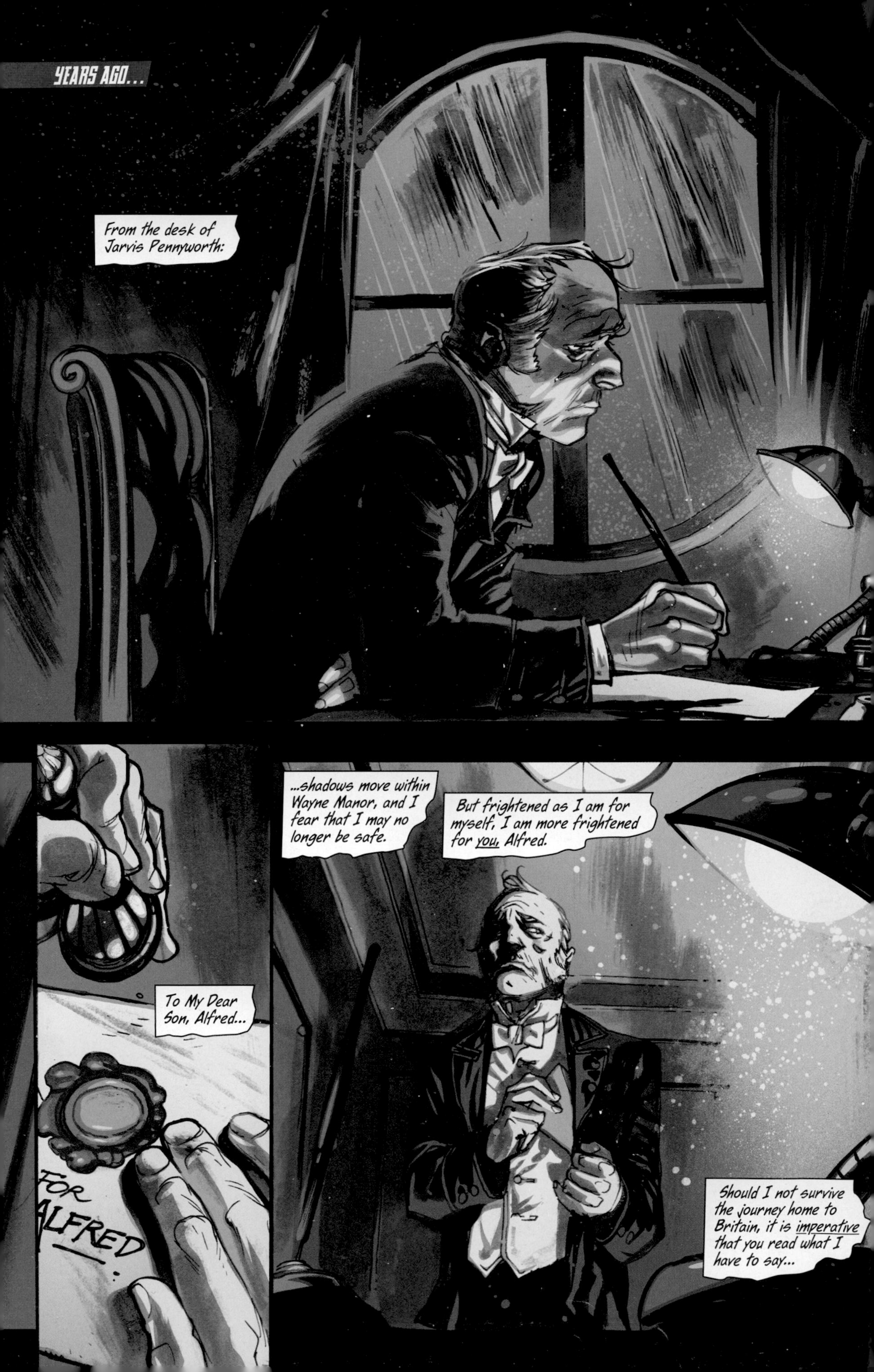
YEARS AGO...
From the desk of Jarvis Pennyworth:
To My Dear Son, Alfred...
FOR ALFRED
...shadows move within Wayne Manor, and I fear that I may no longer be safe.
But frightened as I am for myself, I am more frightened for you, Alfred.
Should I not survive the journey home to Britain, it is imperative that you read what I have to say...

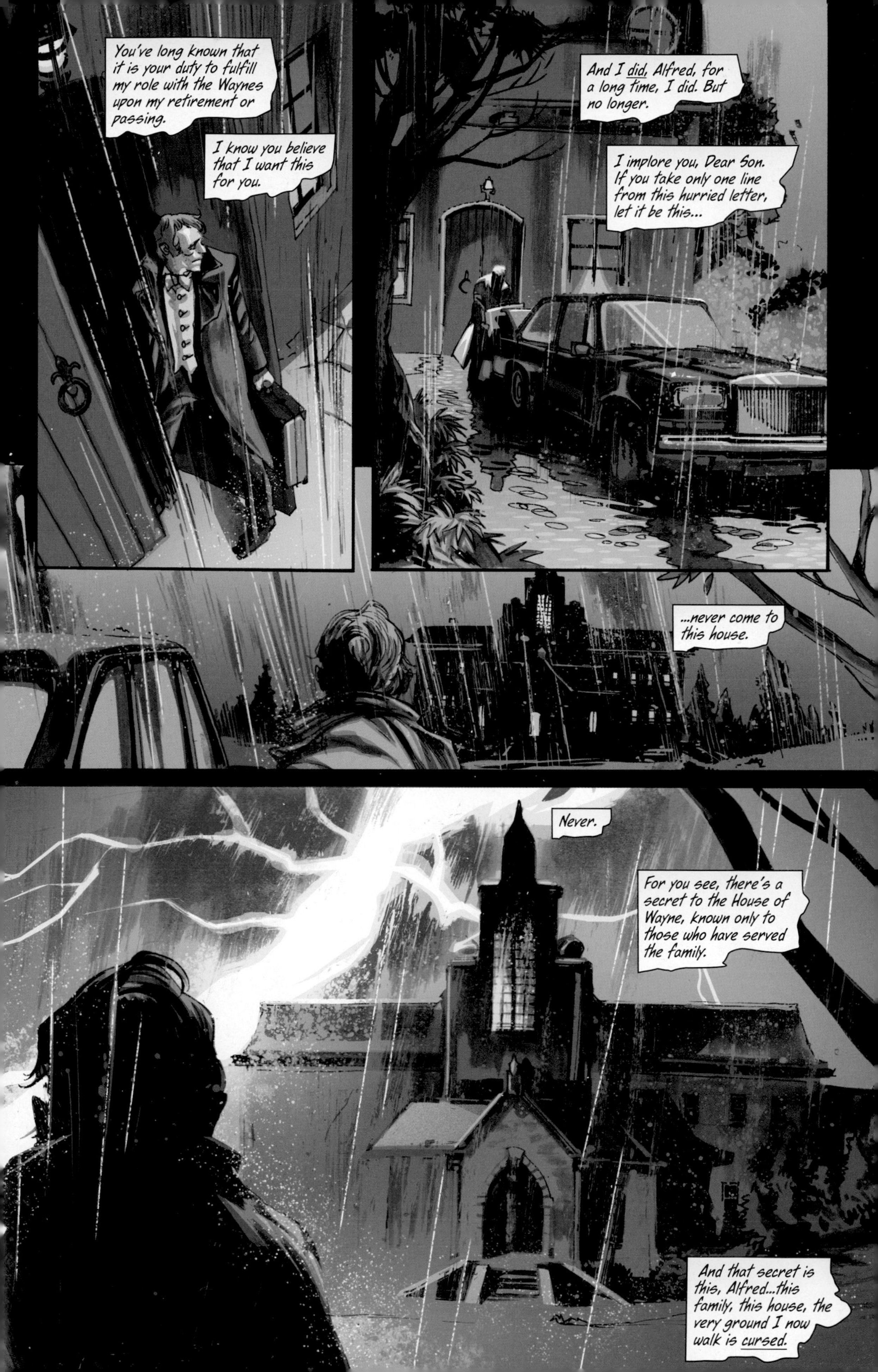
You've long known that it is your duty to fulfill my role with the Waynes upon my retirement or passing.
I know you believe that I want this for you.
And I did, Alfred, for a long time, I did. But no longer.
I implore you, Dear Son. If you take only one line from this hurried letter, let it be this...
...never come to this house.
Never.
For you see, there's a secret to the House of Wayne, known only to those who have served the family.
And that secret is this, Alfred...this family, this house, the very ground I now walk is cursed.

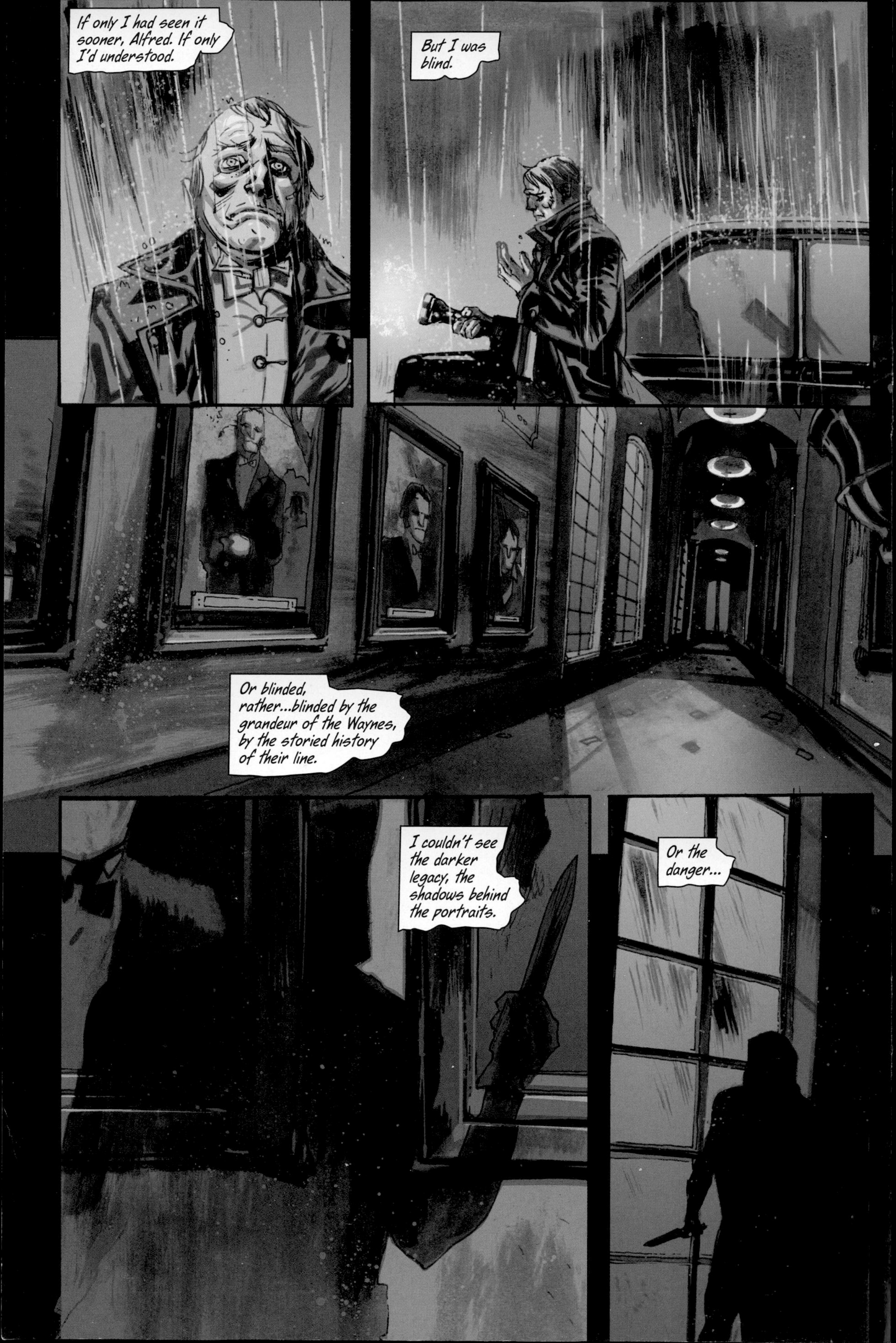
If only I had seen it sooner, Alfred. If only I'd understood.
But I was blind.
Or blinded, rather...blinded by the grandeur of the Waynes, by the storied history of their line.
I couldn't see the darker legacy, the shadows behind the portraits.
Or the danger...

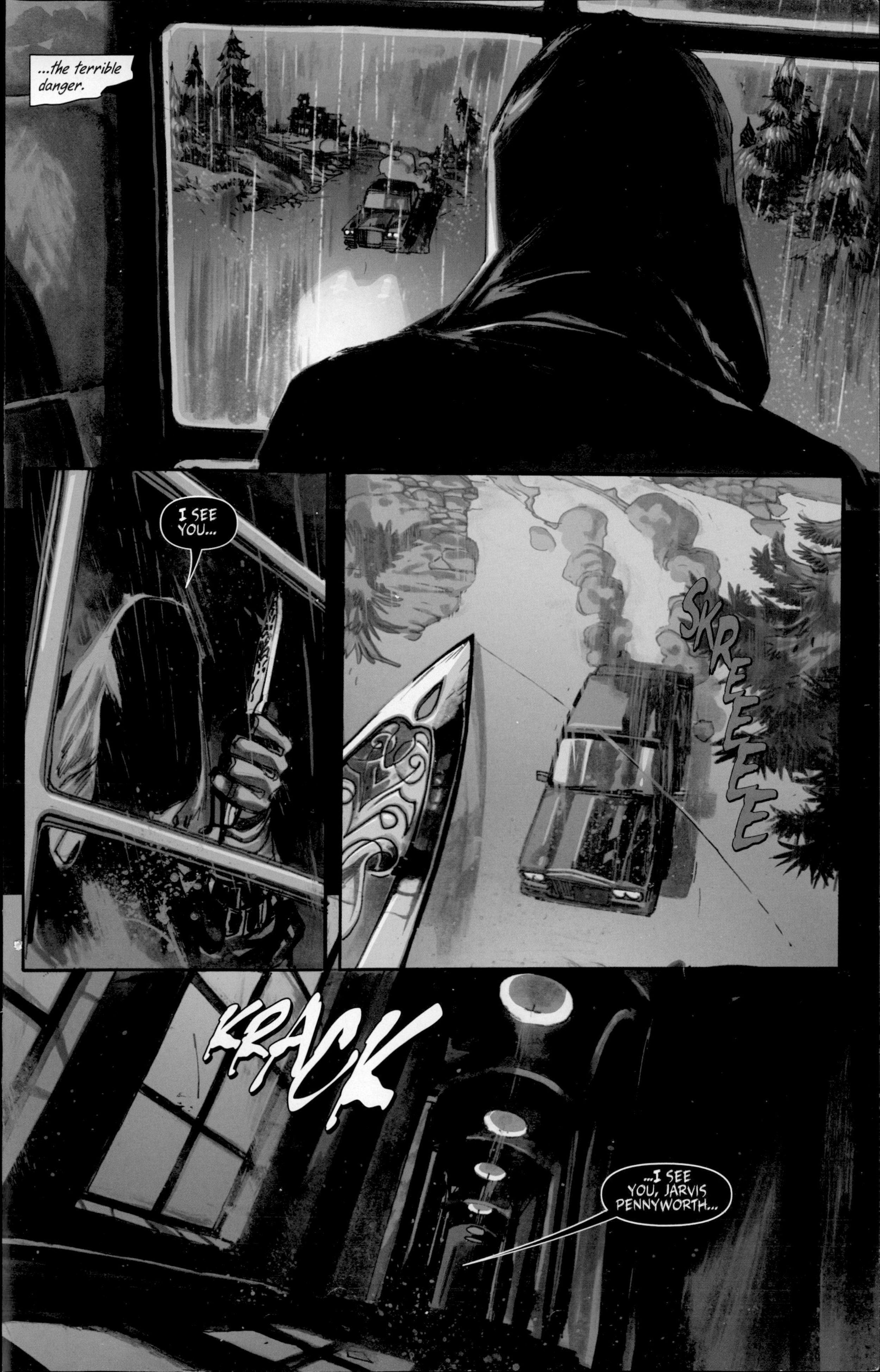
...the terrible danger.
I SEE YOU...
SKREEEEE
KRACK
...I SEE YOU, JARVIS PENNYWORTH...

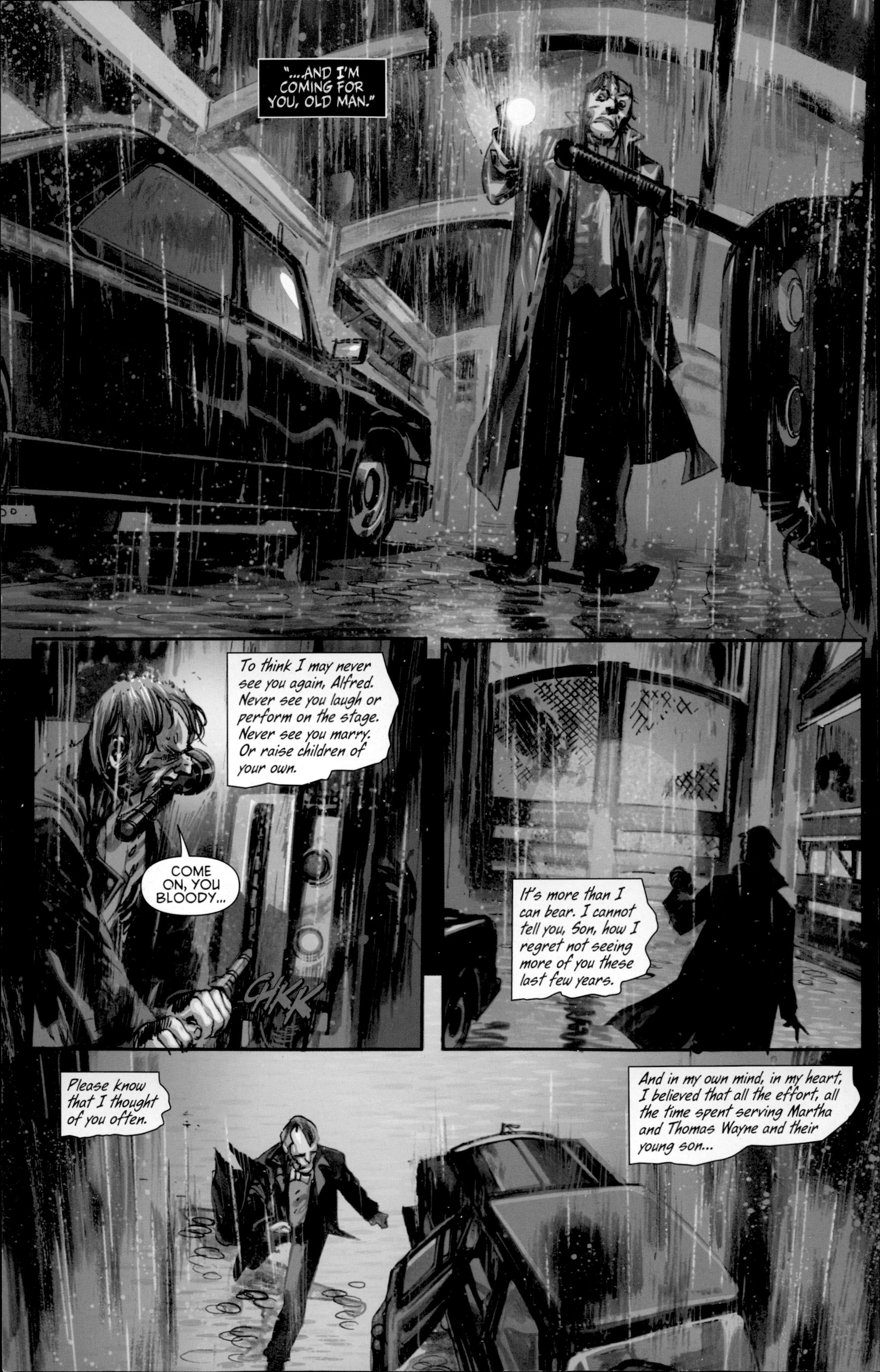
"...AND I'M COMING FOR YOU, OLD MAN."
To think I may never see you again, Alfred. Never see you laugh or perform on the stage. Never see you marry. Or raise children of your own.
COME ON, YOU BLOODY...
CHKK
It's more than I can bear. I cannot tell you, Son, how I regret not seeing more of you these last few years.
Please know that I thought of you often.
And in my own mind, in my heart, I believed that all the effort, all the time spent serving Martha and Thomas Wayne and their young son...

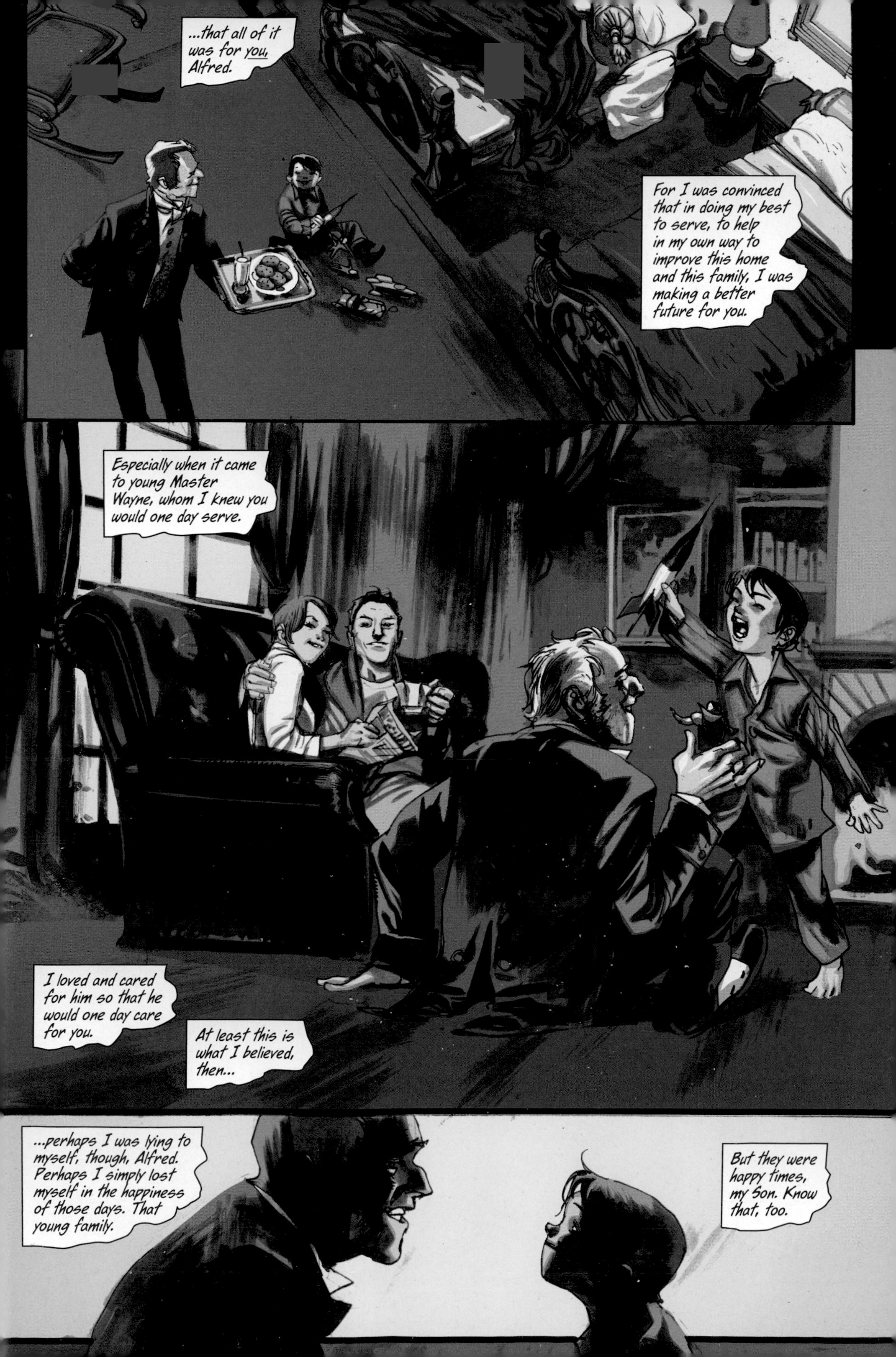
...that all of it was for you, Alfred.
For I was convinced that in doing my best to serve, to help in my own way to improve this home and this family, I was making a better future for you.
Especially when it came to young Master Wayne, whom I knew you would one day serve.
I loved and cared for him so that he would one day care for you.
At least this is what I believed, then...
...perhaps I was lying to myself, though, Alfred. Perhaps I simply lost myself in the happiness of those days. That young family.
But they were happy times, my Son. Know that, too.

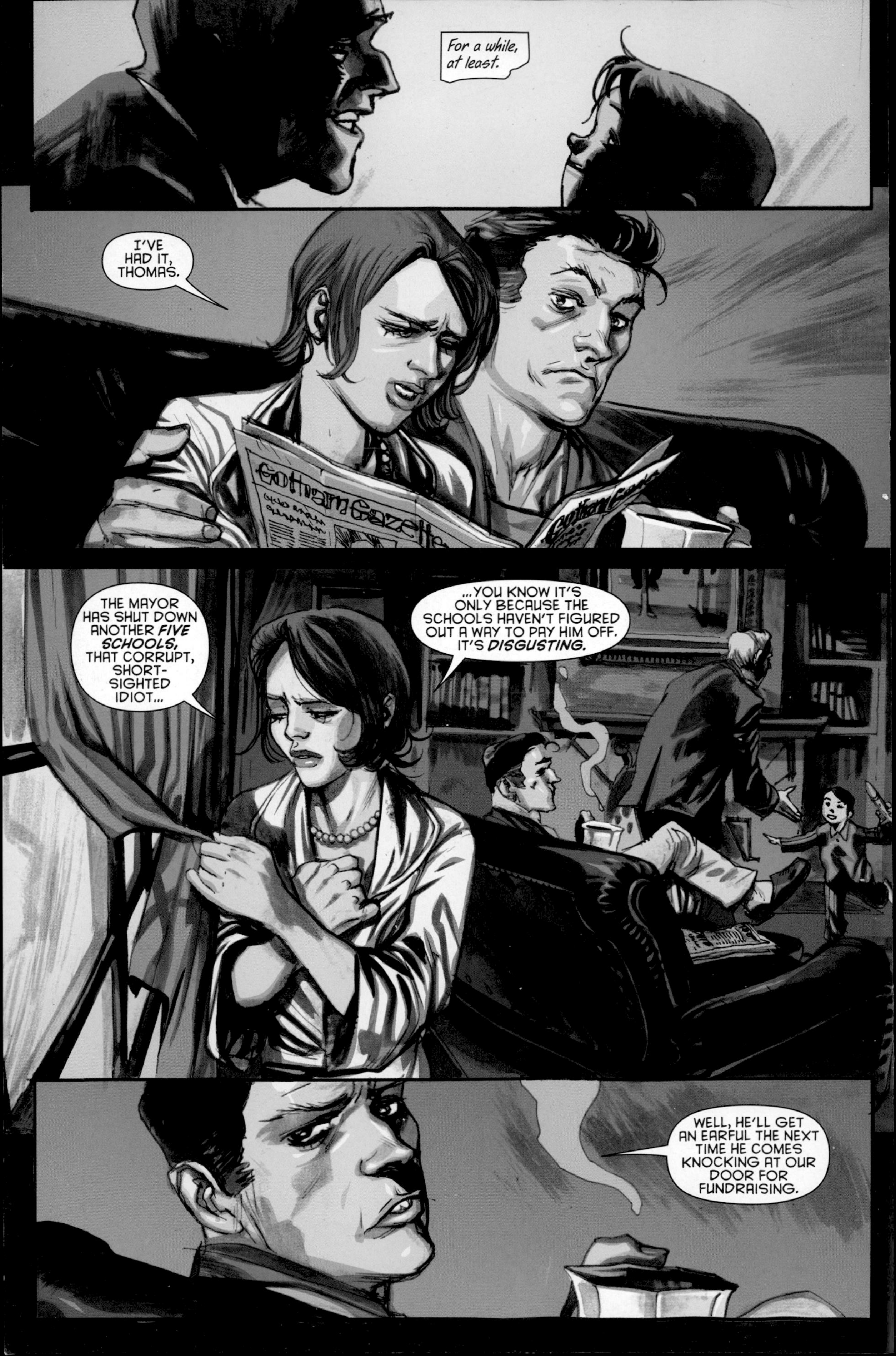
For a while, at least.
I'VE HAD IT, THOMAS.
THE MAYOR HAS SHUT DOWN ANOTHER *FIVE SCHOOLS,* THAT CORRUPT, SHORT-SIGHTED IDIOT...
...YOU KNOW IT'S ONLY BECAUSE THE SCHOOLS HAVEN'T FIGURED OUT A WAY TO PAY HIM OFF. IT'S *DISGUSTING.*
WELL, HE'LL GET AN EARFUL THE NEXT TIME HE COMES KNOCKING AT OUR DOOR FOR FUNDRAISING.

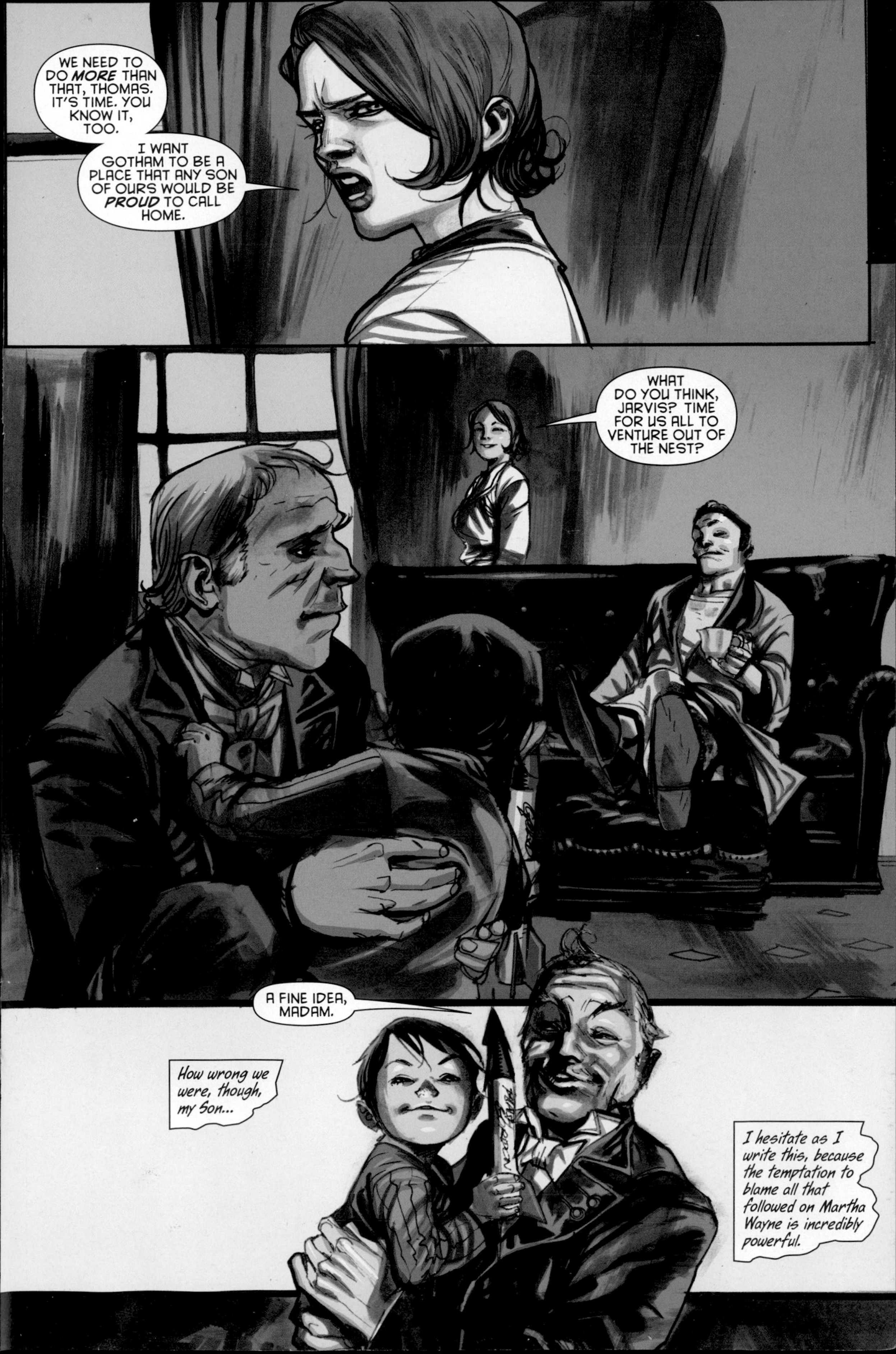
WE NEED TO DO MORE THAN THAT, THOMAS. IT'S TIME. YOU KNOW IT, TOO.
I WANT GOTHAM TO BE A PLACE THAT ANY SON OF OURS WOULD BE PROUD TO CALL HOME.
WHAT DO YOU THINK, JARVIS? TIME FOR US ALL TO VENTURE OUT OF THE NEST?
A FINE IDEA, MADAM.
How wrong we were, though, my Son...
I hesitate as I write this, because the temptation to blame all that followed on Martha Wayne is incredibly powerful.

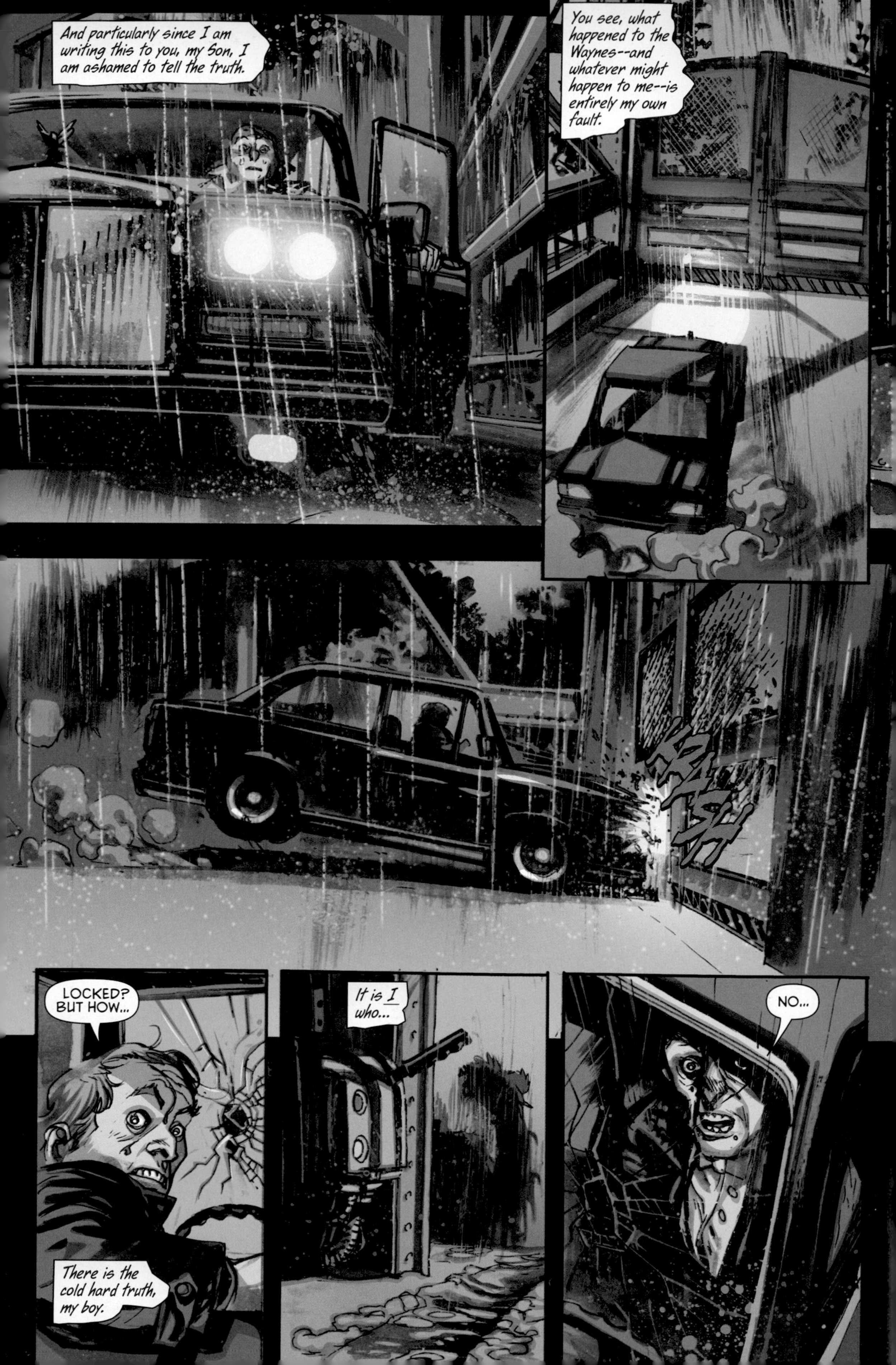
And particularly since I am writing this to you, my Son, I am ashamed to tell the truth.
You see, what happened to the Waynes--and whatever might happen to me--is entirely my own fault.
KRASH
LOCKED? BUT HOW...
There is the cold hard truth, my boy.
It is I who...
NO...

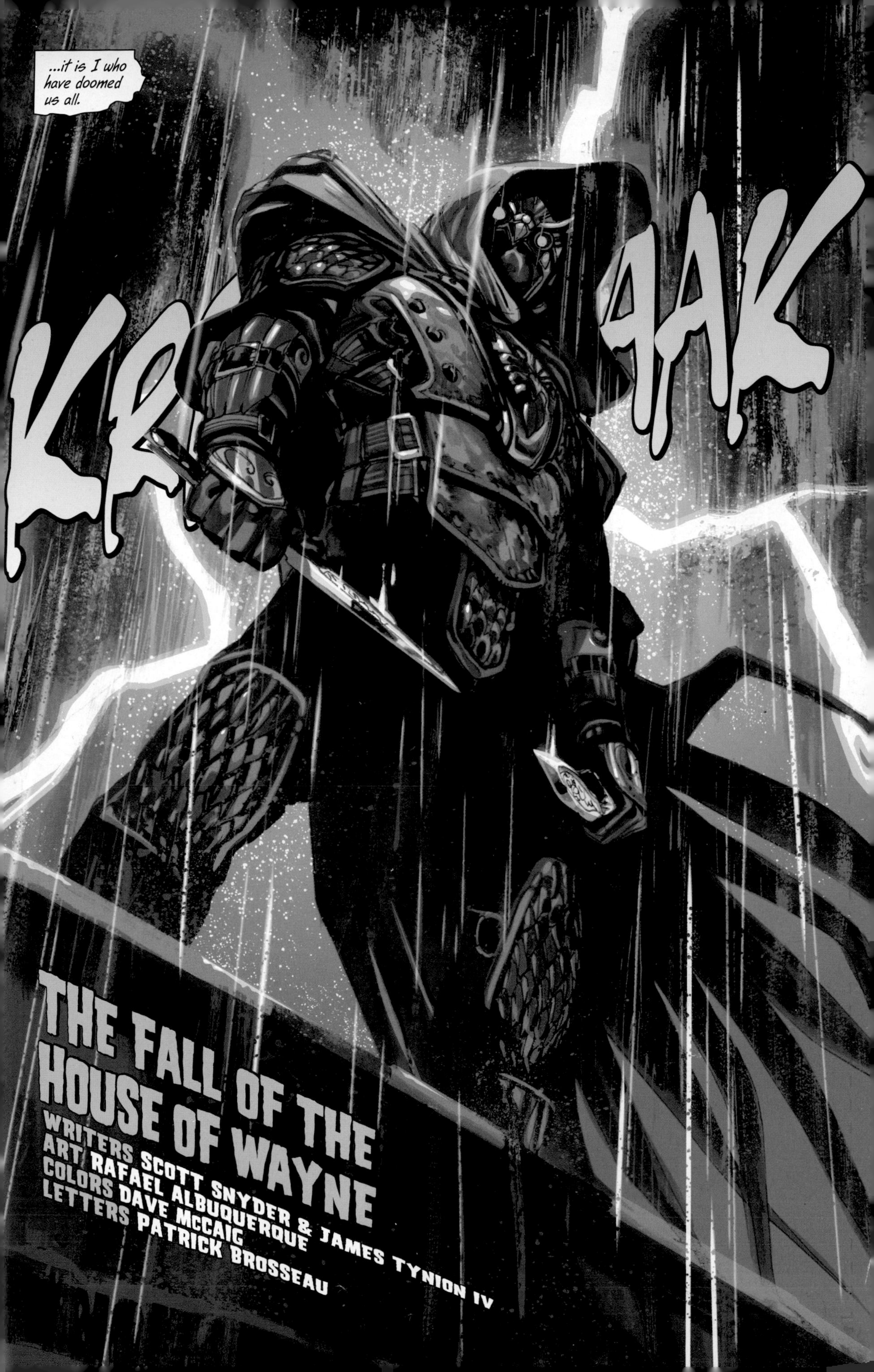
...it is I who have doomed us all.
KR
AAK
THE FALL OF THE HOUSE OF THE HOUSE OF WAYNE
WRITERS SCOTT SNYDER & JAMES TYNION IV
ART RAFAEL ALBUQUERQUE
COLORS DAVE McCAIG
LETTERS PATRICK BROSSEAU

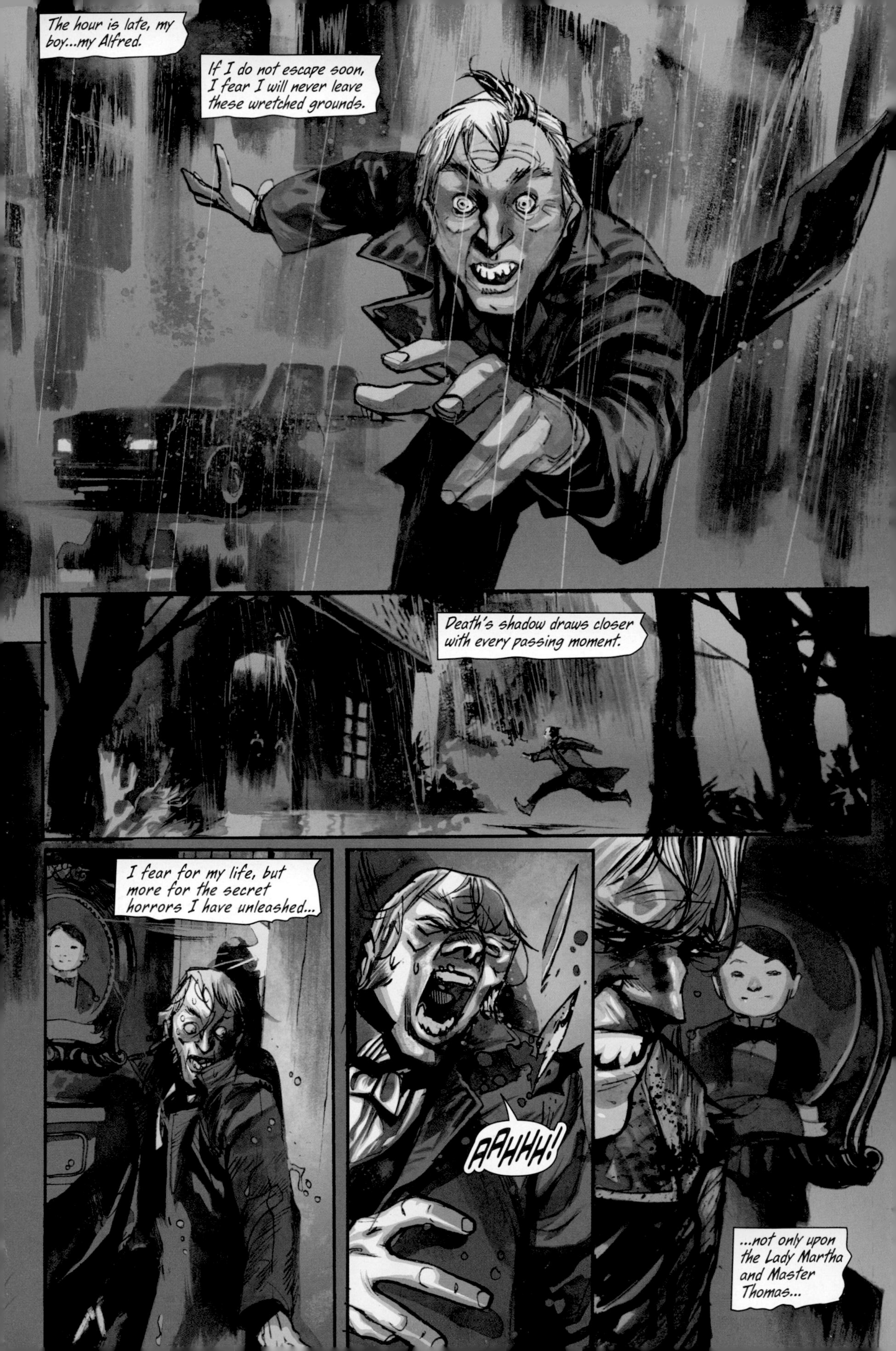
The hour is late, my boy...my Alfred.
If I do not escape soon, I fear I will never leave these wretched grounds.
Death's shadow draws closer with every passing moment.
I fear for my life, but more for the secret horrors I have unleashed...
AAHHH!
...not only upon the Lady Martha and Master Thomas...

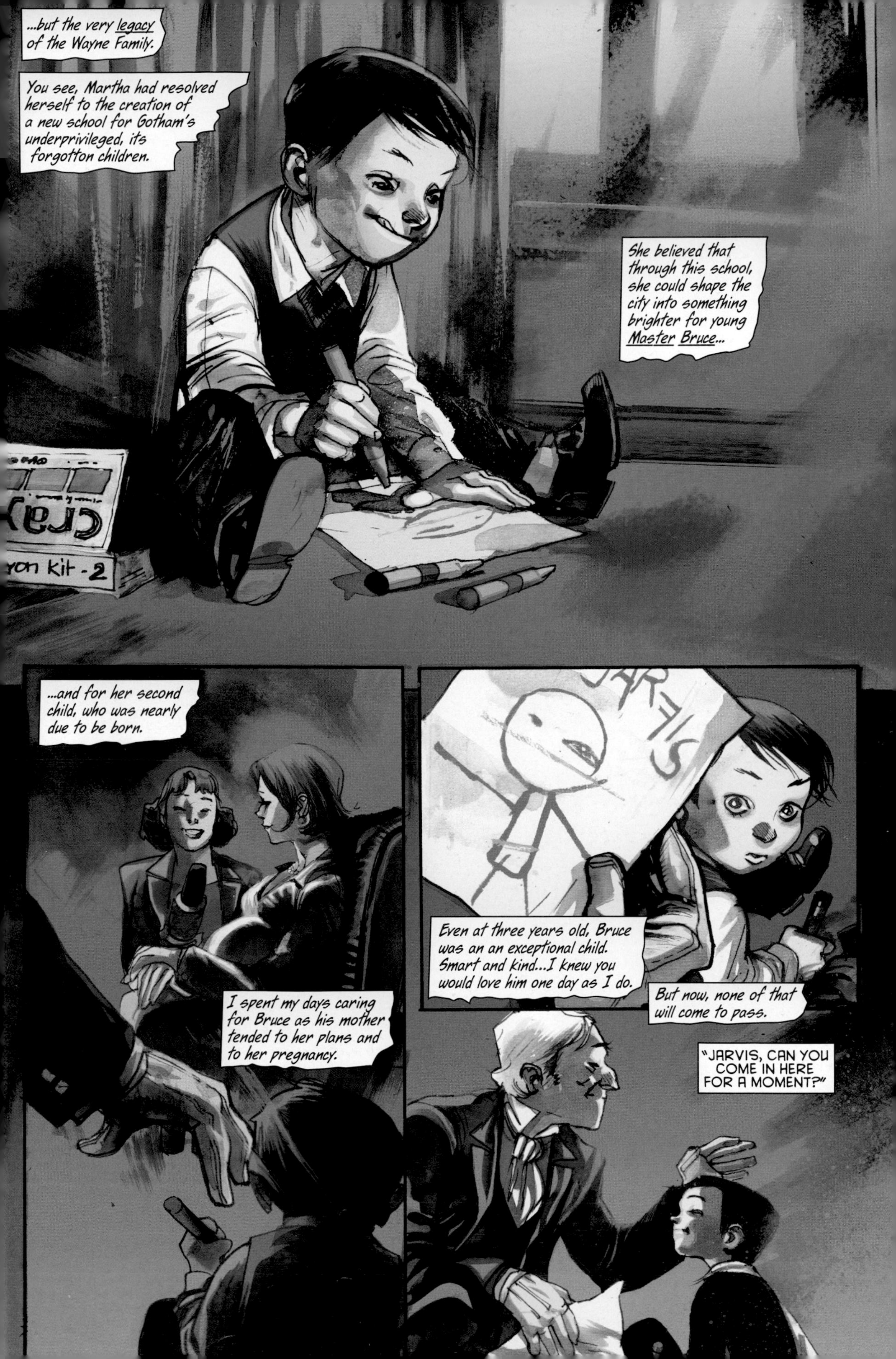
...but the very legacy of the Wayne Family.
You see, Martha had resolved herself to the creation of a new school for Gotham's underprivileged, its forgotton children.
She believed that through this school, she could shape the city into something brighter for young Master Bruce...
...and for her second child, who was nearly due to be born.
I spent my days caring for Bruce as his mother tended to her plans and to her pregnancy.
Even at three years old, Bruce was an an exceptional child. Smart and kind...I knew you would love him one day as I do.
But now, none of that will come to pass.
"JARVIS, CAN YOU COME IN HERE FOR A MOMENT?"

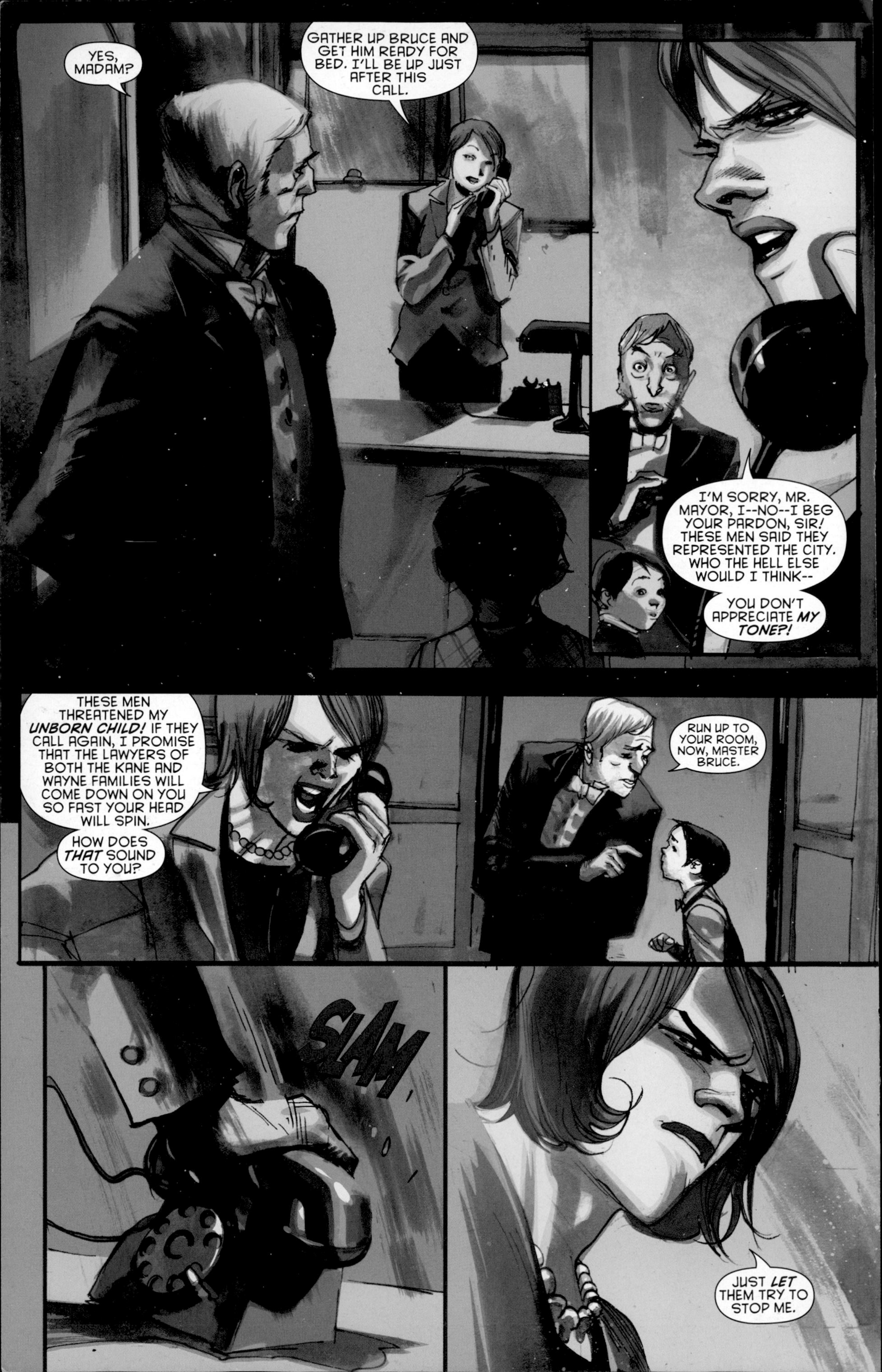
YES, MADAM?
GATHER UP BRUCE AND GET HIM READY FOR BED. I'LL BE UP JUST AFTER THIS CALL.
I'M SORRY, MR. MAYOR, I--NO--I BEG YOUR PARDON, SIR! THESE MEN SAID THEY REPRESENTED THE CITY. WHO THE HELL ELSE WOULD I THINK--
YOU DON'T APPRECIATE *MY TONE?!*
THESE MEN THREATENED MY *UNBORN CHILD!* IF THEY CALL AGAIN, I PROMISE THAT THE LAWYERS OF BOTH THE KANE AND WAYNE FAMILIES WILL COME DOWN ON YOU SO FAST YOUR HEAD WILL SPIN.
HOW DOES *THAT* SOUND TO YOU?
RUN UP TO YOUR ROOM, NOW, MASTER BRUCE.
SLAM
JUST *LET* THEM TRY TO STOP ME.

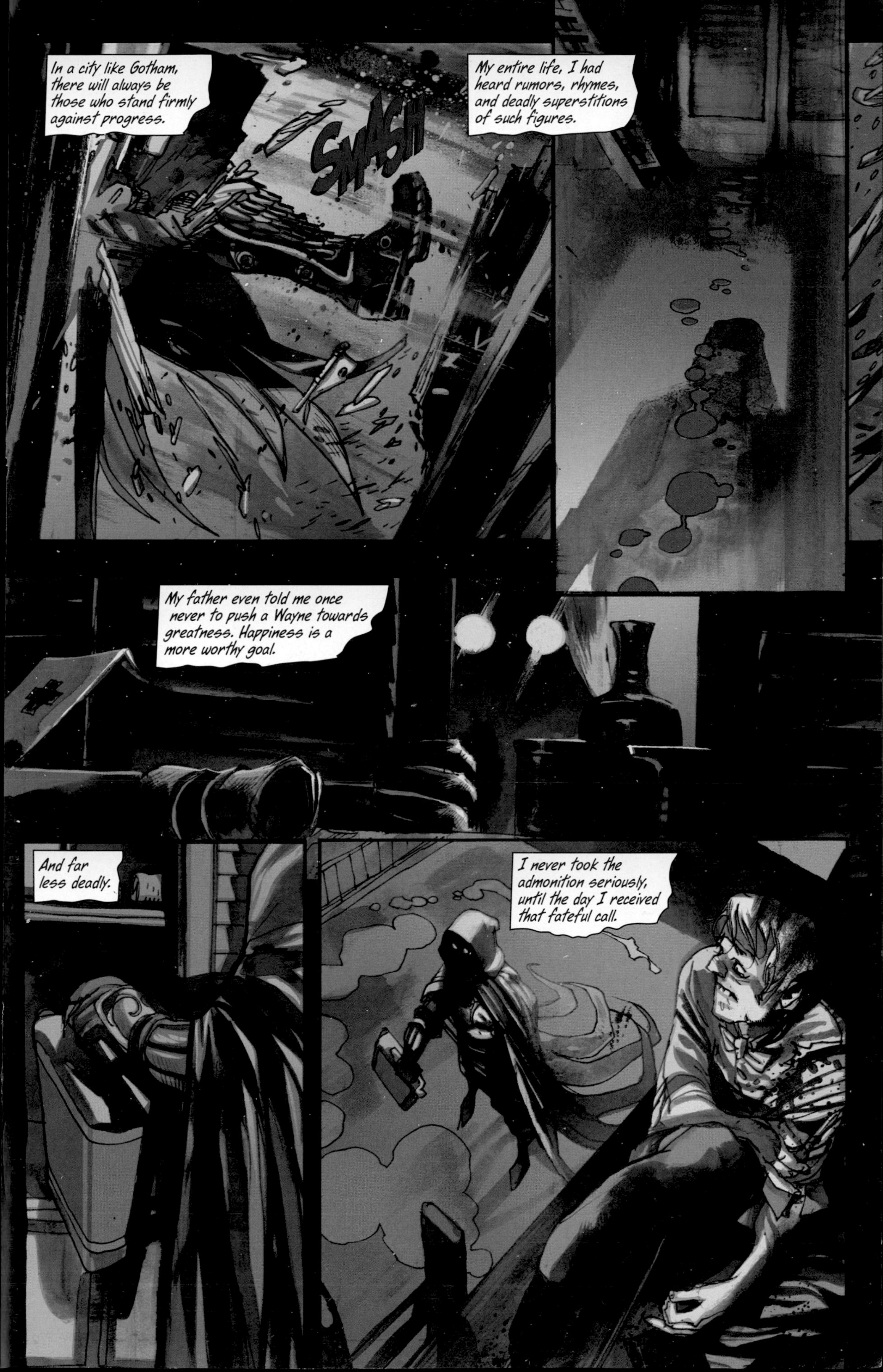
In a city like Gotham, there will always be those who stand firmly against progress.
SMASH
My entire life, I had heard rumors, rhymes, and deadly superstitions of such figures.
My father even told me once never to push a Wayne towards greatness. Happiness is a more worthy goal.
And far less deadly.
I never took the admonition seriously, until the day I received that fateful call.

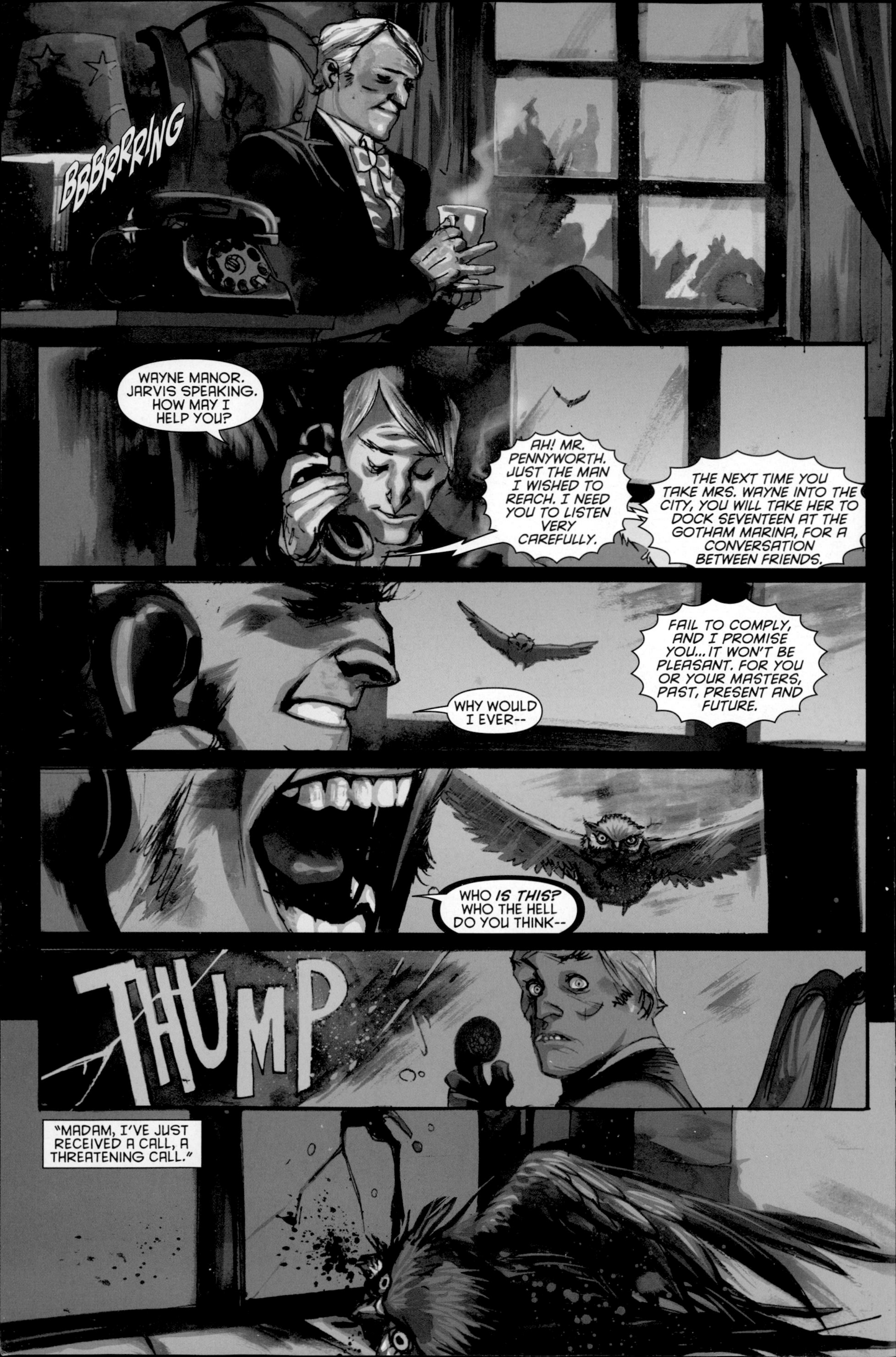
BBBRRRRING
WAYNE MANOR. JARVIS SPEAKING. HOW MAY I HELP YOU?
AH! MR. PENNYWORTH. JUST THE MAN I WISHED TO REACH. I NEED YOU TO LISTEN VERY CAREFULLY.
THE NEXT TIME YOU TAKE MRS. WAYNE INTO THE CITY, YOU WILL TAKE HER TO DOCK SEVENTEEN AT THE GOTHAM MARINA, FOR A CONVERSATION BETWEEN FRIENDS.
WHY WOULD I EVER--
FAIL TO COMPLY, AND I PROMISE YOU... IT WON'T BE PLEASANT. FOR YOU OR YOUR MASTERS, PAST, PRESENT AND FUTURE.
WHO *IS THIS?* WHO THE HELL DO YOU THINK--
THUMP
"MADAM, I'VE JUST RECEIVED A CALL, A THREATENING CALL."

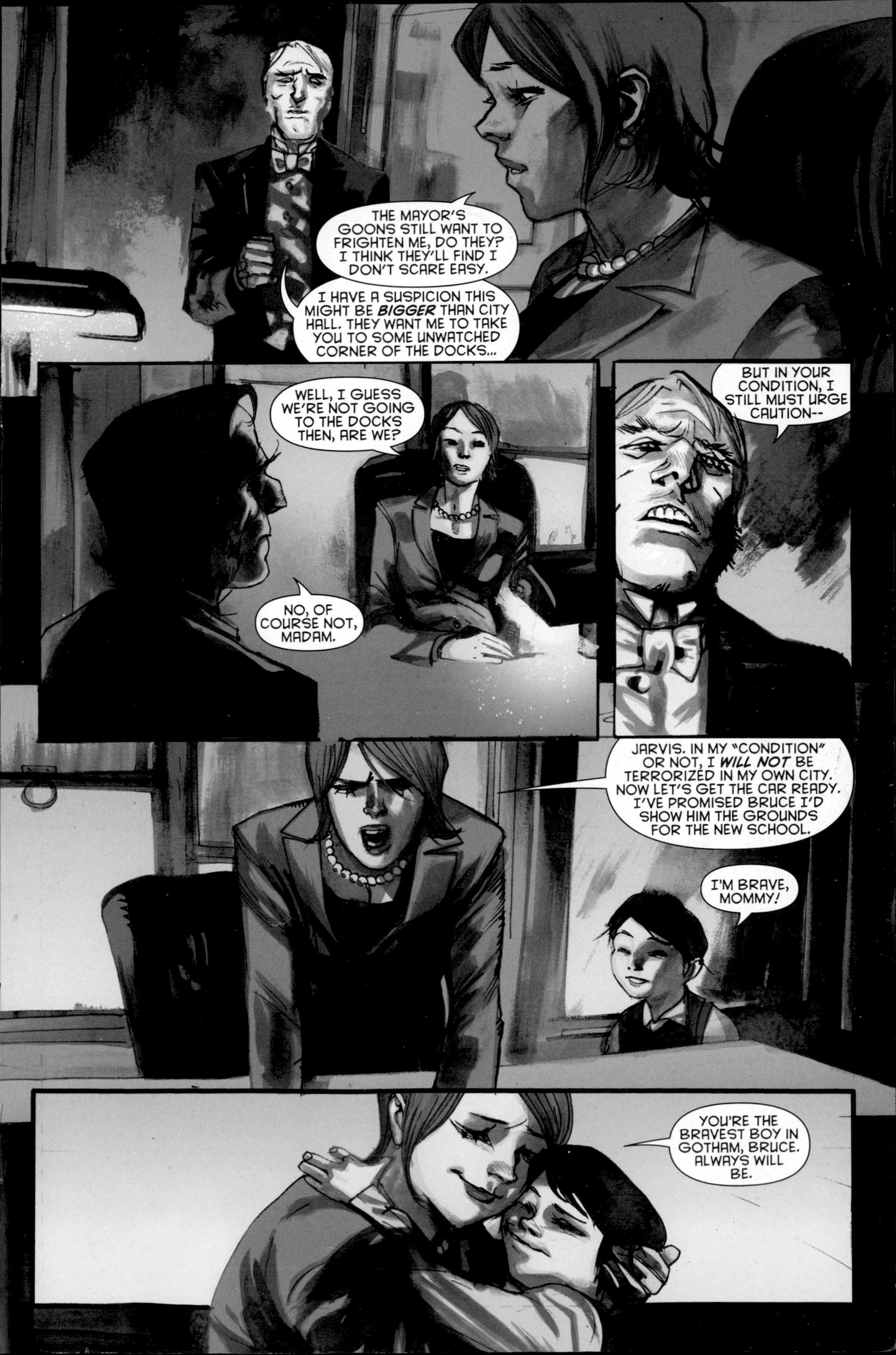
THE MAYOR'S GOONS STILL WANT TO FRIGHTEN ME, DO THEY? I THINK THEY'LL FIND I DON'T SCARE EASY.
I HAVE A SUSPICION THIS MIGHT BE *BIGGER* THAN CITY HALL. THEY WANT ME TO TAKE YOU TO SOME UNWATCHED CORNER OF THE DOCKS...
WELL, I GUESS WE'RE NOT GOING TO THE DOCKS THEN, ARE WE?
NO, OF COURSE NOT, MADAM.
BUT IN YOUR CONDITION, I STILL MUST URGE CAUTION--
JARVIS. IN MY "CONDITION" OR NOT, I *WILL NOT* BE TERRORIZED IN MY OWN CITY. NOW LET'S GET THE CAR READY. I'VE PROMISED BRUCE I'D SHOW HIM THE GROUNDS FOR THE NEW SCHOOL.
I'M BRAVE, MOMMY!
YOU'RE THE BRAVEST BOY IN GOTHAM, BRUCE. ALWAYS WILL BE.

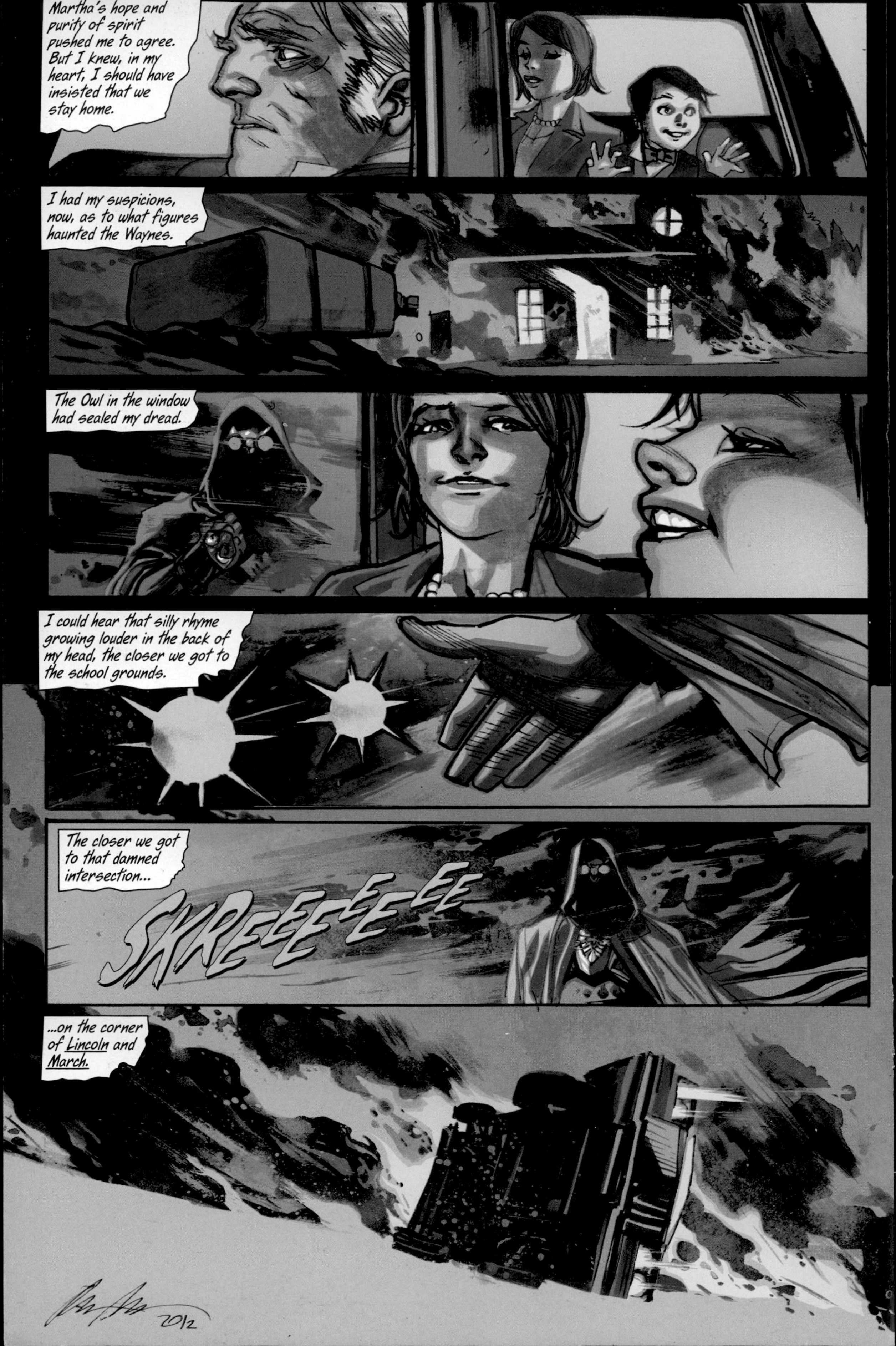
Martha's hope and purity of spirit pushed me to agree. But I knew, in my heart, I should have insisted that we stay home.
I had my suspicions, now, as to what figures haunted the Waynes.
The Owl in the window had sealed my dread.
I could hear that silly rhyme growing louder in the back of my head, the closer we got to the school grounds.
The closer we got to that damned intersection...
SKREEEEEEE
...on the corner of Lincoln and March.

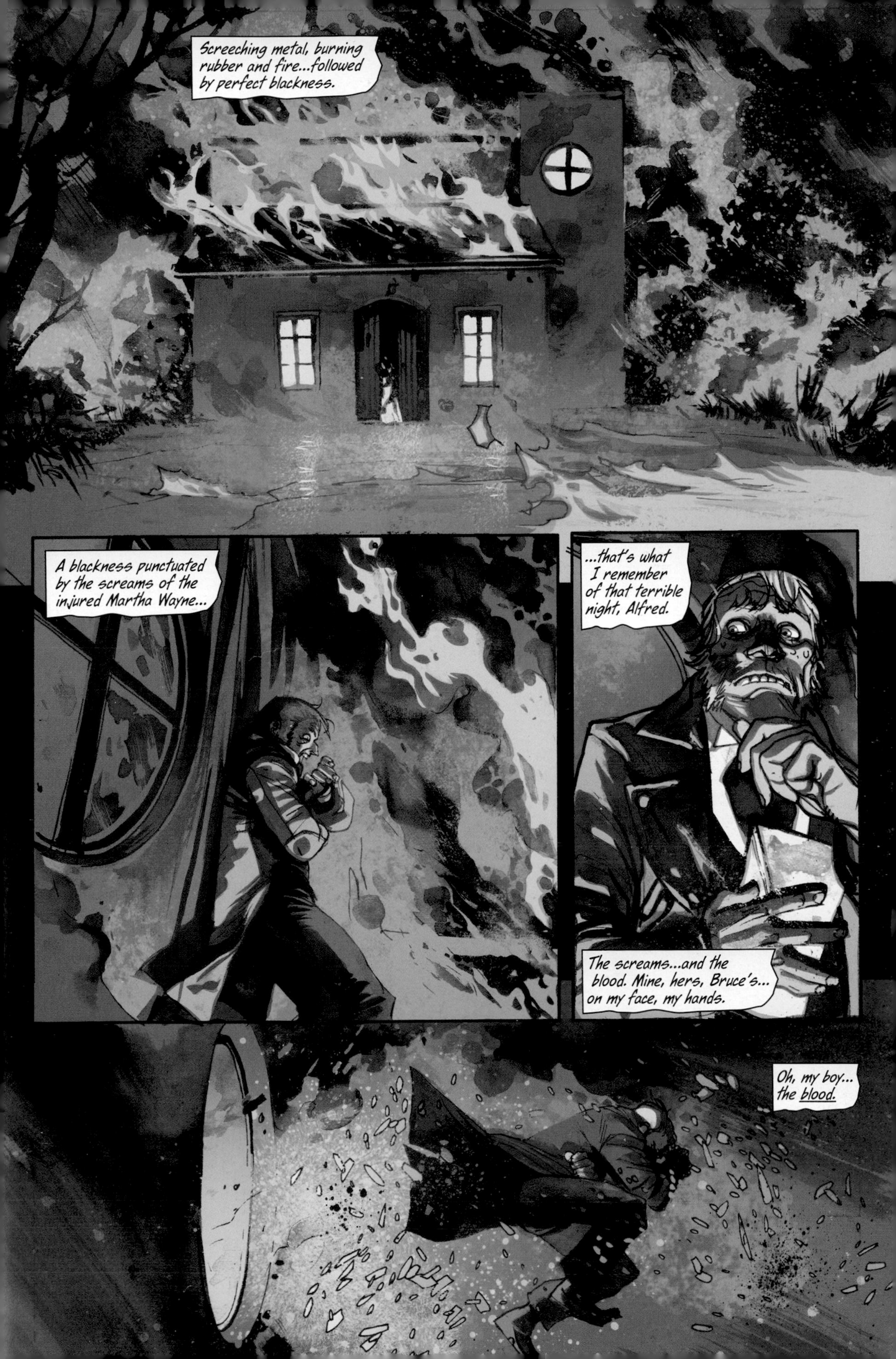
Screeching metal, burning rubber and fire...followed by perfect blackness.
A blackness punctuated by the screams of the injured Martha Wayne...
...that's what I remember of that terrible night, Alfred.
The screams...and the blood. Mine, hers, Bruce's... on my face, my hands.
Oh, my boy... the blood.

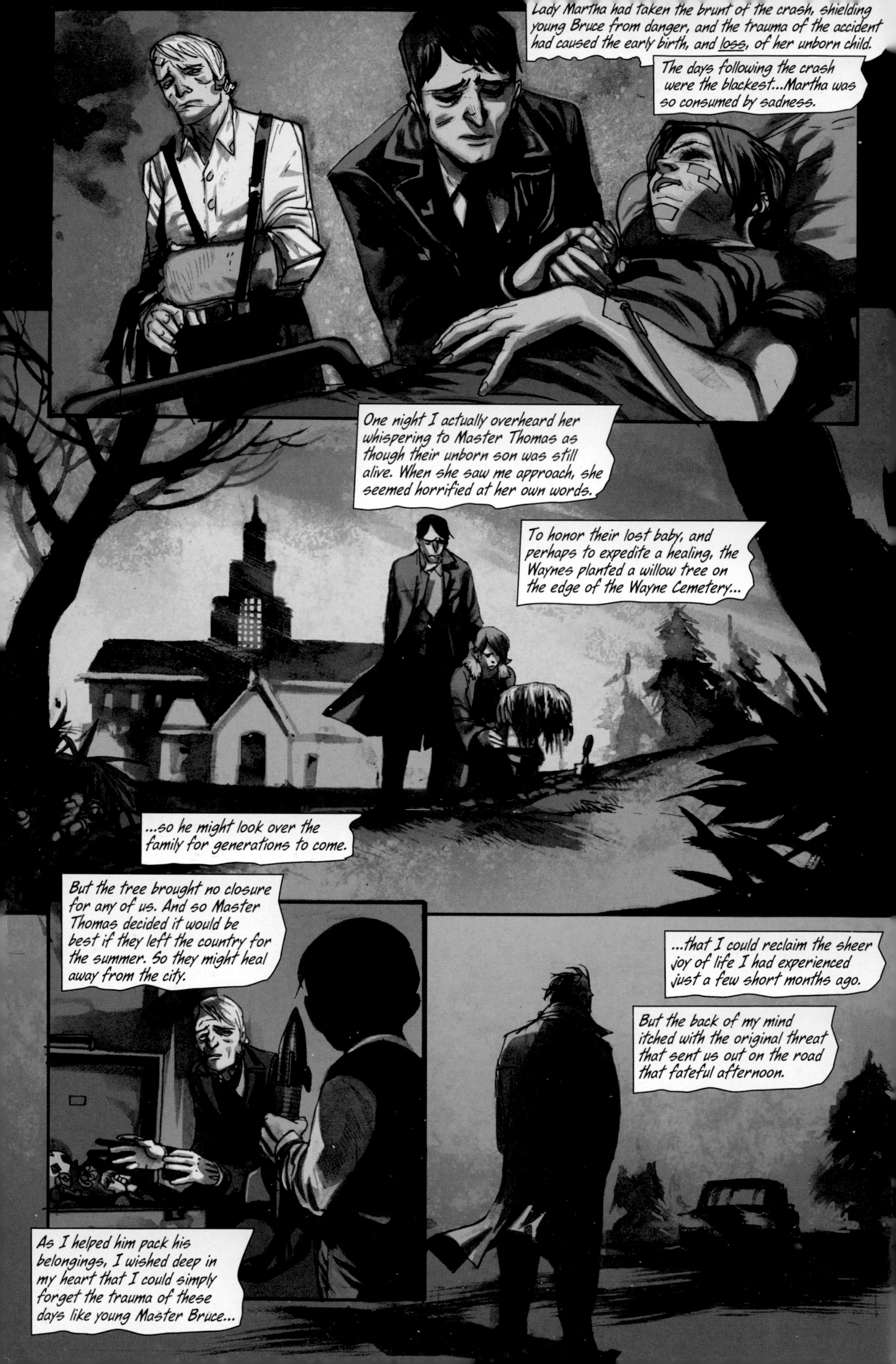

Lady Martha had taken the brunt of the crash, shielding young Bruce from danger, and the trauma of the accident had caused the early birth, and loss, of her unborn child.
The days following the crash were the blackest...Martha was so consumed by sadness.
One night I actually overheard her whispering to Master Thomas as though their unborn son was still alive. When she saw me approach, she seemed horrified at her own words.
To honor their lost baby, and perhaps to expedite a healing, the Waynes planted a willow tree on the edge of the Wayne Cemetery...
...so he might look over the family for generations to come.
But the tree brought no closure for any of us. And so Master Thomas decided it would be best if they left the country for the summer. So they might heal away from the city.
As I helped him pack his belongings, I wished deep in my heart that I could simply forget the trauma of these days like young Master Bruce...
...that I could reclaim the sheer joy of life I had experienced just a few short months ago.
But the back of my mind itched with the original threat that sent us out on the road that fateful afternoon.

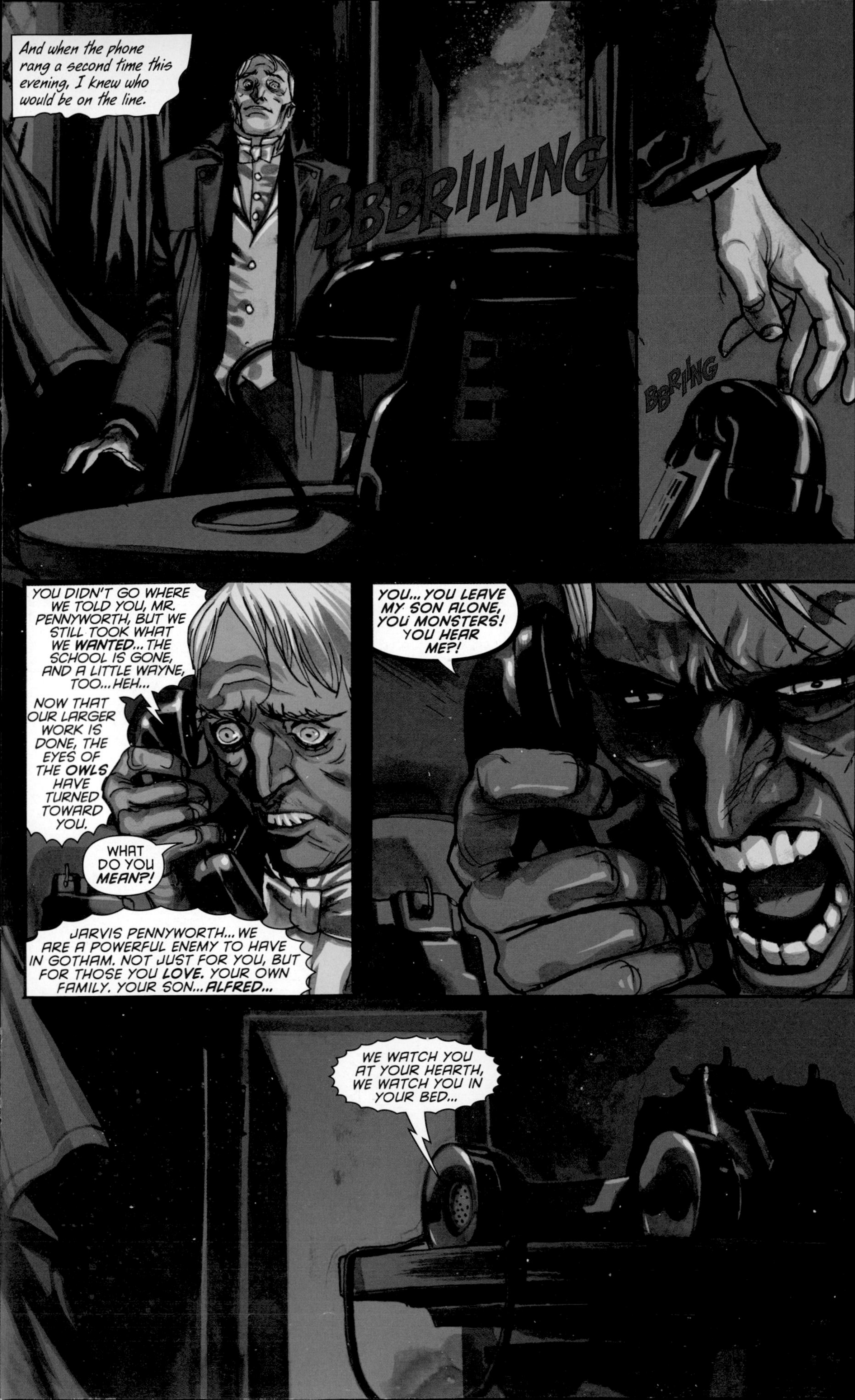
And when the phone rang a second time this evening, I knew who would be on the line.
BBBRIIINNG
BBRIING
YOU DIDN'T GO WHERE WE TOLD YOU, MR. PENNYWORTH, BUT WE STILL TOOK WHAT WE WANTED... THE SCHOOL IS GONE, AND A LITTLE WAYNE, TOO... HEH...
NOW THAT OUR LARGER WORK IS DONE, THE EYES OF THE OWLS HAVE TURNED TOWARD YOU.
WHAT DO YOU MEAN?!
JARVIS PENNYWORTH... WE ARE A POWERFUL ENEMY TO HAVE IN GOTHAM. NOT JUST FOR YOU, BUT FOR THOSE YOU LOVE. YOUR OWN FAMILY. YOUR SON... ALFRED...
YOU... YOU LEAVE MY SON ALONE, YOU MONSTERS! YOU HEAR ME?!
WE WATCH YOU AT YOUR HEARTH, WE WATCH YOU IN YOUR BED...

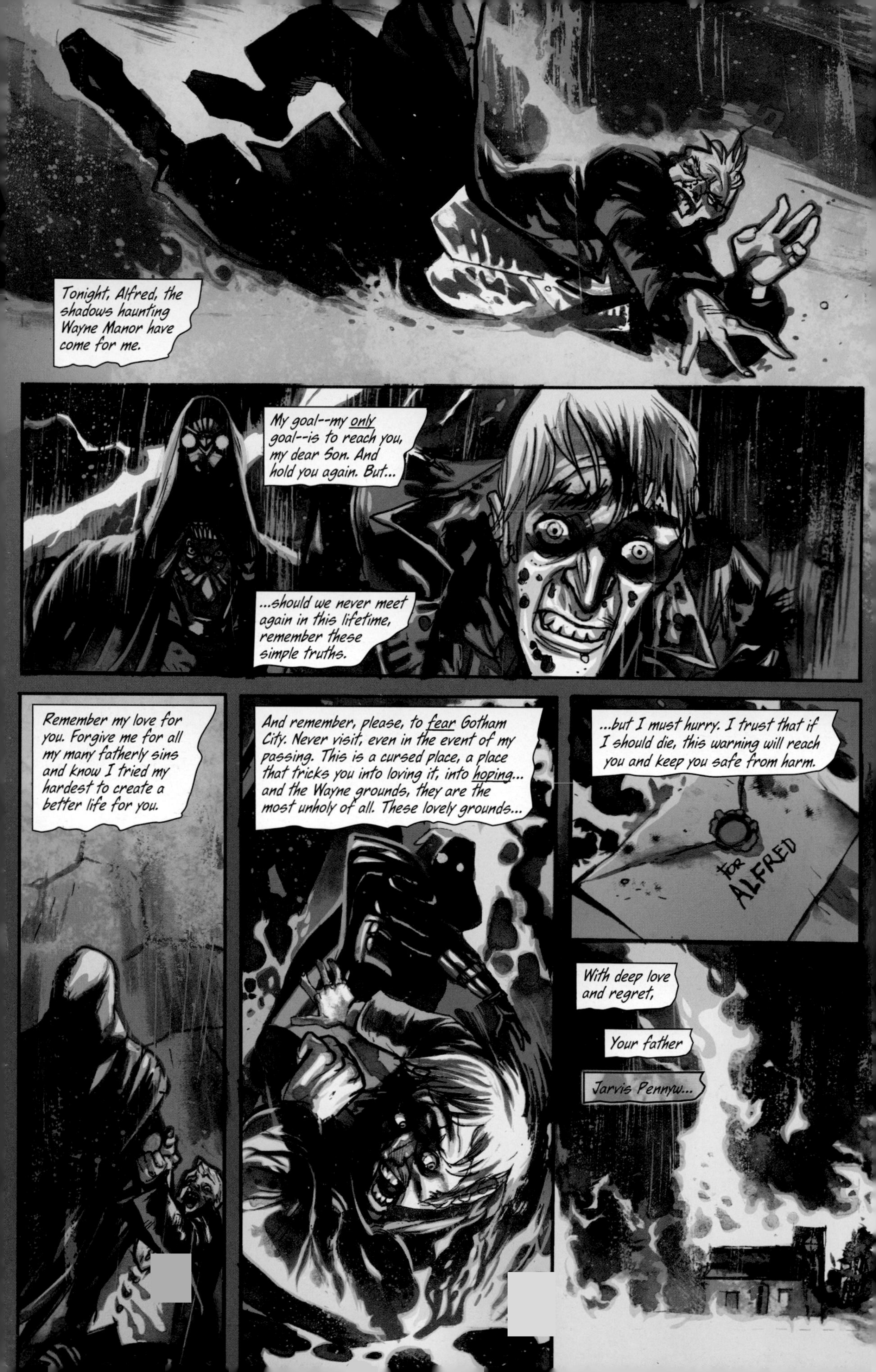

Tonight, Alfred, the shadows haunting Wayne Manor have come for me.
My goal--my only goal--is to reach you, my dear Son. And hold you again. But...
...should we never meet again in this lifetime, remember these simple truths.
Remember my love for you. Forgive me for all my many fatherly sins and know I tried my hardest to create a better life for you.
And remember, please, to fear Gotham City. Never visit, even in the event of my passing. This is a cursed place, a place that tricks you into loving it, into hoping... and the Wayne grounds, they are the most unholy of all. These lovely grounds...
...but I must hurry. I trust that if I should die, this warning will reach you and keep you safe from harm.
FOR ALFRED
With deep love and regret,
Your father
Jarvis Pennyw...

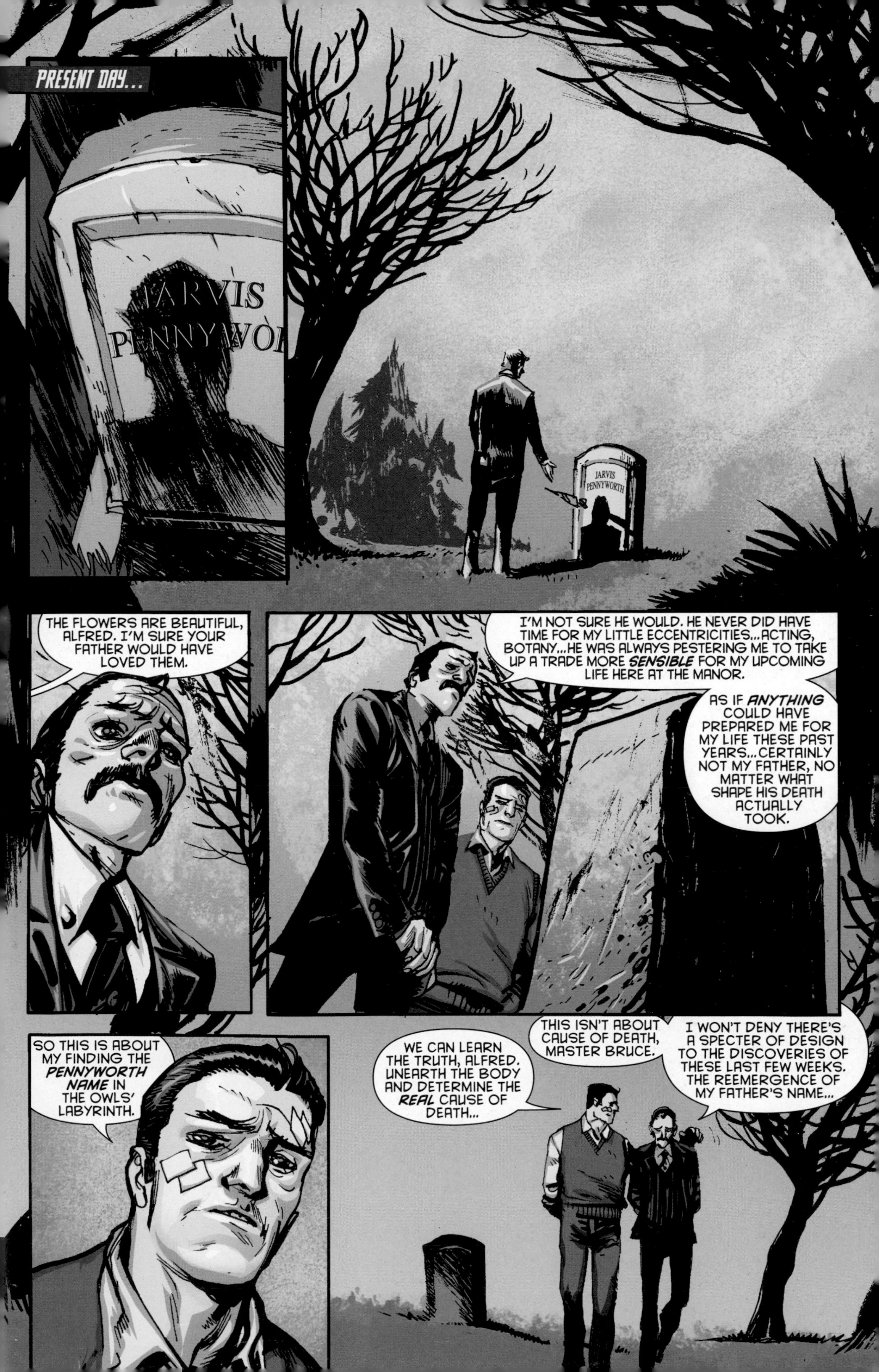
PRESENT DAY...
JARVIS PENNYWOR
JARVIS PENNYWORTH
THE FLOWERS ARE BEAUTIFUL, ALFRED. I'M SURE YOUR FATHER WOULD HAVE LOVED THEM.
I'M NOT SURE HE WOULD. HE NEVER DID HAVE TIME FOR MY LITTLE ECCENTRICITIES...ACTING, BOTANY...HE WAS ALWAYS PESTERING ME TO TAKE UP A TRADE MORE SENSIBLE FOR MY UPCOMING LIFE HERE AT THE MANOR.
AS IF ANYTHING COULD HAVE PREPARED ME FOR MY LIFE THESE PAST YEARS...CERTAINLY NOT MY FATHER, NO MATTER WHAT SHAPE HIS DEATH ACTUALLY TOOK.
SO THIS IS ABOUT MY FINDING THE PENNYWORTH NAME IN THE OWLS' LABYRINTH.
WE CAN LEARN THE TRUTH, ALFRED. UNEARTH THE BODY AND DETERMINE THE REAL CAUSE OF DEATH...
THIS ISN'T ABOUT CAUSE OF DEATH, MASTER BRUCE.
I WON'T DENY THERE'S A SPECTER OF DESIGN TO THE DISCOVERIES OF THESE LAST FEW WEEKS. THE REEMERGENCE OF MY FATHER'S NAME...

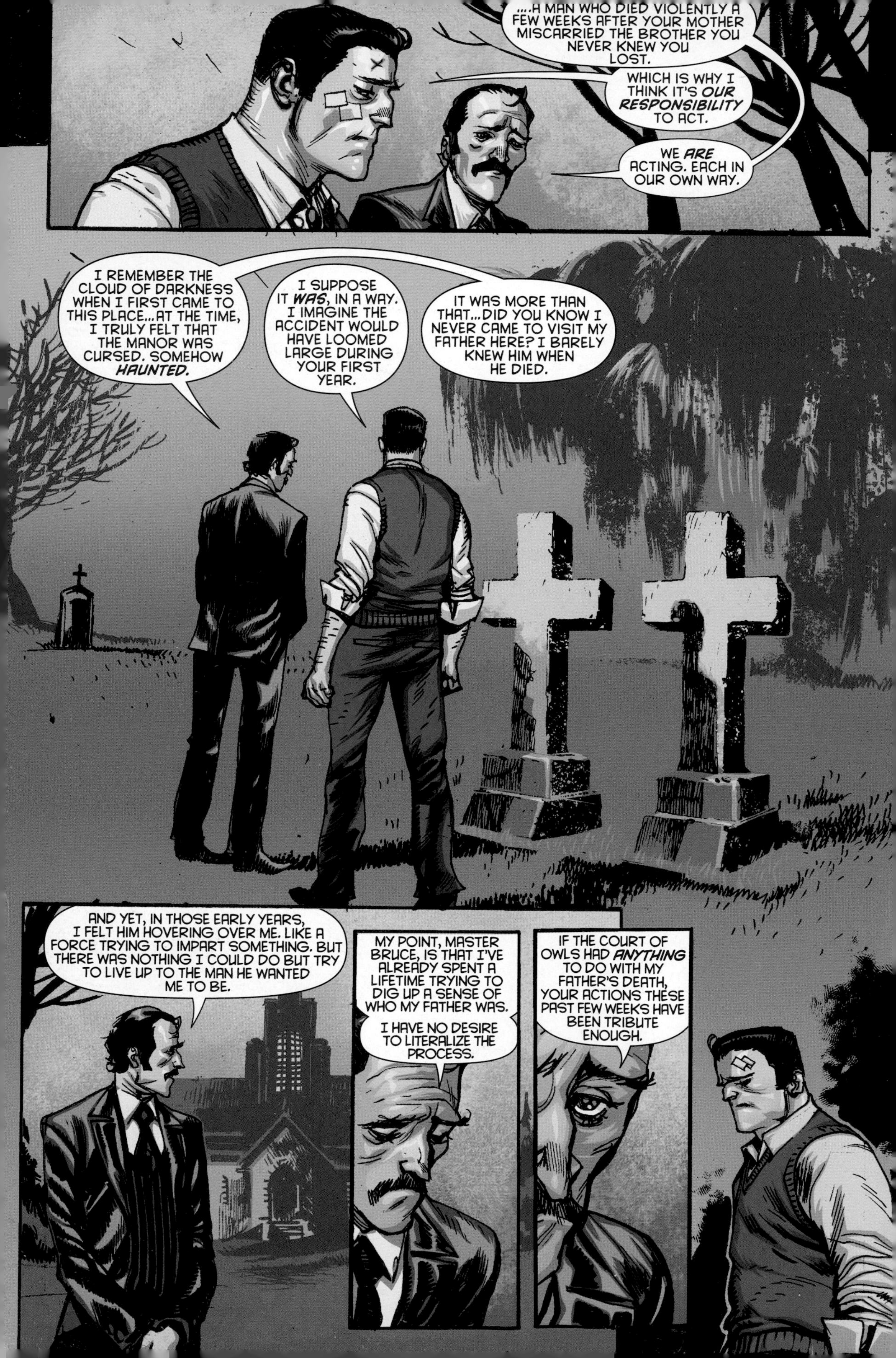
...A MAN WHO DIED VIOLENTLY A FEW WEEKS AFTER YOUR MOTHER MISCARRIED THE BROTHER YOU NEVER KNEW YOU LOST.
WHICH IS WHY I THINK IT'S OUR RESPONSIBILITY TO ACT.
WE ARE ACTING. EACH IN OUR OWN WAY.
I REMEMBER THE CLOUD OF DARKNESS WHEN I FIRST CAME TO THIS PLACE...AT THE TIME, I TRULY FELT THAT THE MANOR WAS CURSED. SOMEHOW HAUNTED.
I SUPPOSE IT WAS, IN A WAY. I IMAGINE THE ACCIDENT WOULD HAVE LOOMED LARGE DURING YOUR FIRST YEAR.
IT WAS MORE THAN THAT...DID YOU KNOW I NEVER CAME TO VISIT MY FATHER HERE? I BARELY KNEW HIM WHEN HE DIED.
AND YET, IN THOSE EARLY YEARS, I FELT HIM HOVERING OVER ME. LIKE A FORCE TRYING TO IMPART SOMETHING. BUT THERE WAS NOTHING I COULD DO BUT TRY TO LIVE UP TO THE MAN HE WANTED ME TO BE.
MY POINT, MASTER BRUCE, IS THAT I'VE ALREADY SPENT A LIFETIME TRYING TO DIG UP A SENSE OF WHO MY FATHER WAS.
I HAVE NO DESIRE TO LITERALIZE THE PROCESS.
IF THE COURT OF OWLS HAD ANYTHING TO DO WITH MY FATHER'S DEATH, YOUR ACTIONS THESE PAST FEW WEEKS HAVE BEEN TRIBUTE ENOUGH.

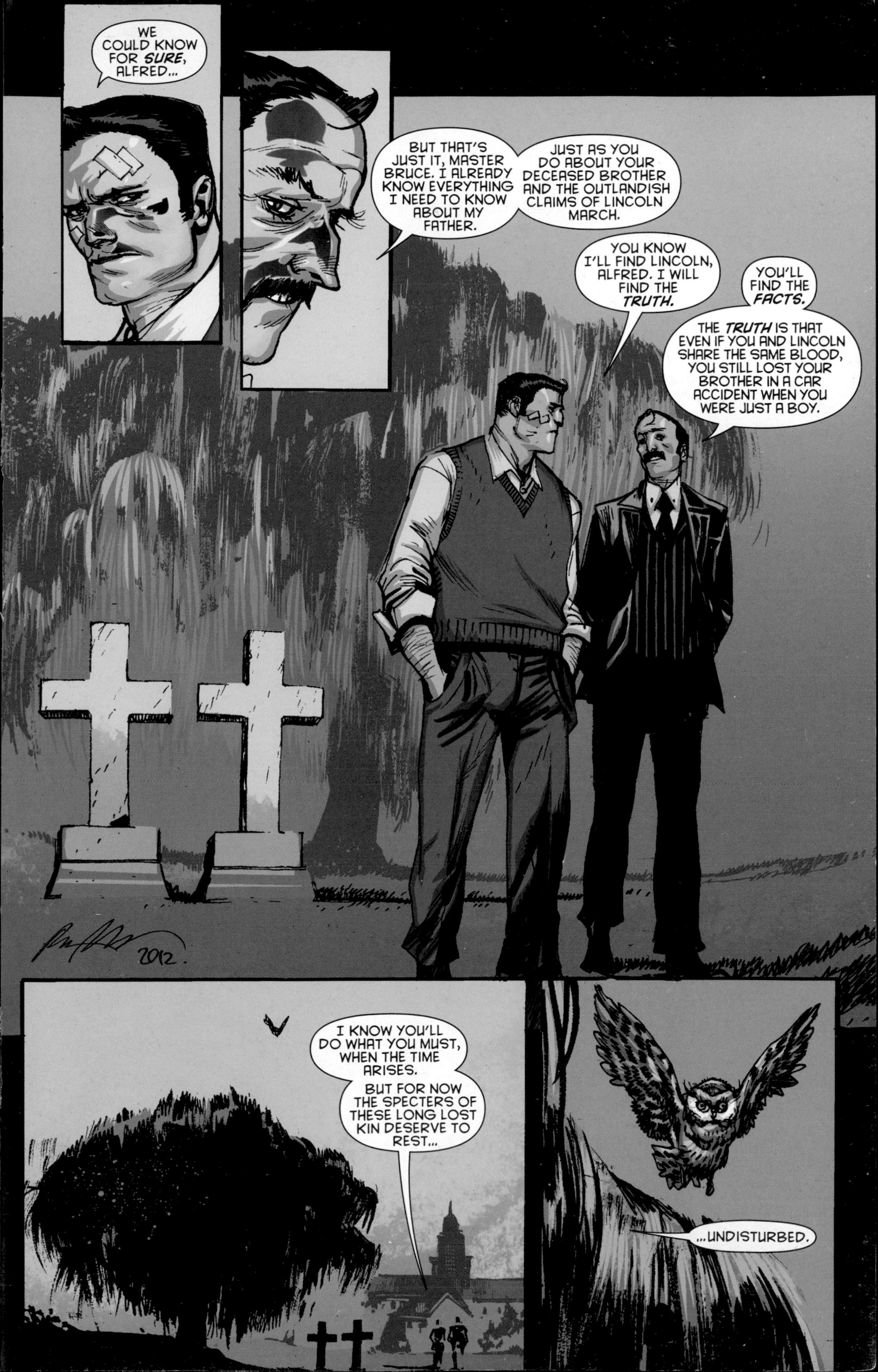

WE COULD KNOW FOR *SURE*, ALFRED...
BUT THAT'S JUST IT, MASTER BRUCE. I ALREADY KNOW EVERYTHING I NEED TO KNOW ABOUT MY FATHER.
JUST AS YOU DO ABOUT YOUR DECEASED BROTHER AND THE OUTLANDISH CLAIMS OF LINCOLN MARCH.
YOU KNOW I'LL FIND LINCOLN, ALFRED. I WILL FIND THE *TRUTH.*
YOU'LL FIND THE *FACTS.*
THE *TRUTH* IS THAT EVEN IF YOU AND LINCOLN SHARE THE SAME BLOOD, YOU STILL LOST YOUR BROTHER IN A CAR ACCIDENT WHEN YOU WERE JUST A BOY.
2012.
I KNOW YOU'LL DO WHAT YOU MUST, WHEN THE TIME ARISES.
BUT FOR NOW THE SPECTERS OF THESE LONG LOST KIN DESERVE TO REST...
...UNDISTURBED.

Batman battle suit armor design

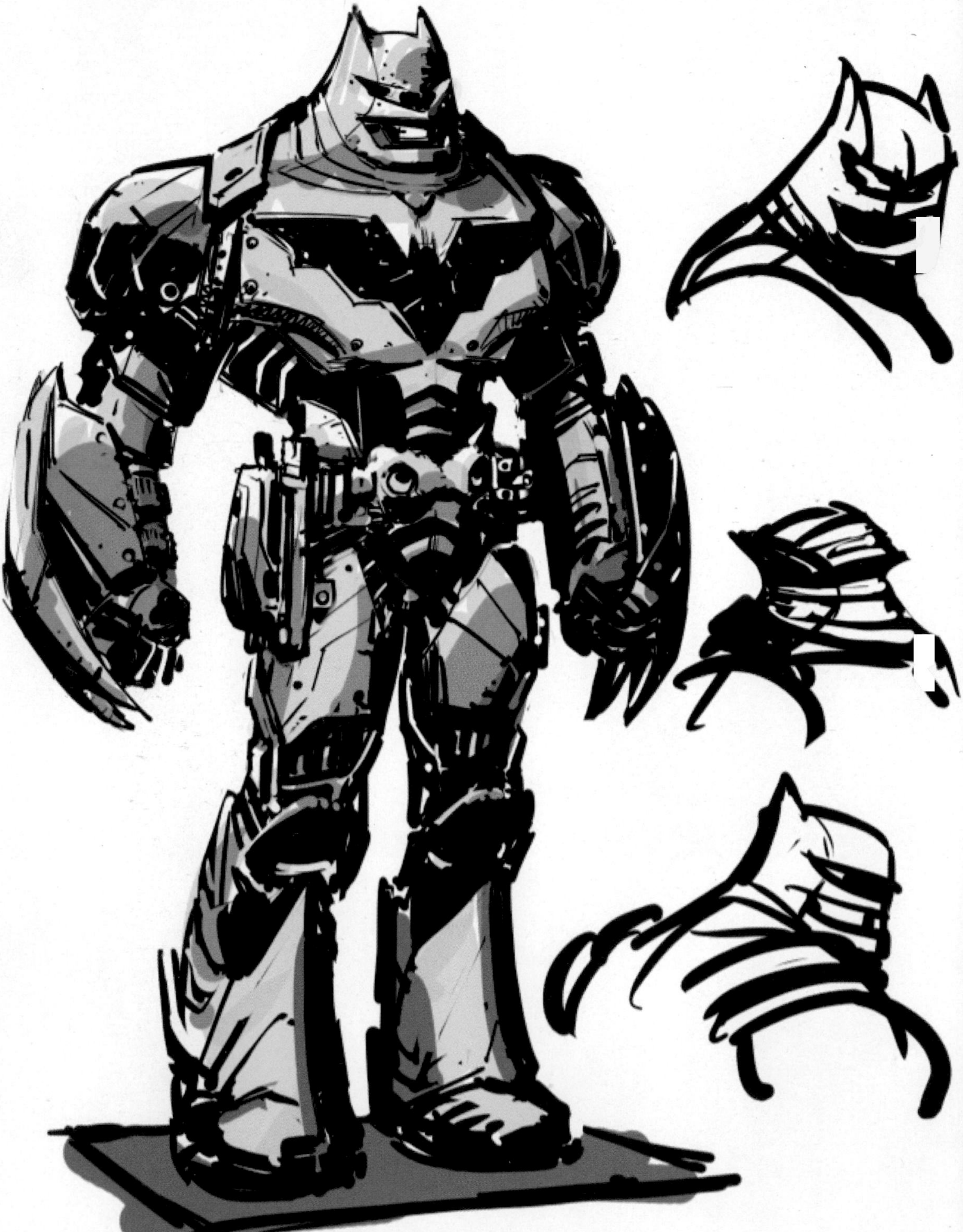

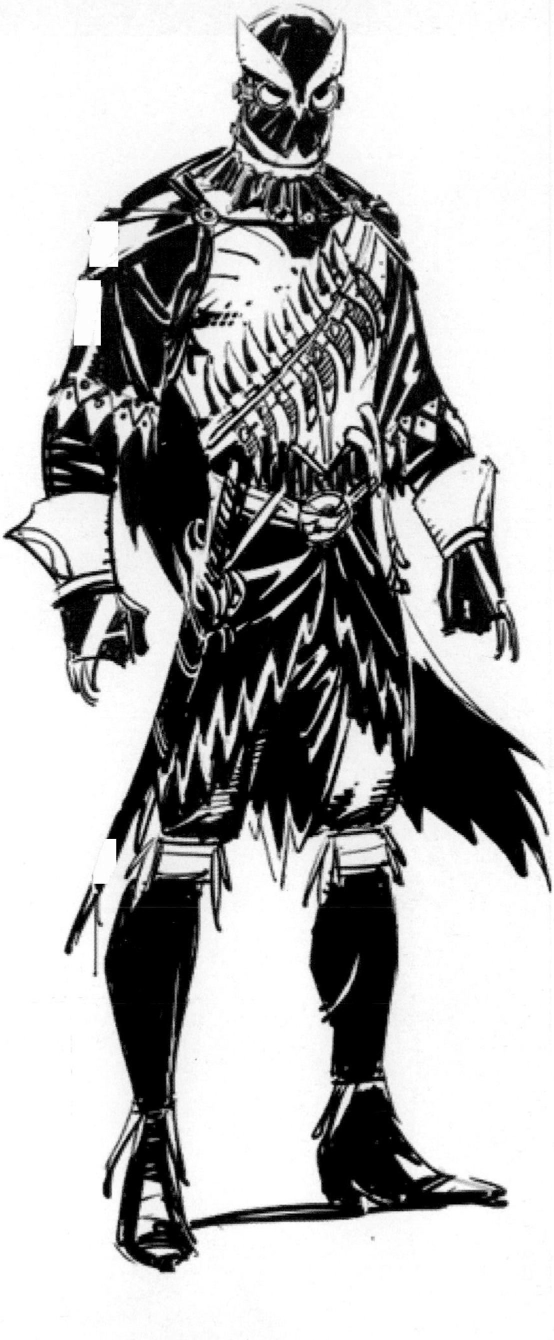

Talon of the 1660s

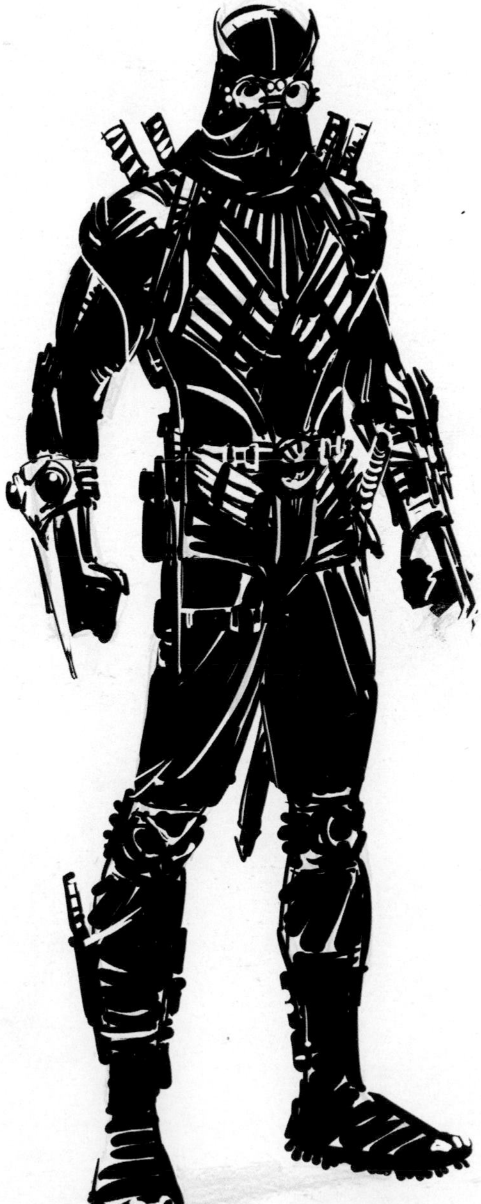

Talon of the 1980s

Talon of the 1700s

Talon of the 1840s

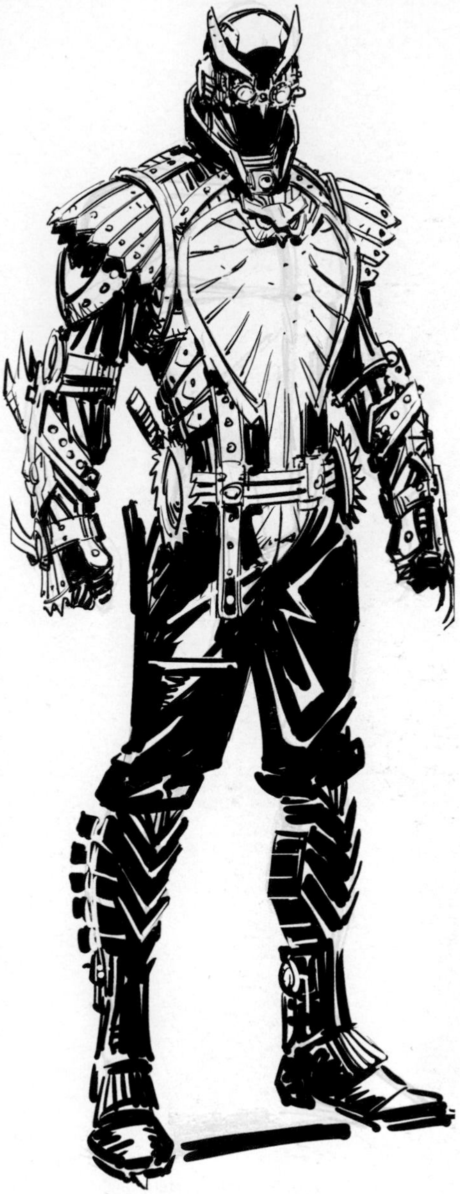

Talon of the 1870s

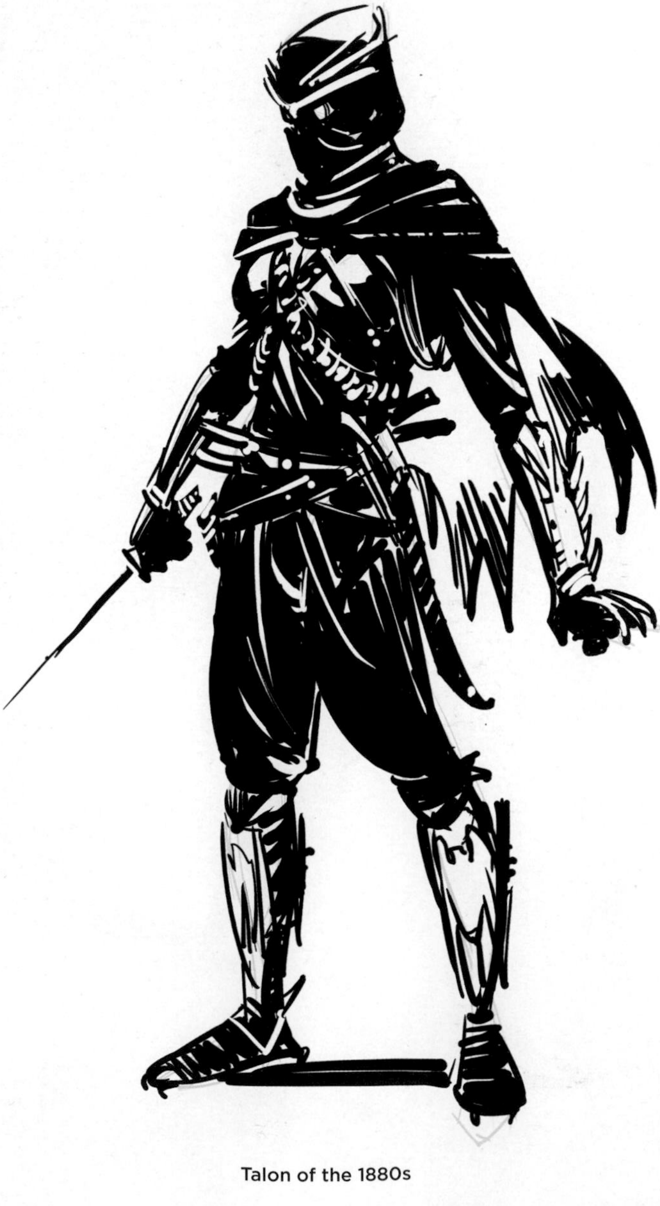

Talon of the 1880s

Talon of the 1940s

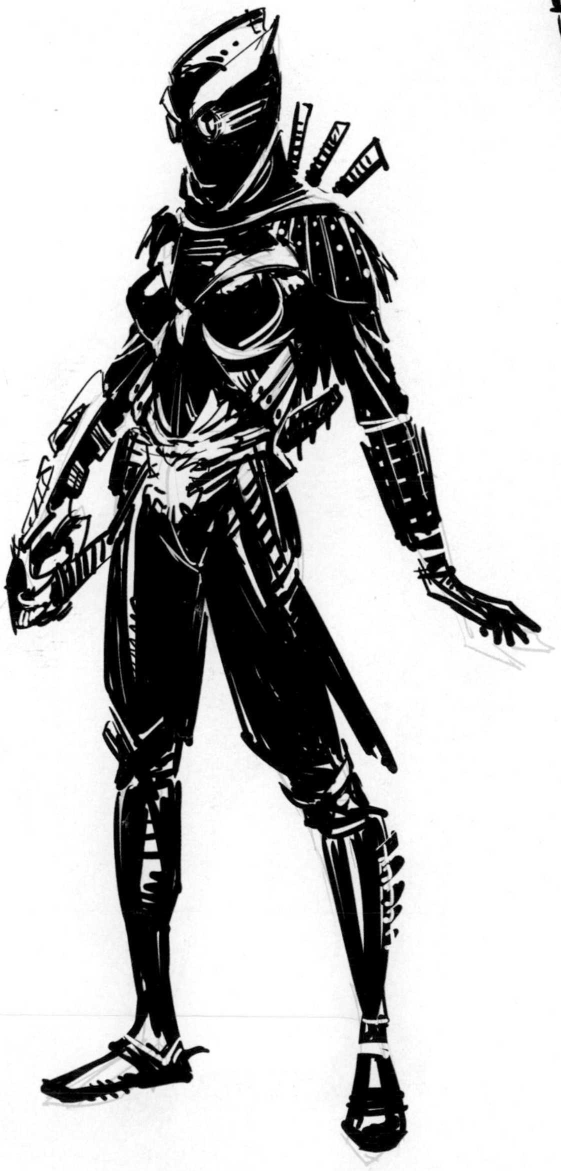

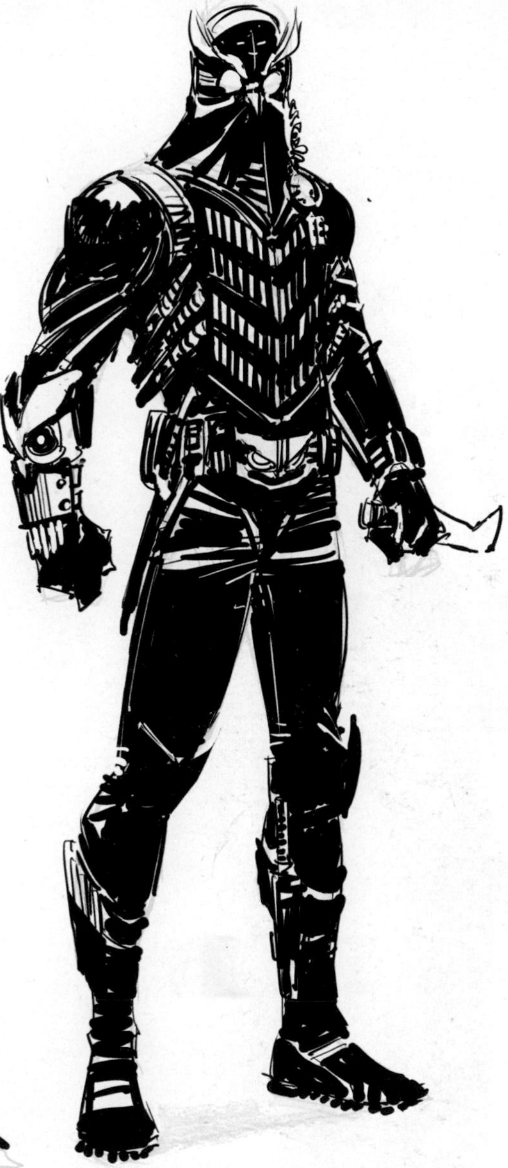

Talon of the 1950s

Talon of the 1880s
Design by MORITAT

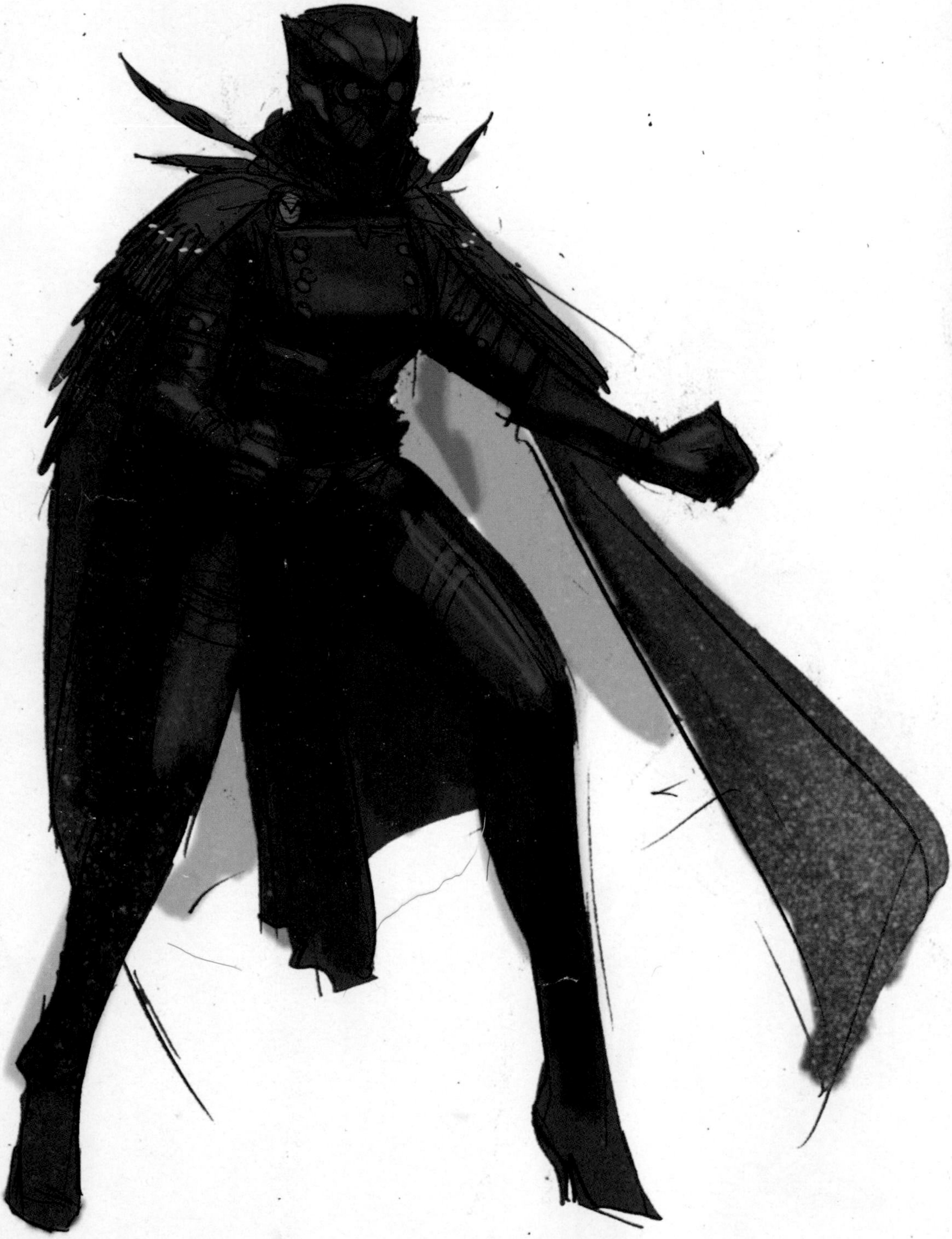